Pattern Matching Algorithms

Edited by
Alberto Apostolico
Zvi Galil

New York   Oxford
Oxford University Press
1997

Oxford University Press

Oxford   New York

Athens   Auckland   Bangkok   Bogota   Bombay   Buenos Aires
Calcutta   Cape Town   Dar es Salaam   Delhi   Florence   Hong Kong
Istanbul   Karachi   Kuala Lumpur   Madras   Madrid   Melbourne
Mexico City   Nairobi   Paris   Singapore   Taipei   Tokyo   Toronto

and associated companies in
Berlin   Ibadan

Library of Congress Cataloging-in-Publication Data
Apostolico, Alberto, 1948–
Pattern matching algorithms / edited by A. Apostolico, Zvi Galil.
p.   cm.
Includes bibliographical references and index.
ISBN 0-19-511367-5
1. Computer algorithms.   2. Combinatorial analysis.
I. Galil, Zvi.   II. Title.
QA76.9.A43A66   1997
006.4—dc21   96-49602

1 3 5 7 9 8 6 4 2

Printed in the United States of America
on acid-free paper

Pattern
Matching
Algorithms

Preface

Issues of matching and searching on elementary discrete structures arise pervasively in Computer Science as well as in many of its applications. Their relevance may be expected to grow even further in the near future as information is amassed, disseminated and shared at an increasing pace. A number of algorithms have been discovered in recent years in response to these needs. Along the way, a number of combinatorial structures and tools have been exposed that often carry intrinsic value and interest. The main ideas that developed in this process concurred to distill the scope and flavor of Pattern Matching, now an established specialty of Algorithmics.

The lineage of Pattern Matching may be traced back for more than two decades, to a handful of papers such as "Rapid identification of repeated patterns in strings, trees, and arrays", by R.M. Karp, R.E. Miller and A.L. Rosenberg, "Automata theory can be useful", by D.E. Knuth and V.R. Pratt, and, in a less direct way, S.A. Cook's "Linear time simulation of deterministic two-way pushdown automata". The outgrowth of these powerful seeds is impressive: I. Simon lists over 350 titles in the current version of his bibliography on string algorithms; A.V. Aho references over 140 papers in his recent survey of string-searching algorithms alone; and advanced workshops and schools, books and special issues of major journals have been already dedicated to the subject and more are planned for the future.

This book attempts a snapshot of the current state of the art in Pattern Matching as seen by specialists who have devoted several years of their study to the field. Without pretending to be exhaustive, the book does cover most basic principles and presents material advanced enough to portray faithfully the current frontier of research in the field. Our intention was to combine a textbook suitable for a graduate or advanced level course with an in-depth source for the specialist as well as the neophyte.

The appearance of this book marks, somewhat intentionally, the Tenth anniversary since "Combinatorial Algorithms on Words". We wish it an equally favorable reception, and possibly even more opportunities to serve, through the forthcoming years, the growth of its useful and fascinating subject.

a.a. and z.g.

Contributors

Amihood Amir, Computer Science Department, Georgia Institute of Technology, Atlanta, GA 30332, USA

Alberto Apostolico, Department of Computer Sciences, Purdue University, CS Building, West Lafayette, IN 47907, USA *and* Dipartimento di Elettronica e Informatica, Università di Padova, Via Gradenigo 6/A, 35131 Padova, Italy

Mikhail J. Atallah, Department of Computer Sciences, Purdue University, CS Building, West Lafayette, IN 47907, USA

Maxime Crochemore, Institut Gaspard Monge, Université de Marne-la-Vallée, 2 rue de la Butte Verte, F-93160 Noisy-le-Grand, France.

Martin Farach, DIMACS, Rutgers University, CoRE Building, Busch Campus, P.O. 1179, Piscataway, NJ 08855-1179, USA

Zvi Galil, Department of Computer Science, Columbia University, New York, NY 10027, USA *and* Department of Computer Science, School of Mathematical Sciences, Tel Aviv University, Tel Aviv, 69978 Israel

Raffaele Giancarlo, Dipartimento di Matematica ed Applicazioni, Università di Palermo, Via Archirafi 34, 90123 Palermo, Italy

Roberto Grossi, Dipartimento di Sistemi e Informatica, Università di Firenze, Via Lombroso 6/17, 50134 Firenze, Italy

Daniel S. Hirschberg, Department of Information and Computer Science, University of California at Irvine, Irvine, CA 92717, USA

Tao Jiang, Department of Computer Science, McMaster University, Hamilton, Ontario L8S 4K1, Canada

Gad M. Landau, Department of Computer Science, Polytechnic University, 6 MetroTech, Brooklyn, NY 11201, USA

Ming Li, Department of Computer Science, University of Waterloo, Waterloo, Ontario N2L 3G1, Canada

Dennis Shasha, Courant Institute of Mathematical Science, New York University, 251 Mercer Street, New York, NY 10012, USA

Uzi Vishkin, Institute for Advanced Computer Studies and Electrical Engineering Department, University of Maryland, College Park, MD 20742, USA. *and* Department of Computer Science, School of Mathematical Sciences, Tel Aviv University, Tel Aviv, 69978 Israel

Ilan Yudkiewicz, Department of Computer Science, School of Mathematical Sciences, Tel Aviv University, Tel Aviv, 69978 Israel
Kaizhong Zhang, Department of Computer Science, University of Western Ontario, London, Ontario N6A 5B7, Canada

Contents

3 On-line String Searching

4 Serial Computations of Levenshtein Distances

Pattern
Matching
Algorithms

1
Off-line Serial Exact String Searching

String searching or string-matching is the problem of locating all occurrences of a string x of length m, called the pattern, in another string t of length n, called the text. The algorithmic complexity of the problem is analyzed by means of standard measures: running time and amount of memory space required by the computations. This chapter deals with solutions in which the pattern only is preprocessed. There are mainly three kinds of methods to solve the problem: sequential methods simulating a finite automaton, practically fast methods, and time-space optimal methods. Alternative solutions based on a preprocessing of the text are described in Chapter 3. Parallel algorithms for the problem, presented in Chapter 2, sometimes also generate new serial algorithms. Finally, methods that search for approximate occurrences of a pattern are the subject of Chapters 4, 5, and 6.

1.1   Searching for strings in texts

The problem is of main importance for several reasons. From a theoretical point of view, it is a paradigm for the design of efficient algorithms, in the same way as are, for instance, sorting methods. From a practical point of view, the algorithms developed in this chapter often serve as basic components in text facility software.

In the whole chapter, x denotes the pattern of length m ($m = |x|$), and t is the text of length n ($n = |t|$). To avoid trivial situations, the pattern is assumed to be a non-empty string ($x \neq \lambda$, $m \neq 0$). Since the problem becomes a simple counting exercise when the alphabet reduces to only one symbol, the reader may consider in the following that the common alphabet Σ of the text and the pattern contains at least two symbols ($|\Sigma| > 1$).

We assume that the pattern is given first. The text is given at search time only. This allows us to preprocess the pattern in order to accelerate the future search in the text. An instance of the problem arises when we try to recognize a specific pattern in various texts or streams of symbols arriving through a communication channel. No preprocessing of the text is possible nor allowed. This contrasts with the problem of locating words in a dictionary, or an entire corpus of fixed texts, problem which is considered in Chapter 3.

We mainly consider algorithms that use comparison of symbols as the basic elementary operation. These comparisons are usually of the kind equal-unequal. But a few algorithms also assume that the alphabet is ordered, which is not a restriction in practice, and therefore profit from comparisons of the kind less-equal-greater. We consider algorithms using branching operations as well, typically used in connection with automata.

Efficient algorithms, as most of those considered in this chapter, have a running time that is linear in the size of the input (i.e. $O(n + m)$). And most algorithms require an additional amount of memory space that is linear in the size of the pattern (i.e. $O(m)$). Information stored in this space is computed during the preprocessing phase, and later used during the search phase. The time spent during the search phase is particularly important. So, the number of comparisons made and the number of inspections executed have been evaluated with great care. For most algorithms, the maximum number of comparisons (or number of inspections) made during the execution of the search is less than $2n$. The minimum number of comparison necessary is $\lfloor n/m \rfloor$, and some algorithms reach that bound in some situations.

The average running time of the search phase is sometimes considered as more significant than the worst-case time complexity. Despite the fact that it is usually difficult to modelize the probability distribution of specific texts, results for a few algorithms (with a hypothesis on what "average" means) are known. Equiprobability of symbols and independence between their occurrences in texts represent a common hypothesis used in this context. It is known that, in this case, the best average time of the search phase is $O(n \log m/m)$. It is even rather simple to design a string searching algorithm working in this time span, and this chapter contains a practical implementation of an algorithm having this performance.

We consider three classes of string searching algorithms. In the first class, the text is searched sequentially, one symbol at a time from the beginning to the end. Thus all symbols of the text (except perhaps $m - 1$ of them at the end) are inspected. The algorithms simulate a recognition process using a finite automaton. The second class contains algorithms that are practically fast. The time complexity of the search phase can even be sublinear, under the assumption that text and pattern reside in the main memory. Algorithms of the first two classes usually require $O(m)$ extra memory space. Algorithms of the third class show that the additional space can be reduced to a few integers stored in a constant amount of memory space.

The complexity of the string searching problem is given by the following theorem. The proof is based on space-economical methods (Section 1.4). Linear time is however illustrated by almost all algorithms of the chapter.

---

put window at the beginning of text;
while window on text **do**
begin
 scan: **if** window = pattern **then** report it;
 shift: shift window to the right and
 memorize some information for use during next scans and shifts;
end;

Fig. 1.1. The sliding window strategy: scan-and-shift mechanism

Note that in the "O" notation the coefficient is independent of the alphabet size.

Theorem 1.1. *The string searching problem, locating all occurrences of a pattern x in a text t, can be solved in linear time, $O(|t| + |x|)$, with a constant amount of additional memory space.*

The above classification can be somehow refined by considering the way the search phases of algorithms work. It is convenient to consider that the text is examined through a *window*. The window is assimilated to the subword of the text it contains and has (usually) the length of the pattern. It runs along the text from the beginning to the end. This scheme is called the *sliding window* strategy and is described as an algorithm in Figure 1.1.

During the search, the window on the text is periodically shifted to the right according to rules that are specific to each algorithm. When the window is placed at a certain position on the text, the algorithms check whether the pattern occurs there, i.e., if the pattern equals the content of the window. This is the *scan* operation during which the algorithm acquires from the text information which are often used to determine the next shift of the window. Part of the information can also be kept in memory after the shift operation. This information is then used for two purposes: first, saving time during next scan operations, and, second, increasing the length of further shifts. Thus, algorithms operate a series of alternate scans and shifts.

The simplest implementation of the scan-and-shift scheme is given in Figure 1.2, as a procedure called NAIVE_SEARCH. After each scan operation, the strategy consists here in sliding the window one place to the right, which obviously generates a correct algorithm (as far as scans are correctly implemented). In the algorithm, the value of the variable *pos* is the current position of the window on the text. And variable i points successively to symbols of the pattern (see Figure 1.8). The symbol $x[i]$ is aligned with the symbol of the text at position $pos + i - 1$.

The NAIVE_SEARCH algorithm has several advantages: it needs no preprocessing of any kind on the pattern, and it requires only a fixed amount

procedure NAIVE_SEARCH(x, t: *string*; m, n: *integer*);
begin
    {it is assumed that $m = |x|$ and $n = |t|$}
    pos := 1;
    while *pos* $\leq n - m + 1$ **do begin**
        $i := 1$;
        while $i \leq m$ **and** $x[i] = t[pos + i - 1]$ **do** $i := i + 1$;
        if $i = m + 1$ **then** writeln('x occurs in t at position ', *pos*);
        pos := *pos* + 1;
    end;
end;

Fig. 1.2. Naive string searching algorithm

of extra memory space (few registers). However, its maximum running time is $O(n.m)$ (for instance if σ^n is searched for all occurrences of σ^m, $\sigma \in \Sigma$). On the average, if all symbols have the same probability wherever they are in strings, it is simple to see that the number of symbol comparisons NAIVE_SEARCH makes, is less than $2n$. This bound, while it could look quite small, is indeed very high compared to the lower bound on expected time, $O(n \log m/m)$, that is reached by the fastest algorithms (see Section 1.3).

The way the algorithms scan the content of the window influence greatly their design and performance. Five types of scans are considered here. Scans are based on different notions, which are generally used to compare strings and that leads, indeed, to distances between strings. The scan operations considered in this chapter are based on these elements:

- longest common prefix,
- longest prefix of the window, subword of the pattern,
- longest common suffix,
- longest suffix of the window, prefix of the pattern,
- pattern factorization.

The first two notions lead to algorithms that operate sequential searches (see Section 1.2). The next two notions produce the practically-fastest known algorithms (see Section 1.3). Combining the first and third notions produces the two-way scan scheme based on the fifth notion and yields time-space optimal algorithms (see Section 1.4). Many other scanning strategies are possible, and some of them are discussed at the end of the chapter or in exercises.

For the exposition of a string searching algorithm, it is simpler to present its preprocessing phase separately from its search phase. It is however sometimes possible to incorporate the preprocessing phase inside the search

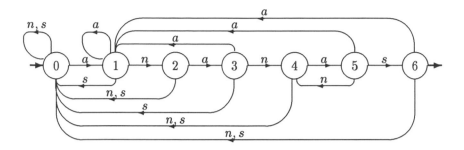

Fig. 1.3.   String-matching automaton of pattern *ananas*

phase, getting then a *lazy preprocessing* of the pattern. Such implementation details are left to the reader.

1.2   Sequential searches

In the sliding window scheme for searching for x in t, it is rather natural to scan the window from left to right. This is the way NAIVE-SEARCH algorithm of Figure 1.2 proceeds. There are even situations in which it is recommended to do so, such as when scanning a stream of symbols arriving through a channel of communication. The present section describes efficient variants of this strategy.

1.2.1   STRING-MATCHING AUTOMATON

Checking whether pattern x is a subword of text t can be equivalently stated as a membership question: is t member of the language $\Sigma^{\star}x\Sigma^{\star}$? Or, stated differently, is there a prefix of t member of the language $\Sigma^{\star}x$? The languages $\Sigma^{\star}x\Sigma^{\star}$ and $\Sigma^{\star}x$ are both rational languages, so we can expect that the problem translates into a decision procedure on automata representing the languages. Consider, for instance, a deterministic automaton recognizing $\Sigma^{\star}x$. Then, while reading the text through the automaton, an occurrence of the pattern x is discovered each time a final state of the automaton is met. The position of the occurrence can then be reported (see Figure 1.4).

Recall that a deterministic automaton $\mathcal{A}$ is a sequence $(Q, \Sigma, initial, T, \delta)$ where Q is the finite set of states, *initial* the initial state, T the set of terminal states, and δ is the transition function. For a state $q \in Q$ and a symbol $\sigma \in \Sigma$, $\delta(q, \sigma)$ is the state reached from q by transition of symbol σ. The transition function extends to words, and $\delta(q, w)$ denotes, if it exists, the state reached after reading the word w in the automaton from the state q. The automaton $\mathcal{A}$ recognizes the language $\{w \in \Sigma^{\star}/\delta(initial, w) \in T\}$.

The minimal (deterministic) automaton for the language $\Sigma^{\star}x$ is denoted

```
procedure SEARCH(x, t: string; m, n: integer);
begin
    { (Q, Σ, initial, {terminal}, δ) is the automaton SMA(x) }
    q := initial;
    if q = terminal then report an occurrence of x in t;
    while not end of t do begin
        σ := next symbol of t;
        q := δ(q, σ);
        if q = terminal then report an occurrence of x in t;
    end;
end;
```

Fig. 1.4. String searching with automaton

```
function SMA(x: string): automaton;
begin
    let initial be a new state;
    Q := {initial}; terminal := initial;
    for all σ in Σ do δ(initial, σ) := initial;
    while not end of x do begin
        τ := next symbol of x; r := δ(terminal, τ);
        add new state s to Q; δ(terminal, τ) := s;
        for all σ in Σ do δ(s, σ) := δ(r, σ);
        terminal := s;
    end;
    return (Q, Σ, initial, {terminal}, δ);
end;
```

Fig. 1.5. Construction of a string-matching automaton

by $\mathcal{A}(x)$, and called the *String-Matching Automaton of x*. Figure 1.3 shows an example of string-matching automaton for the pattern *ananas* ("ananas" is the French word for pineapple). The number of states of $\mathcal{A}(x)$ is $m + 1$. The construction of $\mathcal{A}(x)$ can be done, starting with a straightforward non-deterministic version, with the standard procedures which determinize and minimize automata. However, it is remarkable that the direct construction of $\mathcal{A}(x)$ is simple, and takes optimal time (proportional to its size). The algorithm is given in Figure 1.5 as procedure SMA(x) that produces $\mathcal{A}(x)$. The construction is on-line. At a given step, it is assumed that the string-matching automaton $\mathcal{A}(u)$ for a prefix u of pattern x has already been built. The automaton has exactly one initial state, *initial*, and one terminal state,

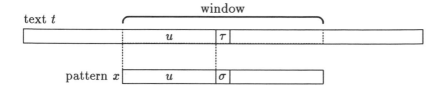

Fig. 1.6. Left-to-right scan: mismatch situation ($\sigma \neq \tau$)

terminal. Its transition function is denoted by δ, and Q is the set of states. Let τ be the next symbol of the pattern ($u\tau$ is a prefix of x). The work done during the processing of symbol τ remains to "unwind" the transition that starts from the terminal state and labeled by τ. This means that, after the operation, the target of the transition leads to a "clone" of the former target. The new state also becomes the new unique terminal state.

The time complexity of procedure SMA is $O(m|\Sigma|)$. This is true, in fact, if transitions are computed in constant time. An array representation of the function δ can be used for this purpose. The associated search phase (Figure 1.4) then produces a real-time algorithm that works in $O(n)$ time with $O(m|\Sigma|)$ extra space.

The main inconvenience with the approach described in this section is that the complexity of the algorithm we get depends on the cardinality of the alphabet. This makes the method almost useless in practical applications. However, this is certainly the best sequential method for small alphabets, and also when comparisons are better replaced by branchings. Furthermore, the method is the base for several other algorithms described in the next subsection. There, the algorithms all implicitly contain a compact representation of the automaton $\mathcal{A}(x)$.

Finally, note that the construction of $\mathcal{A}(x)$ does not need to be done before the search phase starts. It is possible and certainly is a more clever implementation to make a lazy construction of $\mathcal{A}(x)$ while searching t. This remark is also valid for all other methods based on automata, and especially those described in the following sections.

1.2.2 FORWARD PREFIX SCAN

KMP algorithm is the classical algorithm that implements efficiently the left-to-right scan strategy. In this section, we first describe a slightly simpler version called MP algorithm. And then, after the presentation of KMP algorithm, we describe another algorithm that we call MPS. This latter slightly improves on KMP string searching algorithm. The three algorithms, MP, KMP, and MPS, can be regarded as implementations by symbol comparisons of the search based on the string-matching automaton (algorithm in Figure 1.4).

---

while window on text **do**
begin
    $u :=$ longest common prefix of window and pattern;
    if $u =$ pattern **then** report a match;
    shift window $period(u)$ places to right;
    memorize $border(u)$;
end;

Fig. 1.7.   Scheme of MP algorithm

The important current situation for searching algorithms that implement a left-to-right scan is shown in Figure 1.6. It is when the window on text t contains a string $u\tau y$, and pattern x is equal to $u\sigma z$ (where u, y, z are words on Σ, and τ, σ are distinct symbols of Σ). This is the *mismatch situation*. An analogue situation is met when the window contains the pattern itself. Indeed, we can also consider that this is a mismatch situation, as if the pattern x were right-marked by a symbol not occurring in the text t. In either case, the window is shifted to the right, and the process continues its series of scans and shifts.

Consider a mismatch situation and a closest position of the window (to the right) that can possibly contain pattern x. This position is at most $|u\tau|$ places to the right of the present position of the window, because no symbol of the text to the right of symbol τ has been examined so far. This implies that, after the shift, the prefix u of x overlaps the occurrence of $u\tau$ in the text (or, at least, is adjacent to it). Thus, the distance between the present position of the window and the next position that needs to be considered is $period(u\tau)$. The period corresponds to the longest possible overlap of $u\tau$ over itself, namely the border $border(u\tau)$. Then, the length of the smallest safe shift of the window is the smallest period of $u\tau$. Computing all periods $period(u\tau)$ (for prefixes u of x and symbols τ) amounts to consider the minimal deterministic automaton recognizing the language $\Sigma^* x$, as described in Section 1.2.1.

There are two solutions to reduce down to $O(m)$ the extra space used by the algorithms. The first solution is to approximate periods of the words $u\tau$'s. It is implemented by MP and KMP algorithms that we describe first in the following. The second solution is to store only significant periods of the possible $u\tau$'s. It is implemented by MPS algorithm, presented at the end of the section.

MP algorithm   The scheme of MP algorithm is given in Figure 1.7. In a mismatch situation (see Figure 1.6), the length of the shift performed during the search phase of MP algorithm is $period(u)$. This is obviously not greater than $period(u\tau)$, so that no occurrence of the pattern can be

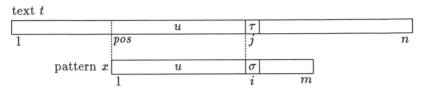

Fig. 1.8. Variables i and j used in MP algorithm ($pos = j - i + 1$)

---

procedure MP(x, t: *string*; m, n: *integer*);
begin
    $i := 1; j := 1$;
    while $j \leq n$ **do begin**
        while ($i = m + 1$) **or** ($i > 0$ **and** $x[i] \neq t[j]$) **do** $i := MP\_next[i]$;
        $i := i + 1; j := j + 1$;
        if $i = m + 1$ **then** writeln('x occurs in t at position ', $j - i + 1$);
    end;
end;

Fig. 1.9. MP search algorithm

missed. This argument proves the correctness of the search scheme. But it is remarkable that the approximation on shifts realized by MP algorithm still leads to a linear search for the pattern. Indeed, the entire algorithm, including the preprocessing phase, runs in linear time, and requires only $O(m)$ extra space to store all periods of prefixes of x.

A detailed version of MP searching algorithm is given in Figure 1.9. Variables of MP algorithm are shown in Figure 1.8. The algorithm uses only two variables i and j. The former runs through positions of x, and the latter through positions of t. The current position of the window is not explicitly represented, as in NAIVE_SEARCH, but has value $j - i + 1$. Shifting the window p places to the right remains to decrement the pointer i on the pattern by the quantity $period(u)$, leaving j unchanged. Indeed, next values of i's are precomputed and stored in a table called MP_next by the algorithm of Figure 1.11.

The precomputation of table MP_next used in MP algorithm is similar to the computation of borders of pattern prefixes, that is presented first. The computation of borders is based on the fact: "a border of a border of a word w is a border of w". More precisely, it relies on the following remark:

if the border of $u\sigma$ is not empty ($u\sigma$ prefix of x with σ in Σ), then it is of the form $v\sigma$ where v is a border of u.

---

procedure COMPUTE_BORDERS(x: *string*; m: *integer*);
begin
    $Border[0] := -1$;
    for $i := 1$ **to** m **do begin**
      $j := Border[i-1]$;
      while $j \geq 0$ **and** $x[i] \neq x[j+1]$ **do** $j := Border[j]$;
      $Border[i] := j + 1$;
    end;
end;

Fig. 1.10.   Computation of borders of pattern prefixes

---

procedure COMPUTE_MP_NEXT(x: *string*; m: *integer*);
begin
    $MP\_next[1] := 0$; $j := 0$;
    for $i := 1$ **to** m **do begin**
      { at this point, we have $j = MP\_next[i]$ }
      while $j > 0$ **and** $x[i] \neq x[j]$ **do** $j := MP\_next[j]$;
      $j := j + 1$;
      $MP\_next[i + 1] := j$;
    end;
end;

Fig. 1.11.   Computation of table *MP_next*

Thus, the word v is the longest border of u followed by σ (i.e. such that $v\sigma$ is prefix of u). Procedure COMPUTE_BORDERS in Figure 1.10 implements this rule to compute the borders of all prefixes of the pattern x. The procedure produces the lengths of the borders in a table called *Border*: the value $Border[i]$ is the length of $border(x[1:i])$. For the empty prefix that has no border, the length is set to -1 ($Border[0] = -1$), a convention which is compatible with the algorithm. Prefixes are processed in order of increasing lengths. To compute the border of a given prefix, variable j runs through the lengths of borders of the preceding prefix in decreasing order until the above condition is met.

    The table *MP_next* used by MP algorithm is defined by $MP\_next[1] = 0$, and, for $2 \leq i \leq m + 1$, by

$$MP\_next[i] = i - period(x[1:i-1]),$$

corresponding to a shift of $period(x[1:i-1])$ positions. The quantity

$i - period(x[1 : i - 1])$ is also $Border[i - 1] + 1$, and thus can be computed after $Border$:

$$MP\_next[i] = Border[i - 1] + 1.$$

Indeed, the precomputation of table MP_next can be realized directly, without first computing borders of pattern prefixes. It should be noted that the precomputation, which is described in Figure 1.11, is designed in the same fashion as MP searching algorithm itself. This phenomenon is specific to string searching algorithms of the present section. The preprocessing remains to search for the pattern x inside x itself starting at the second position.

Theorem 1.2. *MP string searching algorithm runs in time $O(|x| + |t|)$. It executes at most $2|t| - 1$ symbol comparisons during the search phase, and at most $2|x| - 3$ symbol comparisons during the preprocessing phase. MP algorithm requires $O(|x|)$ extra memory space.*

Proof Consider the expression $2j - i$ in MP algorithm (Figure 1.9). Each symbol comparison strictly increases its value: positive comparisons increase both i and j by 1, negative comparisons increase $j - i$, the position of the window, leaving j unchanged. The final value of $2j - i$ is not greater than $2n + 1$. This is reached only when final values of i and j are 1 and $n + 1$ respectively. But then their previous values were 0 and n respectively, which shows that the last incrementation has been done after no symbol comparison. So, we can consider that the final value of $2j - i$ is $2n$, and since its initial value is 1, the number of symbol comparisons made during the search phase is not greater than $2n - 1$. This value is reached by text $\sigma^{m-1}\tau$ and pattern σ^m. With the remark immediately preceding the theorem the preprocessing phase is equivalent to the search inside a text of length $m - 1$. The number of symbol comparisons at preprocessing phase is thus $2(m - 1) - 1 = 2m - 3$. Finally, $O(m)$ extra space is used to store the table MP_next. □

From the precomputation phase of MP algorithm, one can easily deduce an algorithm to compute all the periods of pattern x (recall that we assume $x \neq \lambda$), and not only its smallest period. These periods, in increasing order, are quantities $m - Border[m], m - Border^2[m], \ldots, m - Border^k[m]$, where k is the smallest integer for which $border^k(x)$ is the empty word.

KMP algorithm KMP algorithm is a slight improvement on MP algorithm. The difference only lies in the computation of shifts (see Figure 1.12). Therefore, the precomputation phase only is modified. In a mismatch situation (see Figure 1.6), where $u\tau$ is a prefix of the window, and $u\sigma$ a prefix of the pattern, the length of the produced shift is *interrupt_period(u)* in KMP algorithm, instead of *period(u)* in MP algorithm.

---

while window on text **do**
begin
    $u :=$ longest common prefix of window and pattern;
    if $u =$ pattern **then** report a match;
    shift window $interrupt\_period(u)$ places to the right;
    memorize $strict\_border(u)$;
end;

Fig. 1.12.   Scheme of KMP algorithm

The quantity is a period of u which, in addition, is not incompatible with the mismatch symbol τ of the text. It satisfies

$$period(u) \leq interrupt\_period(u) \leq period(u\tau).$$

The later inequality implies the correctness of the search phase of KMP algorithm.

We explain the modification brought by KMP algorithm. Let u be the word $x[1 : i - 1]$, and assume that

$$period(x[1 : i - 1]) = period(x[1 : i]) = p.$$

Then, since by definition of MP_next, the distance between i and $MP\_next[i]$ is the period p, the same symbol σ occurs at positions i and $MP\_next[i]$ in the pattern. So, a mismatch at position i in x with a symbol of the text recurs at position $MP\_next[i]$. This means that instruction "$i := MP\_next[i]$" in MP algorithm is not optimized. The solution proposed by KMP algorithm is to consider the smallest *interrupted period* of u, that is, the smallest period of u which is not a period of $x[1 : i] = u\sigma$ (see Figure 1.13). Note that this may not be defined (in which case we give it value $|u| + 1$), and that the notion is related only to proper prefixes of x. We additionally define for the pattern itself $interrupt\_period(x)$ as $period(x)$. Interrupted periods correspond to the dual notion of *strict borders*. When $u\sigma$ is a prefix of x, a strict border of u is any border v of u not followed by σ (i.e. such that $v\sigma$ is not a prefix of u). We denote by $strict\_border(u)$ the longest strict border of u. And, for the pattern x itself, we define $strict\_border(x)$ as $border(x)$. Note that $strict\_border$ is not defined for all prefixes of x, simply because a given prefix can have no strict border at all.

KMP search algorithm works as MP algorithm. The only difference is that it uses the table KMP_next instead of MP_next. The precomputation of KMP_next is given in Figure 1.14. The algorithm relies on the following observation. Let $k = MP\_next[i]$ for some position i in x. Then:

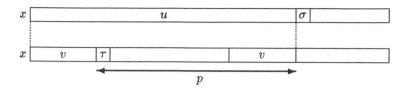

Fig. 1.13. Interrupted period p of u, and strict border v of u ($\sigma \neq \tau$)

---

procedure COMPUTE_KMP_NEXT(x: *string*; m: *integer*);
begin
 $KMP\_next[1] := 0; j := 0$;
 for $i := 1$ **to** m **do begin**
  { at this point, we have $j = MP\_next[i]$ }
  while $j > 0$ **and** $x[i] \neq x[j]$ **do** $j := KMP\_next[j]$;
  $j := j + 1$;
  if $i = m$ **or** $x[i+1] \neq x[j]$ **then** $KMP\_next[i+1] := j$
  else $KMP\_next[i+1] := KMP\_next[j]$;
 end;
end;

Fig. 1.14. Computation of table KMP_next

$$KMP\_next[i] = \begin{cases} k, & \text{if } x[i] \neq x[k] \text{ or if } i = m, \\ KMP\_next[k], & \text{if } x[i] = x[k]. \end{cases}$$

This recursively defines KMP_next, though the algorithm implements it with an iterative computation. The algorithm is very similar to the pre-computation of MP_next. An additional test in the main loop serves to eventually find the current value of $KMP\_next[i]$.

For MP and KMP search algorithms we can define a notion of *delay*. This is related to the time that elapses between the reading of two consecutive symbols of the text. Since the time is proportional to the number of comparisons done on a symbol of the text (internal while loop of MP algorithm), we define the delay as the maximum number of symbol comparisons made at a given position in the text. In the case of MP and KMP algorithms, considering how the algorithms work, the delay is also one unit more (except when an occurrence of the pattern is found) than the maximum length of border sequences used by the algorithms (ordinary borders, or strict borders, respectively). The delay for MP algorithm is simple to evaluate. It is less than m, and, indeed, this bound is tight. It is reached, for instance, when searching for σ^m inside $(\sigma^{m-1}\tau)^k$ (σ and τ different symbols, $n = k.m$). On occurrences of symbol τ of the text, MP algorithm makes exactly m comparisons, one on each symbol of the pattern. And the number of borders of σ^{m-1} is exactly $m-1$. The delay of KMP algorithm is logarithmic in the size of the pattern (Theorem 1.4 below). Before proving the result, we first state an intermediate property of strict borders.

Lemma 1.3. *Let w be a prefix of pattern x. Assuming that both words are defined, let $u = strict\_border(w)$ and $v = strict\_border(u)$. Then, we have $|w| > |u| + |v| + 1$.*

Proof Since u and v are proper prefixes of x, we can consider the symbols $\sigma = x[|u| + 1]$ and $\tau = x[|v| + 1]$. By definition of v, we have $\sigma \neq \tau$. Since u and v are borders of w, $p = |w| - |u|$ and $q = |w| - |v|$ are both periods of w. Assume that $|w| \leq |u| + |v| + 1$ holds. It implies $p + q - 1 \leq |w|$. The periodicity lemma then shows that $q - p$ is also a period of w. But this is obviously false because the above occurrences of different symbols σ and τ are precisely at distance $q - p$. The conclusion follows.   □

Theorem 1.4. *The delay of KMP string searching algorithm is bounded by $\log_\Phi(|x| + 1)$, where Φ is the golden ratio, $(1 + \sqrt{5})/2$.*

Proof Let $k > 0$ be the delay of KMP algorithm when searching for pattern x. The quantity k is the length of the longest sequence associated to a prefix w of x:

$$(w, \; strict\_border(w), \; strict\_border^2(w), \ldots, \; strict\_border^{k-1}(w))$$

assuming that $strict\_border^k(w)$ is undefined. Note that we can consider that w is shorter than x, because the number of symbol comparisons related to an occurrence of x in t is the same as the number of symbol comparisons related to a mismatch just after an occurrence of $border(x)$, which is a proper prefix of x.

    We prove, by induction on k, that if the sequence associated to w has length k, then $|w| \geq F_{k+2} - 2$ (recall that F_k is the k-th Fibonacci number: $F_0 = 0$, $F_1 = 1$, and $F_k = F_{k-1} + F_{k-2}$, for $k > 1$).

    The inequality obviously holds for $k = 1$ because $F_3 - 2 = 0$. It holds for $k = 2$ because both $F_4 - 2 = 1$ and the equality is reached for w of length 1. Assume that $k \geq 3$. Then, $u = strict\_border(w)$ and $v = strict\_border(u)$ exist. The induction hypothesis applies to both of them. This gives $|u| \geq F_{k+1} - 2$ and $|v| \geq F_k - 2$, respectively. The above lemma then gives

$$|w| \geq |u| + |v| + 2 \geq F_{k+1} - 2 + F_k - 2 + 2 = F_{k+2} - 2.$$

Which ends the induction.

    Applying then a classic inequality on Fibonacci numbers ($F_k \geq \Phi^{k-2}$) we get $|w| \geq \Phi^k - 2$. Thus, $m + 1 \geq \Phi^k$, or, equivalently $k \leq \log_\Phi(m + 1)$. □

while window on text **do**
begin
    $u :=$ longest common prefix of window and pattern;
    if $u =$ pattern **then** report a match;
    let τ be the symbol following u in text;
    shift window $period(u\tau)$ places to the right;
    memorize $tagged\_border(u, \tau)$;
end;

Fig. 1.15.   Scheme of MPS algorithm

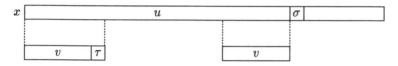

Fig. 1.16.   String v is a border of prefix u tagged by τ $(\sigma \neq \tau)$

As an example of words for which the maximum delay of KMP algorithm is reached, we consider the prefix of length $F_{k+2} - 1$ of the $(k + 2)$-th Fibonacci word. (Fibonacci words are defined by induction: $f_1 = b$, $f_2 = a$, and $f_k = f_{k-1}f_{k-2}$, for $k > 1$.) Let us denote the prefix by w_{k+2}. For instance, we have $w_8 = abaababaabaababaabab$. If during the search for w_{k+2} a mismatch occurs on the rightmost symbol of it with a symbol in the text not occurring in w_{k+2}, then the delay at that step is exactly k, the maximum possible. On the example w_8, if a mismatch occurs on the rightmost occurrence of b with a symbol σ distinct from both a and b, then KMP algorithm compares σ with the following occurrences of underlined letters of w_8: _aba_aba_baaba_aba_babaaba_b_, making exactly 6 comparisons before reading the next letter of the text.

MPS algorithm   MPS algorithm can be considered as a further refinement of MP algorithm. Here, the general scheme with the left-to-right scan applies the most accurately as possible: in a mismatch situation (see Figure 1.6), where $u\tau$ is the shortest prefix of the window that is not prefix of the pattern, MPS algorithm makes a shift of length $period(u\tau)$. The clue to avoid quadratic space, is to consider only non trivial periods of all the $u\tau$'s, and to precompute them before the search phase starts. Trivial periods of $u\tau$'s are those that satisfy $period(u\tau) = |u\tau|$. Equivalently, the period of $u\tau$ is not trivial if there is a border v of u followed by symbol τ (in the sense that $v\tau$ is a prefix of u). The border v is then said to be a border *tagged* by symbol τ (see Figure 1.16), and the longest such border is

```
text      ......a b a a b a c.........
              a b a a b a a
                  a b a a b a a
                      a b a a b a a
                      a b a a b a a
     (i) MP search. 4 comparisons on symbol c.


text      ......a b a a b a c.........
              a b a a b a a
                      a b a a b a a
                      a b a a b a a
     (ii) KMP search. 3 comparisons on symbol c.


text      ......a b a a b a c.........
              a b a a b a a
                      a b a a b a a
     (iii) MPS search. 2 comparisons on symbol c.
```

Fig. 1.17. Behaviors of MP, KMP and MPS

denoted by $tagged\_border(u, \tau)$. By the duality between periods and borders, we have then $period(u\tau) = |u| - |v|$. Note that $tagged\_border(u, \tau)$ is not always defined; moreover, for our purpose it is useless to define it when $u\tau$ is a prefix of x. Regarding Lemma 1.5, it is defined for at most m pairs (u, τ) (u prefix of pattern x, $\tau \in \Sigma$), while the number of possible pairs is $(m + 1)|\Sigma|$. Figure 1.15 describes the scheme of MPS algorithm. Figure 1.17 illustrates different behaviors of the three algorithms MP, KMP, and MPS in a mismatch situation.

Lemma 1.5. *The maximum number of tagged borders of all prefixes of x is $|x|$.*

Proof We show that there is a one-to-one correspondence between tagged borders and periods of prefixes of x. Let $v = tagged\_border(u, \tau)$, and $w = tagged\_border(r, \sigma)$, for u, r prefixes of x, and τ, σ two symbols. By assumption, neither $u\tau$ nor $r\sigma$ are prefixes of x. But, by definition of tagged borders, $v\tau$ and $w\sigma$ are prefixes of x.

Assume that $period(u\tau) = period(r\sigma) = p$. Then, v and w have occurrences that start at the same position $p + 1$ in x. Thus, one of them is a prefix of the other. But, since neither $u\tau$ nor $r\sigma$ are prefixes of x, this can happen only if $v = w$. Therefore, different tagged borders correspond to different periods of x. Thus, since periods p are integers running from 1 to m, there are at most m distinct tagged borders for all prefixes of x.

procedure MPS(x, t: *string*; m, n: *integer*);
begin
    $i := 0$; $j := 1$;
    while $j \leq n$ **do begin**
        $q := head[i]$;
        repeat
            $i := list\_element[q]$; $q := q + 1$;
        until $i = 0$ **or** $x[i] = t[j]$;
        if $i = m$ **then** writeln('x occurs in t at position ', $j - m + 1$);
        $j := j + 1$;
    end;
end;

Fig. 1.18.   MPS algorithm – search phase

Words of the form $\sigma \tau \sigma^{m-2}$ reach the upper bound.   □

It is clear that MPS algorithm is correct, as MP and KMP algorithms are. It also seems obvious that MPS search is faster than MP and KMP searches. But this somehow depends on what representation of non trivial periods (for the $u\tau$'s) is chosen. Preprocessing time and extra space required by MPS algorithm both relies on Lemma 1.5.

MPS algorithm may be regarded as a particularly efficient method to implement the string-matching automaton $\mathcal{A}(x)$. The method is unfortunately strongly dependent on the specific features of the automaton $\mathcal{A}(x)$, so that it cannot be generalized easily to other kinds of automata. Tagged borders, or equivalently non-trivial periods, correspond in the automaton to *backward arcs* not arriving on the initial state. Lemma 1.5 equivalently says that there are at most m such arcs in the automaton $\mathcal{A}(x)$. For example, there are five backward edges in the automaton of Figure 1.3, namely, the edges $(1, a, 1), (3, a, 1), (5, a, 1), (6, a, 1), (5, n, 4)$.

MPS algorithm can be implemented as follows. To each position i on the pattern x is attached the list of tagged borders of $x[1 : i - 1]$. This list contains the positions in x defined as follows: if v is a border of $x[1 : i-1]$ tagged by symbol τ (hence, $\tau \neq x[i]$), then $|v| + 1$ is in the list. There is no need to put symbol τ itself in the list because, by definition of tagged borders, $\tau = x[|v| + 1]$. In the implementation used in Figures 1.18 and 1.19 lists are stored in an array called *list_element*. Each list is stored in a segment of the array. The starting position is given by the array *head*. The list associated with position i starts with position $i + 1$ (when $i < m$) and ends with 0. Doing so, the computation of transitions is realized by comparisons of symbols, in the same model of computation as MP and KMP algorithms. In some sense, lists considered by MPS algorithm in

```
procedure COMPUTE_MPS_LISTS(x: string; m: integer);
{ head is an array of size m + 1, list_element is an array of size 3m + 1 }
begin
    head[0] := 0; list_element[0] := 1; list_element[1] := 0;
    i := 0; p := 1;
    for j := 1 to m do begin
        { computation of transitions from state j }
        { i is the length of the border of x[1 : j] }
        head[j] := p + 1;
        if j < m then begin
            p := p + 1; list_element[p] := j + 1;
        end;
        q := head[i]; i := 0;
        repeat
            k := list_element[q]; q := q + 1;
            if k ≠ 0 and j < m and x[k] = x[j + 1] then i := k
            else begin
                p := p + 1; list_element[p] := k;
            end;
        until k = 0;
    end;
end;
```

Fig. 1.19.   MPS algorithm – preprocessing phase

the "forward prefix scan" strategy are the shortest possible. In particular, they are generally shorter than lists implicitly managed by MP and KMP algorithms.

The implementation of lists of positions considered here additionally satisfies the property: each list is in decreasing order of its positions. It is then rather obvious to note that comparisons executed at search phase are also comparisons executed by KMP and MP searching algorithms. We then get the same worst-case time and space complexities as these algorithms. The improvement is on the delay, which is obviously not greater than the size of pattern alphabet. Furthermore, it can be proved that the delay is not greater than $1 + \log_2 m$, which improves on the delay of KMP (and MP) algorithm. The preprocessing of lists of tagged borders is an easy exercise. Since MPS implements the automaton $\mathcal{A}(x)$, the preprocessing phase can be adapted from the construction of it (Figure 1.5). It is presented in Figure 1.19. We sum up remarks on MPS algorithm in the following theorem.

Theorem 1.6. *MPS algorithm runs in time $O(|x| + |t|)$. The searching algorithm makes less than $2|t| - 1$ symbol comparisons. The delay of the search is at most $min(1 + \log_2 |x|, |\Sigma|)$. In the comparison $(= / \neq)$ model, this bound is optimal for sequential searching algorithm.*

When the size of the alphabet Σ is 2, each list considered by MPS algorithm has size at most 3 (because all lists end with 0). The time between readings of two consecutive text symbols is thus bounded by a constant (the delay is bounded by 2). The search for x in t becomes a *real-time* search. Indeed, under the same assumption, KMP searching algorithm is also a real-time algorithm (this is not true for MP algorithm). On larger alphabets of given size, the real-time property still holds for MPS search algorithm but no longer holds for KMP algorithm. However, there is a general method to transform the three searching algorithms MP, KMP, and MPS into real-time algorithms (see bibliographic notes).

1.2.3   FORWARD SUBWORD SCAN

The algorithms MP and KMP of Section 1.2.2 make use of a general method to implement automata with a small amount of memory space. In the present section we first describe more generally what are failure functions. Then, we describe another efficient application of the method to string-matching. It is based on an automaton representing all subwords of the pattern as opposed to the string-matching automaton.

Failure functions   Tables *MP_next* and *KMP_next* of the previous section are particular implementations of what is known as *failure functions*. This kind of functions is generally used to reduce the memory space required to store transition functions of automata.

Consider a deterministic automaton $\mathcal{A} = (Q, \Sigma, initial, T, \delta)$ with the notation of Section 1.2.1. A failure function may avoid the use of a trivial matrix representation of δ in $O(|Q||\Sigma|)$ space. In the case of the string-matching automaton $\mathcal{A}(x)$, the function *MP_next*, for instance, serves to reduce the space to $O(m)$ (instead of $O(m|\Sigma|)$), quantity which does not depend on the size of the alphabet. The price of this advantage is a slower computation of transitions of the automaton, which is reported by the delay of algorithms. The next table summarizes the tradeoff between space and time. Search time is everywhere proportional to the length of the text, independently of the size of the alphabet. The main difference between the various implementations of the string-matching automaton lies in the delay or the branching time they realize. Preprocessing time is used to compute the information stored in the extra space (transition matrix, or failure function).

Note that at the second line of the table the required space is quadratic while preprocessing time is linear. This corresponds to an implementation

---

function transition(q: *state*; σ: *symbol*): *state*;
begin
    while $\zeta(q,\sigma)$ undefined **and** $s(q)$ defined **do** $q := s(q)$;
    if $\zeta(q,\sigma)$ defined **then** **return**($\zeta(q,\sigma)$)
    else **return**(*initial*);
end;

Fig. 1.20.   Computing a transition with a failure function

of the transition matrix of the automaton $\mathcal{A}(x)$ for which only transitions not going to the initial state are effectively computed. This can be done with the general technique to represent sparse matrices without having to initialize them.

	Extra space	Preproces-sing time	Search time	Branching time
computation of addresses				
Matrix	$O(|\Sigma||x|)$	$O(|\Sigma||x|)$	$O(|t|)$	$O(1)$
Sparse matrix	$O(|\Sigma||x|)$	$O(|x|)$	$O(|t|)$	$O(1)$
comparison model of computation				
MP	$O(|x|)$	$O(|x|)$	$O(|t|)$	$O(|x|)$
KMP	$O(|x|)$	$O(|x|)$	$O(|t|)$	$O(\log_\Phi |x|)$
MPS	$O(|x|)$	$O(|x|)$	$O(|t|)$	$O(\min(\log_2 |x|, |\Sigma|))$

Failure functions can be defined more generally as follows. We say that a pair (ζ, s) represents the transition δ of the automaton $\mathcal{A}$ if:

- ζ is a sub-transition of δ,
- s is a partial function from Q to Q,
- $\delta(q,\sigma) = \delta(s(q),\sigma)$, whenever $\zeta(q,\sigma)$ is not defined but $\delta(q,\sigma)$ and $s(q)$ are.

The function s is the failure function of the representation. Each state $s(q)$ is a stand-in of state q. State $s(q)$ helps to compute transitions on q that are not directly defined on it.

Computing a transition in $\mathcal{A}$ with a representation (ζ, s) for δ may be done by the function in Figure 1.20. For a particular failure function we have to insure that the algorithm stops. This often comes from the fact that failure functions induce a tree structure on the set of states. Each application of the failure link s gives a state closer to the root of the tree. The structure of the algorithm in Figure 1.20 is similar to that of MP algorithm. The representation of $\mathcal{A}(x)$ implicitly used by MP algorithm is given by the failure function *border*. The sub-transition associated with this failure function defines the straightforward automaton recognizing the prefixes of pattern x.

while window on text **do**
begin
    $u :=$ longest prefix of window, subword of pattern;
    if $u =$ pattern **then** report a match;
    $v :=$ longest suffix of u, occurring in a different right context
        inside the pattern;
    shift window $|u| - |v|$ places to the right;
    memorize v;
end;

Fig. 1.21.   Scheme of FS algorithm

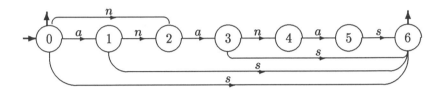

Fig. 1.22.   The suffix automaton of word *ananas*

Common subwords The main idea in the "Forward Subword" (FS) algorithm is that during the scan operation of the searching algorithm we can search for the longest prefix of the window that is a subword of the pattern, and not only a prefix of it. During such a scan, more information on prefixes of the window are collected at a time, and this finally leads to a natural sequential string searching algorithm. The time between two readings of consecutive text symbols is $O(\Sigma)$, which makes the search real-time on fixed alphabets. The scheme of FS algorithm is given in Figure 1.21.

An efficient implementation of the FS scheme relies on the compact representation of suffixes of the pattern, called the suffix automaton of the pattern. The scheme can also be implemented with suffix trees, or analogue data structures.

We first describe the suffix automaton features required to implement the FS string searching algorithm. Let $\mathcal{S}(x) = (Q, \Sigma, i, T, \delta)$ be the minimal deterministic automaton recognizing all suffixes of pattern x. The transition function δ is partially defined, in the sense that there is no sink state in the automaton. An example of such automaton is shown in Figure 1.22. A natural failure function that we call s, is defined on states of $\mathcal{S}(x)$. It is, in fact, an important notion to design an efficient algorithm that builds $\mathcal{S}(x)$. We explain how the failure function is defined. Let u be a non-empty subword of x, and let $q = \delta(i, u)$. Let v be the longest proper suffix of u

procedure FS(x, t: *string*; m, n: *integer*);
begin
    $l := 0$; $q := initial$;
    for $j := 1$ **to** n **do begin**
        if $\delta(q, t[j])$ defined **then begin**
            $l := l + 1$; $q := \delta(q, t[j])$;
        end else begin
            while $\delta(q, t[j])$ undefined **and** $r(q)$ defined **do** $q := r(q)$;
            if $\delta(q, t[j])$ defined **then begin**
                $l := Length(q) + 1$; $q := \delta(q, t[j])$;
            end else begin
                $l := 0$; $q := initial$;
            end
        end;
        if $l = m$ **then** writeln('x occurs in t at position ', $j - m + 1$);
    end;
end;

Fig. 1.23. Forward subword string searching algorithm

such that $\delta(i, v) \neq q$. Then we define $s(q)$ precisely as state $p = \delta(i, v)$. It can be shown that the definition is correct, which means that $s(q)$ does not depend on the choice of the word u such that $q = \delta(i, u)$. Note that $s(q)$ is defined on all states of $\mathcal{S}(x)$ except on the initial state (which corresponds to the word $u = \lambda$).

In the above definition of function s, it can be proved that the word v is the longest word for which $p = \delta(i, v)$. This property is crucial, and FS algorithm partially relies on it. We denote by $Length(p)$ the length of the longest word w such that $p = \delta(i, w)$. Function $Length$ is used in the implementation of FS scheme to detect occurrences of the pattern in the searched text. Contrary to the algorithm based on string-matching automata, this detection cannot be done by terminal states only. This is realized by a simultaneous computation of the length of the current subword of x found in t. Function $Length$ is precisely used to reset properly the current length after following a failure link.

Lemma 1.7. *Let u be any word such that $q = \delta(i, u)$ in the suffix automaton $\mathcal{S}(x)$. Let v be the longest suffix of u such that $\delta(i, v) \neq q$. Then, v is the longest word w such that $\delta(i, w) = s(q)$, or equivalently $|v| = Length(\delta(i, v))$.*

We define the sequence of lengths, $\{l_k / 0 \leq k \leq n\}$, related to the pattern x and the text t by

$$l_k = \max\{|u|/u \text{ subword of } x \text{ and } u \text{ suffix of } t[1:k]\}.$$

In other words, l_k is the maximum length of subwords of x ending at position k in t. Thus, whenever $l_k = m$, the word x itself occurs at position $k - m + 1$ in the text t.

The basis of FS string searching algorithm is a sequential computation of lengths l_k. This is realized with the automaton $\mathcal{S}(x)$, together with its failure function s and its function $Length$, both defined on the set of states.

Indeed, instead of the failure function s, we rather use another failure function r that optimizes the delay of the search. Its definition is based on output transitions of states. The follow set of a state q of $\mathcal{S}(x)$ is

$$FOLLOW(q) = \{\sigma \in \Sigma / \delta(q, \sigma) \text{ is defined}\}.$$

Then, $r(q)$ is defined as follows:

$$r(q) = \left\{ \begin{array}{ll} s(q), & \text{if } FOLLOW(s(q)) \not\subseteq FOLLOW(q), \\ r(s(q)), & \text{otherwise.} \end{array} \right.$$

The definition of r parallels the definition of KMP_next introduced after the notion of strict borders. Note that $r(q)$ can be left undefined with this definition.

There is also a second remark that simplifies the computation of r. In the suffix automaton we always have $FOLLOW(q) \subseteq FOLLOW(s(q))$. The inclusion holds because $s(q)$ corresponds to a suffix v of some word u for which $q = \delta(i, u)$. Then, any symbol following u in x also follows v, and the property transfers to follow sets of q and $s(q)$ respectively. With this remark, the definition of the failure function r can be equivalently stated as:

$$r(q) = \left\{ \begin{array}{ll} s(q), & \text{if } |FOLLOW(s(q))| \neq |FOLLOW(q)|, \\ r(s(q)), & \text{otherwise.} \end{array} \right.$$

Thus, computation of r has only to consider outdegrees of states of the automaton $\mathcal{S}(x)$.

FS algorithm is given in Figure 1.23. The core of FS algorithm is the computation of transitions with the failure table r, similarly as in the general method described in Figure 1.20. The structure of FS algorithm is analogue to that of KMP algorithm (or MP algorithm). Transitions in FS algorithm replace symbol comparisons made in KMP algorithm. Search time is linear for a fixed alphabet. Otherwise it depends on the branching time in the automaton $\mathcal{S}(x)$. It is $\log \Sigma$ if we want to achieve linear size for $\mathcal{S}(x)$. The same argument applies for the construction of $\mathcal{S}(x)$: it is linear for fixed alphabets.

Theorem 1.8. *FS string searching algorithm executes less than $2|t|$ tests* *on transitions in the automaton $\mathcal{S}(x)$. It requires $O(|x|)$ extra space.*

The proof of the first point is similar to the evaluation of the time complexity of MP algorithm. The space complexity heavily depends on a remarkable property of suffix automata: the size of $\mathcal{S}(x)$ is $O(m)$. Moreover, this is independent of the alphabet size.

Optimization from s to r in FS algorithm is similar to the improvement of KMP on MP. The improvement is on the delay between two consecutive readings on the text. The delay is proportional to the number of failure links traversed during a continuous series of failures. The property of follow sets mentioned above shows that the delay is $O(|\Sigma|)$, where Σ can be restricted to the alphabet of the pattern. Thus, on a fixed alphabet, the procedure FS finds all occurrences of x inside t in real-time.

Lemma 1.9. *The delay of FS string searching algorithm is bounded by the size of the pattern alphabet.*

Proof This is a consequence of the fact already mentioned: $FOLLOW(q)$ is strictly included in $FOLLOW(r(q))$.　　　　　　　　□

A straightforward adaptation of FS algorithm provides a linear time algorithm to compute the maximum length $LCF(x,t)$ of a common subword of x and t, or to compute the *subword distance* between two strings:

$$d(x,t) = |x| + |t| - 2.LCF(x,t).$$

1.3　Practically fast searches

In this section, we describe string searching algorithms that are considered as the fastest in practice. The algorithms apply when text and pattern both reside in main memory. We thus do not take into account the time to read them. Under this assumption, some algorithms have a sublinear behavior. The common feature of these algorithms is that they scan the window in the reverse direction, from right to left.

1.3.1　REVERSE-SUFFIX SCAN

BM algorithm The classical string searching algorithm that scans the window in reverse direction is BM algorithm. At a given position in the text, the algorithm first identifies the longest common suffix u of the window and the pattern. A match is reported if it equals the pattern. After that, the algorithm shifts the window to the right. Shifts are done in such a way that the occurrence of u in the text remains aligned with an equal subword of the pattern, and are often called *match shifts*. The length of the shift is determined by what is called the *displacement* of u inside x, and denoted by $d(u)$. The scheme of BM algorithm is displayed in Figure 1.24. Function d depends only on the pattern x so that it can be precomputed

while window on text **do**
begin
    u := longest common suffix of window and pattern;
    if u = pattern **then** report a match;
    shift window $d(u)$ places to the right;
end;

Fig. 1.24.   Scheme of BM algorithm

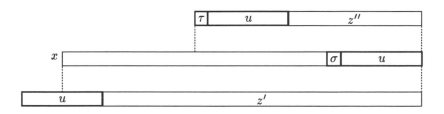

Fig. 1.25.   Two possible z's in the definition of $d(u)$ $(\sigma \neq \tau)$

before the search starts. In BM algorithm a heuristics on mismatch symbols of the text is also usually used. This yields another displacement function used in conjunction with d. It is presented in Section 1.5, as a general method that may improve almost all algorithms in certain practical situations.

We now precisely define the displacement function of suffixes of x. For the pattern x, suffix of itself, $d(x) = period(x)$. Consider now a proper suffix u of x. Let σ the symbol preceding suffix u in x (σu is also a suffix of x). In a mismatch situation (see Figure 1.26), what is wanted is an occurrence of a subword τu in x to align with the text. Symbol τ must be different from σ to avoid another immediate mismatch. If τu is a subword of x, its rightmost occurrence is used to define $d(u)$ (see Figure 1.25). If τu is not a subword of x, the displacement associated with u is defined with the longest prefix of x that is also a suffix of u. In the latter case, $d(u)$ is a period of the whole pattern x. It even is the smallest period p of x such that $p + |u| \geq m$. This remark is used in the algorithm that computes d. The formal definition of $d(u)$, for a suffix u of x, is:

$$d(u) = \min\{|z| > 0/(x \text{ suffix of } uz) \text{ or } (\tau uz \text{ suffix of } x$$
$$\text{and } \tau u \text{ not suffix of } x, \text{ for } \tau \in \Sigma)\}.$$

Note that, if z is the suffix of x of length $d(u)$, $d(u)$ is a period of the word uz, simply because u is a border of this string.

In BM search algorithm a precomputed table D is used to represent function d. It is defined by

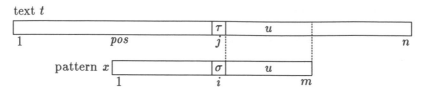

Fig. 1.26.   Variables *pos* and *i* in BM algorithm $(j = pos + i - 1)$

---

procedure BM(x, t: *string*; m, n: *integer*);
begin
    $pos := 1$;
    while $pos \leq n - m + 1$ **do begin**
        $i := m$;
        while $i > 0$ **and** $x[i] = t[pos + i - 1]$ **do** $i := i - 1$;
        if $i = 0$ **then** writeln('x occurs in t at position ', *pos*);
        $pos := pos + D[i]$;
    end;
end;

Fig. 1.27.   Memoryless BM algorithm

$$D[i] = d(x[i + 1 : m]), \text{ for } i = 0, .., m.$$

BM search algorithm is shown in Figure 1.27. Figure 1.26 illustrates the meaning of variables *pos* and *i* used in the algorithm. The algorithm is memoryless in the sense that, after a shift, it starts scanning the window from scratch. No information about previous matches is kept in memory.

The precomputation of table D is given in Figure 1.28. It is certainly the most delicate point in the design of BM algorithm. Historically, it took some time before its first correct computation appeared. The computation uses the notion of borders already considered in MP algorithm. It is composed of two steps. The first step of the algorithm is devoted to the computation of borders of pattern suffixes. The table R_next, computed during the first step, is the exact analogue of the table MP_next adjusted to the reverse pattern. Implementation of this part is a straightforward adaptation of the algorithm COMPUTE-MP-NEXT of Section 1.2.2. During the first step (first "for" loop in Figure 1.28), the table D is partially computed. Values $D[i]$ are related to strict borders, and correspond to the second part in the definition of d (u suffix of x):

$$\min\{|z| / \tau u z \text{ suffix of } x \text{ and } \tau u \text{ not suffix of } x, \text{ for } \tau \in \Sigma\}.$$

---

procedure COMPUTE_D(x: *string*; m: *integer*);
begin
    { R_next is the reverse version of MP_next table }
    $R\_next[m] := m + 1$; $j := m + 1$;
    for $i := m$ **downto** 1 **do begin**
        { at this point, we have $j = R\_next[i]$ }
        while $j \leq m$ **and** $x[i] \neq x[j]$ **do begin**
            if $D[j]$ undefined **then** $D[j] := j - i$;
            $j := R\_next[j]$;
        end;
        $j := j - 1$; $R\_next[i - 1] := j$;
    end;
    { values of p run through all periods of x, in increasing order }
    $p := R\_next[0]$;
    for $j := 0$ **to** m **do begin**
        if $D[j]$ undefined **then** $D[j] := p$;
        if $j = p$ **then** $p := R\_next[p]$;
    end;
end;

Fig. 1.28. Linear computation of the displacement table D

The second step of the algorithm (second "for" loop in Figure 1.28), computes those $D[i]$'s that are left undefined after the first step. Computed values correspond to the first part of the definition of d (u suffix of x):

$$\min\{|z| > 0/x \text{ suffix of } uz\}.$$

The values of z's are periods of the whole pattern, and table R_next is used to run through all these periods.

The order of steps, as well as the order in which j's are considered in the last step, are important to eventually get the correct values. The time linearity of the algorithm COMPUTE_D is essentially a consequence of the linearity of algorithm COMPUTE_MP_NEXT.

When algorithm BM is applied to find all occurrences of a^m inside a^n, the search time becomes O(mn). The reason for the quadratic behavior is that no memory is used at all. It is however very surprising that BM algorithm turns out to be linear when search is limited to the first occurrence of the pattern. By the way, the original algorithm has been designed for that purpose. Only very periodic patterns may increase the search time to a quadratic quantity, as shown by the next theorem. The bound it gives is the best possible. So, only a modified version of BM algorithm can make less than $2n$ symbol comparisons at search time.

Theorem 1.10. *Assume that pattern x satisfies $period(x) > |x|/2$. Then, BM searching algorithm performs at most $3|t| - |t|/|x|$ symbol comparisons.*

The theorem also suggests that only little information about configurations encountered during the process has to be kept in memory in order to get a linear time search for any kind of patterns. This is achieved, for instance, if prefix memorization is performed each time an occurrence of the pattern is found. But this is also achieved with a better bound by the algorithm of the next section called TURBO_BM. This modification of BM algorithm forgets all the history of the search, except the most recent one. Analysis becomes simpler, and the maximum number of comparisons at search phase becomes less than $2n$.

Turbo_BM algorithm The main feature of TURBO_BM algorithm is that it memorizes the last match (only when a match shift is applied). The technique, storing the last matched subword, is an extension of the prefix memorization used to improve on the worst-case behavior of BM algorithm (see bibliographic notes). This has two advantages: first, this allows to skip a part of the text during the next scan; second, it is used to increase the length of the next shift. Both features are important to get the final time complexity of the algorithm.

TURBO_BM algorithm performs two kinds of shifts: the match shifts of BM algorithm, and, what we call *turbo-shifts*. A third kind of shift, based on mismatch symbols, can be added to TURBO_BM, in the same way as it can be added to the original BM algorithm. This is described in Section 1.5. Turbo-shifts are defined by a simple rule that needs no extra preprocessing of the pattern. So, TURBO_BM algorithm has exactly the same preprocessing phase as BM algorithm.

We now precisely explain what is a turbo-shift. Consider the situation at the end of a scan operation containing no skip, and following immediately a match shift. In such a situation the last scanned suffix of x that matches the text is memorized, and the shift is applied. Pattern x can be decomposed into $ywvu$, where w, the memory, matches the text at the new position of the window, and u, the current match, is the longest common suffix of the window and the pattern (Figure 1.29). Assume furthermore that u is shorter than w. Then, the length of the turbo-shift is defined as $|w| - |u|$.

The validity of turbo-shifts can be analyzed as follows. Let v be written $v_0\sigma$ for $\sigma \in \Sigma$ (note that v is non-empty). Since both u is shorter than w and w is a suffix of x, σu is a suffix of w. Thus, $\sigma u v_0 \sigma u$ is a suffix of x. It is aligned with a subword of the text of the form $\sigma u v_1 \tau u$, where $\sigma \neq \tau$ and $|v_0| = |v_1|$. Occurrences of different symbols σ and τ in the text show that subwords containing the two occurrences do not have period $|vu|$. But, by definition of the shift in BM algorithm, as already mentioned, $d(w) = |vu|$

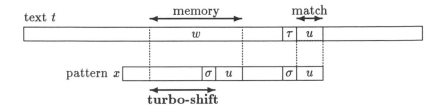

Fig. 1.29.   Turbo-shift defined from the two previous matches w and u

---

procedure TURBO_BM(x, t: *string; m, n: integer*);
begin
    $pos := 1; memory := 0; shift := m$;
    while $pos \leq n - m + 1$ **do begin**
        $i := m$;
        while $i > 0$ **and** $x[i] = t[pos + i - 1]$ **do begin**
            $i := i - 1$; **if** $i = m - shift$ **then** $i := i - memory$;
        end;
        if $i = 0$ **then** writeln('x occurs in t at position ', pos);
        $match := m - i$; $turbo\_shift := memory - match$;
        $shift := \max(D[i], turbo\_shift)$;
        if $shift < D[i]$ **then**
            $memory := \min(m - shift, match)$;
        else begin
            $shift := \max(shift, match + 1)$; $memory := 0$;
        end;
        $pos := pos + shift$;
    end;
end;

Fig. 1.30.   Reverse-suffix string-matching with memory

is a period of wvu. So, no occurrence of wvu can include the occurrences of σ and τ in the text. This shows that the turbo-shift, of length $|w| - |u|$ is safe: it cannot miss an occurrence of x in t.

A somewhat similar argument shows that turbo-shifts can be made greater than the length of the current match u. Indeed, the same rule also applies if occurrence shifts are considered by the algorithm (see Section 1.5).

In TURBO_BM algorithm (see Figure 1.30) we use the notation:

$$memory = |w|, \quad match = |u|.$$

The meaning of the variables is explained in Figure 1.29.

Theorem 1.11. *The algorithm* TURBO_BM *(search phase) is linear. It makes less than* $2|t|$ *symbol comparisons.*

Proof We decompose the search into stages. Each stage is itself divided into the two operations: scan and shift. At stage k we call Suf_k the suffix of the pattern that matches the text and suf_k its length. It is preceded by a letter that does not match the aligned letter in the text (in the case Suf_k is not x itself). We also call $shift_k$ the length of the shift done at stage k. Consider three types of stages according to the nature of the scan, and of the shift:

(i) stage followed by a stage with jump,
(ii) no type (i) stage with long shift,
(iii) no type (i) stage with short shift.

We say that the shift at stage k is short if $2shift_k < suf_k + 1$. The idea of the proof is to amortize comparisons with shifts. We define $cost_k$ as follows:

— if stage k is of type (i), $cost_k = 1$,
— if stage k is of type (ii) or (iii), $cost_k = suf_k + 1$.

In the case of a type (i) stage, the cost corresponds to the mismatch comparison. Other comparisons made during the same stage are reported to the cost of next stage. So, the total number of comparisons executed by the algorithm is the sum of costs. We want to prove (Σ all costs) $<$ $2 \cdot (\Sigma$ all shifts). In the second sum, the length of the last shift is replaced by m. Even with this assumption, we have (Σ all shifts) $\leq n$, and, if the above inequality holds, we get the result (Σ all costs) $< 2n$.

For stage k of type (i), $cost_k$ is trivially less than $2shift_k$, because $shift_k > 0$. For stage k of type (ii), $cost_k = suf_k + 1 \leq 2shift_k$, by definition of long shifts. We still have to consider stages of type (iii). Since in this situation, we have $shift_k < suf_k$, the only possibility is that a BM_shift is applied at stage k. This leads to a potential turbo-shift at stage $k + 1$. The situation at stage $k + 1$ is the general situation when a turbo-shift is possible (see Figures 1.31 and 1.32).

We first consider two cases and establish inequalities (on the cost of stage k) that are used later.

Case (a) $suf_k + shift_k > m$ By definition of the turbo-shift, we have $suf_{k+1} + shift_k + shift_{k+1} \geq m$. Then,

$$cost_k \leq m \leq 2shift_k - 1 + shift_{k+1}.$$

Case (b) $suf_k + shift_k \leq m$ By definition of the turbo-shift, we have $suf_k - suf_{k+1} \leq shift_{k+1}$. Thus,

$$cost_k = suf_k + 1 \leq suf_k + 1 + shift_{k+1} + 1 \leq shift_k + shift_{k+1}.$$

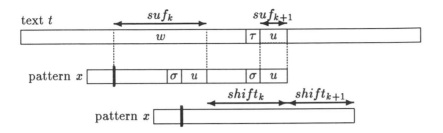

Fig. 1.31. Cost amortized by turbo-shift: Case (a)

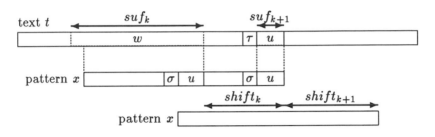

Fig. 1.32. Cost amortized by turbo-shift: Case (b)

We can consider that at stage $k + 1$ case (a) occurs, because this gives the higher bound on $cost_k$ (this is true if $shift_k \geq 2$; the case $shift_k = 1$ can be treated directly).

If stage $k+1$ is of type (i), then $cost_{k+1} = 1$, and then $cost_k + cost_{k+1} \leq 2shift_k + shift_{k+1}$, an even better bound than expected.

If $suf_{k+1} \leq shift_{k+1}$ (which includes the case where stage $k + 1$ is of type (ii)), we get what expected, $cost_k + cost_{k+1} \leq 2shift_k + 2shift_{k+1}$.

The last situation to consider is when with $suf_{k+1} > shift_{k+1}$, which implies that stage $k+1$ is of type (iii). This means, as previously mentioned, that a BM_shift is applied at stage $k + 1$. Thus, the above analysis also applies at stage $k + 1$, and, since only case (b) can occur then, we get $cost_{k+1} \leq shift_{k+1} + shift_{k+2}$. We finally get

$$cost_k + cost_{k+1} \leq 2shift_k + 2shift_{k+1} + shift_{k+2}.$$

The last argument proves the first step of an induction: if all stages k to $k + j$ are of type (iii) with $suf_k > shift_k, \ldots, suf_{k+j} > shift_{k+j}$, then

$$cost_k + \cdots + cost_{k+j} \leq 2shift_k + \cdots + 2shift_{k+j} + shift_{k+j+1}.$$

Let k' be the first stage after stage k (including k) such that $suf_{k'} \leq shift_{k'}$. Integer k' exists because the contrary would produce an infinite

> **while** window on text **do**
> **begin**
> u := longest suffix of window that is prefix of pattern;
>   **if** u = pattern **then** report a match;
>   shift window $|pattern| - |u|$ places to the right;
>   memorize u;
> **end**;

Fig. 1.33.   Scheme of RP algorithm

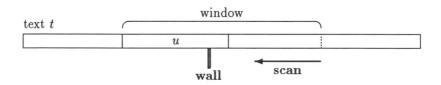

Fig. 1.34.   Scan for a prefix of the pattern is limited by *wall* inside the last prefix found u

sequence of shifts with decreasing lengths. We then get

$$cost_k + \cdots + cost_{k'} \le 2shift_k + \cdots + 2shift_{k'},$$

which shows that $\Sigma cost_k \le 2\Sigma shift_k$, as expected, and ends the proof of the theorem.   □

1.3.2 REVERSE-PREFIX SCAN

The algorithm described in the present section, called RP algorithm, is the analogue counterpart of FS algorithm (Section 1.2.3). The idea of the algorithm is to search for a prefix of the pattern by scanning the right part of the window in the reverse direction. This approach leads to an average-optimal string searching algorithm on fixed alphabets (within logarithmic factor otherwise): the expected time of the search phase is $O(n \log m/m)$.

As FS algorithm, RP algorithm uses the same data structure. The search phase is based on a fast computation of the longest suffix u of the window that is prefix of the pattern. The rule for the shift just amounts to align the pattern with the prefix of the pattern found in the text. This prefix is kept in memory to save on further work. This prefix memorization avoids a quadratic running time, but does not significantly affect the expected time complexity. The scheme of RP is given in Figure 1.33.

Memorization of prefix u at search phase, serves to limit the next scan of the window. During the next scan, it is as if we put a *wall* in the window, at distance $|u| - period(u)$ from the left end (see Figure 1.34). No scan is done to the left of the wall. With the use of more sophisticated data structures, it is even possible to avoid scanning twice the prefix u itself, but we do not describe this variant here. So, only the part of the window on the left of the wall (of size $|u| - period(u)$) is not scanned again. And just the occurrence in the text of the suffix of u of length $period(u)$ can be scanned twice. The time complexity of RP algorithm is thus easy to analyze. But this somehow also depends on the implementation technique used to search for prefixes of the pattern.

In order to rapidly find the longest suffix of the window which is prefix of the pattern, the suffix automaton data structure is used. In fact, we consider the automaton recognizing deterministically all prefixes of x read from right to left. It is the suffix automaton for the reversed pattern. The data structure contains information that can be used to compute lengths of shifts.

The version of RP algorithm presented in Figure 1.35 conceptually uses two elements in addition to the suffix automaton: periods of prefixes of the pattern, and the displacement function dis of subwords of the pattern. Periods of prefixes are stored in a table called *Period* and defined by $Period[i] = period(x[1:i])$, for $0 < i \leq m$, and by $Period[0] = 0$. The algorithms of Section 1.2.2 show that the precomputation of *Period* takes linear time. It is however possible to compute periods dynamically during the search. The displacement function, dis, is similar to the one considered for BM algorithm. It is defined only for subwords of pattern x. Let v be a subword of x. Then,

$$dis(v) = \min\{|z|/vz \text{ suffix of } x\}.$$

Function dis is not implemented separately from the data structures used by the algorithm. Its values are computed on the fly during the search thanks to information precomputed during the first phase, and contained in the suffix automaton.

The RP algorithm works as follows. It scans the window from right to left until either the current suffix goes out of subwords of x, or the wall stops the process. In the former case, the last prefix of x encountered while scanning the window determines the shift of the window. In the latter case, if the scanned suffix of the window is also a suffix of the pattern, an occurrence of the pattern is found in the text, and it is reported. In any case, the shift is computed with the help of the function dis. In the latter situation, we have to know what is the longest prefix of x found in the window without scanning the window at the left of the wall. The next lemma gives a property used for that purpose, i.e. to compute the prefix

```
procedure RP(x, t: string; m, n: integer);
begin
    pos := 1; wall := 0;
    while pos ≤ n − m + 1 do begin
        i := m;
        while i > wall and t[pos + i − 1 : pos + m − 1] subword of x do
            i := i − 1;
        if i = wall and dis(t[pos + i : pos + m − 1]) = 0 then
            writeln('x occurs in t at position ', pos);
        if i = wall then
            shift := max(dis(t[pos + i : pos + m − 1]), Period[m])
        else begin
            u := longest prefix of x that is also
                suffix of t[pos + i : pos + m − 1];
            shift := m − |u|;
        end;
        pos := pos + shift; wall := m − shift − Period[m − shift];
    end;
end;
```

Fig. 1.35.   Reverse-prefix string searching algorithm

of x, and thus the length of the shift. The correctness of RP algorithm readily comes after the lemma.

Lemma 1.12. (Key lemma) *Let $w = u_1 u_2 v$ with the following conditions: $|w| = |x|$, $u_1 u_2$ is a prefix of x, $u_2 v$ is a subword of x, and $|u_2| \geq period(u_1 u_2)$. Let u be the longest prefix of x that is suffix of w. Then $|u| = |x| − dis(u_2 v)$, or otherwise stated, $dis(u) = dis(u_2 v)$.*

Proof Since $u_2 v$ is a subword of x, x can be written $u_3 u_2 v v'$ with $|v'| = dis(u_2 v)$. A length argument shows that u_3 is not longer than u_1. Since words $u_1 u_2$ and $u_3 u_2$ coincide on a common suffix u_2 of length not smaller than their period, one of them is a suffix of the other. Which implies that u_3 is a suffix of u_1. Thus, the prefix $u_3 u_2 v$ of x is a suffix of w. The maximality of its length is straightforward from hypothesis, and then $u = u_3 u_2 v$. The conclusion follows: $|u| = |x| − dis(u_2 v)$, or, equivalently, $dis(u) = dis(u_2 v)$. □

Theorem 1.13. *RP searching algorithm makes at most $2|t|$ inspections of text symbols.*

Proof If u is the longest prefix of x, suffix of the window, then at most $period(u)$ symbols of u are scanned again. This is amortized by the next shift that has a length not smaller than *period(u)* (because the shift is compatible with the occurrence of *u* in the text). Therefore, the total number of all these extra inspections is not greater than the sum of lengths of all shifts, bounded by *n*. Globally, we get the 2*n* bound. □

We analyze the average running time of RP algorithm in the situation where the text is random. The probability that a specified symbol occurs at any position in the text is $1/|\Sigma|$. And this does not depend on the context of the symbol.

Theorem 1.14. *Let $c = |\Sigma| > 1$. Under independent equiprobability condition, the expected number of inspections made by RP search algorithm is $O(|t| \log_c |x|/|x|)$.*

Proof We first count the expected number of symbol inspections necessary to shift the window (of size *m* on the text) *m*/2 places to the right. We show that $O(\log_c m)$ inspections, on the average, are sufficient to achieve that goal. Since there are 2*n*/*m* segments of text of length *m*/2, we get the expected time $O(n \log_c m/m)$.

Let $r = 3\lfloor \log_c m \rfloor$. There are more than m^3 possible values for the word $t[pos + m - r - 1 : pos + m - 1]$. But, the number of subwords of length $r + 1$ ending in the right half of the pattern is at most *m*/2 (provided *m* is large enough). The probability that $t[pos+m-r-1 : pos+m-1]$ matches a subword of the pattern, ending in its right half, is then $1/(2m^2)$. This is also the probability that the corresponding shift has length less than *m*/2. In this case, we bound the number of inspections by *m*(*m*/2) (worst behavior of the algorithm making shifts of length 1). In the other case, the number of inspections is bounded by $3 \log_c m$.

The expected number of inspections that lead to a shift of length at least *m*/2 is thus less than

$$3 \log_c m (1 - \frac{1}{2m^2}) + m(m/2)\frac{1}{2m^2} \ ,$$

which is $O(\log_c m)$. This achieves the proof. □

1.4 Space-economical methods

This section is devoted to the presentation of a *time-space optimal* string-matching algorithm, which provides a proof of Theorem 1.1. The main interest in the *two-way algorithm* (TW algorithm) presented in this section is theoretical. The additional requirement is on the memory space used by string searching algorithms. Previous sections present several algorithms running in time linear in the size of the input words *x* and *t*. They all require extra memory space to store precomputed information about the pattern. Except for the algorithm using the SMA automaton, extra space

---

compute a critical factorization (x_l, x_r) of pattern x;
while window on text **do**
begin
  $u :=$ longest common prefix of both x_r and
    the right part of the window aligned with it;
  if $u = x_r$ **then begin**
    if x_l prefix of the window **then** report a match;
    shift window $period(x)$ places to the right;
  end else
    shift window $|u| + 1$ places to the right;
end;

Fig. 1.36. Scheme of TW search algorithm

is proportional to the size of the pattern. It is shown in this section that the extra space can be reduced to a constant amount of memory without increasing the asymptotic time complexity of the overall algorithm. This yields a time-space optimal string searching algorithm. Several proofs of the result exist, based on different algorithmic methods. The present algorithm has the further advantage of having an efficient search phase: the number of symbol comparisons it makes is less than the "canonical" $2n$ bound. Preprocessing phase assumes an ordering on the alphabet of the pattern. This ordering seems to have nothing to do with the string searching problem, but its consideration strongly helps both to prove the combinatorial property used by the algorithm, and to preprocess the pattern.

We first describe the search phase of TW algorithm, and then show how the pattern is preprocessed. The overall is realized in linear time with only constant extra memory space.

1.4.1 CONSTANT-SPACE SEARCHING ALGORITHM

The preprocessing phase of TW algorithm partly consists in computing a factorization $x_l x_r$ of the pattern x having a specific property described hereafter. The search for x divides into both the search for x_r first, and then the search for x_l. The search for x_r is simple, due to the property of the decomposition. The search for x_l is only done when x_r is found at the current position in the text, and leads to shifts of length $period(x)$, due also to the property of the decomposition. The scheme of TW searching algorithm is displayed in Figure 1.36.

Before describing deeper the TW search phase, we first explain what decomposition $x_l x_r$ of the pattern x is considered. Let (y, z) be a factorization of x (i.e. $yz = x$). A *repetition at* (y, z) is a non-empty word w such that both conditions hold:

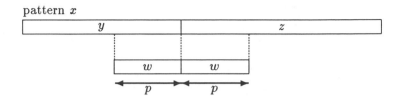

Fig. 1.37. Repetition w and local period p at the factorization (y, z); it is a critical factorization if $p = period(x)$

(i) w is a suffix of y or conversely y is a suffix of w,
(ii) w is a prefix of z or conversely z is a prefix of w.

The case where w is both a suffix of y and a prefix of z is displayed in Figure 1.37. The repetition w thus occurs on both sides of the cut between y and z in x, with possible overflow on left and right ends of x. The length of a repetition at (y, z) is called a *local period* at (y, z), and the length of the shortest repetition, denoted by $r(y, z)$, is called *the local period* at (y, z).

Every factorization (y, z) has at least one repetition, namely zy. This shows that we have the inequalities $1 \leq r(y, z) \leq m$. Indeed, one may easily verify that

$$1 \leq r(y, z) \leq period(x).$$

A factorization (y, z) of x such that $r(y, z) = period(x)$ is called a *critical factorization* of x. For instance, the word $x = abaabaa$ has period 3. It has three critical factorizations: $(ab, aabaa)$, $(abaa, baa)$, and $(abaab, aa)$. In other words, if (y, z) is a critical factorization of x, the local period at (y, z) coincides with the global period of x. The TW algorithm considers only critical factorizations that additionally satisfy $|y| < period(x)$. The existence of such a factorization is known as the critical factorization theorem whose proof is given below, in the presentation of the preprocessing phase of TW algorithm.

Let $x_l x_r$ be a critical factorization of x computed by the preprocessing phase of TW algorithm ($|x_l| < period(x)$). The main step of the scan operation during the search for $x = x_l x_r$ in t consists in testing whether x_r is a suffix of the window. The window is scanned from left to right starting at the appropriate position. If a mismatch occurs, the length of the shift that follows is exactly equal to the number of symbol comparisons done at this step (Figure 1.38). If an occurrence of x_r is found in t at the current position, in a second step the algorithm checks whether x_l is a prefix of the window. The following shift slides the window $period(x)$ places to the right (Figure 1.39). Any strategy for scanning the second part of the window is possible. It is usually done from right to left, in the reverse order of the other scan. This is why the algorithm is called *two-way*.

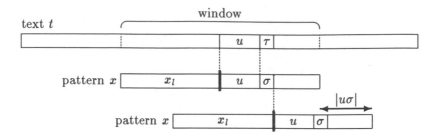

Fig. 1.38.   Shift after a mismatch on the right ($\sigma \neq \tau$)

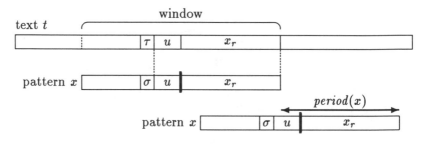

Fig. 1.39.   Shift after a mismatch on the left ($\sigma \neq \tau$)

The detailed implementation of the two-way scheme is given in Figure 1.40. A straightforward implementation of the TW scheme leads to a quadratic algorithm for highly periodic patterns (as for BM algorithm). Quadratic running time is avoided by the *prefix memorization* technique. In case a shift of length $period(x)$ is applied, we keep in memory the prefix of the pattern that matches the text (after the shift is done). This avoids scanning it twice during the next scan. This memorization is necessary to achieve a linear search. Variable *memory* in the TW search algorithm exactly stores the length of the memorized prefix of x. Globally, the TW algorithm obviously requires only a few registers in addition to the pattern and the text. Among them are: the period of the pattern, and the length of x_l, the left part of a critical factorization of the pattern.

The correctness of procedure TW in Figure 1.40 relies on several properties of critical factorizations that are summarized below.

Lemma 1.15. *Let (y, z) be any critical factorization of the non-empty string x.*

(a) If uy is a prefix of x, $period(x)$ divides $|u|$.

(b) If w is a prefix of z, v is a suffix of w, and wv is a suffix of yw (in this situation w overlaps the cutpoint of the factorization), $period(x)$

procedure TW(x, t: *string*; m, n: *integer*);
{ $p = period(x)$, and $\ell = |x_l|$ where $x_l x_r$ is a critical factorization of x
   that satisfies the condition $\ell < p$ }
begin
   $pos := 1$; $memory := 0$;
   while $pos \leq n - m + 1$ **do begin**
      $i := \max(\ell, memory) + 1$;
      while $i \leq m$ **and** $x[i] = t[pos + i - 1]$ **do** $i := i + 1$;
      if $i = m + 1$ **then begin**
         $j := \ell$;
         while $j > memory$ **and** $x[j] = t[pos + j - 1]$ **do** $j := j - 1$;
         if $j \leq memory$ **then** writeln('x occurs in t at position ', pos);
         $pos := pos + p$; $memory := m - p$;
      end else begin
         $pos := pos + i - \ell$; $memory := 0$;
      end;
   end;
end;

Fig. 1.40. Constant extra space string searching algorithm

divides $|v|$.

The time complexity of TW search algorithm of Figure 1.40 is linear in the length of the text. Indeed, the number of symbol comparisons made during the search is less then $2n$.

Lemma 1.16. *The maximum number of symbol comparisons made during a run of TW search algorithm is less than $2|t|$.*

Proof One can prove that comparisons made during the first main step of the scan (between window and x_r) strictly increase the value of $pos + i$. Since values of the expression form an increasing sequence of integers from $|x_l| + 1$ to n in the worst case, less than n comparisons are made during all these steps.

    When comparisons are made at the second step of the scan (between window and x_l), x is afterward shifted $period(x)$ places to the right. Since, by assumption, the length of x_l is less than $period(x)$, comparisons made during all these steps are made on different occurrences of symbols of t. Then at most n comparisons are made during all second steps of the scan. This proves the result.   □

1.4.2 COMPUTING A CRITICAL FACTORIZATION

The Critical Factorization Theorem, stated below, is a consequence of Theorem 1.18 that additionally provides a simple algorithm for computing critical factorizations. This latter theorem uses an ordering on the alphabet, and reduces the computation to the determination of two lexicographically maximum suffixes of the pattern.

Theorem 1.17. (Critical Factorization Theorem) *Every non-empty string x has at a critical factorization (y, z) that satisfies $|y| < period(x)$.*

Each ordering $\leq$ on the alphabet Σ extends to a lexicographic ordering (also noted $\leq$) on the set of strings Σ^*. It is defined as usual by $u \leq v$ if either u is a prefix of v or $u = f\sigma g$, $v = f\tau h$ with σ, τ two symbols such that $\sigma < \tau$. Let $\leq$ be a lexicographic ordering on Σ^*. We denote by $\widetilde{\leq}$ the lexicographic ordering obtained by reversing the ordering $\leq$ on Σ.

The main remark about orderings $\leq$ and $\widetilde{\leq}$ is that their intersection is the prefix ordering. In other words, if $u \leq v$ and $u \widetilde{\leq} v$ simultaneously hold, then u is a prefix of v. This property is used in the proof of the next theorem.

Theorem 1.18. *Let x be a non-empty string. Let z (resp. z') be the maximum suffix of x according to the ordering $\leq$ (resp. $\widetilde{\leq}$). Let y and y' be such that $x = yz = y'z'$. Then, if $|y| \geq |y'|$, (y, z) is a critical factorization of x. Otherwise (y', z') is a critical factorization of x.*

In addition, we have $|y|, |y'| < period(x)$.

Proof We assume that $|y| \geq |y'|$, and prove that (y, z) is a critical factorization of x. The other case is symmetric.

First note that if x is of the form σ^m, then any factorization, and (y, z) in particular, is critical (in this case we have $y = y' = \lambda$ and $z = z' = x$). So, we can consider that x contains at least two occurrences of different symbols. The choice of z and z' then leads to $z \neq z'$, and thus, $|y| > |y'|$.

Let w be a the shortest repetition at (y, z) (w is a non-empty word). We have to prove that $|w|$, which is the local period $r(y, z)$, is equal to the period of x. Note that, since $|w| \leq period(x)$, we only have to prove that $|w|$ is *any* period of x (this implies that it is then the smallest period). We distinguish four cases according to the definition of repetitions.

Case (a) w is a suffix of y, and z is a prefix of w.

String w can be written zh ($h \in \Sigma^*$). Since w is suffix of y, $wz = zhz$ is a suffix of $yz = x$. But then, the suffix wz of x is obviously greater than z, which contradicts the definition of z. This case is impossible.

Case (b) w is a suffix of y, and w is a prefix of z.

String z can be written wh ($h \in \Sigma^*$). Both strings wh and wwh are suffixes of x. By the definition of $z = wh$, we have $wwh < wh$, which implies $wh < h$. But, since h is also a suffix of x we get a contradiction with the definition of z. This case is impossible.

```
function MAXIMUM_SUFFIX(x: string; m: integer): position;
begin
    i := 0; j := 1; k := 1; p := 1;
    while j + k ≤ m do begin
        σ := x[i + k]; τ := x[j + k];
        if σ < τ then begin
            i := j; j := j + 1; k := 1; p := 1;
        end else if σ = τ then begin
            if k ≠ p then k := k + 1 else begin j := j + p; k := 1; end
        end else begin {σ > τ}
            j := j + k; k := 1; p := j - i;
        end;
    end;
    return(i); {x[i + 1 : m] is the maximum suffix of x}
end;
```

Fig. 1.41. Localization of maximum suffixes

Case (c) y is a suffix of w, and z is a prefix of w.

In this situation, x is a subword of ww. So, $|w|$ is a period of x, and, by the remark above, this shows that (y, z) is a critical factorization of x.
Case (d) y is a suffix of w, and w is a prefix of z.

The suffix z can be written wh ($h \in \Sigma^\star$). We may assume that h is non-empty, because the situation $h = \lambda$ is dealt with by Case (c). We prove that $|w|$ is a period of x by showing that h is a border of z. Since we assume $|y| > |y'|$, for some non-empty string s, $y = y's$ and $z' = sz$. String sh is a suffix of x because s is a suffix of w. By definition of $z' = sz$, we have $sh \widetilde{<} sz$, which implies $h \widetilde{<} z$. But, we have also $h < z$ by definition of z. The two inequalities altogether imply that h is a prefix of z. Therefore, h is a border of z, and w is a period of z. It is also a period of $x = yz$ because y is a suffix of w. This proves that in this situation again (y, z) is a critical factorization of x.

Cases (a) to (d) show that (y, z) is a critical factorization of x, under the hypothesis $|y| \geq |y'|$. In addition, we have $|y| < period(x)$, because both $|w| = period(x)$ and cases (a) and (b) are impossible. The same property holds symmetrically for y'. □

The critical factorization (y, z) provided by Theorem 1.18 is such that the length of y is less than the period of x, condition that is desired for TW searching algorithm. As an example, the theorem gives the factorization $(ab, aabaa)$ for the word $x = abaabaa$. A consequence of the theorem is that the computation of a critical factorization reduces to the localization of lexicographically maximum suffixes of the pattern. Several algorithms

---

procedure COMPLETE_TW(x, t: *string*; m, n: *integer*);
begin
    let (x_l, x_r) be a critical factorization of x
        computed with the help of function MAXIMUM_SUFFIX;
    $p := period(x_r)$ {final value of p in MAXIMUM_SUFFIX};
    if $(|x_l| \leq m/2$ **and** x_l suffix of $x_r[1 : p])$ **then**
        {p is $period(x)$}
        search t for x with TW algorithm
    else
        { $period(x) > \max(|x_l|, |x_r|)$ }
        search t for x with modified TW algorithm: no memory,
        and p replaced by $\max(|x_l|, |x_r|) + 1$;
end;

Fig. 1.42.   Complete time-space optimal string searching algorithm

exist to solve this problem. But the algorithm presented in Figure 1.41 uses only constant extra memory space as required in the present section. When the input is the non-empty string x, which decomposes into yz with maximum suffix z, the function returns $|y|$. The algorithm obviously uses only a fixed number of registers (in addition to x), and it runs in linear time.

The correctness of the function MAXIMUM_SUFFIX is out of the scope of this chapter. It is related to the Lyndon factorization of strings. However, its linearity can be proved by showing that each symbol comparison (of the kind less-equal-greater) strictly increases the value of expression $i + j + k$. And its values form an increasing sequence of integers running from 2 to $2m$ at most. The maximum number of symbol comparisons is thus less than $2m$.

1.4.3 COMPUTING THE PERIOD OF THE PATTERN

The computation of the period $period(x)$ of pattern x is straightforward with the table *Border* of Section 1.2.2. The overall gives a linear time computation of $period(x)$, but requires linear extra space though. There is a time-space optimal algorithm to compute $period(x)$ that can be used to complete the preprocessing phase of TW algorithm. However, we describe here a simpler solution that still gives an overall time-space optimal string searching algorithm, but does not always computes $period(x)$ in all situations.

The complete TW algorithm (Figure 1.42) distinguishes two cases according to whether the period of the pattern is small or not. The algorithm relies on several properties easy to check and that fit perfectly when considered altogether in the scope of TW algorithm.

The complete TW algorithm computes the period of the pattern when it is small, which is the important situation to consider when designing a linear-time algorithm. The first step of the algorithm is to compute a critical factorization (x_l, x_r) of x. It is done, according to Theorem 1.18, by two calls to the function MAXIMUM_SUFFIX (respectively with orderings $\leq$ and $\tilde{\leq}$). It must be noted that the final value of variable p in MAXIMUM_SUFFIX is the period of the maximum suffix of the pattern. This value is an approximation of $period(x)$. A simple test (third instruction in Figure 1.42) is used to decide if $p = period(x)$ (note that if the test fails it is still possible that $p = period(x)$). If so, all precomputed information are present to search for x in t with the TW algorithm of Figure 1.40.

If the test fails, by Lemma 1.19 below, $period(x) > \max(|x_l|, |x_r|)$. The search is then done in this case with the so-modified TW searching algorithm:

no prefix memorization is done, and shifts of length $period(x)$ are replaced by shifts of length $\max(|x_l|, |x_r|) + 1$.

Since the latter quantity is not greater than $period(x)$, the correctness of the modified TW searching algorithm follows from the correctness of the original TW algorithm. A further nice feature of the modified TW searching algorithm is that it runs in linear time. Moreover, the number of symbol comparisons that it makes is less than $2n$. This strongly depends on the value $\max(|x_l|, |x_r|) + 1$, which replaces $period(x)$ for the shifts. The algorithm would also be correct with a value smaller than $\max(|x_l|, |x_r|) + 1$, but this would lead to a slower string searching algorithm.

Lemma 1.19. *Let (x_l, x_r) be a critical factorization of x that satisfies $|x_l| < period(x)$, and let p be the period of x_r. If x_l is not a suffix of $x_r[1 : p]$ then there is no occurrence of x_l in x other than its prefix occurrence, and $period(x) \geq \max(|x_l|, |x_r|) + 1 > |x|/2$.*

Proof Any occurrence of x_l in x that is not a suffix of $x_r[1 : p]$ yields a local period at (x_l, x_r) not greater than $|x_l|$. This contradicts the fact (x_l, x_r) is a critical factorization satisfying $|x_l| < period(x)$. □

All elements discussed in the present section proves Theorem 1.1. The more precise result concerning the complete two-way string searching algorithm is stated in the next theorem. Finally note the time complexity is independent of the alphabet.

Theorem 1.20. *The complete TW string searching algorithm runs in time $O(|x| + |t|)$ with a constant amount of extra memory space. Less than $2|t|$ symbol comparisons are made during the search phase.*

1.5   Heuristics for practical implementations

We discuss in this section a technique commonly used to improve several algorithms of this chapter. The improvement mainly deals with the practical aspect of string searching. It can be considered just as a useful implementation technique, although a few combinatorial properties may depend on it. There are situations (for small alphabets, for example) in which adding it to existing algorithms is almost of no use.

The technique is sometimes called the *occurrence heuristics*. It consists in considering a displacement function (or table) defined on symbols of the alphabet. The function is used in mismatch situations to increase lengths of shifts. Doing so, one changes the model of computation that is no longer based only on symbol comparison as elementary operation. It can even happen that no comparison at all is done in some runs of searching algorithms.

If the alphabet is binary the occurrence heuristics is likely to yield short shifts. It becomes useful, but difficult to analyze, for large alphabets or when the probability distribution is no longer uniform. This is typically the situation in natural languages.

BM algorithm has been first designed with an additional displacement table defined on the alphabet. We call it DA, and for a symbol σ of the alphabet, $DA[\sigma]$ is the position of the rightmost occurrence of σ counted from the right end of the pattern.

More precisely

$$DA[\sigma] = \min(\{|z| > 0 / \sigma z \text{ suffix of } x\} \cup \{m\}).$$

To incorporate table DA in BM algorithm, instruction

$pos := pos + D[i]$

in Figure 1.27 is replaced by

if $i = 0$ **then** $pos := pos + D[i]$
else $pos := pos + \max(D[i], DA[t[pos + i - 1]] - m + i)$.

In BM algorithm, it is the mismatch symbol $t[pos + i - 1]$ of the text that partly guides the shift. But the same table DA can also be used differently, considering $t[pos + m - 1]]$ the rightmost symbol of the window. Indeed, even symbol $t[pos + m]]$ immediately at the right of the window is sometimes considered, because, after the shift, the symbol is inside the window. Such applications of a displacement table on the alphabet can be combined, not only with BM algorithm and its variants, but also with MP, KMP, or MPS algorithms, for instance. It is clear then that the sequential behavior of these latter algorithms drops.

There is also no problem to incorporate table DA in Turbo_BM algorithm. Instruction

$$shift := \max(D[i], turbo\_shift)$$

is just replaced by

$$shift := \max(D[i], DA[t[pos + i - 1]] - m + i, turbo\_shift).$$

The proof of correctness is analogue to that of the original TURBO_BM algorithm, because the same arguments still apply. The worst-case time complexity is unchanged.

In TW algorithm, another displacement table, called DB, can be considered. Let (x_l, x_r) be the critical factorization of pattern x precomputed before the search phase. Then, for a symbol σ of the alphabet, we define

$$DB[\sigma] = \min(\{|z|/\sigma z \text{ suffix of } x_l\} \cup \{|x_l|\}).$$

This is the restriction of table DA to the prefix x_l of x. In TW algorithm (Figure 1.40), where ℓ stands for the length of x_l, instruction

$$pos := pos + i - \ell$$

is changed into

$$pos := pos + i - \ell + DB[t[pos + i - 1]]).$$

This does not affect the correctness nor the maximum time complexity of the algorithm.

Whenever an occurrence heuristics function is added to a string searching algorithm, the time complexity of the preprocessing phase then depends on the alphabet, or at least on pattern alphabet, and typically becomes $O(m + |\Sigma|)$. The extra space for such table also depends on the alphabet.

There are rather few results concerning the analysis of string searching algorithms with occurrence heuristics. However, this has been done, considering different probability distributions of the alphabet, for a searching algorithm called H algorithm. It can be considered as a simplified version of BM algorithm, in which shifts are computed only with the occurrence heuristics applied to the rightmost symbol of the window. The next result gives the expected number of symbol comparisons done during the search. This is to be compared with the expected time, $O(n \log m/m)$, of RP searching algorithm in Section 1.3.2. It shows that the expected searching time is bounded by a quantity independent of the size of the pattern.

Let $C(m, n)$ be the average number (over all patterns of length m) of symbol comparisons done by H search algorithm on a random text of length n.

Theorem 1.21. *Under independent equiprobability distribution on the alphabet of size c, the limit $C(m) = \lim_{n \to \infty} \left(\frac{1}{n} C(m, n) \right)$ exists and satisfies (for $m > c \geq 2$):*

$$\frac{c + 1}{c^2} \leq C(m) \leq \frac{2c - 1}{c(c - 1)}.$$

The limit $C(m)$ is the average number of symbol comparisons per text character done by H search algorithm.

1.6   Exercises

1. In automaton $\mathcal{A}(x)$ almost all transitions go to the initial state. Implement the transition function of the automaton without considering the above trivial transitions with the technique to implement sparse matrices. Show that your algorithms (preprocessing and searching phases) work in linear time.

2. Design an efficient algorithm that builds the minimal automaton recognizing the language $\Sigma^* x \Sigma^*$.

3. The exponent of a non-empty string w, denoted by $exponent(w)$, is the quantity $|w|/period(w)$. Show that $exponent(ww) = 2$ iff w is a primitive word. Design an algorithm to compute the exponents of all non-empty prefixes of x.

4. Give a linear-time algorithm to compute the longest suffix of x which is prefix of y.

5. Show that the algorithm COMPUTE_KMP_NEXT makes almost $3m$ symbol comparisons on the input string aba^{m-2}.
   Design an algorithm that computes the table KMP_next with less than $2m$ comparisons on any input string x of length m.

6. A square is a string of the form uu with $u \neq \lambda$. In a squarefree string, no subword is a square. Design a linear-time algorithm to test whether the product uv of two squarefree strings, u and v, is squarefree. [hint: if uv contains a square centered in v, v has a prefix of the form fgf where g is a non-empty suffix of v].
   Deduce an efficient algorithm to test squarefreeness of a string. (see Main and Lorentz, 1984.)

7. Show that any order for elements in lists considered by MPS algorithm leads to a linear-time search algorithm.
   Prove that the delay of MPS searching algorithm is not larger than $1 + \log_2 m$ (see bibliographic notes).

8. * Assume that x starts with $\sigma^k \tau$ (σ and τ different letters, $k > 0$). Consider the following variant of KMP search algorithm that uses the same failure table for x: search the text as in KMP algorithm but comparing only the symbols of the suffix $x[k + 1 : m]$ of x (from left to right); when an occurrence of the suffix is found in the text, check whether it is preceded by σ^k, and report a match if so.
   Note that symbols of the prefix σ^k of x are compared with symbols in the text only when an occurrence of $x[k + 1 : m]$ is found. Which means that, in some situations, parts of the text are skipped during the search.
   Design a complete string searching algorithm based on the above de-

scription. Show that the search makes less than $1.5n$ comparisons. Show that this quantity becomes $\frac{4}{3}n$ by considering interrupted periodicities. (see Colussi, 1991, or Galil and Giancarlo, 1992.)

9. Design BM algorithm with a variable j instead of $pos + i - 1$. Modify the table D and its preprocessing accordingly.

10. * Prove Theorem 1.10. (see Cole, 1990.)

11. ** Table D considered in BM algorithm can be improved by considering tagged suffixes of the pattern (similarly as tagged borders in MPS algorithm). In the comparison model, is there a computation of tagged suffixes that works in linear time independently of the alphabet size ?

12. ** Give a complete analysis of the expected running time of BM algorithm in a realistic probability model.

13. ** Consider a variant of BM algorithm in which all previous matches inside the current window are memorized. Each window configuration is a state of what is called the Boyer-Moore automaton. Is the maximum number of states of the automaton polynomial ? (see Knuth, Morris, and Pratt, 1977.)

14. What is the maximum number of symbol comparisons made by Turbo-BM algorithm ?

15. Design a variant of RP algorithm where symbols in the text are scanned only once.

16. * Show that there is a logarithmic number of squares of primitive words that are prefixes of a string.
    Produce infinitely many words that reach the upper bound.
    Design a time-space algorithm to test whether a string starts with a k-th power of a non-empty word ($k > 1$). (see Crochemore and Rytter, 1995.)

17. * Design a time-space optimal algorithm to compute all periods of a string. (see Crochemore, 1992.)

1.7   Bibliographic notes

Historically, the first linear-time string searching algorithm, MP algorithm, is by Morris and Pratt (1970). The improvement on MP algorithm, called KMP algorithm is by Knuth, Morris, and Pratt (1977). Theorem 1.4 on the delay of KMP algorithm comes from Duval (1981). Its original statement in (Knuth, Morris, and Pratt, 1977) contains a flaw. The variant of KMP algorithm, called MPS algorithm, is by Simon (1989). It has been published later (Simon, 1993), and the present version is by Hancart (1992) who proved Theorem 1.6. A variant of MPS algorithm makes no more $n(2 - 1/m)$ comparisons, which is an optimal bound (Hancart 1992). The prefix-matching problem, introduced by Breslauer, Colussi, and Toniolo (1992), independently leads to the same result.

Galil (1981) gave a criterion to transform sequential searching algorithm into real-time algorithm. This applies to MP, KMP and MPS algorithms. See also (Slisenko, 1983).

The general notion of failure function is implicit in the table-compression technique for representing automata in (Aho, Sethi and Ullman, 1986, Chapter 3). Perrin (1990) discusses questions related to such representations.

The linearity of the size of the suffix automaton has first been noticed by Blumer *et alii* (1983). The average size of the data structure is analyzed in (Blumer *et alii*, 1989). The linear construction may be found in (Blumer *et alii*, 1985) and (Crochemore, 1986). Algorithm "Forward Subword" is from (Crochemore, 1987). This shows that the longest common subword of two words can be computed in linear time (independently of the alphabet, if quadratic space is allowed) disproving a conjecture of Knuth.

BM algorithm has been designed by Boyer and Moore (1977). The first proof on the linearity of BM algorithm (restricted to the search of the first occurrence of the pattern, as it has been originally designed) is in (Knuth, Morris and Pratt, 1977). It is proved, there, that the number of symbol comparisons of BM algorithm is less than $7n$. Guibas and Odlyzko (1980) have shown that it is less than $4n$, and conjectured a $2n$ bound at the same time. But this was disproved by Cole (1990), who gave the "tight" $3n$ bound. The displacement table D is a modification introduced on the original displacement function by (Knuth, Morris and Pratt, 1977). But, the first correct algorithm for computing D is by Rytter (1980).

The quadratic behavior of BM algorithm (as presented in this chapter to locate all occurrences of the pattern) gave rise to several variants. "Prefix memorization" introduced in BM by Galil (1979) leads to a linear-time searching algorithm. See also (Zhu and Takaoka, 1987). With $O(m)$ extra space to store the whole history of the search, Apostolico and Giancarlo (1986) got a $2n$ bound on the number of symbol comparisons. TURBO_BM, from (Crochemore *et alii*, 1992), reaches the same bound with only constant space in addition to BM algorithm. The algorithm of Colussi (1994) has the same $2n$ bound with a modified displacement function. In this algorithm the scanning operation is driven by the periodicities of pattern suffixes, and is not strictly done from right to left as in BM algorithm.

"Reverse-Prefix" algorithm is from (Lecroq, 1992) and (Crochemore *et alii*, 1992). A similar algorithm has been presented by Park (1992). The article (Crochemore *et alii*, 1992) describes variants of the same approach.

The "time-space optimality" of string searching is by (Galil and Seiferas, 1983). Another analysis of their algorithm may be found in (Crochemore and Rytter, 1995), where it is proved that the search phase makes less than $5n$ comparisons. The two-way algorithm is from (Crochemore and Perrin, 1991). Two other time-space string searching algorithms are presented in (Crochemore, 1992) and (Gąsieniec, W. Plandowski, W. Rytter, 1995). The first one needs no preprocessing and uses an ordering of the alphabet. The second one is based on the fact that non periodic patterns have a long enough non periodic prefix or suffix and packs $\log m$ bits of information into an integer memory cell of the Random Access Machine model.

The general expected time complexity of string matching is given in (Yao, 1979). Horspool (1980) considers the simplified version of BM algorithm (called H algorithm in Section 1.5) including only a displacement function defined on symbols. Such variants of BM algorithm have been later studied and analyzed in several papers, among them are (Schaback, 1988), (Sunday, 1990), (Baeza-Yates, Gonnet, and Régnier, 1990), (Hume and Sunday, 1991). Theorem 1.21 is from (Hancart, 1993). More precise bounds may be found in (Baeza-Yates, Régnier, 1992).

It is shown in (Rivest, 1977) that any string searching algorithm working with symbol comparisons makes at least $n - m + 1$ comparisons in the worst case. The current lower bound is $n + \frac{2}{m+3}(n - m)$ (see Cole et alii, 1995). A simple variant of KMP searching algorithm can be shown to perform less than $1.5n$ symbol comparisons (Apostolico and Crochemore, 1991). Colussi, Galil and Giancarlo (1990) have presented an algorithm that makes less than $n + \frac{1}{3}(n - m)$ comparisons at search phase. This bound has been improved by Cole and Hariharan to $n + \frac{8}{3(m+1)}(n - m)$, but with a quadratic-time preprocessing step. A similar result has been independently discovered by Zwick and Paterson (see Cole et alii, 1995). With a linear-time preprocessing step, the current upper bound is $n + \frac{4\log m + 2}{m}(n - m)$ by Breslauer and Galil (1993).

The string searching problem can be solved by hashing. The main part of the work thus reduces to key comparisons, and symbol are eventually compared in case keys are equal. This has been introduced by Harrison (1971), and later fully analyzed by Karp and Rabin (1987).

The two algorithms of (Baeza-Yates and Gonnet, 1992) and (Wu and Manber, 1992) solve the string matching problem using shifts of memory words as basic operations. Their solutions lead to efficient practical algorithms to locate approximate patterns of small size.

The methods described in the present chapter extend to the search of a finite set of strings in a text. Aho and Corasick (1975) gave an extension of KMP algorithm, based on an adequate use of automata, which is implemented by the "fgrep" command under the UNIX operating system. Commentz-Walter (1979) has designed an extension of BM algorithm to several patterns. It is fully described in (Aho, 1990), and a variant may be found in (Baeza-Yates and Régnier, 1990). The extension of RP algorithm to multi-pattern matching is presented in (Crochemore et alii, 1992).

More algorithms on the string-matching problem may be found in (Crochemore and Rytter, 1994) and (Stephen, 1994).

Bibliography

AHO, A.V. , Algorithms for finding patterns in strings, in (VAN LEEUWEN, J., editor, *Handbook of Theoretical Computer Science*, vol A, *Algorithms and complexity*, Elsevier, Amsterdam, 1990) 255–300.

AHO, A.V., AND M. CORASICK, Efficient string matching: an aid to bibliographic search, *Comm. ACM* **18** (1975) 333–340.

AHO, A.V., R. SETHI, J.D. ULLMAN, *Compilers — Principles, Techniques and Tools*, Addison-Wesley, Reading, Mass., 1986.

APOSTOLICO, A., AND M. CROCHEMORE, Optimal canonization of all substrings of a string, *Information and Computation* **95**:1 (1991) 76–95.

APOSTOLICO, A., AND R. GIANCARLO, The Boyer-Moore-Galil string searching strategies revisited, *SIAM J. Comput.* **15** (1986) 98–105.

BAEZA-YATES, R.A., AND G.H. GONNET, A new approach to text searching, *Comm. ACM* **35**:10 (1992) 74–82.

BAEZA-YATES, R.A., G.H. GONNET, M. RÉGNIER, Analysis of Boyer-Moore type string searching algorithms, in (*Proc. of 1st ACM-SIAM Symposium on Discrete Algorithms*, American Mathematical Society, Providence, 1990) 328–343.

BAEZA-YATES, R.A., M. RÉGNIER, Fast algorithms for two-dimensional and multiple pattern matching, in (R. KARLSSON, J. GILBERT, editors, *Proc. 2nd Scandinavian Workshop in Algorithmic Theory*, Lecture Notes in Computer Science 447, Springer-Verlag, Berlin, 1990) 332–347.

BAEZA-YATES, R.A., AND M. RÉGNIER, Average running time of the Boyer-Moore-Horspool algorithm, *Theoret. Comput. Sci.* **92** (1992) 19–31.

BLUMER, A., J. BLUMER, A. EHRENFEUCHT, D. HAUSSLER, R. MC-CONNELL, Linear size finite automata for the set of all subwords of a word: an outline of results, *Bull. Europ. Assoc. Theoret. Comput. Sci.* **21** (1983) 12–20.

BLUMER, A., J. BLUMER, A. EHRENFEUCHT, D. HAUSSLER, M.T. CHEN, J. SEIFERAS, The smallest automaton recognizing the subwords of a text, *Theoret. Comput. Sci.* **40** (1985) 31–55.

BLUMER, A., A. EHRENFEUCHT, D. HAUSSLER, Average sizes of suffix trees and DAWGS, *Discrete Applied Mathematics* **24** (1989) 37–45.

BOYER, R.S., AND J.S. MOORE, A fast string searching algorithm, *Comm. ACM* **20** (1977) 762–772.

BRESLAUER, D., AND Z. GALIL, Efficient comparison based string matching, *J. Complexity* **9**:3 (1993) 339–365.

BRESLAUER, D., L. COLUSSI, L. TONIOLO, Tight comparison bounds for the string prefix matching problem, *Inf. Process. Lett.* **47**:1 (1993) 51–57.

COLE, R., Tight bounds on the complexity of the Boyer-Moore pattern matching algorithm, in (*2nd annual ACM-SIAM Symp. on Discrete Algorithms*, 1990) 224–233.

COLE, R. AND R. HARIHARAN, Tighter upper bounds on the exact complexity of string matching, *SIAM Journal of Computing* (1995).

COLE, R., R. HARIHARAN, M.S. PATERSON, U. ZWICK, Tighter lower bounds on the exact complexity of string matching, *SIAM Journal of Computing* **24**:1 (1995) 30–45.

COLUSSI, L., Correctness and efficiency of string-matching algorithms, *Information and Computation* **95** (1991) 225–251.

COLUSSI, L., Fastest pattern matching in strings, *J. Algorithms* **16**:2 (1994) 163–189.

COLUSSI, L., Z. GALIL, R. GIANCARLO, On the exact complexity of string matching, in (*Proc. 31st Symposium on Foundations of Computer Science*, IEEE, 1990) 135–143.

COMMENTZ-WALTER, B., A string matching algorithm fast on the average, in (*ICALP*, LNCS, Springer-Verlag, Berlin, 1979) 118–132.

CROCHEMORE, M., Transducers and repetitions, *Theoret. Comput. Sci.* **45** (1986) 63–86.

CROCHEMORE, M., Longest common factor of two words, in (*TAPSOFT'87*, Ehrig, Kowalski, Levi and Montanari, eds, vol 1, LNCS, Springer-Verlag, Berlin, 1987) 26–36.

CROCHEMORE, M., String-Matching on Ordered Alphabets, *Theoret. Comput. Sci.* **92** (1992) 33–47.

CROCHEMORE, M., A. CZUMAJ, L. GĄSIENIEC, S. JAROMINEK, T. LECROQ, W. PLANDOWSKI, W. RYTTER, Speeding up two string matching algorithms, *Algorithmica* **12** (1994) 247–267.

CROCHEMORE, M., A. CZUMAJ, L. GĄSIENIEC, S. JAROMINEK, T. LECROQ, W. PLANDOWSKI, W. RYTTER, Fast multi-pattern matching, Report IGM 93-3, University of Marne-la-Vallée, 1993.

CROCHEMORE, M., AND D. PERRIN, Two-way string- matching, *J. ACM* **38**:3 (1991) 651–675.

CROCHEMORE, M. AND W. RYTTER, *Text Algorithms*, Oxford University Press, 1994.

CROCHEMORE, M. AND W. RYTTER, Cubes, squares and time-space efficient string searching, *Algorithmica* **13** (1995) 405–425.

DUVAL, J.-P., A remark on the Knuth-Morris-Pratt string searching algorithm, 1981. Unpublished.

DUVAL, J.-P., Factorizing words over an ordered alphabet, *J. Algorithms* **4** (1983) 363–381.

GALIL, Z., On improving the worst case running time of the Boyer-Moore string searching algorithm, *Comm. ACM* **22** (1979) 505–508.

GALIL, Z., String matching in real time, *J. ACM* **28** (1981) 134–149.

GALIL, Z., AND R. GIANCARLO, On the exact complexity of string matching: upper bounds, *SIAM J. Comput.* **21**:3 (1992) 407–437.

GALIL, Z., AND J. SEIFERAS, Time-space optimal string matching, *J. Comput. Syst. Sci.* **26** (1983) 280–294.

GĄSIENIEC, L., W. PLANDOWSKI, W. RYTTER, The zooming method: a recursive approach to time-space efficient string matching, *Theoret. Comput. Sci.* **147** (1995) 19–30.

GUIBAS, L.J., AND A.M. ODLYZKO, A new proof of the linearity of the Boyer-Moore string searching algorithm, *SIAM J. Comput.* **9** (1980) 672–682.

HANCART, C., On Simon's string searching algorithm, *Inf. Process. Lett.* **47** (1992) 95–99.

HANCART, C., Analyze exacte et en moyenne d'algorithmes de recherche d'un motif dans un texte, Rapport IGM 93–11, Université de Marne-la-Vallée, 1993.

HARRISON, M.C., Implementation of the substring test by hashing, *Comm. ACM* **14**:12 (1971) 777–779.

HORSPOOL, R.H., Practical fast searching in strings, *Software — Practice and Experience* **10** (1980) 501–506.

HUME, A. AND D.M. SUNDAY, Fast string searching, *Software — Practice and Experience* **21**:11 (1991) 1221–1248.

KARP, R.M., AND M.O. RABIN, Efficient randomized pattern matching algorithms, *IBM J. Res.Dev.* **31** (1987) 249–260.

KNUTH, D.E., J.H. MORRIS Jr, V.R. PRATT, Fast pattern matching in strings, *SIAM J. Comput.* **6** (1977) 323–350.

LECROQ, T., A variation on the Boyer-Moore algorithm, *Theoret. Comput. Sci.* **92** (1992) 119–144.

MAIN, M.G., AND R.J. LORENTZ, An $O(n \log n)$ algorithm for finding all repetitions in a string, *J. Algorithms* **5** (1984) 422–432.

MORRIS, J.H. JR, AND V.R. PRATT, A linear pattern-matching algorithm, Report 40, University of California, Berkeley, 1970.

PARK, K., communication at the British Colloquium of Theoret. Comput. Sci., 1992. Unpublished.

PERRIN, D., Finite automata, in (*Handbook of Theoretical Computer Science*, J. van Leeuwen, ed., vol B, *Formal models and semantics*, Elsevier, Amsterdam, 1990) 1–57.

RIVEST, R.L., On the worst case behavior of string searching algorithms, *SIAM J. Comput.* **6**:4 (1977) 669–674.

RYTTER, W., A correct preprocessing algorithm for Boyer-Moore string searching, *SIAM J. Comput.* **9** (1980) 509–512.

SCHABACK, R.. On the expected sublinearity of the Boyer-Moore string searching algorithm, *SIAM J. Comput.* **17** (1988) 648–658.

SIMON, I., personal communication (1989).

SIMON, I., String matching algorithms and automata, in (*First American Workshop on String Processing*, Baeza-Yates and Ziviani, eds, Universidade Federal de Minas Gerais, 1993) 151–157.

SLISENKO, A.O., Detection of periodicities and string-matching in real time, *J. Sov. Math.* **22**:3 (1983) 1326–1387.

STEPHEN, G.A., *String Searching Algorithms*, World Scientific, 1994.

SUNDAY, D.M., A very fast substring search algorithm, *Comm. ACM* **33**:8 (1990) 132–142.

WU, S., AND U. MANBER, Fast text searching allowing errors, *Comm. ACM* **35**:10 (1992) 83–91.

YAO, A.C., The complexity of pattern matching for a random string, *SIAM J. Comput.* **8** (1979) 368–387.

ZHU, R.F., AND T. TAKAOKA, On improving the average case of the Boyer-Moore string matching algorithm, *J. Inf. Process.* **10**:3 (1987) 173–177.

2
Off-line Parallel Exact String Searching

The string matching problem is defined as follows: given a string $P_0 \ldots P_{m-1}$ called the pattern and a string $T_0 \ldots T_{n-1}$ called the text find all occurrences of the pattern in the text. The output of a string matching algorithm is a boolean array MATCH$[0..n-1]$ which contains a *true* value at each position where an occurrence of the pattern starts. Many sequential algorithms are known that solve this problem optimally, i.e., in a linear $O(n)$ number of operations, most notable of which are the algorithms by Knuth, Morris and Pratt and by Boyer and Moore. In this chapter we limit ourselves to *parallel algorithms*.

2.1 Preliminaries

All algorithms considered in this chapter are for the parallel random access machine (PRAM) computation model.

In the design of parallel algorithms for the various PRAM models, one tries to optimize two factors simultaneously: the number of processors used and the time required by the algorithm. The total number of operations performed, which is the time-processors product, is the measure of optimality. A parallel algorithm is called *optimal* if it needs the same number of operations as the fastest sequential algorithm. Hence, in the string matching problem, an algorithm is optimal if its time-processor product is linear in the length of the input strings. Apart from having an optimal algorithm the designer wishes the algorithm to be the fastest possible, where the only limit on the number of processors is the one caused by the time-processor product. The following fundamental lemma given by Brent is essential for understanding the tradeoff between time and processors :

Lemma 2.1. *(**Brent***): Any PRAM algorithm of time t that consists of x elementary operations can be implemented on p processors in $O(x/p + t)$ time.*

Using Brent's lemma, any algorithm that uses a large number x of processors to run very fast can be implemented on $p < x$ processors, with the same total work, however with an increase in time as described.

A basic problem in the study of parallel algorithms for strings and arrays is finding the maximal/minimal position in an array that holds a certain value. The best algorithm for this problem was found by Fich, Ragde and Wigderson. It works in constant time using n processors on the CRCW-PRAM , where n is the size of the array. We use this algorithm throughout this chapter.

Another issue that we should consider is the operations we may perform on the symbols in the strings. These are chosen from some set which is called *alphabet*. The weakest assumption about the symbols, termed the *general alphabet* assumption, is that the only operations we can perform on them are comparisons which result in an equal or unequal answer. Most of the algorithms we describe in this Chapter work using only this assumption. However, stronger assumptions on the set of symbols may lead to different results. One possible assumption, usually called the *fixed alphabet* assumption maintains that the symbols are integers from a fixed range. These symbols can be used as indices of an array or in another case many of them can be packed together in one register.

Given a pattern of length m and a text of length n, we assume that $n = c \cdot m$, where $c > 1$ is a constant. In certain algorithms we choose a specific constant c as we see fit for a clearer presentation. This is possible since the text string can be broken to overlapping blocks of length $c \cdot m$ and all the blocks can be searched in parallel. In some cases we describe a parallel algorithm that has the claimed time bound using n processors (not optimal). The optimal version, using $O(n/t)$ processors, can be derived using standard techniques. In many places in our exposition we use quantities like $\log m$, $\log \log m$, $\sqrt{m}$, and $m/2$ as integers. It is easy to check that any way of rounding them suffices. In the following we describe some of fastest algorithms known for the string matching problem in the various parallel machine models (EREW, CREW, CRCW), as well as the lower bound proof for the *general alphabet* case.

In the description of the algorithms we use the following terminology: A position in the text which is a possible start of an occurrence of the pattern is called a *candidate*. Candidates are *eliminated* when it is proved that an occurrence of the pattern cannot start in them. Candidates *survive* when an attempt to eliminate them does not succeed (we call them *survivors*). A *naive* check of a candidate is one where m text positions starting from the candidate are simultaneously compared with all m corresponding pattern positions. This naive check takes $O(1)$ time and $O(m)$ processors per candidate. Many algorithms partition the strings to disjoint consecutive blocks of equal size: a *k-block* is such a block of size k. Such a block starts at position ik for some i. All the algorithms work in two main phases:

- A *preprocessing* phase in which the pattern is analyzed and useful information is extracted from it. This information is saved in convenient data structures to be used in the following phase.

- A *search* phase, which usually works in several rounds. In this phase the text is searched using the data structures created in the first phase. The set of candidates is maintained containing initially all the text positions. The number of candidates is decreased in every round until it permits a naive check of each one of them.

This chapter is organized as follows: In Section 2 we provide some background by describing two techniques that are used by fast but not the fastest parallel algorithms. In Section 3 we describe some basic properties of strings and the concept of witnesses that is used in the recent fastest parallel algorithms for the string matching problem. We also describe in this section the lower bound proof for the problem. In Section 4 we describe the concept of a deterministic sample that proved crucial for the fastest parallel search algorithms now known. Section 5 is devoted to the fastest optimal algorithm for the CRCW-PRAM and in Section 6 we describe the optimal algorithm for the EREW-PRAM and CREW-PRAM . In Section 7 we discuss the application of the string matching concepts to solving parallel two-dimensional pattern matching. Section 8 contains some conclusions and open questions that still exist.

2.2 Application of sequential techniques

Karp, Miller and Rosenberg defined an equivalence relation on the set of positions of the input strings and use it to obtain a relatively fast sequential algorithm for the string matching problem. Their method is also used by other algorithms that manipulate strings and arrays. In the parallel application of their algorithm we use the assumption that the symbols belong to $[0, .., m]$, i.e., it's a *fixed alphabet*. (m replaces all symbols in the text that do not appear in the pattern). This assumption is required by any optimal application of their technique, and a small modification can handle an alphabet of polynomial size. Two positions of the input string are k-equivalent if the substrings of length k starting at those positions are equal. The algorithm's main task is to assign unique names to each position in the same equivalence class. These names, in turn, represent the substrings corresponding to the equivalence classes in the subsequent comparisons required by the problem at hand. Consider the input as one string of length $l = n + m$ which is made of a text of length n concatenated with a pattern of length m. The goal is to find all positions which are in the same m-equivalence class as the position where the pattern starts. The following observation is the basis for the entire algorithm:

Fact 1. *For integers i, j, a, b we have: i is $(a + b)$-equivalent to j if and only if i is a-equivalent to j and $i + a$ is b-equivalent to $j + a$.*

This observation shows that we can combine equivalences of short substrings to obtain larger ones using only the naming information we already computed. We describe a logarithmic time implementation of the Karp, Miller and Rosenberg method on an n-processor arbitrary CRCW-PRAM. We denote by $n_j(i)$ the unique name assigned to the substring of length j starting at position i of the input string; assume $n_j(i)$ is defined only for $i+j \leq l$ and the names are integers in the range $0 \cdots m$. Suppose $n_r(i)$ and $n_s(i)$ are known for all positions i of the input string. One can combine these names to obtain $n_{r+s}(i)$ for all positions i in constant time using l processors as follows: Assume a two dimensional array of size $(m+1) \times (m+1)$ is available; assign a processor to each position of the input string. Each processor tries to write the position number it is assigned to in the entry at row $n_r(i)$ and column $n_s(i+r)$ of the matrix. If more than one processor attempts to write the same entry, an arbitrary one succeeds. Now $n_{r+s}(i)$ is assigned the value written in row $n_r(i)$ and column $n_s(i+r)$ of the matrix. That is, $n_{r+s}(i)$ is a position of the input string, not necessarily i, which is $(r+s)$-equivalent to i.

The algorithm starts with $n_1(i)$ as the symbol at position i of the string. Recall that we assume that input symbols are in $[0..m]$. It proceeds with $O(\log m)$ steps computing $n_2(i)$, $n_4(i)$, $\cdots n_{2^j}(i)$ for $j \leq \log_2 m$, by merging names of two 2^j-equivalence classes into names of 2^{j+1}-equivalence classes. In another $O(\log m)$ steps it computes $n_m(i)$ by merging a subset of the names of powers-of-two equivalence classes computed before, and reports all positions which are in the same m-equivalence class as the starting position of the pattern.

This algorithm requires $O(m^2)$ space which can be reduced to $O(m^{1+\epsilon})$ using a time-space tradeoff as described in the suffix tree construction algorithm of Apostolico et al..

Another technique that translates into a simple parallel algorithm is the randomized algorithm of Karp and Rabin. We describe here a parallel version of their algorithm that works with the assumption that the alphabet is binary (the set $\{0, 1\}$) and translates the input symbols into 2×2 non-singular matrices. Similarly to the previous algorithm, this algorithm computes names to all the text substrings which are of the same size as the pattern and then simply compares these names to find the occurrences of the pattern. However, here, the names are not simply symbols from some finite set, but they correspond directly to the symbols that construct the substrings. The name of a given substring is the product of the matrices representing it.

The following representation is used, which assures a unique name for any string as a product of the matrices representing it.

$$f(0) = \begin{pmatrix} 1 & 0 \\ 1 & 1 \end{pmatrix} \qquad\qquad f(1) = \begin{pmatrix} 1 & 1 \\ 0 & 1 \end{pmatrix}$$

$$f(s_1 s_2 \cdots s_i) = f(s_1) f(s_2) \cdots f(s_i)$$

Most of the work in the algorithm is performed using a well known method for parallel prefix computation summarized in the following theorem.

Theorem 2.2. *(Folklore): Suppose a sequence of n elements $x_1, x_2, \cdots, x_n$ are drawn from a set with an associative operation $*$, computable in constant time. Let $p_i = x_1 * x_2 * \cdots x_i$, usually called a prefix sum. Then an EREW-PRAM can compute all p_i $i = 1 \cdots n$, in $O(\log n)$ time using $\frac{n}{\log n}$ processors.*

Karp and Rabin's algorithm first multiplies the matrices representing the pattern to get a single matrix which is the name of the pattern (they use the term *fingerprint*). By Theorem 2.2 this can be done by an $\frac{m}{\log m}$-processor EREW-PRAM in $O(\log m)$ time. The text string is also converted to the same representation and matches can be reported based only on comparison of two matrices; the name of the pattern and the name of each text position. To compute the name of a text position j, which is the product of the matrices representing the substring of size m starting from position j, first compute all prefix products for the matrix representation of the text and call them $\bar{T}_i$. Then compute the inverse of each $\bar{T}_i$; the inverse exists since each $\bar{T}_i$ is a product of invertible matrices. The name for a position j, $0 \le j \le n - m - 1$ is given by $\bar{T}_{j-1}^{-1} \bar{T}_{j+m-1}$; the name of position 0 is $\bar{T}_m$. By Theorem 2.2 the prefix products also take optimal $O(\log n)$ time on the EREW-PRAM. Since the remaining work can be done in constant optimal time, the algorithm works in optimal $O(\log n)$ total time.

However, there is a problem with the algorithm described above. The entries of those matrices may grow too large to be represented in a single register; so the numbers are truncated modulo some random prime p. All computations are done in the field $\mathcal{Z}_p$ which assures that the matrices are still invertible.

This truncated representation does not assure uniqueness, but Karp and Rabin show that the probability of their algorithm erroneously reporting a nonexisting occurrence is very small if p is chosen from a range which is large enough. For a long time this algorithm was the only parallel algorithm which worked in optimal logarithmic time on the EREW-PRAM. Only the latest algorithm that is described in Section 2.6.1 achieves the same time bound, but it is a deterministic algorithm.

2.3 Periodicities and Witnesses.

A string u is called a *period* of string w if w is a prefix of u^k for some positive integer k or equivalently if w is a prefix of uw. The shortest period of a string w is called *the period* of w. In addition, p is the length of a period of the string if and only if all the positions i, $i \ge p$ of the string satisfy $w_i = w_{i-p}$. For example, the period of the string *dobidobido* is *dobi*, *dobidobi* is also a period (but not the shortest one).

If a pattern P occurs in positions i and j of some string and $0 < j - i < |P|$ then the occurrences must overlap. This implies that P has a period of length $j - i$. The following lemma provides some limitations on the existence of periods in strings.

Lemma 2.3. (GCD) *If w has periods of lengths p and q and $|w| \geq p + q$ then w has a period of length $\gcd(p, q)$.*

Proof: Exercise.   □

Corollary 1. *Let p be the length of the period of a pattern P, and let i, j ($i < j$) be occurrences of this pattern in a text string T of length n. Then $p \leq j - i$ and there are no more then n/p occurrences of P in T.*

As we mentioned in Section 1, the algorithms we are about to describe attempt to reach a stage in the search phase where naive checks can be applied to the surviving candidates. We need m processors to perform a naive check of a single candidate hence we cannot perform more than $O(n/m)$ naive checks in $O(1)$ time using $O(n)$ processors. It is implied by Corollary 1 that the number of candidates that might survive depends on the period length of the pattern, and could be larger than $O(n/m)$. Therefore we need to identify strings with relatively small period length and treat them differently. If the period of string w is shorter than a half (fourth) of w, w is called *periodic* (*4-periodic*).

Two other corollaries of the GCD Lemma can be stated as follows.

Corollary 2. *Let u be the period of a string w. The prefix of w of length $2|u| - 1$ is nonperiodic.*

Corollary 3. *Let w be a nonperiodic string of length m. For any l, $l < m/2$ there exists a nonperiodic substring of w of length l.*

Proof: Consider the prefix of w of length l. If it is periodic with period u, find the first position k in P such that $w_{k-|u|} \neq w_k$. This position exists since w is nonperiodic. The substring $w_{k-l+1}, \ldots, w_k$ is nonperiodic and has length l.   □

From now on let p be the length of the period of the pattern P. In case P is periodic, we would first look for occurrences of its nonperiodic prefix z of size $2p - 1$. The period u of P is also the period of z. We first find all occurrences of z. (We will show how to handle nonperiodic patterns next.) We then check naively which of the occurrences of z extends to an occurrence of uu. The positions starting such occurrences are the current survivors.

Then, by counting the number of consecutive matches of u starting at each survivor, we can locate all the occurrences of the entire pattern P.

In the next paragraph we describe how we can perform this counting step efficiently.

Vishkin showed how to count these matches in optimal $O(\log m)$ time on the EREW-PRAM using ideas which are similar to prefix computation. Breslauer and Galil showed how it can be done in optimal constant time on the CRCW-PRAM (and also in $O(\log m)$ time on the EREW-PRAM). We call an occurrence of u at position i an *initial occurrence* if there is no occurrence of uu at position $i - p$ and a *final occurrence* if there is no occurrence of uu at position $i + p$.

Assume without loss of generality that the text is of length $n \leq \frac{3}{2}m$ and the pattern is $u^k v$ where u is the period of the pattern and v is a proper prefix of u. There is at most one initial occurrence which can start an actual occurrence of the pattern: The rightmost initial occurrence in the first $\frac{m}{2}$ positions. Any initial occurrence to the left of it cannot have enough consecutive occurrences of the period following it to make an occurrence of the full pattern. This is also the case with an initial occurrence starting in a position greater then $\frac{m}{2}$ (the text is not long enough). The corresponding final occurrence is the leftmost final occurrence to the right of the initial occurrence. By subtracting the positions of the initial and final occurrences and verifying the occurrence of v to the right of the final occurrence, one can compute the number of times that the period is repeated and which of the survivors (the occurrences of uu) are actual occurrences of the pattern. All the parts above, except for finding the occurrences of z can be easily done in constant time on the CRCW-PRAM using n processors.

From now on we assume without loss of generality that during the text search the pattern is not periodic, i.e., it is shorter than twice its period. During the preprocessing phase we will find whether the pattern is periodic or not by computing $r = min(m/2, p)$, where p is the length of the period of P.

2.3.1 WITNESSES

Recall that p is the length of the period of the pattern P. For every i, $0 < i < p$ there exist at least one position h, $h > i$ in P such that $P_h \neq P_{h-i}$. We call such a position a *witness* against i (being a period of P). Vishkin introduced this concept and suggested that in the preprocessing of the pattern an array of such witnesses should be prepared. Consequently, in the preprocessing phase we compute $r = min(m/2, p)$ and for every i, $0 < i < r$, we compute $witness[i] = h$, where h is a position such that $P_h \neq P_{h-i}$.

Using this witness information Vishkin suggested a method which he called a *duel* to eliminate at least one of two close candidates.

Suppose i and j are candidates and $0 < j - i < p$. Then, $h = witness[j - i]$ is defined. Since $P_h \neq P_{h+i-j}$, at most one of them is equal to T_{i+h} (see

Fig. 2.1. $X \neq Y$ and therefore we cannot have $Z = X$ and $Z = Y$.

Figure 1) and at least one of the candidates can be eliminated. (As in a real duel sometimes both are eliminated.)

The concept of witnesses is useful in the fastest optimal algorithms now known. The *witnesses* array is used in the search phase to eliminate many candidates concurrently. Next we describe the algorithm suggested by Vishkin for the computation of witnesses and for the search phase. This algorithm takes optimal $O(\log m)$ time. The search phase can also be implemented optimally on the CREW-PRAM .

Recall that $r = min(p, m/2)$ where p is the period of the pattern. First we describe the text search phase which works in stages. There are $\log r$ stages. At stage i the text string is partitioned into consecutive k_i-blocks, where k_i is 2^i. The algorithm maintains that each such block contains at most one surviving candidate. We start at stage 0 where we have 1-blocks, and each position of the string is a candidate.

At stage i, consider a k_{i+1}-block which consists of two k_i-blocks. It contains at most two surviving candidates, one in each k_i-block. A duel is performed between these two candidates, leaving at most one in the k_{i+1}-block.

At the end of $\log r$ stages, we are left with at most n/r candidates which can be verified in constant-time using n processors. Note that the total number of operations performed is $O(n)$ and the time is $O(\log m)$. By Brent's Lemma an optimal implementation is possible.

The pattern preprocessing phase is similar to the text search phase. It takes $\log m$ stages. We use the term *source* for a position for which a witness has not yet been computed. The description below outlines a logarithmic time implementation using m processors.

The *witnesses* array which we used in the text processing phase is computed incrementally. At stage i we first compute witnesses to all the sources except one in a prefix of the pattern. Then we use these witnesses, performing the duel described below between surviving "close" sources along the whole pattern.

Let i and j be two positions in the pattern such that $i < j \leq m/2$. If $s = witness\,[j - i]$ is already computed then we can find at least one of $witness[i]$ or $witness[j]$ using a duel on the pattern as follows.

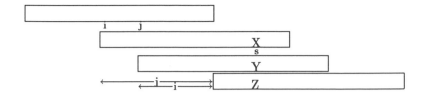

Fig. 2.2. $X \neq Y$ and therefore we cannot have $Z = X$ and $Z = Y$.

- If $s + i \leq m$ then $s + i$ is also a witness either against i or against j.

- If $s + i > m$ then either s is a witness against j or $s - j + i$ is a witness against i (see Figure 2).

The pattern preprocessing proceeds as follows. At stage i the pattern is partitioned into consecutive k_i-blocks. Each block has at most one source left. The only source in the first block is always 0. At stage i, consider the first k_{i+1}-block. It has at most one other source left, say position j. We first try to compute a witness against this source by comparing all pairs of positions that are j apart. This can be easily done in constant time on the CRCW-PRAM with m processors. If a witness is not found, then j is the period length of the pattern and the pattern preprocessing terminates. If a witness was found, a duel is performed in each k_{i+1}-block between the two remaining sources in each such block. It results in each k_{i+1}-block having at most one source left. After $\log r$ stages witness[i] is computed against every i, $0 < i < r = min(p, m/2)$ and the algorithm can proceed with the text search.

The version above is not optimal because in each stage the computation of the witness against the source in the leftmost block takes $O(m)$ work. This step could be also stated as the verification of the period corresponding to that source. The optimal implementation of the pattern preprocessing is very similar to Galil's original algorithm: instead of verifying the period for the whole pattern, we do it only for a prefix of the pattern of size 2^{i+1} as described below.

We compare all pairs of positions that are j apart only in the first k_{i+1}-block. If a mismatch is found it can be used as a witness against the source and we are done. If no mismatch has been found, we continue to a *periodic* stage $i + 1$ in which we try to verify the same period length in a block of double length. At some point either a mismatch is found or the period length is verified for the whole string and the pattern preprocessing is terminated. If a mismatch is found, it can be easily shown that it can be used as a witness value for all remaining sources in the first block; and the algorithm can catch up to stage $i + 1$ (with the current value of i) by performing duels.

2.3.2   COMPUTING AND USING WITNESSES IN $O(\log \log M)$ TIME

Breslauer and Galil used the witness information to obtain an optimal $O(\log \log m)$ time algorithm for general alphabet. They observed that duels work like maximum, i.e., that the outcome of performing a duel is that at least one of the candidates is eliminated, and sometimes both of them. Hence, they were able to use a method based on an algorithm for finding the maximum suggested by Valiant for the comparison model and implemented by Shiloach and Vishkin on the CRCW-PRAM . Next we provide a brief description of their algorithm, which has some similarities to Vishkin's algorithm. We start by describing the search phase. Recall that we assumed that in the text search the pattern is nonperiodic.

Partition the text into disjoint consecutive m-blocks and consider each one separately. In each block consider each position as a candidate. Assuming we had m^2 processors for each such block, a duel can be performed between each pair of candidates resulting in at most one occurrence in each block. Since we have only m processors for each block, partition the m-blocks into $\sqrt{m}$-blocks and repeat recursively. The recursion bottoms out with one processor per 1-block. When we are done with the recursive call we are left with at most one candidate in each $\sqrt{m}$-block, thus at most $\sqrt{m}$ candidates per m-block. Then in constant time we make all m duels. We are left with at most a single candidate in each m-block. We can naively check the survivors for occurrences of the full pattern.

To make the text search phase run in optimal $O(\log \log m)$ time we start with an $O(\log \log m)$ time sequential algorithm which runs in parallel, performing duels, in all $\log \log m$-blocks, and leaves only $m/\log \log m$ candidates in each block. Then we proceed with the above procedure starting with the reduced number of candidates.

The pattern preprocessing can also be performed in optimal $O(\log \log m)$ time. We do not describe the full pattern preprocessing phase here, since it is similar to the $O(\log m)$ algorithm described in Section 2.3. Here, using the approach described above for the search phase, we have only $O(\log \log m)$ stages and we choose the increasing block lengths to be of the form: $k_i = m^{1-2^{-i}}$, $k_0 = 1$.

Breslauer and Galil went on to show a $\Omega(\log \log m)$ lower bound for parallel string matching over general alphabet. We show in later sections that this lower bound can be limited to the preprocessing phase.

2.3.3   A LOWER BOUND FOR THE CRCW-PRAM

The model Breslauer and Galil used for the lower bound proof is similar to Valiant's parallel comparison tree model. We assume the only access the algorithm has to the input strings is by comparisons which check whether two symbols are equal or not. The algorithm is allowed m comparisons in each round, after which it can proceed to the next round or terminate with

the answer. We give a lower bound on the minimum number of rounds
necessary in the worst case. On a PRAM the algorithms also have to
perform some computations for allocating processors, deciding which comparisons to make, etc.; these actions come free of charge in the comparison
model. Therefore, a lower bound for the number of rounds in the parallel
comparison model immediately translates into a lower bound for the time
of the CRCW-PRAM .

The lower bound of $\Omega(\log \log m)$ rounds is proved first for a closely related problem of computing the period length of a string and it is shown
how it can be translated to the original problem. However, given the witnesses, we will later show that the search phase can be performed optimally
in constant time. Thus, the lower bound holds only for the preprocessing
phase. Moreover, the lower bound does not hold for CRCW-PRAM when
fixed alphabet is assumed, and it is still an open problem whether parallel string pattern matching over a fixed alphabet can be done in less than
$O(\log \log m)$ time. Similarly, finding the maximum in the parallel decision
tree model has exactly the same lower bound, but for small integers the
maximum can be found in constant time on the CRCW-PRAM .

Breslauer and Galil gave a strategy for an adversary to answer
$\frac{1}{4} \log \log m$ rounds of comparisons after which it still has the choice of fixing
the input string S in two ways: in one the resulting string has a period of
length smaller than $m/2$ and in the other it does not have any such period.
This implies that any algorithm which terminates in fewer rounds can be
fooled.

We say that an integer k is a possible period length if we can fix S
consistently with answers to previous comparisons in such a way that k is
a period length of S. For such k to be a period length we need each residue
class modulo k to be fixed to the same symbol, thus if $l \equiv j \mod k$ then
$S_l = S_j$.

At the beginning of round i the adversary maintains an integer k_i which
is a possible period length. The adversary answers the comparisons of
round i in such a way that some k_{i+1} is a possible period length and few
symbols of S are fixed. Let $K_i = m^{1-4^{-(i-1)}}$. The adversary maintains the
following invariants which hold at the beginning of round number i.

1. k_i satisfies $\frac{1}{2}K_i \leq k_i \leq K_i$.
2. If S_l was fixed, then for every $j \equiv l \mod k_i$, S_j was fixed to the same
   symbol.
3. If a comparison was answered as equal, then both symbols compared
   were fixed to the same value.
4. If a comparison was answered as unequal, then
   a. it was between symbols in positions belonging to different residue
      classes modulo k_i.

    b. if the symbols were already fixed then they were fixed to different values.

5. The number of fixed symbols f_i satisfies $f_i \leq K_i$.

Note that invariants 3 and 4 imply consistency of the answers given so far. Invariants 2, 3 and 4 imply that k_i is a possible period length: if we fix all symbols in each unfixed residue class modulo k_i to a new symbol, a different symbol for different residue classes, we obtain a string consistent with the answers given so far that has a period length k_i.

We start at round number 1 with $k_1 = K_1 = 1$. It is easy to see that the invariants hold initially. We show how to answer the comparisons of round i and how to choose k_{i+1} so that the invariants still hold. We call the multiples of k_i in the range $\frac{1}{2}K_{i+1} \ldots K_{i+1}$ candidates for k_{i+1}. For a choice of k_{i+1}, comparison $S_l = S_j$ must be answered as equal if $l \equiv j \mod k_{i+1}$. We say that k_{i+1} *forces* this comparison. Breslauer and Galil showed, using elementary number theory, that at every stage there exists a candidate for k_{i+1} in the range $\frac{1}{2}K_{i+1} \ldots K_{i+1}$ that forces very few (at most $\frac{4mK_i \log m}{K_{i+1}}$) comparisons, thus not fixing many positions. The adversary chooses such a k_{i+1}. Next we show how the adversary can answer the comparisons in round i so that the invariants also hold at the beginning of round $i + 1$.

For each comparison that is forced by k_{i+1} and is of the form $S_l = S_j$ where $l \equiv j \mod k_{i+1}$ the adversary fixes the residue class modulo k_{i+1} to the same new symbol (a different symbol for different residue classes). The adversary answers comparisons between fixed symbols based on the value to which they are fixed. All other comparisons involve two positions in different residue classes modulo k_{i+1} (and at least one unfixed symbol) and are always answered as unequal.

Since k_{i+1} is a multiple of k_i, the residue classes modulo k_i split; each class splits into $\frac{k_{i+1}}{k_i}$ residue classes modulo k_{i+1}. Note that if two positions are in different residue classes modulo k_i, then they are also in different residue classes modulo k_{i+1}; if two positions are in the same residue class modulo k_{i+1}, then they are also in the same residue class modulo k_i. It is not difficult to prove that the invariants still hold.

Theorem 2.4. *Any comparison-based parallel algorithm for finding the period length of a string $S_0 \ldots S_{m-1}$ using m comparisons in each round requires at least $\frac{1}{4} \log \log m$ rounds.*

Proof: Fix an algorithm which finds the period of S and let the adversary described above answer the comparisons. After $i = \frac{1}{4} \log \log m$ rounds $f_{i+1}, k_{i+1} \leq m^{1 - 4^{-\frac{1}{4} \log \log m}} = \frac{m}{2\sqrt{\log m}} \leq \frac{m}{2}$. The adversary can still fix S to have a period length k_{i+1} by fixing each remaining residue class modulo k_{i+1} to the same symbol, different symbol for each class. Alternatively, the adversary can fix all unfixed symbols to different symbols. Note that this choice is consistent with all the the comparisons answered so far by invariants 3 and 4, and the string does not have any period length smaller than $\frac{m}{2}$. Consequently, any algorithm which terminates in less than $\frac{1}{4} \log \log m$ rounds can be fooled.   □

Theorem 2.5. *The lower bound holds also for any comparison-based string matching algorithm when $n = O(m)$.*

Proof: Fix a string matching algorithm. We present to the algorithm a pattern $P_0 \ldots P_{m-1}$ which is $S_0 \ldots S_{m-1}$ and a text $T_0 \ldots T_{2m-2}$ which is $S_1 \ldots S_{2m-1}$, where S is a string of length $2m$ generated by the adversary in the way described above. (We use the same adversary that we used in the previous proof; the adversary sees all comparisons as comparisons between symbols in S.) After $\frac{1}{4} \log \log 2m$ rounds the adversary still has the choice of fixing S to have a period length smaller than m, in which case we have an occurrence of P in T, or to fix all unfixed symbols to completely different characters, which implies that there would be no such occurrence. Thus, the lower bound holds also for any such string matching algorithm. □

The combination of the algorithm in Section 3.2 and the lower bound proof above provide the following tight bounds for the time complexity for both, testing whether a given string is periodic and for string matching in case $n = 2m - 1$. In both cases the bound is $\Theta(\lceil m/p \rceil + \log \log_{1+p/m} 2p)$.

In the lower bound proof above we can see that the limitation lies within the pattern preprocessing phase; faster text searches were indeed achieved as we show next.

2.4   Deterministic samples

Another useful concept is the *deterministic sample*, DS for short, introduced by Vishkin. Let P be a nonperiodic pattern string of length m. A DS of P for k shifts ($k \leq m/2$) is an ordered set A of positions of the pattern and a number f, such that if the positions are verified to match a candidate i in the text, then all other candidates in the interval $[i - f + 1, i + k - f]$ can be eliminated. The elimination of these candidates is possible because a mismatch is guaranteed to exist with at least one of the DS positions that matched i. If the DS positions, when checked, do not match a certain candidate then this candidate can be trivially eliminated. The *size* of a DS is the size of the ordered set A.

The DS is crucial for very fast string matching algorithms since a very small DS (of size $\log m$ for $m/2$ shifts) can be found. Let the text string T be partitioned to disjoint consecutive h-blocks. We say that T is *h-good*

```
0  1  1  1  0  1  0 │ 1  0  1  1  1  0  1  1 │ 0
   0  1  1  1  0  1 │ 0  1  0  1  1  1  0  1 │ 1  0
      0  1  1  1  0 │ 1  0  1  0  1  1  1  0 │ 1  1  0
         0  1  1  1 │ 0  1  0  1  0  1  1  1 │ 0  1  1  ...
            0  1  1 │ 1  0  1  0  1  0  1  1 │ 1  0  1  ...
   x ⟶       0  1 │ 1  1  0  1  0  1  0  1 │ 1  1  0  ...
               0 │ 1  1  1  0  1  0  1  0 │ 1  1  1  ...
                 │ 0  1  1  1  0  1  0  1 │ 0  1  1  ...
```

Fig. 2.3. A 2-size DS of x for 8 shifts: $A = 2, 4$ and $f = 6$.

if all the h-blocks have at most two candidates left in them. The optimal elimination of candidates using DS is best expressed by the following lemma.

Lemma 2.6. *If text T is h-good and an h-size DS for k shifts is given, then T can be made k-good in optimal constant-time on an n-processor CRCW-PRAM .*

Proof: Let A be the ordered set of the h-size DS. For each k-block, there are initially at most $2k/h$ candidates and $h/2$ processors are available per candidate. For each candidate in the k-block, make h comparisons with the positions of A. If a candidate has a mismatch, it provides a witness against the candidate. Find the leftmost (ls) and rightmost (rs) survivors in the k-block. By the definition of DS, every survivor i in the middle has at least one mismatch in the DS positions aligned with ls and rs. For each such i find a mismatch by making $2h$ comparisons with the DS positions aligned with ls and rs. Only ls and rs survive. □

The current way of using the DS in the search phase was originally called the principle of *diet* by Galil. It follows from Lemma 3 that if we can make $T \log m$-good (reduce the number of surviving candidates to at most two per $\log m$-block), we can apply the $\log m$-size DS to eliminate most of the candidates in constant time, so that we are left with at most two surviving candidates in every $m/2$-block, and these can be checked naively. Obviously we would first have to compute the $\log m$-size DS. It means that it suffices to look for a nonperiodic substring z of the original pattern of length $\log m$. In the preprocessing we can easily find such a z and its first occurrence in the pattern (see Corollary 3). In the text search we look for the occurrences of z in the text. We are able to eliminate all the candidates that do not have an occurrence of z in an offset corresponding its first occurrence in the pattern. Since z is nonperiodic, there is at most one survivor per $\log m/2$-block; i.e., as needed above for using DS and finishing the search. Thus, the diet reduces the size of the pattern from m to $\log m$ and can be repeated to reduce it even further. Having to search for z we need a DS for z, which we also compute in the preprocessing phase and

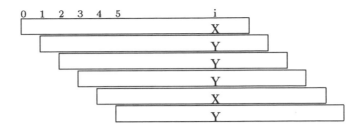

Fig. 2.4. Aligned copies of the pattern and a column i.

during the text search phase we have only to make $T \log\log m$-good. We next prove the existence of DS of size $\log m$ for $m/2$ shifts and a method to compute it.

Lemma 2.7. *For any nonperiodic pattern of length m, a deterministic sample of size $\log t$ for $t \le m/2$ shifts exists.*

Proof: Consider t copies of the pattern placed under each other, each shifted ahead by one position with respect to its predecessor. Thus copy number k is aligned at position k of copy number one. Call the symbols of all copies aligned over position number i of the first copy *column i* (see Figure 4). Since we assume that the pattern is shorter than twice its period length and there are $t \le m/2$ copies, for any two copies there is a witness to their mismatch.

Take the first and last copies and a witness to their mismatch. The column of the mismatch has at least two different symbols and thus one of the symbols in that column, in either the first or the last copy, appears in the column in at most half of the copies. Keep only the copies which have the same symbol in that column to get a set of at most half the number of original copies, which all have the same symbol at the witness column. This procedure can be repeated at most $\log t$ times until there is a single copy left, say copy number f. Note that all columns chosen hit copy number f. The deterministic sample consists of the positions in copy number f of the columns considered. There are at most $\log t$ such columns. If this sample is verified for position i of a text string no other occurrence is possible at positions $i - f + 1$ to $i - f + t$. $\square$

One can find such a deterministic sample in parallel by the constructive proof of Lemma 2.7. This way of DS computation takes $O(\log^2 m/\log\log m)$ time with an optimal number of processors.

2.4.1   FASTER TEXT SEARCH USING DS

Vishkin developed an optimal $O(\log^* m)^1$ time search phase algorithm. The preprocessing in Vishkin's algorithm takes $O(\log^2 m/\log\log m)$ as described above. He uses a DS of size $\log m$ for $m/2$ shifts. In his algorithm Vishkin compares simultaneously increasing subsets of the positions of the single $\log m$ DS. Initially, he compares the first position of the DS and eliminates at least half of the candidates, as follows from the construction of the DS. Then he has more processors than candidates, and he can use them to verify the next two positions of the DS concurrently, etc. The method used, creating exponential acceleration, is called the *accelerating cascade design* principle by Cole and Vishkin.

Galil gave a constant time search phase algorithm. He used the idea of diet described above, reducing the text search to the goal of making the text $\log\log m$-good. In the following paragraphs we use the concept of *segments* which was introduced by Galil for improving the Boyer-Moore algorithm.

Definition: Let u be the period of some periodic substring z of the pattern P that we look for in the text T. A *segment* is a maximal substring of T containing z having the same period length as z. We call an occurrence of z at position i an *initial occurrence* if there is no occurrence of z at position $i - |u|$ and a *final occurrence* if there is no occurrence of z at position $i + |u|$.

Fact 2. *Given an occurrence of a periodic string z in T and the length of the period of z, one can find the initial (final) z in its segment in constant time with linear number of processors on the CRCW-PRAM .*

Galil used the following technique for making the text $\log\log m$-good. Without loss of generality, he considered a text string of size $\frac{5}{4}m$. In this case any occurrence of the pattern must start in the first $\frac{1}{4}m$ positions, and since the pattern is non-periodic only **one** occurrence is possible. His method was based on choosing a specific, very small substring z of size $O(\log\log m)$ from the second or third quarter of the pattern. Assuming there is an occurrence of the pattern in the text, each occurrence of z in the second or third quarter of the text (assumed to have five quarters) corresponds to an occurrence of z in one of the first three quarters of the pattern. He showed that we can find, in constant time and $O(m)$ processors, **one** occurrence of z in the second or third quarters of the text. This single occurrence in the text, termed the *found z*, was used to eliminate all but $O(m/\log\log m)$ candidates.

- If z is non periodic, it is easy to see that it could appear only $O(m/\log\log m)$ times in the pattern. The found z must correspond

---

[1] The function $\log^* m$ is defined as the smallest k such that $\log^{(k)} m \leq 2$, where $\log^{(1)} m = \log m$ and $\log^{(i+1)} m = \log\log^{(i)} m$.

to one of the occurrences of z in the pattern. In the preprocessing we find all the occurrences of z in the pattern. Thus, after finding the occurrence of z in the text we can mark as survivors only the candidates for which the found z corresponds to an occurrence of z in the pattern. Subsequently, there is at most one survivor in each $\log\log m/2$-block in the text.

- If z is periodic, the same approach may not work because there can be too many occurrences of z in the pattern. Instead we look at the segments in which z is found both in the pattern and in the text. Two segments of z in a string can overlap by at most $\frac{|z|}{2}$, otherwise the periodicity continues and they must be part of the same segment. Let α be the segment of the found z in the text and let β be the corresponding segment in the pattern. Either the initial occurrences of z in α and β correspond to each other or the final occurrences in α and β do . In the preprocessing we find all the segments of z in the pattern and all their initial and final occurrences of z (see Fact 2) and we store them in different processors. After locating the found z in the text we find the initial and final z in its segment α. Again, we mark as survivors all candidates for which the initial (final) z in α corresponds to an initial (final) z in a segment in the pattern. Since the segments cannot overlap by more than $\frac{|z|}{2}$ there cannot be more than one survivor in each $\log\log m/2$-block.

The z chosen is the most frequent substring of length $\log\log m$ in the second quarter of the pattern. The actual finding of the single occurrence of z inside the text is a bit more involved and it is divided into different cases according to the size of the alphabet. We use a *hitting set* which is a set of positions in the second and third quarters of the text such that if there is an occurrence of the pattern in the text, at least one position in the set must be a position of an occurrence of z. The choice of z guarantees the existence of the hitting set. The latter is computed in the preprocessing phase. We do not give the details here.

The preprocessing time in Galil's algorithm was dominated by the computation of the $\log m$ size DS, which at that time required $O(\log^2 m/\log\log m)$ time and is worse than the preprocessing time in Breslauer and Galil's $O(\log\log m)$ algorithm. Goldberg and Zwick first provided a solution with $O(\log m)$ preprocessing and constant search utilizing larger deterministic samples. However, a solution that combines the constant time search phase with a very fast $O(\log\log m)$ preprocessing is possible and it is described in the next section.

2.5 The fastest known CRCW-PRAM algorithm

Here we describe algorithms that reach two main goals in the area of parallel string matching.

- An $O(\log \log m)$ preprocessing phase, combined with a simple constant time search phase algorithm.
- A constant expected time Las Vegas algorithm for computing the period of the pattern and all witnesses. This suffices, as we shall see, for solving the full string matching problem in constant expected time.

These goals were reached mainly by providing new methods for computing DS for sufficiently long substrings of the pattern, and for computing witness information. One idea that prompted the discovery of the new methods is an observation following Breslauer and Galil's $O(\log \log m)$ algorithm: If one precomputes the witnesses, it is enough to find DS for a nonperiodic substring of size $r = m^{1/3}$ in which case $m = r^3$ processors and space are available for the task. This is because one can use such DS to decrease the number of candidates to one in every $r/2$-block and can then apply a constant number of rounds of duels to obtain an $m/2$-good text. Another idea was that if we find a sufficiently large substring that is periodic with period length $p < r/2$ (which we call *periodicity*), we can take just two elements (the end of this periodicity and a shift by p) to serve as a deterministic sample.

2.5.1   COMPUTING DETERMINISTIC SAMPLES IN CONSTANT TIME

Let x be a nonperiodic string of length r (a substring of the pattern in our algorithms). We first show how to construct a constant-size DS of x for $\log \log r$ shifts in constant time with $r^2 \log \log r$ processors. This constant-size DS is later used as the first step in the text search phase. Recall that our definition of DS includes a position f which defines the interval around a candidate that survived the DS in which other candidates are eliminated.

1. If there exists a position i in x such that $x_i \neq x_{i+j}$ (or $x_i \neq x_{i-j}$) for every $1 \leq j \leq \log r$, then we take $A = \{i\}$ and $f = \log r$ (or $A = \{i\}$ and $f = 1$) as the DS for $\log r$ shifts.

2. Otherwise, every symbol in x occurs very often (with distance shorter than $\log r$ between neighboring occurrences). So every symbol occurs at least $r/\log r$ times in x, which implies that there are at most $\log r$ different symbols in x. Consider all disjoint $\log \log r$-blocks in the first half of x. Since there are $(\log r)^{\log \log r}$ different strings of size $\log \log r$ over $\log r$ symbols and $(\log r)^{\log \log r} < r/(2 \log \log r)$, some non overlapping $\log \log r$-blocks are identical in the first half of x. Find such a block y in constant time using $r^2 \log \log r$ processors. Let z be the substring between the two copies of y (z could be the null string). The substring yzy has a period $p = |yz| < r/2$, this substring is our desired periodicity. Since x is nonperiodic, period p has a mismatch in x. Let q be the smallest (largest) position such that $x_q \neq x_{p+q}$ to the right (left) of the first copy of y. Then $A = \{q, q+p\}$

and $f = 1$ ($A = \{q, q + p\}$ and $f = \log \log r$) is the constant-size DS for $\log \log r$ shifts.

Next we show how to construct a $\log k$-size DS of string x for k shifts, $k \leq r/2$, in constant time using r^3 processors and r^2 space. Here too we look for a periodicity by looking for a repetition of a large enough block. This time we consider k-blocks starting at positions i for $0 \leq i < k$.

Using $k^3 < r^3$ processors, the algorithm checks in constant time if x has a periodicity, i.e, if a k-block appears at least twice. If we find such a repetition, hence a periodicity, we are done. As described above for the constant size DS, we take the two elements marking the end (start) of the periodicity inside x and we get a constant size DS. If there is no such periodicity, the case is somewhat more complicated, as described next.

Consider (for discussion only) the compacted prefix tree T of all the k k-blocks (each path from the root of T to a leaf corresponds to a block and every internal node has a degree of at least two). Since T has k leaves, there is at least one leaf v of depth $\leq \log k$. The nodes along this path represent $\log k$ positions by which the block corresponding to the leaf is different from all the other k-blocks. We show how to find this block and the $\log k$ positions that serve as the DS.

We first compute a $k \times k$ 0-1 matrix: one row for each block. The matrix is set initially to 0. With r processors per each pair of blocks, we find in constant time the smallest position l such that the two blocks differ at l (a node in T). Set to 1 entry l in the two rows i and j. Now we only have to find a row with no more than $s = \log k$ 1's and compress their positions to an array of size s. We first replace all 1's with their corresponding positions. Then we use the deterministic polynomial approximate compaction (PAC) of Ragde. A d-PAC is an optimal algorithm that compacts an array of size n with at most x nonzero elements into an array of size x^d (assuming that $x^d < n$). Ragde gave a constant-time optimal $(4 + \epsilon)$-PAC and Hagerup a $(1 + \epsilon)$-PAC for any $\epsilon > 0$. (Below we will use also the latter.) Ragde used his PAC to compress an array of length n with at most x items ($=$ nonzero entries) into an array of size x in time $O(\log x / \log \log n)$. In case the number of items is larger than x the algorithm fails. Note that when $\log x = O(\log \log n)$ the time is $O(1)$. We use it here with $x = \log k$ for each row of the matrix, so it takes constant time. This algorithm succeeds at least in one of the rows in the matrix (at all those with $\leq \log k$ elements) and yields the desired DS. Each row corresponds to a k-block in x. Let b be the start position of the k-block corresponding to the block we found. We take the positions in the row to be the required DS with $f = k - b$. For example, consider Figure 3. For the block $B = 11010101$, its start position in x is 2 and f is 6.

2.5.2   APPLYING DS TO OBTAIN THE FASTEST ALGORITHMS

As we have mentioned before, the computation of the DS was the dominating factor in the slow preprocessing phase required for Vishkin's and Galil's fast search phase algorithms. In Galil's algorithm, a computation of the hitting set also took place, but it can be performed in $O(\log \log m)$ time using optimal number of processors if the substring z we look for is short enough. However, the ability to compute DS in constant time for large enough (size $= m^{1/3}$) substrings of the pattern, combined with the **constant size** DS for substrings of size $\leq \log \log m$ solved the problem in a uniform way. The substrings for which these DS are computed are the first nonperiodic substrings of the required length in the pattern P. By Corollary 3 of the GCD Lemma these nonperiodic substrings exist. Let l be the length of one such required nonperiodic substring z. Since we have at least l^2 processors we can find z easily by first checking the periodicity of a prefix of the pattern of size $2l$. We can do this in constant time using m processors. If it is not periodic we are done, otherwise we find the end of the periodicity (as in the DS computation) and use the substring of size l there as our z. The scheme of the constant-time search phase **CONST-SEARCH** is given below. It still needs $O(\log \log m)$ time preprocessing phase, since it requires the witness information.

> **Procedure CONST-SEARCH(P,T)**
>
> 1. Find the first nonperiodic substring x of P of length $r = m^{1/3}$ and the first nonperiodic substring x' of x of length $2 \log r$.
> 2. Use the constant-size DS of x for $\log \log r$ shifts to make T $\log \log r$-good.
> 3. Use the $\log \log r$-size DS of x' for $\log r$ shifts to make T $\log r$-good.
> 4. Use the $\log r$ size DS of x for $r/2$ shifts to make T $r/2$-good.
> 5. Use a few rounds of dueling to make T $m/2$-good. (First to reduce the number of candidates per block to at most one, then by squaring the block size in each round.)
> 6. Check naively the surviving candidates.

2.5.3   A NEW METHOD TO COMPUTE WITNESSES : PSEUDO-PERIODS

The witnesses of a substring P' of P of size $m^{1-2^{-k}}$ can be computed in $O(k)$ time using the first k stages in the preprocessing of Breslauer and Galil $O(\log \log m)$ algorithm. Hence, we derive the following conclusion.

Corollary 4. *Using CONST-SEARCH, we get an $O(k)$-time n-processors algorithm for string matching in case $m = O(n^{1-2^{-k}})$.*

The very fast search algorithm above is used in the preprocessing of a given pattern string. The following definition and fact are required.

Definition: If position i in text T is not an occurrence of a pattern P, a position j such that $T_j \neq P_{j-i}$ is called a *witness* to non-occurrence at i.

There is a strong correlation between witnesses to non-occurrences and witnesses against possible periods which allows us to use our best search algorithms in the preprocessing of the pattern. It is best described by the following fact.

Fact 3. *Let z be a substring of pattern P that occurs in position k in P. Apply a search algorithm for occurrences of z in P and let i be a candidate that was eliminated in this search. The witness to the non-occurrence at i is a witness against $j = i - k$ (being a period of P).*

When we eliminate a candidate i using a duel, we immediately get a witness to the non-occurrence at i. When we eliminate a candidate using DS we can also get a witness to its non-occurrence in constant time: Let the DS be of size k, we have k processors per candidate. If the candidate is eliminated because (at least) one of the DS positions does not match then this position can serve as a witness. If the candidate is eliminated by the first or last surviving candidates in its block, then we can use the k processors assigned to this candidate to check which of the DS positions, aligned with the first or last candidates does not match.

Corollary 4 and Fact 3 can be used to derive an expected constant time Las Vegas algorithm. The scheme is very similar to the lower bound proof given in Section 2.3.3. There the adversary maintained a number representing the smallest possible period length. This number was replaced at each new stage by a larger number that was divisible by its predecessor, allowing the adversary to maintain consistency with his previous answers. The algorithm here uses essentially the same method as in the lower bound proof, only here the algorithm is the one that maintains a number representing the smallest possible period length. We call this number a *pseudo-period* and it is the smallest possible period only in the sense that the pattern may not have a period shorter than this number. It has an operational definition: Given a string P of length m, if we compute witnesses against all $i < m/4$ except for multiples of q, we say that q is a pseudo period of P. It follows from this definition that if P is 4-periodic, q must divide the period p of P. In the following discussion, when we say we compute the period of P we mean computing $r = min(p, m/4)$ and witnesses against positions i, $i < r/4$.

Using Corollary 4 with $k = 1$, we can compute a large pseudo-period in constant time, and witnesses against non-multiples of it. These witnesses are also witnesses against non-multiples of the real period of the pattern.

Procedure PSEUDO-PERIOD(P, m);

1. Look for the first nonperiodic substring z of size $2\sqrt{m}$ in P.
   If such a z does not exist, find q - the period of P ($q \leq \sqrt{m}$) and naively compute witnesses for $i < q$. **return** (q).
   If such a z exists, compute witnesses for it naively, and go to Step 2.

2. Use the optimal constant-time procedure CONST-SEARCH to find all occurrences of z in P and witnesses to non-occurrences. Let t be the start position of z in P. If a witness to non-occurrence was found for position i, then it is a witness against $i - t$ being a period of P (Fact 3).

3. Construct the $(m - |z|)$-bit binary string b such that $b_i = 1$ if i is an occurrence of z, $b_i = 0$ otherwise. Compute q the period of b in case $q < m/4$ and witnesses of b against non-multiples of q. From these compute witnesses of P against the same positions. This computation exploits the special form of b; it contains at most $\sqrt{m}$ 1's with distance of at least $\sqrt{m}$ between them, since z is non-periodic and of length $2\sqrt{m}$. Thus, we can compute witnesses of b by considering only the 1's.

   (a) Divide b into $\sqrt{m}$-blocks. In each such block there is at most one 1.

   (b) Record the position of the 1 in every given block in the first element in that block. (Now every processor can read from the first element of a block the position of the 1 in that block.)

   (c) Let t be the position of the first 1 in b. For positions $i < t$, t is a witness against $t - i$. If $t \geq m/4$ this substep is done.

   (d) Otherwise consider $i \geq 2t$ (i.e., $i - t \geq t$). If $b_i = 0$ then i is a witness against $i - t$. If $b_i = 1$ $i - t$ is a potential period of b since it shifts the first 1 to 1. Use the $\sqrt{m}$ processors for the block of i to check if $i - t$ is a period of b by checking for all k such that $b_k = 1$ that ($b_{k+i-t} = 1$ or $k + i - t > m - z$) and ($b_{k-i+t} = 1$ or $k - i + t < 0$). If all these tests succeed $i - t$ is a period of b. If the test with k failed, $k + i - t$ or k is a witness against $i - t$. Compute q the smallest period of b.

   (e) From the witnesses of b compute witnesses of P. Let w be the witness of b against i. Assume $b_w = 0$ and $b_{w-i} = 1$. (The other case is similar.) Let j be the witness to non-occurrence of z at w in P. One can verify that $w + t + j$ is a witness of P against i.

Procedure PSEUDO-PERIOD can be performed in constant time and $O(m)$ processors on the CRCW-PRAM. It computes a q which satisfies:
P1. If $q \leq \sqrt{m}$, q is the real period of P.
P2. If $q > \sqrt{m}$, then q is a pseudo period of P.

Given q integers, let $\mathrm{LCM}(k, q)$ be the minimum of $k/4$ and the LCM of the q integers. Given a $k \times q$ array B of symbols and for every column c its pseudo period $q_c < k/4$ and witnesses against non-multiples of q_c, Procedure FIND-LCM computes $\mathrm{LCM}(k, q)$ of the pseudo periods and witnesses against non-multiples of $\mathrm{LCM}(k, q)$ smaller than $k/4$ in constant time with kq processors.

Procedure FIND-LCM(k, q):

1. Construct a $(k/4 - 1) \times q$ array B': in the c-th column of B', write 1 in the multiples of the pseudo period q_c and 0 in other places.
2. For each row that is not all 1's, any entry 0 provides a witness against the row number.
3. If there is a row with all entries 1's, return the smallest row, otherwise return $k/4$.

Recall that the main problem is to compute the period and the witnesses of the pattern P. We describe next an $O(\log \log m)$ time algorithm for the main problem. The algorithm consists of rounds and maintains a variable q that is increased in every round. The invariant at the end of a round is that q is a pseudo period of P. Initially, $q = 1$, We describe one round of the algorithm. A witness against i found during the round is a witness against iq in P.

1. Divide P into q-blocks and make an array B of $k = m/q$ rows and q columns, where column j contains all P_i for all $i \equiv j \mod q$.
2. For each column c of B, find q_c, its pseudo period, and witnesses against non-multiples of q_c using PSEUDO-PERIOD. If all pseudo periods are $\leq \sqrt{k}$, all pseudo periods are real periods. Using FIND-LCM, compute $\mathrm{LCM}(k, q)$ and witnesses against non-multiples of $\mathrm{LCM}(k, q)$ smaller than $k/4$. The period of P that we compute is $q \cdot \mathrm{LCM}(k, q)$. (Recall that by computing the period we mean computing $\min(m/4, p)$.) Stop.
3. Otherwise, choose such a column c with $q_c > \sqrt{k}$. Witnesses against non-multiples of q_c were computed in Step 2. $q \leftarrow q \cdot q_c$.
4. If $q < m/4$, then go to the next round; else stop.

Note that in the first round we have one column and we compute a pseudo period of P by PSEUDO-PERIOD. In subsequent rounds $q \cdot q_c$ is a pseudo period because we compute witnesses for all non-multiples of $q \cdot q_c$. Since the new value k is at most $\sqrt{k}$, there are at most $O(\log \log m)$ rounds.

This algorithm follows the structure of the lower bound proof. In that proof the 'possible period length' is maintained, which is the minimum number that can still be a period based on the results of **all** the comparisons so far. The lower bound argument maintains a possible period length $q \leq m^{1-4^{-i}}$ in round i and forces any algorithm to have at least $\frac{1}{4} \log \log m$

rounds. Here, the number maintained q is a pseudo period. q may not be a period length but it must divide the period if the pattern is 4-periodic.

2.5.4   A CONSTANT EXPECTED TIME ALGORITHM

We present a constant expected time algorithm for computing witnesses, based on the pseudo-period technique. Using CONST-SEARCH this algorithm yields a constant expected time algorithm for the full parallel pattern matching algorithm.

First we execute three rounds of the deterministic algorithm and then execute Round 4 until it stops. At the beginning of Round 4, q is a pseudo period and B is the $k \times q$ array, $k = m/q$, created by Step 1 of the deterministic algorithm. We have $q > m^{7/8}$ and $k = m/q < m^{1/8}$.

Round 4:

1. Randomly choose $s = m/k^2$ columns from B and find the period of each chosen column naively with k^2 processors. Using naive comparisons also compute witnesses against nonperiods. Using FIND-LCM, compute $h = \text{LCM}(k, s)$ and witnesses against non-multiples of h.

2. If $h = k/4$, the pattern P is not 4-periodic. Stop.

3. Otherwise, check if h is a period of each column of B. If h is a period in all columns, qh is the period of P; Stop. Otherwise, Let C be the set of columns where h is not a period. One can show that $|C| \leq m^{1/2}$ with high probability.

4. Using Hagerup's $(1 + \epsilon)$-PAC, try to compact C into the set C' of size $m^{3/4}$. (If $|C| \leq m^{1/2}$, the compaction will succeed.) If the compaction fails, try again Round 4 starting from Step 1.

5. If the compaction is successful, compute all periods of columns in C' naively (we have enough processors because $m^{3/4}k^2 < m$). Using naive comparisons also compute witnesses against nonperiods. Using FIND-LCM, compute $h' = \text{LCM}(k, m^{3/4})$ of these periods and witnesses against non-multiples of h'. The period of P that we compute is $\min(m/4, q \cdot \text{LCM}(h, h'))$.

The probability that the PAC will fail is very small, and the expected number of rounds is smaller than 5. Thus, we presented above a constant expected time algorithm for computing witnesses of a string and using CONST-SEARCH also for the general parallel string matching. In fact, we can prove a somewhat stronger property of the algorithm: it has constant time with very high probability (probability exponentially close to 1).

2.6   Fast optimal algorithms on weaker models

The results presented in the previous sections provide the foundation for fast optimal algorithms on CREW-PRAM , EREW-PRAM and even a hypercube . There exist general simulations for any CRCW-PRAM algorithm on the CREW or EREW models. However, these simulations suffer from a $O(\log p)$ loss in time and optimality, where p is the maximum number of processors working in any single stage of the CRCW-PRAM algorithm. A lower bound of $\Omega(\log n)$ for computing a Boolean AND of n input bits on any CREW-PRAM implies an $\Omega(\log n)$ lower bound for string matching in this parallel computation model, as well as the weaker EREW-PRAM . No algorithm of those mentioned so far (except Vishkin's $O(\log m)$ search phase) could have been translated to an optimal $O(\log m)$ time algorithm on these models. Czumaj et al. came up with a new simple method for computing witnesses, a method that allowed them to tackle successfully the problems raised by these models.

Their method is a modification of the pseudo-period technique presented in Section 5. It consists of a divide and conquer approach to the period computation problem. They observed that once we found a pseudo-period for the pattern and divided the pattern to the 'equivalence classes' modulo the pseudo-period, we actually have to solve the original problem (finding the period and witnesses against non-multiples of the period) in every equivalence class separately. Using the FIND-LCM procedure, the various real periods that we get can be combined to form the real period of the full pattern. This is, in fact, a recursive form of the previous algorithm and it can be stated formally as follows.

procedure FIND-PERIOD(P, m)

1. q:=PSEUDO-PERIOD(P, m). If $q \leq \sqrt{m}$, Stop: q is a real period.
2. Divide pattern P into q substrings $c_i = P_i P_{i+q} \ldots$ for all $i = 1, \ldots, q$.
3. For all substrings c_i in parallel do:
$$\text{FIND-PERIOD}(c_i, m/q)$$
4. Use FIND-LCM to collect witnesses from the recursively processed c_i's and to find the period of the input string; A witness against j in one of the c_i's is a witness against jq in P.

The recursion representing the time complexity of this procedure in the CRCW-PRAM model is as follows.

$$(1) \qquad T(m) \leq T(\sqrt{m}) + O(1)$$

The solution of this recursion is $T(m) = O(\log \log m)$.

On the CREW-PRAM (and also the EREW-PRAM) one can perform the nonrecursive part in $O(\log m)$ (instead of $O(1)$). We get the recursion

$$(2) \qquad T'(m) \leq T'(\sqrt{m}) + O(\log m)$$

whose solution is $T'(m) = O(\log m)$.

The algorithm presented above (FIND-PERIOD) is not optimal. It can be made optimal using the following modification, which works well on all PRAM models. The idea is to use the algorithm to compute period and witnesses for large enough substring of P such that the total work is still linear, and to use the obtained information with the same technique (pseudo-period) to obtain witnesses and period for the whole pattern. Let t be the time of the preprocessing on the relevant model (on CRCW-PRAM $t = O(\log \log m)$ and on the other models $t = O(\log m)$).

procedure OPTIMAL-PREP (P, m)

1. Use FIND-PERIOD to preprocess the prefix z of size $2m/t$ of P. If it is non periodic, compute all witnesses and continue to Step 2. Otherwise, look for the end of the periodicity. If the periodicity doesn't end, then the pattern P is periodic with the period found for the prefix; Stop. Otherwise, use the nonperiodic substring of size $2m/t$ at the end of the periodicity as z. Use FIND-PERIOD to compute all witnesses for this z. The total work done in this stage is $O(m)$ and the time is $O(t)$ (Using general simulations on CREW-PRAM and EREW-PRAM).

2. Use **one** step of PSEUDO-PERIOD with the above z (instead of a z of length $2\sqrt{m}$) implemented on m/t processors. For the search of z inside P use the optimal search algorithm as described for each model. The pseudo period q that is found is of length at least $|z|/2$, since z is nonperiodic. Divide pattern p into q substrings $c_i = P_i P_{i+q} \ldots$ for all $i = 1, \ldots, q$. Each substring c_i is of length $< t$.

3. Let s be the smallest number such that $s \cdot |c_i| > t$. Assign a processor to each s c_i's. Since $s \cdot |c_i| < 2t$, m/t processors suffice. Each processor processes s c_i's sequentially, computing the period and witnesses for each c_i in $O(t)$ time.

4. Collect witnesses from the processed c_i's: a witness against j in one of the c_i's is a witness against jq in P.

For the text search on the CREW, we use the simple optimal algorithm of Vishkin. For the preprocessing we use the above OPTIMAL-PREP algorithm. Note that we use the algorithm for the search phase also in Step 2 of OPTIMAL-PREP , inside PSEUDO-PERIOD, to search for z with an optimal number of processors. We do not need DS. The last step in PSEUDO-PERIOD which involves finding the period of a $0, 1$ b-string can also be performed in optimal $O(\log m)$ time on the CREW-PRAM and EREW-PRAM .

2.6.1   OPTIMAL ALGORITHM ON THE EREW-PRAM

We assume here that $\log n = O(\log m)$; i.e. n is polynomial in m. Otherwise the search phase is dominated by $O(\log(n/m)) = O(\log n)$ which is the minimal time it takes to spread $O(n/m)$ copies of the pattern to all non overlapping m-blocks in the text.

The text search has a similar scheme to the one used for the CRCW-PRAM , but here we take care of read and write conflicts. It is constructed from a constant number of stages each taking $\Omega(\log m)$ time. We first make the text T $\log m$-good by processing $\log m$-blocks sequentially with $n/\log m$ processors. Then we apply DS to surviving candidates, item by item, avoiding read and write conflicts. The last stage includes performing duels concurrently until naive checks are possible. This last step which included squaring the sizes of k-blocks needs a more complex schedule in order to avoid read conflicts. Reading by processors can be considered as requests from memory. If the number of requests is m^c for some $c < 1$ then they can be answered in optimal $O(\log m)$ on the EREW-PRAM . This is true since in this case we can use sorting in $O(\log m)$ time and $O(m)$ work on the EREW-PRAM . We refer to this as *sparse sorting*. Instead of squaring we use an expansion step: from k-good blocks we move only to $k^{4/3}$-good blocks. This supports sparse sorting of read/write requests from the shared memory. The number of requests (symbol testing) during every expansion step is small ($O(m^d)$ for a constant $d < 1$).

The scheme of the EXPANSION procedure is given below, followed by the description of optimal $O(\log m)$-time text searching.

procedure EXPANSION(k,4/3)

1. In every k-block we have at most one candidate. It has an offset l in the block which we distribute into the first $k^{1/3}$ positions of the k-block.

2. Now the j-th processor from the i-th block reads the i-th position of the j-th block (no read/write conflicts here).

3. Every duel must get a proper witness, they are read from global array of witnesses. Every duel sends a request for the proper witness position. In each $k^{4/3}$-block we have $(k^{1/3})^2 = k^{2/3}$ requests (duels). There are $m/k^{4/3}$ such blocks and the total number of requests is bounded by $k^{2/3} \cdot m/k^{4/3} = m/k^{2/3}$ which is $O(m^d)$ if $k = m^c$ (where $c, d < 1$). To avoid read conflicts we can use the simple EREW-PRAM sparse sorting.

4. When all duels know their text positions they send requests to get a text symbol from the proper text position. The scheme of getting text symbols is the same as in Step 3. Any lost duel determines a witness against the corresponding candidate. Again, to record the new witness, we have to simulate a concurrent write by sparse sorting. If all duels are won for a given $k^{4/3}$-block, this candidate survives.

Expansion can be applied similarly if initially we have at most two candidates per k-block.

procedure OPT-SEARCH (P,T)

1. Process duels sequentially in every $\log m$-block in the text to make T $\log m$-good.
2. Use $\log m$-size DS to make T $k = (m^{1/3})$-good.
3. call EXPANSION(k,4/3) a few times (with increasing k) to make T $m/2$-good.
4. Check naively surviving candidates.

The pattern preprocessing is essentially the same as the one for the CREW-PRAM . One needs to verify that no concurrent reads are used.

The above algorithms for the EREW-PRAM were also modified to work on a hypercube . For this model, they show that string matching on general alphabet requires $\Omega(\log m)$ time and $\Omega(n \log m)$ work. They give an algorithm that matches these lower bounds.

2.7   Two dimensional pattern matching

The notions of witnesses and DS, developed for the one dimensional case, are used also in solving the two dimensional (2D) pattern matching problem. Similarly to the one dimensional case, the algorithms for the 2D problem work in two main phases: a *preprocessing* phase and a *search* phase. We use the search phase description to demonstrate the application of the above notions in the 2D case. We do not discuss here the preprocessing phase since it is quite involved.

We show how to find all occurrences of a 2D pattern P of size $m \times m$ in a text T of size $n \times n$ in $O(1)$ time and $O(n^2)$ work following the preprocessing of the pattern. We use here the notion of *h-periodicity* (or horizontal periodicity), which is string periodicity generalized to 2D along the horizontal dimension.

Definitions: A period of the pattern is a vector v such that if we place a copy of the pattern over itself shifted by this vector then no mismatches exist in the overlapped region. A horizontal period is a horizontal such vector. A witness against period v is a pair of positions $(a, a + v)$ in the pattern that the characters in them do not match. A candidate is a location in the text which can serve as the top left corner of an occurrence of the pattern. The range of a candidate is the area covered by an occurrence of the pattern if it starts in this candidate. Two candidates are *compatible* if the pattern occurrences assigned to them match wherever they overlap (their difference is a period). If two candidates are not compatible then we can eliminate at least one of the two by a duel using the witness against their difference being a period. The pattern P is *h-periodic* if it has a horizontal period vector of length l, $l < m'$ where $m' = \frac{m}{2}$.

We assume that P is not h-periodic; as in the one dimensional case the algorithm can be generalized to handle the h-periodic case. The following lemmas are crucial for the algorithm.

Lemma 2.8. *Some row of P (considered as a string) has a period of length $\geq \frac{\log m}{2}$.*

Proof: Assume all the rows have periods with length $< \frac{\log m}{2}$. The LCM of these periods must be smaller then $m/2$ and it is a horizontal period of P, a contradiction. □

The following lemma extends the notion of DS to two dimensions.

Lemma 2.9. *There exist a set of at most $\log m$ positions in P and a number f (a DS) such that if they are verified to match a candidate $q = (i, j)$ in the text, then all other candidates in the same row as q in the horizontal interval $[j - f + 1, j + m' - f]$ can be eliminated, i.e., they do not start an occurrence of the pattern.*

Proof: Let P' be a one-dimensional string that is constructed by concatenating the columns of P. As in Vishkin's construction for a string of length m, we put $m/2$ copies of P' one on top of the other, with m positions between neighboring copies, and compute DS of size $\log m$. This DS of P' gives a DS of P due to the obvious correspondence. □

The search phase consists of four stages, each takes $O(1)$ time and uses $O(n^2)$ operations. The text is divided into disjoint blocks of size $m' \times m'$, $m' = m/2$. All text blocks are processed in parallel. The description that follows is for a single text block B.

1. All the rows of B are processed in parallel. Let row r be the row of P given by Lemma 2.8. We find all occurrences of r beginning in B using the fast optimal one dimensional algorithm in $O(1)$ time and $O(m'^2)$ work. Only candidates such that r rows below them there is an occurrence of row r survive. Since row r has a period of size at least $\frac{\log m'}{2}$, at most $\frac{2m'}{\log m'}$ candidates survive in each row of B

2. All the rows of B are processed in parallel. At most two candidates in every row survive this step. Consider a row r' in B.
   For each surviving candidate c in r', we compare in parallel the characters of the DS, properly aligned. We eliminate candidates for which a mismatch was found. We find the first and last candidates in r' that survived the DS matching and eliminate all other candidates in r' (according to Lemma 2.9, similar to the one dimensional algorithms). This takes $O(1)$ time and $O(m')$ work for each row r'.

3. We have at most two survivors in each row of B for a total of $O(m')$ following Step 2. All pairs of surviving candidates in B are dueled in parallel in $O(1)$ time and $O((m')^2)$ work. Now all surviving candidates in B are mutually compatible.

4. Each text position that is in the range of at least one candidate is assigned one such candidate. (All of these candidates expect the same text symbol.) Comparisons are performed with the corresponding pattern positions. For any mismatch found, we need to eliminate all candidates such that the mismatch falls in their ranges. This is done by assigning to each candidate one of the mismatches in its region and eliminating those candidates to which a mismatch is assigned. The two assignments are quite simple and we omit the details here.

The text search algorithm described above works in optimal constant time. The computation of the DS can also be performed in optimal constant time. The rest of the preprocessing (computation of witnesses) can be performed in optimal $O(\log \log m)$ time.

2.8   Conclusion and open questions

We tried to demonstrate that a few basic concepts constitute the core of the parallel string matching algorithms. The progress achieved in the study of these algorithms resulted from a better understanding of these concepts and the finding of better ways to compute the corresponding information.

In Section 4, we showed a tight bound of $\Theta(\lceil m/p \rceil + \log \log_{1+p/m} 2p)$ for the problems of testing whether a given string is periodic and for string matching in case $n = 2m - 1$. Here we complete the analysis for the (unrestricted) string matching problem.

Theorem 2.10. *The time complexity of the string matching problem on the* CRCW-PRAM *is* $\Theta(\lceil n/p \rceil + \log \log_{1+p/m} 2p)$.

Proof: Upper   bound: Compute   witnesses   in $O(\lceil m/p \rceil + \log \log_{1+p/m} 2p)$, and then search in $O(\lceil n/p \rceil)$ using the algorithm described in Section 5.

Lower bound: Assume we can do string matching in time T. Obviously $T \geq \lceil n/p \rceil$. Now note that we can use string matching to test whether a given string w is periodic as follows. Find all occurrences of the first half of w starting at its first half. If there is only one occurrence (at 0), then w is not periodic. If there is another one, test if the periodicity extends to the end of w. w is periodic if and only if this test succeeds. So we have $T \geq \Omega(m/p + \log \log_{1+p/m} 2p)$.

□

Since the lower and upper bounds have been matched, only few questions remain open.

- String matching over a fixed alphabet. The lower bound of Section 2.3.3 assumes that the input strings are drawn from general alphabet and the only access to them is by comparisons. The lower and upper bounds for the string matching problem over general alphabet are identical to those for comparison based maximum finding algorithm obtained by Valiant. A constant time algorithm can find the maximum of integers in a restricted range which suggests the possibility of a faster string matching algorithm in case of constant alphabet.

- Deterministic sample computation. Finding a deterministic sample quickly with an optimal number of processors proved crucial for the fastest parallel string matching algorithm presented in this Chapter. The constant-time algorithms for computing DS use a polynomial number of processors, hence it can be applied only to a small substring of the original pattern. The other optimal algorithm for computing DS takes $O(\log^2 m / \log \log m)$ time. Are there algorithms that bridge this gap? Computing DS for the whole pattern in $O(\log \log m)$ time and an optimal number of processors may be still possible.

2.9   Exercises

1. Prove the GCD lemma.
2. In the proof of Corollary 3 we demonsrate how nonperiodic substrings of (almost) any length can be found. Prove that the strings we find are indeed nonperiodic.
3. In the periodic stage of the optimal $O(\log m)$ algorithm, show that the mismatch found is a witness against all remaining sources in the first block.
4. Given the following string : 1011101011111010, find a DS of size 2 for 8 shifts.
5. Write a program that computes witnesses for a given input string.
6. In the last stage of the two-dimension search we have to assign positions in the text to candidates. Show how this can be performed in constant time with n^2 processors.

2.10   Bibliographic notes

The sequential string matching problem has many optimal solutions, most notable of which are the algorithms by Knuth, Morris and Pratt [1977] and by Boyer and Moore [1977]. Karp, Miller and Rosenberg [1972] found the general technique of naming that was used by Crochemore and Rytter [1990] and Kedem, Landau and Palem [1989] for solving the parallel string matching problem. Karp and Rabin [1987] provided a randomized algorithm that solved the parallel string matching problem on the EREW-PRAM in $O(\log n)$ time.

Fich, Ragde and Wigderson [1984] described the algorithm for finding the leftmost one in an array of 1's and 0's, in constant time. This algorithm is used by most of the advanced string matching algorithms.

Galil [1985] designed an optimal $O(\log m)$ time algorithm for fixed alphabet. Vishkin [1985] introduced the concepts of witnesses and duels and used them in an optimal $O(\log m)$ time algorithm for general alphabet. Subsequently, Breslauer and Galil [1990] improved Vishkin's techniques and obtained an optimal $O(\log \log m)$ time algorithm for general alphabet. Breslauer and Galil [1992] went on to prove the lower bound for the problem. Vishkin [1990] introduced the concept of deterministic sample and used it to obtain an $O(\log^* m)$ time search phase. Galil followed with a constant time search phase using deterministic samples. These two very fast algorithms for the search phase required preprocessing in $O(\log^2 m / \log \log m)$ time.

Goldberg and Zwick [1994] first provided a solution with $O(\log m)$ preprocessing and constant search time utilizing larger deterministic samples. Cole et al. [1993] achieved two main goals in the area of parallel string matching: an $O(\log \log m)$ preprocessing phase with a constant time search, and a constant expected time for both the preprocessing and the search. In their algorithm they use the deterministic polynomial approximate compaction (PAC) of Ragde [1993] and its improvement by Hagerup [1992]. The same techinques were also used in their optimal algorithm for pattern matching in two dimensions. Czumaj et al. [1993] recently showed how the algorithms for preprocessing and text search in one and two dimensions can be transformed into optimal algorithms on the CREW-PRAM and the EREW-PRAM . They also showed how to transform them into algorithms on the hypercube with best possible work and time.

Bibliography

APOSTOLICO, A., C. ILIOPOULOS, , G.M. LANDAU, B., SCHIEBER, AND U. VISHKIN, Parallel construction of a suffix tree with applications, *Algorithmica* 3 (1988), 347-365.

BOYER, R. S., AND J.S. MOORE, A fast string searching algorithm, *Comm. ACM* 20 (1977), 762-772.

BRENT, R. P., The parallel evaluation of general arithmetic expressions, *J. ACM* 21 (1974), 201-206.

BRESLAUER, D., AND Z. GALIL, An optimal $O(\log \log n)$ parallel string matching algorithm, *SIAM J. Comput.* 19 (1990), 1051-1058.

BRESLAUER, D., AND Z. GALIL, A lower bound for parallel string matching, *SIAM J. on Comput.* 21 (1992), 856-862.

COLE, R., Parallel merge sort, *SIAM J. Comput.* 17 (1988), 770-785 .

COLE, R., M. CROCHEMORE, Z. GALIL, L. GĄSIENIEC, R. HARIHARAN, S. MUTHUKRISHNAN, K. PARK, AND W. RYTTER, Optimally fast parallel algorithms for preprocessing and pattern matching in one and two dimensions, *Proc. 34th IEEE Symp. Found. Computer Science* (1993), 248-258.

COLE, R., AND U. VISHKIN, Deterministic coin tossing and accelerating cascades: micro and macro techniques for designing parallel algorithms, *Proc. 18th ACM Symp. Theory Of Computing*(1986), 206-219.

COOK, S. A., C. DWORK, AND R. REISCHUK, Upper and lower time bounds for parallel random access machines without simultaneous writes, *SIAM J. Comput.* 15 (1986), 87-97.

CROCHEMORE, M., AND W. RYTTER, Parallel computations on strings and arrays, *Proc. 7th Symp. on Theoretical Aspects of Comp. Science*(1990), 109-125.

CZUMAJ, A., Z. GALIL, L. GĄSIENIEC, K. PARK, AND W. PLANDOWSKI, Work-time optimal parallel algorithms for string problems on the CREW-PRAM , the EREW-PRAM and the Hypercube, *manuscript*, (1993).

FICH, F. E., R.L. RAGDE, AND A. WIGDERSON, Relations between concurrent-write models of parallel computation, *SIAM J. Comput.* 17 (1988) 606-627.

GALIL, Z., On improving the worst case running time of the Boyer-Moore string matching algorithm, *Comm. ACM* 22 (1979), 505-508.

GALIL, Z., Optimal parallel algorithms for string matching, *Information and Control* 67 (1985), 144-157.

GALIL, Z., A constant-time optimal parallel string-matching algorithm, *Proc. 24th ACM Symp. Theory Of Computing* (1992), 69-76

GOLDBERG, T., AND U. ZWICK, Faster parallel string matching via larger deterministic samples, *Journal of Algorithms* 16 (1994), 295-308.

HAGERUP, T., On a compaction theorem of Ragde, *Inform. Process. Lett.* 43 (1992), 335-340.

JÁJÁ, J., *An Introduction to Parallel Algorithms*, Addison-Wesley, 1992

KARP, R.M., R.E. MILLER, AND A.L. ROSENBERG, Rapid identification of repeated patterns in strings, trees and arrays, *Proceedings of the 4th ACM Symp. Theory Of Computing* (1972), 125-136.

KARP, R.M., AND M.O. RABIN, Efficient randomized pattern matching algorithms, *IBM J. Res. Develop.* 31 (1987), 249-260.

KEDEM, Z., G. LANDAU, AND K. PALEM, Optimal parallel suffix-prefix matching algorithm and application, *Proc. 1st ACM Symp. on Parallel Algorithms and Architectures* (1989), 388-398.

KNUTH, D.E., J.H. MORRIS, AND V.R. PRATT, Fast pattern matching in strings, *SIAM J. Comput.* 6 (1977), 322-350.

LANDER, R. E., AND M.J. FISCHER, Parallel Prefix Computation, *J. ACM* 27 (1980), 831-838.

LYNDON, R.C., AND M.P. SCHUTZENBERGER, The equation $a M = b Nc P$ in a free group, *Michigan Math. J.* 9 (1962), 289-298.

RAGDE, P., The parallel simplicity of compaction and chaining, *J. Algorithms* 14 (1993), 371-380

SCHIEBER, B., Design and analysis of some parallel algorithms, *PhD. the-*

sis, Dept. of Compter Science, Tel Aviv Univ.(1987).

SHILOACH, Y., AND U. VISHKIN, Finding the maximum, merging and sorting in a parallel computation model, *J. Algorithms* 2 (1981), 88-102.

VALIANT, L.G., Parallelism in comparison models, *SIAM J. Comput.* 4 (1975), 348-355.

VISHKIN, U., Optimal parallel pattern matching in strings, *Information and Control* 67 (1985), 91-113.

VISHKIN, U., Deterministic sampling - A new technique for fast pattern matching, *SIAM J. Comput.* 20 (1990), 22-40.

3
On-line String Searching

In the previous two chapters, we have examined various serial and parallel methods to perform exact string searching in a number of operations proportional to the total length of the input. Even though such a performance is optimal, our treatment of exact searches cannot be considered exhausted yet: in many applications, searches for different, a-priorily unknown patterns are performed on a same text or group of texts. It seems natural to ask whether these cases can be handled better than by plain reiteration of the procedures studied so far. As an analogy, consider the classical problem of searching for a given item in a table with n entries. In general, n comparisons are both necessary and sufficient for this task. If we wanted to perform k such searches, however, it is no longer clear that we need kn comparisons. Our table can be sorted once and for all at a cost of $O(n \log n)$ comparisons, after which binary search can be used. For sufficiently large k, this approach outperforms that of the k independent searches.

In this chapter, we shall see that the philosophy subtending binary search can be fruitfully applied to string searching. Specifically, the text can be pre-processed once and for all in such a way that any query concerning whether or not a pattern occurs in the text can be answered in time proportional to the length of the pattern. It will also be possible to locate all the occurrences of the pattern in the text at an additional cost proportional to the total number of such occurrences. We call this type of search *on-line*, to refer to the fact that as soon as we finish reading the pattern we can decide whether or not it occurs in our text. As it turns out, the auxiliary structures used to achieve this goal are well suited to a host of other applications.

3.1 Subword trees

There are several, essentially equivalent digital structures supporting efficient on-line string searching. Here, we base our discussion on a variant known as suffix tree. It is instructive to discuss first a simplified version of suffix trees, which we call *expanded suffix tree*. This version is not the most efficient from the standpoint of complexity, but it serves a few pedagogical

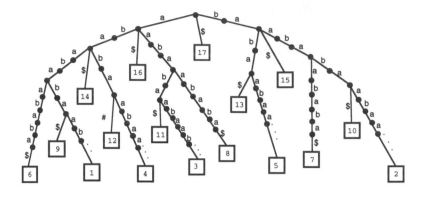

1	2	3	4	5	6	7	8	9	10	11	12	13	14	15	16	17
a	b	a	a	b	a	b	a	a	b	a	a	b	a	b	a	$

Fig. 3.1.   An expanded suffix tree

purposes, among which that of clearly exposing the relationship between
subword trees and finite automata.

Let x be a string of $n - 1$ symbols over some alphabet Σ and $ an
extra character not in Σ. The *expanded suffix tree* T_x associated with x is
a digital search tree collecting all suffixes of x. Specifically, T_x is defined
as follows.

1. T_x has n leaves, labeled from 1 to n.
2. Each arc is labeled with a symbol of $\Sigma \cup \{\$\}$. For any i, $1 \le i \le n$,
   the concatenation of the labels on the path from the root of T_x to
   leaf i is precisely the suffix $suf_i = x_i x_{i+1} ... x_{n-1}\$$.
3. For any two suffixes suf_i and suf_j of $x\$$, if w_{ij} is the longest common
   prefix that suf_i and suf_j have in common, then the path in T_x relative
   to w_{ij} is the same for suf_i and suf_j.

An example of expanded suffix tree is given in Figure 3.1.

The tree can be interpreted as the state transition diagram of a deterministic finite automaton where all nodes and leaves are final states, the
root is the initial state, and the labeled arcs, which are assumed to point
downwards, represent part of the state-transition function. The state transitions not specified in the diagram lead to a unique non-final *sink* state.
Our automaton recognizes the (finite) language consisting of all substrings
of string x. This observation clarifies also how the tree can be used in an
on-line search: letting y be the pattern, we follow the downward path in
the tree in response to consecutive symbols of y, one symbol at a time.
Clearly, y occurs in x if and only if this process takes to a final state. In
terms of T_x, we say that the *locus* of a string y is the node α, if it exists,
such that the path from the root of T_x to α is labeled y.

> **procedure** BUILDTREE (x, T_x)
> **begin**
> $T_0 \leftarrow \bigcirc$;
> **for** $i = 1$ **to** n **do** $T_i \leftarrow$ INSERT(suf_i, T_{i-1});
> $T_x = T_n$;
> **end**

Fig. 3.2.   Building an expanded suffix tree

Fact 1. *A string y occurs in x if and only if y has a locus in T_x.*

The implementation of Fact 1 takes $O(t \cdot |y|)$ character comparisons, where t is the time necessary to traverse a node, which is constant for a finite alphabet. Note that this only answers whether or not y occurs in x.

Fact 2. *If y has a locus α in T_x, then the occurrences of y in x are all and only the labels of the leaves in the subtree of T_x rooted at α.*

Thus, if we wanted to know where y occurs, it would suffice to visit the subtree of T_x rooted at node α, where α is the node such that the path from the root of T_x to α is labeled y. Such a visit requires time proportional to the number of nodes encountered, and the latter can be $\Theta(n^2)$ on the expanded suffix tree. This is as bad as running an offline search naively, but we will see shortly that a much better bound is possible.

An algorithm for the construction of the expanded T_x is readily organized (see Figure 3.2). We start with an empty tree and add to it the suffixes of $x\$$ one at a time. Conceptually, the insertion of suffix suf_i ($i = 1, 2, ..., n$) consists of two phases. In the first phase, we search for suf_i in T_{i-1}. Note that the presence of $\$$ guarantees that every suffix will end in a distinct leaf. Therefore, this search will end with failure sooner or later. At that point, though, we will have identified the longest prefix of suf_i that has a locus in T_{i-1}. Let $head_i$ be this prefix and α the locus of $head_i$. We can write $suf_i = head_i \cdot tail_i$ with $tail_i$ nonempty. In the second phase, we need to add to T_{i-1} a path leaving node α and labeled $tail_i$. This achieves the transformation of T_{i-1} into T_i.

We will assume that the first phase of INSERT is performed by a procedure FINDHEAD, which takes suf_i as input and returns a pointer to the node α. The second phase is performed by a procedure ADDPATH, which receives such a pointer and directs a path from node α to leaf i. The details of these procedures are left for an exercise.

Theorem 3.1. *The procedure BUILDTREE takes time $\Theta(n^2)$ and linear space.*

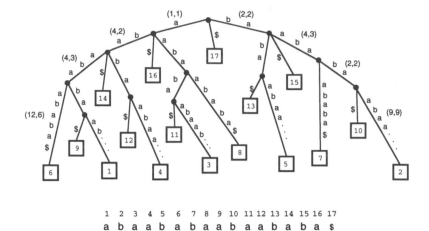

1 2 3 4 5 6 7 8 9 10 11 12 13 14 15 16 17
a b a a b a b a a b a a b a b a $

Fig. 3.3. A suffix tree in compact form

Proof: The procedure performs n calls to INSERT. The ith such call requires time proportional to the length $n - i + 1$ of suf_i. Hence the total charge is proportional to $\sum_{i=1}^{n}(n + 1 - i) = \sum_{i=1}^{n} i = n(n + 1)/2$. □

It is instructive to examine the cost of BUILDTREE in terms of the two constituent procedures of INSERT. If the symbols of x are all different, then T_x contains $\Theta(n^2)$ arcs. The procedure FINDHEAD only charges linear time overall, and the heaviest charges come form ADDPATH. At the other extreme, consider $x = a^{n-1}$. In this case, ADDPATH charges linear time overall and the real work is done by FINDHEAD.

It is easy to reduce the work charged by ADDPATH by resorting to a more compact representation of T_x. Specifically, we can collapse every chain formed by nodes with only one child into a single arc, and label that arc with a substring, rather than with a symbol of $x\$$. Such a *compact* version of T_x has at most n internal nodes, since there are $n + 1$ leaves in total and every internal node is branching. The compact version of the tree of Figure 3.1 is in Figure 3.3. Clearly, the two versions are equivalent for our purposes, and it takes little to adapt the details of BUILDTREE in order to fit the new format.

With the new convention, the tree for a string formed by all different symbols only requires 1 internal node, namely, the root. Except for arc-labeling, the construction of such a tree is performed in linear time, since ADDPATH spends now constant time per suffix. However, there is no improvement in the management of the case $x = a^{n-1}$, in which FINDHEAD still spends $\Theta(n^2)$ time.

While the topology of the tree requires now only $O(n)$ nodes and arcs, each arc is labeled with a substring of $x\$$. We have seen that the lengths of these labels may be $\Theta(n^2)$ (think again of the tree for a string formed by all different symbols). Thus, as long as this labeling policy is maintained, T_x will require $\Theta(n^2)$ space in the worst case, and it is clearly impossible to build a structure requiring quadratic space in less that quadratic worst-case time. Fortunately, a more efficient labeling is possible which allows us to store T_x in linear space. For this, it is sufficient to encode each arc label into a suitable pair of pointers in the form $[i, j]$ to a single common copy of x. For instance, pointer i denotes the starting position of the label and j the end. Now T_x takes linear space and it makes sense to investigate its construction in better than quadratic time.

As already seen, the time consuming operation of INSERT is in the auxiliary procedure FINDHEAD. For every i, this procedure starts at the the root of T_{i-1} and essentially locates the longest prefix $head_i$ of suf_i that is also a prefix of suf_j for some $j < i$. Note that $head_i$ will no longer necessarily end at a node of T_{i-1}. When it does, we say that $head_i$ has a *proper locus* in T_{i-1}. If $head_i$ ends inside an arc leading from some node α to some node β, we call α the *contracted locus* and β the *extended locus* of $head_i$. We use the word *locus* to refer to the proper or extended locus, according to the case. It is trivial to upgrade FINDHEAD in such a way that the procedure creates the proper locus of $head_i$ whenever such a locus does not already exist. Note that this part of the procedure only requires constant time.

3.2 McCreight's algorithm

The discussion of the previous section embodies the obvious principle that the construction of a digital search tree for an arbitrary set of words $\{w_1, w_2, ..., w_k\}$ cannot be done in time better than the $\sum_{i=1}^{k} |w_i|$ in the worst case. This seems to rule out a better-than-quadratic construction for T_x, even when the tree itself is in compact form. However, the words stored in T_x are not unrelated, since they are all suffixes of a same string. This simple fact has the following imporant consequences.

Lemma 3.2. *For any* i, $1 \leq i \leq n$, $|head_{i+1}| \geq |head_i| - 1$

Proof: Assume the contrary, i.e., $|head_{i+1}| < |head_i| - 1$. Then, $head_{i+1}$ is a substring of $head_i$. By definition, $head_i$ is the longest prefix of suf_i that has another occurrence at some position $j < i$. Let $x_j x_{j+1}...x_{j+|head_i|-1}$ be such an occurrence. Clearly, any substring of $head_i$ has an occurrence in $x_j x_{j+1}...x_{j+|head_i|-1}$. In particular, $x_{j+1} x_{j+2}...x_{j+|head_i|-1} = x_{i+1} x_{i+2}...x_{i+|head_i|-1}$, hence $x_{i+1} x_{i+2}...x_{i+|head_i|-1}$ must be a prefix of $head_{i+1}$. $\square$

Lemma 3.3. *Let* $w = ay$, *with* $a \in \Sigma$ *and* $y \in \Sigma^*$. *If* w *has a proper locus in* T_x, *so does* y.

Proof: Since every node of T_x is branching, then the fact that w has a proper locus in T_x means that there are at least substrings of x in the form wa and wb with $a, b \in \Sigma$ and $a \neq b$. But then ya and yb are also substrings of x. □

Note that the converse of Lemma 3.3 is not true. Lemmas 3.2 and 3.3 are very helpful. Assume we have just inserted suf_i into T_{i-1}. Because $suf_i = head_i \cdot tail_i$ with $tail_i$ nonempty, we are guaranteed that $head_i$ has a proper locus, say, α in T_i. Let $head_i = ay_i$. Clearly, there is a path labeled y_i in T_i. Assume that we can reach instantaneously the end of this path. This might be at a node or in the middle of an arc. Lemma 3.2 tells us that $head_{i+1}$ is not shorter than this path. Once we are at that point we only need go further into the tree in response to the symbols of suf_{i+1} that follow y_i, until we fall off the tree again. Let $head_{i+1} = y_i z_{i+1}$, where z_{i+1} is possibly empty. Clearly, we only need to do work proportional to z_{i+1}. Having found $head_{i+1}$, we can invoke the same principle and write $head_{i+1} = a' y_{i+1}$ so that $head_{i+2} = y_{i+1} z_{i+2}$, and so on.

Lemma 3.4. $\sum_{i=1}^{n+1} |z_i| = n$

Proof: The z_i's are non-overlapping. □

Lemma 3.4 suggests that FINDHEAD be regarded as consisting of two stages. With reference to the insertion of suf_{i+1}, Stage 1 consists of finding the end of the path to y_i, and Stage 2 consists of identifying z_{i+1}. For reasons that will become apparent in the sequel, we refer to Stage 2 as the *scanning*. Lemma 3.4 shows that all executions of scanning take amortized linear time. Thus the main task is to perform Stage 1 with the same amortized efficiency as Stage 2.

Let us add to the structure of T_x some new links called *suffix links* and defined as follows: For every string $w = ay$ having a proper locus in T_x, there is a link directed from the locus of w to the locus of y. It would be nice to have that, at the inception of every iteration of BUILDTREE, every node of the tree produced thus far has a defined suffix link. In fact, assume that, upon completion of the insertion of suf_i, both $head_i$ and y_i had proper loci in T_i. Following the suffix link assigned to the locus α of $head_i$ we would reach instantaneously the locus of y_i. In other words, Stage 1 would require constant time per iteration.

Unfortunately, there are two difficulties. The first one is that lemma 3.3 tells us that y_i has a proper locus in T_x, but it says nothing of T_i. In other words, y_i is not guaranteed to have a proper locus in T_i. The second difficulty is that, upon completion of T_i, even if y_i had a proper locus in T_i, it might be impossible to reach it immediately from the locus α of $head_i$, for the simple reason that α was just created as part of the ith iteration of BUILDTREE. In conclusion, we cannot maintain as an invariant that every node of T_i has a defined suffix link. However, we can maintain the next best thing, namely:

Invariant 1. *In T_i, every node except possibly the locus of $head_i$ has a defined suffix link.*

At the beginning, the suffix link of the root points to the root itself. Assume that we have just found the locus of $head_i$. By Invariant 1, Father[α] has a defined suffix link. Let $head_i = ay_i = aw_is_i$ where aw_i is the (possibly empty) prefix of y_i having Father[α] as its proper locus. By following the suffix link from Father[α], we thus reach the proper locus γ of w_i. Once at node γ, we know that we need to go down in the tree for at least $|s_i|$ symbols, by virtue of Lemma 3.2. This phase is called *rescanning*, since we have already seen the symbols of s_i. Before examining the mechanics of rescanning, we point out that it may end up in one of two possible ways:

1. $y_i = w_is_i$ has a proper locus in T_i.
2. $y_i = w_is_i$ has an extended locus in T_i.

Case 1 is relatively easy. All we have to do is to set the suffix link from α to the locus γ of y_i, and initiate the scanning from this node. Case 2 is more elaborate. Note that Invariant 1 prescribes that at the end of this pass there be a suffix link defined from α to the proper locus of y_i. Since such a locus did not exist, we have to introduce it at this moment. But we are in the middle of an arc, and splitting an arc with a node having only one child might infringe our convention on the structure of T_x! The following lemma ensures that no such infringement will take place.

Lemma 3.5. *If y_i does not have a proper locus in T_i, then $head_{i+1} = y_i$.*

Proof: Exercise. □

In principle, we may design the rescanning along the same lines as the scanning. Unlike the z_i substrings involved in scanning, however, the s_i substrings involved in rescanning present mutual overlaps. This is undesirable, since it plays havoc with the linear time complexity. A closer look reveals a significant difference between scanning and rescanning: in rescanning, we know beforehand the length of the substring s being rescanned. This allows us to rescan in time proportional to the number of nodes traversed in rescanning, rather than to the length $|s|$ itself. At first sight, it is not clear how this would induce a savings, since the number of such nodes can be $\Theta(|s|)$. However, we will show that the *total* number of nodes involved in rescanning is linear in $|x|$. Before getting to that point, let us refine the details of rescanning.

Suppose we reached node γ, the locus of w_i, and let $\bar{a}$ be the first symbol of s_i. There is precisely one arc leaving γ with a label that starts with $\bar{a}$. Let γ_1 be the child of γ along this arc. By comparing $|s_i|$ and the length of the label of the arc (γ, γ_1) we can decide in constant time whether the locus of $y_i = w_i s_i$ is in the middle of this arc, precisely on γ_1 or further below. In the first two cases the rescanning is finished, in the third case, we move to γ_1 having rescanned a prefix of s_i, and need still to rescan a suffix s_i' of s_i. We proceed in the same way from γ_1, thus finding a descendant γ_2 of γ_1, and so on. The time spent at each of the nodes $\gamma, \gamma_1, \gamma_2, \ldots$ is constant, whence rescanning takes time linear in the number of nodes traversed.

Lemma 3.6. *The number of intermediate nodes encountered in rescanning thru all iterations of BUILDTREE is $O(n)$.*

Proof: Let res_i be defined as the shortest suffix of $x\$$ to which the rescanning and scan operations are confined during the ith iteration of BUILDTREE. Observe that for every intermediate node γ_f encountered during the rescan of s_i, there will be a nonempty string which is contained in res_i but not in res_{i+1}. Therefore, $|res_{i+1}|$ is at most $|res_i| - int_i$, where int_i is the number of intermediate nodes encountered while rescanning at iteration i. By repeated substitutions we see that $\sum_{i=1}^{n+1} int_i$ is at most n, since $|res_{n+1}| = 0$ and $|res_0| = 0$. Thus, the number of nodes encountered during the rescanning is at most n. $\square$

In conclusion, we can formulate the following

Theorem 3.7. *The suffix tree in compact form for a string of n symbols can be built in $O(t \cdot n)$ time and $O(n)$ space, where t is the time needed to traverse a node.*

3.3   Storing suffix trees

When the alphabet Σ is a constant independent of n, the factor t in Theorem 3.7 is also a constant. It is desirable to detail how the constructions of the previous sections handle the cases where $|\Sigma|$ is not a constant. For this purpose, we must address the issue of the memory allocations of suffix trees. This is done in this section.

In some applications, T_x needs only be traversed bottom-up. This occurs, for instance, in connection with computations of the *squares* in a string, or in computing substring statistics, etc. In all these cases, a satisfactory representation of the tree is achieved by letting each node have precisely one pointer, directed to its father. This node format does not pose any problem in allocation irrespective of the size of Σ.

For problems like on-line searches, which we used as motivation in our discussion, we need to traverse the tree downwards from the root, and thus we need that edges be directed from each node to its children. The number of edges leaving a node is bounded above by $|\Sigma|$, and $|\Sigma|$ can be $\Theta(n)$.

In other words, even though there are $O(n)$ arcs in T_x irrespective of the size of Σ, the number of arcs leaving a specific node can assume any value from 2 to $\Theta(n)$. This poses a problem of efficiently formatting the nodes of T_x. Before addressing this point, we recall that, in addition to the edges leaving it, each node of T_x must also store appropriate *branching* labels for all the downward edges originating from it. Such labels are needed during the construction of T_x, and they also drive, e.g., the downward search in T_x of any string w. Earlier in this Chapter, we stipulated that each edge be labeled with a pair of integers pointing to a substring of x. In order to leave a node towards one of its children, however, we need to know the first character of such a substring. To fix the ideas, let (i, j) be the label of an edge (α, β). We may use our knowledge of i to access the character x_i. Alternatively, we could add to the pair (i, j) the symbol of Σ that corresponds to x_i. The two approaches are different, since we need $\log |\Sigma|$ bits to identify a symbol and $\log n$ bits to identify a position of x.

The set of branching labels leaving each internal node of T_x can be stored using a linear list, a binary trie, or an array.

Resorting to arrays supports, say, searching for a word w in T_x in time $O(|w|)$, but requires space $\Theta(|\Sigma|n)$ or $\Theta(n^2)$, depending on the labeling convention adopted, to store T_x. Note that the initialization of the overall space allocated seems to require quadratic time. Fortunately, techniques are available to initialize only the space which is actually used. We leave this as an exercise. Lists or binary tries require only linear space for T_x. However, the best time bounds for searching w under the two labeling conventions become $O(|w| \log |\Sigma|)$ and $O(|w| \log n)$, respectively. Such bounds refer to the implementation with binary tries. For ordered alphabets, the bound $O(|w| \log |\Sigma|)$ extends also to the list implementation of the symbol-based downward labels. To summarize our discussion, the multiplicative factor t appearing in Theorem 3.7 and in on-line search is a logarithm, the argument of which can be made to be either $|\Sigma|$ or n. Clearly, we would choose $|\Sigma|$ when Σ is finite.

3.4   Building suffix trees in parallel

We address now the parallel construction of the suffix tree T_x associated with input string x. We adopt the concurrent-read concurrent-write (CRCW) parallel random access machine (PRAM) model of computation described in the first Chapter of the book. We use n processors which can simultaneously read from and write to a common memory with $\Theta(n^2)$ locations. When several processors attempt to write simultaneously to the same memory location, one of them succeeds but we do not know in advance which. Note that an algorithm takes care in general of initializing the memory it uses. In this particular case, however, we will show that a memory location is read by some processor only after that processor attempted to write to it. Thus, we do not need to initialize this space. The overall *processors* × *time* cost of our algorithm is $O(n \log n)$, which is optimal when $|\Sigma|$ is of the same order of magnitude as n. It is left as an exercise to show that the space can be reduced to $O(n^{1+\epsilon})$, for any chosen $0 < \epsilon \le 1$, with a corresponding slow-down proportional to $1/\epsilon$.

From now on, we will assume w.l.o.g. that $n - 1$ is a power of 2. We also extend x by appending to it $n - 1$ instances of the symbol $. We use $x\#$ to refer to this modified string. Our idea is to start with a tree D_x which consists simply of a root node with n children, corresponding to the first n suffixes of $x\#$, and then produce $\log n$ consecutive *refinements* of D_x such that the last such refinement coincides with T_x up to a reversal of the direction of all edges. The edges in D_x and each subsequent refinement point from each node to its parent. Throughout, information is stored into the nodes and leaves. Specifically, each leaf or internal node of a refinement of D_x is labeled with the descriptor of some substring of $x\#$ having starting positions in $[1,n]$. We adopt pairs in the form (i, l), where i is a position and l is a length, as descriptors. Thus, the root of D_x is the locus of the empty word. The root has n sons, each one being the locus of a distinct suffix of x.

We use n processors $p_1, p_2, ..., p_n$, where i is the *serial number* of processor p_i. At the beginning, processor p_i is assigned to the i-th position of $x\#$, $i = 1, 2, ..., n$.

Our computation consists of a preprocessing phase followed by a processing phase. They are described next.

3.4.1   PREPROCESSING

The preprocessing consists of partitioning the substrings of $x\#$ of length $2^q (q = 0, 1, ..., \log n)$ into equivalence classes, in such a way that substrings that are identical end in the same class. For this, each processor is assigned $\log n + 1$ cells of the common memory. The segment assigned to p_i is called ID_i. By the end of the preprocessing, $ID_i[q]$ $(i = 1, 2, ...n; q = 0, 1, ..., \log n)$ contains (the first component of) a descriptor for the substring of $x\#$ of length 2^q which starts at position i in $x\#$, in such a way that all the occurrences of the same substring of x get the same descriptor. For convenience, we extend the notion of ID to all positions $i > n$ through the convention: $ID_i[q] = n + 1$ for $i > n$. We will use a *bulletin board* (BB) of $n \times (n + 1)$ locations in the common memory. According to our convention, all processors can simultaneously attempt to write to BB and simultaneously read from it. In the following, we call $winner(i)$ the index of the processor which succeeds in writing to the location of the common memory attempted by p_i.

The initializations are as follows. In parallel, all processors initialize their ID arrays filling them with zeroes. Next, the processors partition themselves into equivalence classes based on the symbol of Σ faced by each. Treating symbols as integers, processors that face the same symbol attempt to write their serial number in the same location of BB. Thus, if $x_i = s \in \Sigma$, processor p_i attempts to write i in $BB[1, s]$. Through a second reading from the same location, p_i reads $j = winner(i)$ and sets $ID_i[0] \leftarrow j$. Thus $(j, 1)$ becomes the descriptor for every occurrence of symbol s.

We now describe *iteration* q, $q = 1, 2, ..., \log n$, which is also performed synchronously by all processors. Processor p_i, $i = 1, 2, ..., n$ first grabs $ID_{i+2^q}[q])$ and then attempts to write i in $BB[ID_i[q], ID_{i+2^q}[q]]$. Finally, p_i sets: $ID_i[q + 1] \leftarrow winner(i)$, $i = 1, 2, ..., n$. Note that, since no two n-symbol substrings of $x\#$ are identical, p_i $(i = 1, 2, ..., n)$ must be writing its own number into $ID_i[\log n]$ at the end of the computation. Note that a processor reads from a location of BB only immediately after attempting to write to that location. Our discussion of preprocessing establishes the following theorem.

Theorem 3.8. *There is an algorithm to compute the ID tables in $O(\log n)$ time and $\Theta(n^2)$ space with n processors in a CRCW.*

3.4.2 STRUCTURING D_X

We need some conventions regarding the allocation of D_x and of its subsequent refinements. For this purpose, we assign to each processor another segment of the common memory, also consisting of $\log n + 1$ cells. The segment assigned to p_i is called $NODE_i$. Like the ID tables, $NODE_i$ is made empty by p_i at the beginning. Our final construction takes as input the string $x\#$, a location of the common memory called $ROOT$, and the arrays $ID_i[q]$; $(i = 1, 2, ..., n, q = 0, 1, ..., \log n)$, and computes the entries of the arrays $NODE_i[q]$ $(i = 1, 2, ..., n, q = 0, 1, ..., \log n)$. By the end of the computation, if, for some value of $q \leq \log n$, $NODE_i[q]$ is not empty, then it represents a node μ created with the kth refinement of D_x, where $k = \log n - q$, with the following format: the field $NODE_i[q].LABEL$ represents $label(\mu)$, and the field $NODE_i[q].PARENT$ points to the $NODE$ location of Father$[\mu]$. The initialization consists of setting:

$$NODE_i[\log n].PARENT \leftarrow address(ROOT);$$
$$NODE_i[\log n].LABEL \leftarrow (ID_i[\log n], n)$$

Hence $NODE_i[\log n]$ becomes the locus of suf_i.

Note that $NODE_i[\log n]$ stores the leaf labeled (i, n) and thus is not empty for $i = 1, 2, ..., n$.

To familiarize with the $NODE$ tables, we consider the process that produces the first refinement of D_x. Essentially, we want to partition the edges of D_x into equivalence classes, putting edges labeled with the the same first $n/2$ symbols in the same class. For every such class, we want to funnel all edges in that class through a new internal node, which is displaced $n/2$ symbols from the root.

We do this as follows. Assume one row known to all processors, say, row r of BB is assigned to $ROOT$. Then, processors facing the same label in $ID[\log n - 1]$ attempt to write their serial number in the same location of this row of BB. Specifically, if $ID_i[\log n - 1] = k$, processor p_i attempts to write i in $BB[r, k]$. Through a second reading from the same location, p_i reads $j = winner(i)$. This elects $NODE_j[\log n - 1]$ to be the locus in the new tree of strings having label $(j, n/2)$. Processor p_j copies this pair into $NODE_j[\log n - 1].LABEL$ and sets a pointer to $ROOT$ in $NODE_j[\log n - 1].LABEL$.

For all i such that $winner(i) = j$, processor p_i sets:

$$NODE_i[\log n - 1].PARENT \; \leftarrow \; address(NODE_j[\log n - 1])$$
$$NODE_i[\log n - 1].LABEL \; \leftarrow \; ID_{i+n/2}[\log n - 1]$$

We shall see shortly that some additional details need to be fixed before this refinement of D_x can be deemed viable. For instance, nodes having a single child must be forbidden in any of the refinements. This means that, whenever a node μ is created that has no siblings, then the pointer from Father$[\mu]$ must be removed and copied back into μ. Taking care of this problem is not difficult. A more serious problems is the following one. Recall that we started out with the processors sitting on locations of the $NODE$ arrays that correspond to the leaves of D_x. As a result of the first refinement, we have now internal nodes other than the root. In order to proceed with our scheme, we need to equip these internal nodes each with its own processor. Since we avoid the formation of unary nodes we will need no more tha $2n$ processors at any point of our computation. However, there is no way to predict which $NODE$ locations will host the newly inserted nodes, and there are $\Theta(n \log n)$ such locations. Thus, the main difficulty is designing a scheme that assigns dynamically processors to nodes in such a way that every node gets its processor.

3.4.3   REFINING D_X

We concentrate now on the task of producing $\log n$ consecutive refinements of $D_x = D^{(\log n)}$. The q-th such refinement is denoted by $D^{(\log n - q)}$. The last refinement $D^{(0)}$ is identical to T_x except for the edge directions, which are reversed.

We will define our sequence of refinements by specifying how $D^{(\log n - q)}$ is obtained from $D^{(\log n - q + 1)}$, for $q = 1, 2, ..., \log n$. Three preliminary notions are needed in order to proceed.

A *nest* is any set formed by all children of some node in $D^{(k)}$. Let (i, l) and (j, f) be the labels of two nodes in some nest of $D^{(k)}$. An integer t, $0 < t \leq \min[l, f]$, is a *refiner* for (i, l) and (j, f) iff $x\#[i, i + t - 1] = x\#[j, j + t - 1]$. A nest of $D^{(k)}$ is *refinable* if 2^{k-1} is a refiner for every pair of labels of nodes in the nest.

Assume now that all refinements down to $D^{(k)}$, $\log n \leq k < 0$, have been already produced, and that $D^{(k)}$ meets the following *condition(k)*:

(i) $D^{(k)}$ is a rooted tree with n leaves and no unary nodes;
(ii) Each node of $D^{(k)}$ is labeled with a descriptor of some substring of x; each leaf is labeled, in addition, with a distinct position of $x\$$; the concatenation of the labels on the path from the root to leaf j describes suf_j.
(iii) No pair of labels of nodes in a same nest of $D^{(k)}$ admits a refiner of size 2^k.

Observe that *condition*($\log n$) is met trivially by D_x. Moreover, part (iii) of *condition*(0) implies that reversing the direction of all edges of $D^{(0)}$ would change $D^{(0)}$ into a digital-search tree that stores the collection of all suffixes of $x\$$. Clearly, such a trie fulfills precisely the definition of T_x.

We now define $D^{(k-1)}$ as the tree obtained by transforming $D^{(k)}$ as follows. Let $(i_1, l_1), (i_2, l_2), ..., (i_m, l_m)$ be the set of all labels in some nest of $D^{(k)}$. Let ν be the parent node of that nest. The nest is refined in two steps.

STEP 1. Use the *LABEL* and *ID* tables to modify the nest rooted at ν, as follows. With the child node labeled (i_j, l_j) associate the *contracted* label $ID_{i_j}[k-1]$, $j = 1, 2, ..., m$. Now partition the children of ν into equivalence classes, putting in the same class all nodes with the same contracted label. For each non-singleton class which results, perform the following three operations.

(1) Create a new parent node μ for the nodes in that class, and make μ a son of ν.
(2) Set the *LABEL* of μ to $(i, 2^{(k-1)})$, where i is the contracted label of all nodes in the class.
(3) Consider each child of μ. For the child whose current *LABEL* is (i_j, l_j), change *LABEL* to $(i_j + 2^{k-1}, l_j - 2^{k-1})$.

STEP 2. If more than one class resulted from the partition, then stop. Otherwise, let C be the unique class resulting from the partition. It follows from assumption (i) on $D^{(k)}$ that C cannot be a singleton class. Thus a new parent node μ as above was created for the nodes in C during STEP 1. Make μ a child of the parent of ν and set the *LABEL* of μ to $(i, l + 2^{k-1})$, where (i, l) is the label of ν.

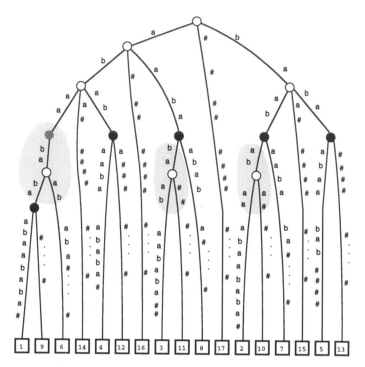

Fig. 3.4.   One step in the parallel refinement

The following lemma shows that our definition of the series of refine-ments $D^{(k)}$ is unambiguous.

Lemma 3.9. *The synchronous application of Steps 1 and 2 to all nests of $D^{(k)}$ produces a tree that meets condition$(k-1)$.*

Proof: Properties (ii-iii) of *condition*$(k-1)$ are easily established for $D^{(k-1)}$. Thus, we concentrate on property (i). Since no new leaves were inserted in the transition from D^k to $D^{(k-1)}$, property (i) will hold once we prove that $D^{(k-1)}$ is a tree with no unary nodes.

Since $|\{\$\} \cup \Sigma| > 1$, then the nest of the children of the root cannot end in a singleton class for any $k > 0$. Thus for any parent node ν of a nest of $D^{(k)}$ involved in STEP 2, Father$[\nu]$ is defined. By *condition*(k), node ν has more than one child, and so does Father$[\nu]$. Let $\bar{D}^{(k)}$ be the structure resulting from application of Step 1 to $D^{(k)}$.

If, in $D^{(k)}$, the nest of Father$[\nu]$ is not refinable, then ν is a node of $D^{(k-1)}$, and ν may be the only unary node in $\bar{D}^{(k)}$ between any child of ν in $D^{(k)}$ and the parent of ν in $D^{(k)}$. Node ν is removed in STEP 2, unless ν is a branching node in $\bar{D}^{(k)}$. Hence no unary nodes result in this part of $D^{(k-1)}$.

Assume now that, in $D^{(k)}$, both the nest of ν and that of Father$[\nu]$ are refinable. We claim that, in $\bar{D}^{(k)}$, either the parent of ν has not changed and it is a branching node, or it has changed but still is a branching node. Indeed, by definition of $D^{(k)}$, neither the nest of ν nor that of Father $[\nu]$ can be refined into only one singleton equivalence class. Thus, by the end of STEP 1, the following alternatives are left.

1. The Father of ν in $\bar{D}^{(k)}$ is identical to Father$[\nu]$ in $D^{(k)}$. Since the nest of Father$[\nu]$ could not have been refined into only one singleton class, then Father$[\nu]$ must be a branching node in $D^{(k-1)}$. Thus this case reduces to that where the nest of Father$[\nu]$ is not refinable.

2. The parent of ν in $\bar{D}^{(k)}$ is not the parent of ν in $D^{(k)}$. Then Father$[\nu]$ in $\bar{D}^{(k)}$ is a branching node, and also a node of $D^{(k-1)}$. If ν is a branching node in $\bar{D}^{(k)}$, then there is no unary node between ν and Father$[\nu]$ in $\bar{D}^{(k)}$, and the same holds true between any node in the nest of ν and ν. If ν is an unary node in $\bar{D}^{(k)}$, then the unique child of ν is a branching node. Since the current parent of ν is also a branching node by hypothesis, then removing ν in STEP 2 eliminates the only unary node existing on the path from any node in the nest of ν to the closest branching ancestor of that node. □

If the nest of $D^{(k)}$ rooted at ν had a row r of BB all to itself, then the transformation undergone by this nest in Step 1 can be accomplished by m processors in constant time, m being the number of children. Each processor handles one child node. It generates the contracted label for that node using its $LABEL$ field and the ID tables. Next, the processors use the row of BB assigned to the nest and the contracted labels to partition themselves into equivalence classes: each processor in the nest whose contracted label is i competes to write the address of its node in the ith location of r. A *representative* processor is elected for each class in this way. Singleton classes can be trivially spotted through a second concurrent write restricted to losing processors (after this second write, a representative processor which still reads its node address in r knows itself to be in a singleton class). The representatives of each nonsingleton class create now the new parent nodes, label them with their contracted label, and make each new node accessible by all other processors in the class. To conclude STEP 1, the processors in the same class update the labels of their nodes.

For STEP 2, the existence of more than one equivalence class needs to be tested. This is done through a competition of the representatives which uses the root of the nest as a common write location, and follows the same mechanism as in the construction of D_x. If only one equivalence class was produced in STEP 1, then its representative performs the adjustment of label prescribed by STEP 2.

We conclude that once each node of $D^{(k)}$ is assigned a distinct processor, $D^{(k-1)}$ can be produced in constant time. The difficulty, however, is how to assign in constant time additional processors to the nodes created anew in $D^{(k-1)}$. It turns out that bringing fewer processors into the game leads to a crisp processor (re-)assignment strategy. The basic idea is to perform the manipulations of Steps 1-2 using $m-1$ processors, rather than m for a nest of m nodes. The only prerequisite for this is that all $m-1$ processors have access to the unique node which lacks a processor of its own. Before starting STEP 1, the processors elect one of them to serve as a substitute for the missing processor. After each elementary step, this simulator "catches-up" with the others. This can be used also to assign the rows of BB to the nodes of $D^{(k)}$: simply assign the i-th row to processor p_i. Then, whenever p_i is in charge of the simulation of the missing processor in a nest, its BB row is used by all processors in that nest. In summary, we stipulate the following

Invariant 2. *In any refinement of D_x, if a node other than ROOT has m children, then precisely $m-1$ of the children have been assigned a processor. Moreover, each one of the $m-1$ processors knows the address of the unique sibling without a processor.*

For any given value of k, let a *legal* assignment of processors to the nodes of $D^{(k)}$ be an assignment that enjoys Invariant 2.

Lemma 3.10. *Given a legal assignment of processors for $D^{(k)}$, a legal assignment of processors for $D^{(k-1)}$ can be produced in constant time.*

Proof: We give first a constant-time policy that re-allocates the processors in each nest of $D^{(k)}$ on the nodes of $\bar{D}^{(k)}$. We show then that our policy leads to a legal assignment for $D^{(k-1)}$.

Let then ν be the parent of a nest of $D^{(k)}$. A node to which a processor has been assigned will be called *pebbled*. By hypothesis, all but one of the children of ν are pebbled. Also, all children of ν are nodes of $\bar{D}^{(k)}$. In the general case, some of the children of ν in $D^{(k)}$ are still children of ν in $\bar{D}^{(k)}$, while others became children of newly inserted nodes $\mu_1, \mu_2, ..., \mu_t$. Our policy is as follows. At the end of STEP 1, for each node μ_r of $\bar{D}^{(k)}$ such that all children of μ_r are pebbled, one pebble (say, the representative processor) is chosen among the children and passed on to the parent. In STEP 2, whenever a pebbled node ν is removed, then its pebble is passed down to the (unique) son μ of ν in $\bar{D}^{(k)}$.

Clearly, our policy can be implemented in constant time. To prove its correctness, we need to show that it generates a legal assignment for $D^{(k-1)}$.

It is easy to see that if node ν is removed in the transition from $\bar{D}^{(k)}$ to $D^{(k-1)}$, then the unique son μ of ν in $\bar{D}^{(k)}$ is unpebbled in $\bar{D}^{(k)}$. Thus, in STEP 2, it can never happen that two pebbles are moved onto the same node of $D^{(k-1)}$.

By definition of $D^{(k)}$, the nest of node ν cannot give rise to a singleton class. Thus at the end of STEP 1, either (Case 1) the nest has been refined in only one (nonsingleton) class, or (Case 2) it has been refined in more than one class, some of which are possibly singleton classes.

Before analyzing these two cases, define a mapping f from the children in the nest of the generic node ν of $D^{(k)}$ into nodes of $D^{(k-1)}$, as follows. If node μ is in the nest of ν and also in $D^{(k-1)}$ then set $\mu' = f(\mu) = \mu$; if instead μ is not in $D^{(k-1)}$, let $\mu' = f(\mu)$ be the (unique) son of μ in $\bar{D}^{(k)}$.

In Case 1, exactly one node μ is unpebbled in $\bar{D}^{(k)}$. All the nodes μ''s are siblings in $D^{(k-1)}$ and, by our policy, μ' is pebbled in $D^{(k-1)}$ iff μ is pebbled in $D^{(k)}$.

In Case 2, node ν is in $D^{(k-1)}$. Any node μ in the nest of ν is in $\bar{D}^{(k)}$. At the end of STEP 2, the pebble of node μ will go untouched unless μ is in a nonsingleton equivalence class. Each such class generates a new parent node, and a class passes a pebble on to that node only if all the nodes in the class were pebbled. Thus, in $D^{(k-1)}$, all the children of ν except one are pebbled by the end of STEP 1. Moreover, for each nonsingleton equivalence class, all nodes in that class but one are pebbled. At the end of STEP 2, for each node μ which was in the nest of ν in $D^{(k)}$, node μ' is pebbled iff μ was pebbled at the end of STEP 1, which concludes the proof. $\square$

3.4.4 REVERSING THE EDGES

In order to transform $D^{(0)}$ into a suffix tree we need only to reverse the direction of all edges. For simplicity, we retain the format according to which edge labels are assigned to the child, rather than to the father node in an edge. We must still add to each node a branching label of the kind discussed in Section 3.3. As seen in that section, there are various ways of implementing these labels. We will limit our description to the trie implementations of symbol-based branching labels and the array implementation of ID-based branching labels, since all the others can be derived from one of these two quite easily.

To implement symbol-based labels with tries, we need to replace each original internal node of $D^{(0)}$ with a binary trie indexing to a suitable subset of Σ. This transformation can be obtained in $O(\log |\Sigma|)$ time using the legal assignment of processors that holds on $D^{(0)}$ at completion. We outline the basic mechanism and leave the details as an exercise. We simply perform $\log |\Sigma|$ further refinements of $D^{(0)}$, for which the ID tables are not needed. In fact, the best descriptor for a string of $\log |\Sigma|$ bits or less is the string itself. Thus, we let the processors in each nest partition their associated nodes into finer and finer equivalence classes, based on the bit-by-bit inspection of their respective symbols. Clearly, a processor occupying a node with label (i, l) will use symbol x_i in this process. Whenever a new branching node ν is created, one of the processors in the current nest of ν climbs to $\mu = \text{Father}[\nu]$ and assigns the appropriate branching label to μ. At the end, the processors assign branching labels to the ultimate fathers of the nodes in the nest.

For the array implementation of ID-based branching labels, we assign a vector of size n, called OUT_ν, to each node ν of $D^{(0)}$. The vector OUT_ν stores the branching label from ν as follows. If μ is a son of ν and the label of μ is (i, l), a pointer to μ is stored in $OUT_\nu[ID_i[0]]$. It as an easy exercise to show that n processors legally assigned to $D^{(0)}$, and equipped with $\Theta(n)$ locations each, can construct this implementation of T_x in constant time. In fact, the same can be done with any $D^{(k)}$, but the space needed to accommodate OUT vectors for all refinements $D^{(k)}$ would become $\Theta(n^2 \log n)$. Observe that, since n processors cannot initialize $\Theta(n^2)$ space in $O(\log n)$ time, the final collection of OUT vectors will describe in general a graph containing T_x plus some garbage. T_x can be separated from the rest by letting the processors in each nest convert the OUT vector of the parent node into a linked list. This task is accomplished trivially in extra $O(\log n)$ time, using prefix computation.

Theorem 3.11. *The suffix tree in compact form for a string of n symbols can be built in $O(\log n)$ steps by n processors in a CRCW-PRAM, using $O(n^2)$ auxiliary space without need for initialization.*

Proof: The claim is an obvious consequence of Theorem 3.8, lemmas 3.9 and 3.10 and the discussion above. $\square$

As we see shortly, T_x alone is not enough to carry out on-line string searching in parallel. For this, we shall need the entire series of $D^{(k)}$'s as implemented by OUT vectors.

3.5   Parallel on-line search

Assume that, in the course of the construction of the suffix tree associated with string $x\#$, we saved the following entities: (1) The $\log n$ bulletin boards used in the construction of the ID tables. (2) All the intermediate trees $D^{(k)}$, $k = \log n, ..., 0$, each implemented by the vectors OUT_ν, defined the previous section. Note that this assumption presupposes $O(n^2 \log n)$ space. We show, that, with this information available, m processors can answer in $O(\log m)$ steps whether a pattern $y = y_1 y_2 ... y_m$ occurs in x. Formally, we list the following

Theorem 3.12. *Let x be a string of n symbols. There is an $O(n \log n)$-work preprocessing of x such that, for any subsequently specified pattern $y = y_1 y_2 ... y_m$, m processors in a CRCW can find whether y occurs in x in time $O(\log m)$.*

Proof: We give an explicit construction that meets the claim, assuming conditions (1) and (2) above were satisfied during preprocessing. We perform our on-line search in three main steps, as follows.

Step 1. Recall that we computed $ID_i[q]$ $(i = 1, ..., n; q = 0, ..., \log n)$ for the string $x\#$. The value $ID_i[q]$ is a label for the substring $x_i, ..., x_{i+2^q-1}$, such that $ID_i[q] = ID_j[q]$ if $x_i, ..., x_{i+2^k-1} = x_j, ..., x_{j+2^k-1}$. The first step of the on-line search for y consists of labeling in a similar way some of the substrings in the pattern y. For $q = 0, ..., \log m$, the substrings we assign labels to are all substrings whose length is 2^q and starting at every position i such that i is a multiple of 2^q and $i + 2^q \le m$. These new labels are stored in the vectors $PID_i[q]$, so that $PID_i[q]$ stores the label of the substring $y_i, ..., y_{i+2^q-1}$. PID labels are assigned in such a way that whenever two substrings of length 2^q, one in y and the other in $x\#$, are equal then their labels are equal too. For this, we follow a paradigm similar to that used in deriving the ID labels, but we do not compute the PID labels from scratch. Instead, we just copy appropriate entries of the bulletin boards (BBs) used in deriving the ID labels. Since the BB tables were not initialized, then every time we copy an entry of a BB table, we need to check the consistency of such an entry with the corresponding entry of an ID table. Should we find no correspondence at any step of this process, we can conclude that there is a substring of the patterns that never occurs in the text, whence the answer to the query is NO.

Step 2. Let $PID_1[\log m]$ (that is, the name of the prefix of y whose length is $2^{\log m}$) be h. Observe that if none of $ID_i[\log m]$ is equal to h then the prefix of y whose length is $2^{\log m}$ does not occur in x. We conclude that y does not occur in x whence the answer to the query is NO.

Suppose $h = ID_i[\log m]$ for some $1 \le i \le n - 1$. We check whether $NODE_h[\log m]$ appears in $D^{(\log n-1)}$. Note that $NODE_h[\log m]$ will not appear in $D^{(\log n-1)}$ if and only if all the substrings of x whose prefix of length $2^{\log m}$ is the same as the prefix of y have also the same prefix of length $2^{\log m+1}$. If $NODE_h[\log m]$ appears in $D^{(\log n-1)}$ then we are guaranteed that it will appear also in $D^{(\log m)}$ and we proceed to Step 3. In fact, all the refinements $D^{(\log n-1)}, ..., D^{(\log m)}$ deal only with substrings whose length is greater than $2^{\log m}$. Otherwise, i.e., $NODE_h[\log m]$ does not appear in $D^{(\log n-1)}$, we check whether y is equal to $x_h, ..., x_{k+h-1}$ symbol by symbol. This can be done in $\log m$ time using $m/\log m$ processors. The answer to the query is YES if and only if the two strings are equal.

Step 3. We find a node ν in T_x such that y is a prefix of the string having ν as its locus (if such a node exists). For this, we use the vectors $PID_i[q]$, of Step 1 and the $D^{(q)}$ trees, $q = \log m-1, ..., 0$, of the preprocessing. Node ν is found thru a "binary search" of $\log m$ iterations, as follows.

Iteration q ($q = \log m - 1, ..., 0$). Let ν and y' be the input parameters of iteration q. (For iteration $\log m - 1$, $\nu = NODE_k[\log m]$ and y' is the suffix of y starting at position $2^{\log m} + 1$.) The invariant property satisfied in all the iterations is that ν is a node in $D^{(q+1)}$ and y' is a substring whose length is less than 2^{q+1}. Our goal is to check whether y' follows an occurrence of $W(\nu)$. We work on $D^{(q)}$. There are two possibilities:

(*Possibility*1) The node ν appears in $D^{(q)}$. Possibility 1 has two sub-possibilities. (*Possibility* 1.1) 2^q is larger than the length of y'. In this case we do nothing and the input parameters of the present iteration become the input parameters of the next iteration. (*Possibility* 1.2) 2^q is less than or equal to the length of y'. Assume that y' starts at position j of y and b is the value stored in $PID_j[q]$. If the entry $OUT_\nu[b]$ is empty then y does not occur in x. Otherwise, the input parameters of the next iteration will be the suffix of y' starting at position $2^q + 1$ and the node pointed to by $OUT_\nu[b]$.

(*Possibility* 2) The node ν does not appear in $D^{(q)}$. This means that ν had only one son in $\bar{D}^{(q+1)}$ and so it was omitted from $D^{(q)}$ (in Step 2 of refining $\bar{D}^{(q+1)}$). Let μ be the single son of ν in $\bar{D}^{(q+1)}$. Possibility 2 has two subpossibilities. (*Possibility* 2.1) 2^q is larger than the length of y'. Assume that the $LABEL$ of μ in $D^{(q)}$ is (i, l). In this case y' occurs in x if and only if y' is a prefix of $x_{i+l-2^q+1}, ..., x_{i+l}$. We check this letter by letter in $\log m$ time using $m/\log m$ processors. (*Possibility* 2.2) 2^q is less or equal to the length of y'. We compare $ID_{i+l-2^q+1}[q]$ (the unique name of $x_{i+l-2^q+1}, ..., x_{i+l}$) to the unique name of the prefix of y' whose length is 2^q. If these names are different then y does not occur in x. Otherwise, the input parameters of the next iteration will be the suffix of y' starting at position $2^q + 1$ and the node μ.

As a final remark, observe that we did not initialize the vectors OUT_ν, therefore it could be that we will get a wrong positive answer. To avoid mistakes, every time we get a positive answer we need to explicitly check whether y really appears in x at the position given in the answer. This can be done in $\log m$ time using $m/\log m$ processors as a last step. □

3.6   Exhaustive on-line searches

Given T_x in compact form and Fact 2 of Section 3.1, one can find, for any pattern y, *all* the occurrences of *any substring* w of y in x in serial time $O(|w| + l)$, l being the total number of occurrences of w in x. This application is a special case of the following broader problem. Assume we are given a set of strings W upon which we want to perform many *substring queries*, as follows. In each query, we specify arbitrarily a substring w' of some string w in W (possibly, $w' = w$) as the *pattern*, ad also a set $W' = \{\bar{w}_1, \bar{w}_2, ..., \bar{w}_t\}$ of *textstrings*, where each $\bar{w}$ is a string from W or a substring of one such string. The result of the query is the set of *all* the occurrences of w' in W'. The quantity $\bar{n} = \sum_{h=1}^{t} |\bar{w}_h| + |w'|$ is the *size* of the query. This kind of queries arise naturally in sequence data banks, and they have obvious (off-line) serial solution taking time linear in $\bar{n}$. We investigate now their efficient on-line parallel implementation.

It can be proved that the strings in a data bank can be preprocessed once and for all in such a way that any subsequent substring query on the bank takes constant time on a CRCW PRAM with a number of processors linear in the size of the query. Preprocessing a string x costs $O(\log |x|)$ CRCW-PRAM steps and $O(|x| \log |x|)$ total work and space. Note that the methods used in off-line parallel searches depend crucially on the specific pattern being considered and thus do not support instantaneous substring queries. For space limitations, we will describe only part of the method, suitable for a restricted class of inputs. But our discussion will suffice to display an interesting fact, namely, that assuming an arbitrary order on the input alphabet may lead to efficient solutions to problems on strings to which the notion of alphabet order is totally extraneous.

Let then the alphabet Σ be ordered according to the linear relation $<$. This order induces a lexicographic order on Σ^+, which we also denote by $<$. Given two words u and v, we write $u \ll v$ or $v \gg u$ to denote that there are two symbols a and a' with $a < a'$, and a word $z \in \Sigma^*$ such that za is a prefix of u and za' is a prefix of v. Thus, $u < v$ iff either $u \ll v$ or u is a prefix of v.

Fact 3. *Let $u \ll v$. Then, for any w and z in A^*, we have $uw \ll vz$.*

If $x = vwy$, then the integer $1 + |v|$, where $|v|$ is the length of v is the *(starting) position* in x of the *substring* w of x. Let $I = [i, j]$ be an interval of *positions* of a string x. We say that a substring w of x *begins* in I if I contains the starting position of w, and that it *ends* in I if I contains the position of the last symbol of w.

We recall few notions from the introductory chapter. A string w is *primitive* if it is not a power of another string (i.e., writing $w = v^k$ implies $k = 1$). A primitive string w is a *period* of another string z if $z = w^c w'$ for some integer $c > 0$ and w' a possibly empty prefix of w. A string z is *periodic* if z has a period w such that $|w| \leq |z|/2$. It is a well known fact of combinatorics on words that a string can be periodic in only one period. We refer to the shortest period of a string as *the* period of that string. A string w is a *square* if it can be put in the form vv in terms of a primitive string v (v is the *root* of the square). A string is *square-free* if none of its substrings is a square. Our implementation of fast substring queries will be discussed under the very restrictive assumption that all strings we handle are square-free. In the general method, this assumption can be waived without any penalty in efficiency.

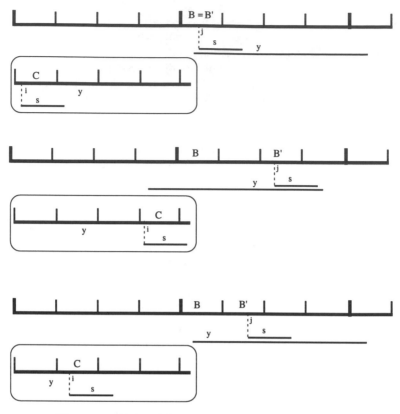

Fig. 3.5.   Left-, right-seeded, and balanced patterns

We can explain the basic criterion used in our construction in terms of the standard, single-pattern string searching problem. Let then y s.t. $|y| \geq 4$ be this pattern and x a text string, as in Figure 3.5. Consider the ordered set S of all *positioned* substrings of y having length $c = 2^{(\lfloor \log |y| \rfloor - 2)}$, and let (i, s) be the one such substring such that s is a lexicographic minimum in S and i the smallest starting position of s in y. Substring (i, s) is called the *seed* of y. Pattern y is *left-seeded* if $i < c$, *right-seeded* if $i > |y| - 2c + 1$, *balanced* in all other cases.

Let now the positions of x be also partitioned into *cells* of equal *size* $c = 2^{(\lfloor \log |y| \rfloor - 2)}$, and assume that there is at least one occurrence of y in x, starting in some cell B. In principle, every position of B is equally qualified as a candidate starting position for an occurrence of y. However, the same is not true for the implied occurrences of the seed of y. This seed will start in a cell B' that is either B itself or a close neighbor of B. Consider the set of all substrings of x which start in B' and have length $|s|$. It is not difficult to see then that the one such positioned substring corresponding to (i, s) has the property of being a lexicographic minimum

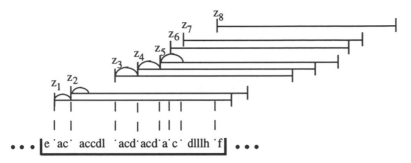

Fig. 3.6. Left stubs in a block

among all such substrings originating in B' and to its right, or originating in B' and to its left, or both, depending on whether y is left-, right-seeded, or balanced. Once we have a candidate position for s in B', it is possible to check in constant time with s processors whether this actually represents an occurrence of y, since $|y| \leq 8|s|$. The problem is thus to identify such a candidate position. Note that, although we know that the seed of, say, a left-seeded pattern must be lexicographically least with respect to all substrings of equal length that begin in B' and to its right, there might be up to $|s| = |B'|$ substrings with this property. Even if we were given the starting positions of all such substrings, checking all of them simultaneously might require $|s|^2$ processors.

Throughout the rest of this discussion, we concentrate on the management of left-seeded patterns, but it shall be apparent that the case of right-seeded patterns is handled by symmetric arguments.

3.6.1 LEXICOGRAPHIC LISTS

Let $B = [h, h + m]$, where $m \leq n/2$ and $h \leq (n - 2m + 1)$, be a cell of size m on out string x ($|x| = n$). A *stub* of B is any positioned substring (i, z) of x of length $|z| = m$ and $i \in B$. Stub (i, z) is a *left stub* of B if $i = h + m$ or, for any other stub (i', z') of B with $i < i'$, we have $z \leq z'$. We use $\mathcal{L}(B) = \{(i_1, z_1), (i_2, z_2), ..., (i_k, z_k)\}$ to denote the sequence of left stubs of B, and call the ordered sequence $\{i_1, i_2, ..., i_k\}$, where $(i_1 < i_2 < ... < i_k)$, the *left list* of B.

As an example, let the substring of x in block B be

$$eacaccdlacdacdacdlllhf,$$

as in Figure 3.6, and assume for simplicity that the positions of x falling within B be in $[1,22]$.

We have 8 left stubs in B, beginning with the rightmost such stub $(22, z_8) = f...$. Since h and l are both larger than f, the next left stub is $(17, z_7) = dlllhf...$. We immediately have $(16, z_6) = cdlllhf...$ and

$(15, z_5) = acdlllhf...$. Since d and c are both larger than a, there will not be a left stub until $(12, z_4) = acdacdlllhf...$. We similarly have $(9, z_3) = acdacdacdlllhf...$. Finally, we have $(4, z_2) = accdlacdacdacdlllhf...$ and $(2, z_1) = acaccdlacdacdacdlllhf...$. Note that the prefix of z_1 of length $2 = i_2 - i_1$ matches the corresponding prefix of z_2. Similarly, the prefix of z_3 of length $3 = i_4 - i_3$ matches a prefix of z_4, and the prefix of z_4 of length $3 = i_5 - i_4$ matches a prefix of z_5. We say that z_1 and z_2 are in a *run*, and so are z_3, z_4 and z_5. Obviously, there can be no runs in a square-free string.

Lemma 3.13. *Assume that x is square-free, and let (i, z) and $(j, \bar{z})$ be two consecutive left stubs from $\mathcal{S}(B)$. Then, $i < j$ implies $z' \ll \bar{z}'$, where z' and $\bar{z}'$ are the prefixes of z and $\bar{z}$ of length $|j - i|$.*

Proof: Straightforward. $\square$

Let now $\mathcal{L}(B) = (i_1, z_1), (i_2, z_2), ..., (i_k, z_k)$ be the ordered sequence of left stubs in $\mathcal{S}(B)$. If $k = 1$, then define $\mathcal{I}(B)$ as the singleton set containing only (i_1, z_1). Assume henceforth $k > 1$. For $f = 1, 2, ..., k - 1$, let l_f be the prefix of z_f such that $|l_f| = i_{f+1} - i_f$. We use $\mathcal{I}(B)$ to denote the ordered sequence $(i_1, l_1), (i_2, l_2)..., (i_{k-1}, l_{k-1})$. With each $(i_f, l_f) \in \mathcal{I}(B)$, we associate its *shadow* (i_{f+1}, l'_f), where l'_f is the prefix of z_{f+1} having the same length as l_f. The ordered sequence of shadows of the members of $\mathcal{I}(B)$ is denoted by $\mathcal{I}'(B)$. By construction, we have that $l_f \le l'_f$ for each f in $[1, k - 1]$. If, in addition, x is square-free, then Lemma 3.13 ensures that $l_f \ll l'_f$ for each f in $[1, k - 1]$. We now use the elements of $\mathcal{I}(B) \cup \mathcal{I}'(B)$ to construct the ordered sequence $\bar{\mathcal{I}}(B) = (i_1, \bar{l}_1), (i_2, \bar{l}_2), ..., (i_k, \bar{l}_k)$ defined as follows (cf. Figure 3.7).

First, we set $\bar{l}_1 = l_1$ and $\bar{l}_k = l'_{k-1}$. Next, for $1 < f < k$, we set $\bar{l}_f = l'_{f-1}$ if $i_{f+1} - i_f < i_f - i_{f-1}$, and $\bar{l}_f = l_f$ otherwise. Sequence $\bar{\mathcal{I}}(B)$ plays an important role in our constructions, due to the following lemmas.

Lemma 3.14. *If x is square-free, then the word terms in $\bar{\mathcal{I}}(B)$ form a lexicographically strictly increasing sequence.*

Proof: We prove that, for $k > 1$, we must have $\bar{l}_1 \ll \bar{l}_2 \ll ... \ll \bar{l}_k$. This is easily seen by induction. By Lemma 3.13, $\bar{l}_1 = l_1 \ll l'_1$. By our definition of $\bar{l}_2$, we have $|\bar{l}_2| \ge |l'_1|$, i.e., l'_1 is a prefix of $\bar{l}_2$. By Fact 2, we get then that $\bar{l}_1 \ll \bar{l}_2$. Assuming now that the claim holds for all values of f up to $f = h < k$, the same argument leads to establish that $\bar{l}_h \ll \bar{l}_{h+1}$. $\square$

Lemma 3.15. *The sum of the lengths of the word terms in $\bar{\mathcal{I}}(B)$ is bounded above by $4|B|$.*

Proof: Each $\bar{l}$ derives its length either from a distinct l or from a distinct l'. Since the l's do not mutually overlap, then their total length is bounded by $2m$, and the same is true of the l''s. $\square$

Lemmas 3.14 and 3.15 justify our interest in $\bar{\mathcal{I}}(B)$. In fact, Lemma 3.14 states that if x is square-free, then there is at most one member $(i, \bar{l})$ of $\bar{\mathcal{I}}(B)$ such that $\bar{l}$ is a prefix of seed w. Note that this is not true for the elements of $\mathcal{I}(B)$, since we may have that, for some f, l_{f+1} is a prefix of l_f. For example, let $...adbcadc$ be the last 7 symbols of x that fall in B. Then z_k starts with c, while z_{k-1} and z_{k-2} start, respectively, with adc and $adbcadc$. We have $l_{k-1} = ad$, which is a prefix of $l_{k-2} = adbc$. Lemma 3.15 is a handle to check all these prefixes against (i, s) simultaneously and instantaneously, with $O(|s|)$ processors.

Observe that given a copy of x, the set $\mathcal{I}(B) \cup \mathcal{I}'(B)$ is completely specified by the ordered sequence of starting positions of the members of $\mathcal{I}(B)$, which we called the left list of B. Clearly, the left list of any cell B enumerates also the starting positions of all elements of $\bar{\mathcal{I}}(B)$.

3.6.2 BUILDING LEXICOGRAPHIC LISTS

We show now how a generic square-free string w is preprocessed. Without loss of generality, we assume $|w|$ a power of 2. The basic invariant stating that w is square-free will be called henceforth *Property 1*. The preprocessing consists of performing approximately $\lfloor \log |w| \rfloor$ stages, as follows. At the beginning of stage t $(t = 1, 2, ...)$ of the preprocessing the positions of w are partitioned as earlier into $|w|/2^{t-1}$ disjoint cells each of size 2^{t-1}. Starting with the first cell $[1, 2^{t-1}]$, we give now all cells consecutive ordinal numbers. For $t = 1, 2, ...$, stage t handles simultaneously and independently every pair (B_{od}, B_{od+1}) of cells such that od is an odd index. The task of a stage is to build the lexicographic list relative to every cell $B_d \cup B_{d+1}$, using the lexicographic lists of B_{od} and B_{od+1}). The crucial point is to perform each stage in constant time with $|w| = n$ processors.

We need to make some preliminary arrangements for inter-processor communication.

Let our n processors be $p_1, p_2, ..., p_n$ where p_i $(i = 1, 2, ..., n)$ has *serial number i*. The input w is stored into an array of consecutive locations of the common memory, and processor p_i is assigned to the i-th symbol w_i of w $(i = 1, 2, ..., n)$.

The first position of each cell is called the *cell head* and is assigned a few special memory locations. In our construction, cell heads are used as bulletin boards for sharing information among processors. For example, cell heads are used to record the starting position of the lexicographically least among the stubs that begin in that cell. We use $ls(B)$ to denote this least stub of a cell B. Property 0 ensures that $ls(B)$ is unique. Since the partition of the positions of x into cells is rigidly defined for each stage, then the position of any cell head can be computed by any processor in constant time. Throughout our scheme, we need to maintain some invariant conditions that are given next.

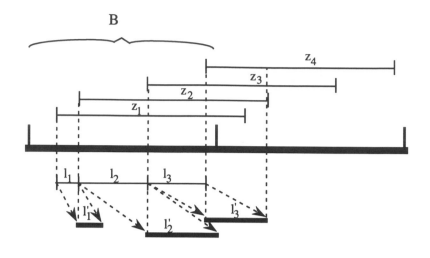

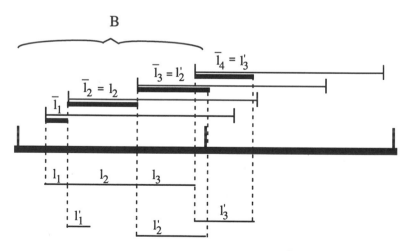

Fig. 3.7. Building a sequence $\bar{\mathcal{I}}$

Invariant 3. *At the beginning of each stage and for every cell, the starting position of the ls of that cell is stored in the cell head.*

We also need that the processors in every cell know the organization of the left list of that cell. The processors use this information in order to compute the sequence $\bar{\mathcal{I}}$ defined earlier. This information is stored according to the invariant properties that are given next. The processor assigned to the starting position of a left stub is called a *stub representative*.

Invariant 4. *If processor p is assigned to a symbol of a member (i, l) of some sequence $\mathcal{I}$ then p knows the serial number of the stub representative of l.*

Invariant 5. *Every stub representative knows the address of its immediate predecessor in its left list, if the latter exists. Similarly, every stub representative knows the address of its immediate successor in its left list, if the latter exists.*

Note that the first element of the left list of a cell is always the starting position of the ls of that cell. Therefore, Property 3 ensures also that the starting position of the first element in the left list of B is stored in the cell head of B. Finally, the last element of the left list of a cell is, by construction, always the last position in that cell.

Theorem 3.16. *Let w be a square-free string, and (B_d, B_{d+1}) two consecutive cells in a partition of w. Given the left lists of B_d and B_{d+1}, the left list of $\bar{B} = B_d \cup B_{d+1}$ can be produced by a CRCW PRAM with $|\bar{B}|$ processors in constant time, preserving invariants 3, 4 and 5.*

Proof: Consider first the computation $ls(\bar{B})$. This could be done by straightforward lexicographic pairwise comparisons of appropriate extensions of the current ls's in adjacent cells. Such extensions consist of the substrings starting with the current ls's and having size $|\bar{B}|$. Thus, we compare the extended ls's of B_{od} and B_{od+1}. By Property 0, only one of these extensions will survive in the comparison, and the winner coincides with $ls(\bar{B})$. Note that in order to know the result of a *lexicographic* comparison, the processors need to find the leftmost position where the two strings being compared mismatch. A technique to achieve this in constant time was discussed in the introductory chapter.

Our main task, however, is that of combining the two left lists of B_{od} and B_{od+1} into the left list for cell $\bar{B} = B_{od} \cup B_{od+1}$. This is more elaborate than the computation of $ls(\bar{B})$, but it yields $ls(\bar{B})$ as a by-product. The basic observation is that, as a consequence of Property 0, the left list of B_{od+1} is a suffix of the left list of $\bar{B}$. Thus, the issue is how to identify the prefix of the left list of B_{od} to which the left list of B_{od+1} is to be appended.

Let i' be the smallest element of the left list of B_{od+1}, and let z' be the substring of w having length 2^t and starting position i'. We use now $(i_1, \bar{l}_1), (i_2, \bar{l}_2), ..., (i_k, \bar{l}_k)$ to denote the sequence $\bar{\mathcal{I}}(B_{od})$. For $f = 1, 2, ..., k$, let $shadow(\bar{l}_f)$ be the prefix of z' of length $|\bar{l}_f|$. Since (cf. Lemma 3.14) $\bar{l}_1 \ll \bar{l}_2 \ll ... \ll \bar{l}_k$, then precisely one of the following cases must apply.

A) $\bar{l}_k \ll shadow(\bar{l}_k)$.

B) $\bar{l}_1 \gg shadow(\bar{l}_1)$.

C) There are two consecutive elements $(i_h, \bar{l}_h)$ and $(i_h, \bar{l}_{h+1})$ of $\bar{\mathcal{I}}(B_{od})$ such that $\bar{l}_h \ll shadow(\bar{l}_h) \ll \bar{l}_{h+1}$.

D) There is precisely one element $(i_h, \bar{l}_h)$ in $\bar{\mathcal{I}}(B_{od})$ such that $\bar{l}_h = shadow(\bar{l}_h)$.

In case (A), the left list for the combined cell $\bar{B}$ consists of the concatenation of the left lists of B_{od} and B_{od+1}. If case (B) applies, then the left list of $\bar{B}$ coincides with the left list of B_{od+1}. In case (C), the left list of $\bar{B}$ is obtained by appending the left list of B_{od+1} to the sequence of the first h elements of the left list of B_{od}. We are thus left with case (D). Let i_h be the starting position in w of $\bar{l}_h$, and z the substring of length 2^t of w having starting position i_h. By Property 0, we must have that either $z \ll z'$ or $z \gg z'$. In the first case, the left list of $\bar{B}$ is obtained by appending the left list of B_{od+1} to the sequence of the first h elements in the left list of B_{od}. In the second case, from $\bar{l}_{h-1} \ll \bar{l}_h$ and $\bar{l}_h = shadow(\bar{l}_h)$ we derive $\bar{l}_{h-1} \ll z'$, whence the left list of $\bar{B}$ results from appending the left list of B_{od+1} to the sequence of the first $h-1$ members of the left list of B_{od}.

This concludes our case analysis. We have to show next that, using the invariants, our $|\bar{B}|$ processors can perform the computation in constant time.

The preliminary identification of $\bar{\mathcal{I}}(B_{od})$ is easily performed by the stub representatives: using Invariant 5, each such representative p can infer the length of its associated word $\bar{l}$ by comparison of the absolute differences of its own serial number to the serial numbers of its predecessor and successor in the left list, respectively. We want now the processors to compare, in overall constant time, every word $\bar{l}$ from $\bar{\mathcal{I}}(B_{od})$ to the prefix of length $|\bar{l}|$ of $ls(B_{od+1})$. For every $\bar{l}$, we need $|\bar{l}|$ processors for the comparison that involves $\bar{l}$ as one of the terms. This cannot be solved by just letting the $|\bar{l}|$ processors assigned to the symbols of $\bar{l}$ do the work. In fact, $\bar{l}$ may overlap with one or more of its successors in $\bar{\mathcal{I}}(B_{od})$, in which case these successors would simultaneously claim part of the processors of $\bar{l}$ for comparing their own symbols. One way around this difficulty is to arrange for each $\bar{l}$ that overlaps its successor to "borrow" at some point the processors needed for the comparison from its own predecessor in $\bar{\mathcal{I}}(B_{od})$. In fact, our construction of $\bar{\mathcal{I}}(B_{od})$ guarantees for any f that, if $\bar{l}_f$ overlaps with $\bar{l}_{f+1}$, then $|\bar{l}_{f-1}| = |\bar{l}_f|$. Since processors are only lent (if needed) to an immediate right successor in the left list, this policy does not generate conflicts. In conclusion, this part of the computation is performed in two substeps. In the first substep, processors assigned to $\bar{l}$'s that have no overlap with their successors perform their required lexicographic comparison in a normal way. In the second substep, the representatives of the $\bar{l}$'s that overlap send for help from their respective predecessors in the left list, and such predecessors arrange for the comparisons.

The remaining details of a comparison are as follows. Let w_d be a symbol of a word $\bar{l}_f$ from $\bar{\mathcal{I}}(B_{od})$, and assume that $\bar{l}_f$ does not overlap with its successor. Then, $\bar{l}_f = l_f$, where l_f is the word in the f-th element of $\mathcal{I}(B_{od})$. Processor p_d uses invariants 4 and 5 to compute $|\bar{l}_f|$ and the offset off_d of position d from the starting position of l_f. Combined with the information stored in the head of cell B_{od+1} (cf. Invariant 3), this offset yields the position d' having offset off_d from the starting position of $ls(B_{od+1})$. Thus, p_d knows that it is assigned to compare x_d with $w_{d'}$. If p_d detects a mismatch, it turns off a switch assigned to the starting position of l_f. The case of an overlapping $\bar{l}_f$ is handled similarly by the processors borrowed from $\bar{l}_{f-1}$. At the end, at most one stub representative will have a switch still in the "on" position. If this is the case, such representative will identify itself by writing in the cell head. This concludes the description of the combination of left lists, which takes clearly constant time with $\Theta(|\bar{B}|)$ processors. Propagation of the invariants to $\bar{B}$ is trivial. $\square$

Reasoning symmetrically, it is easy to introduce *right stubs* and *right lists* and so on in every cell partition of w. This leads to establish a dual of Theorem 3.16. We use the term *lexicographic* lists refer to the collection of left and right lists. Theorem 3.16 and its dual admit the following corollary.

Corollary 1. *For any string w and integer $\ell \leq |w|$, a CRCW PRAM with $|w|$ processors can compute the lexicographic lists relative to the first $\log \ell$ stages of the preprocessing of w in $O(\log \ell)$ time and using linear auxiliary space per stage.*

Proof: Straightforward. $\square$

3.6.3 STANDARD REPRESENTATIONS FOR CONSTANT-TIME QUERIES

A square-free string w together with the first $(\ell \leq \lfloor \log |w| \rfloor - 2)$ lexicographic lists is said to be in *ℓ-standard form*. When $\ell = \lfloor \log |w| \rfloor - 2$, we simply say that w is in *standard* form. We are now ready to show that searching for a string in standard form into another string also in standard form is done instantaneously with a linear number of processors. With y denoting a square-free pattern and x a square-free text, we revisit the informal discussion at the beginning of Section 3.6.

Clearly, retrieving the seed (i, s) of y from its $|s|$-standard form is immediate. In fact, consider the partition of y into cells of size $|s|$ and let C be the cell of this partition which contains i.

Fact 4. *Stub (i, s) is the first element of $\mathcal{H}(C)$.*

Fact 4 is the handle to identify the position i of s in y. Since there are at most 4 cells in the partition of the positions of y, and each such cell contributes one known candidate, mutual comparison of the substrings of length $|s|$ starting at these candidate positions is all is needed. This is easily done in constant time with $|y|$ processors. There are of course more direct ways of computing the seed of y within these bounds, but reasoning uniformly in terms of standard forms has other advantages in our context.

Assume to fix the ideas that y is left-seeded, and that there is an occurrence of y beginning in a cell B of the partition of x into cells of size $|s|$. Let B' be the cell of x where the corresponding occurrence of the seed s begins (cf. Fig. 3.5). The identification of the position j of s within B' is quite similar to the combination of adjacent left lists discussed earlier. In fact, j is clearly the position of a left stub in $\mathcal{L}(B')$. Lemma 3.14 of the previous section tells us that, if we consider the sequence, say, $\bar{\mathcal{I}}(B')$, then we can find at most one term $\bar{l}_f$ such that $\bar{l}_f$ is a prefix of s. We thus search in $\bar{\mathcal{I}}(B')$ for a term $\bar{l}_f$ such that, letting $\tilde{s}$ be the prefix of s of length $|\bar{l}_f|$, we have that $\tilde{s} = \bar{l}_f$. Lemma 3.15 and the discussion of Theorem 3.16 tell us that $O(|B|)$ processors are enough to match, simultaneously, each $\bar{l}_f$-term against a corresponding prefix $\tilde{s}$ of s. The details are easily inferred from the preceding discussion and can be omitted.

Let now y' be a substring of y, and consider the $(\log\lfloor |y'| \rfloor - 2)$-th lexicographic list for y. Clearly, y' is embedded in a set of at most 9 consecutive cells in the associated cell partition of y. The same holds for every occurrence of y' in any substring x' of x such that $|x'| \geq |y'|$. Again, assume to fix the ideas that y' is left-seeded. Note that if y' and its seed (i', s') start in the same cell, say, C' on y, it is no longer necessarily true that (i', s') is the first term in the head list of C'. However, (i', s') must still be a left stub in C'. Since the starting position f of y' in y is known, all we need to do is to identify the leftmost left stub in $\mathcal{L}(C')$ that starts at f or to the right of f. This takes constant time with the priority-write emulation discussed in the introduction, after which we have a suitable substitute for Fact 4. From this point on, the search for y' into x' involves only minor variations with respect to the above description, and so does the search for y' in any set of substrings of a given set of strings.

3.7   Exercises

1. Write detailed programs implementing the sequential procedure INSERT for a suffix tree both in expanded and compact form.

2. Adapt the programs of the previous exercise to implement serial on-line search for a pattern in a suffix tree both in expanded and compact form. Expand your programs so that each finds now all occurrences of the pattern.

3. Give a counterexample to the converse of Lemma 3.3.

4. Prove Lemma 3.5.

5. Design detailed space implementations for an expanded and compact suffix tree.

6. Show that it is possible to implement the nodes of a suffix tree as

arrays of size Σ that do not need initialization.

7. Design an efficient serial algorithm that transforms the suffix tree for x into the suffix tree for $x'wx''$ where $x'x'' = x$ and w is an arbitrary string.

8. Design serial and parallel algorithms to find the longest common substring of two gives strings. Discuss the generalization of this problem to the case of $k > 2$ strings.

9. A *palindrome* is a string that reads the same forward and backward, i.e., w is a palindrome iff $w = w^R$. A palindrome substring w of a string x is *maximal* if either w is a prefix or suffix of x, or extending w with the two symbols that precede and follow it in x does not generate a palindrome. Design an efficient sequential algorithm based on the notion of suffix tree that finds all maximal palindromes in a string.

10. * Design an efficient algorithm that builds the smallest (i.e., with fewest states) finite automaton recognizing all and only the substrings of a given string x. Note that the arcs in the transition diagram of the automaton must be labeled by a single symbol. (Hint: all nodes which are roots of identical subtrees of T_x can be collapsed into a single node.)

11. Show that the space required in the parallel construction of a suffix tree can be reduced to $O(n^{1+\epsilon})$, for any chosen $0 < \epsilon \leq 1$, with a corresponding slow-down proportional to $1/\epsilon$.

12. Show that the technique used in on-line parallel search can be extended to find:
    (a) the number of occurrences of z in x;
    (b) in case of more than one occurrence, what is the starting position of the first or last occurrence;
    (c) what is the longest prefix of z that occurs in x.

13. Expand the discussion of Section 3.6 to handle the cases of balanced and right-seeded patterns, respectively.

14. Assume that the input alphabet is of finite size. Show that, under this hypothesis, the number of processors needed in both constructions of Section 3.6 can be reduced by a factor of $\log n$.

15. * Design a parallel algoritm based on lexicographic lists that tests whether a string is square-free.

16. * Generalize the method used in exhaustive on-line searches to the case of general (i.e., not necessarily square-free) strings.

3.8 Bibliographic notes

Suffix trees are a special kind of the *PATRICIA* trees introduced by Morrison [1968]. The serial suffix tree construction presented in this chapter is due to McCreight [1976]. An earlier construction, due to Weiner [1973] builds a variant of the tree known as *position tree* (cf. Aho, Hopcroft and Ullmann [1974]). Weiner's construction gave, as a trivial by-product, a linear-time method for finding the longest repeated substring in a string over a finite alphabet. Not long before, D. Knuth had posed the problem of whether such a problem could be solved in better than $O(n^2)$ time. Weiner's and McCreight's constructions are equivalent at the outset, but they have notable intrinsic differences. Weiner's construction scans the input string from right to left, but does not need to know all of it before it can start. Conversely, McCreight's construction scans x from left to right, but it needs the entire string before starting. The duality inherent to these two constructions was exposed by Chen and Seiferas [1985].

Subsequent constructions approach the problem of building the tree on-line or in real time (Majster and Majer [1985], Ukkonen [1992], Kosaraju [1994]), and build several variants such as inverted textfiles (Blumer et al., [1987]), factor transducers (Crochemore [1985], Blumer et al. [1985]), suffix arrays (Manber and Myers [1990]), etc. A recent comparative discussion of suffix tree algorithms and implementations is in Giegerich and Kurtz [1995].

The parallel construction of suffix trees presented in this chapter is adapted from Apostolico et al. [1988]. Constructions achieving linear total work are found in Hariharan [1994] on the CREW , and Sahinalp and Vishkin [1994] on the CRCW. It is an open problem whether a construction can be carried out optimally in linear space an/or with $n/\log n$ processors when the alphabet is finite. The treatment of exhaustive on-line searches follows Apostolico [1992].

Suffix trees and their companion structures have found applications in many areas, including approximate string searching, data compression, computations of substring statistics and detection of squares and other regularities in strings. Some such applications were discussed in Apostolico [1985], and elsewhere in Apostolico and Galil [1985]. Many more are found in other chapters of the present volume.

Bibliography

AHO, A. V., J. E. HOPCROFT, AND J. D. ULLMAN[1984]. *The Design and Analysis of Computer Algorithms*, Addison-Wesley, Reading, Mass.

APOSTOLICO, A.[1985]. "The Myriad Virtues of Suffix Trees", pp.85-96 in [AG].

APOSTOLICO, A.[1992]. "Efficient CRCW-PRAM Algorithms for Universal Substring Searching", *Theoretical Computer Science* **1277**, to appear.

APOSTOLICO, A. AND Z. GALIL (eds.) [1985]. *Combinatorial Algorithms on Words*, Springer-Verlag ASI F12.

APOSTOLICO, A., C. ILIOPOULOS, G. LANDAU, B. SCHIEBER, AND U. VISHKIN [1988]. "Parallel construction of a suffix tree, with applications", *Algorithmica* **3** (Special Issue on Parallel and Distributed Computing), 347-365.

APOSTOLICO, A. AND F.P. PREPARATA[1983]. "Optimal off-line detection of repetitions in a string", *Theoretical Computer Science*, **22**, 297-315.

BLUMER A., J. BLUMER, A. EHRENFEUCHT, D. HAUSSLER, M.T. CHEN, AND J. SEIFERAS[1985]. "The smallest automaton recognizing the subwords of a text", *Theoretical Computer Science*, **40**, 31-55.

BLUMER, A., J. BLUMER, A. EHRENFEUCHT, D. HAUSSLER, AND R. McCONNELL [1987]. "Complete inverted files for efficient text retrieval and analysis", *Journal of the ACM* **34**, (3), 578-595.

CHEN, H.T., AND J. SEIFERAS [1985]. "Efficient and elegant subword tree construction", pp. 97-109 in [AG].

CROCHEMORE, M. [1985]. "Optimal factor transducers", pp. 31-43 in [AG].

GIEGERICH, R. AND S. KURTZ [1995]. "A comparison of imperative and purely functional suffix tree constructions", *Science of Computer Programming* **25**, 187-218.

HARIHARAN, R. [1994]. "Optimal parallel suffix tree construction", *Proc. 26th ACM Symp. on Theory of Computing*, 290-299.

KARP, R.M., R.E. MILLER AND A.L. ROSENBERG[1972]. "Rapid identification of repeated patterns in strings, trees and arrays", *Proceedings of the 4th ACM Symposium on the Theory of Computing*, 125-136.

KNUTH, D.E., J.H., MORRIS AND V.R. PRATT [1976]. "Fast pattern matching in strings", *SIAM Journal on Computing* **6**, 2, 323-350.

KOSARAJU, S.R. [1994]. "Real-time pattern matching and quasi real time construction of suffix trees", *Proc. 26th ACM Symp. on Theory of Computing*, 300-309.

MAJSTER, M.E., AND A. REISNER[1980]. "Efficient on-line construction and correction of position trees", *SIAM Journal on Computing* **9**, 4, 785-807.

MANBER, U. AND E. MYERS [1990]. "Suffix arrays: a new method for on-line string searches", *Proceedings of the 1st Symposium on Discrete Algorithms*, 319-327.

McCREIGHT, E.M.[1976]. "A space economical suffix tree construction algorithm", *Journal of the ACM* **23**, (2), 262-272.

MORRISON, D.R., [1968]. "PATRICIA - practical algorithm to retrieve information coded in alphanumeric", *Journal of the ACM* **15**, (4), 514-534.

SAHINALP, S.C. AND U. VISHKIN [1994]. "Symmetry breaking for suffix tree construction", *Proc. 26th ACM Symp. on Theory of Computing*, 300-309.

UKKONEN, E., [1992]. "Constructin suffix trees on-line in linear time", *Proceedings of Information Processing 92* , Vol. 1, 484-492.

WEINER, P.[1973] Linear pattern matching algorithms, *Proceedings of the 14th Annual Symposium on Switching and Automata Theory*, 1-11.

4
Serial Computations of Levenshtein Distances

In the previous chapters, we discussed problems involving an exact match of string patterns. We now turn to problems involving similar but not necessarily exact pattern matches.

There are a number of similarity or distance measures, and many of them are special cases or generalizations of the Levenshtein metric. The problem of evaluating the measure of string similarity has numerous applications, including one arising in the study of the evolution of long molecules such as proteins. In this chapter, we focus on the problem of evaluating a longest common subsequence, which is expressivcly equivalent to the simple form of the Levenshtein distance.

4.1   Levenshtein distance and the LCS problem

The Levenshtein distance is a metric that mcasures the siinilarity of two strings. In its simple form, the Levenshtein distance, $D(x, y)$, between strings x and y is the minimum number of character insertions and/or deletions (indels) required to transform string x into string y. A commonly used generalization of the Levenshtein distance is the minimum cost of transforming x into y when the allowable operations are character insertion, deletion, and substitution, with costs $\delta(\lambda, \sigma), \delta(\sigma, \lambda)$, and $\delta(\sigma_1, \sigma_2)$, that are functions of the involved character(s).

There are direct correspondences between the Levenshtein distance of two strings, the length of the shortest *edit sequence* from one string to the other, and the length of the *longest common subsequence* (LCS) of those strings. If D is the simple Levenshtein distance between two strings having lengths m and n, SES is the length of the shortest edit sequence between the strings, and L is the length of an LCS of the strings, then $SES = D$ and $L = (m + n - D)/2$. We will focus on the problem of determining the length of an LCS and also on the related problem of recovering an LCS.

Another related problem, which will be discussed in Chapter 6, is that of approximate string matching, in which it is desired to locate all positions within string y which begin an approximation to string x containing at most D errors (insertions or deletions).

procedure CLASSIC(x, m, y, n, C, p):
begin
    $L[0{:}m, 0] \leftarrow 0$;
    $P[0{:}m, 0] \leftarrow 1$;
    $L[0, 0{:}n] \leftarrow 0$;
    $P[0, 0{:}n] \leftarrow 2$;
    for $i \leftarrow 1$ **until** m **do**
        for $j \leftarrow 1$ **until** n **do**
            if $x_i = y_j$ **then** $L[i, j] \leftarrow 1 + L[i-1, j-1]$
            else if $L[i-1, j] > L[i, j-1]$ **then** $L[i, j] \leftarrow L[i-1, j]$
                else $L[i, j] \leftarrow L[i, j-1]$;
            if $x_i = y_j$ **then** $P[i, j] \leftarrow 3$
            else if $L[i-1, j] > L[i, j-1]$ **then** $P[i, j] \leftarrow 1$
                else $P[i, j] \leftarrow 2$;
    $p \leftarrow L[m, n]$;
    $(i, j) \leftarrow (m, n)$;
    $k \leftarrow p$;
    while $k > 0$ **do**
        if $P[i, j] = 3$ **then**
            begin
                $C[k] \leftarrow x_i$;
                $k \leftarrow k - 1$;
                $(i, j) \leftarrow (i-1, j-1)$;
            end
        else
            if $P[i, j] = 1$ **then** $i \leftarrow i - 1$
            else $j \leftarrow j - 1$
end

Fig. 4.1.   Classic LCS algorithm

4.2   Classical algorithm

Let the two input strings be $x = x_1 x_2 ... x_m$ and $y = y_1 y_2 ... y_n$ and let $L(i, j)$ denote the length of an LCS of $x[1{:}i]$ and $y[1{:}j]$. A simple recurrence relation exists on L:

$$L(i, j) = \begin{cases} 0, & \text{if either } i = 0 \text{ or } j = 0 \\ 1 + L(i-1, j-1), & \text{if } x_i = y_j \\ \max\{L(i-1, j), L(i, j-1)\}, & \text{if } x_i \neq y_j \end{cases} \qquad (4.1)$$

This forms the basis for a dynamic programming algorithm that determines the length of an LCS. We fill matrix $L[0{:}m, 0{:}n]$ with the values of the L-function. We first set the values stored in the boundary cells ($L[0, \bullet]$ and $L[\bullet, 0]$) to 0. By sweeping the matrix in an order calculated to visit a cell only when its precedents (as defined by the recurrence) have already been valuated, we iterate setting the value stored in $L[i, j]$ to the value of $L(i, j)$ using the recurrence relation. (See Figure 4.1.) Storing pointers $P[i, j]$ that indicate which L-entry contributed to the value of $L(i, j)$ (change of coordinate 1, 2, or both), enables the recovery of an LCS by tracing these threads from (m, n) back to (0,0). A solution LCS, having length $p = L(m, n)$, will be placed in array C. This method requires $O(mn)$ time and space.

The recurrence relation on L can be revised to enable computation of the generalized Levenshtein distance, $D(i, j)$ between $x[1{:}i]$ and $y[1{:}j]$, where insertions, deletions and substitutions have costs that are a function, δ, of the symbols involved. A similar dynamic programming algorithm will evaluate D.

$$D(i,j) = \begin{cases} 0, & \text{if } i = 0 \text{ and } j = 0 \\ D(0, j-1) + \delta(\lambda, y_j), & \text{if } i = 0 \text{ and } j > 0 \\ D(i-1, 0) + \delta(x_i, \lambda), & \text{if } i > 0 \text{ and } j = 0 \\ D(i-1, j-1), & \text{if } x_i = y_j \\ \min \left\{ \begin{array}{l} D(i, j-1) + \delta(\lambda, y_j), \\ D(i-1, j) + \delta(x_i, \lambda), \\ D(i-1, j-1) + \delta(x_i, y_j) \end{array} \right\}, & \text{if } x_i \neq y_j \end{cases}$$

$$(4.2)$$

4.3   Non-parameterized algorithms

A number of algorithms developed for solving the LCS problem have execution times dependent upon either the nature of the input (beyond merely the sizes of the two input strings) or the nature of the output. Such algorithms are referred to as input- or output-sensitive. Before discussing such algorithms, we first describe two LCS algorithms of general applicability whose performance is not parameterized by other variables.

4.3.1   LINEAR SPACE ALGORITHM

The space complexity of determining the length of an LCS can be reduced to $O(n)$ by noting that each row of L depends only on the one immediately preceding row of L. The length of an LCS of strings $x[1{:}m]$ and $y[1{:}n]$ will be returned in $L[n]$ after invoking FINDROW(x, m, y, n, L). (See Figure 4.2.)

Recovering an LCS using only linear space is not as simple. The "curve" that recovers an LCS was obtained by following threads through the L matrix after it was computed in its entirety. Instead, we first determine the middle point of an LCS curve and then, applying the procedure recursively, we determine the quartile points, etc.

procedure FINDROW(x, m, y, n, L):
begin
    $L[0 : n] \leftarrow 0$;
    for $i \leftarrow 1$ **until** m **do**
        begin
            for $j \leftarrow 1$ **until** n **do**
                if $x_i = y_j$ **then** $L_{new}[j] \leftarrow 1 + L[j-1]$
                else $L_{new}[j] \leftarrow \max\{L_{new}[j-1], L[j]\}$;
            for $j \leftarrow 1$ **until** n **do** $L[j] \leftarrow L_{new}[j]$
        end
end

Fig. 4.2. FINDROW algorithm

There are several ways to determine the middle point of an LCS curve. We outline two methods, one that is conceptually simple and the other that is easier and more efficient to implement.

The simple method computes the middle row of L and then continues computing additional rows $L[i, \bullet]$, retaining for each element (i, j) a pointer to that element of the middle row through which the LCS curve from (0,0) to (i, j) passes. The pointer retained by (m, n) indicates the middle point of an LCS. (See Figure 4.3.)

A more efficient method is to use the linear space FINDROW algorithm to compute the middle row of L and also the middle row of the solution matrix L^R for the problem of the reverses of strings x and y. It can be shown that their sum is maximized at points where LCS curves intersect with the middle row. It is in this manner that the middle point of an LCS curve is determined. Applying this procedure recursively, the quartile intersections can be recovered, etc. (See Figure 4.4.) Each iteration uses linear space, and it can be shown that the total time used is still quadratic, though about double what it was before.

This paradigm to recover an LCS, requiring only linear space, by using divide-and-conquer with algorithms that only evaluate the length of an LCS, can also be applied to many other algorithms for the LCS problem.

4.3.2 SUBQUADRATIC ALGORITHM

A subquadratic time algorithm for this problem, that applies to the case of a finite alphabet of size s, uses a "Four Russians" approach. Essentially, instead of calculating the matrix L, the matrix is broken up into boxes of some appropriate size, k. The "high" sides of a box (the $2k - 1$ elements of L on the edges of the box with largest indices) are computed from L-values known for boxes adjacent to it on the "low" side and from the relevant

function FINDMID(x, m, y, n):
begin
    $L[0:n] \leftarrow 0$;
    $mid \leftarrow \lceil m/2 \rceil$;
    for $i \leftarrow 1$ **until** mid **do**
        begin
            for $j \leftarrow 1$ **until** n **do**
                if $x_i = y_j$ **then** $L_{new}[j] \leftarrow 1 + L[j-1]$
                else $L_{new}[j] \leftarrow \max\{L_{new}[j-1], L[j]\}$;
            for $j \leftarrow 1$ **until** n **do** $L[j] \leftarrow L_{new}[j]$
        end;
    for $j \leftarrow 0$ **until** n **do** $P[j] \leftarrow j$;
    for $i \leftarrow mid + 1$ **until** m **do**
        begin
            for $j \leftarrow 1$ **until** n **do**
                begin
                    if $x_i = y_j$ **then** $L_{new}[j] \leftarrow 1 + L[j-1]$
                    else $L_{new}[j] \leftarrow \max\{L_{new}[j-1], L[j]\}$;
                    if $x_i = y_j$ **then** $P_{new}[j] \leftarrow P[j-1]$
                    else if $L_{new}[j-1] > L[j]$ **then**
                        $P_{new}[j] \leftarrow P_{new}[j-1]$
                      else $P_{new}[j] \leftarrow P[j]$
                end;
            for $j \leftarrow 1$ **until** n **do** $L[j] \leftarrow L_{new}[j]$;
            for $j \leftarrow 1$ **until** n **do** $P[j] \leftarrow P_{new}[j]$
        end;
    return $P[n]$
end

Fig. 4.3.   FINDMID algorithm

symbols of x and y by using a lookup table that was precomputed.

There are $2k + 1$ elements of L adjacent to a box on the "low" side. Two adjacent L-elements can differ by either zero or one. There are thus 2^{2k} possibilities in this respect. The symbols of x and y range over an alphabet of size s for each of the $2k$ elements, yielding a multiplicative factor of s^{2k} and the total number of boxes to be precomputed is therefore $2^{2k(1+\log s)}$. Each such box can be precomputed in time $O(k^2)$ for a total precomputing time of $O(k^2 2^{2k(1+\log s)})$.

The sides of a box can be stored as "steps" consisting of 0's and 1's indicating whether adjacent elements of the side differ by 0 or 1. A box can therefore be looked up in time $O(2k)$. There are $(n/k)^2$ boxes to be

procedure LINEARSPACE(x, m, y, n, C, p):
begin
  if $n = 0$ **then** $p \leftarrow 0$
  else
    if $m = 1$ **then**
      if $\exists j \leq n$ with $y_j = x_1$ **then**
        begin
          $p \leftarrow 1$;
          $C[1] \leftarrow x_1$
        end
      else $p \leftarrow 0$
    else
      begin
        $i \leftarrow \lceil m/2 \rceil$;
        FINDROW(x, i, y, n, L);
        let x^R be the reverse of string x;
        let y^R be the reverse of string y;
        FINDROW(x^R, $m - i$, y^R, n, L^R);
        determine a k in the range $0 \ldots n$
            that maximizes $L[k] + L^R[n - k]$;
        LINEARSPACE(x, i, y, k, C, q);
        let $x'[1 : m - i]$ consist of elements $x[i + 1 : m]$;
        let $y'[1 : n - k]$ consist of elements $y[k + 1 : n]$;
        LINEARSPACE(x', $m - i$, y', $n - k$, C', r);
        $p \leftarrow q + r$;
        let $C[q + 1 : p]$ consist of elements $C'[1 : r]$
      end
end

Fig. 4.4. Linear space LCS algorithm

looked up, for a total time of $O(n^2/k)$.

  The total execution time will therefore be $O(k^2 2^{2k(1+\log s)} + n^2/k)$. If we let $k = (\log n)/(2 + 2\log s)$, we see that the total execution time will be $O(n^2/\log n)$. This algorithm can be modified for the case when the alphabet is of unrestricted size, with the resulting time complexity of $O(n^2(\log \log n)/\log n)$.

  We note that this method works only for the classical Levenshtein distance metric but not for generalized cost matrices.

4.3.3 LOWER BOUNDS

The $O(n^2/\log n)$ algorithm is the asymptotically fastest known. It is an open question as to whether this algorithm is asymptotically best possible.

If we consider algorithms for solving the LCS problem that are restricted to making symbol comparisons of the form "$\sigma_1 = \sigma_2$?" then any such algorithm must make $\Omega(n^2)$ comparisons for alphabets of unrestricted size and $\Omega(ns)$ comparisons for alphabets of size restricted to s. In particular, if $T(n,s)$ is the minimum number of "equal-unequal" comparisons under the decision tree model needed to find an LCS of two strings of length n when the total number of distinct symbols that can appear in the strings is s, then

$$T(n,2) = 2n - 1$$
$$T(n,s) \geq ns/2 + s^2/4, \quad \text{for } s \leq n$$
$$T(n,s) \geq 3ns/4, \qquad\quad \text{for } n \leq s \leq 4n/3$$
$$T(n,s) = n^2, \qquad\qquad \text{for } s \geq 4n/3$$

If we consider algorithms that may make symbol comparisons of the form "$\sigma_1 \leq \sigma_2$?" then any such algorithm that solves the LCS problem must make $\Omega(n \log m)$ symbol comparisons for alphabets of unrestricted size. The proofs of these lower bounds generally have relied on exhibiting a path of requisite length in decision trees that support such algorithms by using adversary arguments. We present a sketch of the $\Omega(n \log m)$ lower bound.

Let the adversary's response to a comparison $p : q$ be as follows. If p and q are both positions in string x (say, x_i and x_j) then if $i < j$ return "less than"; otherwise, return "greater than".

If p and q are not both positions in string x then let R be the number of relative orderings of positions of strings x and y that are consistent with the results of comparisons made thus far and that are consistent with $x_1 < x_2 < ... < x_m$. Let R_1 be the subset of R consistent with $p < q$ and let R_2 be the subset of R consistent with $p > q$. If $|R_1| > |R_2|$ then return "less than"; otherwise, return "greater than".

Define positions p and q to be *comparable* with respect to a sequence of comparisons if it can be logically deduced from the results of the comparisons that $p < q$ or that $p > q$.

Lemma 4.1. *The algorithm must perform sufficient comparisons so that all positions in x are comparable to all positions in y.*

Each y_j in string y can be in any one of $m + 1$ distinct states:

$$y_j \leq x_1,$$
$$x_i < y_j \leq x_{i+1}, [i = 1, ..., m - 1],$$
$$x_m < y_j$$

Thus, there are $(m + 1)^n$ possible relative orderings of the elements of y with respect to the elements of x and it will take $\log(m + 1)^n \geq n \log m$ comparisons to distinguish which states the elements of y are in.

There are many algorithmic techniques that are not modeled by decision trees and for which these lower bounds would not apply. Examples of such techniques include array indexing (as used by the subquadratic algorithm of Section 4.3.2) and hashing.

4.4   Parameterized algorithms

In this section, we discuss several algorithms for the LCS problem whose performance is parameterized by variables other than the sizes of the two input strings. Before describing these algorithms, we define some notation.

Consider the $(m + 1) \times (n + 1)$ lattice of points corresponding to the set of prefix pairs of x and y, allowing for empty prefixes. We refer to the first coordinate of a point as its i-value and to the second coordinate as its j-value. We say that point (i, j) *dominates* point (i', j') if $i' \leq i$ and $j' \leq j$. A *match* point is a point (i, j) such that $x_i = y_j$. The point $(0, 0)$ is specially designated as also being a match point. Point (i, j) has rank k if $L(i, j) = k$. Point (i, j) is k-dominant if it has rank k and it is not dominated by any other point of rank k. Analagously, a point (i, j) is k-minimal if it has rank k and it does not dominate any other point of rank k. Note that if a point is k-dominant or k-minimal then it must be a match point.

The dominance relation defines a partial order on the set of match points. The LCS problem can be expressed as the problem of finding a longest chain in the poset of match points, modified to exclude links between match points that share the same i-value or j-value. Most known approaches to the LCS problem compute a minimal antichain decomposition for this poset, where a set of match points having equal rank is an antichain. These approaches typically either compute the antichains one at a time, or extend partial antichains relative to all ranks already discovered.

Let r be the number of match points, excluding $(0, 0)$, and let d be the total number of dominant points (all ranks). Then $0 \leq p \leq d \leq r \leq mn$.

4.4.1   *PN* ALGORITHM

We describe an algorithm that solves the LCS problem by computing the poset antichains one at a time, iteratively determining the set of k-minimal points for successively larger values of k. This algorithm requires time $O(pn + n \log n)$. If the expected length of an LCS is small, this algorithm will be faster than the classic algorithm.

The k-minimal points, if ordered by increasing i-value, will have their j-values in decreasing order. The algorithm detects all minimal match points of one rank by processing the match points across rows.

procedure PN(x, m, y, n, C, p):
begin
    $\forall \sigma \in x$, build ordered MATCHLIST(σ) of y-positions containing σ;
    $M[0, 0{:}m] \leftarrow 0$;
    $first \leftarrow 0$;
    for $k \leftarrow 1$ **step** 1 **do**
        begin
            $prev \leftarrow first$;
            $low \leftarrow M[k-1, prev]$;
            $high \leftarrow n+1$;
            for $i \leftarrow prev + 1$ **until** m **do**
                begin
                    $t \leftarrow \min\{j \in \text{MATCHLIST}(x_i) \mid j > low\}$;
                    if $t < high$ **then**
                        $M[k, i] \leftarrow high \leftarrow t$
                    else $M[k, i] \leftarrow 0$;
                    if $M[k, i] > 0$ and $first = prev$ **then** $first \leftarrow i$;
                    if $M[k-1, i] > 0$ **then** $low \leftarrow M[k-1, i]$
                end;
            comment $M[k, 0{:}m]$ contains the set of k-minimal points;
            if $first = prev$ **then goto** recover
        end;
recover:
    $p \leftarrow k - 1$;
    $k \leftarrow p$;
    for $i \leftarrow m$ **step** -1 **until** 0 **do**
        if $M[k, i] > 0$ **then**
            begin
                $C[k] \leftarrow x_i$;
                $k \leftarrow k - 1$
            end
end

Fig. 4.5. Sketch of pn LCS algorithm

Define $low_k(i)$ to be the minimum j-value of match points having rank $k-1$ whose i-value is less than i. Define $high_k(i)$ to be the minimum j-value of match points having rank k whose i-value is less than i ($n + 1$ if there are no such points). The following lemma is essential to the algorithm.

Lemma 4.2. (i, j) *is a k-minimal point iff j is the minimum value such that $x_i = y_j$ and $low_k(i) < j < high_k(i)$.*

A sketch of the $O(pn)$ algorithm is given in Figure 4.5. The algorithm obtains its efficiency by the use of three simple data structures. First, a collection of balanced binary search trees provides a mapping of alphabet symbols to the integers $\{1, \ldots, |\Sigma|\}$. Second, for each $\sigma \in x$, MATCHLIST(σ) contains the ordered list of positions in y in which symbol σ occurs. Third, array M maintains the set of k-minimal points ordered by the i-values of the points. For each value of k, an iteration of the outer loop determines the set of k-minimal points in linear time. A crucial observation is that the evaluation of variable t, the minimum element in MATCHLIST(x_i) satisfying the *low* and *high* bounds, can be accomplished by iteratively decrementing a pointer to that MATCHLIST. The total number of decrementations to that MATCHLIST cannot exceed the size of that MATCHLIST, and the sum of the lengths of all MATCHLISTs is n.

4.4.2   HUNT-SZYMANSKI ALGORITHM

We now describe an algorithm, due to J. Hunt and T. Szymanski, for solving the LCS problem in $O((r + n)\log n)$ time and $O(r + n)$ space. (See Figure 4.6.) This algorithm is particularly efficient for applications where most positions of one sequence match relatively few positions in the other sequence. Examples of such applications include finding the longest ascending subsequence of a permutation of the integers $\{1 \ldots n\}$ and file differencing in which a line of prose is considered atomic.

The algorithm detects dominant match points across all ranks by processing the match points row by row. For each i, the ordered list MATCHLIST(i) is set to contain the descending sequence of positions j for which $x_i = y_j$. This initializing process can be performed in time $O(n\log n)$ by stably sorting a copy of sequence y while keeping track of each element's original position, and counting the number of elements of each symbol value. MATCHLIST(i) can be implemented with a count of the size and a pointer to the last of the now contiguous subset of elements having symbol x_i. Then, iteratively for each row i, the algorithm evaluates the *threshhold* function $T(i, k)$ defined to be the smallest j such that $L(i, j) \geq k$. This function satisfies the recurrence relation

$$T(i, k) = \begin{cases} \text{smallest } j \text{ such that } x_i = y_j \\ \qquad \text{and } T(i-1, k-1) < j \leq T(i-1, k) \\ T(i-1, k), \text{ if no such } j \text{ exists} \end{cases} \qquad (4.3)$$

By maintaining the T values in a one-dimensional array THRESH and considering the j in MATCHLIST(i) in descending order, the k for which $T(i, k)$ differs from $T(i-1, k)$ can be determined in $O(\log n)$ time by using binary search on the THRESH array.

Variations of the Hunt-Szymanski algorithm have improved complexity. The basic algorithm can be implemented with flat trees to achieve time

procedure HUNT(x, m, y, n, C, p):
begin
    for $i \leftarrow 1$ **until** m **do**
        begin
            comment initialize THRESH values;
            THRESH[i] $\leftarrow n + 1$;
            set MATCHLIST[i] to be the descending sequence
                of positions j s.t. $x_i = y_j$;
        end
    THRESH[0] $\leftarrow 0$;
    LINK[0] $\leftarrow \lambda$;
    comment compute successive THRESH values
        THRESH[k] $= T(i - 1, k)$ (initially) and $T(i, k)$ (finally);
    for $i \leftarrow 1$ **until** m **do**
        for each j in MATCHLIST[i] **do**
            begin
                use binary search on the THRESH array to find k
                    such that THRESH[$k - 1$] $< j \leq$ THRESH[k];
                if $j <$ THRESH[k] **then**
                    begin
                        THRESH[k] $\leftarrow j$;
                        create a list node *new* whose fields contain:
                            i, LINK[$k - 1$];
                        LINK[k] $\leftarrow new$
                  end
            end
    $t \leftarrow$ largest k such that THRESH[k] $\neq n + 1$;
    $last \leftarrow$ LINK[t];
    $p \leftarrow 0$;
    while $last \neq \lambda$ **do**
        begin
            comment recover LCS in reverse order;
            $(i, prev) \leftarrow$ fields of list node $last$;
            $p \leftarrow p + 1$;
            $S[p] \leftarrow x_i$;
            $last \leftarrow prev$
        end;
    $C[1 : p] \leftarrow$ the reverse of the sequence of elements $S[1 : p]$
end

Fig. 4.6. Hunt-Szymanski LCS algorithm

complexity $O(r \log \log n + n \log n)$ over an unbounded alphabet and $O((r + n) \log \log n)$ over a fixed-size alphabet. However, since the use of flat trees imposes a large multiplicative constant, this improvement is of theoretical interest only.

By concentrating attention on the d dominant points (a subset of the r match points), the basic algorithm can be modified to have $O(m \log n + d \log(mn/d))$ time complexity and $O(d + n)$ space complexity. The time complexity can be theoretically further improved to $O(n + d \log \log(mn/d))$ by application of Johnson's improvement to flat trees.

4.4.3 ND ALGORITHM

Let D be the difference in length between x and $\text{LCS}(x, y)$; $D = m - p$. We now describe an $O(nD)$-time LCS algorithm. (See Figure 4.7.) This algorithm is based on evaluating the function $M(k, i)$ defined to be the largest j such that $x[i : m]$ and $y[j : n]$ have an LCS of size $\geq k$. This function is symmetric to the threshhold function (Equation 4.3 of Section 4.4.2) and satisfies the following recurrence relation.

$$M(k, i) = \begin{cases} \text{largest } j > M(k, i+1) \text{ such that } x_i = y_j, \text{ and} \\ \qquad \qquad \text{if } k > 1, \ j < M(k-1, i+1) \qquad (4.4) \\ M(k, i+1), \text{ if no such } j \text{ exists} \end{cases}$$

The efficiency of this algorithm derives from the procedure of avoiding calculating elements of M which cannot induce an LCS. The elements of M are evaluated along diagonals, one diagonal at a time. The first diagonal $(diag = m)$ is $M[1, m]$ through $M[m, 1]$; successive diagonals (smaller values of $diag$) are $M[1, diag]$ through $M[diag, 1]$. No further elements of M are evaluated beyond diagonal p. We know that we have encountered the last required diagonal when the length, p, of the longest found CS equals the diagonal number. Each diagonal requires only linear time since the y index, j, has range at most 1 to n. Therefore the total time required is $O(n(m - p))$.

The algorithm, as given, uses m^2 space for the M array. However, by using the simple mapping of $M[k, i]$ to an element of a one-dimensional array, it is straightforward to use space $O(mD)$. The space-saving technique, discussed earlier, can be applied to this algorithm, resulting in an algorithm with $O(nD)$ time and linear space complexity.

4.4.4 MYERS ALGORITHM

Myers developed an $O(nD)$ time algorithm that can be executed using linear space. Under a basic stochastic model, his algorithm has expected time complexity $O(n + D^2)$. A non-practical variation, using suffix trees, has $O(n \log n + D^2)$ worst-case time complexity.

```
procedure NAKATSU( x, m, y, n, C, p ):
begin
     diag ← m;
     p ← 0;
     while p < diag do
           begin
                 i ← diag;
                 len ← 1;
                 jₘₐₓ ← n + 1;
                 comment evaluate M[k, i] along one diagonal;
                 while i ≠ 0 and jₘₐₓ ≠ 0 do
                       begin
                             comment clear an element of M
                                          for uniform handling;
                             if diag = m or len > p then M[len, i + 1] ← 0;
                             jₘᵢₙ ← max{1, M[len, i + 1] };
                             j ← jₘₐₓ − 1;
                             comment calculate one M[k, i];
                             while j ≥ jₘᵢₙ and xᵢ ≠ yⱼ do j ← j − 1;
                             if j ≥ jₘᵢₙ then jₘₐₓ ← j
                             else jₘₐₓ ← M[len, i + 1];
                             M[len, i] ← jₘₐₓ;
                             if jₘₐₓ = 0 then len ← len − 1;
                             if len > p then p ← len;
                             len ← len + 1;
                             i ← i − 1
                       end;
                 diag ← diag − 1
           end;
     comment recover an LCS, the length of which is p;
     if jₘₐₓ = 0 then i ← i + 2
     else i ← i + 1;
     k ← p;
     while k > 0 do
           begin
                 while M[k, i] = M[k, i + 1] do
                       i ← i + 1;
                 C[p + 1 − k] ← xᵢ;
                 i ← i + 1;
                 k ← k − 1
           end
end
```

Fig. 4.7. nD LCS algorithm

```
function MYERS( x, m, y, n ):
begin
    DOMI[1] ← 0;
    comment look for dominant D-deviation points;
    for D ← 0 until m + n do
        for k ← −D step 2 until D do
            begin
                comment diagonals are 2 apart;
                if k = −D or (k ≠ D and
                        DOMI[k − 1] <DOMI[k + 1]) then
                        i ← DOMI[k + 1]
                else i ← DOMI[k − 1] + 1;
                j ← i − k;
                comment until non-match is found
                        increment both coordinates;
                while i < m and j < n and x[i + 1] = y[j + 1] do
                    (i, j) ← (i + 1, j + 1);
                comment store i-value
                        of diagonal k dominant D-deviation;
                DOMI[k] ← i;
                comment if we found minimum adequate deviation
                        then return length of LCS;
                if i = m and j = n then
                    return (i + j − D)/2;
            end
end
```

Fig. 4.8.   Myers LCS algorithm

The LCS trace will not deviate from the main diagonal more than the difference between the two input sequences. The essence of Myers' algorithm is to avoid evaluating unnecessary parts of the L matrix. Associated with each point (i, j) having rank k is its diagonal number, $i - j$, and its deviation, $i + j - 2k$. There is only one 0-dominant point, $(0, 0)$, and it has deviation 0. The set of dominant 0-*deviation* points lie on the 0-diagonal from $(0, 0)$ through $(i - 1, i - 1)$, where i is the minimum index such that $x_i \neq y[i]$. The algorithm iterates calculating the set of dominant points having successively higher deviation. Each dominant $(D + 1)$-deviation point can be found by starting at a dominant D-deviation point, traversing one unit orthogonally (adding one to exactly one coordinate), and iteratively incrementing both coordinates until just before the first non-match point is encountered. The algorithm terminates when point (m, n) is reached.

Implementation is made easier by the fact that there will be exactly one dominant D-deviation point for every other diagonal (that is, half the diagonals) in the range $-D$ to $+D$.

The code shown in Figure 4.8 returns the length of an LCS. In this code, DOMI[k] stores the i-value of the dominant D-deviation point located on diagonal k. Therefore, that point is (DOMI[k],DOMI[k] $- k$).

In order to recover an LCS, either the sequence of all encountered dominant points (all successive values of array DOMI) are retained, necessitating the usage of $O(nD)$ space or, by using a space-saving method similar to that used earlier, linear space will suffice at a cost of increasing the time requirements by a factor of about two.

A linear space version is enabled by determining the midpoint of an SES (shortest edit sequence) curve. This can be done by alternately calculating dominant D-deviation points for the two reverse problems (x,y and x^R,y^R) for iteratively larger values of D until a member of one of the two sets of dominant deviation points meets or passes a member of the other set along their common diagonal. A first point of meeting or passage will be an SES midpoint.

4.5 Exercises

1. Implement the classical algorithm to recover the sequence of edit operations (insert, delete, substitute) that will result in minimum total cost. Assume that substituting one symbol for another incurs cost 1.5 while insertion or deletion of a symbol incurs unit cost.

2. A string insertion (deletion) consists of inserting (deleting) a string of any length at one location. Implement an algorithm that determines the minimum cost sequence of character and string insertions and deletions required to transform string x into string y under the constraint that no substring of an inserted string may subsequently be deleted. Assume that single character insertions and deletions have unit cost, and that each string insertion and deletion has cost $1 +$ stringlength/2.

3. What can you say about the complexity of the above problem without the constraint disallowing subsequent partial deletion of inserted strings.

4. Show that the sum of the middle rows of L and L^R is maximized at points where LCS curves intersect with the middle row.

5. How many nested levels of iterations are required by the Linear Space Algorithm? Show that the total time used is quadratic.

6. Implement the pn LCS algorithm.

7. Prove the recurrence relation on threshhold values.

8. Show the relation between the T function defined in Section 4.4.2, and the M function defined in Section 4.4.3. What, if any, is the relation

between the T function and the *low* and *high* functions defined in Section 4.4.1?

9. Implement a linear space version of Myers algorithm that recovers an LCS.

10. Implement a cubic-time and quadratic-space algorithm that recovers a longest subsequence common to three strings.

4.6   Bibliographic notes

Levenshtein [1966] introduced measures of distance between strings based on indels. Applications of the LCS and related problems are discussed in more detail in Sankoff and Kruskal [1983]. The string-to-string edit problem is described and solved in Wagner and Fisher [1974]. Approximate string matching is discussed in Ukkonen [1985], Galil and Giancarlo [1988], Landau and Vishkin [1988], and Galil and Park [1990]. Chin and Poon [1994] analyze some heuristics for computing an LCS. Gotoh [1982] exhibits an $O(mn)$ time algorithm to compute the edit distance between two strings under a generalized Levenshtein distance in which indels of substrings have cost linear in the indel length. The linear space algorithm for the LCS problem is due to Hirschberg [1975]. The conceptually simple linear space method of determining the middle of an LCS curve is due to Eppstein (unpublished).

The "Four Russians" are Arlazarov, Dinic, Kronrod, and Faradzev [1970]. Their approach is also discussed in Aho, Hopcroft, and Ullman [1974]. The subquadratic time algorithm for restricted size alphabet is from Masek and Paterson [1980]. A discussion for the case of unrestricted size alphabet can be found in Hunt and Szymanski [1977].

Lower bounds for the LCS problem are proven in Aho, Hirschberg, and Ullman [1976], Wong and Chandra [1976], and Hirschberg [1978]. The description of LCS algorithmic approaches in terms of poset antichains was first explicated in Apostolico, Browne, and Guerra [1992]. An LCS algorithm with time complexity $O(pn+n\log n)$ is in Hirschberg [1977]. The $O((r+n)\log n)$ time Hunt-Szymanski algorithm is described in Hunt and Szymanski [1977]. Apostolico [1986] improves its worst-case performance. The notion of flat trees is from van Emde Boas [1975]; they are improved in Johnson [1982]. Modifications to the Hunt-Szymanski algorithm are discussed in Hsu and Du [1984a] (but see Apostolico [1987]), Apostolico and Guerra [1987] and Eppstein, Galil, Giancarlo, and Italiano [1990]. Other algorithms are discussed in Chin and Poon [1990] and Rick [1995].

The $O(nD)$-time algorithm is due to Nakatsu, Kambayashi, and Yajima [1982]. The code in Figure 4.7 is from their paper, with changes in the variable names. The linear space version of Nakatsu's algorithm is shown in Kumar and Rangan [1987].

Myers algorithm is from Myers [1986]. The code in Figure 4.8 is from

Myers [1986], with changes in the variable names. Wu, Manber, Myers, and Miller [1990] obtain a slightly faster $O(nP)$ algorithm, where P is the number of deletions in the shortest edit script.

The LCS problem can be generalized to the problem of determining a longest sequence common to N strings. Maier [1978] shows that if the number of strings, N, is not a constant then the N-LCS problem is NP-complete. However, for fixed values of N, the N-LCS problem can be solved using extensions of the algorithms in this chapter for the 2-LCS problem. Itoga [1981] shows that the extension of the classical algorithm has time and space complexity proportional to the product of the number of strings and the strings' lengths which, in the case of N strings each of length n, is $\theta(Nn^N)$. Other algorithms for the N-LCS problem are shown in Hsu and Du [1984b] and Irving and Fraser [1992].

Bibliography

AHO, A. V., D. S. HIRSCHBERG, AND J. D. ULLMAN [1986]. "Bounds on the complexity of the longest common subsequence problem," *Jour. ACM* **23**, 1-12.

AHO, A. V., J. E. HOPCROFT, AND J. D. ULLMAN [1974]. *The Design and Analysis of Computer Algorithms*, Addison-Wesley, Reading, Mass.

APOSTOLICO, A. [1986]. "Improving the worst-case performance of the Hunt-Szymanski strategy for the longest common subsequence of two strings," *Info. Processing Letters* **23**, 63-69.

APOSTOLICO, A. [1987]. "Remark on Hsu-Du New Algorithm for the LCS Problem," *Info. Processing Letters* **25**, 235-236.

APOSTOLICO, A., S. BROWNE, AND C. GUERRA [1992]. "Fast linear-space computations of longest common subsequences," *Theoretical Computer Science* **92**, 3-17.

APOSTOLICO, A., AND C. GUERRA [1987]. "The longest common subsequence problem revisited," *Algorithmica* **2**, 315-336.

ARLAZAROV, V. L., E. A. DINIC, M. A. KRONROD, AND I. A. FARADZEV [1970]. "On economical construction of the transitive closure of a directed graph," *Dokl. Akad. Nauk SSSR* **194**, 487-488 (in Russian). English translation in *Soviet Math. Dokl.* **11**, 1209-1210.

CHIN, F. Y. L., AND C. K. POON [1990]. "A fast algorithm for computing longest common subsequences of small alphabet size," *Jour. of Info. Processing* **13**, 463-469.

CHIN, F., AND C. K. POON [1994]. "Performance analysis of some simple heuristics for computing longest common subsequences," *Algorithmica* **12**, 293-311.

VAN EMDE BOAS, P. [1975]. "Preserving order in a forest in less than logarithmic time," *Proc. 16th FOCS*, 75-84.

EPPSTEIN, D., Z. GALIL, R. GIANCARLO, AND G. ITALIANO [1990]. "Sparse dynamic programming," *Proc. Symp. on Discrete Algorithms*, San Francisco CA, 513-522.

GALIL, Z., AND R. GIANCARLO [1988]. "Data structures and algorithms for approximate string matching," *Jour. Complexity* 4, 33-72.

GALIL, Z., AND K. PARK [1990]. "An improved algorithm for approximate string matching," *SIAM Jour. Computing* 19, 989-999.

GOTOH, O. [1982]. "An improved algorithm for matching biological sequences," *Jour. Mol. Biol.* 162, 705-708.

HIRSCHBERG, D. S. [1975]. "A linear space algorithm for computing maximal common subsequences," *Commun. ACM* 18, 341-343.

HIRSCHBERG, D. S. [1977]. "Algorithms for the longest common subsequence problem," *Jour. ACM* 24, 664-675.

HIRSCHBERG, D. S. [1978]. "An information theoretic lower bound for the longest common subsequence problem," *Info. Processing Letters* 7, 40-41.

HSU, W. J., AND M. W. DU [1984a]. "New algorithms for the LCS problem," *Jour. of Computer and System Sciences* 29, 133-152.

HSU, W. J., AND M. W. DU [1984b]. "Computing a longest common subsequence for a set of strings," *BIT* 24, 45-59.

HUNT, J. W., AND T. G. SZYMANSKI [1977]. "A fast algorithm for computing longest common subsequences," *Commun. ACM* 20, 350-353.

IRVING, R. W., AND C. B. FRASER [1992]. "Two algorithms for the longest common subsequence of three (or more) strings," Proc. of the 3rd Annual Symp. on Combinatorial Pattern Matching, *Lecture Notes in Computer Science* 644, 214-229.

ITOGA, S. Y. [1981]. "The string merging problem," *BIT* 21, 20-30.

JOHNSON, D. B. [1982]. "A priority queue in which initialization and queue operations take $O(\log \log D)$ time," *Math. Systems Theory* 15, 295-309.

KUMAR, S. K., AND C. P. RANGAN [1987]. "A linear space algorithm for the LCS problem," *Acta Informatica* 24, 353-362.

LANDAU, G. M., AND U. VISHKIN [1988]. "Fast string matching with k differences," *Jour. Comp. and System Sci.* 37, 63-78.

LEVENSHTEIN, V. I. [1966]. "Binary codes capable of correcting deletions, insertions, and reversals," *Cybernetics and Control Theory* 10 (1966), 707-710.

MAIER, D. [1978]. "The complexity of some problems on subsequences and supersequences," *Jour. ACM* 25, 322-336.

MASEK, W. J., AND M. S. PATERSON [1980]. "A faster algorithm for computing string edit distances," *Jour. Comput. System Sci.* 20, 18-31.

MYERS, E. W. [1986]. "An $O(ND)$ difference algorithm and its variations," *Algorithmica* 1, 251-266.

NAKATSU, N., Y. KAMBAYASHI, AND S. YAJIMA [1982]. "A longest common subsequence algorithm suitable for similar text strings," *Acta Informatica* **18**, 171-179.

RICK, C. [1995]. "A new flexible algorithm for the longest common subsequence problem," Proc. of the 6th Annual Symp. on Combinatorial Pattern Matching, *Lecture Notes in Computer Science* **937**, 340-351.

SANKOFF, D., AND J. B. KRUSKAL [1983]. *Time Warps, String Edits, and Macromolecules*, Addison-Wesley, Reading, Mass.

UKKONEN, E. [1985]. "Finding approximate patterns in strings," *Jour. Algorithms* **6**, 132-137.

WAGNER, R. A., AND M. J. FISCHER [1974]. "The string-to-string correction problem," *Jour. ACM* **21**, 168-173.

WONG, C. K., AND A. K. CHANDRA [1976]. "Bounds for the string editing problem," *Jour. ACM* **23**, 13-16.

WU, S., U. MANBER, E. W. MYERS, AND W. MILLER [1990]. "An $O(NP)$ sequence comparison algorithm," *Info. Processing Letters* **35**, 317-323.

5
Parallel Computations of Levenshtein Distances

This chapter discusses parallel solutions for the string editing problem introduced in Chapter 5. The model of computation used is the synchronous, shared - memory machine referred to as PRAM and discussed also earlier in this book. The algorithms of this chapter are based on the CREW and CRCW variants of the PRAM. In the CREW - PRAM model of parallel computation concurrent reads are allowed but no two processors can simultaneously attempt to write in the same memory location (even if they are trying to write the same thing). The CRCW - PRAM differs from the CREW - PRAM in that it allows many processors to attempt simultaneous writes in the same memory location: in any such common-write contest, only one processor succeeds, but it is not known in advance which one.

The primary objective of PRAM algorithmic design is to devise algorithms that are both *fast* and *efficient* for problems in a particular class called NC. Problems in NC are solvable in $O(\log^{O(1)} n)$ parallel time by a PRAM using a polynomial number of processors. In order for an algorithm to be both fast and efficient, the product of its time and processor complexities must fall within a polylog factor of the time complexity of the best sequential algorithm for the problem it solves. This goal has been elusive for many simple problems, such as topological sorting of a directed acyclic graph and finding a breadth-first search tree of a graph, which are trivially in NC. For some other problems in NC, it seems counter-intuitive at first that any fast and efficient algorithm may exist, due to the overwhelming number of simultaneous subproblems that arise at some point of the computation. Such is the case of the string-editing problem. This chapter will show that string editing can be solved in $O((\log n)^2)$ time and $O(n^2/\log n)$ processors on the CREW-PRAM, and in $O(\log n \log \log n)$ time and $O(n^2/\log \log n)$ processors on the CRCW-PRAM.

Throughout, it will be convenient to analyze our algorithms using the time and work (i.e., number of operations) complexities. The processor complexity is deduced from these by using Brent's theorem, which states that any synchronous parallel algorithm taking time T that consists of a total of W operations can be simulated by P processors in time $O((W/P)+$

T). There are actually two qualifications to Brent's theorem before one can apply it to a PRAM: (i) at the beginning of the i-th parallel step, we must be able to compute the amount of work W_i done by that step, in time $O(W_i/P)$ and with P processors, and (ii) we must know how to assign each processor to its task. Both qualifications (i) and (ii) to the theorem will be satisfied in our algorithms.

5.1   Edit distances and shortest paths

Let x be a string of $|x|$ symbols on some alphabet I. We consider three *edit operations* on x, namely, *deletion* of a symbol from x, *insertion* of a new symbol in x and *substitution* of one of the symbols of x with another symbol from I. We assume that each edit operation has an associated nonnegative real number representing the *cost* of that operation. More precisely, the cost of deleting from x an occurrence of symbol a is denoted by $D(a)$, the cost of inserting some symbol a between any two consecutive positions of x is denoted by $I(a)$ and the cost of substituting some occurrence of a in x with an occurrence of b is denoted by $S(a, b)$. An *edit script* on x is any consistent (i.e., all edit operations are viable) sequence σ of edit operations on x, and the cost of σ is the sum of all costs of the edit operations in σ.

Now, let x and y be two strings of respective lengths $|x|$ and $|y|$. The *string editing problem* for input strings x and y consists of finding an edit script σ' of minimum cost that transforms x into y. The cost of σ' is the *edit distance from x to y*. As seen in Chapter 6, the problem is solved by a serial algorithm in $\Theta(|x||y|)$ time and space, through dynamic programming, and such a performance represents a lower bound when the queries on symbols of the string are restricted to tests of equality. Many important problems are special cases of string editing, including the *longest common subsequence* problem and the problem of *approximate matching* between a pattern string and text string. Clearly, any solution to the general string editing problem implies similar bounds for all these special cases.

It is worthwhile to review the criterion that subtends the computation of edit distances by dynamic programming. For this, let $C(i, j)$, $(0 \le i \le |x|,\ 0 \le j \le |y|)$ be the minimum cost of transforming the prefix of x of length i into the prefix of y of length j. Let s_k denote the kth symbol of string s. Then $C(0, 0) = 0$, and

$$C(i,j) = \min\{C(i{-}1,j{-}1){+}S(x_i,y_j),\ C(i{-}1,j){+}D(x_i),\ C(i,j{-}1){+}I(y_j)\}$$

for all i, j, $(1 \le i \le |x|; 1 \le j \le |y|)$. Hence $C(i, j)$ can be evaluated row-by-row or column-by-column in $\Theta(|x||y|)$ time. Observe that, of all entries of the C-matrix, only the three entries $C(i-1, j-1)$, $C(i-1, j)$, and $C(i, j-1)$ are involved in the computation of the final value of $C(i, j)$. Such interdependencies among the entries of the C-matrix induce an $(|x| + 1) \times (|y| + 1)$ *grid* directed acyclic graph (grid DAG for short) associated

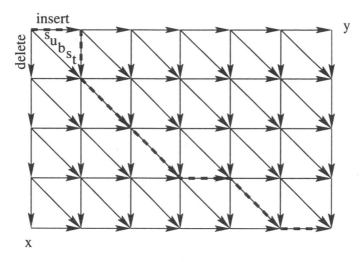

Fig. 5.1. Example of a 5 × 7 grid DAG.

with the string editing problem. We will see that in fact the string editing problem, can be viewed as a shortest-paths problem on a grid DAG.

Definition 5.1. *An $l_1 \times l_2$ grid DAG is a directed acyclic graph whose vertices are the $l_1 l_2$ points of an $l_1 \times l_2$ grid, and such that the only edges from grid point (i, j) are to grid points $(i, j+1)$, $(i+1, j)$, and $(i+1, j+1)$.*

Figure 5.1 shows an example of a grid DAG and also illustrates our convention of drawing the points such that point (i, j) is at the ith row from the top and jth column from the left. Note that the top-left point is $(0, 0)$ and has no edge entering it (i.e., is a *source*), and that the bottom-right point is (m, n) and has no edge leaving it (i.e., is a *sink*).

We now review the correspondence between edit scripts and grid graphs. We associate an $(|x| + 1) \times (|y| + 1)$ grid DAG G with the string editing problem in the natural way: the $(|x| + 1)(|y| + 1)$ vertices of G are in one-to-one correspondence with the $(|x| + 1)(|y| + 1)$ entries of the C-matrix, and the *cost* of an edge from vertex (k, l) to vertex (i, j) is equal to $I(y_j)$ if $k = i$ and $l = j - 1$, to $D(x_i)$ if $k = i - 1$ and $l = j$, to $S(x_i, y_j)$ if $k = i - 1$ and $l = j - 1$. We can restrict our attention to edit scripts which are not wasteful in the sense that they do no obviously inefficient moves such as: inserting then deleting the same symbol, or changing a symbol into a new symbol which they then delete, etc. More formally, the only edit scripts considered are those that apply at most one edit operation to a given symbol occurrence. Such edit scripts that transform x into y or vice versa are in one-to-one correspondence to the weighted paths of G that originate at the source (which corresponds to $C(0, 0)$) and end on the sink (which corresponds to $C(|x|, |y|)$). Thus, any complexity bounds we establish for

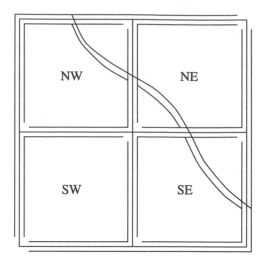

Fig. 5.2. Illustrating how the problem is partitioned.

the problem of finding a shortest (i.e., least-cost) source-to-sink path in an $m \times n$ grid DAG G, extends naturally to the string editing problem. The *left boundary* of G is the set of points in its leftmost column. The *right, top,* and *bottom* boundaries are analogously defined. The *boundary* of G is the union of its left, right, top, and bottom boundaries.

5.2   A monotonicity property and its use

Assume for now that $m = n$, i.e., G is an $m \times m$ grid DAG.

Let $DIST_G$ be a $(2m) \times (2m)$ matrix containing the lengths of all shortest paths that begin at the top or left boundary of G, and end at the right or bottom boundary of G. Our parallel algorithms (both CREW-PRAM and CRCW-PRAM) work as follows: divide the $m \times m$ grid into four $(m/2) \times (m/2)$ grids NW, SW, NE, SE, as shown in Fig. 5.2 (where N, S, E, W are mnemonics for North, South, East, West, respectvely). In parallel, recursively solve the problem for each of the four grids NW, SW, NE, SE, obtaining the four distance matrices $DIST_{NW}$, $DIST_{SW}$, $DIST_{NE}$, $DIST_{SE}$. Then obtain from these four matrices the desired matrix $DIST_G$. The main problem we face, is how to perform the "combine" step efficiently, in parallel.

Suppose that we manage to show that $DIST_G$ can be obtained from $DIST_{NW}$, $DIST_{SW}$, $DIST_{NE}$, $DIST_{SE}$ in parallel in time $O(\log m)$ for the CREW-PRAM, or in $O(\log \log m)$ for the CRCW-PRAM, in both cases doing $O(m^2)$ work. Then the time and work complexities of the overall algorithm would obey the following recurrences:

$$T_{CREW}(m) \leq T_{CREW}(m/2) + c_1 \log m \qquad (for\ CREW-PRAM),$$

$$T_{CRCW}(m) \le T_{CRCW}(m/2) + c_2 \log\log m \qquad (for\ CRCW - PRAM),$$

$$W_{CREW}(m) \le 4W_{CREW}(m/2) + c_3 m^2 \qquad (for\ CREW - PRAM),$$

$$W_{CRCW}(m) \le 4W_{CRCW}(m/2) + c_4 m^2 \qquad (for\ CRCW - PRAM),$$

with boundary conditions $T_{CREW}(4) = c_5$, $T_{CRCW}(4) = c_6$, $W_{CREW}(4) = c_7$, $W_{CRCW}(4) = c_8$, where $c_1, \ldots, c_8$ are constants. This would imply that $T_{CREW}(m) = O((\log m)^2)$, $T_{CRCW}(m) = O(\log m \log\log m)$, with both $W_{CREW}(m)$ and $W_{CRCW}(m)$ being $O(m^2 \log m)$.

Therefore, we only need to concern ourselves with establishing the "combine" bounds, that is, showing that $DIST_G$ can be obtained from $DIST_{NW}$, $DIST_{SW}$, $DIST_{NE}$, $DIST_{SE}$ in $O(\log m)$ time for the CREW-PRAM, in $O(\log\log m)$ time for the CRCW-PRAM, with $O(m^2)$ work for both models.

Let $DIST_{NW \cup SW}$ be the $(3m/2) \times (3m/2)$ matrix containing the lengths of shortest paths that begin on the top or left boundary of $NW \cup SW$ and end on its right or bottom boundary. Let $DIST_{NE \cup SE}$ be analogously defined for $NE \cup SE$. Our procedure for obtaining $DIST_G$ performs the following three steps:

1) Use $DIST_{NW}$ and $DIST_{SW}$ to obtain $DIST_{NW \cup SW}$.
2) Use $DIST_{NE}$ and $DIST_{SE}$ to obtain $DIST_{NE \cup SE}$.
3) Use $DIST_{NW \cup SW}$ and $DIST_{NE \cup SE}$ to obtain $DIST_G$.

We only show how step 1 is done. The procedures for steps 2 and 3 are similar. First, note that the entries of $DIST_{NW \cup SW}$ that correspond to shortest paths that begin and end on the boundary of NW (respectively, SW) are already available in $DIST_{NW}$ (respectively, $DIST_{SW}$), and therefore we need worry only about the entries of $DIST_{NW \cup SW}$ for paths that begin on the top or left boundary of NW and end on the right or bottom boundary of SW. For any such v-to w path, we have:

$$DIST_{NW \cup SW}(v, w) = \min_{p \in C}(Dist_{NW}(v, p) + Dist_{SW}(p, w)), \qquad (5.1)$$

where C denotes the boundary common to NW and SW. Using the above equation 5.1 to compute $DIST_{NW \cup SW}(v, w)$ for a given v, w pair is trivial to do in $O(\log m)$ CREW-PRAM time or $O(\log\log m)$ CRCW-PRAM time by using $O(m)$ work for each such v, w pair, but that would require an unacceptable $O(m^3)$ total work since there are $O(m^2)$ such pairs. We next prove a property that will be useful in decreasing the amount of work done.

Definition 5.2. *If X denotes a subset of the points on the left or top boundary of NW, Y denotes a subset of the points on the bottom or right boundary of SW, and Z denotes a subset of the points on the common boundary of NW and SW, then for every $v \in X$ and $w \in Y$, we define*

point $\theta_{X,Z,Y}(v,w)$ to be the leftmost $p \in Z$ *which minimizes* $Dist_{NW}(v,p)+$
$Dist_{SW}(p,w)$. *Equivalently,* $\theta_{X,Z,Y}(v,w)$ *is the leftmost point* $p \in Z$ *that
is traversed by a shortest v-to-w path that is constrained to go through Z.*

In the case where Z is the whole boundary common to NW and SW
(i.e., $Z = C$), knowing $\theta_{X,C,Y}(v,w)$ is like knowing the desired quantity
$DIST_{NW \cup SW}(v,w)$, because the above definition implies that

$$DIST_{NW \cup SW}(v,w) =$$

$$DIST_{NW}(v, \theta_{X,C,Y}(v,w)) + DIST_{SW}(\theta_{X,C,Y}(v,w), w).$$

Therefore computing this θ function would essentially solve the problem
of obtaining the $DIST_{NW \cup SW}$ matrix from the $DIST_{NW}$ and $DIST_{SW}$
matrices. This is what we henceforth seek to achieve.

Let X, Y, Z be as in the above Definition 5.2. We also introduce a
linear ordering $<_X$ on the points in X, such that they are encountered in
increasing order of $<_X$ by a walk that starts at the leftmost point of the
lower boundary of NW and ends at the top of the right boundary of NW.
The linear orderings $<_Y$ on Y and $<_Z$ on Z are defined analogously. Then
the following holds.

Lemma 5.3. (Monotonicity Lemma) *For any $v \in X$ and $w_1, w_2 \in Y$,*

$$\text{if } w_1 <_Y w_2 \text{ then } \theta_{X,Z,Y}(v,w_1) \leq_Z \theta_{X,Z,Y}(v,w_2). \tag{5.2}$$

For any $w \in Y$ and $v_1, v_2 \in X$,

$$\text{if } v_1 <_X v_2 \text{ then } \theta_{X,Z,Y}(v_1,w) \leq_Z \theta_{X,Z,Y}(v_2,w). \tag{5.3}$$

Proof: We prove the first part of the claim, by contradiction (the proof of
the second part of the claim is similar and omitted). Since X, Z, Y and v are
understood, we use $\theta(w_1)$ as a shorthand for $\theta_{X,Z,Y}(v,w_2)$. Suppose that
we have $w_1 <_Y w_2$ and $\theta(w_2) <_Z \theta(w_1)$, as shown in Fig. 5.3. By definition
of the function θ there is a shortest path from v to w_1 going through $\theta(w_1)$
(call this path α), and one from v to w_2 going through $\theta(w_2)$ (call it β).
Since $w_1 <_Y w_2$ and $\theta(w_2) <_Z \theta(w_2)$, the two paths α and β must cross
at least once somewhere in the region SW: let z be such an intersection
point. See Fig. 5.3. Let $prefix(\alpha)$ (respectively, $prefix(\beta)$) be the portion
of α (respectively, β) that goes from v to z. We obtain a contradiction in
each of two possible cases:

Case 1. The length of $prefix(\alpha)$ differs from that of $prefix(\beta)$. Without loss of generality, assume it is the length of $prefix(\beta)$ that is the
smaller of the two. But then, the v-to-w_1 path obtained from α by replacing $prefix(\alpha)$ by $prefix(\beta)$ is shorter than α, a contradiction.

Case 2. The length of $prefix(\alpha)$ is same as that of $prefix(\beta)$. In α,
replacing $prefix(\alpha)$ by $prefix(\beta)$ yields another shortest path between v

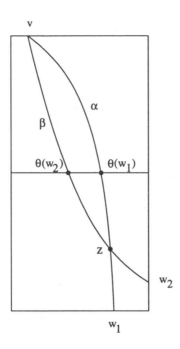

Fig. 5.3.   The Monotonicity Lemma

and w_1, one that crosses Z at a point to the left of $\theta(w_1)$, contradicting the definition of the function θ. $\qquad\qquad\qquad\qquad\qquad\qquad\qquad\square$

Lemma 5.3 is the basis for the following definitions (we use the θ symbol in the notation of the definitions that follow, rather than introduce a previously unused symbol, because this new usage of θ is closely related to the previous one and the context will leave no room for confusion).

Definition 5.4. *For any $m \times n$ matrix A, let θ_A be the m-vector such that, for every row index r $(1 \leq r \leq m)$, $\theta_A(r)$ is the smallest column index c that minimizes $A(r, c)$ (that is, among all c's that minimize $A(r, c)$, $\theta_A(r)$ is the smallest). If θ_A satisfies the following* sorted *property:*

$$\theta_A(r) \leq \theta_A(r+1),$$

and if for every submatrix A' of A, $\theta_{A'}$ also satisfies the sorted property, then matrix A is said to be totally monotone. *Given a totally monotone matrix A, the problem of computing the θ_A array is known as that of "computing the row minima of a totally monotone matrix".*

Now, in equation 5.1, if we fix v and define the matrix A by the equation $A(w, p) = DIST_{NW}(v, p) + DIST_{SW}(p, w)$, then Lemma 5.3

implies that A is totally monotone. Furthermore, knowing the θ_A matrix is like knowing row v of the desired matrix $DIST_{NW \cup SW}$, since $DIST_{NW \cup SW}(v, w) = DIST_{NW}(v, \theta_A(w)) + DIST_{SW}(\theta_A(w), w)$. Since there are m possible choices for v, our problem amounts to m computations of row minima of totally monotone matrices (one for each possible choice for v). Solving the problem in this way turns out *not* to be the best approach, since these m row minima computations are not independent of each other, a fact that will be exploited later on and that motivates the following definition.

Definition 5.5. *Suppose we have an $n_1 \times n_2 \times n_3$ matrix A and we wish to compute, for every $1 \leq i \leq n_1$ and $1 \leq j \leq n_3$, the $n_1 \times n_3$ matrix θ_A such that $\theta_A(i, j)$ is the smallest index k that minimizes $A(i, k, j)$ (that is, among all k's that minimize $A(i, k, j)$, $\theta_A(i, j)$ is the smallest). If θ_A satisfies the following* sorted *property:*

$$\theta_A(i, j) \leq \theta_A(i, j + 1),$$

$$\theta_A(i, j) \leq \theta_A(i + 1, j),$$

and if for every submatrix A' of A, $\theta_{A'}$ also satisfies the above sorted property, then we say that A is totally monotone. *Given such a matrix A, computing its θ_A matrix is known as the problem of "computing the tube minima of a totally monotone matrix".*

Now, in equation 5.1, if we define the matrix A by the equation

$$A(v, p, w) = DIST_{NW}(v, p) + DIST_{SW}(p, w),$$

then Lemma 5.3 implies that A is totally monotone. Furthermore, knowing the θ_A matrix is like knowing the desired matrix $DIST_{NW \cup SW}$, since $DIST_{NW \cup SW}(v, w) = DIST_{NW}(v, \theta_A(v, w)) + DIST_{SW}(\theta_A(v, w), w)$. Therefore the "combine" stage of our divide and conquer scheme amounts to a tube minima computation. To establish the CREW-PRAM and CRCW-PRAM bounds we had claimed for the computation of the $DIST_G$ matrix, it therefore suffices to give algorithms that perform the tube minima computation in logarithmic time for the CREW-PRAM, doubly logarithmic time for the CRCW-PRAM, and with quadratic work in either case. This is what the rest of this chapter seeks to establish.

Throughout, we refer to the first (resp., second, third) index of an entry of A as its *row* (resp., *column*, *height*) index. Thus an A that is $n_1 \times n_2 \times n_3$ has n_1 row indices, n_2 column indices, and n_3 height indices.

5.3   A sequential algorithm for tube minima

Both the CREW-PRAM and the CRCW-PRAM algorithms for tube minima will need, as a subroutine, a sequential $O(m^2)$ time algorithm for the tube minima of an $m \times m \times m$ totally monotone matrix. (Note that a quadratic time sequential algorithm for $DIST_G$ is *not* automatically obtained from the quadratic time sequential algorithms for string editing, since these deal with the computation of only one shortest path in the grid graph — the source-to-sink one.)

Let A' be the $(m/2) \times (m/2)$ submatrix obtained from A by considering only the odd row, column, and height indices of A. Let A'' be the $(m/2) \times (m/2)$ submatrix obtained from A by considering only the odd row indices, the *even* column indices, and the odd height indices. First, we recursively solve the problem for A' and A'', obtaining the arrays $\theta_{A'}$ and $\theta_{A''}$. If we could show that θ_A can be obtained from $\theta_{A'}$ and $\theta_{A''}$ in $O(m^2)$ time, then the recurrence for the time complexity would be $T(m) = 2T(m/2) + c_1 m^2$, $T(4) = c_2$, werer c_1, c_2 are constants. This would imply that $T(m) = O(m^2)$, as required. Hence we next show how θ_A can be obtained from $\theta_{A'}$ and $\theta_{A''}$ in $O(m^2)$ time:

1. For all odd i and all odd j, compute $\theta_A(i,j)$. This takes $O(1)$ time for each such pair i, j, because $\theta_A(i,j)$ is either $\theta_{A'}(i,j)$ or $\theta_{A''}(i,j)$, both of which are available.

2. For all odd i and even j, compute $\theta_A(i,j)$. This takes $O(m)$ time for a fixed odd i and all even j, by the following analysis. For a fixed odd row index a, let $Z_{a,1}, Z_{a,2}, \ldots, Z_{a,m/2}$ be the partition of the column indices of A that is induced by the set of values

$$\{ \theta_A(a,b) \mid b \text{ is odd } \}.$$

   Monotonicity implies that $\theta_A(i,j) \in Z_{i,(j/2)+1} \cup \{\theta_A(i,j-1), \theta_A(i,j+1)\}$, and hence computing $\theta_A(i,j)$ can be done in $O(1 + |Z_{i,(j/2)+1}|)$ time. Summing the time (for the fixed i) over all even j, gives $O(m)$ time because $|Z_{i,1}| + |Z_{i,2}| + \cdots + |Z_{i,m/2}| = m$. Therefore the total time taken by this step is $O(m^2)$.

3. For all even i and all odd j, compute $\theta_A(i,j)$. This takes $O(m^2)$ time, by an analysis similar to the one given for previous step (interchanging the roles of i and j, of rows and heights).

4. For all even i and all even j, compute $\theta_A(i,j)$. This takes $O(m^2)$ time (the method is essentially the same as for the previous two steps).

5.4 Optimal EREW-PRAM algorithm for tube minima

Our strategy consists of two stages: First, we attack the row minima problem, giving a logarithmic time, linear processor solution in the EREW-PRAM model. Then we use the row minima solution to establish a logarithmic time, quadratic work bound for tube minima in the EREW model. In the last subsection of this section, we explain why these EREW-PRAM bounds for tube minima imply similar CREW-PRAM (not EREW-PRAM) bounds for the combining stage of the parallel divide and conquer for string editing.

5.4.1 EREW-PRAM COMPUTATION OF ROW MINIMA

The main result of this subsection is an EREW-PRAM algorithm of time complexity $O(\log n)$ and processor complexity $O(n)$ for computing the row minima of an $n \times n$ matrix A.

Theorem 5.6. *The row minima (that is, the array θ_A) of an $m \times n$ totally monotone matrix A can be computed in $O(\log m + \log n)$ time with $O(m+n)$ processors in the EREW-PRAM model.*

In fact we prove a somewhat stronger result: that an implicit description of θ_A can be computed, within the same time bound as in the above theorem, by $O(n)$ processors. From this implicit description, a single processor can obtain any particular $\theta_A(r)$ value in $O(\log n)$ time.

Subsection 5.4.1 gives a preliminary result that is a crucial ingredient of the scheme of Subsection 5.4.1: an $O(\max(n, \log m))$ time algorithm using $\min(n, \log m)$ processors in the EREW-PRAM model. Subsection 5.4.1, which contains the heart of our CREW method, uses a kind of sampling and pipelining, where samples are evenly spaced (and progressively finer) *clusters* of elements and where the "help" for computing the information at a node comes from its children and from some of its subtree's leaves. Subsection 5.4.1 transforms the CREW algorithm of Subsection 5.4.1 into an EREW algorithm by relying on (i) storing each leaf solution in a suitable parallel data structure, and (ii) re-defining the nature of the information stored at the internal nodes.

Recall that the EREW-PRAM is the parallel model where the processors operate synchronously and share a common memory, but no two of them are allowed simultaneous access to a memory cell (whether the access is for reading or for writing in that cell). The CREW-PRAM differs from the EREW-PRAM in that simultaneous reading is allowed (but simulateous writing is still forbidden).

Preliminaries In this subsection we introduce some notation, terminology, and conventions.

Since the matrix A is understood, we henceforth use θ as a shorthand for θ_A. Throughout the section, R will denote the set of m row indices of A, and C will denote its n column indices. To avoid cluttering the exposition, we assume that m and n are powers of two (the scheme can easily be modified for the general case).

An *interval* of rows or columns is a non-empty set of *contiguous* (row or column) indices $[i, j] = \{i, i + 1, \cdots, j\}$. We imagine row indices to lie on a horizontal line, so that a row is *to the left of* another row if and only if it has a smaller index (similarly "left of" is defined for columns). We say that interval I_1 is to the left of interval I_2, and I_2 is to the right of I_1, if the largest index of I_1 is smaller than the smallest index of I_2. (Note: for rows, it might seem more appropriate to say "above" rather than "to the left of", but the latter is in fact quite appropriate because we shall later map the rows to the leaves of a tree.)

Let I be a column interval, and let A_I be the $m \times |I|$ submatrix of A consisting of the columns of A in I. We use θ_I as a shorthand for θ_{A_I}. That is, if r is a row index, then $\theta_I(r)$ denotes the smallest $c \in I$ for which $A(r, c)$ is minimized. Note that $\theta_I(r)$ usually differs from $\theta(r)$, since we are minimizing only over I rather than C.

Throughout the section, instead of storing θ_I directly, we shall instead store a function π_I which is an implicit description of θ_I.

Definition 5.7. *For any column interval I and any column index c, $\pi_I(c)$ is the row interval such that, for every row index r in that interval, we have $\theta_I(r) = c$; $\pi_I(c)$ is empty if no such r exists.*

Note that the monotonicity of A implies that, if $c_1 < c_2$, then $\pi_I(c_1)$ is to the left of $\pi_I(c_2)$.

Note that each $\pi_I(c)$ can be stored in $O(1)$ space, since we need only store the beginning and end of that row interval. Throughout the section, we shall use π_I as an implicit description of θ_I. The advantage of doing so is that we use $O(|I|)$ storage instead of the $O(|R|)$ that would be needed for explicitly storing θ_I. The disadvantage is that, given a row index r, a processor needs to binary search in the π_I array for the position of row index r in order to determine $\theta_I(r)$. Had we stored directly θ_I, $\theta_I(r)$ would be readily available in constant time. From now on, we consider our problem to be that of computing the π_C array. Once we have π_C, it is easy to do a postprocessing computation that obtains (explicitly) θ from π_C with m processors: each column c gets assigned $|\pi_C(c)|$ processors which set $\theta(r) = c$ for every $r \in \pi_C(c)$. Therefore Theorem 5.6 would easily follow if we can establish the following.

Theorem 5.8. *π_C can be computed in $O(\log m + \log n)$ time and $O(n)$ processors in the EREW-PRAM model.*

The rest of this section proves the above theorem.

Definition 5.9. *The s-sample of the set R of row indices is obtained by choosing every s-th element of R (i.e., every row index which is a multiple of s). For example, the 4-sample of R is $(4, 8, \cdots, m)$. For $k \in [0, \log m]$, let R_k denote the $(m/2^k)$-sample of R.*

For example, $R_0 = (m)$, $R_3 = (m/8,\ m/4, 3m/8,\ m/2, 5m/8, 3m/4, 7m/8, m)$, and $R_{\log m} = (1, 2, \cdots, m) = R$. Note that $|R_k| = 2^k = 2|R_{k-1}|$.

A $\log m$ Processor Algorithm This subsection gives an algorithm which is needed as an important ingredient in the algorithm of the next subsection. It has the feature that its complexity bounds depend on the number of columns in a stronger way than on the number of rows.

Lemma 5.10. *The π_C array can be computed in $O(\max(n, \log m))$ time with $\min(n, \log m)$ processors in the EREW-PRAM model.*

The bounds of the above lemma might look unappealing at first sight, but their significance lies in the fact that m can be much larger than n. In fact we shall use this lemma, in the next subsection, on problems of size $m \times (\log n)$. The rest of this subsection proves the lemma. Simple-minded approaches like "use one processor to binary search for $\pi_C(c)$ in parallel for each $c \in C$" do not work, the difficulty being that we do not know which $\pi_C(c)$'s are empty. In fact, if we knew which $\pi_C(c)$'s are empty then we could easily achieve $O(\log m)$ time with n processors (by using the above-mentioned straightforward binary search—e.g., binary search for the right endpoint of $\pi_C(c)$ by doing $\log m$ comparisons involving the two columns c and c', where c' is the nearest column to the right of c having a nonempty $\pi_C(c')$).

We shall compute the π_C array by computing two arrays, *LeftExtend* and *RightExtend*, whose significance is as follows.

Definition 5.11. *For any column c, let $LeftExtend(c)$ be the left endpoint of row interval $\pi_{[1,c]}(c)$. That is, $LeftExtend(c)$ is the minimum row index r such that, for any $c' < c$, $A(r, c) < A(r, c')$. Let $RightExtend(c)$ be the right endpoint of row interval $\pi_{[c,n]}(c)$. That is, $RightExtend(c)$ is the maximum row index r such that, for any $c' > c$, $A(r, c) \leq A(r, c')$.*

Intuitively, $LeftExtend(c)$ measures how far to the left (in R) column c can "extend its influence" if the only competition to it came from columns to its left. The intuition for $RightExtend(c)$ is analogous, with the roles of "left" and "right" being interchanged. Note that $LeftExtend(c)$ (resp., $RightExtend(c)$) might be undefined, which we denote by setting it equal to the nonexistent row $m + 1$ (resp., 0).

Once we have the *RightExtend* and *LeftExtend* arrays, it is easy to obtain the π_C array, as follows. If either $LeftExtend(c) = m + 1$ or $RightExtend(c) = 0$ then obviously $\pi_C(c)$ is empty. Otherwise we distinguish two cases: (i) if $RightExtend(c) < LeftExtend(c)$ then $\pi_C(c)$ is empty, and (ii) if $LeftExtend(c) \leq RightExtend(c)$ then interval $\pi_C(c)$ is not empty and has $LeftExtend(c)$ and $RightExtend(c)$ as its two endpoints. Hence it suffices to compute the *RightExtend* and *LeftExtend* arrays. The rest of this subsection explains how to compute the *LeftExtend* array (the computation of *RightExtend* is symmetrical and is therefore omitted). Furthermore, for the sake of definiteness, we shall describe the scheme assuming $n \geq \log m$ (it will be easy for the reader to see that it also works if $n < \log m$). Thus we have $\min\{n, \log m\} = \log m$ processors and wish to achieve $O(\max\{n, \log m\}) = O(n)$ time performance. We shall show how to use the $\log m$ processors to compute the *LeftExtend* array in $n + \log m$ $(= O(n))$ time steps. To simplify the presentation we assume, without loss of generality, that $A(m, 1) > A(m, 2) > \cdots > A(m, n)$ (one can always add a "dummy" last row to A in order to make this hold— obviously this does not destroy the monotonicity of A). This assumption simplifies the presentation because it causes every *LeftExtend*(c) to be $\leq m$ (i.e., it is defined).

We first give a rough overview of the scheme. Imagine that the row indices R are organized as a complete binary search tree T_R: the leaves contain R sorted by increasing order, and each internal node v contains the row index r of the largest leaf in the subtree of v's left child (in which case we can simply refer to v as "internal node r" rather than the more cumbersome "the internal node that contains r"). Note that a row index $r < m$ appears exactly twice in T_R: once at a leaf, and once at an internal node (m appears only once, as the rightmost leaf). Having only $\log m$ processors, we clearly cannot afford to build all of T_R. Instead, we shall build a portion of it, starting from the root and expanding downwards along n root-to-leaf paths $P_1, \cdots, P_n$. Path P_c is in charge of computing *LeftExtend*(c), and does so by performing a binary search for it as it traces a root-to-leaf path in the binary search tree T_R. If path P_c exits at leaf r then *LeftExtend*(c) $= r$. The tracing of all the P_i's is done in a total of $n + \log m$ time steps. Path P_c is inactive until time step c, at which time it gets assigned one processor and begins at the root, and at each subsequent step it makes one move down the tree, until it exits at some leaf at step $c + \log m$. Clearly there are at most $\log m$ paths that are simultaneously active, so that we use $\log m$ processors. At time step $n + \log m$ the last path (P_n) exits a leaf and the computation terminates. If, at a certain time step, path P_c wants to go down to a node of T_R not traced earlier by a $P_{c'}$ ($c' < c$), then its processor builds that node of T_R (we use a pointer representation for the traced portion of T_R— we must avoid indexing since we cannot afford using m space). During path P_c's root-to-leaf trip, we shall maintain the property that, when P_c is at node r of T_R, *LeftExtend*(c) is guaranteed to be one of the leaves in r's subtree (this property is obviously true when P_c is at the root, and we shall soon show how to maintain it as P_c goes from a node to one of its children). It is because of this property that the completion of a P_c (when it exits from a leaf of T_R) corresponds to the end of the computation of *LeftExtend*(c).

The above overview implies that at each time step, the lowermost nodes of the $\log m$ active paths are "staggered" along the levels of T_R in that they are at levels $1, 2, \cdots, \log m$ respectively. Hence at each time step, at most one processor is active at each level of T_R, and the computation of exactly one *LeftExtend*(c) gets completed (at one of the leaves).

We have omitted a crucial detail in the above overview: what additional information should be stored in the traced portion of T_R in order to aid the downward tracing of each P_c (such information is needed for P_c to know whether to branch left or right on its trip down). The idea is for each path to leave behind it a trail of information that will help subsequent paths. Note that $LeftExtend(c)$ depends upon columns $1, 2, \cdots, c-1$ and is independent of columns $c+1, \cdots, n$. Before specifying the additional information, we need some definitions.

Definition 5.12. *Let c and c' be column indices, r be a row index. We say that c is better than c' for r (denoted by $c <_r c'$) iff one of the following holds: (i) $A(r, c) < A(r, c')$, or (ii) $A(r, c) = A(r, c')$ and $c < c'$.*

Note that for any columns c, c' and row r, we must have either $c <_r c'$ or $c' <_r c$. When the algorithm compares $A(r, c)$ to $A(r, c')$ in order to determine whether $c <_r c'$ or $c' <_r c$, it is useful if the reader thinks of such a comparison as a *competition* between c and c' for r: c wins the competition over c' if the outcome is $c <_r c'$, otherwise it loses r to c'. When a path P_c is at an internal node r, it competes for r with the best column for r among the columns in $[1, c-1]$ (that is, it competes with $\theta_{[1,c-1]}(r)$). If c beats $\theta_{[1,c-1]}(r)$ in this competition for r, then P_c obviously branches down to the left child of r in T_R (its $LeftExtend(c)$ is certainly not greater than r). Otherwise it branches to the right child of r. However, the above assumes that the $\theta_{[1,c-1]}(r)$ values are available when needed. We must now make sure that, when P_c enters node r, it can easily (i.e., in constant time) obtain $\theta_{[1,c-1]}(r)$. Note that we can neither maintain the needed $\theta_{[1,c-1]}(r)$ at r, nor can we carry it down with P_c on its downward trip (it is not hard to see that either one of these two approaches runs into trouble). Instead, we shall use a judicious combination of both: some information is maintained locally in r, some is carried along by P_c. When P_c enters r, P_c combines the information it is carrying, with the information in r, to obtain in constant time $\theta_{[1,c-1]}(r)$. This is made more precise below.

Each internal node r' that has been already visited by a path contains, in a register $label(r')$, the best c' for r' among the subset of columns whose path went through r' (hence $label(r')$ is empty if no path visited r' so far).

When P_c enters internal node r of T_R, it carries with it, in a register $rival(c)$, the largest c' such that $c' < c$ and $LeftExtend(c')$ is smaller than the leftmost leaf in the subtree of r (hence $rival(c)$ is empty when P_c is at the root).

Note that the current $rival(c)$ and $label(r)$ allow P_c to obtain $\theta_{[1,c-1]}(r)$ in constant time, as follows. Recall that $\theta_{[1,c-1]}(r)$ is the best for r (i.e., smallest under the $<_r$ relationship) among the columns in $[1, c-1]$. Now, view $[1, c-1]$ as being partitioned into three subsets: the subset S_1 (resp., S_3) consisting of the columns c' whose $LeftExtend(c')$ is smaller (resp., larger) than the leftmost (resp., rightmost) leaf in the subtree of r, and the subset S_2 of the columns c' whose $LeftExtend(c')$ is in the subtree of r. Now, no column in S_3 can be $\theta_{[1,c-1]}(r)$ (by the definition of S_3). The best for r in S_2 is $label(r)$ (by definition). The best for r in S_1 is $rival(c)$, by the following argument. Suppose to the contrary that there is a $c'' \in S_1$, $c'' < rival(c)$, such that c'' is better for r than $rival(c)$. A contradiction with the monotonicity of A is obtained by observing that we now have: (i) $c'' < rival(c)$, (ii) $LeftExtend(rival(c)) < r$, and (iii) c'' is better than $rival(c)$ for r but not for $LeftExtend(rival(c))$. Hence $rival(c)$ must be the best for r in S_1. Hence $\theta_{[1,c-1]}(r)$ is one of $\{rival(c), label(r)\}$, which can be obtained in constant time from $rival(c)$ and $label(r)$, both of which are available (P_c carried $rival(c)$ down with it when it entered r, and r itself maintained $label(r)$ during the previous time step).

The main problem that remains is how to update, in constant time, the $rival(c)$ and the $label(r)$ registers when P_c goes from r down to one of r's two children. We explain below how P_c updates its $rival(c)$ register, and how r updates its $label(r)$ register. (We need not worry about updating the $label(r')$ of a row r' not currently being visited by a $P_{c'}$, since such a $label(r')$ remains by definition unchanged.)

By its very definition, $label(r)$ depends on all the paths $P_{c'}$ $(c' < c)$ that previously went through r. Since P_c has just visited r, we need to make c compete, for row r, with the previous value of $label(r)$: if c wins then $label(r)$ becomes c, otherwise it remains unchanged.

The updating of $rival(c)$ depends upon one of the following two cases.

The first case is when c won the competition at r, i.e., P_c has moved to the left child of r (call it r'). In that case by its very definition $rival(c)$ remains unchanged (since the leftmost leaf in the subtree of r' is the same as the leftmost leaf in the subtree of r).

The second case is when c lost the competition at r, i.e., P_c has moved to the right child of r (call it r''). In that case we claim that it suffices to compare the old $label(r)$ to the old $rival(c)$: the one which is better for r'' is the new value of $rival(c)$. We now prove the claim. Let r_1 (resp., r_2) be the leftmost leaf in the subtree of r (resp., r''). Let C' (resp., C'') be the set of paths consisting of the columns β such that $\beta < c$ and $LeftExtend(\beta) < r_1$ (resp., $LeftExtend(\beta) < r_2$). By definition, the old (resp., new) value of $rival(c)$ is the largest column index in C' (resp., C''). The claim would follow if we can prove that the largest column index in $C'' - C'$ is the old $label(r)$ (by "old $label(r)$" we mean its value before updating, i.e., its value when P_c first entered r). We prove this by contradiction: let $\hat{c}$ denote the old $label(r)$, and suppose that there is a $\gamma \in C'' - C'$ such that $\gamma > \hat{c}$. Since both γ and $\hat{c}$ are in $C'' - C'$, their respective paths went from r to the left child of r. However, P_γ did so *later* than $P_{\hat{c}}$ (because $\gamma > \hat{c}$). This in turn implies that γ is better for r than $\hat{c}$, contradicting the fact that $\hat{c}$ is the old $label(r)$. This proves the claim.

Concerning the implementation of the above scheme, the assignment of processors to their tasks is trivial: each active P_c carries with it its own processor, and when it exits from a leaf it releases that processor which gets assigned to $P_{c+\log m}$ which is just beginning at the root of T_R.

The Tree-Based Algorithm   This subsection builds on the algorithm of the previous subsection and establishes the CREW version of Theorem 5.8 (the next subsection will extend it to EREW). It is useful to think of the computation as progressing through the nodes of a tree T which we now proceed to define.

Partition the column indices into $n/\log n$ adjacent intervals $I_1, \cdots,$ $I_{n/\log n}$ of size $\log n$ each. Call each such interval I_i a *fat column*. Imagine a complete binary tree T on top of these fat columns, and associate with each node v of this tree a *fat interval* $I(v)$ (i.e., an interval of fat columns) in the following way: the fat interval associated with a leaf is simply the fat column corresponding to it, and the fat interval associated with an internal node is the union of the two fat intervals of its children. Thus a node v at height h has a fat interval $I(v)$ consisting of $|I(v)| = 2^h$ fat columns. The storage representation we use for a fat interval $I(v)$ is a list containing the indices of the fat columns in it; we also call that list $I(v)$, in order to avoid introducing extra notation. For example, if v is the left child of the root, then the $I(v)$ array contains $(1, 2, \cdots, n/(2 \log n))$. Observe that $\sum_{v \in T} |I(v)| = O(|T| \log |T|) = O((n/\log n) \log n) = O(n)$.

The ultimate goal is to compute $\pi_C(c)$ for every $c \in C$.

Let *leaf problem* I_i be the problem of computing $\pi_{I_i}(c)$ for all $c \in I_i$. Thus a leaf problem is a subproblem of size $m \times \log n$. From Lemma 5.10 it follows that a leaf problem can be solved in $O(\log n + \log m)$ time by $\min\{\log n, \log m\}$ ($\leq \log n$) processors. Since there are $n/\log n$ leaf problems, they can be solved in $O(\log n + \log m)$ time by n processors. We assume that this has already been done, i.e., that we know the π_{I_i} array for each leaf problem I_i. The rest of this subsection shows that an additional $O(\log n + \log m)$ time with $O(n)$ processors is enough for obtaining π_C.

Definition 5.13. *Let $J(v)$ be the interval of original columns that belong to fat intervals in $I(v)$ (hence $|J(v)| = |I(v)| \cdot \log n$). For every $v \in T$, fat column $f \in I(v)$, and subset R' of R, let $\psi_v(R', f)$ be the interval in R' such that, for every r in that interval, $\theta_{J(v)}(r)$ is a column in fat column f. We use "$\psi_v(R', *)$" as a shorthand for "$\psi_v(R', f)$ for all $f \in I(v)$)".*

We henceforth focus on the computation of the $\psi_{root(T)}(R, *)$ array, where $root(T)$ is the root node of T. Once we have the array $\psi_{root(T)}(R, *)$, it is easy to compute the required π_C array within the prescribed complexity bounds: for each fat column f, we replace the $\psi_{root(T)}(R, f)$ row interval by its intersection with the row intervals in the π_{I_f} array (which are already available at the leaf I_f of T). The rest of this subsection proves the following lemma.

Lemma 5.14. $\psi_v(R, *)$ *for every* $v \in T$ *can be computed by a CREW-PRAM in time* $O(height(T) + \log m)$ *and* $O(n)$ *processors, where* $height(T)$ *is the height of* T $(= O(\log n))$.

Proof. Since $\sum_{v \in T}(|I(v)| + \log n) = O(n)$, we have enough processors to assign $|I(v)| + \log n$ of them to each $v \in T$. The computation proceeds in $\log m + height(T) - 1$ *stages*, each of which takes constant time. Each $v \in T$ will compute $\psi_v(R', *)$ for progressively larger subsets R' of R, subsets R' that double in size from one stage to the next of the computation. We now state precisely what these subsets are. Recall that R_i denotes the $(m/2^i)$-sample of R, so that $|R_i| = 2^i$.

At the t-th stage of the algorithm, a node v of height h in T will use its $|I(v)| + \log n$ processors to compute, in constant time, $\psi_v(R_{t-h}, *)$ if $h \leq t \leq h + \log m$. It does so with the help of information from $\psi_v(R_{t-1-h}, *)$, $\psi_{LeftChild(v)}(R_{t-h}, *)$, and $\psi_{RightChild(v)}(R_{t-h}, *)$, all of which are available from the previous stage $t - 1$ (note that $(t - 1) - (h - 1) = t - h$). If $t < h$ or $t > h + \log m$ then node v does nothing during stage t. Thus before stage h the node v lies "dormant", then at stage $t = h$ it first "wakes up" and computes $\psi_v(R_0, *)$, then at the next stage $t = h + 1$ it computes $\psi_v(R_1, *)$, etc. At stage $t = h + \log m$ it computes $\psi_v(R_{\log m}, *)$, after which it is done.

The details of what information v stores and how it uses its $|I(v)| + \log n$ processors to perform stage t in constant time are given below. In the description, tree nodes u and w are the left and right child, respectively, of v in T.

After stage t, node v (of height h) contains $\psi_v(R_{t-h}, *)$ and a quantity $Critical_v(R_{t-h})$ whose significance is as follows.

Definition 5.15. *Let* R' *be any subset of* R. $Critical_v(R')$ *is the largest* $r \in R'$ *that is contained in* $\psi_v(R', f)$ *for some* $f \in I(u)$; *if there is no such* r *then* $Critical_v(R') = 0$.

The monotonicity of A implies that for every $r' < Critical_v(R')$ (resp., $r' > Critical_v(R')$), r' is contained in $\psi_v(R', f)$ for some $f \in I(u)$ (resp., $f \in I(w)$).

We now explain how v performs stage t, i.e., how it obtains

$$Critical_v(R_{t-h})$$

and

$$\psi_v(R_{t-h}, *)$$

using $\psi_u(R_{t-h}, *)$, $\psi_w(R_{t-h}, *)$, and $Critical_v(R_{t-1-h})$ (all three of which were computed in the previous stage $t - 1$). The fact that the $|I(v)| +

$\log n$ processors can do this in constant time is based on the following observations, whose correctness follows from the definitions.

Observation 1. 1. $Critical_v(R_{t-h})$ is either the same as $Critical_v(R_{t-1-h})$, or the successor of $Critical_v(R_{t-1-h})$ in R_{t-h}.
2. If $f \in I(u)$, then $\psi_v(R_{t-h}, f)$ is the portion of interval $\psi_u(R_{t-h}, f)$ that is $\leq Critical_v(R_{t-h})$.
3. If $f \in I(w)$, then $\psi_v(R_{t-h}, f)$ is the portion of interval $\psi_w(R_{t-h}, f)$ that is $> Critical_v(R_{t-h})$.

The algorithmic implications of the above observations are discussed next.

Computing $Critical_v(R_{t-h})$. Relationship (1) of Observation 1 implies that, in order to compute $Critical_v(R_{t-h})$, all v has to do is determine which of $Critical_v(R_{t-1-h})$ or its successor in R_{t-h} is the correct value of $Critical_v(R_{t-h})$. This is done as follows. If $Critical_v(R_{t-1-h})$ has no successor in R_{t-h} then $Critical_v(R_{t-1-h}) = m$ (the last row) and hence $Critical_v(R_{t-h}) = Critical_v(R_{t-1-h})$. Otherwise the updating is done in the following two steps. For conciseness, let r denote $Critical_v(R_{t-1-h})$, and let s denote the successor of r in R_{t-h}.

- The first step is to compute $\theta_{J(u)}(s)$ and $\theta_{J(w)}(s)$ in constant time. This involves a search in $I(u)$ (resp., $I(w)$) for the fat column $f' \in I(u)$ (resp., $f'' \in I(w)$) whose $\psi_u(R_{t-h}, f')$ (resp., $\psi_w(R_{t-h}, f'')$) contains s. These two searches in $I(u)$ and $I(w)$ are done in constant time with the $|I(v)|$ processors available. We explain how the search for f' in $I(u)$ is done (that for f'' in $I(w)$ is similar and omitted). Node v assigns a processor to each $f \in I(u)$, and that processor tests whether s is in $\psi_u(R_{t-h}, f)$; the answer is "yes" for exactly one of those $|I(u)|$ processors and thus can be collected in constant time. Next, v determines $\theta_{J(u)}(s)$ and $\theta_{J(w)}(s)$ in constant time by using $\log n$ processors to search for s in constant time in the leaf solutions $\pi_{I_{f'}}$ and $\pi_{I_{f''}}$ available at leaves f' and f'', respectively. If the outcome of the search for s in $\pi_{I_{f'}}$ is that $s \in \pi_{I_{f'}}(c')$ for $c' \in I_{f'}$, then $\theta_{J(u)}(s) = c'$. Similarly, $\theta_{J(w)}(s)$ is obtained from the outcome of the search for s in $\pi_{I_{f''}}$.
- The next step consists of comparing $A(s, \theta_{J(u)}(s))$ to $A(s, \theta_{J(w)}(s))$. If the outcome is $A(s, \theta_{J(u)}(s)) > A(s, \theta_{J(w)}(s))$, then $Critical_v(R_{t-h})$ is the same as $Critical_v(R_{t-1-h})$. Otherwise $Critical_v(R_{t-h})$ is s.

We next show how the just computed $Critical_v(R_{t-h})$ value is used to compute $\psi_v(R_{t-h}, *)$ in constant time.

Computing $\psi_v(R_{t-h}, *)$. Relationship (2) of Observation 1 implies the following for each $f \in I(u)$:

- If $\psi_u(R_{t-h}, f)$ is to the left of $Critical_v(R_{t-h})$, then $\psi_v(R_{t-h}, f) = \psi_u(R_{t-h}, f)$.
- If $\psi_u(R_{t-h}, f)$ is to the right of $Critical_v(R_{t-h})$ then $\psi_v(R_{t-h}, f) = \emptyset$.
- If $\psi_u(R_{t-h}, f)$ contains $Critical_v(R_{t-h})$ then $\psi_v(R_{t-h}, f)$ consists of the portion of $\psi_u(R_{t-h}, f)$ up to (and including) $Critical_v(R_{t-h})$.

The above three facts immediately imply that $O(1)$ time is enough for $|I(u)|$ of the $|I(v)|$ processors assigned to v to compute $\psi_v(R_{t-h}, f)$ for all $f \in I(u)$ (recall that the $\psi_u(R_{t-h}, *)$ array is available in u from the previous stage $t - 1$, and $Critical_v(R_{t-h})$ has already been computed).

A similar argument, using relationship (3) of Obervation 1, shows that $|I(w)|$ processors are enough for computing $\psi_v(R_{t-h}, f)$ for all $f \in I(w)$. Thus $\psi_v(R_{t-h}, *)$ can be computed in constant time with $|I(v)|$ processors. This completes the proof of Lemma 5.14.   □

Avoiding Read Conflicts   The scheme of the previous subsection made crucial use of the "concurrent read" capability of the CREW-PRAM. This occurred in the computation of $Critical_v(R_{t-h})$ and also in the subsequent computation of $\psi_v(R_{t-h}, *)$. In its computation of $Critical_v(R_{t-h})$, there are two places where the algorithm of the previous subsection uses the "concurrent read" capability of the CREW (both of them occur during the computation of $\theta_{J(u)}(s)$ and $\theta_{J(w)}(s)$ in constant time). After that, the CREW part of the computation of $\psi_v(R_{t-h}, *)$ is the common reading of $Critical_v(R_{t-h})$. We review these three problems next, using the same notation as in the previous subsection (i.c., u is the left child of v in T, w is the right child of v in T, v has height h in T, s is the successor of $Critical_v(R_{t-1-h})$ in R_{t-h}, etc.).

- Problem 1: This arises during the search in $I(u)$ (resp., $I(w)$) for the fat column $f' \in I(u)$ (resp., $f'' \in I(w)$) whose $\psi_u(R_{t-h}, f')$ (resp., $\psi_w(R_{t-h}, f'')$) contains s. Specifically, for finding (e.g.) f', node v assigns a processor to each $f \in I(u)$, and that processor tests whether s is in $\psi_u(R_{t-h}, f)$; the answer is "yes" for exactly one of those $|I(u)|$ processors and thus can be collected in constant time.
- Problem 2: Having found f' and f'', node v determines $\theta_{J(u)}(s)$ and $\theta_{J(w)}(s)$ in constant time by using $\log n$ processors to search for s, in constant time, in the leaf solutions $\pi_{I_{f'}}$ and $\pi_{I_{f''}}$ available at leaves f' and f'', respectively. There are two parts to this problem: (i) many ancestors of a leaf I_f (possibly all $\log n$ of them) may simultaneously access the same leaf solution π_{I_f}, and (ii) each of those ancestors uses $\log n$ processors to do a constant-time search in the leaf solution π_{I_f} (in the EREW model, it would take $\Omega(\log \log n)$ time just to tell the processors in which leaf to search).

- Problem 3: During the computation of $\psi_v(R_{t-h}, *)$, the common reading of the $Critical_v(R_{t-h})$ value by the fat columns $f \in I(v)$.

Any solution we design for Problems 1–3 should also be such that no concurrent reading of an entry of matrix A occurs. We begin by discussing how to handle Problem 2.

Problem 2.

To avoid the "many ancestors" part of Problem 2 (i.e., part (i)), it naturally comes to mind to make $\log n$ copies of each leaf I_f and to dedicate each copy to one ancestor of I_f, especially since we can easily create these $\log n$ copies of I_f in $O(\log n)$ time and $\log n$ processors (because the space taken by π_{I_f} is $O(\log n)$). But we are still left with part (ii) of Problem 2, i.e., how an ancestor can search the copy of I_f dedicated to it in constant time by using its $\log n$ processors in an EREW fashion. On the one hand, just telling all of those $\log n$ processors which I_f to search takes an unacceptable $\Omega(\log \log n)$ time, and on the other hand a single processor seems unable to search π_{I_f} in constant time. We resolve this by organizing the information at (each copy of) I_f in such a way that we can replace the $\log n$ processors by a single processor to do the search in constant time. Instead of storing a leaf solution in an array π_{I_f}, we store it in a tree structure (call it $Tree(f)$) that enables us to exploit the highly structured nature of the searches to be performed on it. The search to be done at any stage t is not arbitrary, and is highly dependent on what happened during the previous stage $t - 1$, which is why a single processor can do it in constant time (as we shall soon see).

We now define the tree $Tree(f)$. Let $List = [1, r_1], [r_1 + 1, r_2], \cdots, [r_p + 1, m]$ be the list of (at most $\log n$) nonempty intervals in π_{I_f}, in sorted order. Each node of $Tree(f)$ contains one of the intervals of $List$. (It is implicitly assumed that the node of $Tree(f)$ that contains $\pi_{I_f}(c)$ also stores its associated column c.) Imagine a procedure that builds $Tree(f)$ from the root down, in the following way (this is not how $Tree(f)$ is actually built, but it is a convenient way of defining it). At a typical node x, the procedure has available a contiguous subset of $List$ (call it $L(x)$), together with an integer $d(x)$, such that no interval of $L(x)$ contains a multiple of $m/(2^{d(x)})$. (The procedure starts at the root of $Tree(f)$ with $L(root) = List$ and $d(root) = -1$.) The procedure determines which interval of $L(x)$ to store in x by finding the smallest integer $i > d(x)$ such that a multiple of $m/(2^i)$ is in an interval of $L(x)$ (we call i the *priority* of that interval), together with the interval of $L(x)$ for which this happens (say it is interval $[r_k + 1, r_{k+1}]$, and note that it is unique). Interval $[r_k + 1, r_{k+1}]$ is then stored at x (together with its associated column), and the subtree of x is created recursively, as follows. Let L' (resp., L'') be the portion of $L(x)$ to the left (resp., right) of interval $[r_k + 1, r_{k+1}]$. If $L' \neq \emptyset$ then the procedure creates a left child for x (call it y) and recursively goes to y with $d(y) = i$ and with $L(y) = L'$.

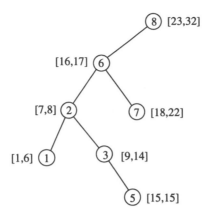

Fig. 5.4. Illustrating $Tree(f)$.

If $L'' \neq \emptyset$ then the procedure creates a right child for x (call it z) and recursively goes to z with $d(z) = i$ and with $L(z) = L''$.

Note that the root of $Tree(f)$ has priority zero and no right child, and that its left child w has $d(w) = 0$ and $L(w) = (List$ minus the last interval in $List)$.

Figure 5.4 shows the $Tree(f)$ corresponding to the case where $m = 32$, $\log n = 8$, and

$$\pi_{I_f} = [1,6]\ [7,8]\ [9,14]\ [\ ]\ [15,15]\ [16,17]\ [18,22]\ [23,32].$$

In that figure, we have assumed (for convenience) that the columns in I_f are numbered $1, \cdots, 8$, and we have shown both the columns c (circled) and their associated intervals $\pi_{I_f}(c)$. For this example, the priorities of the nonempty intervals of π_{I_f} are (respectively) $3, 2, 3, 5, 1, 3, 0$. The concept of priority will be useful for building $Tree(f)$ and for proving various facts about it. The following proposition is an easy consequence of the above definition of $Tree(f)$.

Proposition 5.16. *Let X be an interval in List, of priority i. Let X' (resp., X'') be the nearest interval that is to the left (resp., right) of X in List and that has priority smaller than i. Let i' (resp., i'') be the priority of X' (resp., X''). Then we have the following:*

1. *If $i > 0$ then at least one of $\{X', X''\}$ exists.*
2. *If only one of $\{X', X''\}$ exists, then X is its child in $Tree(f)$ (right child in case of X', left child in case of X'').*
3. *If X' and X'' both exist, then $i' \neq i''$. Furthermore, if $i' > i''$ then X is the right child of X' in $Tree(f)$, otherwise (i.e., if $i' < i''$) X is the left child of X''.*

Proof. The proof refers to the hypothetical procedure we used to define $Tree(f)$. For convenience, we denote a node x of $Tree(f)$ by the interval X that it contains; i.e., whereas in the description of the procedure we used to say "the node x of $Tree(f)$ that contains X" and "list $L(x)$", we now simply say "node X" and "list $L(X)$" (this is somewhat of an abuse of notation, since when the procedure first entered x it did not yet know X).

That (1) holds is obvious.

That (2) holds follows from the following observation. Let X be a child of X' in $Tree(f)$. When the procedure we used to define $Tree(f)$ was at X', it went to node X with the list $L(X)$ set equal to the portion of $L(X')$ before X' (if X is left child of X') or after X' (if X is right child of X'). This implies that the priorities of the intervals between X' and X in $List$ are all larger than the priority of X. This implies that, when starting in $List$ at X and moving along $List$ towards X', X' is the first interval that we encounter that has a lower priority than that of X. Hence (2) holds.

We now prove (3). Note that the proof we just gave for (2) also implies that the parent of X is in $\{X', X''\}$. Hence to prove (3), it suffices to show that one of $\{X', X''\}$ is ancestor of the other (this would imply that they are both ancestors of X, and that the one with the larger priority is the parent of X). We prove this by contradiction: let Z be the lowest common ancestor of X' and X'' in $Tree(f)$, with $Z \notin \{X', X''\}$. Since Z has lower priority than both X' and X'', it cannot occur between X' and X'' in $List$. However, the fact that X' (resp., X'') is in the subtree of the left (resp., right) child of Z implies that it is in the portion of $L(Z)$ before Z (resp., after Z). This implies that Z occurs between X' and X'' in $List$, a contradiction.   □

We now show that $Tree(f)$ can be built in $O(\log m + \log n)$ time with $|List|$ ($\leq \log n$) processors. Assign one processor to each interval of $List$, and do the following in parallel for each such interval. The processor assigned to an interval X computes the smallest integer i such that a multiple of $m/(2^i)$ is in that interval (recall that this integer i is the priority of interval X). Following this $O(\log m)$ time computation of the priorities of the intervals in $List$, the processor assigned to each interval determines its parent in $Tree(f)$, and whether it is left or right child of that parent, by using the above Proposition 5.16. Reading conflicts are easy to avoid during this $O(|List|)$ time computation (the details are trivial and omitted).

Note: Although we do not need to do so, it is in fact possible to build $Tree(f)$ in $O(\log m + \log n)$ time by using only one processor rather than $\log n$ processors, but the construction is somewhat more involved and we refrain from giving it in order not to break the flow of the exposition.

As explained earlier, after $Tree(f)$ is built, we must make $\log n$ copies of it (one for each ancestor in T of leaf I_f).

We now explain how a single processor can use a copy of $Tree(f)$ to perform constant time searching. From now on, if a node of $Tree(f)$ contains interval $\pi_{I_f}(c)$, we refer to that node as either "node $\pi_{I_f}(c)$" or as "node c". We use $RightChild(c)$ and $LeftChild(c)$ to denote the left and right child, respectively, of c in $Tree(f)$.

Proposition 5.17. *Let* $r \in R_k$, r' *be the predecessor of* r *in* R_k. *Let* $r \in \pi_{I_f}(c)$, *and let* $r' \in \pi_{I_f}(c')$. *Then the predecessor of* r *in* R_{k+1} *(call it* r''*) is in* $\pi_{I_f}(c'')$ *where* $c'' \in \{c', RightChild(c'), LeftChild(c), c\}$.

Proof. If $c'' \in \{c', c\}$ then there is nothing to prove, so suppose that $c'' \notin \{c, c'\}$. This implies that $c \neq c'$ (since $c = c'$ would imply that $c'' = c$). Then $\pi_{I_f}(c')$, $\pi_{I_f}(c'')$ and $\pi_{I_f}(c)$ are distinct and occur in that order in $List$ (not necessarily adjacent to one another in $List$). Note that $\pi_{I_f}(c')$ and $\pi_{I_f}(c)$ each contains a row in R_k, that $\pi_{I_f}(c'')$ contains a row in R_{k+1} but no row in R_k, and that all the other intervals of $List$ that are between $\pi_{I_f}(c')$ and $\pi_{I_f}(c)$ do not contain any row in R_{k+1}. This, together with the definition of the priority of an interval, implies that $\pi_{I_f(c')}$ and $\pi_{I_f(c)}$ have priorities no larger than k, that $\pi_{I_f}(c'')$ has a priority equal to $k + 1$, and that all the other intervals of $List$ that are between $\pi_{I_f}(c')$ and $\pi_{I_f}(c)$ have priorities greater than $k + 1$. This, together with proposition 5.16, implies that $c'' \in \{RightChild(c'), LeftChild(c)\}$.   □

Proposition 5.18. *Let* $r \in R_k$, r' *be the successor of* r *in* R_k. *Let* $r \in \pi_{I_f}(c)$, *and let* $r' \in \pi_{I_f}(c')$. *Then the successor of* r *in* R_{k+1} *(call it* r''*) is in* $\pi_{I_f}(c'')$ *where* $c'' \in \{c, RightChild(c), LeftChild(c'), c'\}$.

Proof. Similar to that of Proposition 5.17, and therefore omitted.   □

Now recall that, in the previous subsection, the searches done by a particular v in a leaf solution at I_f had the feature that, if at stage t node $v \in T$ asked which column of I_f contains a certain row $r \in R_k$, then at stage $t + 1$ it is asking the same question about r' where r' is either the successor or the predecessor of r in R_{k+1}. This, together with Propositions 5.17 and 5.18, implies that a processor can do the search (in $Tree(f)$) at stage $t + 1$ in constant time, so long as it maintains, in addition to the node of $Tree(f)$ that contains the current r, the two nodes of $Tree(f)$ that contain the predecessor and (respectively) successor of r in R_k. These are clearly easy to maintain.   □

We next explain how Problems 1 and 3 are handled.

Problems 1 and 3.

Right after stage $t - 1$ is completed, v stores the following information (recall that the height of v in T is h). The fat columns $f \in I(v)$ for which interval $\psi_v(R_{t-1-h}, f)$ is not empty are stored in a doubly linked list. For each such fat column f, we store the following information: (i) the row interval $\psi_v(R_{t-1-h}, f) = [\alpha_1, \alpha_2]$, and (ii) for row α_1 (resp., α_2), a pointer to the node, in v's copy of $Tree(f)$, whose interval contains row α_1 (resp.,

α_2). In addition, v stores the following. Let z be the parent of v in T, and let s' be the successor of $Critical_z(R_{t-1-(h+1)})$ in $R_{t-(h+1)}$, with s' in $\psi_v(R_{t-1-h}, g)$ for some $g \in I(v)$. Then v has g marked as being its *distinguished fat column*, and v also stores a pointer to the node, in v's copy of $Tree(g)$, whose interval contains s'. Of course, information similar to the above for v is stored in every node x of T (including v's children, u and w), with the height of x playing the role of h. In particular, in the formulation of Problem 1, the fat columns we called f' and f'' are the distinguished fat columns of u and (respectively) w, and thus are available at u and (respectively) w, each of which also stores a pointer to the node containing s in its copy of $Tree(f')$ (for u) or of $Tree(f'')$ (for w).

Assume for the time being that we are able to maintain the above information in constant time from stage $t-1$ to stage t. This would enable us to avoid Problem 1 because instead of searching for the desired fat column f' (resp., f''), node u (resp., w) already has it available as its distinguished fat column. Problem 3 would also be avoided, because now only the distinguished fat columns of u and w need to read from v the $Critical_v(R_{t-h})$ value (whereas previously all of the fat columns in $I(u) \cup I(w)$ read that value from v). It therefore suffices to show how to maintain, from stage $t-1$ to stage t, the above information (i.e., v's linked list and its associated pointers to the $Tree(f)$s of its elements, v's distinguished fat column g, and the pointer to v's copy of $Tree(g)$). We explain how this is done at v.

First, v computes its $Critical_v(R_{t-h})$: since we know from stage $t-1$ the distinguished fat columns f' and f'' of u and (respectively) w, and their associated pointers to u's copy of $Tree(f')$ and (respectively) w's copy of $Tree(f'')$, v can compare the two relevant entries of matrix A (i.e., $A(s, \theta_{J(u)}(s))$ and $A(s, \theta_{J(w)}(s))$) and it can decide, based on this comparison, whether $Critical_v(R_{t-h})$ remains equal to $Critical_v(R_{t-1-h})$ or becomes equal to s, its successor in R_{t-h}. But since this is done in parallel by all v's, we must show that no two nodes of T (say, v and v') try to access the same entry of matrix A. The reason this does not happen is as follows. If none of $\{v, v'\}$ is ancestor of the other then no read conflict in A can occur between v and v' because their associated columns (that is, $J(v)$ and $J(v')$) are disjoint. If one of v, v' is ancestor of the other, then no read conflict in A can occur between them because the rows they are interested in are disjoint (this is based on the observation that v is interested in rows in $R_{t-h} - \cup_{i=0}^{t-1-h} R_i$ and hence will have no conflict with any of its ancestors).

As a side effect of the computation of $Critical_v(R_{t-h})$, v also knows which fat column $\hat{f} \in \{f', f''\}$ is such that $\psi_v(R_{t-h}, \hat{f})$ contains $Critical_v(R_{t-h})$. It uses its knowledge of $\hat{f}$ to update its linked list of nonempty fat columns (and their associated row intervals) as follows (we distinguish two cases):

1. $\hat{f} = f'$. In that case v's new linked list consists of the portion of u's old (i.e., at stage $t - 1$) linked list whose fat columns are $< f'$ (the row intervals associated with these fat columns are as in u's list at $t - 1$), followed by f' with an associated interval $\psi_v(R_{t-h}, f')$ equal to the portion of $\psi_u(R_{t-h}, f')$ up to and including $Critical_v(R_{t-h})$, followed by f'' with an associated interval $\psi_v(R_{t-h}, f'')$ equal to the portion of $\psi_w(R_{t-h}, f'')$ larger than $Critical_v(R_{t-h})$ if that portion is nonempty (if it is empty then f'' is not included in v's new linked list), followed by the portion of w's old (i.e., at stage $t - 1$) linked list whose fat columns are $> f''$ (the row intervals associated with these fat columns are as in w's list at $t - 1$).

2. $\hat{f} = f''$. Similar to the first case, except that $Critical_v(R_{t-h})$ is now in the interval associated with f'' rather than f'.

It should be clear that the above computation of v's new linked list and its associated intervals can be implemented in constant time with $|I(v)|$ processors (by copying the needed information from u and w, since these are at height $h-1$ and hence at stage $t-1$ already "knew" their information relative to $R_{t-1-(h-1)} = R_{t-h}$).

In either one of the above two cases (1) and (2), for each endpoint α of a $\psi_v(R_{t-h}, f)$ in v's linked list, we must compute the pointer to the node, in v's copy of $Tree(f)$, whose interval contains that α. We do it as follows. If f was not in v's list at stage $t - 1$, then we obtain the pointer from u or w, simply by copying it (more specifically, if in u or w it points to a node of u's or w's copy of $Tree(f)$, then the "copy" we make of that pointer is to the same node but in v's own copy of $Tree(f)$). On the other hand, if f was in v's list at stage $t - 1$, then we distinguish two cases. In the case where α was also an endpoint of $\psi_v(R_{t-1-h}, f)$, we already have its pointer (to v's copy of $Tree(f)$) available from stage $t - 1$. If α was not an endpoint of $\psi_v(R_{t-1-h}, f)$ then α is predecessor or successor of an endpoint of $\psi_v(R_{t-1-h}, f)$ in R_{t-h}, and therefore the pointer for α can be found in constant time (by using Propositions 5.16 and 5.17).

Finally, we must show how v computes its new distinguished fat column. It does so by first obtaining, from its parent z, $Critical_z(R_{t-(h+1)})$ that z has just computed. The old distinguished fat column g stored at v had its $\psi_v(R_{t-1-h}, g)$ containing the successor s' of $Critical_z(R_{t-1-(h+1)})$ in $R_{t-(h+1)}$. It must be updated into a $\hat{g}$ such that $Critical_v(R_{t-h}, \hat{g})$ contains the successor s'' of $Critical_z(R_{t-(h+1)})$ in $R_{t+1-(h+1)}$. We distinguish two cases.

1. $Critical_z(R_{t-(h+1)}) = Critical_z(R_{t-1-(h+1)})$. In that case s'' is the predecessor of s' in $R_{t+1-(h+1)}$, and the fat column $\hat{g} \in I(v)$ for which $\psi_v(R_{t-h}, \hat{g})$ contains s'' is either the same as g or it is the predecessor

of g in the linked list for v at stage t (which we already computed). It is therefore easy to identify $\hat{g}$ in constant time in that case.

2. $Critical_z(R_{t-(h+1)}) = s'$. In that case s'' is the successor of s' in $R_{t+1-(h+1)}$, and the fat column $\hat{g} \in I(v)$ for which $\psi_v(R_{t-h}, \hat{g})$ contains s'' is either the same as g or it is the successor of g in the linked list for v at stage t (which we already computed). It is therefore easy to identify $\hat{g}$ in constant time in that case as well.

In either one of the above two cases, we need to also compute a pointer value to the node, in v's copy of $Tree(\hat{g})$, whose interval contains s''. This is easy if $\hat{g} = g$, because we know from stage $t-1$ the pointer value for s' into v's copy of $Tree(g)$, and the pointer value for s'' can thus be found by using Propositions 5.17 and 5.18 (since s'' is predecessor or successor of s' in R_{t-h}). So suppose $\hat{g} \neq g$, i.e., $\hat{g}$ is predecessor or successor of g in v's linked list of nonempty fat columns at t. The knowledge of the pointer for s' to v's copy of $Tree(g)$ at $t-1$ is of little help in that case, since we now care about v's copy of $Tree(\hat{g})$ rather than $Tree(g)$. What saves us is the following observation: s'' *must be an endpoint* of row interval $\psi_v(R_{t-h}, \hat{g})$. Specifically, s'' is the left (i.e., beginning) endpoint of $\psi_v(R_{t-h}, \hat{g})$ if $\hat{g}$ is the successor of g in v's linked list at stage t (Case 2 above), otherwise it is the right endpoint of $\psi_v(R_{t-h}, \hat{g})$ (Case 1 above). Since s'' is such an endpoint, we already know the pointer for s'' to v's copy of $Tree(\hat{g})$ (because such pointers are available, in v's linked list, for all the endpoints of the row intervals in that linked list).

5.4.2 THE TUBE MINIMA BOUND

This subsection shows that $O(m^2)$ work suffices for computing in $O(\log m)$ time the tube minima of an $m \times m \times m$ matrix, in the EREW-PRAM model. Let X be the set of row indices of A, Z its set of column indices, and Y be its set of height indices. Our task is to compute $\theta_A(v, w)$ for all $v \in X$ and all $w \in Y$. We use $S(L, k)$ to denote the k-sample of a list L.

In the first stage of the computation, for each $v \in S(X, \log m)$, we use the row-minima algorithm to obtain $\theta_A(v, w)$ for all $w \in Y$. This first stage of the computation takes $O(\log m)$ time and $O(m \log m)$ work for each v, hence a total of $O(m \log m (m/ \log m)) = O(m^2)$ work.

In the second stage of the computation, for each $w \in S(Y, \sqrt{\log m})$, we compute $\theta_A(v, w)$ for all $v \in S(X, \sqrt{\log m})$. We now describe how this is done for a particular value of w. Let $X_1, X_2, \ldots, X_{m/\log m}$ be the intervals in the partition of X induced by $S(X, \log m)$. The values $\{\theta_A(v, w) \mid v \in S(X, \log m)\}$, which are known from the first stage, induce a partition of Z into $m/\log m$ intervals $Z_1, Z_2, \ldots, Z_{m/\log m}$. For each $v \in S(X, \sqrt{\log m})$, the monotonicity property implies that, if $v \in X_k$, then $\theta_A(v, w) \in Z_k$ and hence can be computed in $O(\log m)$ time and $O(1+|Z_k|)$ work. Since there are $\sqrt{\log m}$ such v's that are in $X_k \cap S(X, \sqrt{\log m})$, the work for them is

$O(\sqrt{\log m}(1+|Z_k|))$. Summing over all k, $1 \leq k \leq m/\log m$, gives the work needed to compute $\theta_A(v, w)$ for that fixed w and all $v \in S(X, \sqrt{\log m})$:

$$\sum_{1 \leq k \leq m/\log m} \sqrt{\log m}(1+|Z_k|) =$$

$$O((m/\sqrt{\log m}) + m\sqrt{\log m}) = O(m\sqrt{\log m}),$$

where the fact that $\sum_k |Z_k| = m$ was used. Since there are $m/\sqrt{\log m}$ such w's in $S(Y, \sqrt{\log m})$, the total work for stage two is $O(m\sqrt{\log m}(m/\sqrt{\log m})) = O(m^2)$.

The third stage of the computation "fills in the blanks" by actually computing $\theta_A(v, w)$ for all $v \in X$ and $w \in Y$. Let $X_1, X_2, \ldots, X_{m/\sqrt{\log m}}$ be the intervals in the partition of X induced by $S(X, \sqrt{\log m})$. Similarly, let $Y_1, Y_2, \ldots, Y_{m/\sqrt{\log m}}$ be the intervals in the partition of Y induced by $S(Y, \sqrt{\log m})$. Let Z_{ij}, $1 \leq i, j \leq m/\sqrt{\log m}$, be the interval of Z that is defined by the set of $\theta_A(v, w)$ such that $v \in X_i$ and $w \in Y_j$. Of course we already know the beginning and end of each such interval Z_{ij} (from the second stage of the computation). We then solve the problem defined by each $X_i, Z_{i,j}, Y_j$, as follows. If $|Z_{ij}| \leq \sqrt{\log m}$ then a single processor can solve the problem sequentially in $O((\sqrt{\log m})^2) = O(\log m)$ time. If $|Z_{ij}| > \sqrt{\log m}$ then we partition Z_{ij} into $|Z_{ij}|/\sqrt{\log m}$ pieces $J_1, J_2, \ldots$ of size $\sqrt{\log m}$ each. We assign to each J_k one processor which solves sequentially the sub-problem defined by X_i, J_k, Y_j, i.e. it computes for each $v \in X_i$ and $w \in Y_j$ the smallest $p \in J_k$ that minimizes $A(v, p, w)$. This sequential computation takes $O(\log m)$ time because $|X_i| = |J_k| = |Y_j| = \sqrt{\log m}$. The work done so far for a particular pair of intervals X_i, Y_j is, of course, $O((\log m)(1 + |Z_{ij}|/\sqrt{\log m})) = O(\log m + |Z_{ij}|\sqrt{\log m})$. To finish the job for such a pair of intervals X_i, Y_j we must still determine, for each v, w with $v \in X_i$ and $w \in Y_j$, the best answer for it among the $|Z_{ij}|/\sqrt{\log m}$ possibilities returned by each of the above-mentioned sequential computations. This takes logarithmic time and $O(|Z_{i,j}|/\sqrt{\log m})$ work for a particular v, w pair, hence a total (for all such v, w pairs) of $O(|X_i||Y_j||Z_{ij}|/\sqrt{\log m}) = O(|Z_{ij}|\sqrt{\log m})$ work. Summing over all i, j gives, for this third stage, a total amount of work equal to $O(m^2)$ because of the following:

Lemma 5.19. $\sum_{i=1}^{m/\sqrt{\log m}} \sum_{j=1}^{m/\sqrt{\log m}} |Z_{ij}| = O(m^2/\sqrt{\log m})$.

Proof. First, observe that Z_{ij} and $Z_{i+1,j+1}$ are adjacent intervals that are disjoint except for one possible common endpoint (the rightmost point in Z_{ij} and the leftmost point in $Z_{i+1,j+1}$ may coincide). This observation implies that for any given integer δ ($0 \leq |\delta| \leq m/\sqrt{\log m}$), we have: (It is understood that $|Z_{ij}| = 0$ if $j < 1$ or $j > m/\sqrt{\log m}$.)

$$\sum_{i=1}^{m/\sqrt{\log m}} |Z_{i,i+\delta}| = O(m).$$

The lemma follows from the above simply by re-writing the summation in the lemma's statement:

$$\sum_{\delta=-m/\sqrt{\log m}}^{m/\sqrt{\log m}} \sum_{i=1}^{m/\sqrt{\log m}} |Z_{i,i+\delta}|. \quad \square$$

This completes the description of the optimal EREW-PRAM algorithm for tube minima.

5.4.3 IMPLICATIONS FOR STRING EDITING

The EREW-PRAM bounds for tube minima that were just established imply similar CREW-PRAM (but not necessarily EREW-PRAM) bounds for the combining stage of the parallel divide and conquer for string editing. The reason for this is that the matrix A derived from the string editing problem is only implicitly available, described by the equation $A(v, p, w) = DIST_{NW}(v, p) + DIST_{SW}(p, w)$. Thus simultaneous reading of $A(v_1, p, w)$ by processor x and of $A(v_2, p, w)$ by processor y requires common reading of $DIST_{SW}(p, w)$ by both processors x and y, whereas the development of the EREW-PRAM bounds for tube minima assumed that x and y would not have such a "read conflict" (because the matrix A was assumed to be explicitly available).

5.5 Optimal CRCW-PRAM algorithm for tube minima

The main result of this section is a CRCW-PRAM algorithm, for tube minima, of time complexity $O(\log \log n)$ and $O(n^2 / \log \log n)$ processor complexity.

Theorem 5.20. *The $n \times n$ matrix θ_A of an $n \times n \times n$ matrix A can be computed in $O(\log \log n)$ time with $O(n^2 / \log \log n)$ processors in the CRCW-PRAM model.*

Before going into the details fo the proof, we point out that a major ingredient in the approach consists of the judicious use of an "aspect ratio condition": Intuitively, the idea is to allow the aspect ratio of the subproblems solved recursively to deteriorate, but not too much, and in a controlled fashion (this is made precise later in the section). Although aspect ratios play a crucial role in establishing Theorem 1, once we have that theorem we can use it to solve problems of *arbitrary* aspect ratios, as we later show.

In Section 5.5.1 we give a preliminary algorithm for the case where A is $\ell \times h \times \ell$ and $h \leq \ell^2$. That algorithm runs in $O(\log \log \ell)$ time and does

$O((\ell h + \ell^2)(\log \ell)^2)$ work. Section 5.5.2 uses that preliminary algorithm to establish the above theorem. Section 5.5.3 concludes with further remarks.

5.5.1 A PRELIMINARY ALGORITHM

This section gives a preliminary algorithm that has the right time complexity, but does too much work (hence uses too many processors).

The procedure is recursive, and requires that A be $\ell \times h \times \ell$ with $h \le \ell^2$. We call this last condition the *aspect ratio* requirement; we assume it to be true initially, and we maintain it through the recursion (doing so without damaging the time complexity or the work complexity is, in fact, the main difficulty in this preliminary algorithm). The preliminary CRCW-PRAM algorithm runs in $O(\log \log \ell)$ time and has work (that is, number of operations) complexity $O((\ell h + \ell^2)(\log \ell)^2)$.

Before describing the algorithm, we need a few definitions and a review of some properties.

Let X (resp., Y) be a subset of the row (resp., height) indices of A, and let Z be a contiguous interval of the column indices of A. The *problem induced by the triplet* (X, Z, Y) is that of finding $\theta_{A'}$ for the $|X| \times |Z| \times |Y|$ submatrix A' of A induced by X, Z and Y. That is, it consists of finding, for each pair u, v with $u \in X$ and $v \in Y$, the smallest index $k \in Z$ such that $A(u, k, v)$ is minimized. This k need not equal $\theta_A(u, v)$ since we are minimizing only over Z. However, the following property holds. Assume X (resp., Y) is a contiguous interval of row (resp., height) indices of A. Let x, z, y (resp., x', z', y') be the smallest (resp., largest) indices in X, Z, Y respectively. If $\theta_A(x, y) = z$ and $\theta_A(x', y') = z'$, then the solution to the triplet (X, Y, Z) gives the correct value of $\theta_A(u, v)$ for all $u \in X$ and $v \in Y$ (this follows from the sortedness of θ_A).

The first stage of the computation partitions the row indices of A into $\ell^{1/3}$ contiguous intervals $X_1, X_2, \cdots, X_{\ell^{1/3}}$ of size $\ell^{2/3}$ each. Similarly, the height indices of A are partitioned into $\ell^{1/3}$ contiguous intervals $Y_1, Y_2, \cdots, Y_{\ell^{1/3}}$ of size $\ell^{2/3}$ each. An *endpoint* of an interval X_i (resp., Y_i) is the largest or smallest index in it. For each pair v, w such that v is an endpoint of X_i and w is an endpoint of Y_j, we assign $h^{1+(1/6)}$ processors which compute, in constant time, the index $\theta_A(v, w)$. (Computing the minimum of h entries using $h^{1+(1/6)}$ processors is easily shown to take constant time.) The total number of processors used in this step of the algorithm is $O(\ell^{1/3}\ell^{1/3}h^{1+(1/6)})$, which is $O(\ell h)$ because $h \le \ell^2$.

Let x (resp., x') be the smallest (resp., largest) index in X_i, and let y (resp., y') be the smallest (resp., largest) index in Y_j. Let $Z_{i,j}$ be the interval $[a, b]$ where $a = \theta_A(x, y)$ and $b = \theta_A(x', y')$. In the future, when we want to define such a $Z_{i,j}$, we shall simply say "let $Z_{i,j}$ denote the interval of column indices of A defined by the set $\theta_A(v, w)$ such that $v \in X_i$ and $w \in Y_j$"; we do so for simplicity of expression, although it is an abuse of language (because $Z_{i,j}$ might include an index k that is not the $\theta_A(u, v)$ of any pair $u \in X_i, v \in Y_j$).

After the above stage of the computation we know the beginning and end of each such interval $Z_{i,j}$. As already observed, for any pair of indices u, v where $u \in X_i$ and $v \in Y_j$, we have $\theta_A(u, v) \in Z_{i,j}$. Thus it suffices to solve all of the subproblems defined by triplets $(X_i, Z_{i,j}, Y_j)$. However, some of these triplets might violate the aspect ratio condition because their $Z_{i,j}$ is too large (larger than $|X_i|^2 = \ell^{4/3}$): each such troublesome triplet (we call it a *bad* triplet) will be further partitioned into $k_{i,j} = \lceil |Z_{i,j}|/\ell^{4/3} \rceil$ smaller subproblems, by partitioning $Z_{i,j}$ into $k_{i,j}$ pieces of size $\ell^{4/3}$ each (except that possibly the $k_{i,j}$-th piece might be smaller). Specifically, if $Z_{i,j}^{(k)}$ denotes the k-th piece from this partition of $Z_{i,j}$, then the k-th sub-problem *spawned* by the bad triplet $(X_i, Z_{i,j}, Y_j)$ is $(X_i, Z_{i,j}^{(k)}, Y_j)$. Of course such a spawned subproblem $(X_i, Z_{i,j}^{(k)}, Y_j)$ no longer has the property that $\theta_A(u, v) \in Z_{i,j}^{(k)}$ for $u \in X_i$ and $v \in Y_j$. However, the answer returned by solving such an $(X_i, Z_{i,j}^{(k)}, Y_j)$ is not meaningless: we can obtain $\theta_A(u, v)$ for $u \in X_i$ and $v \in Y_j$ by choosing the best among the $k_{i,j}$ candidates returned by the $k_{i,j}$ subproblems $(X_i, Z_{i,j}^{(k)}, Y_j)$, $1 \le k \le k_{i,j}$. We are now ready to give the details of the second stage of the computation.

The second stage of the computation "fills in the blanks" by doing one parallel recursive call on a number of problems, defined as follows. In what follows, we describe these problems one at a time, but one should keep in mind that they are all solved in parallel. The first class of problems to be solved recursively are the good ones, those defined by triplets $(X_i, Z_{i,j}, Y_j)$ where $|Z_{i,j}| \le \ell^{4/3}$. The $Z_{i,j}$ of such a good problem is not large enough to violate the aspect ratio constraint (because it satisfies $|Z_{i,j}| \le |X_i|^2$). The second class of problems to be solved recursively are those spawned by the bad triplets $(X_i, Z_{i,j}, Y_j)$, namely subproblems $(X_i, Z_{i,j}^{(k)}, Y_j)$, $1 \le k \le k_{i,j}$. By definition, each such $(X_i, Z_{i,j}^{(k)}, Y_j)$ satisfies the aspect ratio requirement. When these recursive calls return, we need not do further work for the good triplets, but for the bad ones we only have the answers for the $k_{i,j}$ subproblems they spawned. We can use these $k_{i,j}$ subanswers to get the correct answers in constant time, however. For each bad triplet $(X_i, Z_{i,j}, Y_j)$, we need to compute, for every pair $u \in X_i$ and $v \in Y_j$, the minimum among $k_{i,j}$ entries. We do so by using $k_{i,j} h^{1/6}$ processors for each such pair $u \in X_i$ and $v \in Y_j$ (this is enough, since we are then computing the minimum of $k_{i,j}$ entries using $\ge k_{i,j}^{1+(1/6)}$ processors). Since there are $\ell^{4/3}$ such u, v pairs per bad triplet, the total work done for this "bad triplet postprocessing" is upper-bounded by $\ell^{4/3} h^{1/6} \sum_{i,j} k_{i,j}$; now, since

$$\sum_{i,j} k_{i,j} = \sum_{\beta=-\ell^{1/3}+1}^{\ell^{1/3}-1} \sum_{i} k_{i,i+\beta} \leq \sum_{\beta=-\ell^{1/3}+1}^{\ell^{1/3}-1} (2h/\ell^{4/3}) = O(h/\ell),$$

this work is $O(\ell^{4/3}h^{1/6}h/\ell) = O(h\ell)$ (where the fact that $h \leq \ell^2$ was used).

The bottom of the recursion is as usual: we stop when ℓ is some small enough constant (note that, by the aspect ratio condition, a constant ℓ implies a constant h, since $h \leq \ell^2$).

The above description did not address the processor allocation problem: how processors are assigned, in constant time, to the subproblems they will solve recursively. We postpone discussing this issue until after we analyze the time and work complexities of the above algorithm (the machinery developed during that analysis will be used in the solution to the processor allocation problem).

Analysis Before we analyze the complexity of the above algorithm, we make a sraightforward observation that is needed in the analysis. Let $\delta_{i,j}$ equal one if $|Z_{i,j}| > \ell^{4/3}$, zero otherwise. Consider the sum:

$$H = \sum_{\delta_{i,j}=0} |Z_{i,j}| + \sum_{\delta_{i,j}=1} \sum_{1 \leq k \leq k_{i,j}} |Z_{i,j}^{(k)}|.$$

This can be rewritten as follows, by changing the summation indices from i, j to i, β:

$$II = \sum_{\delta_{i,i+\beta}=0} |Z_{i,i+\beta}| + \sum_{\delta_{i,i+\beta}=1} \sum_{1 \leq k \leq k_{i,i+\beta}} |Z_{i,i+\beta}^{(k)}|.$$

Let H_β be the value of the above sum for a given value of β, that is, fixing β and summing over i (hence $H = \sum_\beta H_\beta$). It is not hard to see that H_β is upper-bounded by $h + \ell^{1/3}$. Since there are $2\ell^{1/3} - 1$ possible choices for β, H is upper-bounded by $2h\ell^{1/3} + 2\ell^{2/3}$. This fact will be used in the analysis below.

The time and work complexities of the algorithm satisfy the recurrences:

$$T(\ell, h) \leq T(\ell^{2/3}, h') + c_1,$$

$$W(\ell, h) \leq c_2 \ell h + \sum_{\delta_{i,j}=0} W(\ell^{2/3}, |Z_{i,j}|) + \sum_{\delta_{i,j}=1} \sum_{1 \leq k \leq k_{i,j}} W(\ell^{2/3}, |Z_{i,j}^{(k)}|),$$

where c_1 and c_2 are constants, and $h' \leq \ell^{4/3}$. The time recurrence clearly implies that $T(\ell, h) = O(\log \log \ell)$. We now prove, by induction on ℓ, that the work recurrence implies that $W(\ell, h) \leq c(\ell h + \ell^2)(\log \ell)^2$ for a constant *c.* The basis of the induction is trivial. For the induction step, using the induction hypothesis in the above recurrence gives

$$W(\ell, h) \le c_2 \ell h + \sum_{\delta_{i,j}=0} c(\ell^{2/3}|Z_{i,j}| + \ell^{4/3})(\log(\ell^{2/3}))^2 +$$

$$\sum_{\delta_{i,j}=1} \sum_{1 \le k \le k_{i,j}} c(\ell^{2/3}|Z_{i,j}^{(k)}| + \ell^{4/3})(\log(\ell^{2/3}))^2.$$

Using the definition of H, the above inequality can be re-written as

$$W(\ell, h) \le c_2 \ell h + (4c/9)\ell^{2/3}(\log \ell)^2 H + (4c/9)\ell^{4/3}(\log \ell)^2 \Big(\sum_{\delta_{i,j}=0} 1 + \sum_{\delta_{i,j}=1} k_{i,j} \Big).$$

Using the facts that $H \le 2h\ell^{1/3} + 2\ell^{2/3}$ and that $\sum_{i,j} k_{i,j} \le c'h/\ell$ for a constant c', the above inequality implies

$$W(\ell, h) \le c_2 \ell h + (8c/9)\ell h(\log \ell)^2 + (8c/9)\ell^{4/3}(\log \ell)^2 +$$

$$(4c/9)\ell^2(\log \ell)^2 + (4c/9)c'\ell^{1/3}h(\log \ell)^2.$$

This clearly implies that $W(\ell, h) \le c(\ell h + \ell^2)(\log \ell)^2$ for a suitably chosen constant c.

It should be clear from the above that a somewhat better bound for $W(\ell, h)$ can be obtained with a sharper analysis, but we choose not bother with it; in fact the rest of this section can establish Theorem 1 even if we had a somewhat worse bound than the above one for $W(\ell, h)$, namely $W(\ell, h) = O((\ell h + \ell^2)(\log \ell)^\alpha)$ is enough so long as α is constant (i.e., even if $\alpha > 2$). This will become clear in Section 5.5.2.

Processor Allocation We now turn our attention to the issue of how the processors are allocated, in constant time, to the subproblems that must be solved recursively. The details of how this is done mimic the above analysis of the work complexity, and are somewhat tedious but not particularly difficult (they do involve some subtle points, however).

Imagine partitioning the subproblems to be solved recursively into *classes*, where class β consists of the subproblems of the form $(X_i, Z_{i,i+\beta}, Y_{i+\beta})$ or $(X_i, Z_{i,i+\beta}^{(k)}, Y_{i+\beta})$. (Hence $-\ell^{1/3} + 1 \le \beta \le \ell^{1/3} - 1$.) The work to be done within class β is

$$Work_\beta \le c\Big(\sum_{\delta_{i,i+\beta}=0} (\ell^{2/3}|Z_{i,i+\beta}| + \ell^{4/3}) +$$

$$\sum_{\delta_{i,i+\beta}=1} \sum_{1 \le k \le k_{i,i+\beta}} (\ell^{2/3}|Z_{i,i+\beta}^{(k)}| + \ell^{4/3}) \Big)(\log \ell)^2.$$

Re-arranging the above and using the definition of H_β gives

$$Work_\beta \leq c(\ \ell^{2/3} H_\beta + \sum_{\delta_{i,i+\beta}=0} \ell^{4/3} +$$

$$\sum_{\delta_{i,i+\beta}=1} k_{i,i+\beta} \ell^{4/3}\ )(\log \ell)^2 = c(\ell^{2/3} H_\beta + \ell^{5/3} + 2h)(\log \ell)^2.$$

Therefore the number of processors we assign to class β must be at least

$$(\ell^{2/3} H_\beta + \ell^{5/3} + 2h)(\log \ell)^2 (\log \log \ell)^{-1},$$

to within a constant factor (in fact the constant factor can be taken to be unity, since we can trade a constant factor in the number of processors for a corresponding one in the time complexity). Since $H_\beta \leq h + \ell^{1/3}$, we can assign to class β a number of processors equal to

$$\zeta(\ell, h) = (h\ell^{2/3} + \ell + \ell^{5/3} + 2h)(\log \ell)^2 (\log \log \ell)^{-1}.$$

This is easy to do in constant time, since the number of processors we assign to class β does not depend on β. What remains to be shown is how, within class β, these $\zeta(\ell, h)$ processors are assigned to the various subproblems of that class. That is, in constant time, each subproblem $(X_i, Z_{i,i+\beta}, Y_{i+\beta})$ or $(X_i, Z_{i,i+\beta}^{(k)}, Y_{i+\beta})$ must be assigned the correct number of processors.

Within a class β, there is a natural left-to-right ordering of the subproblems: a subproblem is *to the left* of another one iff either (i) its row interval is to the left of the other's row interval, or (ii) in case they both have same row interval, its column interval is to the left of the other's column interval. For example, subproblem $(X_i, Z_{i,i+\beta}^{(k)}, Y_{i+\beta})$ is to the left of subproblem $(X_{i'}, Z_{i',i'+\beta}^{(k')}, Y_{i'+\beta})$ iff either (i) $i < i'$, or (ii) $i = i'$ and $k < k'$. Two subproblems of class β are *neighbours* iff one of them is immediately to the left of the other.

For a subproblem of the form $(X_i, Z_{i,i+\beta}, Y_{i+\beta})$, the number of processors to be assigned to it can be written as $f(\ell)|Z_{i,j}| + g(\ell)$ where $f(\ell) = \ell^{2/3}(\log \ell)^2(\log \log \ell)^{-1}$ and $g(\ell) = \ell^{4/3}(\log \ell)^2(\log \log \ell)^{-1}$. For a subproblem of the form $(X_i, Z_{i,i+\beta}^{(k)}, Y_{i+\beta})$, the number of processors to be assigned to it can be written as $f(\ell)|Z_{i,i+\beta}^{(k)}| + g(\ell)$. In either case, we call the $g(\ell)$ portion *fixed* since it is the same for every subproblem, whereas the $f(\ell)|Z_{i,i+\beta}|$ or $f(\ell)|Z_{i,i+\beta}^{(k)}|$ portion is called *variable*.

In what follows, we first discuss how to tentatively assign the variable portions, then we discuss the tentative assigment of the fixed portions (they are easier to handle), and finally how to use these two tentative assignments to obtain the final assignment. In the final assignment, we must be careful to make sure that the processors assigned to a particular subproblem form a contiguous interval of processor numbers (this is necessary because it is not enough for a set of processors to know that they are assigned to a certain subproblem; these processors must also have contiguous numbers).

Summed over all subproblems in class β, the total variable portion for class β is $f(\ell)H_\beta$, and hence is at most $f(\ell)(h + \ell^{1/3})$ processors (because $H_\beta \leq h + \ell^{1/3}$). These $f(\ell)(h + \ell^{1/3})$ processors are partitioned into two groups, one of size $f(\ell)h$ (call it group G_1) and one of size $\ell^{1/3}f(\ell)$ (call it group G_2).

The $f(\ell)h$ processors of group G_1 are tentatively assigned as follows. Imagine associating, with each of the h column indices, $f(\ell)$ processors, and view each column index as being the *leader* of the $f(\ell)$ processors assigned to it. Specifically, the $f(\ell)h$ processors of group G_1 are partitioned into h chunks of size $f(\ell)$ each, and each chunk is associated with a column index (the j-th chunk with the j-th column index, which acts as its leader). We would like to assign all of the chunks whose leaders are in a column interval $Z_{i,i+\beta}$ or $Z_{i,i+\beta}^{(k)}$ to the subproblem corresponding to that interval, but there is a difficulty with this approach, in that a *conflict* can arise: a column index j might belong to *two* neighbouring subproblems, and we must then arbitrarily give the j-th chunk to one of them and thus deprive the other subproblem. Observe that the only way for such a conflict over a column index j to arise is when, for some i, j is the right endpoint of $Z_{i,i+\beta}$ or $Z_{i,i+\beta}^{(k_i,i+\beta)}$, and is simultaneously the left endpoint of $Z_{i+1,i+1+\beta}$ or $Z_{i+1,i+1+\beta}^{(1)}$. In particular, no such conflict can arise between a $Z_{i,i+\beta}^{(k)}$ and the neighbouring $Z_{i,i+\beta}^{(k+1)}$, since these two column intervals are (by definition) disjoint.

Now suppose that, whenever such a conflict occurs, we break the tie in favor of the leftmost of the two neighbouring subproblems involved. Each subproblem that loses a conflict thus has a deficit of $f(\ell)$ processors. However, note that each such subproblem "with deficit" is of the form $(X_i, Z_{i,i+\beta}, Y_{i+\beta})$ or $(X_i, Z_{i,i+\beta}^{(1)}, Y_{i+\beta})$, $i > 1$; hence there are at most $\ell^{1/3}$ such subproblems, with a deficit of $f(\ell)$ processors each. We counteract these deficits by giving $f(\ell)$ of the processors of group G_2 to each subproblem of the form $(X_i, Z_{i,i+\beta}, Y_{i+\beta})$ or $(X_i, Z_{i,i+\beta}^{(1)}, Y_{i+\beta})$, $i > 1$ (note that some of these subproblems get the extra $f(\ell)$ processors without even having a deficit, i.e., even if they did not lose a conflict to their right neighbour).

Note that, if a column does not belong to any column interval $Z_{i,i+\beta}$ or $Z_{i,i+\beta}^{(k)}$, then the chunk of processors associated with it simply remains unclaimed.

It is now easy to replace the above assignments for G_1 and G_2 with another assignment for $G_1 \cup G_2$ which, although also tentative, is better in that it assigns to each particular subproblem a variable portion consisting of processors having consecutive numbers. First, observe that the subset of that variable portion coming from group G_1 is already contiguous, and so is the subset coming from group G_2. It clearly suffices to show that a subproblem also knows the ranks, in each of G_1 and G_2, of the first processor assigned to it. That this holds for G_2 is trivial: the rank ν_2 for a subproblem of the form $(X_i, Z_{i,i+\beta}, Y_{i+\beta})$ or $(X_i, Z_{i,i+\beta}^{(1)}, Y_{i+\beta})$, $i > 1$, is simply $(i-2)f(\ell) + 1$. For G_1, if we let j be the smallest column index in a subproblem's column interval, then the rank is $\nu_1 = (j-1)f(\ell) + 1$.

This completes the tentative assigment of the variable portion of the processors needed by each subproblem. We now turn to the problem of tentatively assigning the fixed portion, that is, assigning $g(\ell)$ processors to each subproblem.

Subproblems having a column interval of the form $Z_{i,i+\beta}$ or $Z_{i,i+\beta}^{(k_i,i+\beta)}$ are the easiest to handle, by assigning $g(\ell)$ processors to every index i, $1 \le i \le \ell^{1/3}$: if $(X_i, Z_{i,i+\beta}, Y_{i+\beta})$ is a good triplet then the $g(\ell)$ processors for index i get assigned to it, otherwise (if it is a bad triplet) they get assigned to the $k_{i,i+\beta}$-th subproblem spawned by that bad triplet.

For subproblems having a column interval of the form $Z_{i,i+\beta}^{(k)}$ where $k < k_{i,i+\beta}$, we exploit the fact that $|Z_{i,i+\beta}^{(k)}| = \ell^{4/3}$, as follows. Imagine marking every column index that is a multiple of $(h/\ell^{4/3})$ as being "special", and associating with each special column $g(\ell)$ processors. Since $|Z_{i,i+\beta}^{(k)}| = \ell^{4/3}$, column interval $Z_{i,i+\beta}^{(k)}$ contains exactly one special column. Detecting this column is trivial to do in constant time (it is the unique multiple of $\ell^{4/3}$ within column interval $Z_{i,i+\beta}^{(k)}$).

This completes the tentative assigment of the fixed portion of the processors needed by each subproblem.

We now discuss how the final assignment of processors is obtained from the above two tentative ones. Let G be the group of processors assigned to class β, and let G' (resp., G'') be the total fixed (resp., variable) portion of G (hence $G = G' \cup G''$). Since each subproblem knows, as a byproduct of the above tentative assignments, the rank within G' (resp., G'') of the first processor assigned to it in G' (resp., G''), it can easily find out the rank of the first processor to be assigned to it in G. Once that rank is known, the processors that were tentatively assigned to the subproblem from G' and G'' can "mark", in constant time, a contiguous interval of processors in G that get assigned to that subproblem. This concludes the discussion of the processor assignment issue.

5.5.2 DECREASING THE WORK DONE

Let us go back to the original goal of computing the θ_A matrix for an $n \times n \times n$ matrix A, in $O(\log \log n)$ time and $O(n^2/\log \log n)$ processors.

Let $ALGO_0$ denote the algorithm of the previous section (recall that it has the right time complexity but does a factor of $(\log n)^2$ too much work). There is more than one way to decrease the work done. The way we do it in this section has the advantage of being self-contained (in Section 5.5.3 we sketch another way, one that uses as a subroutine the CREW-PRAM algorithm.

Using algorithm $ALGO_0$, we shall create an algorithm $ALGO_1$ that runs in $O(\log \log n)$ time with $O(n^2(\log \log n)^2)$ work. Then, using $ALGO_1$, we shall create an algorithm $ALGO_2$ that runs in $O(\log \log n)$ time with $O(n^2(\log \log \log \log n)^2)$ work. Finally, using $ALGO_2$, we shall create an algorithm $ALGO_3$ that runs in $O(\log \log n)$ time with $O(n^2)$ work.

The method for obtaining $ALGO_k$ from $ALGO_{k-1}$ is similar for $k = 1, 2, 3$, and uses the following lemma.

Lemma 5.21. *Let $ALGO'$ and $ALGO''$ be two algorithms for computing θ_A, running in time (respectively) $T'(n)$ and $T''(n)$, and doing work (respectively) $W'(n)$ and $W''(n)$. Then for any $1 \leq s \leq n$, we can construct a third algorithm for computing θ_A that runs in time $O(T'(n/s)+T''(s)+ \log \log s + \log \log(n/s))$ and does work $O(sW'(n/s) + (n/s)^2W''(s) + n^2)$.*

Proof. We give an algorithm that makes use of $ALGO'$ and $ALGO''$. The row indices of A get partitioned into n/s intervals $X_1, \cdots, X_{n/s}$ of length s each. The height indices of A get partitioned into n/s intervals $Y_1, \cdots, Y_{n/s}$ of length s each. The column indices of A get partitioned into s intervals $Z_1, \cdots, Z_s$ of length n/s each. Let E_X (resp., E_Y) be the set of $2(n/s)$ endpoints of the X_i's (resp., Y_i's). Then we do the following:

1. We run, in parallel, s copies of $ALGO'$ one on each of the s triplets $(E_X, Z_1, E_Y), \cdots, (E_X, Z_s, E_Y)$. This takes time $T'(n/s)$ and work $sW'(n/s)$.

2. For each $u \in E_X$ and $v \in E_Y$, we compute the correct $\theta_A(u, v)$ value by taking the best among the s answers for the pair u, v returned by the solutions to the s triplets of the previous stage. We do so in $O(\log \log s)$ time and $O(s)$ work for each such pair u, v. Since there are $O((n/s)^2)$ such pairs u, v, the total work done is $O(n^2/s) = O(n^2)$. If we let $Z_{i,j}$ denote the interval of column indices of A defined by the set $\theta_A(v, w)$ such that $v \in X_i$ and $w \in Y_j$, then after this stage of the computation we know the beginning and end of each such interval $Z_{i,j}$.

3. For every $Z_{i,j}$ such that $|Z_{i,j}| \leq s$, we solve the triplet $(X_i, Z_{i,j}, Y_j)$ by using $ALGO''$. However, algorithm $ALGO''$ assumes unit aspect ratio ("square" matrices), whereas here we might have $|Z_{i,j}| < |X_i|$. We get around this problem simply by making the matrices square (padding with dummy $+\infty$ entries that cannot alter the correctness of the answer returned). Of course this means that we now do $W''(s)$

work for each such triplet. However, since there are at most $(n/s)^2$ such triplets, the total work for this stage is $(n/s)^2 W''(s)$. The time is, of course, $T''(s)$.

4. For every $Z_{i,j}$ such that $|Z_{i,j}| > s$, we partition $Z_{i,j}$ into $k_{i,j} = \lceil |Z_{i,j}|/s \rceil$ intervals $Z_{i,j}^{(1)}$, $Z_{i,j}^{(2)}$, $\cdots$, $Z_{i,j}^{(k_{i,j})}$, of size s each (except that $Z_{i,j}^{(k_{i,j})}$ might be smaller). Then we solve each triplet $(X_i, Z_{i,j}^{(k)}, Y_j)$ by using $ALGO''$ (if $k = k_{i,j}$ then we might need to "pad" the matrix in order to make it square, as in the previous stage). The time is $T''(s)$, and the work per subproblem is $W''(s)$. Since there are at most $\sum_{i,j} k_{i,j}$ such subproblems, and since $\sum_{i,j} k_{i,j} = O((n/s)^2)$, the total work for this stage is $O((n/s)^2 W''(s))$.

5. For every $Z_{i,j}$ such that $|Z_{i,j}| > s$, we compute the right answer for each pair $u \in X_i$ and $v \in Y_j$ from among the $k_{i,j}$ possibilities available from the previous stage. We do this in $O(\log \log k_{i,j}) = O(\log \log(n/s))$ time and $O(k_{i,j})$ work for each such pair u, v. Since there are s^2 such pairs u, v for each such $Z_{i,j}$, the total work for this stage is $O(s^2 \sum_{i,j} k_{i,j}) = O(s^2 (n/s)^2) = O(n^2)$.

It is clear that the above procedure proves the lemma. $\square$

To obtain $ALGO_1$, we use Lemma 5.21 with $s = (\log n)^2$ and with $ALGO' = ALGO'' = ALGO_0$.

To obtain $ALGO_2$, we use Lemma 5.21 with $s = (\log \log n)^2$ and with $ALGO' = ALGO'' = ALGO_1$.

To obtain $ALGO_3$, we use Lemma 5.21 with $s = (\log \log \log n)^2$, with $ALGO' = ALGO_2$, and using for $ALGO''$ the quadratic time sequential algorithm (so that both $W''(s)$ and $T''(s)$ are $O(s^2)$).

Brent's theorem then implies an $O(n^2/\log \log n)$ processor bound for $ALGO_3$, thus establishing Theorem 1. We do not give the details of the processor allocation schemes, since they are very similar to those in Section 2 — in fact here we could even afford to assign processors in $O(\log \log n)$ time rather than in constant time, since the above scheme for obtaining $ALGO_k$ from $ALGO_{k-1}$, $1 \leq k \leq 3$, did not involve any recursive calls to $ALGO_k$.

5.5.3 FURTHER REMARKS

Using algorithm $ALGO_3$, we can tackle problems having different aspect ratios from those considered so far. By way of example, suppose A is $\ell \times h \times \ell$ where $h > \ell^2$, i.e., the aspect ratio condition is violated. For that case, we can get an $O(\log \log \ell + \log \log(h/\ell))$ time, $O(\ell h)$ work algorithm as follows. Let X (resp., Y) be the set of all row (resp., height) indices of A. Partition the column indices of A into $q = \lceil h/\ell \rceil$ intervals of size ℓ each (the q-th interval may be smaller). Let these q intervals be $Z_1, \cdots, Z_q$. Use q copies of $ALGO_3$ to solve in parallel all the (X, Z_i, Y) triplets. This takes $O(\log \log \ell)$ time and $O(q\ell^2) = O(\ell h)$ work. Then, for each pair $u \in X$ and

$v \in Y$, we assign q processors to compute the correct $\theta_A(u, v)$ in $O(\log \log q)$ time (this involves taking the min of q quantities). The total work for this "postprocessing" is $O(\ell^2 q) = O(\ell h)$, and the time is $O(\log \log(h/\ell))$.

We also note that, even if $ALGO_0$ had done a polylog factor more work than the $ALGO_0$ we gave in Section 2, we would still have been able to design an $ALGO_k$ that runs in $O(\log \log n)$ time and does only quadratic work. We would simply have had to use Lemma 5.21 a few more times, and end up with an $ALGO_k$ with $k > 3$.

An alternative method of decreasing the work done consists of using Lemma 5.21 with $ALGO' = ALGO_0$ and with $ALGO'' =$ the optimal CREW-PRAM algorithm for that problem.

This completes the description of the $O(\log \log n)$ time, $O(n^2/\log \log n)$ processor for computing the tube minima of an $n \times n \times n$ totally monotone matrix in the CRCW-PRAM model.

These bounds can easily be shown to be optimal among quadratic-work algorithms for this model (this follows from the $\Omega(\log \log n)$ lower bound for computing the minimum of n entries with $O(n)$ work).

5.6   Exercises

1. Extend the algorithm of Section 5.2 to the general case where $m \leq n$.

2. Design CREW and CRCW algorithms for the following variant of the string editing problem: each edit operation has unit cost; given two strings and an integer k, decide whether there is an edit script transforming one of the strings into the other using at most k edit operations.

3. Design a fast and efficient parallel algorithm that finds the all-pairs longest chains for a set of points in the plane, where a chain is a sequence of points such that each point's successor in the sequence has larger x and y coordinates than that point.

4. ** Design a fast and efficient parallel algorithm for the problem of finding a longest ascending subsequence in a permutation of the first n integers.

5. Assume unit cost for all edit operations. Design parallel algorithms for the following *approximate string searching* problem. Given a *textstring* x, a *pattern* z and an integer k, find all position in x at which substrings having a distance of at most k from z begin.

6. ** Design PRAM algorithms for the string editing problem with a *time* $\times$ *processors* bound matching the time complexity of the best serial algorithm for the problem.

5.7 Bibliographic notes

For the recurrence of C in Section 5.1, see, e.g., Wagner and Fischer [74]. The asymptotically fastest serial algorithms are due to Masek and Paterson [1980]. Lower bounds on the string editing problem were given by Aho et al. [1976] and Wong et al. [1976]. The correspondence between edit scripts and grid graphs is in Sankoff and Krushkal [1980]. Aggarval et al. [1987] and Aggarwal and Park [1988] introduced the notions of "tube maxima" and "row maxima" and are useful references for the myriad of their other applications. The exposition of this Chapter follows mainly Apostolico et al. [1990], Atallah [1993], and Atallah and Kosaraju [1992]. Aggarwal and Park [1988, 1989] gave an $O(\log m \log n)$ time, $O(mn/\log m)$ processor CREW-PRAM algorithm, and an $O(\log n (\log \log m)^2)$ time, $O(mn/(\log \log m)^2)$ processor CRCW - PRAM algorithm; the main difference between those algorithms and this chapter is in the use of different methods for the "combine" stage of the divide and conquer (in the tube minima computation, the cascading divide-and-conquer scheme is not used). A property similar to Equation 5.3 was proved in Fuchs et al. [1977]. Aggarwal and Park [1988] traced this simple observation back to G. Monge, in 1781.

Ranka and Sahni [1988] designed a hypercube algorithm for $m = n$ that runs in $O(\sqrt{n \log n})$ time with n^2 processors. Mathies [1988] obtained a CRCW-PRAM algorithm for the edit distance that runs in $O(\log n \log m)$ time with $O(mn)$ processors if the weight of every edit operation is smaller than a given constant integer.

Many important problems are special cases of string editing, including the *longest common subsequence* problem and the problem of *approximate matching* between a pattern string and text string. Landau and Vishkin [1986], Sellers [1974, 1980], and Ukkonen [1985] are some good sources for the notion of approximate pattern matching and its connection to the string editing problem.

Bibliography

AHO, A.V., D.S. HIRSCHBERG AND J.D. ULLMAN [1976], "Bounds on the complexity of the longest common subsequence problem", *J. Assoc. Comput. Mach.*, **23** 1-12.

AGGARWAL, A., M. KLAWE, S. MORAN, P. SHOR AND R. WILBER [1987], "Geometric applications of a matrix searching algorithm", *Algorithmica*, **2** 209-233.

AGGARWAL, A. AND J. PARK [1988], "Notes on searching in multidimensional monotone arrays", in Proc. 29th Annual IEEE Symposium on Foundations of Computer Science, 1988, IEEE Computer Society, Washington, DC, pp. 497–512.

AGGARWAL, A. AND J. PARK [1989], "Parallel searching in multidimensional monotone arrays", unpublished manuscript, May 31, 1989.

AHO, A.V., J.E. HOPCROFT AND J.D. ULLMAN [1974], *The Design and Analysis of Computer Algorithms*, Addison-Wesley, Reading, MA, (1974).

APOSTOLICO, A., M.J. ATALLAH, L.L. LARMORE AND S. McFADDIN [1990], "Efficient parallel algorithms for string editing and related problems", *SIAM Journal on Computing* **19**, 968-988.

APOSTOLICO, A. AND C. GUERRA [1987], "The longest common subsequence problem revisited", *Algorithmica*, **2**, 315-336.

ATALLAH, M.J. [1993] "A Faster Parallel Algorithm for a Matrix Searching Problem", *Algorithmica*, **9**, 156-167.

Computing the All-Pairs Longest Chains in the Plane, (with D.Z. Chen). *Proc. 1993 Workshop on Algorithms and Data Structures*, Montreal, Canada, 1993. Springer Verlag Lecture Notes in Computer Sci.: 709, 1993, pp. 1-13.

ATALLAH, M.J. AND CHEN, D.Z. [1993], "Computing the All-Pairs Longest Chains in the Plane," in Proc. 1993 Workshop on Algorithms and Data Structures, Montreal, Canada, 1993, 1-13.

ATALLAH, M.J., R. COLE, AND M.T. GOODRICH [1989], "Cascading divide-and-conquer: a technique for designing parallel algorithms", *SIAM J. on Computing*, **18**, 499-532.

ATALLAH, M.J. AND KOSARAJU, S.R. [1992], "An Efficient Parallel Algorithm for the Row Minima of a Totally Monotone Matrix", *J. of Algorithms*, **13**, 394-413.

ATALLAH, M.J. AND McFADDIN, H.S. [1991], "Sequence Comparison on the Connection Machine", *Concurrency: Practice and Experience*, **3**, 89-107.

BRENT, R.P. [1974], "The parallel evaluation of general arithmetic expressions", *J. Assoc. Comput. Mach.*, **21**, 201-206.

COLE, R. [1986], "Parallel merge sort", in Proc. 27th Annual IEEE Symposium on Foundations of Computer Science, IEEE Computer Society, Washingotn, DC, 1986, 511-516.

FICH, F.E., R.L. RADGE, AND A. WIDGDERSON [1984], "Relation between concurrent-write models of parallel computation", in Proc. 3rd Annual ACM Symposium on Distributed Computing, Association for Computing Machinery, New York, 1984, pp. 179-189.

FUCHS, H., Z.M. KEDEM, AND S.P. USELTON [1977], "Optimal surface reconstruction from planar contours", *Communications of the Assoc. Comput. Mach.*, **20** 693-702.

GALIL Z. AND R. GIANCARLO [1987], "Data structures and algorithms for approximate string matching", Tech. Report, Department of Computer Science, Columbia University, NY, 1987.

IVANOV, A.G., [1985], "Recognition of an approximate occurrence of words on a turing machine in real time", *Math. USSR Izv.*, **24**, 479–522.

KEDEM, Z.M., AND H. FUCHS [1980], "On finding several shortest paths in certain graphs", in Proc. 18th Allerton Conference on Communication, Control, and Computing, October 1980, pp. 677–683.

LADNER, R.E., AND M.J. FISCHER [1980], "Parallel prefix computation", *J. Assoc. Comput. Mach.*, **27** 831–838.

LANDAU. G. AND U. VISHKIN, "Introducing efficient parallelism into approximate string matching and a new serial algorithm", in Proc. 18th Annual ACM Symposium on Theory of Computing, Association for Computing Machinery, New York, 1986, pp. 220-230.

LEVENSHTEIN, V.I. [1966], "Binary codes capable of correcting deletions, insertions and reversals", Soviet Phys. Dokl., 10 (1966), pp. 707–710.

H. M. MARTINEZ, ED. [1984], "Mathematical and computational problems in the analysis of molecular sequences", Bull. Math. Bio. (Special Issue Honoring M. O. Dayhoff), 46 (1984).

MASEK, W.J. AND M. S. PATERSON, "A faster algorithm computing string edit distances", J. Comput. System Sci., 20 (1980), pp. 18–31.

MATHIES, T.R. [1988], *A fast parallel algorithm to determine edit distance*, Tech. Report CMU-CS-88-130, Department of Computer Science, Carnegie Mellon University, Pittsburgh, PA, April 1988.

NEEDLEMAN, R.B. AND C.D. WUNSCH [1973], "A general method applicable to the search for similarities in the amino-acid sequence of two proteins", *J. Molecular Bio.*, 48 (1973), pp.443–453.

RANKA, S. AND S. SAHNI [1988], "String editing on an SIMD hypercube multicomputer", Tech. Report 88-29, Department of Computer Science, University of Minnesota, March 1988, *J. Parallel Distributed Comput.*, submitted.

SANKOFF, D.[1972], "Matching sequences under deletion-insertion constraints", Proc. Nat. Acad. Sci. U.S.A., 69 (1972), pp.4–6.

SANKOFF, D. AND J. B. KRUSKAL, EDS. [1983], *Time Warps, String Edits and Macromolecules: The Theory and Practice of Sequence Comparison*, Addison-Wesley, Reading, MA 1983.

SELLERS, P.H. [1974], "An algorithm for the distance between two finite sequences", *J. Combin. Theory*, **16** 253–258.

SELLERS, P.H. [1980], "The theory and computation of evolutionary distance: pattern recognition", **J. Algorithms**, **1** 359–373.

SHILOACH, Y. AND U. VISHKIN [1981], "Finding the maximum, merging and sorting in a parallel model of computation", *J. Algorithms*, **2** 88–102.

UKKONEN, E. [1985], "Finding approximate patterns in strings", *J. Algorithms* **6** 132–137.

VALIANT, L.E. [1985], "Parallelism in comparison problems", *SIAM J. Comput.*, **4** 348–355.

WAGNER, R.A. AND M. J. FISCHER [1974], "The string to string correction problem", *J. Assoc. Comput. Mach.*, **21**, 168–173.

WONG, C.K. AND A.K. CHANDRA [1976], "Bounds for the string editing problem", *J. Assoc. Comput. Mach.*, **23**, 13–16.

6
Approximate String Searching

Consider the string searching problem, where differences between characters of the pattern and characters of the text are allowed. Each difference is due to either a mismatch between a character of the text and a character of the pattern, or a superfluous character in the text, or a superfluous character in the pattern. Given a text of length n, a pattern of length m and an integer k, serial and parallel algorithms for finding all occurrences of the pattern in the text with at most k differences are presented. For completeness we also describe an efficient algorithm for preprocessing a rooted tree, so that queries requesting the *lowest common ancestor* of every pair of vertices in the tree can be processed quickly.

Problems:
Input form. Two arrays: $A = a_1, ..., a_m$ - the pattern, $T = t_1, ..., t_n$ - the text and an integer k (≥ 1).

In the present chapter we will be interested in finding all occurrences of the pattern string in the text string with at most k differences.

Three types of differences are distinguished:
(a) A character of the pattern corresponds to a different character of the text - a *mismatch* between the two characters. (Item 2 in Example 1, below.)
(b) A character of the pattern corresponds to "no character" in the text. (Item 4).
(c) A character of the text corresponds to "no character" in the pattern. (Item 6).
Example 1. Let the text be *abcdefghi* , the pattern *bxdyegh* and $k = 3$. Let us see whether there is an occurrence with $\leq k$ differences that ends at the eighth location of the text. For this the following correspondence between *bcdefgh* and *bxdyegh* is proposed. 1. b (of the text) corresponds to b (of the pattern). 2. c to x. 3. d to d. 4. Nothing to y. 5. e to e. 6. f to nothing. 7. g to g. 8. h to h. The correspondence can be illustrated as

$$b \; x \; d \; y \; e \quad g \; h$$
$$b \; c \; d \quad \; e \, f \; g \; h$$

In only three places the correspondence is between non-equal characters. This implies that there is an occurrence of the pattern that ends at the eighth location of the text with 3 differences as required.

So, the main problem we consider is:

String searching with k differences (the $k-differences$ problem, for short): Find all occurrences of the pattern in the text with at most k differences of type (a),(b) and (c).

The case $k = 0$ in the both problems is the string searching problem, which is discussed in Chapter 2. In this Chapter algorithms for the k differences problem are given. The "k mismatches problem" is simpler than the k differences problem (there, occurrences of the pattern in the text with at most k differences of type (a) only are allowed); however, there are no known algorithms for the k mismatches problem that are faster than the algorithms for the k differences problem, on the other hand the algorithms for the k differences problem solve the k mismatches problem as well.

The model of computation used in this chapter is the random-access-machine (RAM) for the serial algorithms, and the concurrent-read concurrent-write (CRCW) parallel random access machine (PRAM) for the parallel algorithms. A PRAM employs p synchronous processors, all having access to a common memory. A CRCW PRAM allows simultaneous access by more than one processor to the same memory location for read and write purposes. In case several processor seek to write simultaneously at the same memory location, one of them succeeds and it is not known in advance which one.

The k-differences problem is not only a basic theoretical problem. It also has a strong pragmatic flavor. In practice, one often needs to analyze situations where the data is not completely reliable. Specifically, consider a situation where the strings that are the input for the problem contain errors, as in reality, and one still needs to find all possible occurrences of the pattern in the text. The errors may include a character being replaced by another character, a character being omitted, or a superfluous character being inserted. Assuming some bound on the number of errors would clearly yield the k-differences problem.

Note that the measure of the quality of a match between the pattern and a substring of the text depends on the application. The k differences problem defines one possible measure. In many applications in molecular biology a penalty table is given. This table assigns a penalty value for the deletion and insertion of each letter of the alphabet, as well as a value for matching any pair of characters. In the simplest case the score of a match is simply the sum of the corresponding values in the penalty matrix. In some cases however gaps (successive insertions or deletions) get penalties that are different from the sum of the penalties of each insertion (deletion).

The serial algorithm is given in Section 6.1. The parallel algorithm is described in Section 6.2. Both, the serial and parallel, algorithms use, as a procedure, an algorithm for the LCA problem. The problem and the algorithm are given in Section 6.3.

6.1 The serial algorithm

In this section, an efficient algorithm for the k-differences problem is presented. As a warm-up, the section starts with two serial $O(mn)$ time algorithms for this problem. The first one is a simple dynamic programming algorithm. The second algorithm follows the same dynamic programming computation in a slightly different way, that will help explain the efficient algorithm. Subsection 6.1.3 gives the efficient serial algorithm.

6.1.1 THE DYNAMIC PROGRAMMING ALGORITHM.

A matrix $D_{[0,...,m;0,...,n]}$ is constructed, where $D_{i,\ell}$ is the minimum number of differences between $a_1, ..., a_i$ and any contiguous substring of the text ending at t_ℓ.

If $D_{m,\ell} \leq k$ then there must be an occurrence of the pattern in the text with at most k differences that ends at t_ℓ.

Example 2.

Let the text be $GGGTCTA$, the pattern $GTTC$ and $k = 2$. The matrix $D_{[0,...4;0,...,7]}$ (Table 6.1) is computed to check whether there are occurrences of the pattern in the text with $\leq k$ differences.

		G	G	G	T	C	T	A
	0	0	0	0	0	0	0	0
G	1	0	0	0	1	1	1	1
T	2	1	1	1	0	1	1	2
T	3	2	2	2	1	1	1	2
C	4	3	3	3	2	1	2	2

Table 6.1.

There are occurrences of the pattern in the text with $\leq k$ differences ending at t_4, t_5, t_6 and t_7.

The following algorithm computes the matrix $D_{[0,...,m;0,...,n]}$

Initialization
        for all $\ell, 0 \leq \ell \leq n$, $D_{0,\ell} := 0$
        for all $i, 1 \leq i \leq m$, $D_{i,0} := i$
    for $i := 1$ to m do
        for $\ell := 1$ to n do

$$D_{i,\ell} := \min \left(D_{i-1,\ell} + 1, D_{i,\ell-1} + 1, D_{i-1,\ell-1} \text{ if } a_i = t_\ell \text{ or} \right.$$
$$\left. D_{i-1,\ell-1} + 1 \text{ otherwise}\right)$$

($D_{i,\ell}$ is the minimum of three numbers. These three numbers are obtained from the predecessors of $D_{i,\ell}$ on its column, row and diagonal, respectively.)

Complexity. The algorithm clearly runs in $O(mn)$ time.

6.1.2 AN ALTERNATIVE DYNAMIC PROGRAMMING COMPUTATION

The algorithm computes the same information as in the matrix D of the dynamic programming algorithm, using the diagonals of the matrix. A *diagonal d* of the matrix consists of all $D_{i,\ell}$'s such that $\ell - i = d$.

For a number of differences e and a diagonal d, let $L_{d,e}$ denote the largest row i such that $D_{i,\ell} = e$ and $D_{i,\ell}$ is on diagonal d. The definition of $L_{d,e}$ clearly implies that e is the minimum number of differences between $a_1, ..., a_{L_{d,e}}$ and any substring of the text ending at $t_{L_{d,e}+d}$. It also implies that $a_{L_{d,e}+1} \neq t_{L_{d,e}+d+1}$. For the k-differences problem one needs only the values of $L_{d,e}$'s, where e satisfies $e \leq k$.

Example 2 (continued)

Let us demonstrate the $L_{d,e}$ values for diagonal 3 (Table 6.2).

		G	G	G	T	C	T	A
				0				
G					1			
T						1		
T							1	
C								2

Table 6.2.

$L_{3,0} = 0$, $L_{3,1} = 3$ and $L_{3,2} = 4$.

If one of the $L_{d,e}$'s equals m, for $e \leq k$, it means that there is an occurrence of the pattern in the text with at most k differences that ends at t_{d+m}.

The $L_{d,e}$'s are computed by induction on e. Given d and e it will be shown how to compute $L_{d,e}$ using its definition. Suppose that for all $x < e$ and all diagonals y, $L_{y,x}$ was already computed. Suppose $L_{d,e}$ should get the value i. That is, i is the largest row such that $D_{i,\ell} = e$, and $D_{i,\ell}$ is on the diagonal d. The algorithm of the previous subsection reveals that $D_{i,\ell}$ could have been assigned its value e using one (or more) of the following data:

(a) $D_{i-1,\ell-1}$ (which is the predecessor of $D_{i,\ell}$ on the diagonal d) is $e - 1$ and $a_i \neq t_\ell$. Or, $D_{i,\ell-1}$ (the predecessor of $D_{i,\ell}$ on row i which is also on

the diagonal "below" d) is $e - 1$. Or, $D_{i-1,\ell}$ (the predecessor of $D_{i,\ell}$ on column ℓ which is also on the diagonal "above" d) is $e - 1$.
(b) $D_{i-1,\ell-1}$ is also e and $a_i = t_\ell$.

This implies that one can start from $D_{i,\ell}$ and follow its predecessors on diagonal d by possibility (b) till the first time possibility (a) occurs.

The following algorithm "inverts" this description in order to compute the $L_{d,e}$'s. $L_{d,e-1}$, $L_{d-1,e-1}$, and $L_{d+1,e-1}$ are used to initialize the variable row, which is then increased by one at a time till it hits the correct value of $L_{d,e}$.

The following algorithm computes the $L'_{d,e}s$

Initialization
      for all $d, 0 \le d \le n$, $L_{d,-1} := -1$
      for all $d, -(k+1) \le d \le -1$, $L_{d,|d|-1} := |d|-1$, $L_{d,|d|-2} := |d|-2$
      for all $e, -1 \le e \le k$, $L_{n+1,e} := -1$
  2. for $e:=0$ to k do
      for $d:=-e$ to n do
         3. $row := \max [L_{d,e-1} + 1, \; L_{d-1,e-1}, \; L_{d+1,e-1} + 1]$
           $row := \min(row, m)$
         4. while $row < m$ and $row+d < n$ and $a_{row+1} = t_{row+1+d}$
         do
           $row := row + 1$
         5. $L_{d,e} := row$
         6. if $L_{d,e} = m$ then
           print *THERE IS AN OCCURRENCE ENDING AT t_{d+m}*

Remarks. (a) For every i, ℓ, $D_{i,\ell} - D_{i-1,\ell-1}$ is either zero or one.
(b) The values of the matrix D on diagonals d, such that $d > n - m + k + 1$ or $d < -k$ will be useless for the solution of the k-differences problem.
(c) The Initialization step is given for completeness of this presentation. The values entered in this step are meaningless. It is easy to check that these values properly initialize the $L_{d,e}$ values on the boundary of the matrix.

Correctness of the algorithm
Claim. $L_{d,e}$ gets its correct value.
Proof. By induction on e. Let $e = 0$. Consider the computation of $L_{d,0}$, $(d \ge 0)$. Instruction 3 starts by initializing row to 0. Instructions 4 and 5 find that $a_1, ..., a_{L_{d,0}}$ is equal to $t_{d+1}, ..., t_{d+L_{d,0}}$, and $a_{L_{d,0}+1} \ne t_{d+L_{d,0}+1}$. Therefore, $L_{d,0}$ gets its correct value. To finish the base of the induction the reader can see that for $d < 0$, $L_{d,|d|-1}$ and $L_{d,|d|-2}$ get correct values in the Initialization.

Let $e = \ell$. Assume that all $L_{d,\ell-1}$ are correct. Consider the computation of $L_{d,e}$, $(d \ge -e)$. Following Instruction 3, row is the largest row on diagonal d such that $D_{row,d+row}$ can get value e by possibility (a). Then Instruction 4 finds $L_{d,e}$. □

Complexity. The $L_{d,e}$'s for $n + k + 1$ diagonals are evaluated. For each diagonal the variable row can get at most m different values. Therefore, the computation takes $O(mn)$ time.

6.1.3 THE EFFICIENT ALGORITHM

The efficient algorithm has two steps:
Step I. Concatenate the text and the pattern to one string $t_1, ..., t_n$ $a_1, ..., a_m$. Compute the "suffix tree" of this string.
Step II. Find all occurrences of the pattern in the text with at most k differences.

Step I.   The construction of the suffix tree is given in Section 4.

Upon construction of the suffix tree the following is required. For each node v of the tree, a contiguous substring $c_{i+1}, ..., c_{i+f}$ that defines it will be stored as follows: $START(v) := i$ and $LENGTH(v) := f$.
Complexity. The computation of the suffix tree is done in $O(n)$ time when the size of the alphabet is fixed. This is also the running time of Step I for fixed size alphabet. If the alphabet of the pattern contains x letters then it is easy to adapt the algorithm (and thus Step I) to run in time $O(n \log x)$. In both cases the space requirement of Step I is $O(n)$.

Step II.   The matrix D and the $L_{d,e}$'s are exactly as in the alternative dynamic programming algorithm. This alternative algorithm is used with a very substantial change. The change is in Instruction 4, where instead of increasing variable row by one at a time until it reaches $L_{d,e}$, one finds $L_{d,e}$ in $O(1)$ time!

For a diagonal d, the situation following Instruction 3 is that $a_1, ..., a_{row}$ of the pattern is matched (with e differences) with some substring of the text that ends at t_{row+d}.   One wants to find the largest q for which $a_{row+1}, ..., a_{row+q}$ equals $t_{row+d+1}, ..., t_{row+d+q}$. Let $LCA_{row,d}$ be the lowest common ancestor (in short LCA) of the leaves of the suffixes $t_{row+d+1}, ...$ and $a_{row+1}, ...$ in the suffix tree.   The desired q is simply $LENGTH(LCA_{row,d})$.   Thus, the problem of finding this q is reduced to finding $LCA_{row,d}$. An algorithm for the LCA problem is described in Section 6.3.
Example 2 (continued).

Let us explain how one computes $L_{3,1}$ (Table 6.3). For this, $L_{2,0}$, $L_{3,0}$ and $L_{4,0}$ are used. Specifically $L_{2,0} = 2$, $L_{3,0} = 0$ and $L_{4,0} = 0$.
The algorithm (Instruction 3) initializes row to $max(L_{2,0}, L_{3,0} +1, L_{4,0} +1)$ $= 2$. This is reflected in the box in which "Initially $row = 2$" is written. From the suffix tree one gets that $q = 1$. (Since $a_3 = t_6 = T$ and $a_4 \neq t_7$.) Therefore, $L_{3,1} := 3$.

		G	G	G	T	C	T	A
				0 $(L_{3,0})$	0 $(L_{4,0})$			
G								
T					0 $(L_{2,0})$	(Initially row = 2)		
T							1 $(L_{3,1})$	
C								

Table 6.3.

Complexity. In this section we are interested in the *static lowest common ancestors* problem; where the tree is static, but queries for lowest common ancestors of pair of vertices are given on line. That is, each query must be answered before the next one is known. The suffix tree has $O(n)$ nodes. In Section 6.3 an algorithm for the LCA problem is described. It computes LCA queries as follows. First it preprocesses the suffix tree in $O(n)$ time. Then, given an LCA query it responds in $O(1)$ time. For each of the $n + k + 1$ diagonals, $k + 1$ $L_{d,e}$'s are evaluated. Therefore, there are $O(nk)$ LCA Queries. It will take $O(nk)$ time to process them. This time dominates the running time of Step II.

Complexity of the serial algorithm. The total time for the serial algorithm is $O(nk)$ time for an alphabet whose size is fixed and $O(n(\log m + k))$ time for general input.

6.2 The parallel algorithm

The parallel algorithm described below runs in $O(\log n + k)$ time. At the end of this section, an explanation how to modify it to run in $O(\log m + k)$ time is given. The parallel algorithm has the same two steps as the efficient serial algorithm. Specifically:

Step I. Concatenate the text and the pattern to one string $(t_1, ..., t_n a_1, ..., a_m)$. Then, compute, in parallel, the suffix tree of this string (see Chapter 4).

Step II. Find all occurrences of the pattern in the text with at most k differences. This step is done in a similar way to Step II in the serial algorithm.

The matrix D and the $L_{d,e}$'s are exactly as in the serial algorithm. The parallel algorithm employs $n + k + 1$ processors. Each processor is assigned to a diagonal d, $-k \leq d \leq n$. The parallel treatment of the diagonals is the source of parallelism in the algorithm.

For a diagonal d the situation following Instruction 3 is that $a_1, ..., a_{row}$ of the pattern is matched (with e differences) with some substring of the text that ends at t_{row+d}. One wants to find the largest q for which $a_{row+1}, ..., a_{row+q}$ equals $t_{row+d+1}, ..., t_{row+d+q}$. As in the serial algorithm one gets this q from the suffix tree. Let $LCA_{row,d}$ be the lowest common ancestor (in short LCA) of the leaves of the suffixes $t_{row+d+1}, ...$ and $a_{row+1}, ...$ in the suffix tree. The desired q is simply $LENGTH(LCA_{row,d})$. Thus, the problem of finding this q is reduced to finding $LCA_{row,d}$.

The parameter d is used and the *pardo* command for the purpose of guiding each processor to its instruction.

The parallel algorithm

1. *Initialization* (as in Subsection 6.1.2)
2. for $e := 0$ to k do
   for $d := -e$ to n pardo
   3. $row := \max \left[(L_{d,e-1} + 1), (L_{d-1,e-1}), (L_{d+1,e-1} + 1) \right]$
      $row := \min (row, m)$
   4. $L_{d,e} := row + LENGTH(LCA_{row,d})$
   5. if $L_{d,e} = m$ and $d + m \leq n$ then
      print *THERE IS AN OCCURRENCE ENDING AT t_{d+m}*

Complexity. In Chapter 4 it is shown how one may compute the suffix tree in $O(\log n)$ time using n processors. This suffix tree algorithm has the same time complexity for fixed alphabet and for general alphabet. This is also the running time of Step I. As in the serial case, one is interested in the *static lowest common ancestors* problem: where the tree is static, but queries for lowest common ancestors of pair of vertices are given on line. That is, each query must be answered before the next one is known. The suffix tree has $O(n)$ nodes. The parallel version of the serial algorithm, which is given in Section 6.3, for the LCA problem works as follows. It preprocesses the suffix tree in $O(\log n)$ time using $n/\log n$ processors. Then, an LCA query can be processed in $O(1)$ time using a single processor. Therefore, x parallel queries can be processed in $O(1)$ time using x processors. In the second step $n + k + 1$ processors (one per diagonal) are employed. Each processor computes at most $k + 1$ $L_{d,e}$'s. Computing each $L_{d,e}$ takes $O(1)$ time. Therefore, the second step takes $O(k)$ time using $n+k+1$ processors. Simulating the algorithm by n processors, instead of $n + k + 1$ still gives $O(k)$ time. The total time for the parallel algorithm is $O(\log n + k)$ time, using n processors.

Lastly, an explanation how one can modify the algorithm to get $O(\log m + k)$ time using $O(n)$ processors is given. Instead of the above problem $\lceil n/m \rceil$ smaller problems will be solved, in parallel. The first subproblem will be as follows. Find all occurrences of the pattern that end in locations $t_1, ..., t_m$ of the text. Subproblem $i, 1 \leq i \leq \lceil n/m \rceil$ will be:

Find all occurrences of the pattern that end in locations $t_{(i-1)m+1}, ..., t_{im}$ of the text. The input for the first subproblem will consist of the sub-string $t_1, ..., t_m$ of the text and the pattern. The input for subproblem i will consist of the substring $t_{(i-2)m-k+2}, ..., t_{im}$ of the text and the pattern. Clearly, the solution for all these subproblems give a solution for the above problem. Finally, note that one can apply the parallel algorithm of this section to solve each subproblem in $O(\log m + k)$ time using $O(m)$ processors, and all $\lceil n/m \rceil$ subproblems in $O(\log m + k)$ time using $O(n)$ processors. Simulating this algorithm by n processors still gives $O(\log m + k)$ time.

6.3   An algorithm for the LCA problem

The lowest-common-ancestor (LCA) problem

Suppose a rooted tree T is given for preprocessing. The preprocessing should enable to process quickly queries of the following form. Given two vertices u and v, find their lowest common ancestor in T.

The input to this problem is a rooted tree $T = (V, E)$, whose root is some vertex r. The *Euler tour technique* enables efficient parallel computation of several problems on trees. We summarize only those elements of the technique which are needed for presenting the serial lowest common ancestor algorithm below. Let H be a graph which is obtained from T as follows: For each edge $(v \rightarrow u)$ in T we add its anti-parallel edge $(u \rightarrow v)$. Since the in-degree and out-degree of each vertex in H are the same, H has an Euler path that starts and ends in the root r of T. This path can be computed, in linear time, into a vector of pointers D of size $2|E|$, where for each edge e of H, $D(e)$ gives the successor edge of e in the Euler path.

Let $n = 2|V| - 1$. We assume that we are given a sequence of n vertices $A = [a_1, ..., a_n]$, which is a slightly different representation of the Euler tour of T, and that we know for each vertex v its level, $LEVEL(v)$, in the tree.

The *range-minima problem* is defined as follows:
Given an array A of n real numbers, preprocess the array so that for any interval $[a_i, a_{i+1}, ..., a_j]$, the minimum over the interval can be retrieved in constant time.

Below we give a simple reduction from the LCA problem to a restricted-domain range-minima problem, which is an instance of the range-minima problem where *the difference between each two successive numbers for the range-minima problem is exactly one*. The reduction takes $O(n)$ time. An algorithm for the restricted-domain range-minima problem is given later, implying an algorithm for the LCA problem.

6.3.1   REDUCING THE LCA PROBLEM TO A RESTRICTED-DOMAIN RANGE-MINIMA PROBLEM

Let v be a vertex in T. Denote by $l(v)$ the index of the leftmost appearance of v in A and by $r(v)$ the index of its rightmost appearance. For each vertex v in T, it is easy to find $l(v)$ and $r(v)$ in $O(n)$ time using the following (trivial) observation:

$l(v)$ is where $a_{l(v)} = v$ and $LEVEL(a_{l(v)-1}) = LEVEL(v) - 1$.

$r(v)$ is where $a_{r(v)} = v$ and $LEVEL(a_{r(v)+1}) = LEVEL(v) - 1$.

The claims and corollaries below provide guidelines for the reduction.

Claim 1: Vertex u is an ancestor of vertex v iff $l(u) < l(v) < r(u)$.

Corollary 1: Given two vertices u and v, one can find in constant time whether u is an ancestor of v.

Vertices u and v are unrelated (namely, neither u is an ancestor of v nor v is an ancestor of u) iff either $r(u) < l(v)$ or $r(v) < l(u)$.

Claim 2 . Let u and v be two unrelated vertices. (By Corollary 2, we may assume without loss of generality that $r(u) < l(v)$.) Then, the LCA of u and v is the vertex whose level is minimal over the interval $[r(u), l(v)]$ in A.

The reduction. Let $LEVEL(A) = [LEVEL(a_1), LEVEL(a_2), \ldots, LEVEL(a_n)]$. Claim 2 shows that after performing the range-minima preprocessing algorithm with respect to $LEVEL(A)$, a query of the form $LCA(u, v)$ becomes a range minimum query. Observe that the difference between the level of each pair of successive vertices in the Euler tour (and thus each pair of successive entries in $LEVEL(A)$) is exactly one and therefore the reduction is to the restricted-domain range-minima problem as required.

Remark. The observation that the problem of preprocessing an array so that each range-minimum query can be answered in constant time is equivalent to the LCA problem was known. This observation has led to a linear time algorithm for the former problem using an algorithm for the latter. This does not look very helpful: we know to solve the range-minima problem based on the LCA problem, and conversely, we know to solve the LCA problem based on the range-minima problem. Nevertheless, using the restricted domain properties of our range-minima problem we show that this cyclic relationship between the two problems can be broken and thereby, lead to a new algorithm.

6.3.2   A SIMPLE SEQUENTIAL LCA ALGORITHM

In this subsection we outline a sequential variant of the restricted-domain range-minima problem where k, the difference between adjacent elements, is one. Together with the reduction of Section 6.3.1, this gives a sequential algorithm for the LCA problem.

We first describe two preprocessing procedures for the range-minima problem: (i) Procedure I takes $O(n \log n)$ time, for an input array of length n. No assumptions are needed regarding the difference between adjacent elements. (ii) Procedure II takes exponential time. Following each of these preprocessing procedures, query retrieval takes constant-time. Second, the sequential linear-time range-minima preprocessing algorithm is described. Finally, we show how to retrieve a range-minimum query in constant time. *Procedure I.* Build a complete binary tree whose leaves are the elements of the input array A. Compute (and keep) for each internal node all prefix minima and all suffix minima with respect to its leaves.

Procedure I clearly runs in $O(n \log n)$ time. Given any range $[i, j]$, the range-minimum query with respect to $[i, j]$ can be processed in constant time, as follows. (1) Find the lowest node u of the binary tree such that the range $[i, j]$ falls within its leaves. This range is the union of a suffix of the left child of u and a prefix of the right child of u. The minima over these suffix and prefix was computed by Procedure I. (2) The answer to the query is the minimum among these two minima.

Procedure II. We use the assumption that the difference between any two adjacent elements of the input array A is exactly one. A table is built as follows. We assume without loss of generality that the value of the first element of A is zero (since, otherwise, we can subtract from every element in A the value of the first element without affecting the answers to range-minima queries). Then, the number of different possible input arrays A is 2^{n-1}. The table will have a subtable for each of these 2^{n-1} possible arrays. For each possible array, the subtable will store the answer to each of the $n(n-1)/2$ possible range queries. The time to build the table is $O(2^n n^2)$ and $O(2^n n^2)$ space is needed.

The linear-time range-minima preprocessing algorithm follows.

- For each of the subsets $a_{i \log n + 1}, \ldots, a_{(i+1) \log n}$ for $0 \leq i \leq n / \log n - 1$ find its minimum and apply Procedure I to an array of these $n / \log n$ minima.

- Separately for each of the subsets $a_{i \log n + 1}, \ldots, a_{(i+1) \log n}$ for $0 \leq i \leq n / \log n - 1$ do the following. Partition such subset to smaller subsets of size $\log \log n$ each, and find the minimum in each smaller subset; apply Procedure I to these $\log n / \log \log n$ minima.

- Run Procedure II to build the table required for an (any) array of size $\log \log n$. For each of the subsets $a_{i \log \log n + 1}, \ldots, a_{(i+1) \log \log n}$ for $0 \leq i \leq n / \log \log n - 1$ identify its subtable.

The time (and space) for each step of the preprocessing algorithm is $O(n)$.

Consider a query requesting the minimum over a range $[i, j]$. We show how to process it in constant time. The range $[i, j]$ can easily be presented as the union of the following (at most) five ranges: $[i, x_1], [x_1 + 1, y_1], [y_1 + 1, y_2], [y_2 + 1, x_2]$ and $[x_2 + 1, j]$; where: (1) $[i, x_1]$ (and $[x_2 + 1, j]$) falls within a single subset of size $\log \log n$ – its minimum is available in its subtable, (2) $[x_1 + 1, y_1]$ (and $[y_2 + 1, x_2]$) is the union of subsets of size $\log \log n$ and falls within a single subset of size $\log n$ – its minimum is available from the application of Procedure I to the subset of size $\log n$, and (3) $[y_1 + 1, y_2]$ is the union of subsets of size $\log n$ – its minimum is available from the first application of Procedure I. So, the minimum over range $[i, j]$ is simply the minimum of these five minima.

6.4 Exercises

1. Show how can you use the Knuth, Morris and Pratt algorithm to solve the "string searching with one difference" problem.
2. Develop an algorithm for the k-mismatches problem that is based only on the suffix tree data structure and the LCA algorithm.
3. Develop an algorithm for the k-differences problem when mismatches are not allowed, only insertions and deletions are legal.
4. Given a text T, a pattern P, and a character c. First run the Efficient Algorithm, for the k-differences problem, (Section 6.1.3) for T and P. Then show how can you use the $L'_{d,e}s$, that were computed by the efficient algorithm for T and P, to solve the k-differences problem twice, once for the text cT and the pattern P and then for the text Tc and the pattern P, both with equal efficiency.

6.5 Bibliographic notes

Levenshtein [1966] was the first to define the three types of differences. The random-access-machine (RAM)is described in Aho et al. [1974]. Several books, AKL [1989], Gibbons and Rytter [1988], JáJá [1992], and Reif [1992], and a few review papers, Eppstein and Galil [1988], Karp and Ramachandran [1990], Kruskal et al. [1990], Vishkin [1991], can be used as references for PRAM algorithms. A discussion on gaps is given in Galil and Giancarlo [1989] and Myers and Miller [1988].

The reader is referred to Sankoff and Kruskal [1983], a book which is essentially devoted to various instances of the k-differences problem. The book gives a comprehensive review of applications of the problem in a variety of fields, including: computer science, molecular biology and speech recognition. Quite a few problems in Molecular Biology are similar to the k difference problem. Definitions of the problems and algorithms that solve these problems can be found, for example, in Doolittle [1990] and Waterman [1989].

The dynamic programming algorithm (Section 6.1.1) was given independently by 9 different papers; a list of these papers can be found in Sankoff and Kruskal [1983]. The algorithm given in Section 6.1.2 was presented by Ukkonen [1983]. The algorithms given in Sections 6.1.3 and 6.2 were presented in Landau and Vishkin [1989].

The serial algorithm of Harel and Tarjan [1984] was the first to solve the LCA problem. It preprocesses the tree in linear time and then responses to each query in $O(1)$ time. The algorithms of Schieber and Vishkin [1988] and Berkman and Vishkin [1989] compute it in parallel; these algorithms can be used in the serial case, as well, and are simpler than the one of Harel and Tarjan [1984]. The serial algorithm in Section 6.3 was presented in Berkman and Vishkin [1989] where one can find the parallel version of it. The remark in Section 6.3 was observed in Gabow et al. [1984]. A procedure similar to Procedure I in Section 6.3 was used in Alon and Schieber [1987]. For more on the Euler tour technique see Tarjan and Vishkin [1985] and Vishkin [1985].

Other algorithms for the k mismatches problem were given in Galil and Giancarlo [1986], Galil and Giancarlo [1987] and Landau and Vishkin [1986], and for the k-differences problem in Galil and Park [1990], Landau, Myers and Schmidt [1996], Landau and Vishkin [1988], Ukkonen [1985] and Wu and Manber [1992]. In Galil and Giancarlo [1988] a survey was given. Algorithms for approximate multi-dimensional array matching are given in Amir and Landau [1991].

Bibliography

AHO, A.V., J.E. HOPCROFT AND J.D. ULLMAN [1974], *The Design and Analysis of Computer Algorithms*, Addison-Wesley, Reading, MA.

AKL, S.G. [1989], *The Design and Analysis of Parallel Algorithms*, Prentice Hall, Engelwood Cliffs, New Jersey.

AMIR, A., AND G.M. LANDAU [1991], "Fast parallel and serial multi dimensional approximate array matching", *Theoretical Computer Science*, **81**, 97–115.

ALON, N., AND B. SCHIEBER[1987], "Optimal preprocessing for answering on-line product queries," approximate array matching," TR 71/87, The Moise and Frida Eskenasy Institute of Computer Science, Tel Aviv University.

BERKMAN, O. AND U. VISHKIN [1989], "Recursive star-tree parallel data-structure," *SIAM J. Computing*, **22**, 221–242.

EPPSTEIN, D. AND Z. GALIL [1988], "Parallel algorithmic techniques for combinatorial computation," *Ann. Rev. Comput. Sci.*, **3**, 233–283.

DOOLITTLE, R. F.,, (editor) [1990], *Methods in Enzymology*, **183**: Molecular Evolution: Computer Analysis of Protein and Nucleic Acid Sequences.

GABOW, H. N., J. L. BENTLEY AND R. E. TARJAN [1984], "Scaling and related techniques for geometry problems," *Proc. 16th ACM Symposium on Theory of Computing*, pp. 135-143.

GALIL, Z. AND R. GIANCARLO [1986], "Improved string matching with k mismatches," *SIGACT News*, **17**, 52–54.

GALIL, Z. AND R. GIANCARLO [1987], "Parallel string matching with k mismatches," *Theoretical Computer Science,* **51**, 341–348.

GALIL, Z. AND R. GIANCARLO [1988], "Data Structures and algorithms for approximate string matching," *J. Complexity,* **4**, 33–72.

GALIL, Z. AND R. GIANCARLO [1989], "Speeding up dynamic programming with applications to molecular biology," *Theoretical Computer Science,* **64**, 107–118.

GALIL, Z. AND Q. PARK [1990], "An improved algorithm for approximate string matching," *SIAM J. Computing,* **19**, 989–999.

GIBBONS, A. AND W. RYTTER [1988], *Efficient Parallel Algorithms,* Cambridge University Press, Cambridge.

HAREL, D. AND R.E. TARJAN [1984], "Fast algorithms for finding nearest common ancestors," *SIAM J. Computing,* **13**, 338–355.

KARP, R.M. AND V. RAMACHANDRAN [1990], "A survey of parallel algorithms for shared-memory machines," *Handbook of Theoretical Computer Science: Volume A, Algorithms and Complexity* (Editor J. van Leeuwen), MIT Press/Elsevier, 869–942.

KNUTH, D.E., J.H. MORRIS AND V.R. PRATT [1977] "Fast pattern matching in strings," *SIAM J. Computing,* **6**, 323–350.

KRUSKAL, C.P., L. RUDOLPH, AND M. SNIR [1990], "A complexity theory of efficient parallel algorithms," *Theoretical Computer Science,* **71**, 95–132.

JÁJÁ, J. [1992], *Introduction to Parallel Algorithms,* Addison-Wesley, Reading, MA.

LEVENSHTEIN, V. I. [1966], "Binary Codes Capable of Correcting, Deletions, Insertions and Reversals," *Soviet Phys. Dokl* **10**, *SIAM J. Computing,* to appear. 707–710.

LANDAU, G. M., E. W. MYERS, AND J. P. SCHMIDT [1996], "Incremental String Comparison." *SIAM J. Computing,* to appear.

LANDAU, G.M. AND U. VISHKIN [1986], "Efficient string matching with k mismatches," *Theoretical Computer Science,* **43**, 239–249.

LANDAU, G.M. AND U. VISHKIN [1988], "Fast string matching with k differences," *JCSS,* **37**, 63–78.

LANDAU, G.M. AND U. VISHKIN [1989], "Fast parallel and serial approximate string matching," *Journal of Algorithms,* **10**, 157–169.

MYERS, E. W., AND W. MILLER [1988], "Sequence Comparison with Concave Weighting Functions," *Bulletin of Mathematical Biology,* **50**, 97–120.

REIF, J.H. (editor) [1992], *Synthesis of Parallel Algorithms,* Morgan Kaufmann, San Mateo, California.

SANKOFF, D. AND J.B. KRUSKAL (editors) [1983], *Time Warps, String Edits, and Macromolecules: the Theory and Practice of Sequence Comparison,* Addison-Wesley, Reading, MA.

SCHIEBER, B. AND U. VISHKIN [1988], "On finding lowest common ancestors: simplification and parallelization," *SIAM J. Computing,* **17**, 1253–1262.

TARJAN, R. E. AND U. VISHKIN [1985], "An efficient parallel biconnectivity algorithm," *SIAM J. Computing,* **14**, 862–874.

UKKONEN, E. [1983], "On approximate string matching," *Proc. Int. Conf. Found. Comp. Theor.,* Lecture Notes in Computer Science 158, Springer-Verlag, pp. 487–495.

UKKONEN, E. [1985], "Finding approximate pattern in strings," *J. of Algorithms,* **6**, 132–137.

VISHKIN [1985], "On efficient parallel strong orientation," *Information Processing Letters,* **20**, 235–240.

VISHKIN, U. [1991], "Structural parallel algorithmics," *Proc. of the 18th Int. Colloquium on Automata, Languages and Programming,* Lecture Notes in Computer Science 510, Springer-Verlag, pp. 363-380.

WATERMAN, M. S. (editor) [1989], *Mathematical Methods for DNA Sequences,* CRC Press.

WU, S. AND U. MANBER [1992], "Fast Text Searching Allowing Errors," *Comm. of the ACM,* **35**, 83–91.

7
Dynamic Programming: Special Cases

In this Chapter we present some general algorithmic techniques that have proved to be useful in speeding up the computation of some families of dynamic programming recurrences which have applications in sequence alignment, paragraph formation and prediction of RNA secondary structure. The material presented in this chapter is related to the computation of Levenshtein distances and approximate string matching that have been discussed in the previous three chapters.

7.1 Preliminaries

Dynamic programming is a general technique for solving discrete optimization (minimization or maximization) problems that can be represented by decision processes and for which the principle of optimality holds. We can view a decision process as a directed graph in which nodes represent the states of the process and edges represent decisions. The optimization problem at hand is represented as a decision process by decomposing it into a set of subproblems of smaller size. Such recursive decomposition is continued until we get only trivial subproblems, which can be solved directly. Each node in the graph corresponds to a subproblem and each edge (a, b) indicates that one way to solve subproblem a optimally is to solve first subproblem b optimally. Then, an optimal solution, or policy, is typically given by a path on the graph that minimizes or maximizes some objective function. The correctness of this approach is guaranteed by the principle of optimality which must be satisfied by the optimization problem:

Principle of Optimality: An optimal policy has the property that whatever the initial node (state) and initial edge (decision) are, the remaining edges (decisions) must be an optimal policy with regard to the node (state) resulting from the first transition.

Another consequence of the principle of optimality is that we can express the optimal cost (and solution) of a subproblem in terms of optimal costs (and solutions) of problems of smaller size. That is, we can express optimal costs through a recurrence relation. This is a key component of dynamic programming, since we can compute the optimal cost of a sub-problem only once, store the result in a table, and look it up when needed.

It follows from the preceding discussion that dynamic programming solutions have two features in common:

(1) a table (where we store optimal costs of subproblems);
(2) the entry dependency of the table (given by the recurrence relation).

When we are interested in the design of efficient algorithms for dynamic programming, a third feature emerges:

(3) the order to fill in the table (the algorithm).

We notice that feature (2) can be translated into an algorithm in an obvious way and, sometimes, the time performance of this algorithm is optimal under some model of computation (consider, for instance, the algorithm for the edit distance problem). However, some other times, one can use some properties of the problem at hand (not accounted for in its dynamic programming formulation) to change the order in which (2) is computed to obtain better algorithms.

Let n be the input size of a problem. We classify dynamic programming problems by the table size and entry dependency: A dynamic programming problem is called a tD/eD problem if its table size is $O(n^t)$ and a table entry depends on $O(n^e)$ other entries.

We now present the recurrences that come out from dynamic programming formulations of many optimization problems on strings. We need some notation. We use the term *matrices* for tables. Let A be an $n \times m$ matrix. $A[i, j]$ denotes the element in the ith row and the jth column. A_i denotes the ith row of A. A^j denotes the jth column of A. $A[i : i', j : j']$ denotes the submatrix of A which is the intersection of rows $i, i+1, \ldots, i'$ and columns $j, j + 1, \ldots, j'$. $A[i, j : j']$ is a shorthand notation of $A[i : i, j : j']$. Throughout this chapter, we assume that the elements of a matrix are distinct (ties can be broken consistently).

Problem 1 (1D/1D): Given a real-valued function $w(i, j)$ defined for integers $0 \le i < j \le n$ and $D[0]$, compute

$$E[j] = \min_{0 \le i < j} \{D[i] + w(i, j)\} \quad \text{for } 1 \le j \le n, \tag{7.1}$$

where $D[i]$ is easily computed from $E[i]$, i.e., in constant time.

Problem 2 (2D/0D): Given $D[i, 0]$ and $D[0, j]$ for $0 \le i, j \le n$, compute

$$E[i,j] = \min\{D[i-1,j] + x_i, D[i,j-1] + y_j, D[i-1,j-1] + z_{i,j}\}, \quad (7.2)$$

for $1 \leq i, j \leq n$, where x_i, y_j, and $z_{i,j}$ can be obtained in constant time, and $D[i,j]$ is easily computed from $E[i,j]$ (again, in constant time).

Problem 3 (2D/2D): Given $w(i,j)$ for $0 \leq i < j \leq 2n$, and $D[i,0]$ and $D[0,j]$ for $0 \leq i, j \leq n$, compute

$$E[i,j] = \min_{\substack{0 \leq i' < i \\ 0 \leq j' < j}} \{D[i',j'] + w(i'+j', i+j)\} \quad \text{for } 1 \leq i, j \leq n, \quad (7.3)$$

where $D[i,j]$ is easily computed from $E[i,j]$.

In the applications from which Problems 1 and 3 have been distilled off, the cost function w is either convex or concave. In the applications of Problems 2 and 3 the problems may be sparse, i.e., we need to compute $E[i,j]$ only for a sparse set of points. Exploiting these conditions we can design more efficient algorithms than the obvious ones.

7.2 Convexity and Concavity

7.2.1 MONGE CONDITIONS

Convexity or concavity is a crucial property of the cost function w that can be exploited to design fast dynamic programming algorithms. We define it in terms of the *Monge* conditions. w is *convex* if and only if it satisfies the convex Monge condition:

$$w(a,c) + w(b,d) \leq w(b,c) + w(a,d) \quad \text{for all } a < b \text{ and } c < d. \quad (7.4)$$

w is *concave* if and only if it satisfies the concave Monge condition:

$$w(a,c) + w(b,d) \geq w(b,c) + w(a,d) \quad \text{for all } a < b \text{ and } c < d. \quad (7.5)$$

An important notion related to Monge conditiond is total monotonicity of an $m \times n$ matrix A. A is *convex totally monotone* if and only if

$$A[a,c] \geq A[b,c] \quad \Longrightarrow \quad A[a,d] \geq A[b,d]. \quad (7.6)$$

for all $a < b$ and $c < d$.

Similarly, A is *concave totally monotone* if and only if

$$A[a,c] \leq A[b,c] \quad \Longrightarrow \quad A[a,d] \leq A[b,d]. \quad (7.7)$$

for all $a < b$ and $c < d$.

It is easy to check that if w is seen as a two-dimensional matrix, the convex (resp., concave) Monge condition implies convex (resp., concave) total monotonicity of w. Notice that the converse is not true. Total monotonicity and Monge condition of a matrix A are relevant to the design of algorithms because of the following observations. Let r_j denote the row index such that $A[r_j, j]$ is the minimum value in column j. Convex total monotonicity implies that the minimum row indices are nondecreasing, i.e., $r_1 \leq r_2 \leq \cdots \leq r_m$. Concave total monotonicity implies that the minimum row indices are nonincreasing, i.e., $r_1 \geq r_2 \geq \cdots \geq r_m$. We say that an element $A[i, j]$ is *dead* if $i \neq r_j$ (i.e., $A[i, j]$ is not the minimum of column j). A submatrix of A is dead if all of its elements are dead.

7.2.2   MATRIX SEARCHING

Let A be an $m \times n$ matrix and assume that we can compute or access each $A[i, j]$ in constant time, for any i, j. We want to compute the *row maxima* of A. We give an algorithm, nicknamed $SMAWK$ in the literature, that solves this problem in $O(n)$ time when $m \leq n$ and A is totally monotone with respect to row maxima. That is, for all $a < b$ and $c < d$,

$$A[a, d] \geq A[a, c] \quad \Longrightarrow \quad A[b, d] \geq A[b, c]. \tag{7.8}$$

Notice that in the previous subsection we have defined convex and concave total monotonicity in terms of column minima of A. However, with minor modifications, the $SMAWK$ algorithm can find the column minima of an $n \times m$ convex or concave totally monotone matrix in $O(n)$ time, when $n \geq m$. In what follows, we refer to all those versions of the same algorithm as SMAWK (it will be clear from the context which one we will refer to). We give details for the one that finds row maxima.

The hearth of the algorithm is the subroutine $REDUCE$. It takes as input an $m \times n$ totally monotone matrix A with $m \leq n$ and returns an $m \times m$ matrix G which is a submatrix of A such that G contains the columns of A which have the row maxima of A.

Let k be a column index of G with initial value of 1. $REDUCE$ maintains the invariant on k that $G[1 : j - 1, j]$ is dead, for all $1 \leq j \leq k$. (See Fig. 7.1). Also, only dead columns are deleted. The invariant holds trivially when $k = 1$. If $G[k, k] > G[k, k+1]$ then $G[1 : k, k+1]$ is dead by total monotonicity. Therefore, if $k < m$, we increase k by 1. If $k = m$, column $k + 1$ is dead and k is unchanged. If $G[k, k] \leq G[k, k + 1]$ then $G[k : m, k]$ is dead by total monotonicity. Since $G[1 : k - 1, k]$ was already dead by the invariant, column k is dead; k is decreased by 1, if it was greater than 1.

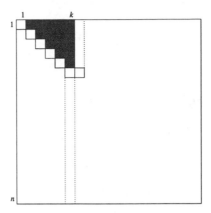

Fig. 7.1. Matrix G (the shaded region is dead)

PROCEDURE $REDUCE(A)$
$G \leftarrow A$;
$k \leftarrow 1$;
    while   *number of columns of G larger than* m **do**
       begin
          case
            $G[k, k] > G[k, k + 1]$ **and** $k < m$: $k \leftarrow k + 1$;
            $G[k, k] > G[k, k+1]$ **and** $k = m$: **delete column**
$k + 1$;
            $G[k, k] \leq G[k, k + 1]$: **delete column** k; $k \leftarrow$
$\min(1, k - 1)$;
          endcase
       end
    return(G);

For the time analysis of $REDUCE$, let a, b, and c denote, respectively, the number of times the first, second, and third branches of the **case** statement are executed. Since a total of $n - m$ columns are deleted and a column is deleted only in the last two branches, we have $b + c = n - m$. Let c' be the number of times k decreases in the third branch. Then $c' \leq c$. Since k starts at 1 and ends no larger than m, $a - c \leq a - c' \leq m - 1$. We have time $t = a + b + c \leq a + 2b + c \leq 2n - m - 1$.

The row maxima of an $m \times n$ totally monotone matrix A with $m \leq n$ are found as follows. We first use $REDUCE$ to get an $m \times m$ matrix G, and then recursively find the row maxima of the submatrix of G which is composed of even rows of G. After having found the row maxima of even rows, we compute the row maxima in odd rows. The procedure $ROWMAX$ shows the algorithm.

PROCEDURE *ROWMAX(A)*
$G \leftarrow REDUCE(A)$;
if $m = 1$ **then** *output the maximum and return*;
$P \leftarrow \{G_2, G_4, \ldots, G_{2\lfloor m/2 \rfloor}\}$;
ROWMAX(P);
from the positions (now known) of the maxima in the
even rows of G,
    find the maxima in its odd rows;

Let $T(m, n)$ be the time taken by *ROWMAX* for an $m \times n$ matrix. The call to *REDUCE* takes time $O(n)$. Notice that P is an $m/2 \times m$ totally monotone matrix, so the recursive call takes time $T(m/2, m)$. Once the positions of the maxima in the even rows of G have been found, the maximum in each odd row is restricted to the interval of maximum positions of the neighboring even rows. Thus, finding all maxima in the odd rows can be done in $O(m)$ time. For some constants c_1 and c_2, the time satisfies the following inequality

$$T(m, n) \leq c_1 m + c_2 n + T(m/2, m), \qquad (7.9)$$

which gives the solution $T(m, n) \leq 2(c_1 + c_2)m + c_2 n = O(n)$, since $m \leq n$. The bookkeeping for maintaining row and column indices also takes linear time.

For completeness, we remark that, when $m > n$, the row maxima can be found in $O(n(1 + \log(m/n)))$ time (see Exercises). In alternative, we can do the same thing in $O(m)$ time by extending the matrix to an $m \times m$ matrix with $-\infty$ in the columns we have added. This matrix is totally monotone if the original matrix is totally monotone. We can now apply *ROWMAX* to the new matrix. Therefore, we can find the row maxima of an $m \times n$ matrix in $O(n + m)$ time.

7.3   The One-Dimensional Case (1D/1D)

We consider algorithms for the computation of recurrence (7.1) both when the cost function w is concave and when it is convex. We present first algorithms that organize the list of candidates for the minimum at a given step into a stack (concave case) or queue (convex case). Then, we describe algorithms that use *SMAWK* as a subroutine. The first set of algorithms is very simple and likely to perform quite well in practice while the other set of algorithms display a better asymptotic time performance. We remark that if $D[i] = E[i]$ and $w(i, i) = 0$ in recurrence (7.1), then we have a shortest path problem with a trivial solution. In what follows, we rule out such case.

Let $B[i, j] = D[i] + w(i, j)$ for $0 \leq i < j \leq n$. We say that $B[i, j]$ is *available* if $D[i]$ is known and therefore $B[i, j]$ can be computed in constant time. That is, $B[i, j]$ is available only when the column minima for columns $1, 2, \ldots, i$ have been found. We say that B *on-line*, since its entries become available as the computation proceed. A matrix is *off-line* if all of its entries are given at the beginning.

The 1D/1D problem is to find the column minima in an on-line upper triangular matrix B. One can easily show that when w satisfies the concave (convex) Monge condition B is totally monotone.

7.3.1   A STACK OR A QUEUE

The algorithms presented here find column minima one at a time and process available entries so that they keep only possible candidates for future column minima. In the concave (resp., convex) case, we use a stack (resp., queue) to maintain the candidates. We discuss the concave case first. The algorithm can be sketched as follows (the discussion following it provides the missing details and a proof of its correctness as well):

> **PROCEDURE** *concave* 1D/1D
> **initialize stack with row** 0;
> **for** $j = 2$ **to** n **do**
>   **begin**
>   **find minimum at column** j;
>   **update stack with row** $j - 1$;
>   **end**
> **end**

For each j, $2 \leq j \leq n$, we find the minimum at column j as follows. Assume that $(i_1, h_1), \ldots, (i_k, h_k)$ are on the stack ((i_1, h_1) is at the top of the stack). Initially, $(0, n)$ is on the stack. The invariant on the stack elements is that in submatrix $B[0 : j - 2, j : n]$ row i_r, for $1 \leq r \leq k$, is the best (gives the minimum) in the column interval $[h_{r-1} + 1, h_r]$ (assuming $h_0 + 1 = j$). By the concave total monotonicity of B, $i_1, \ldots, i_k$ are nonincreasing (see Fig. 7.2). Thus the minimum at column j is the minimum of $B[i_1, j]$ and $B[j - 1, j]$.

Now we update the stack with row $j - 1$ as follows.

(1) If $B[i_1, j] \leq B[j-1, j]$, row $j-1$ is dead by concave total monotonicity. If $h_1 = j$, we pop the top element because it will not be useful.

(2) If $B[i_1, j] > B[j - 1, j]$, we compare row $j - 1$ with row i_r at h_r (i.e., $B[i_r, h_r]$ vs. $B[j - 1, h_r]$), for $r = 1, 2, \ldots$, until row i_r is better than row $j - 1$ at h_r. If row $j - 1$ is better than row i_r at h_r, row i_r cannot give the minimum for any column because row $j - 1$ is better than row i_r for column $l \leq h_r$ and row i_{r+1} is better than row i_r for column $l > h_r$. We pop the element (i_r, h_r) from the stack and continue to compare row $j - 1$ with row i_{r+1}. If row i_r

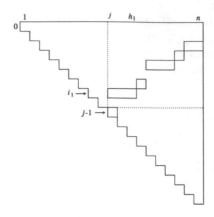

Fig. 7.2.   Matrix B and stack elements at column j

is better than row $j-1$ at h_r, we need to find the border of the two rows $j-1$ and i_r, which is the largest $h < h_r$ such that row $j-1$ is better than row i_r for column $l \leq h$; i.e., finding the zero z of
$$f(x) = B[j-1, x] - B[i_r, x] = w(j-1, x) - w(i_r, x) + (D[j-1] - D[i_r]),$$
then $h = \lfloor z \rfloor$. If $h \geq j+1$, we push $(j-1, h)$ into the stack.

As for the time analysis, we notice that popping stack elements takes amortized constant time (the total number of pop operations cannot be greater than n). When one can compute the border h in constant time, we say that w satisfies the *closest zero property*. For instance $w(i, j) = \log(j - i)$ satisfies the closest zero property. For those functions, the time of the algorithm is $O(n)$. For more general w we can compute h by a binary search in $O(\log n)$ time. Therefore, in general, the total time is $O(n \log n)$.

The convex case is similar. We use a queue instead of a stack to maintain the candidates. Assume that $(i_1, h_1), \ldots, (i_k, h_k)$ are in the queue at column j ((i_1, h_1) is at the front and (i_k, h_k) is at the rear of the queue). The invariant on the queue elements is that in $B[0 : j-2, j : n]$ row i_r for $1 \leq r \leq k$ is the best in the interval $[h_r, h_{r+1} - 1]$ (assuming $h_{k+1} - 1 = n$). By the convex total monotonicity of B, $i_1, \ldots, i_k$ are nondecreasing. Thus the minimum at column j is the minimum of $B[i_1, j]$ and $B[j-1, j]$. One property satisfied by the convex case only is that if $B[j-1, j] \leq B[i_1, j]$, the whole queue is emptied by convex total monotonicity. This property is crucial to design a linear time algorithm for the convex case (which will be discussed shortly).

7.3.2 THE EFFECTS OF *SMAWK*

There are two problems in trying to apply the *SMAWK* algorithm directly to the $1D/1D$ problem. One is that B is not rectangular. In the convex case, we can take care of this difficulty by putting $+\infty$ in the lower half of

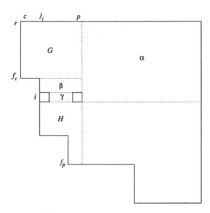

Fig. 7.3. Staircase matrix B'

B. The resulting matrix is totally monotone. However, this "patch" is of no use for the concave case. However, the really serious problem is that the matrix A on which $SMAWK$ works is off-line, while B is on-line. That is, $B[i,j]$ is available only after the column minima for columns $1, \cdots, i$ have been found. The notion of staircase matrix (see Fig. 7.3) helps in solving those problems. We define it in terms of columns. An $n \times m$ matrix S is staircase if

- (1) there are integers f_j for $j = 1, 2, \ldots, m$ associated with S such that $1 \leq f_1 \leq f_2 \leq \cdots \leq f_m \leq n$, and
- (2) $S[i,j]$ is a real number if and only if $1 \leq i \leq f_j$ and $1 \leq j \leq m$. Otherwise, $S[i,j]$ is undefined.

We say that column j a *step-column* if $j = 1$ or $f_j > f_{j-1}$ for $j > 2$, and we say that S has t steps if it has t step-columns.

We now consider the generalization of recurrence (7.1):

$$E[j] = \min_{0 \leq i \leq f_j} \{D[i] + w(i,j)\} \quad \text{for } 1 \leq j \leq n, \qquad (7.10)$$

where $0 \leq f_1 \leq \ldots \leq f_n < n$. For $i = 0, \ldots, f_1$, $D[i]$ is given and, for $i = f_{j-1} + 1, \ldots, f_j$ $(j > 1)$, $D[i]$ is easily computed from $E[j-1]$. This problem occurs as a subproblem in a solution of the $2D/2D$ problem. It becomes recurrence (7.1), if $f_j = j - 1$.

Let $B[i,j] = D[i] + w(i,j)$ again. Now B is an on-line staircase matrix and we need to compute its column minima. We describe first an algorithm for the convex case.

As we compute E from $E[1]$ to $E[n]$, we reduce the matrix B to successively smaller staircase matrices B'. For each staircase matrix B' we maintain two indices r and c: r is the first row of B', c its first column.

That is, $B'[i, j] = B[i, j]$ if $i \geq r$ and $j \geq c$, $B'[i, j]$ is undefined for all other cases. We use an array $N[1 : n]$ to store interim column minima before row r; i.e., $N[j] = B[i, j]$ for some $i < r$ (its use will be clear shortly). At the beginning of each stage the following invariants hold:

(a) $E[j]$ for all $1 \leq j < c$ have been found.
(b) $E[j]$ for $j \geq c$ is $\min(N[j], \min_{i \geq r} B'[i, j])$.

Invariant (a) means that $D[i]$ is known for all $0 \leq i \leq f_c$. Therefore $B'[r : f_c, c : n]$ is available. Initially, the invariants are satisfied by setting $r = 0$, $c = 1$, and $N[j] = +\infty$ for all $1 \leq j \leq n$.

Let $p = \min(f_c + c - r + 1, n)$. We construct a matrix G which consists of $N[c : p]$ as its first row and $B'[r : f_c, c : p]$ as the other rows. G is a square matrix except when $n < f_c + c - r + 1$. G is convex totally monotone and so we can find its column minima $F[c : p]$ using the SMAWK algorithm. Let c' be the first step-column after c, and H be the part of B' below G.

(1) If $c' > p$ (i.e., H is empty), we have found column minima $E[c : p]$ which are $F[c : p]$ by invariant (b).

If $c' \leq p$, column minima $E[c : c' - 1]$ have been found. We need to process H to obtain the other column minima. For each row in H we make two comparisons: one with its first entry, the other with its last entry until either case (2) or (3) occurs. Let i be the current row of H, and j_i the first column of row i. Initially, $i = f_c + 1$. Assume inductively that the part of H above row i is dead (β in Fig. 7.3).

(2) If $B'[i, j_i] \leq F[j_i]$, then rows $r, \ldots, i-1$ of B' are dead (by the convex total monotonicity of B' - it corresponds to emptying the queue in the algorithm sketched in the previous subsection).
(3) If $B'[i, j_i] > F[j_i]$ and $B'[i, p] \leq F[p]$, then $B'[r : i - 1, p + 1 : n]$ is dead (α is in Fig. 7.3).
    Though G is not dead, we can store $F[j_i : p]$ into $N[j_i : p]$ and remove rows $r, \ldots, i - 1$.
(4) Otherwise, $B'[i, j_i : p]$ (γ in Fig. 7.3) is dead (again by convex total monotonicity). We move to the next row of H.

If case (4) is repeated until the last row of H, we have found column minima $E[c : p]$. This case will be called (4'). Note that whenever a new step-column starts, column minima for previous columns have been found, so all entries involved in the computation above become available. If either case (2) or (3) occurs, we start a new stage with $r = i$ and $c = j_i$. Otherwise, we start a new stage with $c = p + 1$ (r is unchanged). The two invariants hold at the beginning of new stages.

Let i' be the last row of B' which was involved in the computation. (e.g., $i' = f_c = f_p$ in case (1) and $i' = f_p$ in case (4')). Each stage takes time $O(i' - r)$. This time can be amortized against the rows or columns that are removed, for a total of $O(n)$.

We now briefly sketch the algorithm for the off-line concave case which has an $O(n\alpha(n))$ time complexity. It can be modified to work for the on-line problem. Consider the matrix B transposed. Then, finding column minima in B becomes finding row minima in the transposed matrix. We will concentrate on this latter problem.

We say that a staircase matrix has *shape* (t, n, m) if it has at most t steps, at most n rows, and at most m columns. The main idea is to reduce the number of steps of a staircase matrix to two (the row minima of a staircase matrix with two steps can be found in linear time using the SMAWK algorithm). We first reduce a staircase matrix of shape (n, n, m) to a staircase matrix of shape $(n/(\alpha(n))^3, n/(\alpha(n))^2, m)$ in $O(m\alpha(n) + n)$ time. Then we successively reduce the staircase matrix to staircase matrices with fewer steps as follows: a staircase matrix of shape $(n/L_s(n), n, m)$ is reduced to a set of staircase matrices $G_1, \ldots, G_k$ in $O(m + n)$ time, where G_i is of shape $(n_i/L_{s-1}(n_i), n_i, m_i)$, $\sum_{i=1}^{k} n_i \leq n$, and $\sum_{i=1}^{k} m_i \leq m + n$. It can be shown by induction on s that the processing (finding row minima) of a staircase matrix of shape $(n/L_s(n), n, m)$ can be done in $O(sm + s^2 n)$ time. Thus the staircase matrix of shape $(n/(\alpha(n))^3, n/(\alpha(n))^2, m)$ can be processed in $O(m\alpha(n) + n)$.

7.4   The Two-Dimensional Case

We now consider the problem of computing recurrence (7.3). We first discuss the case in which w is a general function. Then, we provide algorithms for the case in which w is either concave or convex.

We need a few definitions. Consider the set of points $\{(i, j) | 0 \leq i, j \leq n\}$. We say that (i', j') *precedes* (i, j), denoted by $(i', j') \prec (i, j)$, if and only if $i' < i$ and $j' < j$. The *domain* $d(i, j)$ of a point (i, j) is defined as the set of points (i', j') such that $(i', j') \prec (i, j)$, and the *diagonal index* of a point (i, j) is defined as $i + j$. Let $d_k(i, j)$ be the set of points (i', j') in $d(i, j)$ whose diagonal index is $k = i' + j'$.

Recurrence (7.3) has the property that the function w depends only on the diagonal index of its two argument points. Thus, when we compute $E[i, j]$ we have only to consider the minimum among the $D[i', j']$ entries in $d_k(i, j)$ where $k = i' + j'$. We can use that fact to compute (7.3) in $O(n^3)$ time without convexity and concavity assumptions as we now outline.

$$H^i[k, j] = \min_{(i', j') \in d_k(i, j)} D[i', j']. \tag{7.11}$$

Then, recurrence (7.3) can be written as

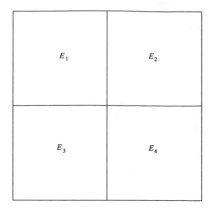

Fig. 7.4.   The partition of matrix E

$$E[i, j] = \min_{k < i+j-1} \{H^i[k, j] + w(k, i + j)\}. \tag{7.12}$$

For each i, j, we compute $H^i[k, j]$ from $H^{i-1}[k, j]$ for all k in $O(n)$ time. Then, $E[i, j]$ is computed in $O(n)$ time. Since we need to compute $O(n^2)$ entries, the overall time is $O(n^3)$. In the following, we assume that w is either convex or concave and discuss how to improve the $O(n^3)$ time bound using those assumptions.

7.4.1   A COARSE DIVIDE-AND-CONQUER

We can combine a divide-and-conquer approach with the matrix searching technique for the computation of recurrence (7.3). The scheme consists of partitioning E into four $n/2 \times n/2$ submatrices E_1, E_2, E_3, and E_4, as shown in Fig. 7.4. We recursively compute E_1 and then we compute the *influence* (a task that is described later) of E_1 on E_2. Then, we recursively compute E_2, taking into account the influence of E_1 on E_2. E_3 is computed in a way similar to E_2. Finally, we compute the influence of E_1, E_2, E_3, respectively, on E_4. Then we recursively compute E_4.

Let $T(n)$ be the time complexity of the algorithm for the problem of size n and assume that the influence of a matrix of size $n \times n$ over a matrix of similar size can be computed in $O(n^2)$ time. Then, the time performance of the algorithm just outlined is given by $T(n) = 4T(n/2) + O(n^2)$. Since $T(1) = O(1)$, we get $T(n) = O(n^2 \log n)$.

What is left to do is to define what is the influence of E_1 on E_2 and how it is computed in $O(n^2)$ time (other influences are defined and computed similarly). Each point $(i, j + n/2)$ in row i of E_2 has the same domain in E_1, and thus depends on the same diagonal minima in E_1. Consequently, consider the matrix $X_i[k, j]$ for $1 \leq j \leq n/2$ and $0 \leq k < i + n/2$ where

$$X_i[k, j] = H^i[k, n/2 + 1] + w(k, i + j + n/2). \tag{7.13}$$

That is, $X_i[k, j]$ contains the influence of E_1 on point $(i, j + n/2)$. Then $E[i, j+n/2]$ is the minimum of two things: $\min_k X_i[k, j]$, and the recursive solution of E_2. The computation of the influence of E_1 on E_2 reduces to compute the column minima of X_i for $1 \le i \le n/2$. Now, X_i is (off-line) totally monotone when w is either convex or concave. As mentioned before, $H^i[k, n/2+1]$ can be computed from $H^{i-1}[k, n/2+1]$ in $O(n)$ time, for all k. Once this has been done, the column minima of X_i can be computed in $O(n)$ time using the $SMAWK$ algorithm. Therefore, the total time for computing the influence is $O(n^2)$.

7.4.2 A FINE DIVIDE-AND-CONQUER

The time bound of $O(n^2 \log n)$ for the computation of recurrence (7.3) can be improved to $O(n^2)$ for the convex case and $O(n^2\alpha(n))$ for the concave case. The algorithm for the two cases is the same. Indeed, the computation of (7.3) is reduced to the computation of a set of on-line $1D/1D$ recurrences. Each of those recurrences is computed by using as a subroutine the best algorithm for the corresponding case.

Without loss of generality, assume that $n + 1$ is a power of two. For $0 \le l \le \log_2(n + 1)$, let a *square of level* l be a $2^l \times 2^l$ square of points whose upper left corner is at the point (i, j) such that both i and j are multiples of 2^l. Let $S^l_{u,v}$ be the square of level l whose upper left corner is at the point $(u2^l, v2^l)$. Let $S^l_{u,*}$ be the set of squares of level l whose upper left corner is in row $u2^l$. Similarly, $S^l_{*,v}$ is the set of squares of level l whose upper left corner is in column $v2^l$. Observe that each square $S^l_{u,v}$ is composed of four squares of level $l-1$. Let $S^l(i, j)$ be the square of level l containing (i, j). We extend the partial order $\prec$ over the squares: $S' \prec S$ if every point in S' precedes every point in S.

For $0 \le l \le \log_2(n + 1)$, let

$$E_l[i, j] = \min\{D[i', j'] + w(i' + j', i + j)|S^l(i', j') \prec S^l(i, j)\}. \qquad (7.14)$$

Note that $E_0[i, j] = E[i, j]$ and, for $l > 0$, $E_l[i, j]$ is an approximation of $E[i, j]$.

Suppose that the matrix D is off-line. Let $E_{\log_2(n+1)}[i, j] = +\infty$ for all (i, j). We compute the matrix E_l given the matrix E_{l+1} for $l = \log_2(n + 1) - 1$ to 0. Consider a point (p, q), and let $S^{l+1}_{u,v} = S^{l+1}(p, q)$. There are four cases depending on the position of the square $S^l(p, q)$ in the square $S^{l+1}(p, q)$.

(1) $S^l(p, q)$ is the upper left subsquare of $S^{l+1}(p, q)$. That is, $S^l(p, q) = S^l_{2u,2v}$. It is easy to see that $E_l[p, q] = E_{l+1}[p, q]$.

(2) $S^l(p, q)$ is the upper right subsquare of $S^{l+1}(p, q)$. That is, $S^l(p, q) = S^l_{2u,2v+1}$. The points in the squares of $S^l_{*,2v}$ that precede the square

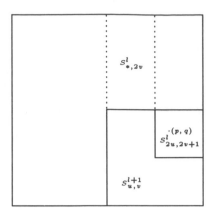

Fig. 7.5. $S^l(p, q)$ is the upper right subsquare of $S^{l+1}(p, q)$

$S^l_{2u,2v+1}$ have to be considered when computing $E_l[p, q]$ (see Fig. 7.5). For the points (i, j) in the squares of $S^l_{*,2v+1}$, we define the *column recurrence*

$$CR^l_v[i, j] = \min\{D[i', j'] + w(i' + j', i + j)\}, \qquad (7.15)$$

where $(i', j') \in S^l_{*,2v}$ and $S^l(i', j') \prec S^l(i, j)$. Then, $E_l[p, q] = \min\{E_{l+1}[p, q], CR^l_v[p, q]\}$.

(3) $S^l(p, q)$ is the lower left subsquare of $S^{l+1}(p, q)$. That is, $S^l(p, q) = S^l_{2u+1,2v}$. The points in the squares of $S^l_{2u,*}$ that precede the square $S^l_{2u+1,2v}$ have to be considered when computing $E_l[p, q]$. For the points (i, j) in the squares of $S^l_{2u+1,*}$, we define the *row recurrence*

$$RR^l_u[i, j] = \min\{D[i', j'] + w(i' + j', i + j)\}, \qquad (7.16)$$

where $(i', j') \in S^l_{2u,*}$ and $S^l(i', j') \prec S^l(i, j)$. Then, $E_l[p, q] = \min\{E_{l+1}[p, q], RR^l_u[p, q]\}$.

(4) $S^l(p, q)$ is the lower right subsquare of $S^{l+1}(p, q)$, i.e., $S^l(p, q) = S^l_{2u+1,2v+1}$. Now, $E_l[p, q] = \min\{E_{l+1}[p, q], CR^l_v[p, q], RR^l_u[p, q]\}$.

Using the fact that the function w depends only on the diagonal index of the points we have the following observations:

(a) The value of $E_l[i, j]$ (also $CR^l_v[i, j]$ and $RR^l_u[i, j]$) is the same for all points in a square of level l which have the same diagonal index $i + j$.

(b) To compute $CR^l_v[i, j]$ (or $RR^l_u[i, j]$) it is sufficient to consider only the minimum $D[i', j']$ among all points in a square of level l which have the same diagonal index $i' + j'$.

By Observation (a) we keep $2^{l+1} - 1$ values for each square of level l (corresponding to the diagonals). Since there are $(n + 1)^2/2^{2l}$ squares at level l, E_l has $O(n^2/2^l)$ values. Thus the overall computation above takes $O(n^2)$ time except for the row and column recurrences. To compute E_l from E_{l+1}, we have to solve $(n + 1)/2^{l+1}$ row recurrences and $(n + 1)/2^{l+1}$ column recurrences. We will show that each recurrence is solved by four instances of Recurrence (7.10). Overall, there are $O(n)$ instances of Recurrence (7.10), which implies $O(n^2)$ time for convex w and $O(n^2\alpha(n))$ for concave w.

Now we show how to compute CR_v^l. The algorithm for the row recurrences is analogous. Each square of level l will be assigned a color, either red or black. The upper left square is red, and all squares of level l are assigned colors in the checkerboard fashion. Consider the diagonals that intersect the squares in $S_{*,2v+1}^l$. Each diagonal intersects at most two squares in $S_{*,2v+1}^l$, one red square and one black square. By Observation (a) the value of $CR_v^l[i, j]$ is the same for a diagonal in a square, but each diagonal intersects two squares. Thus we divide the row recurrence into two recurrences: the *red recurrence* for points in red squares and the *black recurrence* for points in black squares. By Observation (b) we need to consider only the minimum $D[i', j']$ for a diagonal in a square, but again each diagonal in $S_{*,2v}^l$ intersects two squares, one red square and one black square. Thus we divide the red recurrence into two recurrences: the *red-red recurrence* and the *red-black recurrence*. Similarly, the black recurrence is divided into two recurrences. Therefore, each row or column recurrence is solved by four instances of the $1D/1D$ problem.

In the $2D/2D$ problem, however, the matrix D is on-line. It is a simple matter to modify the off-line algorithm described above so that it computes the entries of $E = E_0$ row by row and uses only available entries of D without increasing its time complexity. Therefore, it leads to an $O(n^2)$ time algorithm for the convex case and an $O(n^2\alpha(n))$ time algorithm for the concave case.

7.5   Sparsity

In many application areas, the problems solved by dynamic programming impose constraints on the associated recurrence that make it meaningless (undefined) on some points of its domain. We call such recurrences *sparse*. For the kind of problems we are interested in, the $2D/0D$ and $2D/2D$ recurrences may be sparse. That is, we need to compute E only for a sparse set S of points. Let M be the number of such points. Since the table size is $O(n^2)$ in the two-dimensional problems, $M \leq n^2$. We assume that S is given (usually, it can be obtained by a suitable preprocessing).

7.5.1   THE SPARSE $2D/0D$ PROBLEM

We define the *range* $R(i,j)$ of a point (i,j) to be the set of points (i',j') such that $(i,j) \prec (i',j')$. We also define two subregions of $R(i,j)$: the *upper range* $UR(i,j)$ and the *lower range* $LR(i,j)$. $UR(i,j)$ is the set of points $(i',j') \in R(i,j)$ such that $j' - i' \geq j - i$, and $LR(i,j)$ is the set of points $(i',j') \in R(i,j)$ such that $j' - i' \leq j - i$.

Consider recurrence (7.2). For constants q and u, let $x_i = q$, $y_j = u$, $z_{i,j} = 0$ if $(i,j) \in S$ or $z_{i,j} = q + u$ otherwise , and $E[i,j] = D[i,j]$ (i.e., the edit distance problem when substitutions are not allowed). Then, taking into account the fact that $z_{i,j} = 0$ for $(i,j) \in S$, we can rewrite it as:

$$D[i,j] = \min \begin{cases} D[i_1,j] + q(i - i_1) \\ D[i,j_1] + u(j - j_1) \\ \min_{\substack{(i',j') \prec (i,j) \\ (i',j') \in S}} \{D[i',j'] + q(i - i' - 1) + u(j - j' - 1)\} \end{cases}$$

$$(7.17)$$

where i_1 is the largest row index such that $i_1 < i$ and $(i_1,j) \in S$, and j_1 is the largest column index such that $j_1 < j$ and $(i,j_1) \in S$. Moreover, we can restrict its computation to points $(i,j) \in S$.

The computational bottleneck in Recurrence (7.17) can be modeled as

$$E[i,j] = \min_{\substack{(i',j') \prec (i,j) \\ (i',j') \in S}} \{D[i',j'] + f(i',j',i,j)\} \quad \text{for } (i,j) \in S, \qquad (7.18)$$

where f is a linear function of i', j', i, and j for all points (i,j) in $R(i',j')$. Since $R(i',j')$ is a rectangular region, we refer to (7.18) as the *rectangle case*. We point out that when w is a linear function in the $2D/2D$ problem, it becomes a $2D/0D$ problem and, in case it is sparse, we are dealing with the rectangle case.

Consider now the case of Recurrence (7.2) where $x_i = y_j = q$, $z_{i,j} = 0$ if $(i,j) \in S$; $z_{i,j} = q$ otherwise, and $E[i,j] = D[i,j]$ (i.e., the unit-cost edit distance problem and approximate string matching). Then, taking into account the fact that $z_{i,j} = 0$ for $(i,j) \in S$, we can rewrite it as:

$$D[i,j] = \min \begin{cases} D[i_1,j] + q(i - i_1) \\ D[i,j_1] + q(j - j_1) \\ \min_{\substack{(i',j') \prec (i,j) \\ (i',j') \in S}} \{D[i',j'] + q \times \max(i - i' - 1, j - j' - 1)\} \end{cases}$$

$$(7.19)$$

for $(i,j) \in S$. The main computation in Recurrence (7.19) can also be represented by Recurrence (7.18), where f is a linear function in each of $UR(i',j')$ and $LR(i',j')$. This case will be called the *triangle case* because $UR(i',j')$ and $LR(i',j')$ are triangular regions.

The rectangle case   We show how to compute recurrence (7.18) when
f is a linear function for all points in $R(i', j')$.

Lemma 7.1. *Let P be the intersection of $R(p,q)$ and $R(r,s)$, and (i,j) be
a point in P. If $D[p,q] + f(p,q,i,j) < D[r,s] + f(r,s,i,j)$ (i.e., (p,q) is
better than (r,s) at one point), then (p,q) is better than (r,s) at all points
in P.*

Proof: Use the linearity of f.   □

   By Lemma 7.1, whenever the range of two points intersect, one comparison is enough to decide which point takes over the intersection. So, E can
be partitioned into regions such that for each region P there is a point (i,j)
that is the best for points in P. Obviously, $R(i,j)$ includes P. We refer to
(i,j) as the *owner* of P. The partition of E is not known a priori, but it is
discovered as one proceed row by row. A region P is *active* at row i if P
intersects row i. At a particular row, active regions are column intervals of
that row, and the boundaries are the column indices of the owners of active
regions. We maintain the owners of active regions in a list $ACTIVE$.

   Let $i_1, i_2, \ldots, i_p$ $(p \leq M)$ be the non-empty rows in the sparse set S,
and $ROW[s]$ be the sorted list of column indices representing points of
row i_s in S. The algorithm consists of p steps, one for each non-empty
row. During step s, the points in $ROW[s]$ are processed. Given $ACTIVE$
at step s, the processing of a point (i_s, j) consists of computing $E[i_s, j]$
and updating $ACTIVE$ with (i_s, j). Computing $E(i_s, j)$ simply involves
looking up which region contains (i_s, j). Suppose that (i_r, j') is the owner
of the region that contains (i_s, j). Then $E[i_s, j] = D[i_r, j'] + f(i_r, j', i_s, j)$.
Now $ACTIVE$ needs to be updated to possibly include (i_s, j) as an owner.
Since $R(i_r, j')$ contains (i_s, j), $R(i_r, j')$ includes $R(i_s, j)$. If (i_r, j') is better
than (i_s, j) at $(i_s + 1, j + 1)$, then (i_s, j) will never be the owner of an
active region by Lemma 7.1. Otherwise, we must end the region of (i_r, j')
at column j, and add a new region of (i_s, j) starting at column $j + 1$. In
addition, we need to test (i_s, j) successively against the owners with larger
column indices in $ACTIVE$, to see which is better in their regions. If (i_s, j)
is better, the old region is no longer active, and (i_s, j) conquers the region.
We continue to test against other owners until (i_s, j) is worse (we have
found the end of its region). The algorithm can be outlined as follows.

>   **PROCEDURE** *sparse* 2D/0D
>   **for** $s \leftarrow 1$ **to** p **do**
>   **begin**
>   **for** *each j* *in* $ROW[s]$ **do**
>   **begin**
>   *find in* $ACTIVE$ *the point* (i_r, j') *whose re-*
>   *gion contains* (i_s, j);
> $$E[i_s, j] \leftarrow D[i_r, j'] + f(i_r, j', i_s, j);$$

> update $ACTIVE$ with (i_s, j);
>   end
>   end

For each point in S we perform a lookup operation and an amortized constant number of insertion and deletion operations on the list $ACTIVE$ for a total of $O(M)$ operations. The rest of the algorithm takes time $O(M)$. The total time of the algorithm is $O(M + T(M))$ where $T(M)$ is the time required to perform $O(M)$ insertion, deletion, and lookup operations on $ACTIVE$. If $ACTIVE$ is implemented as a balanced search tree, we obtain $T(M) = O(M \log n)$. Column indices in $ACTIVE$ are integers in $[0, n]$, but they can be relabeled to integers in $[0, \min(n, M)]$ in $O(n)$ time. Since $ACTIVE$ contains integers in $[0, \min(n, M)]$, it may be implemented by van Emde Boas's flat trees (P. van Emde Boas [1977]) to give $T(M) = O(M \log \log M)$. Even better, by using the fact that for each non-empty row the operations on $ACTIVE$ may be reorganized so that we perform all the lookups first, then all the deletions, and then all the insertions, we can use Johnson's version of flat trees (Johnson [1982]) to obtain $T(M) = O(M \log \log \min(M, n^2/M))$ as follows. When the numbers manipulated by the data structure are integers in $[1, n]$, Johnson's data structure supports insertion, deletion, and lookup operations in $O(\log \log D)$ time, where D is the length of the interval between the nearest integers in the structure below and above the integer that is being inserted, deleted, or looked up. With Johnson's data structure, $T(M)$ is obviously $O(M \log \log M)$. It remains to show that $T(M)$ is also bounded by $O(M \log \log(n^2/M))$.

Lemma 7.2. *A homogeneous sequence of $k \leq n$ operations (i.e., all insertions, all deletions, or all lookups) on Johnson's data structure requires $O(k \log \log(n/k))$ time.*

Let m_s for $1 \leq s \leq p$ be the number of points in row i_s. By Lemma 7.2, the total time spent on row i_s is $O(m_s \log \log(n/m_s))$. The overall time is $O(\sum_{s=1}^{p} m_s \log \log(n/m_s))$. Finally, using the concavity of the $\log \log$ function we obtain the claimed bound. Note that the time to compute recurrence (7.18) for the rectangle case is never worse than $O(n^2)$.

The triangle case We show how to compute recurrence (7.18) when f is a linear function in each of $UR(i', j')$ and $LR(i', j')$. Let f_u and f_l be the linear functions for points in $UR(i', j')$ and $LR(i', j')$, respectively.

Lemma 7.3. . *Let P be the intersection of $UR(p, q)$ and $UR(r, s)$, and (i, j) be a point in P. If $D[p, q] + f_u(p, q, i, j) < D[r, s] + f_u(r, s, i, j)$ (i.e., (p, q) is better than (r, s) at one point), then (p, q) is better than (r, s) at all points in P.*

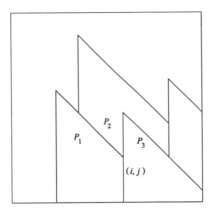

Fig. 7.6.   Regions in the matrix LI

Lemma 7.3 also holds for lower ranges. For each point in S, we divide its range into the upper range and the lower range, and we handle the two ranges separately. Recurrence (7.18) can be written as

$$E[i,j] = \min\{UI[i,j], LI[i,j]\}, \tag{7.20}$$

where

$$UI[i,j] = \min_{\substack{(i',j') \prec (i,j) \\ j'-i' \leq j-i}} \{D[i',j'] + f_u(i',j',i,j)\}, \tag{7.21}$$

and

$$LI[i,j] = \min_{\substack{(i',j') \prec (i,j) \\ j'-i' \geq j-i}} \{D[i',j'] + f_l(i',j',i,j)\}. \tag{7.22}$$

E is computed row by row. The computation of Recurrence (7.21) is as that of the rectangle case except that regions here are bounded by forward diagonals ($d = j - i$) instead of columns. Recurrence (7.22) is a little different since regions are bounded by columns and forward diagonals when we proceed by rows (see Fig. 7.6).

Let $i_1, i_2, \ldots, i_p$ ($p \leq M$) be the non-empty rows in the sparse set S. At step s, we compute LI for row i_s. Assume that we have active regions $P_1, \ldots, P_q$ in sorted order of their appearance on row i_s. We keep the owners of these regions in a doubly linked list $OWNER$. Since there are two types of boundaries, we maintain the boundaries of active regions by two lists $CBOUND$ (column boundaries) and $DBOUND$ (diagonal boundaries). Each boundary in $CBOUND$ and $DBOUND$ has a pointer to an element in $OWNER$. The search for the region containing a point (i_s, j) is carried out by finding the rightmost boundary to the left of (i_s, j) in each boundary list, and choosing among the two boundaries the one that is closer to (i_s, j). Suppose that (i_r, j') is the owner of the region that contains (i_s, j). Then $LI[i_s, j] = D[i_r, j'] + f_l(i_r, j', i_s, j)$. Again, $LR(i_r, j')$ includes $LR(i_s, j)$. If (i_r, j') is better than (i_s, j) at $(i_s + 1, j + 1)$, then (i_s, j) will never be the owner of an active region by Lemma 7.3. Otherwise, we insert (one or two) new regions into $OWNER$, and update $CBOUND$ and $DBOUND$.

One complication in recurrence (7.22) is the following. When we have a region bounded on the right by a column and on the left by a diagonal, we must remove it when the row on which these two boundaries meet is processed (P_2 in Fig. 7.6). If an active region ends at a point, we refer to that point as a *cut* point. We keep lists $cut[i]$, $1 \le i \le n$. $Cut[i]$ contains the cut points of row i. To finish step s, we process all cut points in rows $i_s+1, \ldots, i_{s+1}$. Assume we have processed cut points in rows $i_s+1, \ldots, i-1$. We show how to process $cut[i]$, $i \le i_{s+1}$. If $cut[i]$ is empty, we ignore it. Otherwise, we sort the points in $cut[i]$ by column indices, and process them one by one. Let (i, j) be a cut point in $cut[i]$. Three active regions meet at (i, j). Let P_1, P_2, and P_3 be the three regions from left to right (see Fig. 7.6), and (i_1, j_1) and (i_3, j_3) be the owners of P_1 and P_3, respectively. Note that $j = j_3$ and $j - i = j_1 - i_1$. P_2 is no longer active. If (i_1, j_1) is better than (i_3, j_3) at $(i + 1, j + 1)$, P_1 takes over the intersection of P_1 and P_3. Otherwise, P_3 takes it over.

Lemma 7.4. *The total number of cut points is at most $2M$.*

Proof: Notice that $2M$ boundaries are created in the matrix LI (two for each point in S). For each cut point, two boundaries meet and one of them is removed. Therefore, there can be at most $2M$ cut points. □

$CBOUND$ and $DBOUND$ are implemented by Johnson's data structure. To sort $cut[i]$, we also use Johnson's data structure. The total time is $O(n + M \log\log\min(M, n^2/M))$. So, recurrence (7.22) and recurrence (7.18) for the triangle case are solved in $O(n + M \log\log\min(M, n^2/M))$ time.

7.5.2   THE SPARSE 2D/2D PROBLEM

The sparse 2D/2D problem is also given by recurrence (7.18), where $f(i', j', i, j) = w(i' + j', i + j)$. Suppose that w is either convex or concave.

We need to solve the following subproblem, referred to as dynamic minimization: Let

$$E'[y] = \min_x \{D'[x] + w(x, y)\} \quad \text{for } 1 \le x, y \le 2n, \qquad (7.23)$$

where w is either convex or concave. The values of D' are initially set to $+\infty$. We can perform the following two operations:

(a) Compute the value of $E'[y]$ for some y.

(b) Decrease the value of $D'[x]$ for some x.

Note that operation (b) involving one value of $D'[x]$ may simultaneously change $E'[y]$ for many y's.

Recall that the row indices giving the minima for E' are nondecreasing when w is convex and nonincreasing when w is concave. A row x is *live* if it supplies the minimum for some $E'[y]$. We maintain live rows and their intervals in which rows give the minima using a data structure. Computing $E'[y]$ then reduces to looking up which interval contains y. Decreasing $D'[x]$ involves updating the interval structure: deleting some neighboring live rows and finally performing a binary search at each end. When we use a balanced search tree the amortized time per operation is $O(\log n)$. The bound can be improved to $O(\log \log n)$ with van Emde Boas's data structure for w satisfying the closest zero property.

The $2D/2D$ problem is solved by a divide-and-conquer recursion on the rows of the sparse set S. For each level of the recursion, having t points in the subproblem of that level, we choose a row r such that the numbers of points above r and below r are each at most $t/2$. Such a row always exist, and it can be found in $O(t)$ time. Thus we can partition the points into two sets: those above row r, and those on and below row r. Within each level of the recursion, we will need the points of each set to be sorted by their column indices. To achieve that we initially sort all points, and then at each level of the recursion perform a pass through the sorted list to divide it into the two sets. Thus the order we need will be achieved at a linear cost per level of the recursion. We compute all the minima as follows:

(1) recursively solve the problem above row r,
(2) compute the influence of the points above row r on the points on and below row r, and
(3) recursively solve the problem on and below row r.

Let S_1 be the set of points above row r, and S_2 be the set of points on and below row r. The influence of S_1 on S_2 is an instance of the dynamic minimization problem. points in S_1 and S_2 are processed in order of their column indices. Within a given column we first process the points of S_2, and then the points of S_1. By proceeding along the sorted lists of points in each set, we only spend time on columns that actually contain points. If we use this order, then when we process a point (i, j) in S_2, the points (i', j') of S_1 that have been processed are exactly those with $j' < j$. A point (i, j) in S_1 is processed by performing the operation of decreasing $D'[x]$ to $\min(D'[x], D[i, j])$, where $x = i + j$. A point (i, j) in S_2 is processed by performing the operation of computing $E'[y]$, $y = i + j$.

Since we consider only diagonals that contain points in S, the time per data structure operation is $O(\log M)$ or $O(\log \log M)$ rather than $O(\log n)$ or $O(\log \log n)$.

Thus the influence of S_1 on S_2 can be computed in $O(M \log M)$ or $O(M \log \log M)$ time depending on w. Multiplying by the number of levels of recursion, the total time is $O(n + M \log^2 M)$ in general or $O(n + M \log M \log \log M)$ for simple cost functions. Further improvements are possible by dividing E alternately by rows and columns at the center of the matrix rather than the center of the sparse set (in analogy with the coarse divide-and-conquer for the non-sparse version of the problem). With Johnson's data structure and a special implementation of the binary search, an $O(n + M \log M \log \min(M, n^2/M))$ bound can be obtained. For simple w's, it reduces to $O(n + M \log M \log \log \min(M, n^2/M))$.

We point out, without giving details, that the fine divide-and-conquer for the non-sparse $2D/2D$ problem can be extended to work for the sparse case. Its time complexity is $O(n + M \log \min\{M, n^2/M\})$ time for convex w, and $O(n + M \alpha(M) \log \min\{M, n^2/M\})$ time for concave w.

We also point out that the techniques outlined in this section, suitably combined with matrix searching, can be used to compute recurrence (7.20) in $O(n + M \alpha(M) \log M)$ or $O(n + M \log M)$ time when w is concave or convex, respectively.

7.6 Applications

We discuss some of the applications in which the algorithms presented so far have proved to be useful. The list is not meant to be exaustive since we will concentrate mainly on applications involving strings. Additional problems can be found in the bibliographic references.

7.6.1   SEQUENCE ALIGNMENT

We present dynamic programming recurrences that can be used to solve some sequence alignment problems arising in molecular biology. We also point out where the algorithmic techniques introduced in the preceding sections can be useful in obtaining fast algorithms for their computation.

Recall that sequence alignment seeks to compare two input strings, either to compute a distance between them (similarity) or to find some common sequence (not necessarily a substring) with which each input string shares structural characteristics. It is an important mathematical problem since it has applications in a wide variety of scientific disciplines. For instance, in molecular biology, two protein sequences are compared to identify common functional units. Similar application arise in geology and speech recognition. The problem is also relevant to computer science. Let the two input strings be $x = x[1, m]$ and $y = y[1, n]$.

Our main focus is on fast computation of sequence alignment rather than on establishing how meaningful a given alignment is. For this latter topic, so important for molecular biology, the reader can refer to the excellent book by Waterman [1988] quoted in the references.

We will skip all the discussion that relates to the computation of basic Levenshtein distances, i.e., recurrence (7.2) in problem $2D/0D$, since that topic is dealt with in other chapters. It suffices to mention here that the techniques of Section 7.5 are useful in that context.

We refer to the edit operations of substitution of one symbol for another (point mutations), deletion of a single symbol, and insertion of a single symbol as *basic operations*. Let a *gap* be a consecutive set of deleted symbols in one string or inserted symbols in the other string. With the basic set of operations, the cost of a gap is the sum of the costs of the individual insertions or deletions which compose it. Therefore, a gap is considered as a sequence of homogeneous elementary events (insertion or deletion) rather than as an elementary event itself. But, in molecular biology for instance, it is much more likely that a gap was generated by one single event (a mutation) that deleted all the symbols in the gap, rather than by many individual mutations combined to create the gap. Similar motivations apply to other applications of sequence alignment. Experimental results by Fitch and Smith [1983] indicate that the cost of a gap may depend on its endpoints (or location) and on its length. Therefore we would like to allow gap insertions or deletions to combine many individual symbol insertions or deletions, with the cost of a gap insertion or deletion being some function of the length of the gap. The cost $w(i, j)$ of a generic gap $x[i, j]$ that satisfies such experimental findings must be of the form

$$w(i,j) = f^1(x[i]) + f^2(x[j]) + g(j - i) \qquad (7.24)$$

where f^1 and f^2 are the costs of breaking the string at the endpoints of the gap and g is a function that increases with the gap length.

In molecular biology, the most likely choices for g are linear or concave functions of the gap lengths. With such a choice of g, the cost of a long gap is less than or equal to the sums of the costs of any partition of the gap into smaller gaps. That is, each gap is treated as a unit. Such constraint on g induces a constraint on the function w. Indeed, w must satisfy the following inequality:

$$w(i, j') + w(i', j) \leq w(i, j) + w(i', j') \text{ for all } i < i' \leq j < j', \qquad (7.25)$$

i.e., a restricted version of the concave Monge condition (7.5).

The gap sequence alignment problem can be solved by computing the following dynamic programming equation (w' is a cost function analogous to w):

$$D[i, j] = \min\{D[i - 1, j - 1] + sub(x[i], y[j]), E[i, j], F[i, j]\} \qquad (7.26)$$

where

$$E[i, j] = \min_{0 \le k \le j-1} \{D[i, k] + w(k, j)\}, \qquad (7.27)$$

$$F[i, j] = \min_{0 \le l \le i-1} \{D[l, j] + w'(l, i)\}, \qquad (7.28)$$

with initial conditions $D[i, 0] = w'(0, i)$, $1 \le i \le m$ and $D[0, j] = w(0, j)$, $1 \le j \le n$.

We observe that the computation of recurrence (7.26) consists of $n + m$ interleaved subproblems that have the following general form: Compute

$$E[j] = \min_{0 \le k \le j-1} \{D[k] + w(k, j)\}, \ j = 1, \cdots, n, \qquad (7.29)$$

$D[0]$ is given and for every $k = 1, \cdots, n$, $D[k]$ is easily computed from $E[k]$. That is, $n + m$ instances of the $1D/1D$ problem of Section 7.3.

For general cost functions, (7.26) can be computed in $O(n^2 m)$ time since each $1D/1D$ problem of size s can be solved in $O(s^2)$ time. Assume now that w is either concave or convex. If we compute each instance of the $1D/1D$ subproblem by using the algorithm of Section 7.3.1 corresponding to the convexity of w, then (7.26) can be computed in $O(nm \times \log n)$ time. It can be reduced to $O(nm)$ if w satisfies the closest zero property. In many applications, w satisfies such additional condition; in particular, for the important special case in which w is linear, i.e, w is both concave and convex. If we compute each instance of the $1D/1D$ subproblem by using the algorithms of Section 7.3.2, then (7.26) can be computed in $O(nm)$ or $O(nm\alpha(n))$ time when w is convex or concave, respectively.

An important family of sequence alignment methods for molecular biology applications is based on fragment sequence alignment. The main goal of such methods is to achieve faster computation times giving up some accuracy in the alignment of the two strings. We describe the basic version of such methods. We start by selecting a small number of *fragments*, where each fragment is a triple (i, j, k), k fixed, such that the k-tuple of symbols at positions i and j of the two strings exactly match each other. That is, $x[i, i + k - 1] = y[j, j + k - 1]$. For instance, our set of fragments can be all pairs of matching substrings of length k of the input strings. Such set of fragments can be computed in $O((n + m) \log |\Sigma| + M)$ time, where M denotes the number of such occurrences, by using standard string matching techniques. Then, we can compute an optimal alignment of x and y using only the set of fragments.

For a formal statement of this approach to sequence alignment, we need some definitions. An occurrence of a fragment (i', j', k') is said to be *below* an occurrence of (i, j, k) if $i + k \le i'$ and $j + k \le j'$; i.e., the substrings in fragment (i', j', k') appear strictly after those of (i, j, k) in the input strings. Equivalently, we say that (i, j, k) is *above* (i', j', k'). The *length* of fragment

(i, j, k) is the number k. The *diagonal* of a fragment (i, j, k) is the number $j - i$. An alignment of fragments is defined to be a sequence of fragments such that, if (i, j, k) and (i', j', k') are adjacent fragments in the sequence, either (i', j', k') is below (i, j, k) on a different diagonal (a gap), or the two fragments are on the same diagonal with $i' > i$ (a mismatch). The cost of an alignment is taken to be the sum of the costs of the gaps, minus the number of matched symbols in the fragments. The number of matched symbols may not necessarily be the sum of the fragment lengths, because two mismatched fragments may overlap. Nevertheless, it is easily computed as the sum of fragment lengths minus the overlap lengths of mismatched fragment pairs. The cost of a gap is some function of the distance between diagonals $w(|(j - i) - (j' - i')|)$.

When the fragments are all of length 1, and are taken to be all pairs of matching symbols from the two strings, these definitions coincide with the usual definitions of sequence alignments. When the fragments are fewer, and with longer lengths, the fragment alignment will typically approximate fairly closely the usual sequence alignments, but the cost of computing such an alignment may be much less.

The following recurrence can be used to find an optimal alignment of x and y, given the set of fragments:

$$D[i, j, k] = -k + \min \begin{cases} \min_{(i-l, j-l, k')} D[i - l, j - l, k'] - \max(0, k' - l) \\ \min_{(i', j', k') \text{ above } (i, j, k)} D[i', j', k'] + \beta \end{cases}$$

$$(7.30)$$

where $\beta = w(|(j-i)-(j'-i')|)$. The naive dynamic programming algorithm for this computation takes time $O(M^2)$. If M is sufficiently small, this will be faster than many other sequence alignment techniques. In fact *fastp*, based on the naive computation of recurrence (7.30), is the fastest sequence alignment program available for many biological applications. Therefore, improvements of the algorithm on which *fastp* is based are of considerable practical interest.

We remark that the naive algorithm works for general cost functions w and does not take any advantage of the fact that w's used in practice satisfy linearity or convexity/concavity constraints. We point out that, by suitable transformations, the main part of the computation of recurrence (7.30) can be reduced to the computation of recurrence (7.20). Therefore, if w is linear and we use the techniques presented in Section 7.5.1, (7.30) can be computed in $O((n+m) \log |\Sigma| + M \log \log \min(M, nm/M))$ time (we are including also the time taken to find all pairs of matching substrings of lenght k in the two strings). If we use the techniques presented in Section 7.5.2, together with matrix searching, we can compute (7.30) in $O((n + m) \log |\Sigma| + M \log M \alpha(M))$ or $O((n + m) \log |\Sigma| + M \log M)$ time when w is concave or convex, respectively.

7.6.2 RNA SECONDARY STRUCTURE

We consider some dynamic programming recurrences that can be used to compute the RNA secondary structure. The presentation provided here is very limited in scope, since our main concern is to show how the techniques presented in the previous sections may be of help in this application area. References to a much broader treatment of this topic are given at the end of the chapter. We first discuss an elementary model for the RNA secondary structure. Then, we consider the important special case of the computation of the RNA secondary structure with no multiple loops. Finally, we discuss the impact of sparsity on such computation.

An RNA (ribonucleic acid) is made up of ribonuclosides linked together in a chain by covalent bonds. Each nucleoside comprises one of four different bases. These bases are adenine (A), cytosine (B), guanine (C) or uracil (U). The nucleosides are linked one to the other by a phosphate backbone and are called nucleotides once the phosphate groups are attached. An RNA molecule is uniquely determined by a sequence of bases along the chain. Thus, it can be represented as a string over an alphabet of four symbols, corresponding to the four possible nucleic acid bases. This string or sequence information is known as the *primary structure* of the RNA. Such structure can be determined by gene sequencing experiments. Throughout this chapter, we denote an RNA molecule by a string $y = y[1, n]$ and we refer to its i-th base by $y[i]$.

The linear structure of RNA just described gives a very incomplete picture of the molecule. In the cell, or in vitro, the molecule is folded up in a complicated way like a ball of string. It is this three-dimensional or *ternary structure* which determines the activity of the molecule. The study of this structure is very important, since it controls enzymatic activity of RNA molecules as well as the splicing operations that take place between the time RNA is copied from the parent DNA molecule and the time that it is used as a blueprint for the construction of proteins. Unfortunately, a precise determination of the ternary structure is only possible using very expensive X-ray diffraction methods on cristallized RNA. Further, the only known computational techniques for determining tertiary structure from primary structure involve simulations of molecular dynamics, which require enormous amounts of computing power and therefore can only be applied to very short RNA sequences.

Because of the difficulty in determining the tertiary structures, some biologists have resorted to a simpler model for the study of RNA: The secondary structure, which we now define. In an actual RNA molecule, hydrogen bonding will cause further linkages to form between pairs of bases. Adenine typically pairs with uracil, and cytosine with guanine. Other pairings, in particular between guanine and uracil, may form, but they are much more rare. Each base in the RNA sequence will pair with at most one other base. Paired bases may come from positions of the RNA molecule that are far apart in the primary structure. The set of linkages between bases for a given RNA molecule is known as its *secondary structure*.

Determination of secondary structure also has its own applications: by comparing the secondary structures of two molecules with similar function one can determine how the function depends on the structure. On the other hand, a known or suspected similarity in the secondary structures of two sequences can lead to more accurate computation of the structures themselves, of possible alignments between the sequences, and also of alignments between the structures of the sequences.

We now describe an elementary mathematical model for the secondary structure. A *base pair* is a pair of positions (i, j) where the bases at the positions are adenine and uracil, cytosine and guanine, or possibly guanine and uracil. We write the bases in order by their positions in the RNA sequence; i.e., if (i, j) is a possible base pair, then $i < j$. Each pair has a binding energy determined by the bases making up the pair.

The secondary structure of y can be thought of as a collection S of base pairs minimizing a given cost function. S can be divided into substructures. $S_{i,j}$ is a substructure of S if $S_{i,j} \subset S$ and $S_{i,j}$ is a secondary structure of $y[i, j]$. There are a few types of basic (or elementary) structures from which larger structures can be built.

Let the *loop* of a base pair (i, j) be the set of bases in the sequence between i and j. This structural unit is a basic building block for the determination of secondary structure. In order to somewhat simplify the computation, it is assumed that no two loops cross. That is, if (i, j) and (i', j') are loops in the secondary structure, and some base k is contained in both of them, then either i' and j' are also contained in loop (i, j), or alternately i and j are both contained in loop (i', j'). This assumption is not entirely correct for all RNA, but it works well for the majority of RNA molecules.

A base at position k is *exposed* in loop (i, j) if k is in the loop, and k is not in any loop (i', j') with i' and j' also in loop (i, j). Because of the non-crossing assumption, each base can be exposed in at most one loop. We say that (i', j') is a *subloop* of (i, j) if both i' and j' are exposed in (i, j); if either i' or j' is exposed then by the non-crossing assumption both must be.

Thus, S can be represented as a forest of trees. Indeed, each root of the tree is a loop that is not a subloop of any other loop, and each interior node of the tree is a loop that has some other subloop within it. The possible types of loops are classified according to the subloop relation. A *hairpin* is a loop with no subloops i.e., a leaf in the loop forest. A *single loop* or *interior loop* is a loop with exactly one subloop. Any other loop is called a *multiple loop*.

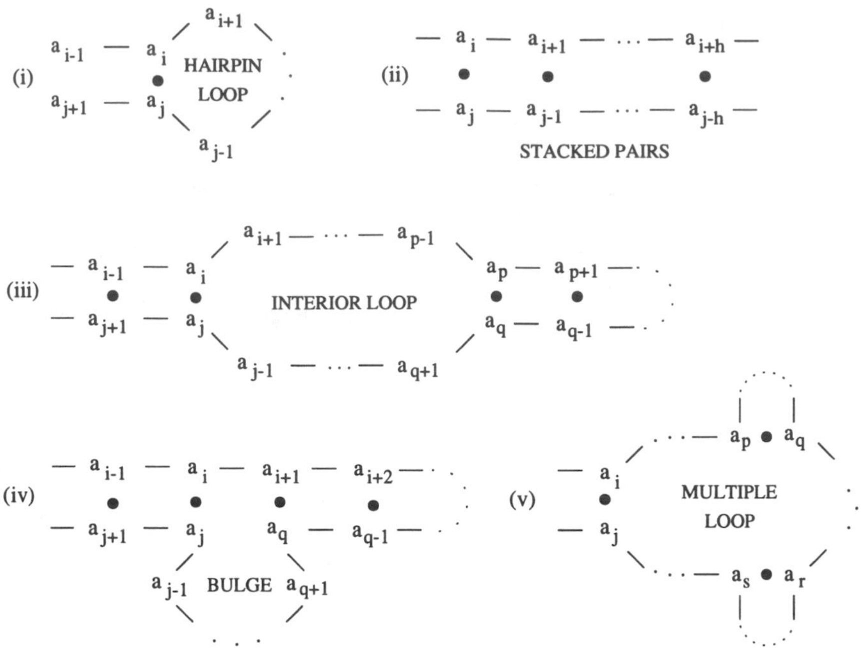

Fig. 7.7.   Building blocks for RNA secondary structure.

Other basic structural units are as follows. A base pair (i, j) such that the two adjacent bases $(i+1, j-1)$ are also paired is called a *stacked pair*. A single loop such that one base of the subloop is adjacent to a base of the outer loop is called a *bulge*. All these units are displayed in Fig. 7.7.

Each base pair in an RNA secondary structure has a binding energy which is a function of the bases in the pair. Also, each loop contributes some energy to the structure, we refer to it as *loop cost*, which is a function of the length of the loop. This length is simply the number of exposed bases in the loop. The loop cost depends on the type of the loop and it is actually different for each of them. Nevertheless, the loop costs in use today for hairpins, bulges and single loops are logarithm-like functions. Sometimes linear functions are also used for the mentioned cost loops.

The total energy of a structure is the sum of the base pair binding energies and loop costs. The optimal RNA secondary structure is then that structure minimizing the total energy.

The optimum secondary structure can be determined in $O(n^4)$ time by computing a three-dimensional dynamic programming recurrence recently discovered by Waterman and Smith [1986]. It is the first polynomial time algorithm obtained for this problem.

Before such an algorithm was found, researchers made further assumptions about the structure in order to obtain polynomial time algorithms.

But, since $O(n^4)$ can be quite large for typical lengths of RNA molecules, the algorithm of Waterman and Smith is mainly of theoretical interest. Many of the older algorithms are still appealing from the practical point of view. In particular, an important special case of RNA secondary structure computation is to obtain the best structure with no multiple loops. This problem appears as a subproblem in various methods for the determination of the RNA secondary structure. Moreover, it is of independent interest since single loop RNA structures could be used to construct a small number of pieces of a structure which could then be combined to find a structure having multiple loops (in this case one sacrifices optimality of the resulting multiple loop structure for efficiency of the structure computation). In what follows, we will consider only the computation of the best structure with no multiple loops. It can be obtained by computing:

$$D[i,j] = \min\{D[i-1,j-1] + b(i,j), H[i,j],$$
$$V[i,j], E[i,j]\} \tag{7.31}$$

where

$$V[i,j] = \min_{0<k<i}\{D[k,j-1] + w'(k,i)\}, \tag{7.32}$$

$$H[i,j] = \min_{0<l<j}\{D[i-1,l] + w'(l,j)\}, \tag{7.33}$$

$$E[i,j] = \min_{\substack{0<k<i-1 \\ 0<l<j-1}}\{D[k,l] + w(k+l,i+j)\}. \tag{7.34}$$

The function w is the energy cost of an internal loop between the two base pairs and w' is the cost of a bulge. Both w and w' typically combine terms for the loop length and for the binding energy of bases i and j. Experimental results show that both w and w' are concave function, i.e., they satisfy inequality (7.25) (and therefore the concave Monge conditions). However, for efficiency reasons, they are sometime approximated by linear functions. The function $b(i,j)$ contains only the base pair binding energy term, and corresponds to the energy gain of a stacked pair.

Notice that recurrence (7.31) is composed of one instance of the $2D/0D$ recurrence (7.2), $2n$ instances of the $1D/1D$ recurrence (7.1) and one instance of the $2D/2D$ recurrence (7.3). For general w and w', its computation seems to require $O(n^4)$ time, the most time consuming part of it being the computation of (7.34). However, it is not hard to find an algorithm that computes (7.31) in $O(n^3)$ time (see Section 7.4). For linear w and w', it is straightforward to obtain an $O(n^2)$ time algorithm computing it.

For concave or convex functions (we consider the convex case only for completeness, since it is not relevant from the practical point of view), recurrences (7.32) and (7.33) can be computed by any of the algorithms computing recurrence (7.1) (see Section 7.3). For concave functions, the best time for computing each of these latter recurrences is $O(n\alpha(n))$ for a total of $O(n^2\alpha(n))$ time. A similar reasoning yields a total of $O(n^2)$ time for convex functions. As for the computation of (7.34), we can use the techniques of Section 7.4 to compute it in $O(n^2\alpha(n))$ or in $O(n^2)$ time when the functions are concave or convex, respectively. These two time bounds are the best known for the computation of (7.31).

We next discuss how some physical constraints of the RNA secondary structure can be used to make (7.31) sparse. (Similar considerations apply to other recurrences for the computation of RNA secondary structure that are not discussed here.) Then, we discuss which algorithmic techniques can be used to efficiently compute the corresponding recurrence.

In recurrence (7.31), the entries in the associated dynamic programming matrix include a term for the binding energy of the corresponding base pair. If the given pair of positions do not form a base pair, this term is undefined, and the value of the cell in the matrix must be taken to be $+\infty$ so that the minimum energies computed for the other cells of the matrix do not depend on that value, and so that in turn no computed secondary structure includes a forbidden base pair.

Further, for the energy functions that are typically used, the energy cost of a loop will be more than the energy benefit of a base pair, so base pairs will not have sufficiently negative energy to form unless they are stacked without gaps at a height of three or more. Thus we could ignore base pairs that cannot be so stacked, or equivalently assume that their binding energy is again $+\infty$, without changing the optimum secondary structure. This observation is similar to that of sparse sequence alignment, in which we only include pairs of matching symbols when they are part of a longer substring match.

The effect of such constraints on the computation of the secondary structure for RNA is twofold. First, they contribute to make the output of the algorithms using them more realistic from the biological point of view. Second, they combine to greatly reduce the number of possible pairs, which we denote by M, that must be considered to a value much less than the upper bound of n^2. For instance, if we required base pairs to form even higher stacks, M would be further reduced. The computation and minimization in this case is taken only over positions (i, j) which can combine to form a base pair. Let S be the set of such positions. We point out that it can be computed in $O(M + n \log |\Sigma|)$ time using standard string matching techniques. We now show how to compute recurrence (7.31) only for points in S, while taking advantage of concavity or convexity assumptions for the cost functions.

We must compute each recurrence (7.32) for each $(i, j) \in S$ taking into account only pairs $(k, j - 1) \in S$ that precede (i, j). (A similar reasoning, which we omit, holds for recurrences (7.33).) Thus, each such recurrence depends only on the points of S in column $j - 1$. Let c_{j-1} be the number of such points. If w is linear, it is straightforward to compute each such recurrence in $O(c_{j-1})$ time for a total of $O(M)$ time. If w is concave or convex (again, we consider convex functions for completeness), we can compute each of them by a simple modification of any of the algorithms computing recurrence (7.1) (see Section 7.3). For concave functions, the best time for computing each of these latter recurrences is $O(c_{j-1}\alpha(M))$ for a total of $O(M\alpha(M))$ time. A similar reasoning yields a total of $O(M)$ time for convex functions.

As for recurrence (7.34), it must be computed for pairs $(i,j) \in S$ taking into account only pairs $(k,l) \in S$ that precede $(i-1, j-1)$. Thus, it is an instance of recurrence (7.18). If w is a linear function, we can use the techniques of Section 7.5.1 to compute it in $O(M \log \log \min(M, n^2/M))$ time. If w is concave or convex, we can use the techniques of Section 7.5.2 to compute it in $O(M\alpha(M) \log \min(M, n^2/M))$ or $O(M \log \min(M, n^2/M))$ time, respectively. Adding $O(n \log |\Sigma|)$ (the time for the determination of S) to each of those time bounds, we obtain the time bound for the computation of (7.31) when w is linear, concave or convex, respectively.

7.7   Exercises

1. Consider recurrence (7.1) of problem $1D/1D$ and let $B[i,j] = D[i] + w(i,j)$. Show that $B[i,j]$ is concave (resp., convex) Monge when w is concave (resp., convex) Monge.

2*. Let A be an $m \times n$ matrix totally monotone with respect to row maxima (see Section 7.2.2). Design an algorithm that finds the row maxima of A in $O(n(1 + \log(m/n)))$ time when $m \geq n$. Show that the algorithm is optimal in the decision tree model of computation.

3. Work out the details of the algorithm for the convex case sketched in Section 7.3.1.

4. Work out the details of the algorithm for the convex case sketched in Section 7.3.2.

5. Show that the off-line algorithms given in Section 7.4.2 for the computation of recurrence (7.3) can be modified to work on-line with no penalty in time performance.

6. Design an algorithm that implements each operation of the dynamic minimazation problem of Section 7.5.2 in amortized $O(\log n)$ time or $O(\log \log n)$ time when w is simple.

7. Show that the algorithms given in Section 7.4.2 can be modified to work for the computation of recurrence (7.18).

8*. Assume that w is concave. Design an algorithm that computes recurrence (7.20) in time $O(n + M\alpha(M) \log M)$.

9**. Can the $O(nm\alpha(n))$ bound of the convex sequence alignment problem be improved? Can a practical algorithm achieve this goal?

10**. Can the space for convex or concave sequence alignment be reduced, similarly to Hirschberg's reduction for linear sequence alignment? The current algorithms require space $O(nm)$, even using Hirschberg's technique, and so new methods would be needed.

11**. Can the bounds for fragment alignment algorithms be reduced? In particular can we achieve the optimal time bounds of $O(M + n)$ for linear and/or convex (concave) cost functions?

12**. Can the space of the algorithms for the computation of single loop RNA structure be reduced below the current $O(n^2)$ bound? Can the space for efficient computation of multiple loop RNA structure with general (or convex or concave) cost functions be reduced below $O(n^3)$?

13**. Is dynamic programming strictly necessary to solve sequence alignment problems? Notice that algorithms based on dynamic programming will take at least $O(mn)$ time in aligning two sequences of length m and n.

7.8   Bibliographic Notes

Dynamic programming and the principle of optimality are due to Bellman [1957], who applied such technique to the analysis of many optimization problems. Part of that work is joint with Dreyfus [1962]. The book by Denardo [1982] provides an excellent reference to additional applications of dynamic programming. Features (1) and (3) of dynamic programming recurrences were observed in Aho et al. [1974], and feature (2) can be found in the literature as dependency graphs (see for instance Bird [1980] and Ukkonen [1985]).

Monge conditions were introduced by Monge [1781], and revived by Hoffman [1961] in connection with a transportation problem. They were rediscovered by F.F. Yao [1980], who used them to speed-up many dynamic programming algorithms with applications to computer science and computational geometry. Bellman [1957] also observed that some dynamic programming problems can be efficiently solved when they satisfy convexity or concavity constraints.

Total monotonicity of matrices, as given by (7.8), was introduced by Aggarwal et al. [1987]   in connection with some problems in computational geometry. The matrix searching algorithm of Section 7.2.2 is also due to them. The notion of staircase totally monotone matrices is due to Aggarwal and Klawe [1990] who applied it to geometric algorithms. The first connection between total monotonicity and dynamic programming is due to Wilber [1988], who cleverly used it to obtain a linear time algorithm for the least weight subsequence problem, improving an earlier algorithm by Hirschberg and Larmore [1987]. Total monotonicity in higher dimensional matrices has been studied by Aggarwal and Park [1988].

Recurrence (7.1) is a generalization of many important subproblems in dynamic programming, all of which satisfy convexity or concavity assumptions. The algorithms of Section 7.3.1 as well as the formulation of the recurrence in the general form given by (7.1) is due to Galil and Giancarlo [1989] (a slightly different algorithm for the concave case, with a more complicated proof of correctness, is due to Miller and Myers [1988]). Generalizing on earlier work by Wilber, Eppstein [1990] obtained the first linear time algorithm for the computation of (7.1) for convex cost functions. He also provided algorithms for mixed concave-convex cost functions. Galil and K. Park [1990] obtained a simpler algorithm (given in Section 7.3.2) that retains the same time bound as the one of Eppstein. Another simple algorithm for the same problem is provided by Klawe [1989]. As for the case of convex cost functions, the best known algorithm (when the cost function does not satisfy the closest zero property) is due to Klawe and Kleitman [1990] and has been presented in Section 7.3.2. In Section 7.6.1 we have discussed sequence alignment with gaps. Its dynamic programming formulation, i.e., recurrence (7.26), was obtained by Waterman et al. [1976]. Later on, Waterman [1984] proposed the use of concave cost functions for that kind of alignment. Moreover, Waterman and Smith [1978] also observed that (a special case of) recurrence (7.1) is useful in the computation of the RNA secondary structure with no multiple loops. We notice that it also appears in recurrences used for the determination of less restricted versions of RNA secondary structure (see for instance Zuker and Stiegler [1981]). Additional problems where instances, or variations, of recurrence (7.1) are used are the following (we provide both references to a description of the problems and to the best algorithms available for them): paragraph formation (Knuth and Plass [1981], Wilber [1988]), economic lot sizing (Denardo [1982], Aggarwal and Park [1990], Federgruen and Tzur [1990]), job shop scheduling (Coffman et al. [1989]).

Recurrence (7.3) is mainly used for the computation of interior loops in RNA folding. It has been obtained by Waterman and Smith [1978]. The same authors [1986] showed that it can be computed in $O(n^3)$ time without any assumptions on the cost function. Later on, Eppstein, Galil and Giancarlo [1988] showed how to compute it in $O(n^2 \log^2 n)$ using convexity or concavity assumptions (usually met in practice) on the weight function. Under the same assumptions, that method was first improved by Aggarwal and J. Park [1988] (the algorithm of Section 7.4.1) and then by Larmore and Schieber [1991] (the algorithm of Section 7.4.2).

The effects of sparsity on the computation of the recurrences in Section 7.5 has been studied, in a unifying framework, by Eppstein et al. [1992a, 1992b] and the material presented in Section 7.5 covers some of that. Earlier results, mostly confined to deal with sparsity in recurrence (7.2) (longest common subsequence) are due to Hirschberg [1977] and Hunt and Szymanski [1977]. Larmore and Schieber [1991] have improved one of the algorithms of Eppstein et al. [1992b] (see Section 7.5.2). The fragment sequence alignment paradigm described in Section 7.6.1 has been studied by Wilbur and Lipman [1983, 1984] . The *fastp* program (D.J. Lipman and W.L. Pearson [1985]), one of the most widely used programs for protein sequence alignment, is based on that paradigm. The description of the RNA secondary structure given in Section 7.6.2 has been abstracted from Sankoff et al. [1983] .

Bibliography

AGGARWAL, A., M.M. KLAWE, S. MORAN, P. SHOR, AND R. WILBER [1987]. "Geometric Applications of a Matrix-Searching Algorithm," *Algorithmica* **2**, 209–233.

AGGARWAL, A., AND J. PARK [1988]. "Searching in Multidimensional Monotone Matrices," *Proc. 29th IEEE Symp. on Foundations of Computer Science*, 497–512.

AGGARWAL, A., AND M.M. KLAWE [1990]. "Applications of Generalized Matrix Searching to Geometric Algorithms," *Discr. Appl. Math.* **27**, 3-24.

AHO, A.V., J. E. HOPCROFT AND J. D. ULLMAN [1974]. *The Design and Analysis of Computer Algorithms,* Addison-Wesley, Reading, Mass.

BELLMAN, R.E. [1957]. *Dynamic Programming,* Princeton University Press, Princeton, N.J.

BELLMAN, R.E., AND S.E. DREYFUS [1962]. *Applied Dynamic Programming,* Princeton University Press, Princeton, N.J.

BIRD, R. [1980]. "Tabulation techniques for recursive programs," *ACM Computing Surveys* **12**, 403-417.

COFFMAN, E.G., A. NOZARI AND M. YANNAKAKIS [1989]. "Optimal scheduling of products with two subassemblies on a single machine," *Operation Research* **37**, 426-436.

DENARDO, E.V. [1982]. *Dynamic Programming: Models and applications,* Prentice-Hall, N.J.

VAN EMDE BOAS, P. [1977]. "Preserving order in a forest in less than logarithmic time," *Info. Processing Letters* **6**, 80-82.

EPPSTEIN, D., Z. GALIL, AND R. GIANCARLO [1988]. "Speeding Up Dynamic Programming," *Proc. 29th IEEE Symp. on Foundations of Computer Science*, 488–496.

EPPSTEIN, D. [1990]. "Sequence Comparison with Mixed Convex and Concave Costs," *Jour. Algorithms* **11**, 85-101.

EPPSTEIN, D., Z. GALIL, R. GIANCARLO, AND G.F. ITALIANO [1992a]. "Sparse Dynamic Programming I: Linear Cost Functions," *Jour. ACM* **39**, 546-567.

EPPSTEIN, D., Z. GALIL, R. GIANCARLO, AND G.F. ITALIANO [1992b]. " Sparse Dynamic Programming II: Convex and Concave Cost Functions," *Jour. ACM* **39**, 568-599.

FEDERGRUEN, A, AND M. TZUR [1990]. "The dynamic lot sizing model with backlogging: A simple $O(n \log n)$ algorithm," Columbia University, Graduate School of Business, New York.

FITCH, W.M., AND T. F. SMITH [1983]. "Optimal Sequence Alignment," *Proc. Nat. Acad. Sci., U.S.A.*, **80**, 1382-1385.

GALIL, Z., AND R. GIANCARLO [1989]. "Speeding Up Dynamic Programming with Applications to Molecular Biology," *Theoretical Computer Science* **64**, 107-118.

GALIL, Z., AND K. PARK [1990]. "A linear-time algorithm for concave one-dimensional dynamic programming," *Info. Processing Letters* **33**, 309-311.

HIRSCHBERG, D.S. [1977]. "Algorithms for the Longest Common Subsequence Problem," *Jour. ACM* **24**, 664-675.

HIRSCHBERG, D.S., AND L.L. LARMORE [1987], "The Least Weight Subsequence Problem," *SIAM Jour. Computing* **16**, 628-638.

HUNT, J.W, AND T.G. SZYMANSKI [1977]. "A Fast Algorithm for Computing Longest Common Subsequences," *Commun. ACM* **20**, 350-353.

JOHNSON, D. B. [1982]. "A priority queue in which initialization and queue operations take $O(\log \log D)$ time," *Math. Systems Theory* **15**, 295-309.

KLAWE, M.M. [1989]. "A simple linear-time algorithm for concave one-dimensional dynamic programming," Dept. of Computer Science, University of British Columbia, Vancouver, CANADA.

KLAWE, M.M., AND D. KLEITMAN [1990]. "An Almost Linear Algorithm for Generalized Matrix Searching," *SIAM Jour. Descrete Math.* **3**, 81-97.

KNUTH, D.E., AND M.F. PLASS [1981]. "Breaking Paragraphs into Lines," *Software Practice and Experience* **11**, 1119-1184.

LARMORE, L.L., AND B. SCHIEBER [1991]. "On-line Dynamic Programming with the Prediction of the RNA Secondary Structure," *Jour. Algorithms* **12**, 490-515.

LIPMAN, D.J., AND W.L. PEARSON [1985]. "Rapid and Sensitive Protein Similarity Searches," *Science* **2**, 1435-1441.

HOFFMAN, A.J. [1961]. "On Simple Linear Programming Problems," *Convexity, AMS Proc. Symp. Pure Math.* **7**, 317-327.

MILLER, W., AND E.W. MYERS [1988]. "Sequence Comparison with Concave Weighting Functions" *Bull. Math. Biol.* **50**, 97-120.

MONGE, G. [1781]. *Déblai et Remblai,* Mémoires de l'Académie des Sciences, Paris.

SANKOFF, D., J.B. KRUSKAL, S. MAINVILLE, AND R.J. CEDERGREN [1983]. "Fast Algorithms to Determine RNA Secondary Structures Containing Multiple Loops," in Sankoff and Kruskal [1983], pp. 93-

120.

SANKOFF, D, AND J.B. KRUSKAL (EDS.) [1983]. *Time Warps, String Edits, and Macromolecules: The Theory and Practice of Sequence Comparison*, Addison-Wesley, Reading, Mass.

UKKONEN, E. [1985]. "Finding Approximate Patterns in Strings," *Jour. Algorithms,* **6**, 132-137.

YAO, F.F. [1980]. "Efficient Dynamic Programming Using Quadrangle Inequalities," *Proc. 12th ACM Symp. on Theory of Computing,* 429–435.

WATERMAN, M.S., T.F. SMITH, AND W.A. BEYER [1976]. "Some Biological Sequence Metrics," *Adv. Math.* **20**, 367-387.

WATERMAN, M.S., AND T.F. SMITH [1978]. "RNA Secondary Structure: A Complete Mathematical Analysis," *Math. Biosciences* **42**, 257-266.

WATERMAN, M.S., [1984]. "Efficient Sequence Alignment Algorithms" *Jour. Theor. Biol.* **108**, 333-336.

WATERMAN, M.S. (ED.) [1988]. *Mathematical Methods for DNA Sequences,* CRC Press, Los Angeles, Ca.

WATERMAN, M.S., AND T.F. SMITH [1986]. "Rapid Dynamic Programming Algorithms for RNA Secondary Structure," *Adv. Appl.Math.* **7**, 455–464.

WILBER, R.E. [1988]. "The Concave Least Weight Subsequence Problem Revisited," *Jour. Algorithms* **9**, 418-425.

WILBUR, W.J., AND D.J. LIPMAN [1983]. "Rapid Similarity Searches of Nucleic Acid and Protein Data Banks" *Proc. Nat. Acad. Sci., U.S.A.,* **80**, 726-730.

WILBUR, W.J., AND D.J. LIPMAN [1984]. "The Context Dependent Comparison of Biological Sequences," *SIAM Jour. Applied Math.* **44**, 557-567.

ZUKER, M., AND P. STIEGLER [1981]. "Optimal Computer Folding of Large RNA Sequences using Thermodynamics and Auxiliary Information," *Nucleic Acids Res.* **9**, 133-138.

8
Shortest Common Superstrings

Given a finite set of strings $S = \{s_1, \ldots, s_m\}$, the *shortest common superstring* of S, is the shortest string s such that each s_i appears as a substring (a consecutive block) of s.

Example. Assume we want to find the shortest common superstring of all words in the sentence "alf ate half lethal alpha alfalfa." Our set of strings is $S = \{$ alf, ate, half, lethal, alpha, alfalfa $\}$. A trivial superstring of S is "alfatehalflethalalphaalfalfa", of length 28. A shortest common superstring is "lethalphalfalfate", of length 17, saving 11 characters.

The above example shows an application of the shortest common superstring problem in data compression. In many programming languages, a character string may be represented by a pointer to that string. The problem for the compiler is to arrange strings so that they may be "overlapped" as much as possible in order to save space. For more data compression related issues, see next chapter.

Other than compressing a sentence about Alf, the shortest common superstring problem has more important applications in DNA sequencing. A DNA sequence may be considered as a long character string over the alphabet of nucleotides $\{A, C, G, T\}$. Such a character string ranges from a few thousand symbols long for a simple virus, to 2×10^8 symbols for a fly and 3×10^9 symbols for a human being. Determining this string for different molecules, or *sequencing* the molecules, is a crucial step towards understanding the biological functions of the molecules. In fact, today, no problem in biochemistry can be studied in isolation from its genetic background. However, with current laboratory methods, such as Sanger's procedure, it is quite impossible to sequence a long molecule directly as a whole. Each time, a randomly chosen fragment of less than 500 base pairs can be sequenced. In general, biochemists "cut", using different restriction enzymes, millions of such (identical) molecules into pieces each typically containing about 200-500 nucleotides (characters). A biochemist "samples" the fragments and Sanger's procedure is applied to sequence the sampled fragment. From hundreds, sometimes millions, of these random fragments, a biochemist has to *assemble* the superstring representing the whole molecule. An algorithm that tries to find a shortest common superstring of a given set of strings (fragments) is routinely used by computers and human being. This algorithm, called Greedy, works as follows: Repeatedly merge a pair of strings with maximum overlap until only one string is left.

The algorithm Greedy, trivial though it may be, occupies a central place in our study. Clearly, Greedy does not always find the shortest superstring. In fact it can be two times off as the following example shows.

Example. Let $S = \{c(ab)^k, (ba)^k, (ab)^k c\}$. Greedy will merge $c(ab)^k$ and $(ab)^k c$ first, and thus output a string almost twice as long as the optimal one, $c(ab)^{k+1}c$.

A popular conjecture is that Greedy achieves linear approximation. More precisely, it is conjectured that the above type of examples is the worst case that can happen to Greedy, $i.e.$, Greedy achieves two times the optimal length. No non-trivial upper bounds on Greedy or, in fact, on any other algorithm for shortest superstring problem have been obtained until recently. We will proceed with our discussion in more or less the historical order. In Section 8.1, we study the related results in the 1980's. These early results lay down the ground work for the approximation solutions to be discussed in Sections 8.2 and 8.3. In Sections 8.2 and 8.3, we present various approximation algorithms and analysis of their performance, including a confirmation of the conjecture that Greedy achieves linear approximation. We prove a negative result on the approximation of shortest superstrings in Section 8.4: we show that the superstring problem is unlikely to have a polynomial-time approximation scheme. Then in Section 8.5, the superstring problem is generalized to also allow the presence of negative strings. Such more general version of the superstring problem arises naturally in practice and studying them may help us better analyze the performance of some approximation algorithms when there are no negative strings. We will present several algorithms and obtain approximation bounds under this more general setting. In Section 8.6, we study the shortest superstring problems from a new perspective: how to learn a string efficiently from randomly sampled substrings. The problem has immediate applications in DNA sequencing. Section 8.7 gives an approximation algorithm and a linear bound for the shortest superstring problem when we allow strings to be flipped in the superstring.

Before we start, we make a few assumptions. Set $S = \{s_1, \ldots, s_m\}$ will always denote our input set, over some fixed alphabet Σ. Without loss of generality, we can assume that S is *substring-free*, $i.e.$, no s_i is a substring of s_j for any $j \neq i$.

8.1   Early results: NP-hardness and some special cases

The study of shortest common superstring problem began in the early 1980's, motivated by its applications in data compression. People soon realized that the problem is hard, that is, NP-hard. As NP-hardness proofs were already a popular subject of study in the early 80's, such a proof comes naturally. Special cases were studied, and it was found that when strings are of length at most 2, there is a polynomial time algorithm. And when we allow strings to have length 3, we again are back to the NP-hardness. The approximation issue was raised in the very first paper on this topic. Although the solution has waited for 10 years to come, some interesting approximation bounds were obtained with respect to the so-called compression measure.

8.1.1   NP-HARDNESS

A reduction from the directed Hamiltonian path problem gives the following theorem.

Theorem 8.1. *Given* $S = \{s_1, \ldots, s_m\}$, *it is NP-hard to find a shortest superstring of* S.

Since later on in Section 8.4 we will prove a stronger result: finding a shortest superstring is MAX SNP-hard, we for the moment omit the proof of this theorem.

The problem remains NP-hard even if

- Each string in S is of length at most 3 with unbounded Σ; or
- $|\Sigma| = 2$. But in this case, some strings in S need to have length about $\Theta(\log \Sigma_{i=1}^{m} |s_i|)$.

8.1.2   A SPECIAL CASE: STRINGS OF LENGTH 2

When strings are allowed to have length 3, our problem is still NP-hard, with unbounded alphabet. Thus the follow theorem is the best we can do in polynomial time.

Theorem 8.2. *Let* $S = \{s_1, \ldots, s_m\}$. *If* $|s_i| \leq 2$ *for all* i, *then a shortest superstring of* S *can be found in polynomial time.*

Proof: We can assume that $|s_i| = 2$ for all i, since any single character is either contained in some other string or it has no overlap with any other string. We can also assume that no string is of the form aa, $a \in \Sigma$, since such strings can always be inserted later either in the place of a single a or at the end.

We now form a directed graph $G = (V, E)$ for the rest of the strings. $V = \Sigma$. For each string $ab \in S$, we add directed edge (a, b) to E. Finding the shortest superstring for S is equivalent to finding a path cover of G with a minimum number of paths. Such a minimal path cover can be easily found by the following strategy: Start from a node with outdegree greater than indegree, travel randomly, deleting each edge traversed, until a node with no outgoing edge. Add this path into the cover. Repeat this until no node has more outdegree, equivalently, indegree equals outdegree for all nodes. Thus we can start from any node, walk randomly, deleting edges along the way, and we must end at the starting node, hence a cycle. If this cycle shares a common node with any path in the cover, then we can open this cycle at this common node, and insert the cycle into the path at this common node properly. Otherwise, we just open the cycle at any node and add this path into the cover. We repeat this until E becomes empty. □

8.1.3 A DETOUR: COMPRESSION MEASURE

Let s be the shortest superstring of $S = \{s_1, \ldots, s_m\}$. Then $d = (\Sigma_{i=1}^{m}|s_i|) - |s|$ is the number of bits that s has saved. While it is hard to prove that Greedy non-trivially approximates s with respect to $|s|$, it turns out that it is easier to show that Greedy approximates s with respect to d, linearly.

Consider any step of Greedy. Assume it merges two strings x and y. Then the overlap of x and y is the maximum among the strings left. With this merge we could have prevented the possible merges on four ends of x and y. But each of such merge would have been shorter than that of x and y. Thus we at least achieves $1/4$ of the compression that could have been done by the optimal compression. Thus if the optimal compression is d bits, Greedy at least compresses $d/4$ bits. In fact, a factor of 2 can be proved, as stated in the following theorem.

Theorem 8.3. *Let s be the shortest superstring of $S = \{s_1, \ldots, s_m\}$. Greedy saves at least $d/2$ bits, where $d = (\Sigma_{i=1}^{m}|s_i|) - |s|$.*

8.2 An $O(n \log n)$ approximation algorithm

DNA sequencing and learning theory have added new interest to the shortest common superstring problem. The renewed interest resulted in solutions to the old open questions. The algorithm Greedy has apparently been used by biologists for a long time. This is after all the first algorithm one would think of. As we will discuss in Section 8.6, provably good approximations to the shortest superstrings imply efficient learning algorithms with few samplings.

The first algorithm achieving any non-trivial approximation bound is Group-Merge which produces a superstring of length $O(n \log n)$. Although linear approximation algorithms have been subsequently found, Group-Merge is still the best approximation when we allow negative strings to be present (to be discussed in Section 8.5). We describe the construction of Group-Merge in this section.

Let s be an optimal superstring of S with $|s| = n$. We order the strings in S by the left ends of their first appearances in s, reading from left to right. We list them according to above ordering: $s_1, ..., s_m$. In the following we identify s_i with its first appearance in s.

The idea behind our algorithm is to merge large groups. Each time, we try to determine two strings such that merging them properly would make many others become substrings of the newly merged string.

For two strings u and u', we use the word *merge* to mean that we put u and u' (and nothing else) together, possibly utilizing some overlaps that they have in common, to construct a superstring of the two. In general there may be more than one way to merge u and u'. There may be two optimal ways, and many other non-optimal ways. For example, if $u = 010$ and $u' = 00200$, we can merge them with u in front optimally as $m_1(u, u') = 0100200$ or with u' in front optimally as $m_2(u, u') = 0020010$; We can also merge them non-optimally as $m_3(u, u') = 01000200$ or $m_4(u, u') = 00200010$. For each way of merge m, we write $m(u, u')$ to denote the resulting superstring. There are at most $2 \min\{|u|, |u'|\}$ ways of merging u and u'. We now present our algorithm.

Algorithm Group-Merge

1. On input $S = \{s_1, ..., s_m\}$, let $T = \emptyset$.
2. Find $s_i, s_j \in S$ such that

$$cost(s_i, s_j) = \min_m \frac{|m(s_i, s_j)|}{weight(m(s_i, s_j))}$$

   is minimized where

$$weight(m(s_i, s_j)) = \sum_{a \in A} |a|,$$

   where A is the set of strings in S that are substrings of $m(s_i, s_j)$.
3. Merge s_i, s_j to $m(s_i, s_j)$ as defined in Step (2). Set $T = T \cup \{m(s_i, s_j)\}$ and $S = S - A$.
4. If $|S| > 0$ then go to (2).
5. Concatenate all strings in T as the final superstring.

Theorem 8.4. *Given a set of strings S, if the length of shortest superstring is n, then algorithm Group-Merge produces a superstring of length $O(n \log n)$.*

Proof: As discussed above, we can assume that in S no string is a substring of another and all strings are ordered by their first appearance in the shortest superstring. Let this order be $s_1, s_2, ..., s_m$. We separate S into groups: The first group G_1 contains $s_1, ..., s_i$ where i, $i \leq m$, is the largest index such that (the first appearances of) s_1 and s_i overlap in s; The second group contains $s_{i+1}, ..., s_j$ where j, $i+1 \leq j \leq m$, is the largest index such that s_j overlaps with s_{i+1} in s; And so on. In general if s_k is the

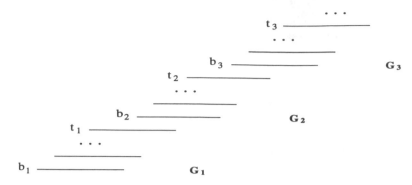

Fig. 8.1.   Grouping of strings.

last element in G_l, then G_{l+1} contains $s_{k+1}, ..., s_p$ where p, $k+1 \leq p \leq m$, is the largest index such that s_{k+1} overlaps with s_p in s. See Figure 8.1.

Assume that there are g groups: $G_1, ..., G_g$. For G_i let b_i and t_i be the first (bottom) and last (top) string in G_i, according to our ordering, respectively. That is, b_i and t_i sandwich the rest of strings in G_i and for some optimal m_i, every string in G_i is a substring of $m_i(b_i, t_i)$.

Lemma 8.5. $\Sigma_{i=1}^{g} |m_i(b_i, t_i)| \leq 2n$, where n is the length of shortest superstring s for S.

Proof: This can easily be seen geometrically: put all the groups $G_1, ..., G_g$ back to their original positions in the optimal arrangement (which gives the shortest superstring s). Then strings in G_i overlap with nothing except strings in G_{i-1} and G_{i+1} (and of course in G_i itself), for $i = 2, ..., g-1$. Thus counting the optimal solution for each G_i separately at most doubles the length of the optimal solution. $\square$

For a set of strings A, let $\|A\| = \sum_{a \in A} |a|$. Let G_i^r be the set of strings remaining in G_i before the rth iteration. Let S_r be the set of strings cancelled at rth iteration of Group-Merge. Let b_r, t_r be the first and last strings in S_r, according to our ordering, respectively. And let m_r be the merge function used in the rth iteration to combine b_r and t_r. Let there be a total of k iterations executed by Group-Merge.

Apparently, at rth iteration, we can properly merge the first and last string in G_j^r such that the result is a superstring of all strings in G_j^r and a substring of $m_j(b_j, t_j)$. Now the length L_j we used to merge strings in G_j can be measured as follows:

$$L_j \leq \sum_{r=1}^{k} \frac{|m_r(b_r, t_r)|}{\|S_r\|} \|G_j^r - G_j^{r+1}\|$$

$$\leq \sum_{r=1}^{k'} \frac{|m_j(b_j, t_j)|}{\|G_j^r\|} \|G_j^r - G_j^{r+1}\|$$

(where $k' \leq k$ indicates the first step $G_j^{k'+1}$ becomes empty)

$$= |m_j(b_j, t_j)| \sum_{r=1}^{k'} \frac{1}{\|G_j^r\|} \|G_j^r - G_j^{r+1}\|$$

$$\leq |m_j(b_j, t_j)| H(\|G_j\|)$$

(where $H(m) = \sum_{i=1}^{m} \frac{1}{i} = \Theta(\log m)$)

$$= |m_j(b_j, t_j)| \Theta(\log \|G_j\|).$$

Hence the total length we use to merge all $G_1, ..., G_g$ is, by Lemma 8.5,

$$\sum_{i=1}^{g} L_i \leq \Theta(\log l) \sum_{i=1}^{g} |m_i(b_i, t_i)|$$

$$\leq \Theta(\log l)2n = \Theta(\log l)n,$$

where $l = \max_i \|G_i\|$. But $O(\log n) = O(\log l)$ since n is only polynomially larger than the number of strings in any G_i and the length of longest string in any G_i. Therefore the algorithm will output a superstring of length at most $O(n \log n)$. □

Remark. Can Group-Merge do better than $O(n \log n)$? The answer is no. See Exercise 3.

8.3 Linear approximation algorithms

Greedy-style algorithms have proven to perform well with respect to the compression measure. For example, we have seen in Section 8.1 that algorithm Greedy can achieve at least half of the optimal compression. Many people suspect that greedy algorithms also work well with respect to the length measure. In fact, it has been conjectured that superstrings produced by Greedy have length at most $2n$. In this section, we first present two new greedy algorithms Mgreedy and Tgreedy, both are simple variants of Greedy, and show that they produce superstrings of length $4n$ and $3n$, respectively. Extending the analysis technique results in an upper bound $4n$ for Greedy, giving a partial affirmative answer to the conjecture.

8.3.1 SOME DEFINITIONS AND SIMPLE FACTS

For two strings s and t, not necessarily distinct, let v be the longest string such that $s = uv$ and $t = vw$ for some *non-empty* strings u and w. We call $|v|$ the (amount of) *overlap* between s and t, and denote it as $ov(s,t)$. Furthermore, u is called the *prefix* of s with respect to t, and is denoted $pref(s,t)$. Finally, we call $|pref(s,t)| = |u|$ the *distance* from s to t, and denote it as $d(s,t)$. The string $uvw = pref(s,t)t$ is obtained by maximally merging s to the left of t and is called the *merge* of s and t. For $s_i, s_j \in S$, we will abbreviate $pref(s_i, s_j)$ to simply $pref(i,j)$. As an example of *self-overlap*, we have for the string $s =$ alfalfa an overlap of $ov(s,s) = 4$. Also, $pref(s,s) =$ alf and $d(s,s) = 3$.

Two strings s and t are said to be *equivalent* if they are cyclic shifts of each other, *i.e.*, if there are strings u,v such that $s = uv$ and $t = vu$. An equivalence class $[s]$ has *periodicity* k $(k > 0)$, if s is invariant under a rotation by k characters (*i.e.*, $s = uv = vu$, where $|u| = k$). Obviously, $[s]$ has periodicity $|s|$. A moment's reflection shows that the minimum periodicity of $[s]$ must equal the number of distinct rotations of s. This is the size of the equivalence class and denoted by $card([s])$ It is furthermore easily proven that if $[s]$ has periodicities a and b, then it has periodicity $\gcd(a,b)$ as well. It follows that all periodicities are a multiple of the minimum one, in particular we have that $|s|$ is a multiple of $card([s])$. For any string s, call $card([s])$ the *period* of s, denoted $period(s)$.

Given a list of strings $s_{i_1}, s_{i_2}, \ldots, s_{i_r}$, we define the superstring $s = \langle s_{i_1}, \ldots, s_{i_r} \rangle$ to be the string $pref(i_1, i_2) \cdots pref(i_{r-1}, i_r)s_{i_r}$. That is, s is the shortest string such that $s_{i_1}, s_{i_2}, \ldots, s_{i_r}$ appear *in order* in that string. For a superstring of a substring-free set, this order is well-defined, since substrings cannot 'start' or 'end' at the same position, and if substring s_j starts before s_k, then s_j must also end before s_k. Define $first(s) = s_{i_1}$ and $last(s) = s_{i_r}$. Note that, if s and t are obtained by maximally merging strings in S, then $ov(s,t)$ in fact equals $ov(last(s), first(t))$, and as a result, the merge of s and t is $\langle first(s), \ldots, last(s), first(t), \ldots, last(t) \rangle$. Also note that there exists a permutation π on the set $\{1, \ldots, m\}$, such that $S_\pi = \langle s_{\pi(1)}, \ldots, s_{\pi(m)} \rangle$ is a shortest superstring for S and every shortest superstring for S equals S_π for some permutation π.

We will consider a traveling salesman problem (TSP) on a weighted directed complete graph G_S derived from S and show that one can achieve a factor of 4 approximation for TSP on that graph, yielding a factor of 4 approximation for the shortest superstring problem. Graph $G_S = (V, E, d)$ has m vertices $V = \{1, \ldots, m\}$, and m^2 edges $E = \{(i,j) : 1 \le i, j \le m\}$. Here we take as weight function the distance $d(,)$: edge (i,j) has weight $w(i,j) = d(s_i, s_j)$, to obtain the *distance graph*. We will call s_i the string *associated* with vertex i, and let $pref(i,j) = pref(s_i, s_j)$ be the string associated to edge (i,j). As an example, the distance graph for the set { ate, half, lethal, alpha, alfalfa } is given in Figure 8.2. All edges not shown have overlap 0.

For any weighted graph G, a *cycle cover* of G is a set of vertex-disjoint cycles, covering all vertices of G. The cycle cover is said to be *optimal* if it

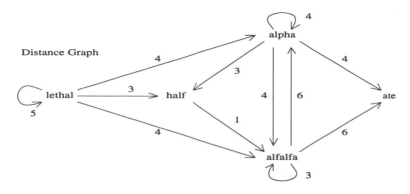

Fig. 8.2. A distance graph.

has the smallest weight. Let $TSP(G_S)$ and $CYC(G_S)$ denote the weight of an optimal Hamiltonian cycle and the weight of an optimal cycle cover of G_S, respectively. It is easy to see that

$$CYC(G_S) \leq TSP(G_S) \leq OPT(S)$$

Also observe that, although finding an optimal Hamiltonian cycle in a weighted graph is in general a hard problem, one can use the well-known Hungarian algorithm to find an optimal cycle cover in polynomial-time.

We now define some notation for dealing with (directed) cycles in G_S. If $c = i_0, \ldots, i_{r-1}, i_0$ is a cycle in G_S with r vertices, we define $strings(c)$ to be the equivalence class $[pref(i_0, i_1) \cdots pref(i_{r-1}, i_0)]$ and $strings(c, i_k)$ the rotation starting with i_k, *i.e.*, the string $pref(i_k, i_{k+1}) \cdots pref(i_{k-1}, i_k)$, where subscript arithmetic is modulo r. Denote the weight of a cycle c as $w(c)$. The following simple facts about cycles in G_S are easy to prove. Let $c = i_0, \cdots, i_{r-1}, i_0$ and c' be two cycles.

Claim 1. *Each string s_{i_j} in c is a substring of s^k for all $s \in strings(c)$ and sufficiently large k.*

Claim 2. *If each of $\{s_{j_1}, \ldots, s_{j_k}\}$ is a substring of s^k for sufficiently large k, then strings $s_{j_1}, \ldots, s_{j_k}$ are contained in a cycle of weight at most $|s|$.*

Claim 3. *The superstring $\langle s_{i_0}, \cdots, s_{i_{r-1}} \rangle$ is a substring of $strings(c, i_0)s_{i_0}$.*

Claim 4. *If $strings(c') = strings(c)$, then there exists a third cycle $\tilde{c}$ with weight $w(c)$ containing all vertices in c and all those in c'.*

Claim 5. *There exists a cycle $\tilde{c}$ of weight $card(strings(c))$ containing all vertices in c.*

8.3.2   A SIMPLE VARIANT OF GREEDY ACHIEVES $4N$

We present an algorithm Mgreedy which finds a superstring of length at most $4n$. The construction proceeds in two stages. We first show that an algorithm that finds an optimal cycle cover on the distance graph G_S, then opens each cycle into a single string, and finally concatenates all such strings together has a performance at most $4n$. We then show that in fact, for distance graphs, a greedy strategy can be used to find optimal cycle covers.

Consider the following algorithm for finding a superstring of the strings in S.

Algorithm Concat-Cycles

1. On input S, create graph G_S and find an optimal cycle cover $C = \{c_1, \ldots, c_p\}$ on G_S.
2. For each cycle $c_i = i_1, \cdots, i_r, i_1$, let $\tilde{s}_i = \langle s_{i_1}, \ldots, s_{i_r} \rangle$ be the string obtained by opening c_i, where i_1 is arbitrarily chosen. The string $\tilde{s}_i$ has length at most $w(c_i) + |s_{i_1}|$ by Claim 3.
3. Concatenate together the strings $\tilde{s}_i$ and produce the resulting string $\tilde{s}$ as output.

Theorem 8.6. *Algorithm Concat-Cycles produces a string of length at most* $4 \cdot OPT(S)$.

Before proving Theorem 8.6, we need a lemma giving an upper bound on the overlap between strings in different cycles of C.

Lemma 8.7. *Let c and c' be two cycles in C with $s \in c$ and $s' \in c'$. Then,* $ov(s, s') < w(c) + w(c')$.

Proof: Let $x = strings(c)$ and $x' = strings(c')$. Since C is an optimal cycle cover, we know by Claim 4 that $x \neq x'$. In addition, by Claim 5, $w(c) \leq card(x)$.

Suppose that s and s' overlap in a string u with $|u| \geq w(c) + w(c')$. Denoting the substring of u starting at the i-th symbol and ending at the j-th as $u_{i,j}$, we have by Claim 1, that $x = [u_{1,w(c)}]$ and $x' = [u_{1,w(c')}]$. From $x \neq x'$ we conclude that $w(c) \neq w(c')$; assume without loss of generality that $w(c) > w(c')$. Then

$$
\begin{aligned}
u_{1,w(c)} &= u_{1+w(c'),w(c)+w(c')} \\
&= u_{1+w(c'),w(c)} u_{w(c)+1,w(c)+w(c')} \\
&= u_{1+w(c'),w(c)} u_{1,w(c')}.
\end{aligned}
$$

This shows that $u_{1,w(c)}$ has periodicity $w(c') < w(c) \leq card(x)$, which contradicts the fact that $card(x)$ is the minimum periodicity. $\square$

Proof of Theorem 8.6. Since $C = \{c_1, \ldots, c_p\}$ is an optimal cycle cover, $CYC(G_S) = \sum_{i=1}^{p} w(c_i) \leq OPT(S)$. A second lower bound on $OPT(S)$ can be determined as follows: For each cycle c_i, let $w_i = w(c_i)$ and l_i denote the length of the longest string in c_i. By Lemma 8.7, if we consider the longest string in each cycle and merge them together optimally, the total amount of overlap will be at most $2 \sum_{i=1}^{p} w_i$. So the resulting string will have length at least $\sum_{i=1}^{p} l_i - 2w_i$. Thus $OPT(S) \geq \max(\sum_{i=1}^{p} w_i, \sum_{i=1}^{p} l_i - 2w_i)$.

The output string $\tilde{s}$ of algorithm Concat-Cycles has length at most $\sum_{i=1}^{p} l_i + w_i$ (Claim 3). So,

$$
\begin{aligned}
|\tilde{s}| &\leq \sum_{i=1}^{p} l_i + w_i \\
&= \sum_{i=1}^{p} l_i - 2w_i + \sum_{i=1}^{p} 3w_i \\
&\leq OPT(S) + 3 \cdot OPT(S) \\
&= 4 \cdot OPT(S).
\end{aligned}
$$

$\square$

We are now ready to present the algorithm Mgreedy, and show that it in fact mimics algorithm Concat-Cycles.

Algorithm Mgreedy

1. Let S be the input set of strings and T be empty.
2. While S is non-empty, do the following: Choose $s, t \in S$ (not necessarily distinct) such that $ov(s,t)$ is maximized, breaking ties arbitrarily. If $s \neq t$, remove s and t from S and replace them with the merged string $\langle s, t \rangle$. If $s = t$, just remove s from S and add it to T.
3. When S is empty, output the concatenation of the strings in T.

We can look at Mgreedy as choosing edges in the graph G_S: When Mgreedy chooses strings s and t as having the maximum overlap (where t may equal s), it chooses the edge $(last(s), first(t))$. Thus, Mgreedy constructs/joins paths, and closes them into cycles, to end up with a cycle cover M. We will call M the cycle cover created by Mgreedy. Now think of Mgreedy as taking a list of all the edges sorted by overlap (resolving ties in some definite way), and going down the list deciding for each edge whether to include it or not. Let us say that an edge e *dominates* another edge f if e precedes f in this list and shares its head or tail with f. Mgreedy includes an edge f if and only if it has not yet included a dominating edge. The following lemma gives a special property of strings and shows that Mgreedy in fact chooses the edges following a *Monge sequence*. (In a minimization problem, a listing of the edges of a graph is called a Monge sequence if it satisfies the following property: For any nodes u, v, s, t such that $u \neq s$ and $v \neq t$, if $w(u,v) + w(s,t) < w(u,t) + w(s,v)$, then either (u,v) or (s,t) precede (u,t) and (s,v).) In Figure 8.3, the vertical bars surround pieces of string that match, showing a possible overlap between s and v, giving an upper bound on $d(s,v)$.

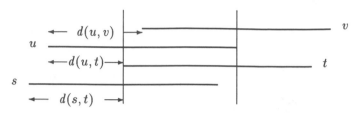

Fig. 8.3. Strings and overlaps

Lemma 8.8. *Let u, v, s, t be strings, not necessarily different, such that $ov(u, t) \geq \max\{ov(u, v), ov(s, t)\}$. Then,*

$$ov(u, t) + ov(s, v) \geq ov(u, v) + ov(s, t)$$

$$d(u, t) + d(s, v) \leq d(u, v) + d(s, t)$$

Theorem 8.9. *The cycle cover created by algorithm Mgreedy is optimal.*

Proof: Among the optimal cycle covers, let C be one that has the maximum number of edges in common with M. We shall show that $M = C$.

Suppose this is not the case, and let e be the edge of maximum overlap in the symmetric difference of M and C, with ties broken the same way as by Mgreedy. Suppose first that this edge is in $C - M$. Since Mgreedy did not include e, it must have included another edge f that dominates e. Edge f cannot be in C, therefore f is in $M - C$, contradicting our choice of the edge e. Suppose that $e = (k, j)$ is in $M - C$. The two C edges (i, j) and (k, l) that share head and tail with e are not in M, and thus are dominated by e. Replacing in C these two edges with $e = (k, j)$ and (i, l) would yield a cycle cover C' that has more edges in common with M and, by Lemma 8.8, has no more weight than C. This would contradict our choice of C. $\square$

Since algorithm Mgreedy finds an optimal cycle cover, the string it produces is no longer than the string produced by algorithm Concat-Cycles. (In fact, it could be shorter since it breaks each cycle in the optimum position.)

8.3.3 IMPROVING TO 3N

Note that in the last step of algorithm Mgreedy, we simply concatenate all the strings in set T without any compression. Intuitively, if we instead try to overlap the strings in T, we might be able to achieve a bound better than $4n$. Let Tgreedy denote the algorithm that operates in the same way as Mgreedy except that in the last step, it merges the strings in T by running Greedy on them. We can show that Tgreedy indeed achieves a better bound: it produces a superstring of length at most $3n$.

Theorem 8.10. *Algorithm Tgreedy produces a superstring of length at most $3n$.*

Proof: Let $S = \{s_1, \ldots, s_m\}$ be a set of strings and s be the superstring obtained by Tgreedy on S. We show that $|s| \leq 3n = 3OPT(S)$.

Let T be the set of all "self-overlapping" strings obtained by Mgreedy on S and M be the cycle cover created by Mgreedy. For each $x \in T$, let c_x denote the cycle in M corresponding to string x, and let $w_x = w(c_x)$ be its weight. Define $w = \sum_{x \in T} w_x$. Note, $w \leq n$. For each $x \in T$, let s_{i_x} be an arbitrary string in cycle c_x. Let $S' = \{s_{i_x} | x \in T\}$, $n' = OPT(S')$, $S'' = \{strings(c_x, i_x)s_{i_x} | x \in T\}$, and $n'' = OPT(S'')$.

By Claim 3, a superstring for S'' is also a superstring for T, so $n_T \leq n''$, where $n_T = OPT(T)$. For any permutation π on elements of T, we have $|S''_\pi| \leq |S'_\pi| + \sum_{x \in T} w_x$, so $n'' \leq n' + w$. Observe that $S' \subseteq S$ implies $n' \leq n$. Summing up, we get

$$n_T \leq n'' \leq n' + w \leq n + w.$$

By Lemma 8.7, the compression achieved in a shortest superstring of T is less than $2w$, i.e., $\|T\| - n_T < 2w$. By the results in Section 8.1, we know that the compression achieved by Greedy on set T is at least half the compression achieved in any superstring of T. That is,

$$\|T\| - |s| \geq (\|T\| - n_T)/2 = \|T\| - n_T - (\|T\| - n_T)/2 > \|T\| - n_T - w.$$

So, $|s| < n_T + w$. Combined with $n_T \leq n + w$, this gives $|s| < n + 2w \leq 3n$. $\square$

8.3.4 A $4N$ UPPER BOUND FOR GREEDY

One would expect that an analysis similar to that of Mgreedy would also work for the original algorithm Greedy. This turns out not to be the case. The analysis of Greedy is severely complicated by the fact that it continues processing the "self-overlapping" strings. Mgreedy was especially designed to avoid these complications, by separating such strings. With a more complicated analysis we can nevertheless show that

Theorem 8.11. *Greedy produces a superstring of length at most $4n$.*

Proof: Here we only sketch the basic idea behind the proof. If we want to relate the merges done by Greedy to an optimal cycle cover, we have to keep track of what happens when Greedy violates the maximum overlap principle, *i.e.*, when some self-overlap is better than the overlap in Greedy's merge. One thing to try is to charge Greedy some extra cost that reflects that an optimal cycle cover on the new set of strings (with Greedy's merge) may be somewhat longer than the optimal cycle cover on the former set (in which the self-overlapping string would form a cycle). If we could just bound these extra costs then we would have a bound for Greedy. Unfortunately, this approach fails because the self-overlapping string may be merged by Greedy into a larger string which itself becomes self-overlapping, and this nesting could go arbitrarily deep. Our proof concentrates on the inner-most self-overlapping strings only. These so called *culprits* form a linear order in the final superstring. We avoid the complications of higher level self-overlaps by splitting the analysis in two parts. In one part, we ignore all the original substrings that connect first to the right of a culprit. In the other part, we ignore all the original substrings that connect first to the left of a culprit. In each case, it becomes possible to bound the extra cost. This method yields a bound of $7n$. By combining the two analyses in a clever way, we can even eliminate the effect of the extra costs and obtain the same $4n$ bound that we found for Mgreedy. □

8.4   A polynomial-time approximation scheme is unlikely

In this section, we prove a negative result on the approximation of shortest superstrings; We show that the superstring problem is *MAX SNP-hard*, where MAX SNP is a class of optimization problems recently introduced by Papadimitriou and Yannakakis, including several variants of maximum satisfiability, the node cover and independent set problem in bounded-degree graphs, max cut, etc. This implies that if there is a polynomial-time approximation scheme for the superstring problem, then there is one also for every member of MAX SNP, which is considered rather unlikely. Note, it is known that every problem in MAX SNP can be approximated within *some* constant factor.

Let A, B be two optimization (maximization or minimization) problems. We say that A *L-reduces* (for *linearly reduces*) to B if there are two polynomial time algorithms f and g and constants α and $\beta > 0$ such that:

1. Given an instance a of A, algorithm f produces an instance b of B such that the cost of the optimum solution of b, $opt(b)$, is at most $\alpha \cdot opt(a)$, and

2. Given any solution y of b, algorithm g produces in polynomial time a solution x of a such that $|cost(x) - opt(a)| \leq \beta|cost(y) - opt(b)|$.

Here are some basic facts about L-reductions. First, the composition of two L-reductions is also an L-reduction. Second, if problem A L-reduces to problem B and B can be approximated in polynomial time with relative error ϵ (i.e., within a factor of $1 + \epsilon$ or $1 - \epsilon$ depending on whether B is a minimization or maximization problem) then A can be approximated with relative error $\alpha\beta\epsilon$. In particular, if B has a polynomial-time approximation scheme, then so does A. A problem is MAX SNP-hard if every problem in MAX SNP can be L-reduced to it.

Theorem 8.12. *Finding a shortest superstring is MAX SNP-hard.*

Proof: The reduction is from a special case of the TSP on directed graphs. Let TSP(1, 2) be the TSP restricted to instances where all the distances are either 1 or 2. We can consider an instance of this problem as being specified by a graph H; the edges of H are precisely those that have length 1 while the edges that are not in H have length 2. We need here the version of the TSP where we seek the shortest Hamiltonian path (instead of cycle), and, more importantly, we need the additional restriction that the graph H be of bounded degree (the precise bound is not important). It has been shown that this restricted version of TSP(1, 2) is MAX SNP-hard.

Let H be a graph of bounded degree D specifying an instance of TSP(1, 2). Our reduction is similar to the one used by Gallant, Maier, and Storer to show the NP-completeness of the superstring decision problem. We have to prove here that it is an L-reduction. For every vertex v of H we have two letters v and v'. In addition there is one more letter #. Corresponding to each vertex v we have a string $v\#v'$, called the *connector* for v. For each vertex v, enumerate the outgoing edges in an arbitrary cyclic order as $(v, w_0), \ldots, (v, w_{d-1})$ (*). Corresponding to the i-th outgoing edge (v, w_i) we have a string $p_i(v) = v'w_{i-1}v'w_i$, where subscript arithmetic is modulo d. We will say that these strings are *associated* with v.

Let n be the number of vertices and m the number of edges of H. If all vertices have degree at most D then $m \leq Dn$. Let k be the minimum number of edges whose addition to H suffices to form a Hamiltonian path. Thus, the optimal cost of the TSP instance is $n - 1 + k$. We shall argue that the length of the shortest common superstring is $2m + 3n + k$. It will follow then that the reduction is linear since m is linear in n.

Let S denote the set of all the strings obtained above. We first discuss how to map a superstring for S to a an ordering of the vertices of H and vice versa. Consider the distance graph G_S for S, and let G_2 be its subgraph with only edges of minimal weight (*i.e.*, 2). Clearly, G_2 has exactly one component for each vertex of H, which consists of a cycle of the associated p strings, and a connector that has an edge to each of these p strings. We need only consider 'standard' superstrings in which all strings associated with some vertex form a subgraph of G_2, so that only the last p string has an outgoing edge of weight more than 2 (*i.e.*, 3 or 4). Namely, if some vertex fails this requirement, then at least two of its associated strings have outgoing edges of weight more than 2, thus we do not increase the length by putting all its p strings directly after its connector in a standard way. A standard superstring naturally corresponds to an ordering of vertices $v_1, v_2, \ldots, v_n$.

For the converse there remains a choice of which string q succeeds a connector $v_i\#v_i'$. If H has an edge from v_i to v_{i+1} and the 'next' edge out of v_i (in (*)) goes to, say v_j, then choosing $q = v_i'v_{i+1}v_i'v_j$ results in a weight of 3 on the edge from the last p string to the next connector $v_{i+1}\#v'_{i+1}$, whereas this weight would otherwise be 4. If H doesn't have this edge, then the choice of q doesn't matter. Let us call a superstring 'Standard' if in addition to being standard, it also satisfies this latter requirement for all vertices.

Now suppose that the addition of k edges to H gives a Hamiltonian path $v_1, v_2, \ldots, v_n$. Then we can construct a corresponding Standard superstring. If the out-degree of v_i is d_i, then its length will be $\sum_{i=1}^{n}(2 + 2d_i + 1) + k + 3 = 3n + 2m + k$.

Conversely, suppose we are given a common superstring of length $3n + 2m + k$. This can then be turned into a Standard superstring of the same length. If $v_1, v_2, \ldots, v_n$ is the corresponding order of vertices, it follows that H cannot be missing more than k of the edges (v_i, v_{i+1}). $\square$

8.5 Dealing with negative strings

Let us consider a more general version of the superstring problem: Given a set of *positive* strings P and a set of *negative* strings N, find a shortest string s such that s contains all strings in P and s does not contain any string in N. The string s is called a *shortest consistent superstring* for (P, N). For simplicity, here we allow a consistent superstring to contain delimiters #, which can be used to prevent a negative string when plain concatenation does not. We still use $n = OPT(P, N)$ to denote the length of shortest consistent superstring for (P, N).

This generalized superstring problem has applications in areas such as string learning and DNA sequencing, as will be discussed in the next section. It turns out that negative strings are very hard to deal with. Although the algorithm Group-Merge described in Section 8.2 can be easily adapted to produce a consistent superstring of length $O(n \log n)$, no linear approximation algorithm is known. It is not hard to show that the algorithm Greedy and its variants do not achieve linear approximation any more.

Theorem 8.13. *For some P and N, Greedy outputs a superstring of length $\Omega(n^{1.5})$.*

Thus, in the following we will consider a special case: we assume that the negative strings do not contain positive strings as substrings. The case is interesting since it corresponds to the situation when restrictions are imposed on the merging of a pair of given strings. In practice, we may want to forbid some 'bad merges' to happen.

8.5.1 A LINEAR APPROXIMATION ALGORITHM

In this special case, there is a polynomial-time algorithm which produces a consistent superstring of length $O(n)$. The algorithm works in a way similar to the algorithm Concat-Cycles described in the previous section and also employs the Hungarian algorithm to find an optimal cycle cover on the distance graph derived from the input strings. A difficulty here is that Lemma 8.7 is no longer valid because of the presence of negative strings. This is resolved by separately processing the *periodic* strings and *non-periodic* strings, which are defined below.

A string s is said to be *i-periodic* if $i \leq \frac{|s|}{period(s)} < i + 1$. A string is *fully periodic* if it is at least 4-periodic. A string s is *prefix-periodic* (or *suffix-periodic*) if s has a fully periodic prefix (or suffix, respectively) of length at least $3|s|/4$. Call a string *periodic* if it is either prefix-periodic or suffix-periodic. Suppose s is a prefix-periodic string and $s = uv$, where u is the longest fully periodic prefix of s. Then u is called the *periodic prefix* of s and v is the *non-periodic suffix* of s. Similarly, if s is a suffix-periodic string and $s = uv$, where v is the longest periodic suffix of s, then v is called the *periodic suffix* of s and u is the *non-periodic prefix* of s. The *factor* of a string s, denoted $factor(s)$, is the prefix of length $period(s)$. Two prefix (or suffix) periodic strings s and t are *compatible* if (i) s or t are fully periodic and their periodic prefixes (suffixes, resp.) have equivalent factors; or (ii) none of s and t are fully periodic, one of their periodic prefixes (suffixes, resp.) is a suffix (prefix, resp.) of the other, and one of their non-periodic suffixes (prefixes, resp.) is a prefix (suffix, resp.) of the other. Informally speaking, two prefix/suffix periodic strings have a "large" overlap if and only if they are compatible.

For example, among the four prefix-periodic strings $s_1 = ababababcd$, $s_2 = abababababa$, $s_3 = babababababc$, and $s_4 = babababacd$, s_1 is compatible with s_2, s_3 but not with s_4, and s_2 is compatible with all s_1, s_3, s_4.

Let $P = \{s_1, \ldots, s_m\}$ and $N = \{t_1, \ldots, t_k\}$. We modify the definition of $m(s_i, s_j)$, $ov(s_i, s_j)$, $pref(s_i, s_j)$, and $d(s_i, s_j)$, taking the negative strings into consideration. For example, now $m(s_i, s_j)$ is the shortest superstring of s_i and s_j (with s_i being in front) that does not contain any string in N and $ov(s_i, s_j)$ represents the maximum overlap between s_i and s_j that is consistent with N. Note that we may need to insert a $\#$ between s_i and s_j in $m(s_i, s_j)$, if all "true" merges of s_i and s_j contain some negative string. A distance graph on strings $s_1, \ldots, s_m$ can be defined as in Section 8.3.1, but using the new distance function. We denote this graph as $G_{P,N}$. Observe that

$$CYC(G_{P,N}) \leq n$$

Before we formally present our algorithm, we need to describe a simple greedy algorithm Greedy 1, which is a straightforward extension of the algorithm Greedy.

Algorithm Greedy 1

1. Choose two (different) strings s and t from P such that $m(s,t)$ does not contain any string in N and $ov(s,t)$ is maximized. Remove s and t from P and replace them with the merged string $m(s,t,)$. Repeat step 1. If such s and t cannot be found, goto step 2.

2. Concatenate the strings in P, inserting delimiters $\#$ if necessary.

Our approximation algorithm combines Greedy 1 and the Hungarian algorithm:

1. Put the prefix-periodic strings in P into set X_1, the suffix-periodic strings into set X_2, and other strings into set Y.

2. Divide X_1 and X_2 further into groups of compatible strings. Run Greedy 1 on each group separately.

3. Construct the graph $G_{Y,N}$ as described above. Find an optimal cycle cover of $G_{Y,N}$. Open each cycle into a path and thus a string.

4. Concatenate the strings obtained in steps 2 and 3, inserting $\#$'s if necessary.

Theorem 8.14. *Given (P, N), where no string in N contains a string in P, the above algorithm produces a consistent superstring for (P, N) of length $O(n)$.*

Proof: (Sketch) We know from the above discussion that the optimal cycle cover found in step 3 has weight $CYC(G_{Y,N}) \leq OPT(Y, N) \leq OPT(P, N) = n$. Since the strings in Y are non-periodic, it is easy to show that their merges are at most 5-periodic. The strings that are at most 5-periodic do not have large self-overlap. More precisely, $ov(s, s) < 5|s|/6$ for any s that is at most 5-periodic. Thus opening a cycle into a path can at most increase its length by a factor of 6. This shows the strings obtained in step 3 have a total length at most $6 \cdot CYC(G_{Y\#}) = O(n)$.

Now we consider the strings produced in step 2. Let $U_1, \ldots, U_r$ be the compatible groups for X_1. (The proof for X_2 is the same.) It follows from the proof of Lemma 8.7 that for any two fully periodic strings x and y, if x and y are incompatible, then $ov(x, y) < period(x) + period(y)$. By our definition of periodicity, for any $u_i \in U_i, u_j \in U_j, i \neq j$, $ov(u_i, u_j) < (|u_i| + |u_j|)/4 + \max\{|u_i|, |u_j|\}/4 < 3\max\{|u_i|, |u_j|\}/4$. Thus, informally speaking, strings belonging to different groups do not have much overlap with each other. It can be shown by a simple calculation that we can afford losing such "small overlaps" in constructing an $O(OPT(X_1, N))$ long consistent superstring for (X_1, N), since replacing each such overlap with a plain concatenation in a shortest consistent superstring for (X_1, N) will at most increase its length by a constant factor. Hence we have the following lemma:

Lemma 8.15. $\sum_{i=1}^{r} OPT(U_1, N) = O(OPT(X_1, N)) = O(n)$.

To complete the proof, it suffices to prove that Greedy 1 produces a consistent superstring of length $O(OPT(U_i, N))$ for each group U_i. A key observation in this proof is that because the strings in U_i are compatible, Greedy 1 performs all merges with large overlaps correctly. (We say a merge is correct if it actually occurs in the construction of a shortest consistent superstring). Greedy 1 ignores all small overlaps (including the correct ones) and replaces them with concatenation. But this is fine as observed before. □.

Remark. Since the Hungarian algorithm runs in $O(m^3)$ time on a graph of m nodes, our algorithm can be made to run in $O(m^3 l_{max})$ time, where l_{max} is the maximum length of the input strings.

8.5.2   A NON-TRIVIAL BOUND FOR A GREEDY SOLUTION

The above algorithm is far more complicated and probably even impractical compared to the greedy algorithms. Thus it would still be interesting to study the performance of greedy algorithms. Although we know that greedy algorithms do not perform well in general, we suspect that they can achieve linear approximation when no negative strings contain positive strings.

In this subsection we show a greedy algorithm which produces a consistent superstring of length $O(n^{4/3})$ in this special case. The algorithm combines Greedy 1 with another algorithm Mgreedy 1, which is a straightforward extension of the algorithm Mgreedy.

Algorithm Mgreedy 1

1. Let (P, N) be the input and T empty.
2. While P is non-empty, do the following: Choose $s, t \in P$ (not necessarily distinct) such that $m(s, t)$ does not contain any string in N and $ov(s, t)$ is maximized. If $s \neq t$, then remove s and t from P and replace them with the merged string $m(s, t,)$. If $s = t$, then just move s from P to T. If such s and t cannot be found, move all strings in P to T.
3. Concatenate the strings in T, inserting delimiters # if necessary.

It is not easy to prove a non-trivial upper bound on the performance of Greedy 1, nor is it easy for Mgreedy 1. The trouble maker again is the periodic strings. So we will consider an algorithm which processes the periodic and non-periodic strings separately:

1. Put the prefix-periodic strings in P into set X_1, the suffix-periodic strings into set X_2, and other strings into set Y.
2. Divide X_1 and X_2 further into groups of compatible strings. Run Greedy 1 on each group separately.
3. Run Mgreedy 1 on set Y.
4. Concatenate the strings obtained in steps 2 and 3, inserting #'s if necessary.

Theorem 8.16. *Given (P, N), where no string in P is a substring of a string in N, the above algorithm returns a consistent superstring of length $O(n^{4/3})$.*

Proof: (Sketch) By the proof of Theorem 8.14, the strings produced in step 2 have total length $O(n)$. So it remains to analyze step 3.

The proof of the $O(n)$ bound for Mgreedy essentially uses the fact that Mgreedy actually selects the edges (representing merges) following a Monge sequence on the distance graph derived from the given strings and finds an optimal cycle cover. However, with the presence of negative strings, a distance graph may or may not have a Monge sequence. (The negative strings lengthen some edges.) Thus we have to use a different strategy.

Our analysis can be roughly stated as follows. Consider the distance graph $G_{Y,N}$ and view Mgreedy 1 as choosing edges in the graph $G_{Y,N}$: When Mgreedy 1 merges strings s and t, it chooses the edge $(last(s), first(t))$. Initially, we fix a path cover C on $G_{Y,N}$ such that the total length of the paths in C is $O(n)$. We analyze Mgreedy 1 on Y with respect to the initial cover C. As Mgreedy 1 merges strings, we update the cover by possibly breaking a path into two or joining two paths into one or turning a path into a cycle. The merges performed by Mgreedy 1 are divided into several classes. A merge is *correct* if it chooses an edge in some current path or cycle. Otherwise the merge is *incorrect*. An incorrect merge is a *jump merge* if it breaks two potential correct merges simultaneously. Suppose in a jump merge Mgreedy 1 chooses an edge (x, y). Let x' be the current successor of x and y' the current predecessor of y, in their respective paths/cycles. That is, the choice of edge (x, y) prevents us from choosing the edges (x, x') and (y', y) in the future. Then the merge is *good* if $m(y', x')$ does not contain any negative string. Otherwise the merge is *bad*. Clearly the type of a merge performed by Mgreedy 1 depends the initial cover C and how we update paths and cycles.

We choose the initial cover C and the updating rule such that (i) Strings in each initial path overlap "a lot"; (ii) Only bad jump merges will increase the total length of the current paths and cycles. Then we can prove an upper bound $O(|C|^{3/2})$ on the total number of bad jump merges, implying an upper bound $O(n^{4/3})$ on the length of the superstring produced by Mgreedy 1. A key fact used in this proof is that the strings in Y do not have a long periodic prefix or suffix and thus, for any two strings there is a unique way of overlapping them to achieve a large amount of overlap. $\square$

8.6 DNA Sequencing and learning of strings

Suppose that we are given a set of strings which are randomly sampled substrings of some unknown string. We would like to infer the unknown string. This is a frequently encountered problem in DNA sequencing. We will formulate this problem in a proper mathematical framework and provide solutions.

8.6.1 MODELLING DNA SEQUENCING VIA LEARNING

We make a few assumptions about DNA sequencing:

- Samples are drawn randomly;
- Each sample is approximately a few hundred base pairs long;
- We are only interested in predicting short fragments of a few hundred base pairs of a DNA sequence, with high probability. It is not our intention to construct the whole molecule precisely.

These assumptions are quite strong. But still the model may find some applications. For example, in practices such as DNA finger printing, we may want to know if some sequence of a few hundred base pairs is present in a patient's (or criminal's) gene.

We have compromised the power of our potential theory. But we can now appeal to Valiant learning model, which is a major learning model in computational learning theory. Our learned DNA sequence will only be good with high probability for short queries about several hundred characters long. Although this only partially captures reality, we are able to fully characterize the world we have captured. This is still meaningful since certain biological functions are encoded by just a few hundred base pairs. One purpose of DNA sequencing is to find the functionality of the genes, there is really no need to insist on recovering the original sequence precisely, especially when this is impossible.

We first describe the so-called *probably approximately correct* (pac) learning model, introduced by L.G. Valiant. We assume that a learning algorithm A has available a black box called EXAMPLES, with two buttons labeled POS and NEG. If POS (NEG) is pushed, a positive (negative) example is generated according to some fixed but unknown probability distribution D^+ (D^-). We assume nothing about the distributions D^+ and D^-, except that $\sum_{s \in POS} D^+(s) = 1$ and $\sum_{s \in NEG} D^-(s) = 1$ (i.e., $\sum_{s \in POS} D^-(s) = 0$ and $\sum_{s \in NEG} D^+(s) = 0$). For discrete domains, the pac learnability can be defined as follows.

Definition 8.17. *Let C and C' be concept classes. C is polynomially learnable from examples by C' if there is a (randomized) algorithm A with access to POS and NEG which, taking inputs $0 < \epsilon, \delta < 1$, for any $c \in C$ and D^+, D^-, halts in polynomial$(size(c), \frac{1}{\delta}, \frac{1}{\epsilon})$ time and outputs a hypothesis $c' \in C'$ that with probability greater than $1 - \delta$ satisfies*

$$\sum_{c'(s)=0} D^+(s) < \epsilon$$

and

$$\sum_{c'(s)=1} D^-(s) < \epsilon,$$

where $c'(s) = 1$ iff s is a positive example of concept c'. We say that A is a learning algorithm of C.

We can now model (a subset of) the DNA sequencing problem as the *string learning problem* under pac learning. Notice that the pac model allows sampling under arbitrary distribution, whereas in our case uniform sampling is sufficient.

Definition 8.18. *String Learning Problem. The concept class C is the set of strings (DNA-molecules to be sequenced) over the 4 letter alphabet $\{A, C, G, T\}$. The positive examples for each concept (i.e. string) c are its substrings; The negative examples are strings that are not substrings of c. Sampling is done at random according to some unknown distributions for positive and negative examples, respectively.*

In DNA sequencing practice, there do appear to be negative examples, due to biological restrictions on what can be combined. We strengthen a useful Occam's Razor theorem by replacing the previous requirement that $size(c') \leq n^\alpha m^\beta$ by that of $K(c'|c) \leq n^\alpha m^\beta$. We omit the proof.

Theorem 8.19. *[Occam's Razor Theorem] Let C and C' be concept classes. Let $c \in C$ with $size(c) = n$. For $\alpha \geq 1$ and $0 \leq \beta < 1$, let A be an algorithm that on input of $m/2$ positive examples of c drawn from D^+ and $m/2$ negative examples of c drawn from D^-, outputs a hypothesis $c' \in C'$ that is consistent with the examples and satisfies $K(c'|c) \leq n^\alpha m^\beta$, where $K(c'|c)$ is the Kolmogorov complexity of c' conditional to c. Then A is a learning algorithm for C by C' for*

$$m = O(max(\frac{1}{\epsilon} \log \frac{1}{\delta}, (\frac{n^\alpha}{\epsilon})^{\frac{1}{1-\beta}})).$$

When $\beta = 0$, and $n > \log \frac{1}{\delta}$, we will use $m = O(\frac{n^\alpha}{\epsilon})$.

By the above theorem, we certainly can trivially learn, with error probability $1/n$, a string of length n by sampling $m = n^3$ examples: the output will be a set of substrings of total length at most n^2 since there are only n^2 substrings and we can merge them into only n substrings. Needless to say, sampling 5000^3 fragments to sequence a DNA-molecule is simply not acceptable. A more careful analysis can bring this down to $O(n \log n/\epsilon)$ by keeping all the strings as the concepts, except merging two strings if one is a substring of another. Since there are at most n^n such concepts (although the total length may be n^2), we need only $O(n \log n/\epsilon)$ examples to learn with error probability ϵ by Theorem 8.19. However, this is still not good enough. For example, we still do not want to sample, say,

$5000 \log 5000$, substrings to identify a virus DNA molecule of 5000 base pairs. A theory must agree with practice. We will show that we need only about $\frac{n \log n \log(n/l)}{l\epsilon}$ fragments, where l is the D^+-expected sample length. This is much closer to the laboratory practice. Notice that the divisor l is around 500 and hence is much more significant than a $\log n$ term for $n \le 3 \times 10^9$. We conjecture that this can be improved to $\frac{6n \log n}{l\epsilon}$.

Our algorithm will depend on a provably good approximation algorithm for shortest superstrings.

8.6.2 LEARNING A STRING EFFICIENTLY

Our concept class $\mathcal{C}$ is the set of strings over $\{A, C, G, T\}$. For each target concept (*i.e.*, string) c, the positive examples are substrings of c distributed according to D^+, which may be uniform in the DNA applications. Negative examples are strings that are not substrings of c, distributed according to D^-. Denote the D^+-expected sample length by l. In the following, we assume that the positive samples have a small deviation (*i.e.*, $\ll l$) in length. This is consistent with real DNA sequencing practice. Let $2^{\mathcal{C}}$ be the class containing all finite sets of strings over $\{A, C, G, T\}$. For any concept $c' \in 2^{\mathcal{C}}$, a positive example of c' is a string that is a substring of some string in c' and a negative example is a string that is not a substring of any string in c'.

Theorem 8.20. $\mathcal{C}$ *is learnable by* $2^{\mathcal{C}}$, *with error probability* ϵ, *using only* $O(\frac{n \log^2 n}{l\epsilon})$ *samples.*

Proof: Given $O(\frac{n \log^2 n}{l\epsilon})$ positive and negative examples, if we output a concept c' such that $K(c'|c) = O(\frac{n \log^2 n}{l})$, then by Theorem 8.19, we have a learning algorithm.

We first change algorithm Group-Merge to also deal with negative examples: At step (2), we now look for a pair of s, s' such that $cost(s, s')$ is minimized under the condition that $m(s, s')$ must not contain a negative example as a substring. The learned concept is

$$c' = \{m(s, s')|m(s, s') \text{ chosen in step (2) of Group-Merge}\}$$

So c' may contain more than one string.

In order to show that the old analysis is still good, we only need to observe one fact: there is always a way to properly combine the first and last strings in each group G_i^r at the rth step such that they contain all strings in G_i^r as substrings and no negative examples as substrings. Hence the analysis of Theorem 8.4 still carries through.

Now we count how many c' are possible outputs of Group-Merge, given the fact that we draw examples using c. c' is constructed by less than $\frac{2n \log n}{l}$ iterations since the total length of c' is $n \log n$ and each positive example is roughly l long. Each step, two possible substrings of c are combined in some way, and this has at most $n^{O(1)}$ choices. So altogether we have $n^{O(\frac{n \log n}{l})}$ potential c'. Therefore

$$K(c'|c) \leq O(\frac{n \log^2 n}{l}).$$

Given a new string, we can decide whether it is a positive or negative example by testing whether it is a substring of some string in c'. By Theorem 8.19, our error probability is at most ϵ. $\square$

The learning algorithm outputs a hypothesis that is in concept class $2^{\mathcal{C}}$ (instead of $\mathcal{C}$). This is necessary since it has been shown that $\mathcal{C}$ is not learnable by $\mathcal{C}$.

In the real life situation of DNA sequencing, there are many restrictions on what can be combined. These conditions may be regarded as negative examples. However, if one prefers to think that *no negative examples are given*, we can still reasonably assume that negative instances are more or less uniformly distributed. And then, we can use the linear approximation in Section 8.3 to obtain the following.

Corollary 1. *Assume a uniform distribution over the negative examples. $\mathcal{C}$ is learnable by $2^{\mathcal{C}}$, with error probability ϵ, using only $\frac{9n \log n}{l\epsilon}$ positive samples.*

Proof: By modifying the arguments of Theorem 8.19 (proof omitted) it is easily seen that our algorithm will still guarantee

$$\sum_{c'(s)=0} D^+(s) \leq \epsilon,$$

On the negative side, because the output length is at most $O(n \log n)$, this will make at most $O((n \log n)^2)$ negative examples positive. Since we have assumed the uniform distribution, the error probability on the negative side is only, for not too small ϵ,

$$O(\frac{(n \log n)^2}{4^n}) < \epsilon.$$

$\square$

8.7   Superstrings with flipping

An interesting variation of the shortest common superstring problem is to allow the strings to be flipped, that is, we want to look for a shortest superstring s such that for every given string t, either t or the reverse of t is a substring of s. The problem may have applications in DNA sequencing practice since in some cases the orientation of a fragment in the target DNA molecule is unknown. It may also be useful in data compression since we may intentionally allow strings to be flipped to achieve better compression. Clearly the problem is still NP-hard. Following the ideas in section 8.3, we can give a simple greedy algorithm achieving $4n$ approximation.

Denote the reverse of a string s as s^R. For convenience, let s^R be null if s is a palindrome. Also define $ov(s, s^R) = 0$ and $d(s, s^R) = |s|$ for any string s. Let $S = \{s_1, \ldots, s_m\}$ and $S^R = \{s_1^R, \ldots, s_m^R\}$. Now a superstring of S is a string s such that for each i, either s_i or s_i^R (maybe both) are contained in s. Again denote the length of a shortest superstring of S as $OPT(S)$. We assume that $S \cup S^R$ is substring free. Observe now a shortest superstring of S must be $\langle s'_{i_1}, \ldots, s'_{i_m} \rangle$ for some permutation $\langle i_1, \ldots, i_m \rangle$, where $s'_{i_j} = s_{i_j}$ or $s_{i_j}^R$. We will consider the distance digraph derived from $S \cup S^R$, still denoted G_S. Now a cycle cover of G_S is a set of vertex-disjoint cycles such that for each $1 \leq i \leq m$, exactly one of s_i and s_i^R is contained in some cycle. Clearly the weight of an optimal cycle of G_S is at most $OPT(S)$.

Our algorithm is actually a simple extension of Mgreedy and will be called Mgreedy 2.

Algorithm Mgreedy 2

1. Let S be the input set of strings and T be empty.
2. While S is non-empty, do the following: Choose $s, t \in S$ (not necessarily distinct) such that $ov(s', t')$ is maximized, breaking ties arbitrarily, where $s' = s$ or s^R and $t' = t$ or t^R. If $s = t$, move s from S to T. If $ov(s', t') = 0$, move all the strings in S to T. If $s \neq t$, remove s, t from S and replace them with the merged string $m(s', t')$.
3. Output the concatenation of the strings in T.

Again we can view Mgreedy 2 as choosing edges in graph G_S.

Lemma 8.21. *Mgreedy 2 creates an optimal cycle cover of G_S.*

Proof: We begin the analysis with an optimal cycle cover of G_S. Generally, when Mgreedy 2 chooses an edge (x, y), we update the cycles to obtain a new cycle cover without increasing the total weight. We need only consider four cases: 1. The current cycles contain x and y; 2. The current cycles contain x and y^R; 3. The current cycles contain x^R and y; and 4. The current cycles contain x^R and y^R.

Since the cases 3 and 4 are really symmetric to cases 2 and 1, respectively, it suffices to consider cases 1 and 2 and show how to update the cycles in each case. Here we discuss Case 2 and leave Case 1 as an exercise. There are two subcases:

Subcase 2.1: x
and y^R are from a same cycle $a, \ldots, b, x, c, \ldots, d, y^R, e, \ldots, a$. Simply

reverse the path $c, \ldots, d, y^R$ in the cycle. This results in a new cycle: $a, \ldots, b, x, y, d^R, \ldots, c^R, e, \ldots, a$.

Subcase 2.2: x and y^R are from two cycles: $a, \ldots, b, x, a$ and $c, \ldots, d, y^R, c$. Merge the two cycles into one: $a, \ldots, b$, $x, y, d^R, \ldots, c^R, a$.

The total weight of the cycle cover is not increased during the above rearrangement by Lemma 8.8. So Mgreedy 2 obtains an optimal cycle cover at the end. □

The following is a straightforward extension of Lemma 8.7.

Lemma 8.22. *Let c and d be two cycles in an optimal weight cycle cover and s and t two strings in c and d, respectively. Then $ov(s, t)$, $ov(s^R, t)$, $ov(s, t^R)$, and $ov(s^R, t^R)$ are less than $w(c) + w(d)$.*

Hence, by the proof of Theorem 8.6, Mgreedy 2 achieves $4 \cdot OPT(S)$.

Theorem 8.23. *Mgreedy 2 produces a superstring of length at most $4 \cdot OPT(S)$.*

8.8   Exercises

1. Show that a linear approximation with compression factor d by Greedy does not necessarily imply any subquadratic approximation with respect to the length of shortest superstring.

2. Prove Theorem 8.3.

3. Show that Group-Merge produces a superstring of length $\Omega(n \log n)$ for some input, where n is the length of shortest superstring.

4. (Theorem 8.13) Give a set of positive and negative strings such that Greedy would return a consistent superstring of length $\Omega(n^{1.5})$. Do the negative strings contain postive strings?

5. Prove that the following problem is NP-complete: Given sets P and N of positive and negative strings over some finite alphabet Σ, find a consistent superstring for (P, N) over over same alphabet Σ.

6. [Shortest common supersequence prolem] If we do not require a string to appear in a superstring *consecutively* then we have at hand the shortest common supersequence problem. Show the following:

   (a) The shortest common supersequence problem is NP-complete.

   (b) ** [Open] Can we find a polynomial time approximation algorithm for the shortest common supersequence problem (independent of alphabet size)?

   (c) Given a set of positive sequences and a set of negative sequences, show that it is NP-hard to find a consistent supersequence s such that s is a supersequence of all positive sequences but of no negative sequences.

7. ** (Open) Prove or disprove that Greedy achieves $2n$ approximation.

8. Obtain an algorithm which can achieve better than $3n$ approximation.

9. ** (Open) If no positive string is a substring of any negative string, can some greedy-style algorithm achieve linear approximation for the shortest consistent superstring problem?

10. ** (Open) Is there a polynomial-time linear approximation algorithm for the general shortest consistent superstring problem? Remark: When the number of negative strings is a constant, a polynomial-time linear approximation algorithm exists.

8.9 Bibliographic notes

The earliest comprehensive study on the superstring problem was by Gallant, Maier, and Storer [1980] who also obtained the results in Sections 8.1.1 and 8.1.2 and first raised the question of approximating shortest superstrings. See also Garey and Johnson [1979] for the NP-completeness result and Storer [1988] and next chapter of this book for related data compression issues. Theorem 8.3 is due to Turner [1989] , and Tarhio and Ukkonen [1988]. The question of finding good approximation algorithms for superstring problem was raised in Gallant et al. [1980], Tarhio and Ukkonen [1988], Timkovsky [1989], Turner [1989]. Discussion on algorithm Group-Merge can be found in Jiang and Li [1993], Li [1990]. Proofs of $O(n)$ upper bounds for algorithms Mgreedy, Tgreedy, and Greedy and the MAX SNP-completeness of the superstring problem in Section 8.3 are taken from Blum, Jiang, Li, Tromp, and Yannakakis [1994]. We thank A. Blum, J. Tromp, and M. Yannakakis for allowing us to include our joint work here. Related material on approximation algorithms and the Hungarian algorithm can be found in Papadimitriou and Steiglitz [1982]. Monge sequences were first studied by Hoffman [1963] . More results on the class MAX SNP and problem TSP(1, 2) are given in Papadimitriou and Yannakakis [1988, 1993]. Approximation algorithms allowing negative strings in Section 8.5 are due to Jiang and Li [1994]. Section 8.6 is extracted from Jiang and Li [1993], and Li [1990]. For a survey on the theory and applications of Kolmogorov complexity, see Li and Vitányi [1993]. Valiant's pac learning theory was proposed in Valiant [1984]. The Occam's Razor theorem is due to Blumer, Ehrenfeucht, Haussler, and Warmuth [1989]. More information relating DNA sequencing and the shortest common superstring problem can be found in Lesk [1988], peltola et al. [1983]. Section 8.7 is from Jiang et al. [1992]. Solutions to Exercises 3 and 4 can be found in Jiang and Li [1993, 1994]. The solution to Exercises 5 and 6(c) are in Jiang anf Li [1993]. Solution to Exercise 6(a) is due to Maier [1978] . Solutions to Exercise 8 are given in Armen et al. [1994], Cszumaj et al. [1994], Jiang and Jiang [1995], Kosaraju et al. [1994], Sweedyk [1995], Teng and Yao [1993]: Teng and Yao [1993] improved the $3n$ bound to $2.89n$; Czumaj, Gasieniec,

Piotrow, and Rytter [1994] to $2.83n$; Kosaraju, Park, and Stein [1994] to $2.79n$; Armen and Stein [1994] to $2.75n$; Jiang and Jiang [1995] to $2.67n$; Sweedyk [1995] to $2.5n$.

Bibliography

ARMEN, C. AND C. STEIN [1994]. "A 2.75 approximation algorithm for the shortest superstring problem". presented at the *DIMACS Workshop on Sequencing and Mapping*, Oct. 1994.

BLUM, A., T. JIANG, M. LI, J. TROMP, M. YANNAKAKIS [1994]. "Linear approximation of shortest superstrings," *Journal of the ACM* 41-4, 630-647.

BLUMER, A., A. EHRENFEUCHT, D. HAUSSLER, AND M. WARMUTH [1989]. "Learnability and Vapnik-Chervonenkis dimension," *Journal of the ACM* 35(4), 929-965.

CZUMAJ, A., L. GASIENIEC, M. PIOTROW, AND W. RYTTER [1994]. "Sequential and parallel approximation of shortest superstrings," *Proc. 4th SWAT*, 95-106.

GALLANT, J., D. MAIER, J. STORER [1980]. "On finding minimal length superstring," *Journal of Computer and System Sciences* 20, 50-58.

GAREY, M. AND D. JOHNSON [1979]. *Computers and Intractability.* Freeman, New York.

HOFFMAN, A. [1963]. "On simple linear programming problems, " *Convexity: Proc. of Symposia in Pure Mathematics, Vol. 7* (V. Klee, Ed.). American Mathematical Society.

JIANG, T. AND Z. JIANG [1995]. "Rotations of periodic strings and short superstrings, " Submitted to *Journal of Algorithms*.

JIANG, T. AND M. LI [1993]. "DNA sequencing and string learning," To appear in *Mathematical System Theory*.

JIANG, T. AND M. LI [1993]. "On the complexity of learning strings and sequences," *Theoretical Computer Science* 119, 363-371.

JIANG, T. AND M. LI [1994]. "Approximating shortest superstrings with constraints, " *Theoretical Computer Science* 134, 73-491

JIANG, T., M. LI AND D. DU [1992]. "A note on shortest common superstrings with flipping," *Information Processing Letters* 44-4, 195-200.

KOSARAJU, R., J. PARK, C. STEIN [1994]. "Long tours and short superstrings, " *Proc. 35th IEEE Symp. on Found. of Comp. Sci.*, 166-177.

LESK, A. (ED.) [1988]. *Computational Molecular Biology, Sources and Methods for Sequence Analysis.* Oxford University Press.

LI, M. [1990]. "Towards a DNA sequencing theory, " *Proc. 31st IEEE Symp. on Found. of Comp. Sci.*, 125-134.

LI, M. AND P.M.B. VITÁNYI [1993]. *An introduction to Kolmogorov complexity and its applications.* Springer-Verlag.

MAIER, D. [1978]. "The complexity of some problems on subsequences and supersequences, " *Journal of the ACM* 25(2), 322-336.

PAPADIMITRIOU, C. AND K. STEIGLITZ [1982]. *Combinatorial Optimization: Algorithms and Complexity.* Prentice-Hall.

PAPADIMITRIOU, C. AND M. YANNAKAKIS [1988]. "Optimization, approximation and complexity classes, " *Proc. 20th ACM Symp. on Theory of Computing*, 229-234.

PAPADIMITRIOU, C. AND M. YANNAKAKIS [1993]. "The traveling salesman problem with distances one and two, " *Mathematics of Operations Research* 18, 1-11.

PELTOLA, H., H. SODERLUND, J. TARHIO, AND E. UKKONEN [1983]. "Algorithms for some string matching problems arising in molecular genetics, " *Information Processing 83 (Proc. IFIP Congress)*, 53-64.

STORER, J. [1988]. *Data Compression: Methods and Theory.* Computer Science Press.

SWEEDYK, E. [1995]. "A $2\frac{1}{2}$ approximation algorithm for shortest common superstrings," *Ph.D Thesis.* Department of Computer Science, University of California at Berkeley.

J. TARHIO AND E. UKKONEN [1988]. "A greedy approximation algorithm for constructing shortest common superstrings," *Theoretical Computer Science* 57, 131-145.

TENG, S. AND F. YAO [1993]. "Approximating shortest superstrings," *Proc. 34th IEEE Symp. on Found. of Comp. Sci.*, 158-165.

TIMKOVSKY, V. [1989]. "The complexity of subsequences, supersequences and related problems, " *Kibernetika* 5, 1-13 (in Russian).

TURNER, J. [1989]. "Approximation algorithms for the shortest common superstring problem, " *Information and Computation* 83, 1-20.

VALIANT, L.G. [1984]. "A theory of the learnable, " *Comm. ACM* 27(11), 1134-1142.

9
Two Dimensional Matching

String matching is a basic theoretical problem in computer science, but has been useful in implementating various text editing tasks. The explosion of multimedia requires an appropriate generalization of string matching to higher dimensions. The first natural generalization is that of seeking the occurrences of a pattern in a text where both pattern and text are *rectangles*.

The last few years saw a tremendous activity in two dimensional pattern matching algorithms. We naturally had to limit the amount of information that entered this chapter. We chose to concentrate on serial deterministic algorithms for some of the basic issues of two dimensional matching.

Throughout this chapter we define our problems in terms of *squares* rather than *rectangles*, however, all results presented easily generalize to rectangles.

9.1 Exact Matching

The *Exact Two Dimensional Matching Problem* is defined as follows:

INPUT: *Text* array $T[n \times n]$ and *pattern* array $P[m \times m]$.
OUTPUT: All locations $[i, j]$ in T where there is an *occurrence* of P, i.e.
$$T[i + k, j + l] = P[k + 1, l + 1] \quad 0 \le k, l \le n - 1.$$

9.1.1 LINEAR REDUCTIONS

A natural way of solving any generalized problem is by reducing it to a special case whose solution is known. It is therefore not surprising that most solutions to the two dimensional exact matching problem use exact string matching algorithms in one way or another. In this section, we present an algorithm for two dimensional matching which relies on reducing a matrix of characters into a one dimensional array.

Let $P'[1 \ldots m]$ be a pattern which is derived from P by setting $P'[i] = P[i, 1]P[i, 2] \cdots P[i, m]$, that is, the ith character of P' is the ith row of P. Let $T_i[1 \ldots n - m + 1]$, for $1 \le i \le n$, be a set of arrays such that $T_i[j] = T[i, j]T[i, j + 1] \cdots T[i, j + m - 1]$. Clearly, P occurs at $T[i, j]$ iff P' occurs at $T_i[j]$.

We can now use any linear time string matching algorithm to find, for each i, the occurrences of P' in T_i. We have, in fact, *linearized* the matrix, that is, we have taken an inherently two dimensional problem and made it into a set of one dimensional problems.

However, string matching algorithms assume that characters can be compared in constant time. A straightforward implementation of the algorithm suggested above would require $O(m)$ to compare two "characters" since the characters of P' and the T_i's are really sequences of m characters from the input alphabet Σ. Thus for each i, it takes $O(nm)$ to find occurrences of P' in T_i, making the total time for two dimensional matching $O(n^2 m)$. This is clearly an improvement over the naive $O(n^2 m^2)$ algorithm, but not good enough. The obvious bottleneck involves comparing pattern rows with length m text subrows. Below is a solution.

An Automaton Based Method Suppose that we take each pattern row and find all its occurrences in the text rows. We now set $T_i[j] = k$ if k is the smallest number such that the kth row of P matches the subrow starting at $T[i,j]$. Similarly, we set $P'[i] = k$ if k is the smallest number such that the ith row of P equals the kth row of P. After such a preprocessing, we can then make constant time "comparisons" between characters of P' and T_i. This second phase takes linear time. It takes $O(n^2)$ time to find occurrences of pattern rows in the text during the preprocessing. There are m such rows, so the complexity is once again $O(n^2 m)$.

Note however, that we can treat the pattern rows as a set of pattern strings. Such a set of pattern strings is called a *dictionary*.

The *Dictionary Matching Problem* is the following:

Preprocess: $D = \{P_i | 1 \leq i \leq k, P_i = P_{i,1} \cdots P_{i,m_i}\}$

Input: Text $T[1, \ldots, n]$.

Output: For each text location i, all $j \in \{1, \ldots, k\}$ such that P_j occurs at T_i.

Let σ be the number of distinct characters that occur in D, and let $d = \sum_{i=1}^{k} |P_i|$. The classical solution, which is a generalization of the Knuth-Morris-Pratt (henceforth KMP)   automaton approach, solves the dictionary matching problem in time $O(d \log \sigma)$, to preprocess the dictionary, and $O(n \log \sigma + tocc)$ to scan the text, where $tocc$, which stands for *total occurrences*, is the size of the output. Note that since all the patterns in our dictionary are the same size, the size of the output is linear. That is, no pattern is a proper prefix of another so two distinct patterns cannot both match at some location.

The details of this algorithm are beyond the scope of this chapter, however, the interested reader is referred to this chapter's conclusion for a reference.

Returning to two dimensional matching, we derive the following algorithm:

1. Let the set of distinct rows in the pattern be a dictionary (if some rows are identical, include only the lowest numbered such row in the dictionary). Construct P'. Use the algorithm for dictionary matching to construct the T_i's.

2. Use any linear time string matching algorithm to find the occurrences of P' in each T_i. For any pair (i, j) such that P' occurs at $T_i[j]$, mark an occurrence of P at $T[i, j]$.

Time: 1. $O(n^2 \log \sigma)$. 2. $O(n^2)$.
Total Time: $O(n^2 \log \sigma)$.

9.1.2 PERIODICITY ANALYSIS

The above two dimensional matching algorithm reduces the problem of two dimensional matching into one dimension. While the complexity achieved is favorable compared to the brute force method, it still contains a term dependent on the alphabet size. In contrast, there are one dimensional string matching algorithms which are linear and do not have an alphabet dependent term, so there is some gap between the complexity of one dimensional matching and two dimensional matching. This gap can be closed somewhat by exploiting the periodicity, or lack thereof, in a two dimensional array.

The periodicity of strings has been well studied and the periodic nature of strings has been used to generate efficient algorithms for string matching. By analyzing the two dimensional periodicity of the pattern and using that knowledge in the text scanning step, we not only obtain a more efficient algorithm, but we will also see that it will prove useful in compressed matching (see §9.3).

A string s can be said to be periodic if there exists a string w such that $s = w^k$ for some $k \geq 2$. This notion of periodicity generalizes nicely to two dimensions if we consider an unbounded pattern which extends in all directions. Then we can define a parallelogram of periodicity with which we can tile the plain to generate the (infinite) pattern. However, for bounded patterns, the notion does not prove as useful since it has been shown that even intuitively periodic patterns may not have such a tiling parallelogram.

In strings, we can equivalently define periodicity in terms of *borders*. A border is a proper prefix of a string which is also a suffix. A string is periodic iff it has a border which is at least half its length. While it is not clear what constitutes a prefix or suffix in a two dimensional pattern, the idea of overlapping regions of pattern can be easily generalized.

The idea of string overlap has been used to derive fast parallel string matching algorithms (see Chapter 2). The well know notion of a *witness* can also be used in the context of two dimensional matching to produce an efficient algorithm for exact matching. For a offset (i, j), the pair (k, l) is a witness if $P[k, l] \neq P[i + k, j + l]$. That is, if the pattern does not overlap with itself when offset by (i, j), then there must be some place where the two copies of the pattern disagree. Any such position of disagreement is a witness, so the witness of an offset need not be unique.

A *witness table* is an array W such that $W[i, j] = (k, l)$ if (k, l) is a witness for offset (i, j). If no such witness exists for (i, j), then $W[i, j]$ is undefined. Such a table can be constructed in time $O(m^2)$. See exercise 1 for a simple version of witness table construction. .

The witness table for the pattern provide some important understanding of its two dimensional structure. This knowledge can be used to provide an alphabet independent $O(n^2)$ text scanning phase.

Alphabet Independent Search   Text processing is accomplished in two stages: Candidate Consistency and Candidate Verification. A *candidate* is a location in the text where the pattern may occur. We denote a candidate starting at text location $T[r, c]$ by (r, c). We say that two candidates (r, c) and (x, y) are *consistent* (denoted $(r, c) \doteq (x, y)$) if they expect the same text characters in their region of overlap (two candidates with no overlap are trivially consistent). Equivalently, two overlapping candidates are consistent if they have no witness.

Initially, we have no information about the text and therefore all text locations are candidates. However, not all text locations are consistent. During the candidate consistency phase, we eliminate candidates until all remaining candidates are pairwise consistent. During the candidate verification phase, we check the candidates against the text to see which candidates represent actual occurrences of patterns. We exploit the consistency of the surviving candidates to rule out large sets of candidates with single text comparisons (since all consistent candidates expect the same text character).

Candidate Consistency   As stated above, the goal of the *candidate consistency algorithm* presented in this subsection is to produce a set of candidates for the given text such that the candidates are all consistent.

We begin with some transitivity lemmas for the $\doteq$ relation.

Lemma 9.1. *For any* $1 \leq r_1 \leq r_2 \leq r_3 \leq n$ *and for any* $1 \leq c_1 \leq c_2 \leq c_3 \leq n$, *if* $(r_1, c_1) \doteq (r_2, c_2)$ *and* $(r_2, c_2) \doteq (r_3, c_3)$, *then* $(r_1, c_1) \doteq (r_3, c_3)$.

Proof: Suppose that $(r_1, c_1) \not\doteq (r_3, c_3)$. Then, there exists an $x \leq m - r_3 + r_1$ and a $y \leq m - c_3 + c_1$ such that $P[x, y] \neq P[x + r_3 - r_1, y + c_3 - c_1]$. But $r_3 \geq r_2$ so $x + r_3 \geq r_2$ and $m \geq x + r_3 - r_1 \geq r_2 - r_1$. Similarly, $m \geq y + c_3 - c_1 \geq c_2 - c_1$. Since $(r_1, c_1) \doteq (r_2, c_2)$, we have that $P[x + r_3 - r_1, y + c_3 - c_1] = P[x + r_3 - r_2, y + c_3 - c_2]$. A similar argument shows that $P[x, y] = P[x + r_3 - r_2, y + c_3 - c_2]$ since $(r_3, c_3) \doteq (r_2, c_2)$. We conclude that $P[x, y] = P[x + r_3 - r_1, y + c_3 - c_1]$. This is a contradiction. Therefore $(r_3, c_3) \doteq (r_1, c_1)$. $\square$

Lemma 9.2. *For any* $1 \leq r_1 \leq r_2 \leq r_3 \leq n$ *and for any* $1 \leq c_3 \leq c_2 \leq c_1 \leq n$, *if* $(r_1, c_1) \doteq (r_2, c_2)$ *and* $(r_2, c_2) \doteq (r_3, c_3)$, *then* $(r_1, c_1) \doteq (r_3, c_3)$.

A one dimensional consistency algorithm: Let c be some column of the text. Initially, all positions in this column are candidates. We would like to remove candidates until all candidates within the column are consistent. Further, we would like to preserve any candidate which might actually represent an occurrence of the pattern in the text. Thus, we will only remove candidates when we find some specific text location with which they mismatch. The idea of algorithm A is the following. Suppose we have eliminated inconsistent candidates from the last i rows of column c. The surviving candidates are placed on a list. Notice that by lemma 9.1, if the candidate in row $n - i$ is consistent with the top candidate on the list, it is consistent with all of them. This check takes constant time using the witness array. This principle is used to produce an $O(n)$ algorithm for column consistency.

Algorithm A. *Eliminate inconsistent candidates within a column*

Step A.1: Get column number, c.

Step A.2: We create a doubly linked list, S, of consistent candidates in column c. Initialize S by adding candidate (n, c) to the top of S.

Step A.3: For row $r = n - 1$ to 1 do:

Step A.3.1: Let (x, c) be the top candidate in S. Test if candidates (r, c) and (x, c) are consistent by reference to the witness arrays:

   o If $(r, c) \doteq (x, c)$, then add (r, c) to the top of S.

If the two candidates under consideration are consistent, then they need not be compared with any other candidates on S. This is because, by lemma 9.1, consistency within a single column is transitive.

   o If $(r, c) \neq (x, c)$ then use the witness character in the text to eliminate one of the candidates. If (x, c) is eliminated, remove it from S and repeat step A.3.1 with the new top candidate in S. If no candidates remain in S, add (r, c) to S.

Clearly, if the two candidates are inconsistent, they can't both match the text. Thus the inappropriate one is eliminated.

Step A.4.3: Return S.

Theorem 9.3. *Algorithm A is correct and runs in time* $O(n)$.

Proof: The correctness of the algorithm follows largely from the comments within the algorithm and from lemma 9.1.

For the complexity bound, note that S can be initialized in constant time. For each row r in the for loop, there is at most one successful test of consistency. For each unsuccessful test, a candidate is eliminated, either the candidate (r, c) or the top candidate in S. Since the number of candidates is bounded by n the total time is $O(n)$. $\square$

A two dimensional consistency algorithm   We use the above algorithm as an initial "weeding out" of candidates so that we get a list for each column of consistent candidates. In the two dimensional consistency algorithm, we start with the rightmost column, which we know to be consistent, and add one column at a time from right to left. We will maintain the following loop invariant:

$$P(i) \equiv \text{the candidates remaining in columns } i, \ldots, n \text{ are all pairwise}$$
$$\text{consistent.}$$

As noted above, by calling Algorithm A with value n we are assured of $P(n)$. The approach of the algorithm below is to quickly insure $P(i)$ once $P(i+1)$ is known. When $P(1)$ holds, we are done. We use a similar idea to that of algorithm A. We first have a phase were we make sure that each candidate is consistent with all candidates above and to the right. A symmetric phase makes sure that candidates below and to the right are consistent, thus assuring $P(i)$. To reduce the work, we note that during the first phase, we need only compare a candidate on column i with the leftmost surviving candidate in each row above it. To further reduce the work, once a candidate in column i is found to be consistent with candidates above it, all lower candidates in column i are also consistent.

Algorithm B. *Candidate Consistency*

> Step B.1: For $i \leftarrow 1$ to n $C_i \leftarrow$ Algo A(i)
> Step B.2: For $i \leftarrow 1$ to n initialize R_i to be an empty list of candidates for each row i.
> Step B.3: Put the candidates on C_n onto their appropriate R_i lists.
> Step B.4: For $i \leftarrow n - 1$ downto 1 do

Add one row at a time, making sure that it is consistent with all candidates added so far.

> Step B.4.1: Call Bottom-Up(i)

Make sure that all candidates in column i are consistent with all candidates below them in columns $i + 1, \ldots, m$.

> Step B.4.2: Call Top-Down(i)

Make sure that all candidates in column i are consistent with all candidates above them in columns $i + 1, \ldots, m$.

Step B.4.3: Add surviving candidates from column i to the appropriate R_j lists.

We describe procedure Bottom-Up only, since procedure Top-Down is symmetric.

Step B1. *Bottom-Up(c)*

Step **B1.1:** Initialize: *cur* gets bottom value from C_c. *row* $\leftarrow n$ is a pointer to the last row

Step **B1.2:** While not at the top of C_c do

Step **B1.2.1:** If *cur* is consistent with leftmost item on R_{row}, then *row* $\leftarrow$ *row* $+ 1$

We compare the current candidate with the leftmost candidate in some row *row* below it. If they are consistent, then by lemma 9.1, all candidates above *cur* on C_c are also consistent with all candidates on R_{row}, *even if cur is later deleted as inconsistent with another candidate*. We need not consider that row again.

Step **B1.2.2:** If *cur* is not consistent with leftmost item on R_{row}, then find a witness to their inconsistency. Check which of them is inconsistent with the text and remove candidate from its list. If *cur* is removed, set *cur* to the previous item on C_c, otherwise do nothing.

We remove the candidate that has a mismatch against the text. If the item in R_{row} is removed, then we still need to check if *cur* is consistent with the remaining candidates in that row. Thus, we don't need to update any pointers. Otherwise, if *cur* is removed, we move up in C_c. We don't need to change *row* because of the comment above. None of the rows below *row* need to be compared against the new candidate *cur* since we already know they are consistent.

Step **B1.2.3:** If the *row* counter points to a row above *cur*'s row, set *cur* to the previous candidate in C_c.

Theorem 9.4. *The Algorithm B is correct and runs in $O(n^2)$.*

Proof: As in algorithm A, no candidate is removed unless a mismatch is found against the text. Therefore, no valid candidates are removed.

To show that at the end of the algorithm, only mutually compatible candidates are left on the R_i lists (and on the C_i), we pick two arbitrary surviving candidates (r_1, c_1) and (r_2, c_2) such that $c_1 < c_2$. We have two cases:

Case $r_1 \leq r_2$: We show this case by induction. Suppose that after processing column $c_1 + 1$ that $P(c_1 + 1)$ holds. The base case is true by Theorem 9.3. Let (r_2, c') be the leftmost candidate such that $c' > c_1$

and c' appears on R_{r_2} after processing column c_1. By lemma 9.1, we need only show that $(r_1, c_1) \doteq (r_2, c')$ since $(r_2, c') \doteq (r_2, c_2)$.

Let (r', c_1) be the last candidate with which (r_2, c') was compared during $BottomUp(c_1)$.

Claim 9.4.1. $r' \geq r_1$ and $(r', c_1) \doteq (r_2, c')$.

Proof: Suppose that $(r', c_1) \not\doteq (r_2, c')$. Then we either delete (r', c_1) or (r_2, c') from the candidate list. If we remove (r_2, c') from the list, then we would compare the next candidate on R_{r_2} with (r', c_1), thus violating the assumption that (r_2, c') was the leftmost candidate compared with a c_1 candidate. If we remove (r', c_1), the we would compare (r_2, c') with the next candidate above (r', c_1), thus violating the assumption that (r', c_1) was the last candidate on column c_1 with with (r_2, c') was compared.

To show that $r' \geq r_1$ we observe that if $r_1 > r'$, then we couldn't have compared (r_2, c') with (r', c_1) without first comparing (r_1, c_1) with (r_2, c'). Since they both survived, they would have had to have been compatible. But then we never would have compared (r_2, c') with (r', c_1) at all. $\square$

Finally, we know that $(r_1, c_1) \doteq (r', c_1)$, $(r', c_1) \doteq (r_2, c')$, $(r_2, c') \doteq (r_2, c_2)$ and that $r_1 \leq r' \leq r_2$ and that $c_1 \leq c' \leq c_2$. So by lemma 9.1, we have proved the case.

Case $r_1 > r_2$: This case is very similar to the one above, however, we refer the reader to procedure $TopDown$ rather than $BottomUp$ and lemma 9.2 rather than lemma 9.1.

The argument that shows the running time to be $O(n^2)$ is similar to the complexity analysis in Theorem 9.3. We observe that during $BottomUp$ (and $TopDown$) in each comparison of candidates results in the removal of a candidate (which can only happen n^2 times in all calls to these procedures), or in the cur pointer being decremented (resp. incremented). This can only happen $O(n)$ time each time $BottomUp$ (resp. $TopDown$) is called, and they are each called $O(n)$ times. Therefore the complexity is $O(n^2)$. $\square$

Source Verification   All remaining candidates are now mutually consistent. Note that each text element $t = T[r, c]$ may be contained by several candidates, and that all candidates agree on their area of overlap. We say a candidate (i, j) is *relevant* to a position (k, l) if $0 \leq k - i \leq m - 1$ and $0 \leq l - j \leq m - 1$, that is, if candidate (i, j) covers position (k, l). This leads to the following crucial observation: Every position in T can be labeled as either *true* or *false*, where *true* means that it equals the unique pattern symbol expected by all relevant candidates, and *false* is all other cases. Thus, every text element needs to be compared to a *single* pattern element, and every candidate source that contains a *false* element within it is not a pattern appearance and can be discarded.

The candidate verification algorithm follows:

Algorithm C. *Candidate Verification*

> Step C.1: Mark every text location $T[r, c]$ with a *pattern coordinate pair* $\langle i, j \rangle$, where $\langle i, j \rangle$ are the coordinates of the pattern element $P[i, j]$ that $T[r, c]$ should be compared with.

There may be several options for some locations, namely, the position of the scanned text element relative to each of its relevant candidates. However, any will do since all candidate sources are now compatible. If a location is not contained in any candidate source it is left unmarked. We will later see how this step is implemented (procedure C1).

> Step C.2: Compare each text location $T[r, c]$ with $P[i, j]$, where $\langle i, j \rangle$ is the pattern coordinate pair of $T[r, c]$. If $T[r, c] = P[i, j]$ then label $T[r, c]$ as *true*, else label it *false*.

> Step C.3: Flag with a *discard* every candidate that contains a *false* location within its bounds.

This flagging is done by the same method as in step C.1.

> Step C.4: Discard every candidate source flagged with a *discard*. The remaining candidates represent all pattern appearances.

Our only remaining task is showing how to mark the text elements with the appropriate pattern coordinate pairs. We adopt the popular sports fans technique - *the wave.*

Starting at the top (left) of each column (row), a wave is propagated going down (to the right) as follows. The first element stands and waves its pattern coordinate pair, if such exists. This nudges the neighbor below (to the right of) it to jump and raise its own pair. If it does not have a pair, it borrows its antecedent's pair, incrementing by 1 its row (column) coordinate, to adjust for its position relative to the same source. If the pair assigned to some position exceeds the size of the pattern, that position is left unmarked.

Thus in two sweeps of the text, column waves and row waves, each text element is given an appropriate pattern coordinate pair. Details of the wave follow:

Step C1. *The Wave*

> Step C1.1: **Initialization:** Mark every candidate with $\langle 1, 1 \rangle$.

> Step C1.2: **Column Waves:** For each column c, and for all positions r from 1 to n in column c do the following step: If $T[r, c]$ does not have

a pair, and $T[r-1, c]$ has pair $\langle i, j \rangle$ with $i < m$ then assign to $T[r, c]$ the pair $\langle i+1, j \rangle$.

Step C1.3: Row Waves: For each row r, and for all positions c from 1 to n in row r do the following step: If $T[r, c]$ does not have a pair, and $T[r, c-1]$ has pair $\langle i, j \rangle$ with $j < m$ then assign to $T[r, c]$ the pair $\langle i, j+1 \rangle$.

A similar version of the wave can be used to flag candidates with *discard*. What is propagated there is the *discard* flag, along with a counter pair to make sure the *discard* flag doesn't get propagated too far.

Theorem 9.5. *Algorithm C is correct and runs in time $O(n^2)$.*

Correctness: The only non-trivial fact is that the wave correctly marks all elements. We need the following terminology. Let (r, c) be a candidate containing position $T[r+i, c+j]$. Then j is the *column distance* between $T[r+i, c+j]$ and (r, c) and i is the *row distance* between $T[r+i, c+j]$ and (r, c). The *column-close* sources containing location $T[r, c]$ are the sources whose column distance to $T[r, c]$ is minimal. The *closest* source containing location $T[r, c]$ is the column-close source whose row distance to $T[r, c]$ is smallest.

Claim: The pattern coordinate pair marked by procedure C1 in location $T[r, c]$ is the pair $\langle i, j \rangle$ where $(r-i+1, c-j+1)$ is the closest source to $T[r, c]$.

Proof: By induction on the column distance of the closest source. For column distance 0 the column wave assures that the marked pair is the distance to the closest source $(+1)$. Assuming that for every text element whose column distance to its closest source is d, the marked pair is the distance to the closest source, the row wave will ensure correct marking of all element with column distance $d+1$ to the source.

Time: Each of the steps of algorithm C is easily implementable in time $O(n^2)$. Note that in each of steps C.1 and C.4 is single call to procedure C1, which clearly takes $O(n^2)$ time. □

9.2 Scaled Matching

An interesting extension of exact matching is exact *scaled matching*. Such a problem is motivated by the fact that one may be interested in matching patterns whose occurrence in the text is of different scale than provided by the pattern. For example, if the text is a newspaper that we would like to scan, then we encounter letters of the alphabet in various sizes.

A "clean" version of the problem may be defined as follows:

The string $aa...a$ where the symbol a is repeated k times (to be denoted a^k), is referred to as 'a' *scaled to k*. Similarly, consider a string $A = a_1 \cdots a_l$. 'A' *scaled to k* (A^k) is the string $a_1^k, ..., a_l^k$.

Let $P[m \times m]$ be a two-dimensional matrix over a finite alphabet Σ. Then P *scaled to k* (P^k) is the $km \times km$ matrix where every symbol $P[i, j]$ of P is replaced by a $k \times k$ matrix whose elements all equal the symbol in $P[i, j]$. More precisely,

$$P^k[i, j] = P[\lceil \tfrac{i}{k} \rceil, \lceil \tfrac{j}{k} \rceil].$$

The problem of *two-dimensional pattern matching with scaling* is defined as follows:

INPUT: Pattern matrix $P[i, j]$ $i = 1, ...m; j = 1, ..., m$ and Text matrix $T[i, j]$ $i = 1, ..., n; j = 1, ..., n$ where $n > m$.

OUTPUT: all locations in T where an occurrence of P scaled to k starts, henceforth a *k-occurence*, for any $k = 1, ..., \lfloor \tfrac{n}{m} \rfloor$.

The basic algorithmic design strategy described below can be viewed as realizing the following approach: For each scale k, try to select only a fraction of $\tfrac{1}{k}$ among the n columns and seek k-occurrences only in these columns. Since each selected column intersects n rows, this leads to consideration of $O(\tfrac{n^2}{k})$ elements. Summing over all scales, we get $O(n^2)$ multiplied by the harmonic sum $\sum_{i=1}^{\frac{n}{m}} \tfrac{1}{i}$, whose limit is $\log \tfrac{n}{m}$, making the total number of elements scanned $O(n^2 \log \tfrac{n}{m})$.

A final intuitive step is to select also a $\tfrac{1}{k}$ fraction of the rows. Since $\sum_{i=1}^{\frac{n}{m}} \tfrac{1}{i^2}$ is bounded by a constant, the number of elements decreases now to

$$O(n^2 \sum_{i=1}^{\frac{n}{m}} \frac{1}{i^2}) = O(n^2).$$

We will show here how to achieve the $O(n^2 \log \tfrac{n}{m})$ bound and hint at the method used to eliminate the logarithmic factor.

9.2.1 STRING SCALED MATCHING

Let us consider the scaled matching problem in one dimension. The solution to this problem will shed light on one aspect of the two dimensional scaled matching problem.

The problem of *one-dimensional string matching with scaling* is the following:

INPUT: Pattern $P = p_1 \cdots p_m$ and text $T = t_1 \cdots t_n$ where $n > m$.

OUTPUT: All positions in T where a k-occurrence of P starts, for any $k = 1, ..., \lfloor \tfrac{n}{m} \rfloor$.

We can use the inherent repetitions in scaled appearances of strings to provide a simple scaled matching algorithm.

Definition: Let $S = \sigma_1 \sigma_2 \cdots \sigma_n$ be a string over some alphabet Σ. The *run length compression* run length compression of string S is the string $S' = \sigma_1'^{r_1} \sigma_2'^{r_2} \cdots \sigma_{\hat{n}}'^{r_{\hat{n}}}$ such that: (1) $\sigma_i' \neq \sigma_{i+1}'$ for $1 \leq i < \hat{n}$; and (2) S can be described as concatenation of the symbol σ_1' repeated r_1 times, the symbol σ_2' repeated r_2 times, ..., and the symbol $\sigma_{\hat{n}}'$ repeated $r_{\hat{n}}$ times.

We denote by $S^\Sigma = \sigma_1' \sigma_2' \cdots \sigma_{\hat{n}}'$, the *symbol part* of S, and by $S^\#$, the vector of natural numbers $r_1, r_2, ..., r_{\hat{n}}$, the *repetition part* of S.

Example 1: For $S = AAABABBCCACAAAA$, $S' = A^3 B^1 A^1 B^2 C^2 A^1 C^1 A^4$,
$S^\Sigma = ABABCACA$ and $S^\# = [3, 1, 1, 2, 2, 1, 1, 4]$.

Algorithm D. *Algorithm for the one dimensional scaled matching problem*

> **Step D.1:** Derive the symbol string T^Σ and the repetition string $T^\#(= t_1, ..., t_{\hat{n}})$ from the text string T. Similarly, derive P^Σ and $P^\#(= p_1, ..., p_{\hat{m}})$ from the pattern string P.

Observation 1. Finding all occurrences of P in T scaled to k is equivalent to finding all locations i that satisfy conditions A and B below.

Condition A. There is an exact occurrence of P^Σ in location i of T^Σ.
Condition B.1. $t_i \geq k p_1$
Condition B.2. $t_{i+1} = k p_2, \dots, t_{i+\hat{m}-2} = k p_{\hat{m}-1}$
Condition B.3. $t_{i+\hat{m}-1} \geq k p_{\hat{m}}$

> **Step D.2:** Suppose $\hat{m} \geq 3$. Derive the *quotient* string $T' = \frac{t_2}{t_1}, \frac{t_3}{t_2}, \dots, \frac{t_{\hat{n}}}{t_{\hat{n}-1}}$ from $T^\#$ and the quotient string $P' = \frac{p_3}{p_2}, \frac{p_4}{p_3}, \dots, \frac{p_{\hat{m}-1}}{p_{\hat{m}-2}}$ from $P^\#$.

Observation 2. Suppose $\hat{m} \geq 3$. Condition B.2 from Observation 1 is satisfied for $k = \frac{t_2}{p_2}$ if and only if an occurrence of string P' starts at location $i + 1$ of string T'.

> **Step D.3.1:** Find all occurrences of string P^Σ in the string T^Σ and all occurrences of the string P' in the string T'.

This is done by applying any linear time string matching algorithm.

> **Step D.3.2:** For each location i in T^Σ, such that P^Σ starts at i and P' starts at location $i + 1$ of T', check whether conditions B.1 and B.3 extend to locations i and $i + \hat{m} - 1$ in T'.

This will take $O(1)$ time per location i.

Comment: Extension to the case where $\hat{m} < 3$ within the same complexity bound as claimed below is trivial.

Time: Step D.1 needs $O(|P| + |T|)$ time. All other steps need $O(|P^\Sigma| + |T^\Sigma|)$ time. If the input is already provided in the run-length form, then the running time of the algorithm will be linear in the length of the compressed input, and possibly sublinear in $|P| + |T|$.

9.2.2 TWO DIMENSIONAL SCALED MATCHING

The main idea behind the $O(n^2 \log \frac{n}{m})$ algorithm is similar to the string matching algorithm presented above. Consider any column j and scale k. If P^k (the pattern scaled to k) starts in column j then every row of the pattern is translated into a k-$block$ of k consecutive equal rows where each row is of length km. The maximum number of possible blocks in a column is $\frac{n}{k}$. Suppose we succeed in dividing column j into b_j^k k-blocks in time $O(b_j^k)(\le O(\frac{n}{k}))$. Finding all appearances of P^k in column j can now be done in time $O(b_j^k)$ by running a KMP-like algorithm where every pattern row is compared only to the first row in the appropriate block (constant time using LCA on suffix trees) and verifying that the number of rows in the block indeed matches the expected number (comparison of numbers, also constant time).

Thus the total time for finding all appearances of P^k is $O(\frac{n^2}{k})$ and the total time for all scales is $O(\sum_{k=1}^{\lfloor \frac{n}{m} \rfloor} \frac{n^2}{k}) = O(n^2 \log \frac{n}{m})$.

We now present a detailed algorithm for scaled pattern matching, assuming that the block division can be done efficiently (we will later show how the block division is done).

Let us first formally define a k-block.

k-**blocks:** Let k be a positive integer. A k-$block$ at *position i_1 of column j_1* of T is a submatrix $T' = T[i_1, ..., i_2; j_1, ..., j_1 + km - 1]$, that satisfies the following:

(1) all rows of T' are equal.

(2) no rows can be added to T' without disrupting condition (1) above (formally, substring $T[i_2; j_1, ..., j_1 + km - 1]$ is not equal to substring $T[i_2 + 1; j_1, ..., j_1 + km - 1]$ and substring $T[i_1; j_1, ..., j_1 + km - 1]$ is not equal to substring $T[i_1 - 1; j_1, ..., j_1 + km - 1]$).

The *height* of a submatrix is its number of rows. The height of such k-block is $i_2 - i_1 + 1$. If a k-block is contained in a k-occurrence then its height must be at least k. (Because each pattern row must appear k successive times.)

Let S_j^k be a list whose elements are lists of consecutive k-blocks in column j. The k-blocks in each list are adjacent and in consecutive order. The last k-block in a list does not have an adjacent k-block below it. The first k-block below it starts the next list. Every list entry is a *starting row* of a k-block and its *height*. The sum of the heights of all blocks in a list is no less than km.

Algorithm E. *Scaled Matching Algorithm*

Pattern analysis: Let $P_1, P_2, ..., P_m$ be the rows of the pattern matrix P. P can be described as row P_{l_1} repeating r_1 times (the block at row l_1), followed by row $P_{l_2}(\ne P_{l_1})$ repeating r_2 times, followed by additional blocks until finally we have row $P_{l_\alpha}(\neq P_{l_{\alpha-1}})$ repeating r_α times, where $l_1 = 1$, $l_k = r_1 + \cdots + r_{k-1} + 1$ and $r_1 + r_2 + \cdots + r_\alpha = m$. The above description is a run-length representation of the sequence $P_1, P_2, \ldots, P_m$ when viewed as a one dimensional string R with m symbols. Formally a pair (P_{l_h}, r_h) is a block of r_h rows at row l_h.

> **Step E.1:** Compress the string R into its run length representation, which is denoted FR.

(This will take time proportional to $|P_1| + |P_2| + \ldots + |P_m|$.)

In the remainder of this presentation we assume that $\alpha > 2$. We leave it to the interested reader to see why there is a solution within the claimed bound for the case $\alpha \leq 2$. Let $\hat{F}R$ be the subsequence of FR that starts at its second element and ends at the predecessor of the last element. That is, $\hat{F}R = (P_{l_2}, r_2)...(P_{l_{\alpha-1}}, r_{\alpha-1})$.

> **Step E.2:** Compute the failure array $FAIL$ for string $\hat{F}R$.

This step is done precisely as in the KMP algorithm with one exception. Comparison of two pairs (P_{l_i}, r_i) and (P_{l_j}, r_j) is done by comparing P_{l_i} and P_{l_j} (using the suffix tree of the concatenated pattern rows, as in Chapter 4) and by comparing the numbers r_i and r_j.

Scanning the text: Scan each *column* j of T separately, as if it was a one-dimensional string. The scan is done in a similar way to KMP, with a few modifications. Most notable is the fact that instead of advancing from a row i to its successive row $i + 1$ in column j, our advancement is guided by the list S_j^k. The other modification is due to the fact that, as in the pattern preprocessing, comparisons between pattern and text symbols are now comparisons between blocks.

Input for Step E.3: Pattern automaton for $\hat{F}R$, lists S_j^k (recall that the elements of S_j^k are lists of consecutive k-blocks).

Output of Step E.3: All indices of T where a copy of rows $P_{l_2}^k...P_{l_{\alpha-1}}^k$ of P^k begins.

In other words, we are ignoring the first and last blocks of P. This is done because all blocks except the first and last are sharply delineated in the text, but the first and last blocks may appear in a text location that has leading and trailing rows equal to the rows in the first and last pattern blocks. Thus, after finding the appearances of P^k without the first and last blocks, we will verify that the beginning and end also match (step E.4). Step E.3 is a modified version of the main loop of KMP. We provide somewhat more detailed psuedocode so emphasize the similarity.

Step E.3:

```
for column col := 1 to n − km + 1 do
    l = start of first list in S^k_{col}
    While l is still a list in S^k_{col} do
    row := l (start of first block in list); h := 2
    last := start of last block in list
    While  row ≤ last do
        if COMPARE(k-block at T[row, col], block at row kl_h of P^k)
        then row := row + kr_h (start of next block in S^k_{col});
        h := h + 1
            if h = α
            then
                Output: there is a match at [row − k(m − l_α) + 1, col] ;
                h := FAIL(h)
            else h := FAIL(h)
        end { while}
        l = next list in S^k_{col}
    end { while}
end { for}
```

Step E.4: For every occurrence of $\hat{F}R$ check whether it extends into an occurrence of the whole pattern.

Time: Assuming that comparisons can be done in constant time, step E.3 is basically the Knuth-Morris-Pratt algorithm. Its time for column col is $O(|S^k_{col}|) \leq O(\frac{n}{k})$. The time for all n columns is $O(\frac{n^2}{k})$. Step E.4 takes constant time per occurrence so its total contribution is also $O(\frac{n^2}{k})$.

We now show how the constant time comparison is achieved.

Step E1. *Compare*

INPUT (1) Block at $T[i, j]$. (The algorithm guarantees that row i is in the list S^k_j.)

(2) The k-block at row kl_h of P^k (represented by the pair (P_{l_h}, r_h)).

OUTPUT Determine in $O(1)$ time whether $T[i; j, j+1, ..., j+km−1] = P_{l_h}$ and the height of the S^k_j block is r_h.

The main tool in comparing the strings $T[i; j, j+1, ..., j+km−1]$ and $P^k_{l_h}$ is an LCA query with respect to the suffix tree ST.

We need to make the suffix tree ST more explicit.

Constructing Suffix Tree ST:

Step E1.1: Form a long string C as follows. Concatenate all rows of T and append to them the following $\lfloor \frac{n}{m} \rfloor$ strings:

* A concatenation of the rows of P.

  * A concatenation of the rows of P, where each row is scaled to 2.
  * For k, $3 \leq k \leq \lfloor \frac{n}{m} \rfloor$, a concatenation of the rows of P, where each row is scaled to k.

The length of string C is equal to

$$|T| + \sum_{j=1}^{m} \sum_{k=1}^{\lfloor \frac{n}{m} \rfloor} |(P_j^k)|$$

which is $O(n^2)$, since

$$|T| = O(n^2)$$

and

$$\sum_{j=1}^{m} \sum_{k=1}^{\lfloor \frac{n}{m} \rfloor} |(P_j^k)| \leq m \sum_{k=1}^{\lfloor \frac{n}{m} \rfloor} km \leq m^2 (\frac{n}{m})^2 = O(n^2)$$

Time: The initial preprocessing of ST is $O(n^2 \log \sigma)$, for effective alphabet size σ. Initial preprocessing for LCA takes also $O(n^2)$ time. Subsequently, every query (i.e. comparison) is constant time.

  Our only remaining task is constructing the lists S_j^k.

9.2.3 PARTITIONING A COLUMN INTO K-BLOCKS

The main idea in constructing list S_j^k is the *power columns*. The algorithm's efficiency is achieved by grouping the n columns of the text into sets of m successive columns each, as follows $\{1, ..., m\}, \{m + 1, ..., 2m\}, ...\{(\lfloor \frac{n}{m} \rfloor - 1)m+1, ..., \lfloor \frac{n}{m} \rfloor m\}$ (possibly followed by a final set of less than m elements $\{\lfloor \frac{n}{m} \rfloor m+1, ..., n\}$). Instead of handling each of the columns separately, the effort for processing all m columns in a set is combined. The key player in each such set is its rightmost column, called *power column*. Columns $m, 2m, ..., \lfloor \frac{n}{m} \rfloor m$ are the *power columns*.

  We now need an additional data structure that enables retrieval of the following queries: *Given a power column c and another column $j \geq c$ (alternatively, $j < c$), find all rows $1 \leq i \leq n-1$ such that rows i and $i+1$ differ between columns c and j (alternatively, between columns j and $c-1$). Formally, $T[i; c, ..., j] \neq T[i+1; c, ..., j]$ (alternatively, $T[i; j, j+1, ..., c-1] \neq T[i + 1; j, j+1, ..., c - 1]$).*

  We would like the time to process this query to be proportional to the length of the output (that is, the number of such rows i). The following data structure will enable such processing.

  Let $[i, c]$ be a position on a power column c in T. Let $B_r[i, c]$ be the largest integer k for which the two strings $T[i; c, c + 1, ..., c + k - 1]$ and $T[i + 1; c, c + 1, ..., c + k - 1]$ are equal. Similarly, let $B_l[i, c]$ be the largest integer k for which the two strings $T[i; c - k, c - (k - 1), ..., c - 1]$ and

$T[i + 1; c - k, c - (k - 1), ..., c - 1]$ are equal. In words, $B_r[i, c]$ gives the longest common prefix of rows i and $i + 1$ starting at column c and $B_l[i, c]$ gives the longest common suffix of rows i and $i + 1$ ending at column $c - 1$.

It is easy to see that $B_r[i, c]$ and $B_l[i, c]$ can be constructed for every row i and power column c in time totalling $O(n^2)$.

Example 2: Let row i in T be $a^3 b^4 c^5 a^2 b^5$ and row $i + 1$ be $c^2 a^1 b^4 c^1 a^1 c^3 b^1 a^1 b^5$. Suppose columns 5, 10 and 15 are power columns. The figure below illustrates rows i and $i + 1$ in T, as well as the power columns:

$$
\begin{array}{ccccccccccccccccc}
a & a & a & b & b & b & b & c & c & c & c & c & a & a & b & b & b & b & b \\
 & & & & | & & & & & | & & & & & | & & & & \\
c & c & a & b & b & b & b & c & a & c & c & c & b & a & b & b & b & b & b
\end{array}
$$

Then $B_r[i, 5] = 4$, $B_r[i, 10] = 3$, $B_r[i, 15] = 5$ and $B_l[i, 5] = 2$, $B_l[i, 10] = 0$, $B_l[i, 15] = 1$.

For a fixed column j and scale k, let c be the power column immediately to the right of j. Consider the arrays $B_r[1, ..., n - 1; c]$ and $B_l[1, ..., n - 1; c]$. Every i where $B_l[i, c] < c - j + 1$ or $B_r[i, c] < km - (c - j + 1)$ indicates a start of a new block. We call such a row a *seam*. We can find the seams using *range minimum queries*.

Definition: Let $L = [l_1, ..., l_n]$ be an array of n numbers.

A *Range Minimum* query is of the form:

Input: Given a range of indices $[i, ..., j]$, where $1 \leq i \leq j \leq n$,

Output: Return an index k $i \leq k \leq j$ such that $l_k = \min\{l_i, ..., l_j\}$.

Following a linear time preprocessing of L, each range minimum query can be processed in $O(1)$ time.

The only difficulty is that we want to find all the k-blocks in time $O(\frac{n}{k})$. Direct use of range minimum queries will find **all** blocks, even the small ones. The time then may exceed the allowed $O(\frac{n}{k})$.

However, since we are only interested in **consecutive** k-blocks, we are assured that, except for the first and last block, all k-blocks have only one seam every k rows. In other words, there are k seamless rows in each side of a seam. This observation leads to the following algorithm.

Algorithm F. *Algorithm for constructing S_j^k*

Step F.1: Divide column j into $\frac{n}{2k}$ intervals of $\frac{k}{2}$ consecutive rows each.

Step F.2: For each interval, do 3 range minimum queries, to find a seam and possibly another seam to its right or left within the interval. If two seams or more are found in an interval it is discarded.

Step F.3: Every single seam interval, followed by non-seam intervals and eventually another single seam interval (with at least k rows between the two seams), defines the beginning of a k-block. Its height is the number of rows between the seams.

Step F.4: Discard all S_j^k entries where the total height of consecutive k-blocks is less than $k(l_{\alpha-1} - l_2)$.

Time: Since there is only a constant amount of work per interval, the time is $O(\frac{n}{k})$ for every column, or $O(\frac{n^2}{k})$ for the entire text.

Total Algorithm Time: We have seen that the time for searching all occurrences of P^k is $O(\frac{n^2}{k})$. Since k ranges over $\{1, \ldots, \lfloor \frac{n}{m} \rfloor\}$ the total time is

$$\sum_{k=1}^{\lfloor \frac{n}{m} \rfloor} \frac{n^2}{k} = O(n^2 \log \frac{n}{m}).$$

Remarks: Note that for scale k, even a list of consecutive k-blocks do not necessarily indicate a possible appearance of P^k. In particular, character changes within rows force upon us the knowledge that a scaled occurrence can appear only within multiples of k from that change (because scale k means that every pattern row now consists of k-length strings, each consisting of a single repeating character). Thus for every scale k it is only necessary to construct the S_j^k for $\frac{n}{k}$ **columns**. This brings the total algorithm time to $O(n^2)$.

9.3 Compressed Matching

Data compression is a well-studied area in information science. The two most common motivations for the study of data compression are:

- *Data storage:* Compression allows more data to be stored on a given device.

- *Data Communications:* Communication links, be they cables, phone lines or satellite channels, are both limited and, usually, slower than the data gathering and data processing ends. Compressing the data prior to transmission, and decompressing on the receiving end can increase the speed (and thus the volume) of the transmission process.

The main thrust in the study of data compression has been to achieve compression that is efficient in packing while also being practical in time and space. Compression of strings has had a long history of study, starting with the naive *run-length* encoding and encompassing such diverse algorithmic methods as the Huffman code, on-line textual substitution methods and stochastic methods. The various methods of string compression generalize to multidimensions. An example of a simple and widely used two-dimensional compression scheme is quadtrees. Other examples include arithmetic methods and textual substitution methods.

In the context of pattern matching, one would like a compression scheme to have the property of allowing pattern matching directly in the *compressed data*. We refer to the problem of finding patterns in compressed text representations as *compressed matching*. If a pattern can be found without the need to decompress the data, noticeable savings in time may arise. For example, in the communications arena, systems of small networked processors could enjoy a boost in efficiency if data could be both *transmitted* and *analysed* in a compressed form, especially if the process requires transmission and analysis of the same data in many nodes.

The *compressed matching problem* is the following: Let $\mathcal{C}$ be a given compression algorithm, let $c(D)$ be the size of the output of $\mathcal{C}(\mathcal{D})$.

INPUT: Compressed text $\mathcal{C}(\mathcal{T})$ and compressed pattern $\mathcal{C}(\mathcal{P})$.

OUTPUT: All locations in T where pattern P occurs.

A compressed matching algorithm is *optimal* if its time complexity is $O(c(T))$. It is *efficient* if for T such that $c(T) \ll |T|$ its time complexity is $o(|T|)$. This definition of *efficient* may seem somewhat strange. It is motivated by the following observation. The size of the compressed data will vary depending on the internal structure of the data. In the worst case it may be $O(|T|)$. Any algorithm that is not optimal would then be worse than first decompressing the text and then matching. However, we implicitly assume that compression is beneficial, i.e. $c(D) \ll |D|$. This leads to our definition of efficient compressed matching. As a further characterization of efficient, we call *almost optimal* any efficient algorithm with complexity $O(c(T)\mathrm{polylog}c(T))$.

In one dimension (strings), an optimal compressed matching algorithm is readily apparent for the run-length compression as defined in section 9.2. Such an algorithm is given by the scaled string matching algorithm by simply considering the 1-occurences in the output of that algorithm.

The run-length compression can be simply generalized to two dimensions by concatenating the run-length compression of all the matrix rows. For simplicity's sake we will refer to this compression as the *two-dimensional run-length compression*, or simply the *run-length compression*.

The classification of two dimensional periodicity has proven to be a powerful tool for this problem, and allowed Amir and Benson to present a $O(c(T) \log |P| + |P|)$ time algorithm for compressed matching in the two-dimensional run-length compression.

For didactic reasons we make some simplifying assumptions and only show this result for the easier, non-periodic case. The more general cases have a similar flavor but need to contend with greater details.

9.3.1 PROBLEM DEFINITION AND ALGORITHM OVERVIEW

The *two-dimensional run-length compressed matching problem* is formally defined as follows:

INPUT: Two-dimensional run-length compressed text matrix T; Compressed two-dimensional pattern matrix P.

OUTPUT: All locations in T where P occurs.

We want the running time of our algorithm to be insensitive to the size of the output, therefore we do not allow trivial patterns. A *trivial matrix* is one in which every element contains the same character. If the text and the pattern are both trivial with the same character, then the output size is $O(|T|)$ which is not efficient for any compression scheme. All other patterns contain a *seam*, that is, an occurence of two different, adjacent characters. Since the number of seams in the text is $O(c(T))$ for run length compression, the output size is optimal. For simplicity's sake we will assume here that *every* pattern *row* contains a seam.

Below is an overview of the algorithm. As in section 9.1, the term *candidate* refers to a location in the *text* that *may* correspond to the element $P[0, 0]$ of an actual occurence of the pattern. Recall that a set of candidates is *compatible* if for any two candidates in the set, the two copies of the pattern originating at the sources overlap without any mismatches.

Algorithm Overview:

Following the scheme of many pattern matching algorithms, this algorithm consists of a *pattern preprocessing* part and a *text scanning* part.

Pattern Preprocessing: As in section 9.1.2 and exercise 1, a witness table is constructed for the pattern. We will assume that the if the (uncompressed) pattern is an $m \times m$ matrix, then there is a witness for every offset (i, j) such that $-m < j < m$ and $0 \leq i \leq m/2$. In a sense, this is equivalent to the condition for aperiodicity in one dimension, in which a string is considered to be to aperiodic if its longest border is less than half the length of the string. A similar (but more complicated) algorithm to the one presented below works for cases in which such an aperiocity assumption is not warranted.

Text Scanning: Performed in three phases:

1) The **restriction phase** is a text scan in which preliminary candidates sources are selected. This phase is not needed in the uncompressed exact matching algorithm because all text locations are assumed to be candidates.

2) The **compatibility phase**, partitions the portion of the text having candidate sources into blocks of size $\frac{m}{2} \times \frac{m}{2}$. Within each block, a single candidate remains, by the aperiodicity assumption.

3) The **verification phase** is a triple scan of the text to determine which of the remaining candidates are actual occurrences of the pattern.

9.3.2 THE COMPRESSED MATCHING ALGORITHM

To simplify the description of the algorithm, we will assume that the uncompressed text is an $n \times n$ array, the pattern is an $m \times m$ array and both

n and m are powers of 2.

Algorithm G. *Text Analysis for Non-Periodic Patterns*

Step G.1: Input Compressed representations of the text and the pattern, and the output from the pattern preprocessing.

Step G.2: Restriction Phase

The goal of the restriction phase is to find potential candidate patterns in the text subject to the restriction that each candidate must contain a pattern characteristic seam (in fact, we are even assuming that each row contains a seam). Because there can be no more seams in the text than $c(T)$, this phase provides an important initial limit on the number of candidates considered in the remaining phases of the algorithm. This step scans through the text computing the source position relative to every seam. The list is then bin-sorted by columns. The remaining candidates are now stored on column lists C_i , where i corresponds to the column of the text in which the candidate source occurs. These lists will be used in the compatibility and verification phases.

Step G.3: Compatibility Phase

Here we partition the text into disjoint, occupied blocks of size $\frac{m}{2} \times \frac{m}{2}$. An *occupied* block contains a candidate source. As a result of the restriction phase, the text is partitioned into occupied blocks of size 1×1 each containing one candidate source. We initially combine vertical pairs of these blocks into blocks of size 2×1 and then combine horizontal pairs of these blocks into blocks of size 2×2. Repeating in a similar fashion for $\log m - 1$ stages, we obtain blocks of size $\frac{m}{2} \times \frac{m}{2}$. Blocks are combined vertically by scanning down one column list (steps 3.1 and 3.2) and horizontally by scanning down two adjacent column lists simultaneously (step 3.3). After each stage, the number of lists is reduced by half, until there are $\frac{2n}{m}$ lists at the end of this phase. More formally, each stage partitions the text into disjoint, occupied j-blocks. A j-*block* is a subarray

$$T[k \cdot 2^j \ldots (k+1)2^j - 1, l \cdot 2^j \ldots (l+1)2^j - 1], \quad k, l = 0 \ldots \frac{n}{2^j} - 1$$

containing 2^j rows and columns. A *half-j-block* is a subarray

$$T[k \cdot 2^j \ldots (k+1)2^j - 1, l \cdot 2^{j-1} \ldots (l+1)2^{j-1} - 1],$$

$$k = 0 \ldots \frac{n}{2^j} - 1, \ l = 0 \ldots \frac{n}{2^{j-1}} - 1$$

containing 2^j rows and 2^{j-1} columns. A *pair of j-blocks* is two j-blocks that form a half $j + 1$-block.

Step G.3: Implementation of Consistency Phase
For $j := 1$ to $\log m - 1$ do:

Step G.3.1: For each column list C_i, $i = 0 \ldots \frac{n}{2^{j-1}} - 1$ scan the list from the top down. If the list contains a pair of occupied $(j-1)$-blocks, look up the witness $w = T[r, c]$ for the candidates in the $Witness$ table from the pattern preprocessing step and put onto the witness list.

The two candidates are *incompatible* and thus have a witness since two compatible sources for non-periodic patterns cannot co-exist within a block of size $\frac{m}{2} \times \frac{m}{2}$ or smaller. As the blocks are combined, we use witness locations from the pattern analysis and refer to the text to eliminate incompatible candidates. Since the text is stored in row lists due to its compressed representation, it is not possible to directly access a witness location in $O(1)$ time. So, for each stage, we first determine all the witness locations, sort them and then do a complete scan of the text to determine which character is in each witness. For each witness, we maintain a pointer to its pair of blocks.

Step G.3.2: Radix sort the witness list. Scan the text to determine the character in each witness and determine which one or both of the candidates mismatches the text character. Eliminate the appropriate candidate(s) from list C_i.

After step 3.2, each list contains half-j-blocks.

Step G.3.3: For each pair of lists C_{2i}, C_{2i+1}, $i = 0 \ldots \frac{n}{2^j} - 1$, scan down both lists simultaneously. If the lists contain two horizontally adjacent occupied half j-blocks, find the witness for the candidates and put on a witness list. Repeat step 3.2 except the remaining candidates are linked onto a new list C_i.

After step 3.3, the number of lists has been reduced by half and each list contains occupied j-blocks.

Step G.4: Verification Phase

In testing the candidates against the text, we employ the following main idea:

- For each segment (run of identical characters) of the text, at most nine candidates contain the first character of the segment.

Step G.4.1: For each segment S of the text, if a candidate C contains the first character of S, then test if S matches the next untested segment of C. If a mismatch occurs, eliminate C.

Consider the first character of a text segment at location $T[r, c]$. Any candidate that overlaps this character must have its source in one of nine contiguous blocks. Let

$$k \cdot \frac{m}{2} \le r < (k+1) \cdot \frac{m}{2}$$

$$l \cdot \frac{m}{2} \le c < (l+1) \cdot \frac{m}{2} \quad k, l = 0 \ldots \frac{2n}{m} - 1$$

Then, the sources for candidates that can contain $T[r, c]$ are in the $\frac{m}{2} \times \frac{m}{2}$ size blocks encompassing text locations

$$T[(k-i) \cdot \frac{m}{2} \ldots (k-i+1) \cdot \frac{m}{2}, (l-j) \cdot \frac{m}{2} \ldots (l-j+1) \cdot \frac{m}{2}] \quad i, j = 0 \ldots 2$$

These blocks are on lists C_{l-j}. Number the blocks consecutively row-by-row from upper left. Then $T[r, c]$ occurs in block B_9. Candidates with sources in blocks $B_4 - B_6$ always overlap row r. Candidates with sources in blocks $B_1 - B_3$ and $B_7 - B_9$ may be, respectively, completely above row r or completely below row r.

Now, compare segment S with first character at $T[r, c]$ and , candidate C with source in one of the nine blocks. Test if S matches the next untested segment in C. (We keep, for each candidate, a pointer to the next untested segment in the compressed representation for P.) On a mismatch, either of character, position or length, eliminate C.

We perform a special test when we begin testing a new row r_C of C, but S is *not* the first segment of that row. C is eliminated unless S matches the second segment of row r_C and the character of the text segment preceding S matches the character of the first segment of row r_C.

We move down each column list C_i as we move down the rows of the text, so there is no time penalty for finding the (possibly) nine candidates to test for each segment.

Theorem 9.6. *The algorithm runs in time $O(c(T) \log |P|)$*

Proof: Restriction Phase: Clearly, $O(c(T))$.

Compatibility Phase: Each stage requires two passes through the text (size $c(T)$) and two passes through the lists C_i (size $O(c(T))$. Sorting the witnesses is done by radix sort in time $O(c(T))$. Each of $\log m$ stages thus requires time $O(c(T))$ and the entire compatibility phase requires time $O(c(T) \log m) = O(c(T) \log |P|)$.

Verification Phase: There are $c(T)$ text segments and $O(c(T))$ candidates. In the scan of the text rows, each segment is tested against at most 9 candidates. The entire verification phase requires time $O(c(T))$.

The total time for the algorithm is therefore $O(c(T) \log |P|)$. $\square$

9.4　Exercises

1. Write a $O(m)$ time algorithm that constructs the witness table of a pattern string $P = p_1 \cdots p_m$. More precisely,

$$WITNESS(i) = \begin{cases} 0, & \text{if } p_{i+j} = p_{1+j}, \quad j = 0, ..., m - i; \\ k, & \text{if } p_k \neq p_{k-i+1}, \text{ for some } i \leq k \leq m. \end{cases}$$

2. Recall the Bird and Baker two dimensional pattern matching algorithm. It first used the Aho and Corasick dictionary matching algorithm to find all pattern rows, and then did a Knuth-Morris-Pratt (KMP) scan vertically, to find all locations were the pattern rows appear consecutively, exactly below each other.

   Using suffix trees, modify the KMP algorithm to find all consecutive appearances of the pattern rows in the text *without needing* the Aho and Corasick algorithm.

3. The two dimensional scaling algorithm presented here had time complexity $O(n^2 \log m)$. Modify the algorithm to achieve time $O(n^2)$. (*Hint:* Assume non-trivial patterns, i.e. patterns with at least two different alphabet symbols. Use symbol changes in the text as "anchors" for possible pattern occurrences.)

4. A *prefix encoding* of string $T = t_1 \cdots t_n$ over alphabet Σ is a mapping $c(T) = c(t_1) \cdots c(t_n)$ where $c : \Sigma \to \{0, 1\}^*$ and where for any $a \neq b$, $a, b \in \Sigma$ $c(a)$ is not a prefix of $c(b)$ and $c(b)$ is not a prefix of $c(a)$. Consider the following compressed matching problem:

   INPUT: Prefix encoding c, $c(T)$, and pattern P.

   OUTPUT: All locations in T where there is an occurrence of P.

   Give a $O(|c(T)| + |P|)$ algorithm for the above problem.

5. In the compressed matching algorithm we assumed that every row (or every column) has a *seam*. In fact, it is sufficient to assume that one row (or column) has a seam. Let us assume that we will encode by run-length of rows if every row has a seam, otherwise, we encode by run-length of columns, if every column has a seam. If there are at least one row and at least one column without a seam (i.e. a *stripe*), then we encode by run-length compression of the rows.

   (a) Prove that if the pattern is non-trivial (has more than one symbol) then there are at least one row and at least one column with a seam.

   (b) Prove that if there are stripes in the compression, then all stripes are of the same "color" (have the same repeating symbol).

6. Generalize the compressed matching algorithm to handle compressions with stripes, by adding a preliminary scan that eliminates all text locations that have a stripe of the wrong color.

9.5 Bibliographic Notes

We have scanned some of the recent results in two dimensional matching. This area is clearly too big to be comprehensively studied in such a brief description. We have therefore concentrated in efficient worst-case sequential deterministic algorithms for exact matching and its variants. Given the long list of modifiers, it is not surprising that a vast amount of work falls outside of the scope of this chapter.

For the interested reader, we can recommend the following papers. For the automata approach described in Section 9.1, see Bird [1977] and Baker [1978]. For the alphabet independent approach of Section 9.1.2, see Amir, Benson and Farach [1994a]. The first $O(m^2)$ witness table construction appeared in Park and Galil [1992]. See Amir, Landau and Vishkin [1992] for a description of the scaled matching algorithm of Section 9.2, and Amir and Calinescu [1996] for an alphabet independent and dictionary scaled matching algorithm. The compressed matching algorithm of Section 9.3 appeared in Amir and Benson [1992], and an improvement can be found in Amir, Benson and Farach [1994b].

See Aho and Corasick [1975] for a description of the the automaton based dictionary matching algorithm. Suffix trees and their contruction are described in Weiner [1973] and McCreight [1976]. The first optimal algorithm for Least Common Ancestor queries appears in Harel and Tarjan [1984]. Gabow, Bentely and Tarjan [1984] discuss range minimum queries and cartesian trees.

Bibliography

AMIR, A., AND G. BENSON [1992]. "Two dimensional periodicity and its application", *Proc. of 3rd Symoposium on Discrete Algorithms, Orlando, Florida*, 440–452.

AMIR, A., G. BENSON, AND M. FARACH [1994a]. "An alphabet independent approach to two dimensional matching", *SIAM J. Comp.*, **23**:2, 313-323.

AMIR, A., G. BENSON, AND M. FARACH [1994b]. "Optimal two-dimensional compressed matching", *Proc. 21st Intl. Col. on Automata, Languages and Programming (ICALP 94)*, Springer-Verlag LNCS 820, 215-226.

AMIR, A., AND G. CALINESCU [1996]. "Alphabet independent and dictionary scaled matching", *Proc. 7th Annual Symposium on Combinatorial Pattern Matching (CPM 96)*, Springer-Verlag LNCS 1075, 320-334.

AHO, A.V., AND M.J. CORASICK [1975]. "Efficient string matching", *C. ACM*, **18**:6, 333-340.

AMIR, A., G.M. LANDAU, AND U. VISHKIN [1992]. "Efficient pattern matching with scaling", *Journal of Algorithms*, **13**:1, 2-32.

BAKER, T.J. [1978]. "A technique for extending rapid exact-match string matching to arrays of more than one dimension", *SIAM J. Comp*, **7**, 533–541.

BIRD, R.S. [1977]. "Two dimensional pattern matching", *Information Processing Letters*, **6**:5, 168–170.

GABOW, H.N., J. L. BENTLEY, AND R. E. TARJAN [1984]. "Scaling and related techniques for geometry problems", *Proc. 16th Symposium on the Theory of Computing (STOC 84)*, 135 – 143.

HAREL, D., AND R.E. TARJAN [1984]. "Fast algorithms for finding nearest common ancestor", *Journal of Computer and System Sciences*, **13**, 338–355.

KNUTH, D.E., J.H. MORRIS, AND V.R. PRATT [1977]. "Fast pattern matching in strings", *SIAM J. Comp.*, **6**, 323–350.

LANDAU, G.M., AND U. VISHKIN [1989]. "Fast parallel and serial approximate string matching", *Journal of Algorithms*, **10**:2, 157–169.

McCREIGHT, E.M. [1976]. "A space-economical suffix tree construction algorithm", *Journal of the ACM*, **23**, 262–272.

MAIN, M.G., AND R.J. LORENTZ [1984]. "An $O(n \log n)$ algorithm for finding all repetitions in a string", *Journal of Algorithms*, 422–432.

PARK, K., AND Z. GALIL [1992]. "Truly alphabet-independent two-dimensional pattern matching", *Proc. 33rd Symposium on the Foundations of Computer Science (FOCS 92)*, 247-256.

WEINER, P. [1973]. "Linear pattern matching algorithm", *Proc. 14 IEEE Symposium on Switching and Automata Theory*, 1–11.

10
Suffix Tree Data Structures for Matrices

We discuss the suffix tree generalization to matrices in this chapter. We extend the suffix tree notion (described in Chapter 3) from text *strings* to text *matrices* whose entries are taken from an ordered alphabet with the aim of solving pattern-matching problems. This suffix tree generalization can be efficiently used to implement low-level routines for Computer Vision, Data Compression, Geographic Information Systems and Visual Databases. We examine the *submatrices* in the form of the text's contiguous parts that still have a matrix shape. Representing these text submatrices as "suitably formatted" strings stored in a compacted trie is the rationale behind suffix trees for matrices. The choice of the format inevitably influences suffix tree construction time and space complexity.

We first deal with *square* matrices and show that many suffix tree families can be defined for the same input matrix according to the matrix's string representations. We can store each suffix tree in *linear* space and give an efficient construction algorithm whose input is both the matrix and the string representation chosen. We then treat *rectangular* matrices and define their corresponding suffix trees by means of some general rules which we list formally. We show that there is a *super-linear* lower bound to the space required (in contrast with the linear space required by suffix trees for square matrices). We give a simple example of one of these suffix trees. The last part of the chapter illustrates some technical results regarding suffix trees for square matrices: we show how to achieve an expected linear-time suffix tree construction for a constant-size alphabet under some mild probabilistic assumptions about the input distribution.

10.1   Suffix trees for square matrices

We begin by defining a wide class of string representations for square matrices. We let Σ denote an ordered alphabet of characters and introduce another alphabet of five special characters, called shapes.

Definition 10.1. A *shape* is one of the special characters taken from set $\{\mathcal{IN}, \mathcal{SW}, \mathcal{NW}, \mathcal{SE}, \mathcal{NE}\}$. Shape $\mathcal{IN}$ encodes the 1×1 matrix generated from the empty matrix by creating a square. The other shapes denote the

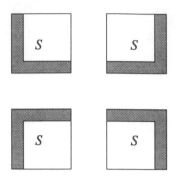

Fig. 10.1.   Shapes $\mathcal{SW}, \mathcal{SE}, \mathcal{NE}, \mathcal{NW}$ (clockwise, from the top left).

extension of a generic $(i-1) \times (i-1)$ matrix S in a larger $i \times i$ matrix that contains S as a submatrix, for any $i > 1$. Shape $\mathcal{SW}$ denotes appending a row of length $i - 1$ to the bottom (South) of S and a column of length i to the left (West) of S. Shapes $\mathcal{SE}, \mathcal{NE}$ and $\mathcal{NW}$ are defined analogously (see Fig. 10.1).

According to Definition 10.1, a string $\mathcal{S}[1:n]$ of shapes, such that $\mathcal{S}[1] = \mathcal{IN}$ and $\mathcal{S}[i] \neq \mathcal{IN}$ for $i > 1$, encodes a partition of a generic $n \times n$ matrix A into subrows and subcolumns: Shape $\mathcal{S}[i]$ denotes the extension of an $(i - 1) \times (i - 1)$ submatrix to a larger $i \times i$ submatrix, for $1 < i \leq n$. Consequently, $\mathcal{S}[1:n]$ can be thought of as a sequence of "onion peeling instructions" used to represent A in one dimension.

Example 10.2. Let us examine the shape string illustrated in Fig. 10.2a, where $\mathcal{S}[1:n] = \mathcal{IN} \, \mathcal{SE} \, \mathcal{NW} \, \mathcal{SE} \, \mathcal{NW} \cdots$. It induces a unique matrix partition by "putting" $\mathcal{IN}$ in the "center" and by then "covering" the matrix subrows and subcolumns with shapes (see Fig. 10.2b).

Let us take A's entries, which are some characters chosen from Σ. We can associate each shape $\mathcal{S}[i]$ with a subrow and a subcolumn because of Definition 10.1. Consequently, we "cover" $2i - 1$ A's entries and concatenate the characters read from these entries clockwise. We obtain a string (representation) that we consider atomic and we therefore call it a *macro character*. We define $\hat{\Sigma} = \cup_{i=1}^{\infty} \Sigma^{2i-1}$ as the set of macro characters: Two macro characters are equal if their string representations are equal; they can be concatenated whenever their string representation lengths are $2i - 1$ and $2i + 1$, respectively, for an integer $i \geq 1$. A *macro string* $\alpha = \alpha[1:n]$ (of length n) is the concatenation of n macro characters according to the above rule, such that the first macro character $\alpha[1] \in \Sigma$. We use common terminology for macro strings α: for example, the *prefix* of length i is $\alpha[1:i]$. However, a macro substring $\alpha[i:j]$ is called a *chunk* to emphasize

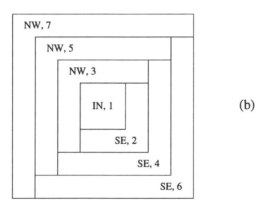

1 2   3   4   5   6   7
IN,SE, NW,SE, NW,SE, NW   (a)

(b)

Fig. 10.2. (a) A sequence of shapes and (b) the partition induced by it.

that $\alpha[i:j]$ is *not* a macro string when $i > 1$ (see Example 10.3). There is a one-to-one correspondence between square matrices and their macro strings.

Example 10.3. A macro string $\alpha[1:n]$ is called *spiral* when $\mathcal{S}[1:n] = \mathcal{IN} \, \mathcal{SE} \, \mathcal{NW} \, \mathcal{SE} \, \mathcal{NW} \cdots$ (see Fig. 10.2). We partition the matrix illustrated in Fig. 10.3a according to $\mathcal{S}$ (see Fig. 10.3b). Each shape covers a matrix subrow and subcolumn and the strings obtained by visiting these shapes clockwise are shown in Fig. 10.3c. At the top, we report the positions the characters are taken from. Fig. 10.3d shows the spiral macro string $\alpha[1:3]$ corresponding to our matrix, in which the macro characters are separated by vertical bars. We wish to point out that $\alpha[1]$ is a character in Σ and $\alpha[1:2]$ is still a spiral macro string, whereas $\alpha[2:3]$ is not. We can represent a macro string in the form of either Fig. 10.3b or Fig. 10.3d.

We would like to build a regular compacted trie (digital search tree) on a set of macro strings and handle their string representations by the method used for suffix trees for regular strings (see Chapter 3). The format induced by the shapes gives us some extra information that we exploit thanks to the notion of compacted trie built *directly on the macro strings in $\hat{\Sigma}^*$* rather than on their string representations in Σ^*.

Given a set of matrices, let us examine the corresponding set $\mathcal{M}$ of their macro strings; we assume that no macro string is a prefix of another one. A trie for macro strings is like a trie for strings except for the following

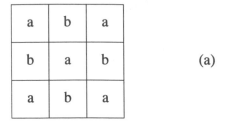

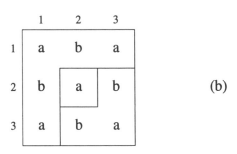

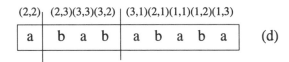

(2,2) (2,3)(3,3)(3,2) (3,1)(2,1)(1,1)(1,2)(1,3)   (c)
  a ; b   a   b ; a   b   a   b   a

(2,2)ᵢ (2,3)(3,3)(3,2) | (3,1)(2,1)(1,1)(1,2)(1,3)

| a | b a b | a b a b a | (d)

Fig. 10.3.   (a) A matrix, (b) its partition into shapes, (c) the strings obtained by visiting the shapes clockwise, and (d) the matrix's macro string.

characteristics (Figs. 10.4a,b): Each arc is labeled by a macro character; all the arcs coming from a node are labeled by different macro characters which originate from the *same shape* and contain the same number of matrix entries; there is a leaf v for each macro string $\alpha \in \mathcal{M}$, such that the concatenation of the labels along the path from the root to v gives α.

Tries for macro strings can have one-child nodes just like tries for strings (Fig. 10.4b). We therefore compact tries for macro strings by taking the maximal paths made up of one-child nodes and compressing them in single

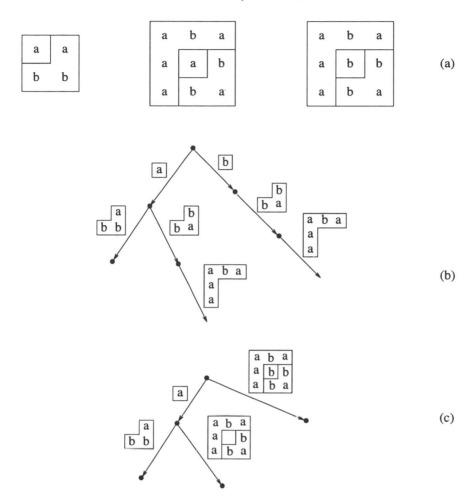

Fig. 10.4. (a) The macro strings for three matrices according to $S[1:3] =$ $\mathcal{IN}\,\mathcal{SE}\,\mathcal{NW}$. (b) The trie for the macro strings. (c) Its compacted version, in which the arcs are labeled by chunks.

arcs. The arcs' new labels are chunks obtained by concatenating the macro characters found along the compressed paths. The resulting data structure is a compacted trie for $\mathcal{M}$ (Fig. 10.4c). Sibling arcs in the compacted trie are labeled by chunks whose first macro characters are distinct.

We use the following terminology when dealing with compacted tries CT. We say that a node u is the *locus* of a macro string α if and only if the labels' concatenation along the downward path leading from the root to u is equal to α. The extension of α is any macro string having a prefix equal to α. The *extended locus* of α is the locus of α's shortest extension having its locus in CT. If the extended locus of a macro string exists, then it is unique.

We can now define the suffix tree for a square matrix A by carefully choosing A's "suffixes", i.e., A's submatrices whose macro strings have to be stored in compacted trie leaves. We closely follow the idea illustrated in Chapter 3 for storing string suffixes in distinct leaves. We aim at defining a compacted trie that represents all of A's square submatrices along the paths by imposing the following two constraints:

Completeness:	For each submatrix B, the extended locus of the macro string representing B is in the compacted trie. Moreover, there is a one-to-one correspondence between A's positions (i, j) and the compacted trie leaves.
Common Submatrix:	If u denotes the extended locus of the macro string representing a submatrix B, then all of u's descendants are extended loci of macro strings representing matrices that contain B as their submatrix.

We now illustrate the suffix tree definition. We define it in terms of an "augmented" square matrix $A\hat{\$}$ (see Fig. 10.5a) whose rows' and columns' numbering ranges from $-n+1$ to $2n$: we set $A\hat{\$}[1:n, 1:n] = A$, while all the other entries $A\hat{\$}[p, q]$ (with $-n + 1 \leq p, q \leq 2n$; $p \notin [1, n]$ or $q \notin [1, n]$) are distinct instances of $\$ \notin \Sigma$. We let the "suffixes" be $n \times n$ matrices denoted by $A_{i,j}$ (with $1 \leq i, j \leq n$), which are $A\hat{\$}$'s submatrices defined in the following way (Fig. 10.5b): $\mathcal{S}[1]$ is put in position (i, j) and $A\hat{\$}$'s subrows and subcolumns around (i, j) are covered by the shapes in $\mathcal{S}[2:n]$. Suffixes $A_{i,j}$ are distinct due to the $\$$ instances and we identify $A_{i,j}$ with its *origin* (i, j). We use $\alpha_{i,j}$ to denote the macro string (of length n) representing $A_{i,j}$ and let $\mathcal{M} = \{\alpha_{i,j} : 1 \leq i, j \leq n\}$ be the set of macro strings to be stored in the compacted trie. When referring to $\alpha_{i,j}$ and $A_{i,j}$, we implicitly assume that $1 \leq i, j \leq n$.

Definition 10.4. The suffix tree T_A for an $n \times n$ matrix A is a compacted trie (over the alphabet $\hat{\Sigma}$) built on $\mathcal{M}$'s macro strings:

(10.4.1) There are n^2 leaves labeled by the pairs $(1, 1), (1, 2), \ldots, (n, n)$ and no internal node having one child (except for the root).

(10.4.2) Each arc is labeled by a chunk so that the labels' concatenations along a root-to-leaf path is equal to one of $\mathcal{M}$'s macro strings. That is, each leaf is the locus of a macro string $\alpha_{i,j}$ and is labeled by the pair (i, j) corresponding to $A_{i,j}$'s origin.

```
     -3 -2 -1 0 1 2 3 4 5 6 7 8
  -3  $ $ $ $ $ $ $ $ $ $ $ $
  -2  $ $ $ $ $ $ $ $ $ $ $ $
  -1  $ $ $ $ $ $ $ $ $ $ $ $
   0  $ $ $ $ $ $ $ $ $ $ $ $
   1  $ $ $ $ b a a b $ $ $ $
   2  $ $ $ $ a b a b $ $ $ $        (a)
   3  $ $ $ $ a b b a $ $ $ $
   4  $ $ $ $ a a a b $ $ $ $
   5  $ $ $ $ $ $ $ $ $ $ $ $
   6  $ $ $ $ $ $ $ $ $ $ $ $
   7  $ $ $ $ $ $ $ $ $ $ $ $
   8  $ $ $ $ $ $ $ $ $ $ $ $
```

$$
A_{1,1} = \begin{array}{|c c c c|}
\$ & \$ & \$ & \$ \\
\$ & b & a & a \\
\$ & a & b & a \\
\$ & a & b & b
\end{array}
\qquad
A_{3,3} = \begin{array}{|c c c c|}
b & a & b & \$ \\
b & b & a & \$ \\
a & a & b & \$ \\
\$ & \$ & \$ & \$
\end{array}
$$

$$
A_{2,2} = \begin{array}{|c c c c|}
b & a & a & b \\
a & b & a & b \\
a & b & b & a \\
a & a & a & b
\end{array}
\qquad
A_{1,4} = \begin{array}{|c c c c|}
\$ & \$ & \$ & \$ \\
a & b & \$ & \$ \\
a & b & \$ & \$ \\
b & a & \$ & \$
\end{array}
\qquad \text{(b)}
$$

$$
A_{3,2} = \begin{array}{|c c c c|}
a & b & a & b \\
a & b & b & a \\
a & a & a & b \\
\$ & \$ & \$ & \$
\end{array}
\qquad
A_{4,4} = \begin{array}{|c c c c|}
b & a & \$ & \$ \\
a & b & \$ & \$ \\
\$ & \$ & \$ & \$ \\
\$ & \$ & \$ & \$
\end{array}
$$

$$
A_{2,4} = \begin{array}{|c c c c|}
a & b & \$ & \$ \\
a & b & \$ & \$ \\
b & a & \$ & \$ \\
a & b & \$ & \$
\end{array}
$$

Fig. 10.5. (a) The matrix $A\hat{\$}$ corresponding to the matrix A (in the center). The $\$$ symbols represent different instances of $\$$. (b) The "suffixes" $A_{i,j}$: we are only showing the ones such that $A\hat{\$}[i,j] = b$. They are partitioned according to $S[1:4] = \mathcal{IN} \, \mathcal{SE} \, \mathcal{NW} \, \mathcal{SE}$.

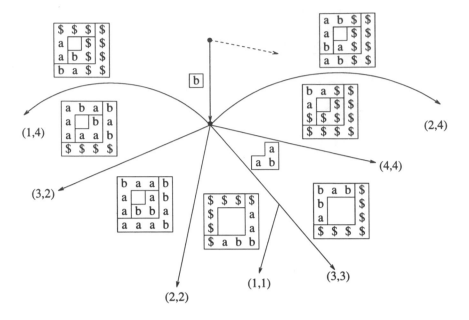

Fig. 10.6.   The suffix tree for the matrix in Fig. 10.5a. We only illustrate the root-to-leaf paths storing the macro string of the matrices shown in Fig. 10.5b.

(10.4.3) The first macro characters in the sibling arcs' labels are *different* and originate from the *same* shape and have the same string representation length.

Example 10.5. We show $A\hat{\$}$ in Fig. 10.5a and let $A = A\hat{\$}[1\!:\!4, 1\!:\!4]$. Let us only examine the suffixes $A_{i,j}$ with $A\hat{\$}[i,j] = b$ (Fig. 10.5b). We obtain T_A's portion in Fig. 10.6. Macro string $\alpha_{i,j}$ has its locus in the leaf labeled (i,j). If two leaves share the same path, then their macro strings share the same prefix that is equal to the macro string represented by the path (e.g., leaves $(1,1)$ and $(3,3)$ and the path from the root to one of their common ancestors).

It is worth noting that Conditions 10.4.1–10.4.3 are reminiscent of Conditions 1–3 in the suffix tree definition for strings (Chapter 3). The Completeness and Common Submatrix constraints mentioned previously are satisfied by T_A because every submatrix is represented by a prefix of a macro string in $\mathcal{M}$.

Fact 10.6. *Let us examine the suffix tree T_A for an $n \times n$ matrix A and take an $s \times s$ matrix B (where $s \leq n$). We have that B is equal to one of A's submatrices if and only if the extended locus of the macro string*

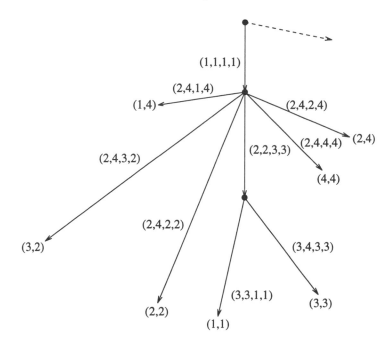

Fig. 10.7. The same tree as the one shown in Fig. 10.6 whose chunks are substituted by descriptors.

representing B is in T_A. All of A's submatrices equal to B can be retrieved in all of T_A's leaves that descend from the extended locus.

Suffix tree T_A has $O(n^2)$ nodes since there are n^2 leaves and every internal node except the root has at least two children. Storing T_A in optimal $O(n^2)$ space requires encoding its labeling chunks by constant-space descriptors. We pick out an arc (u, v) in which v's parent is u and take the arc's label γ. We examine an arbitrary leaf descending from v, i.e., f, and let (i, j) be the pair labeling f. Because of Condition 10.4.2, the labels' concatenation obtained by traversing the path from the root to f must give $\alpha_{i,j} \in \mathcal{M}$. Since (u, v) is along this path, its label γ must appear somewhere in the form of $\alpha_{i,j}$'s chunk. That is, we can find $p, q \in [1, n]$, such that $\alpha_{i,j}[p:q] = \gamma$. We therefore define the constant-space quadruple (p, q, i, j) as γ's *descriptor*. By using (p, q, i, j), we can locate $A\hat{\$}$'s part corresponding to γ in constant time. From now on, we assume that the chunks labeling T_A's arcs are substituted by their appropriate descriptors (Fig. 10.7).

Remark 10.7. Suffix trees for matrices can almost always be used in the same way as suffix trees for strings. For example, we can use T_A to search

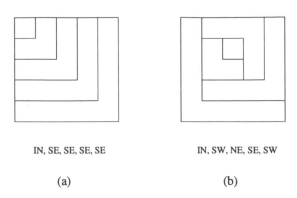

IN, SE, SE, SE, SE   IN, SW, NE, SE, SW

(a)   (b)

Fig. 10.8. (a) The sequence of shapes for Lstrings. (b) Another sequence of shapes.

on-line for pattern matrix B's occurrences in A by using Fact 10.6 (see Exercise 10.1). We can also obtain some *statistics* about A's square sub-matrices by means of some T_A preprocessing (see Exercise 10.2).

Definition 10.4 holds for many macro strings which are well-suited for defining suffix tree families.

Example 10.8. With regard to spiral macro strings, in current literature, their suffix tree is known as *PAT-tree for spiral strings* (see Fig. 10.6). Let us now choose $\mathcal{S}[1:n] = \mathcal{IN}\ \mathcal{SE}\ \mathcal{SE}\ \mathcal{SE} \cdots$ to induce the partition shown in Fig. 10.8a. The resulting macro strings are known in literature as *Lstrings*. The corresponding suffix tree is called an *Lsuffix tree*. An example of an Lsuffix tree is given in Fig. 10.9, where only the paths leading to the leaves labeled (i, i) (for $i = 1, 2, \ldots, 6$) are shown (we ignore some of \$'s instances). The tree satisfies Definition 10.4 and so it can be considered a special case of suffix trees. There are many suffix trees for the same input matrix. For example, if we choose $\mathcal{S}[1:n] = \mathcal{IN}\ \mathcal{SW}\ \mathcal{NE}\ \mathcal{SE}\ \mathcal{SW} \cdots$ (see Fig. 10.8b), we obtain another suffix tree because of Definition 10.4.

In general, an *arbitrary* string of shapes $\mathcal{S}[1:n]$ with $\mathcal{S}[1] = \mathcal{IN}$ and $\mathcal{S}[i] \neq \mathcal{IN}$ for $i > 1$ causes a partition of the input matrix A. Consequently, we can construct the macro string α that represents A according to $\mathcal{S}$ by letting $\mathcal{S}[i]$ "cover" one subrow and one subcolumn. We let $a_1, \ldots, a_{2i-1}$ be the entries in A's subrow and subcolumn covered by shape $\mathcal{S}[i]$ and read them clockwise. We can then make it possible to read these characters in any order (i.e., not only clockwise) by taking a permutation π_{2i-1} of integers $\{1, \ldots, 2i-1\}$ and letting β_i be the string $a_{\pi_{2i-1}(1)} a_{\pi_{2i-1}(2)} \cdots a_{\pi_{2i-1}(2i-1)}$ obtained by permuting $a_1, \ldots, a_{2i-1}$ by means of π_{2i-1}. We set an array $\Pi[1:n]$ to store these permutations (i.e., $\Pi[i] = \pi_{2i-1}$ for $1 \leq i \leq n$). We define A's string representation *according to $\mathcal{S}$ and Π* to be the macro

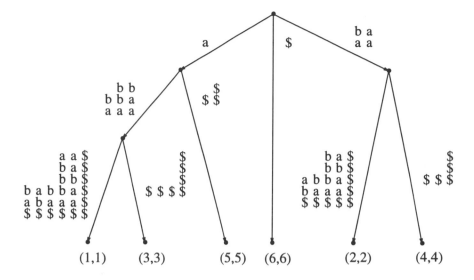

Fig. 10.9. The Lsuffix tree: only the paths corresponding to some "suffixes" are shown, and some $'s are not shown.

string $\beta_1\beta_2\ldots\beta_n$, where each β_i is a macro character. The one-to-one correspondence between macro strings and matrices still holds.

Suffix tree T_A's previous definition still holds even if the choice of the "suffixes" $A_{i,j}$ (and hence their macro strings $\alpha_{i,j}$) can vary because of $\mathcal{S}$ and Π. We can think of $\mathcal{S}$ and Π as producing a suffix tree's concise description independently of A's characters. Since we have 4^{n-1} distinct sequences $\mathcal{S}$ with n shapes, such that $\mathcal{S}[1] = \mathcal{IN}$, and since we can obtain $\Pi_{i=1}^{n}(2i-1)!$ permutation arrays Π from each $\mathcal{S}$, we therefore obtain many suffix trees that can be built on the same text matrix. However, once $\mathcal{S}$ is fixed, the suffix trees obtained by means of the $\Pi_{i=1}^{n}(2i-1)!$ permutation arrays Π are all isomorphic (see Exercise 10.3). This is why we only explicitly treat sequences of shapes $\mathcal{S}$ without specifying Π (by default, we assume that Π contains the identity permutations read clockwise).

10.2   Suffix tree construction for square matrices

Building the suffix tree T_A for an $n \times n$ matrix A and a shape sequence $\mathcal{S}$ can be easily accomplished in $O(n^4)$ time by installing the paths corresponding to all the macro strings $\alpha_{i,j} \in \mathcal{M}$. The bound follows because each $\alpha_{i,j}$ has a string representation of $O(n^2)$ length and the installing procedure is repeated for $1 \le i,j \le n$. However, the expected time of this simple approach is $O(n^2 \log n)$ when using spiral strings, as pointed out by Gonnet. The first $O(n^2 \log n)$ worst-case time solution was obtained by Giancarlo

for the special case of Lstrings by generalizing McCreight's construction
(see Chapter 3). Unfortunately, for all other kinds of macro strings (an
exponential number because of $\mathcal{S}$), Giancarlo's construction does not work
because it does not make clear how the notions of *suffix links* and *rescanning*
(the main components of McCreight's algorithm) can be extended to
our suffix tree families for matrices.

We present an $O(n^2 \log n)$ time construction that works for *all* kinds
of macro strings that can be described by $\mathcal{S}$. We have the additional
advantage of taking *linear* expected time, i.e., $O(n^2)$, for a constant-size
alphabet Σ (see Section 10.5).

Our construction follows the high-level scheme of Apostolico, Iliopoulos,
Landau, Schieber and Vishkin's parallel algorithm (in short, *AILSV*) for
building a suffix tree for strings (see Chapter 3). However, we also need
some techniques tailored to handle macro strings rather than regular strings
efficiently. Instead of employing McCreight's suffix links and rescanning,
Algorithm *AILSV*'s key step is the notion of *refinement*: it produces a
sequence of trees denoted $D^{(r)}$ (for $r = \log n, \ldots, 0$), each one of which is
a better approximation of T_A. We show that refinement can be applied
to matrices when allowing an arbitrary $\mathcal{S}$. Given two chunks $\alpha_{i,j}[p:q]$ and
$\alpha_{i',j'}[p:q']$, we define a *refiner* as an integer ℓ, with $0 \le \ell \le \min(q,q')-p+1$,
such that the first ℓ macro characters of the two chunks are equal (i.e.,
$\alpha_{i,j}[p:p+\ell-1] = \alpha_{i',j'}[p:p+\ell-1]$). It is worth noting that the first macro
characters of both chunks originate from the same shape $\mathcal{S}[p]$ and contain
$2p - 1$ characters each (including $'s).

Definition 10.9. A *refinement tree* $D^{(r)}$ is a labeled tree satisfying the
following constraints (for $0 \le r \le \log n$):

(10.9.1) There are n^2 leaves labeled by the pairs $(1,1),(1,2),\ldots,(n,n)$
and no internal node having one child, except for the root.

(10.9.2) Each node is labeled by a chunk (at least 2^r long) represented
by a descriptor. The labels' concatenation along the downward
path from the root to leaf (i,j) is equal to macro string $\alpha_{i,j} \in
\mathcal{M}$. (An implicit $(1,n,i,j)$ descriptor is associated with this
leaf.) Furthermore, if descriptor (p,q,i,j) labels a node, then
leaf (i,j) is its descendant.

(10.9.3) Any two chunks labeling sibling nodes do not have a refiner 2^r
and their first macro characters originate from the same shape.
(Constraint (10.9.2) allows us to apply the refiner to chunks.)

We wish to point out that $D^{(r)}$'s arcs are stored as child-to-parent
pointers and its nodes are labeled by chunks, while T_A's arcs are parent-to-
child pointers labeled by chunks. At the beginning, $D^{(\log n)}$ is only made
up of the root and the n^2 leaves; at the end, $D^{(0)}$ satisfies T_A's definition

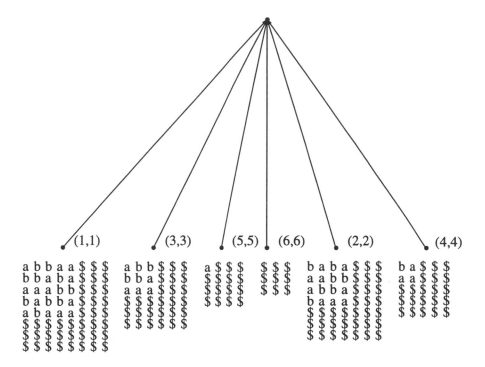

Fig. 10.10. Refinement tree $D^{(2)}$ for the suffix tree in Fig. 10.9. Only some "suffixes" are shown, and some $'s are not shown.

except that the labels must be moved from the nodes to the arcs and the arcs' direction must be inverted.

Example 10.10. Let us choose the Lstrings (Fig. 10.8a) as macro strings in this example and let T_A be the suffix tree partially shown in Fig. 10.9. Refinement tree $D^{(r)}$ (with $r = 1$) is partially illustrated in Fig. 10.11 (we explicitly show the chunks on the arcs rather than their descriptors). No two sibling nodes are labeled by chunks that have a refiner 2^r, i.e., the same $2^r = 2$ initial macro characters. It is worth noting that $D^{(r)}$ can be seen as a "relaxed" version of T_A, in which the chunks can have less than 2^r initial macro characters that are equal. $D^{(\log n)} = D^{(2)}$ is shown in Fig. 10.10 (here, by $\log n$ we mean $\lfloor \log n \rfloor$ because $n = 5$), while $D^{(0)}$ shown in Fig. 10.13 and is isomorphic to T_A (Fig. 10.9).

Once the sequential version of Algorithm $AILSV$ for regular strings is available, we might think that applying a refinement step to macro strings is just an exercise but this is not so (as can be seen below). At the beginning, $D^{(\log n)}$ can be built in $O(n^2)$ time. The next important task is to transform $D^{(r)}$ into $D^{(r-1)}$ by means of the following two steps. We let the children of

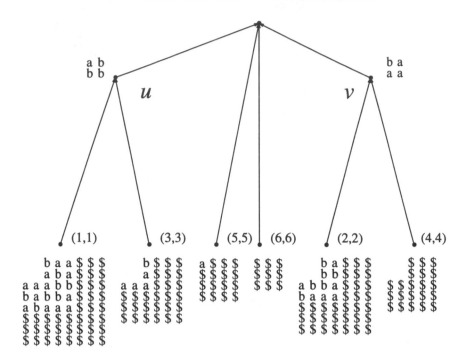

Fig. 10.11. Refinement tree $D^{(1)}$ for the suffix tree in Fig. 10.9. Only some "suffixes" are shown, and some $'s are not shown.

a $D^{(r)}$'s node be referred to as its *nest*. We say that two nodes $u, v \in D^{(r)}$ are *equivalent* if and only if u and v are in the same nest and the chunks labeling them have a refiner 2^{r-1}.

STEP 1.   We partition $D^{(r)}$'s nodes except its root into classes by means of the equivalence relation and refiner 2^{r-1}. For each equivalence class $\mathcal{C}$ with $|\mathcal{C}| > 1$, we create a new node w. The parent u of the nodes in $\mathcal{C}$ becomes w's parent and w becomes the new parent of the nodes in $\mathcal{C}$. If (p, q, i, j) is the descriptor labeling a node in $\mathcal{C}$, then we assign label $(p, p + 2^{r-1} - 1, i, j)$ to w and change the descriptor's first component from p to $p + 2^{r-1}$ for each node in $\mathcal{C}$.

STEP 2.   Let $\tilde{D}^{(r)}$ be the tree resulting from Step 1. For each node u (other than the root) whose nest produced only one equivalence class, we remove u from $\tilde{D}^{(r)}$ and make u's only child w be a child of u's parent. We modify their labels as follows: If (p, q, i, j) and $(q + 1, q', i', j')$ are the descriptors labeling u and w, respectively, then w's descriptor becomes (p, q', i', j'). The resulting tree is $D^{(r-1)}$.

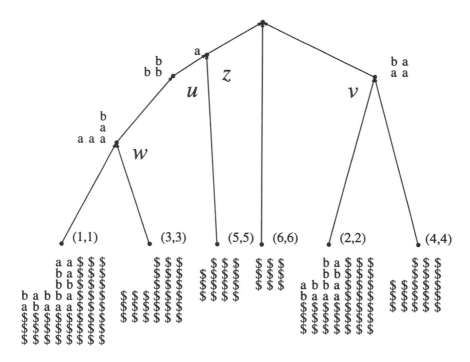

Fig. 10.12. Refinement tree $\tilde{D}^{(1)}$ for the suffix tree in Fig. 10.9, after Step 1. Only some "suffixes" are shown. and some $'s are not shown.

Lemma 10.11. *Steps 1 and 2 correctly transform $D^{(r)}$ into $D^{(r-1)}$.*

Proof: See Exercise 10.13b. □

Example 10.12. We illustrate trees $D^{(2)}, D^{(1)}, \tilde{D}^{(1)}, D^{(0)}$, respectively, by continuing Example 10.10 with reference to Figs. 10.10–10.13 (we explicitly show the chunks rather than the descriptors). We only discuss the refinement from $D^{(1)}$ to $D^{(0)}$. Let us take $D^{(r)} = D^{(1)}$ and execute Step 1 with $r = 1$. The equivalence classes partitioned by refiner $2^{r-1} = 1$ are: $\{(1,1),(3,3)\}, \{u,(5,5)\}, \{(6,6)\}, \{v\}, \{(2,2)\}$ and $\{(4,4)\}$, where pair (i,j) denotes leaf (i,j). The equivalence classes $\mathcal{C}$ with $|\mathcal{C}| > 1$ are: $\mathcal{C}_1 = \{(1,1),(3,3)\}$ and $\mathcal{C}_2 = \{u,(5,5)\}$. We create a new parent for them (i.e., w and z respectively) in the resulting tree $\tilde{D}^{(1)}$ (Fig. 10.12). We then execute Step 2 with $\tilde{D}^{(1)}$, where u is the only node whose nest produced one class (i.e., $\mathcal{C}_1$ in Step 1) and so u has only one child w. We remove u, make z be w's parent and adjust the labels in order to obtain tree $D^{(0)}$ (Fig. 10.13).

At this point, the reader may wonder what makes the computation in Example 10.12 difficult. The answer is that the refinement steps work on

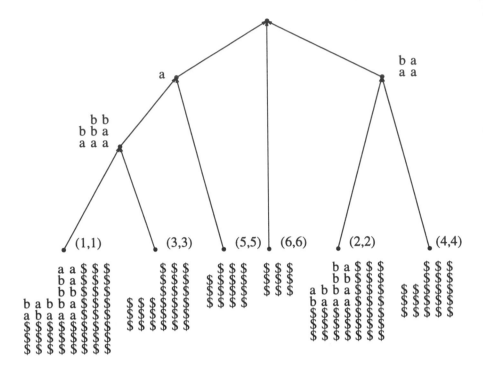

Fig. 10.13.   Refinement tree $D^{(0)}$, which is isomorphic to the suffix tree in Fig. 10.9. Only some "suffixes" are shown, and some $'s are not shown.

macro strings rather than regular strings. The problem we encounter (in Step 1) is how to partition $D^{(r)}$'s nodes into equivalence classes in $O(n^2)$ time. There are $\Theta(n^2)$ nests and each nest requires $O(n^2)$ time to be partitioned with a brute-force approach, while the rest of the operations in Steps 1-2 can be performed in $O(n^2)$ time. This takes a total of $O(n^4)$ time.

We could reduce the time complexity by using Karp, Miller and Rosenberg's pattern-matching technique adapted to macro strings and by following Algorithm $AILSV$ for regular strings. We can briefly describe this approach as follows. In the first place, a label called $name$ is assigned to the chunks (of a power-of-two length) that can be found in the macro strings in $\mathcal{M}$, so that any two chunks are equal if and only if they both have the same length and name. Each of $D^{(r)}$'s nodes also receives a unique integer that identifies it. It is worth noting that both the names and the integers range from 1 to $O(n^2)$. Secondly, pair (η_1, η_2) is assigned to each node u (except the root) where η_1 is the unique integer assigned to u's parent and η_2 is the name assigned to the first 2^{r-1} macro characters in the chunk labeling u. As a result, the equivalent nodes have equal pairs and the node partitioning can be obtained by sorting these pairs lexicographically in $O(n^2)$ time. The drawback to this approach is that it requires $\Omega(n^3 \log n)$ time and space because it may have to assign the names to $\Omega(n^3 \log n)$ *distinct* chunks in $\mathcal{M}$ in the worst case (see Exercise 10.6).

We now show how to partition the nodes in $O(n^2)$ time per refinement step (there are $\log n$ steps), after a preprocessing done in $O(n^2 \log n)$ time. It is worth noting that not all the power-of-two length chunks need names and the ones that need them vary with the refinement step used and the sequence $\mathcal{S}$ chosen. Our preprocessing consists of applying Karp, Miller and Rosenberg's technique to matrices in a standard way by computing the names of $\hat{A\$}$'s submatrices whose side is a power of two (i.e., of shape $s \times s$ for a power of two s). This can be accomplished in $O(n^2 \log n)$ time and space because there are $O(n^2 \log n)$ of these submatrices. We avoid using the names in a straightforward way. For example, we do not take a chunk and split its corresponding $\hat{A\$}$ part into "maximal" square submatrices whose names are known by preprocessing: Since the chunks represent $\hat{A\$}$'s parts that can have irregular shapes (e.g., long and thin), a tuple of $O(n)$ names would be associated with each chunk in the worst case and the total complexity would again be $O(n^3 \log n)$ time (there would be $O(n^2)$ nests in each of the $\log n$ refinement steps, and each nest would contain some tuples of $O(n)$ names).

For these reasons, we introduce the important notion of *capsular matrix* for a chunk, which is defined as the smallest square submatrix that encloses $\hat{A\$}$'s part represented by the chunk. Although two equal chunks do *not* necessarily have equal capsular matrices, this is so in our construction. More specifically, we let α_u denote the first 2^{r-1} macro characters in the chunk labeling a node $u \in D^{(r)}$ (it is well-defined by Condition 10.9.2 of Definition 10.9) and assume that $(p, p + 2^{r-1} - 1, i, j)$ is α_u's descriptor. We define α_u's capsular matrix M_{α_u} to be the one corresponding to the macro string represented by $(1, p + 2^{r-1} - 1, i, j)$, i.e., by partitioning $A_{i,j}$ according to $\mathcal{S}[1:n]$ in order to obtain its submatrix covered by the shapes in $\mathcal{S}[1:p + 2^{r-1} - 1]$ (this submatrix is M_{α_u}).

Example 10.13. We give the capsular matrix when using spiral macro strings. We examine chunk α (see Fig. 10.14c) and show its capsular matrix M_α partitioned according to $\mathcal{S}[1:4] = \mathcal{IN}\,\mathcal{SE}\,\mathcal{NW}\,\mathcal{SE}$ (see Fig. 10.14a). We wish to point out that α can be obtained from M_α by removing the matrix induced by $\mathcal{S}[1:2]$ (see Fig. 10.14b). The capsular matrix's definition applies to any other kind of macro strings and has an interesting property with respect to the chunks that label the refinement trees' nodes. With reference to the Lstrings shown in Fig. 10.11, we examine leaves f and g with labels $(1,1)$ and $(3,3)$, respectively. We let α_f and α_g be the first macro characters of the chunks that label them and let α_f's capsular matrix, i.e.,

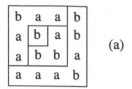

(a)

(b)

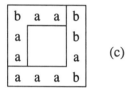

(c)

Fig. 10.14.   Chunk (c) is obtained by removing matrix (b) from matrix (a).

M_f, be obtained by first concatenating chunks from the root to f's parent and then by appending α_f to them (the same holds for M_g and α_g, see Fig. 10.15a). It is worth noting that $M_f = M_g$ because $\alpha_f = \alpha_g$. Let us now examine the leaves f and g that have labels $(1,1)$ and $(3,3)$ shown in Fig. 10.13. The two macro characters and their capsular matrices are shown in Fig. 10.15b. We wish to point out that $\alpha_f \neq \alpha_g$ and $M_f \neq M_g$. The close relationship existing between a chunk and its capsular matrix is usually not verified in general and only holds for the chunks that label the refinement trees' nodes.

Lemma 10.14. (Encapsulation) *Given any two nodes u and v in $D^{(r)}$ (which are distinct and not equal to the root): $M_{\alpha_u} = M_{\alpha_v}$ if and only if u and v are equivalent (i.e., $\alpha_u = \alpha_v$ and u and v are in the same nest).*

Proof: The proof is quite technical and is given as Exercise 10.13c. □

Lemma 10.14 is crucial for dividing the nodes into equivalence classes. For each node $u \in D^{(r)}$ in a nest, we locate its capsular matrix M_{α_u} in constant time. We let $\mathcal{H}$ denote the set of $O(n^2)$ matrices obtained. From Lemma 10.14, it follows that dividing the nodes amounts to grouping their

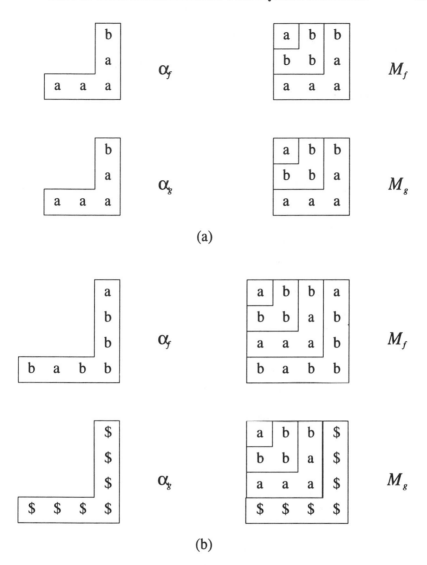

(a)

(b)

Fig. 10.15. Some examples of capsular matrices.

equal capsular matrices together in $\mathcal{H}$. Consequently, we want to identify the equal matrices in $\mathcal{H}$. Since they do not necessarily have a power-of-two side, we associate the following quintuple of integers with each matrix $M \in \mathcal{H}$: its side and the names of the four submatrices covering M (they appear at M's corners, their side is the largest power of two smaller than M's side and their union with the overlaps gives M). It is worth noting that any two matrices are equal if and only if they have the same quintuples and so a standard lexicographic sorting on the quintuples partitions $\mathcal{H}$ in $O(n^2)$ time. We can therefore group equivalent nodes together and perform a refinement step in $O(n^2)$ time.

A simple induction on the refinement steps gives our construction's correctness by Lemma 10.11. We spend $O(n^2 \log n)$ time and space to assign names to the submatrices, $O(n^2)$ time per refinement step and the whole sequence of refinement trees takes a total of $O(n^2)$ space because we only need to store one refinement tree at a time.

Theorem 10.15. *Given an $n \times n$ matrix A, its suffix tree T_A can be built in $O(n^2 \log n)$ time and space.*

We can reduce the space required for suffix tree construction to linear, i.e., $O(n^2)$, without any loss in efficiency (see Section 10.4). For a constant-size alphabet, we can also obtain an expected linear-time construction (see Section 10.5). We now go on to treat the more general case of rectangular matrices. An important remark must be made about their submatrix aspect ratios (the aspect ratio of an $n_1 \times m_1$ submatrix is n_1/m_1 and so square submatrices have aspect ratio 1). Let us fix a single aspect ratio and take all the corresponding (fixed aspect ratio) submatrices into consideration. *Their indexing can be done without any loss in efficiency by the algorithms and data structures examined so far.* In the next section, we therefore assume that submatrix aspect ratios vary.

10.3   Suffix trees for rectangular matrices

The reader may wonder whether the notions and algorithms proposed so far apply to rectangular matrices. In this section, we show that super-linear space is required for indexing rectangular matrices by means of known data structures (in contrast to the linear space required for square matrices). We also give a simple example of a suffix tree for rectangular matrices. As in the case of square matrices (see Section 10.1), we introduce some basic building blocks.

Definition 10.16. A *block character* extends an $n_1 \times m_1$ matrix to a larger matrix by adding a sequence x of characters to it (see Fig. 10.16): Block $(\mathcal{S}, m_1, x)$ denotes appending a row of length m_1 to the bottom (South) and filling this row with x's characters from left to right; blocks $(\mathcal{N}, m_1, x)$, $(\mathcal{E}, n_1, x)$, and $(\mathcal{W}, n_1, x)$ are defined in the same way.

Block characters can be defined for any row's and column's length and two block characters are equal if and only if they are entry-by-entry equal. Block characters are analogous to macro characters (see Section 10.1) except for the fact that the former contain encoded shape information. They can also be concatenated under the obvious constraint of the appended

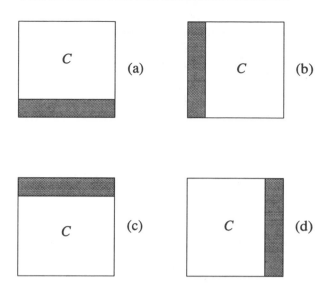

Fig. 10.16. The extensions of C in a matrix that contains C as a submatrix. The shaded rows and columns correspond to the block characters we define.

row's or column's length. Each matrix can be expressed as a sequence of block characters called a *block string* (our definitions of prefix and chunk are analogous to the ones given for macro strings).

Example 10.17. With reference to Fig. 10.17, let us examine matrix B (illustrated in (a)). One of its possible representations as a block string is shown in (b) and its partition in (c): integer i in (c) denotes the i-th block character that appears in the string shown in (b), for $i = 1, 2, \ldots, 6$. Another representation is illustrated in (d) and (e).

An important feature of block strings is that we cannot fix a shape sequence *a priori* for them to describe the submatrices' format for a given input matrix because the submatrices can have various aspect ratios (while we were able to do so for macro strings, because all the square submatrices are characterized by a fixed aspect ratio). We characterize this feature by means of the "submatrix of" relation denoted by $\preceq$. This relation is a total order when restricted to square matrices and can be "translated" into the total order relation "prefix of" by means of macro strings. Unfortunately, $\preceq$ becomes a partial order for rectangular matrices and does not "translate" smoothly into a total order relation like "prefix of" by means of block strings.

We let A be a general $n \times m$ matrix whose entries are taken from an alphabet Σ. We assume that $n \geq m$ without any loss in generality. We define the notion of suffix trees for matrices represented in the form of block strings and then prove that the trees defined in this way require super-

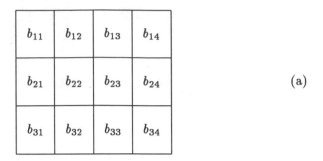

(a)

$(\mathcal{N}, 1, b_{11})\ (\mathcal{S}, 1, b_{21})\ (\mathcal{S}, 1, b_{31})$

$(\mathcal{E}, 3, b_{12}b_{22}b_{32})\ (\mathcal{E}, 3, b_{13}b_{23}b_{33})\ (\mathcal{E}, 3, b_{14}b_{24}b_{34})$

(b)

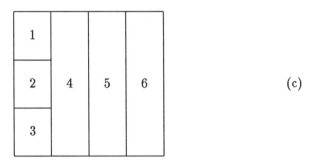

(c)

$(\mathcal{N}, 1, b_{22})\ (\mathcal{S}, 1, b_{32})\ (\mathcal{E}, 2, b_{23}b_{33})$

$(\mathcal{N}, 2, b_{12}b_{13})\ (\mathcal{W}, 3, b_{11}b_{21}b_{31})\ (\mathcal{W}, 3, b_{14}b_{24}b_{34})$

(d)

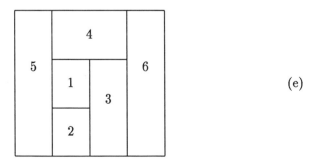

(e)

Fig. 10.17. A matrix and two of its possible representations as block strings.

linear space, i.e., $\Omega(nm^2)$. The following abstract notion of suffix trees is a restatement of the Completeness and Common Submatrix properties given in Section 10.1.

Definition 10.18. An *uncompacted index* I_A for an $n \times m$ matrix A is a rooted tree whose arcs are labeled by block characters:

(10.18.1) No two arcs originating from a node are labeled by equal block characters.

(10.18.2) Let $L(u)$ be the matrix obtained by the labels' concatenation found along the path from the root to a node u. For each submatrix B, there is at least one node u such that $L(u) = B$.

(10.18.3) For any two nodes u and v, if u is v's ancestor, then $L(u)$ is a submatrix of $L(v)$.

The *suffix tree* T_A is an uncompacted index I_A whose maximal paths of one-child nodes are compressed into single arcs.

An uncompacted index topology depends on how we represent A's submatrices in terms of block characters. Let us examine a maximal path p of one-child nodes that goes from a node u to a node v. We compress p in order to obtain a suffix tree by transforming p into a single arc (u, v) whose label is the chunk identified by deleting $L(u)$ from $L(v)$ (by Condition 10.18.2, $L(u)$ is a submatrix of $L(v)$). The chunk can be represented in constant space by the coordinates of its occurrence in A and naturally corresponds to some blocks in the block string representing $L(v)$. See Fig. 10.18 for an example. We do not lose any information in going from the uncompacted index to the suffix tree. We use $L(u)$ to denote the matrix obtained by concatenating the arc labels (now chunks) from the root to a node u. Since we compressed the maximal paths of one-child nodes, A's submatrices are no longer represented by nodes but by arcs instead, i.e., there is at least one arc (u, v) such that $L(u) \preceq B \prec L(v)$ for each submatrix B. The submatrices represented by the same arc are *totally* ordered even if $\preceq$ is a partial order:

Fact 10.19. *Let $A_1, \ldots, A_q$ be the submatrices represented by arc (u, v) (i.e., $L(u) \preceq A_j \prec L(v)$ for $1 \leq j \leq q$). There is a permutation $j_1, \ldots, j_q$ of $1, \ldots, q$, such that $A_{j_1} \preceq A_{j_2} \preceq \cdots \preceq A_{j_q}$.*

We now derive an $\Omega(nm^2)$ lower bound on the number of T_A's nodes and arcs for an arbitrary $n \times m$ matrix A, with $n \geq m$. This also provides us with a lower bound to the time needed to build it. Therefore, for the class of data structures introduced in this Chapter, the problem of building a suffix tree for a general matrix is provably harder than that of building a suffix tree that only represents square submatrices (or fixed aspect ratio submatrices).

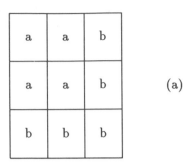

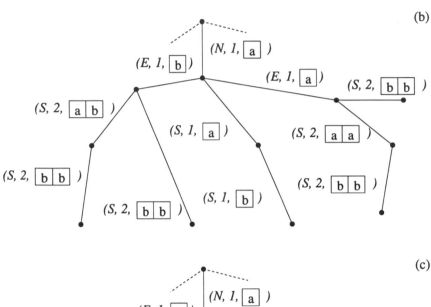

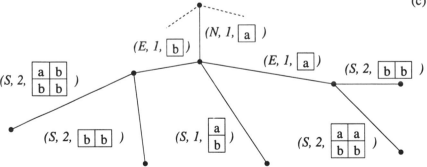

Fig. 10.18. (a) A matrix A and (b) its uncompacted index I_A (only the paths representing the submatrices that contain character a in their upper leftmost entries are shown). (c) Its suffix tree T_A (only the paths corresponding to the ones in (b) are shown).

For an input matrix A, we let $once(A)$ be the number of the submatrices that occur only once in A and let $SIZE(A)$ be the number of arcs and nodes in the smallest suffix tree satisfying Definition 10.18. For given n and m, such that $n \geq m$, we then define $SPACE(n, m)$ as the maximum $SIZE(A)$ taken over all the possible input $n \times m$ matrices A. It is worth noting that there are always some of the smallest suffix trees that contain at least $SPACE(n, m)$ arcs and nodes.

Lemma 10.20. $SPACE(n, m) \geq c \cdot once(A)/n$ for some constant $c > 0$.

Proof: We let $T(A)$ denote the smallest suffix tree for A (i.e., the smallest suffix tree chosen among all possible T_A's satisfying Definition 10.18). For each arc $e_i \in T(A)$, we denote the submatrices that are represented by e_i and only occur once by $A_{i,1} \prec \cdots \prec A_{i,k_i}$ (they are sorted according to the $\preceq$ relation by Fact 10.19). The inequalities must be strict because these submatrices occur once in A and are distinct pairwise. It is worth noting that $k_i \leq 2n$. Indeed, in the uncompacted index yielding $T(A)$, matrix $A_{i,j+1}$ is obtained by appending at least one block character (either a row or a column) to $A_{i,j}$ for $1 \leq j < k_i$, and A_{i,k_i} has $n \times m$ shape at most (it is one of A's submatrices).

We let e be the number of arcs in $T(A)$. Since each submatrix is represented by at least one arc of $T(A)$, we have $\Sigma_{i=1}^{e} k_i \geq once(A)$. But $k_i \leq 2n$, and hence $e \geq once(A)/(2n)$. Therefore, $SPACE(n, m) \geq SIZE(A) = |T(A)| \geq e \geq c \cdot once(A)/n$ for some constant $c > 0$. $\square$

Theorem 10.21. *Let Σ be an alphabet of at least two characters which the characters in A are taken from. For an infinite number of n and m values with $n \geq m$, we obtain $SPACE(n, m) \geq cnm^2$ for some constant $c > 0$.*

Proof: We build an infinite family of matrices A for which $once(A) \geq \Omega(n^2 m^2)$. We pick out $n^2 = 2^k$ (for some $k > 0$) verifying $n \geq 64$ and $n > k$. We also choose an arbitrary m with $0 < m \leq n$. Let us consider a de Bruijn sequence y of length $n\,m$ constructed on two characters of Σ. By de Bruijn sequence definition, each substring of y of length $k = \log(n\,m)$ is distinct, i.e., it only occurs once in y. We transform y into an $n \times m$ matrix A by reading y's characters and putting them in column-major order in A. Let us fix i and j with $1 \leq i \leq n - k + 1$ and $1 \leq j \leq m$. The subcolumn $A[i : i + k - 1, j]$ only appears once in A because it is a substring of length k of the de Bruijn sequence y stored in column-major order in A. As a result, any submatrix that contains the subcolumn in its left must only appear once. Moreover, there are $b_{i,j} = (n - i - k + 2)(m - j + 1)$ of these submatrices. Therefore, $once(A) \geq \Sigma_{i=1}^{n-k+1} \Sigma_{j=1}^{m} b_{i,j}$ because all of these submatrices are distinct pairwise. For $n \geq 64$, this sum is lower bounded by $cn^2 m^2$ for some constant $c > 0$, which means that for the matrix A that we built, $once(A) \geq cn^2 m^2$. The theorem follows from Lemma 10.20. $\square$

We now define a class of suffix trees for $n \times m$ matrices, called *s-trees*. We assume that $n \geq m$ because the definition extends to case $n < m$ by symmetry. We also mention some efficient algorithms for building s-trees.

Let us restrict the block characters in Definition 10.16 to $(\mathcal{S}, d, x)$, where $x \in \Sigma^d$, and d is fixed with $1 \leq d \leq m$. Since we only use one kind of block character and d is fixed, we can drop the encoding $\mathcal{S}$ and d in $(\mathcal{S}, d, x)$ so that the block character becomes a string of length d. As a consequence, the block strings are now strings on the new alphabet Σ^d.

The *s-trees* are a forest of m trees BLT_d, for $1 \leq d \leq m$. For a fixed d, BLT_d represents all the submatrices of width d in the form of block strings on the alphabet Σ^d. This is done as follows:

Let $B_{j,d}$ be the block string of length n that represents $A[1:n, j:j+d-1]$, with $1 \leq j \leq m - d + 1$. That is, the block character $B_{j,d}[i]$ is the row $A[i, j:j+d-1]$. Every submatrix $A[i:k, j:j+d-1]$ corresponds to a substring of $B_{j,d}$ (i.e., $B_{j:d}[i, k] = A[i:k, j:j+d-1]$). Hence, if we build a trie I (for the alphabet Σ^d) on all the block suffixes of $B_{j,d}$, for $1 \leq j \leq m-d+1$, then we represent all of A's submatrices of width d. That is, for each submatrix C of width d, there is a node $u \in I$ such that the concatenation of the labels (block characters) produces C. Moreover, all the submatrices of width d whose prefix is equal to C are in the subtree rooted at u. Therefore, I satisfies the uncompacted index definition (Definition 10.18) when restricted to A's submatrices of width d. By compressing the maximal paths of one-child nodes in I, we obtain BLT_d and therefore satisfy the suffix tree definition when restricted to A's submatrices of width d. By repeating the above process for each width d with $1 \leq d \leq m$, we obtain the s-trees $\{BLT_d : 1 \leq d \leq m\}$.

Theorem 10.22. *The s-trees are suffix trees for matrix A. Moreover, they can be built in $O(nm^2 \log n)$ time and stored in optimal $O(nm^2)$ space.*

Proof: We merge the roots of each BLT_d, $1 \leq d \leq m$, into a single node so that the forest becomes a tree. This, in turn, is a suffix tree for A by the definition of BLT_d.

As far as the time analysis is concerned, each BLT_d is $O(n(m - d + 1))$ size and can be built in $O(n(m - d + 1) \log n)$ time. As a matter of fact, we know that the best algorithm for building a suffix tree for some regular strings with a total length of t (for an alphabet Σ') takes $O(t \min(|\Sigma'|, \log t)) \leq O(t \log t)$ time, provided that we can compare the characters of Σ' in constant time (see Chapter 3). For $\Sigma' = \Sigma^d$, this can be done by some preprocessing of A's rows in $O(nm \log |\Sigma|)$ time in order to find the longest common prefix between any two subrows in constant time (see Chapter 6). $\square$

The s-trees can be used for pattern matching after some preprocessing in $O(nm^2 \log n)$ time (see Exercise 10.9).

10.4   *Linear-space suffix tree construction for square matrices

In Section 10.2, we showed how to build suffix tree T_A for an $n \times n$ matrix A in $O(n^2 \log n)$ time and space. We solved our first problem, namely, that of partitioning the refinement tree nodes into equivalence classes. From now on, we improve time and space complexity and solve the problem of reducing the space required in Theorem 10.15 from $O(n^2 \log n)$ to optimal $O(n^2)$. The overhead space is necessary for storing all the names of the $O(n^2 \log n)$ submatrices having a power-of-two side. We now want to store the names in linear space only, i.e., in $O(n^2)$, while maintaining $O(n^2 \log n)$ time complexity.

We therefore solve the following abstract problem, referred to as *Names on Demand* (in short, NOD). We state it in terms of a generic matrix $F[1{:}p, 1{:}p]$ whose entries are integers in $[1, p^2]$, where p is a power of two. NOD consists of the following two stages:

NOD-*Processing:* We examine F's submatrices whose power-of-two side is no more than p. We group them into equivalence classes, which each contains the equal submatrices.

NOD-*Query:* We choose a subset Q of $O(p^2)$ submatrices on-line from the ones in NOD-processing. A unique integer in $[1, p^2]$ (the *name*) must be assigned *on demand* to each submatrix in Q so that two equal submatrices have equal names assigned. (We say that these names are *consistent*.)

A NOD-query can be repeated with different sets Q and the same submatrix can be assigned two different names in two distinct NOD-queries. Furthermore, we allow some submatrices having different sides to be assigned the same name because they are characterized by their sides.

Remark 10.23. We use the two NOD stages to build the suffix tree (see Section 10.2), assuming that $\Sigma \subseteq \{1, 2, \ldots, n^2\}$ (if this is not so, then we sort and number the n^2 characters in A and encode the \$ instances in $A\hat{\$}$ as integers in $[n^2 + 1, 9n^2]$). We apply NOD-processing, with $F = A\hat{\$}$ and p the power of two nearest to $3n$, before starting the sequence of refinement steps. In each refinement step, we have to partition the set $\mathcal{H}$ of capsular matrices by sorting the quintuples associated with each $M \in \mathcal{H}$, namely M's side and the names of the four submatrices in M's corners. We collect all of these submatrices in set Q, which is therefore contained in the set of the matrices that have been grouped in NOD-processing, where $|Q| = O(n^2)$. We invoke a NOD-query on Q to obtain their names, and finish constructing the suffix tree as in Section 10.2.

The NOD problem can be solved by Karp, Miller and Rosenberg's technique in $O(p^2 \log p)$ time and space for NOD-processing and in $O(p^2)$ time for each NOD-query. However, we can reduce the space to an optimal $O(p^2)$, while maintaining time performance. Let us use shorthand $[\![i,j]\!]^k$ to denote the submatrix $F[i:i+2^k-1, j:j+2^k-1]$ (for $1 \leq i,j \leq p$ and $0 \leq k \leq \log p$). (If some entries of $[\![i,j]\!]^k$ are outside F's boundaries, then we simply assume that they are \$ instances.) Our idea of space reduction is based on the fact that, in NOD-processing, grouping F's submatrices amounts to computing $\log p + 1$ partitions $\Gamma_0, \ldots, \Gamma_{\log p}$ of F's positions. More specifically, we group all the positions (i,j) whose corresponding submatrices $[\![i,j]\!]^k$ are equal together in the same equivalence class by means of the k-th partition Γ_k, for $0 \leq k \leq \log p$. These partitions can be suitably stored as "packed" arrays and require a total of $O(p^2)$ memory cells. Given set $\mathcal{Q}$, a NOD-query consists of "unpacking" a part of the arrays efficiently. Before describing this formally, we wish to give the following example.

Example 10.24. Let $F[1:4, 1:4] = A\$[1:4, 1:4]$, with $p = 4$, where $A\$$ is the matrix shown in Fig. 10.5a. For matrix F, partition Γ_0 groups its 1×1 submatrices into the following two classes (one for characters 'a' and the other for characters 'b'):

$$\{(3,1),(2,1),(1,3),(1,2),(2,3),(3,4),(4,1),(4,2),(4,3)\};$$

$$\{(1,1),(3,3),(3,2),(2,4),(2,2),(1,4),(4,4)\};$$

partition Γ_1 groups the 2×2 submatrices into the following classes:

$$\{(3,1)\}; \quad \{(2,1),(1,3)\}; \quad \{(1,2)\}; \quad \{(2,3)\}; \quad \{(3,4)\}; \quad \{(4,1),(4,2)\}; \quad \{(4,3)\};$$

$$\{(1,1),(3,3)\}; \quad \{(3,2)\}; \quad \{(2,4)\}; \quad \{(2,2)\}; \quad \{(1,4)\}; \quad \{(4,4)\};$$

and partition Γ_2 groups the 4×4 submatrices into singleton classes. Position (i,j) in partition Γ_k represents matrix $[\![i,j]\!]^k$. Let us examine the positions' sequence in Γ_k: we say that position (i,j) has rank l in the partition if (i,j) occupies the l-th position in the sequence. The above partitions are illustrated to highlight the following properties: (1) There is a *ranking* β such that $\beta(i,j) = l$ is (i,j)'s rank in *all* the partitions whatever their classes may be (e.g., $\beta(3,4) = 6$ in Γ_0, Γ_1 and Γ_2). (2) The classes' boundaries can be encoded by $\log p + 1 = 3$ *binary sequences* $B_0, B_1, \ldots, B_{\log p}$ of $p^2 + 1$ bits each, which can be thought of as "characteristic" vectors of the classes. In this example, $B_0 = 1000000010000001$, $B_1 = 11011110110111111$, and $B_2 = 111111111111111$. All the matrices $[\![i,j]\!]^k$ in an equivalence class correspond to ranks $\beta(i,j)$ delimited by two integers: h and h', such that $B_k[h:h'] = 10 \cdots 0 \cdots 01$ and $h \leq \beta(i,j) < h'$. For example, the equivalence class of 1×1 matrices $\{(1,1),(3,3),(3,2),(2,4),(2,2),(1,4),(4,4)\}$ is associated with the binary subsequence $B_0[10:17] = 10000001$, and the class of 2×2 matrices $\{(2,1),(1,3)\}$ is associated with $B_1[2:4] = 101$. Ranking β requires $O(p^2)$ space, and $B_0, \ldots, B_{\log p}$ can be packed in parts of $\Theta(\log p)$ bits each, providing an $O(p^2)$ space representation of partitions $\Gamma_0, \ldots, \Gamma_{\log p}$.

We give a formal description of the ideas illustrated in Example 10.24.

Definition 10.25. A *representation* of the partitions $\Gamma_0, \ldots, \Gamma_{\log p}$ is given by a *ranking* $\beta : [1, p] \times [1, p] \to [1, p^2]$, along with $\log p + 1$ *binary sequences* $B_0, B_1, \ldots, B_{\log p}$ of $p^2 + 1$ bits each:

(10.25.1) Each matrix $[\![i, j]\!]^k$ corresponds to a rank $\beta(i, j)$ that remains the same in all B_k's.

(10.25.2) B_k is a "characteristic" vector of partition Γ_k: the matrices in an equivalence class of Γ_k occupy a contiguous part in B_k whose bits are all set to 0, except where a new equivalence class begins. That is, $[\![i, j]\!]^k = [\![i', j']\!]^k$ if and only if $h \leq \beta(i, j), \beta(i', j') < h'$ for two integers h, h', such that $B_k[h:h'] = 10 \cdots 0 \cdots 01$. (By convention, $B_k[1] = B_k[p^2 + 1] = 1$.)

A *succinct representation* of $\Gamma_0, \ldots, \Gamma_{\log p}$ is obtained by the ranking β and the arrays $\hat{B}_0, \ldots, \hat{B}_{\log p}$ that are produced by packing $B_0, \ldots, B_{\log p}$ (in parts of $\Theta(\log p)$ bits).

From Definition 10.25 it follows that a succinct representation can be stored in $O(p^2)$ space.

10.4.1 NOD-PROCESSING

We use a prefix-sum-like algorithm $Number$, which takes a (not necessarily ordered) sequence $t_1, t_2, \ldots, t_s$ of input keys, and assigns equal integers to adjacent equal keys. That is, it assigns a non-decreasing number n_i to each t_i, such that $n_1 = 1$ and $n_i = n_{i-1} + \delta_i$, for $1 < i \leq s$, where $\delta_i \in \{0, 1\}$ verifies $\delta_i = 0$ if and only if $t_i = t_{i-1}$. This algorithm takes $O(s)$ time. Furthermore, we use a linear-time integer or lexicographic sorting.

In NOD-processing, the simple algorithm described below computes a succinct representation in $O(p^2 \log p)$ time and $O(p^2)$ space. It works by induction on the matrices $[\![i, j]\!]^k$ for $k = 0, 1, \ldots \log p$ by assigning some "temporary names" to them. The temporary names range from 1 to p^2 and are eventually discarded. At the end, the algorithm also outputs ranking β. The k-th inductive step is based on the idea that a matrix's temporary name depends on the temporary names of the four submatrices which the matrix can be decomposed into:

CASE $k = 0$. We sort the matrices $[\![i, j]\!]^0$ according to their characters $F[i, j]$ and then apply Algorithm $Number$ to the sorted matrices (by using their characters as input keys) in order to assign a non-decreasing sequence of temporary names $\eta_1, \eta_2, \ldots, \eta_{p^2}$ to them. All matrices in an equivalence class of Γ_0 now correspond to a sequence $\eta_h, \eta_{h+1}, \ldots, \eta_{h'-1}$ of equal names. The matrices in some other classes of Γ_0 get different names. Entries $B_0[1]$ and $B_0[p^2 + 1]$ are set to 1 and, for $1 < h < p^2 + 1$, entry $B_0[h]$ is set to 1 whenever $\eta_{h-1} \neq \eta_h$. The rest of B_0's entries are set to 0 and B_0 is then packed in $\hat{B}_0$.

CASE $k > 0$. We let $Q_1 = [\![i, j]\!]^{k-1}$, $Q_2 = [\![i + 2^{k-1}, j]\!]^{k-1}$, $Q_3 = [\![i, j + 2^{k-1}]\!]^{k-1}$, and $Q_4 = [\![i + 2^{k-1}, j + 2^{k-1}]\!]^{k-1}$ be the four submatrices of side 2^{k-1} into which we partition $[\![i, j]\!]^k$. We assign the quadruple $q_{i,j} = (\epsilon_1, \epsilon_2, \epsilon_3, \epsilon_4)$ to $[\![i, j]\!]^k$, where ϵ_d is the temporary name assigned to Q_d in step $k - 1$, for $1 \leq d \leq 4$. These names are still available by our inductive assumption (unless Q_d lies completely outside F's boundaries, in which case Q_d is given a unique integer larger than p^2) and can be discarded after use. In analogy with step $k = 0$, we sort the matrices $[\![i, j]\!]^k$ by using the quadruples $q_{i,j}$ as keys. We apply Algorithm $Number$ to the sorted matrices (by using their quadruples as input keys) and obtain their temporary names. We set B_k's entries and then pack B_k in $\hat{B}_k$.

If $k = \log p$, we compute ranking β by setting $\beta(i, j) = l$ where l is (i, j)'s rank in the final list of sorted matrices. This simple algorithm produces a succinct representation that satisfies Definition 10.25.

Lemma 10.26. *NOD-processing correctly computes a succinct representation of the partitions $\Gamma_0, \ldots, \Gamma_{\log p}$ in $O(p^2 \log p)$ time and $O(p^2)$ space.*

We now prove Lemma 10.26. We define a "local" ranking β_k, such that $\beta_k(i, j) = l$ if and only if l is (i, j)'s rank in the sorted list of matrices produced by step k (and so $\beta = \beta_{\log p}$). Let β_k^{-1} be the inverse ranking (i.e., $\beta_k^{-1}(l) = (i, j)$ if and only if $\beta_k(i, j) = l$). We now need Claim 10.27, which states that β_k and B_k correctly represent the equivalence classes in the k-th partition Γ_k.

Claim 10.27. *In step k, NOD-processing correctly produces a partition Γ_k of F's positions into equivalence classes. That is, for each equivalence class, there are two unique integers: h and h', such that $B_k[h\!:\!h'] = 10 \cdots 0 \cdots 01$ and this class is made up of all the matrices $[\![i, j]\!]^k$ that satisfy $(i, j) \in \{\beta_k^{-1}(h), \beta_k^{-1}(h+1), \ldots, \beta_k^{-1}(h' - 1)\}$.*

The proof is left to the reader as Exercise 10.13d. Even though the β_k's are usually distinct pairwise, Claim 10.28 states that $\beta = \beta_{\log p}$ subsumes the information of all the other β_k's and so we can discard all the β_k's except $\beta_{\log p}$.

Claim 10.28. *The equivalence classes created in step k are stable in its subsequent steps $k + 1, k + 2, \ldots, \log p$. That is, if position (i, j) belongs to*

the equivalence class $\{\beta_k^{-1}(h), \beta_k^{-1}(h+1), \ldots, \beta_k^{-1}(h'-1)\}$ *in partition* Γ_k
(described in Claim 10.27), then $h \leq \beta_\ell(i,j) < h'$, *for all* $\ell = k, \ldots, \log p$.

We choose c such that $h \leq c < h'$ to see why Claim 10.28 is true. We let $(i,j) = \beta_k^{-1}(c)$ be a position in an equivalence class of Γ_k. The k-th step assigns an integer η_c to $[\![i,j]\!]^k$ by Algorithm *Number*. However, η_c is the first component ϵ_1 of the quadruple $q_{i,j}$ assigned to $[\![i,j]\!]^{k+1}$ in step $k+1$ and so the positions that are given a rank in $[1, h-1]$ by β_k are still to the left of (i,j) in ranking β_{k+1}, and the positions that are given a rank in $[h', p^2]$ by β_k are still to the right of (i,j) in β_{k+1}. Therefore, in step $k+1$, $[\![i,j]\!]^{k+1}$ can only appear somewhere between the h-th and the $(h'-1)$-st position in the sorted list of matrices. That is, $h \leq \beta_{k+1}(i,j) \leq h'-1$. This process can be repeated for the other steps $k+2, \ldots, \log p$.

We now go back to the proof of Lemma 10.26 and show that ranking β and the characteristic binary sequences B_k computed by the algorithm satisfy Definition 10.25. Assuming that $[\![i,j]\!]^k = [\![i',j']\!]^k$, we notice that (i,j) and (i',j') are in the same equivalence class of Γ_k. By Claim 10.27, there are two integers h and h', such that $h \leq \beta_k(i,j), \beta_k(i',j') < h'$ with $B_k[h:h'] = 10\cdots0\cdots01$. On the other hand, Claim 10.28 and the fact that $\beta_{\log p} = \beta$ imply that $h \leq \beta(i,j), \beta(i',j') < h'$ as well. The reverse of the proof can be proved in the same way.

As for time and space analysis, there are $\log p + 1$ steps and each step requires $O(p^2)$ time and space (we use linear-time sorting). Moreover, the total size of packed arrays $\hat{B}_k$'s is $O(p^2)$ because each array is size $O(p^2/\log p)$ and there are $O(\log p)$ of them. This completes the proof of Lemma 10.26.

10.4.2 *NOD*-QUERIES

We explain how to implement a *NOD*-query in $O(p^2)$ time. As previously mentioned, we want to assign consistent names to a set $\mathcal{Q}$ of $O(p^2)$ submatrices:

STEP 1. We sort the matrices $[\![i,j]\!]^k \in \mathcal{Q}$ by using the pairs $(k, \beta(i,j))$ as keys in order to obtain a list $\mathcal{L}$. We let $\mathcal{L}_k$ be $\mathcal{L}$'s contiguous sublist that contains the submatrices having side 2^k, for a fixed k (by Definition 10.25, equal submatrices are adjacent in $\mathcal{L}_k$ because of ranking β).

STEP 2. For $k = 0, 1, \ldots, \log p$, we use the succinct representation of Γ_k to mark the boundaries between the adjacent equivalence classes in $\mathcal{L}_k$. We then use the boundary marks to assign a distinct integer to each class. The integer is the name of all the matrices in its class.

Step 1 can be easily implemented in $O(p^2)$ time because it sorts all the pairs in range $[0, \log p] \times [1, p^2]$. Step 2 is a little trickier. We show how to carry it out in $O(p^2 \log p)$ time by using B_k, two new binary vectors, C_k and D_k, and a transducer $\mathcal{A}$. By using the so-called Four Russians' trick (see Exercise 10.15), the same computation can be simulated in $O(p^2)$ time on a Random Access Machine (RAM) by using integer vectors $\hat{B}_k$, $\hat{C}_k$ and $\hat{D}_k$ that pack the bits of B_k, C_k and D_k, respectively (Exercise 10.16).

We let the *span* of a given equivalence class in Γ_k be the interval $[h, h' - 1]$ if the class is encoded by $B_k[h{:}h'] = 10\cdots0\cdots01$, where $h = \min\{\beta(i,j)\}$ and $h' = \max\{\beta(i,j)\} + 1$ for all $[\![i,j]\!]^k$ ranging in the class (Condition 10.25.2). We also let C_k be the characteristic vector of $\mathcal{L}_k$, i.e., a binary vector of $p^2 + 1$ bits, such that $C_k[\beta(i,j)] = 1$ if and only if $[\![i,j]\!]^k \in \mathcal{L}_k$. All the other entries in C_k are 0. It can be seen that $[\![i,j]\!]^k$ has the same rank $\beta(i,j)$ in both C_k and B_k and this, together with the definition of span, let $\mathcal{L}_k$'s matrices belonging to the same class in Γ_k be represented by the 1s in $C_k[h, h' - 1]$. They form a *group* induced by B_k (groups are always nonempty). Therefore, we can mark the list $\mathcal{L}_k$ and locate the boundaries between all the adjacent classes by dividing the 1s in C_k into groups by scanning B_k.

For efficiency's sake, we perform the above operation indirectly by using a transducer $\mathcal{A}$ to compute a binary vector D_k. The bits in D_k are considered to be binary colors whose correspondence to the matrices in Γ_k is given by β. D_k is initialized to all 0s. For all q such that $C_k[q] = 1$, $D_k[q]$ is set as follows: The 1s in the leftmost group in C_k are assigned 1 in their homologous positions in D_k. If the previous group in C_k is assigned b, with $b \in \{0, 1\}$, then the 1s in the current group are assigned $\overline{b}$ in their homologous positions in D_k.

Example 10.29. With reference to Example 10.24, we consider the list $\mathcal{L}_1 = \{(1,3), (1,2), (3,4), (4,1), (4,2), (3,3), (3,2), (1,4)\}$ in Step 1. Since the corresponding ranks given by β are $3, 4, 6, 7, 8, 11, 12, 15$, respectively, we have $C_1 = 0011011100110010$. The corresponding groups are induced by $B_1 = 1101111011011111$, i.e., $00\{1\}\{1\}0\{1\}\{11\}00\{1\}\{1\}00\{1\}0$ (the groups are indicated in brackets). The binary colors are alternated every other group and produce $D_1 = 0010010000100010$.

Exercise 10.14 involves verifying that the transducer $\mathcal{A}$ in Fig. 10.21 correctly produces D_k for any given B_k and C_k. In the efficient implementation of iteration k in Step 2, the proper binary colors are assigned to every other class in $\mathcal{L}_k$ by $\mathcal{A}$ and the names are found by running algorithm *Number* on the binary colors in $\mathcal{L}_k$; this is left to the reader as Exercise 10.16.

Lemma 10.30. *A NOD-query correctly assigns consistent names to the matrices in the set $\mathcal{Q}$ in $O(p^2)$ time and space.*

Proof: We only analyze complexity. Step 1 takes $O(p^2)$ time and space by using a linear-time lexicographic sort. In Step 2, we let q_k be the number of matrices in $\mathcal{L}_k$, where $\sum_{k=0}^{\log p} q_k = O(p^2)$. We set C_k and then compute D_k by means of $\mathcal{A}$ so that the matrices in $\mathcal{L}_k$ get the proper binary colors. The operations are simulated by using vectors $\hat{B}_k$, $\hat{C}_k$ and $\hat{D}_k$, rather than B_k, C_k and D_k. In Exercise 10.16, we show that this can be done in $O(p^2/\log p + q_k)$ time and space for each iteration k by means of the Four Russians' trick. The time and space bounds follow because $O(\log p \cdot p^2/\log p + \sum_{k=0}^{\log p} q_k) = O(p^2)$. □

This completes our discussion of NOD queries. By Remark 10.23 and Lemmas 10.26 and 10.30, we can now achieve an optimal space construction of the suffix tree T_A and maintain the same time bound as in Theorem 10.15.

Theorem 10.31. *Given an $n \times n$ matrix A, its suffix tree T_A can be built in $O(n^2 \log n)$ time and $O(n^2)$ space.*

The result obtained in Theorem 10.31 is optimal for a general alphabet Σ because it amounts to sorting Σ's characters. When Σ is constant size, we can use the following algorithm.

10.5 *Linear expected-time suffix tree construction for square matrices

We solve another problem in constructing suffix trees for square matrices stemming from the fact that the required time is not optimal for a constant-size alphabet (unlike suffix trees for strings, which only take linear time). We introduce a variation of our construction that requires optimal $O(n^2)$ expected time for a constant-size alphabet Σ under some mild probabilistic assumptions. We let a repeated submatrix of A be a square submatrix that occurs at least twice. We define A's largest repeated submatrices as the ones having the largest number of entries. Let us assume that the following reasonable hypothesis holds (see the bibliographic notes); we call it the *Logarithmic-Expected-Size* or *L-hypothesis*:

L-Hypothesis: Each of A's largest repeated submatrices is $O(\log n)$ expected size, i.e., the number of its entries is asymptotically smaller than $(cL)^2$ for some constant $c > 1$ (where L is the largest power of two, such that $L^2 \leq \lfloor \log_{|\Sigma|} n^2 \rfloor$).

As far as the L-hypothesis is concerned, let us assume that cL is an integer, without any loss in generality. The L-hypothesis implies that cL is an upper bound to the expected length of the macro strings representing A's repeated submatrices. With regard to the suffix tree T_A, its internal nodes are the ones that store A's repeated submatrices (Exercise 10.2a) and so the extended loci of macro strings longer than cL are expected to be leaves. We call a node *heavy* if it is the locus of a macro string longer than cL; we call it *light* in all other cases. The concept underlying this section is that T_A's part containing light nodes can be built in $O(n^2)$ worst-case time; the rest of T_A's nodes are heavy, and can be installed in $O(n^2)$ expected time. Of course, the worst-case complexity must remain $O(n^2 \log n)$ time; otherwise, adding heavy nodes becomes a trivial task.

A simple analysis shows that we can achieve $O(n^2 \log \log n)$ expected time with the algorithms discussed so far. The refinement trees for T_A have sibling nodes sharing cL macro characters at most and so $D^{(\log n)} = \cdots = D^{(r')}$, for $r' = \lceil \log cL \rceil = O(\log \log n)$. We expect that the remaining $O(\log \log n)$ refinement steps really transform the refinement trees $D^{(r')}, \ldots, D^{(0)}$ in $O(n^2)$ time per step, whereas the previous steps do not modify $D^{(\log n)}$. This $O(n^2 \log \log n)$ analysis can be improved to a better $O(n^2)$ as follows.

A compacted trie CT is said to be *pruned* when it is obtained from T_A by selecting the light nodes; this is done by pruning the subtrees that only contain heavy nodes. More precisely, if $\mathcal{M}$ is the set of macro strings which T_A is built on according to Definition 10.4, then CT is built on the set $\mathcal{M}'$ of distinct cL-length prefixes of $\mathcal{M}$'s macro strings. Let us now assume the following:

(i) We can execute the NOD-processing in $O(n^2)$ expected time (see Exercise 10.18);

(ii) We are able to call a NOD-query in $O(n^2)$ worst-case time (see Exercise 10.19);

(iii) We can build CT in $O(n^2)$ worst-case time (see Section 10.5.1).

As a consequence, T_A can be obtained by installing the heavy nodes in CT by a lazy execution of the refinement steps. This means that CT's leaves must be expanded into T_A's pruned subtrees as follows. We augment CT by creating some new leaves. There is a new leaf, i.e., w, for each macro string in $\mathcal{M}$. This new leaf w's parent is the (light) leaf $v \in CT$, such that the macro string stored in v is a prefix of the macro string associated with w. It follows that the new children of each (light) leaf $v \in CT$ have a one-to-one correspondence with the leaves of T_A's pruned subtree, which must be rooted at v. Therefore, we only have to refine v's nest and remove it when it has one child.

Definition 10.32. For $0 \leq h \leq \log \log n$, let $lazy(h)$ be the sequence of refinement steps $r = 2^h, 2^h - 1, \ldots, 1$ described in Section 10.2 having the following additional characteristics:

(10.32.1) At the beginning, we have $D^{(2^h)}$, which is defined as CT augmented with the new leaves (one new leaf per string in $\mathcal{M}$).

(10.32.2) If a node in $D^{(r)}$ has only one child, then the node is either the root of $D^{(r)}$ or a (light) leaf in CT.

(10.32.3) A refinement step from $D^{(r)}$ to $D^{(r-1)}$ can only be applied to heavy nodes.

Each refinement tree still has $O(n^2)$ nodes because the nodes having at least two children cannot be more than the leaves, i.e., $O(n^2)$, and the one-child nodes cannot be more than CT's nodes, i.e. $O(n^2)$ (by Conditions 10.32.1–10.32.2). Moreover, nest-refining is done almost the same way as in Section 10.2 by Condition 10.32.3 (the one-child nodes are light).

Consequently, $lazy(\log \log n)$ produces T_A correctly as CT's refinement after removing all the one-child nodes except the root from it. It can be seen that $lazy(h)$ produces the compacted trie for the $(cL + O(2^{2^h}))$-length prefixes of $\mathcal{M}$'s macro strings and its cost is $O(2^h n^2)$ time by point (ii). Our strategy relies on applying $lazy(h)$ in stages $h = 0, 1, \ldots, \log \log n$, according to Definition 10.32. We start from stage $h = 0$, and after each stage h, we check to see if tree $D^{(0)}$ has two sibling nodes that make refiner 2^0 possible. This check can be performed in $O(n^2)$ worst-case time by simply running an extra refinement step with $r = 0$. If the result is true, we continue and start stage $h + 1$. If the result is false, we can infer that $lazy(h + 1), \ldots, lazy(\log \log n)$ will do no more refining and therefore we stop executing at stage h.

The worst-case complexity of this execution is still $\sum_{h=0}^{\log \log n} O(2^h n^2) = O(n^2 \log n)$ time and $O(n^2)$ space (see Theorem 10.31). On the other hand, the L-hypothesis implies that we stop executing at stage $h' = O(1)$, such that $cL + O(2^{2^{h'}}) = cL + O(1)$. It follows that no further refining is necessary because T_A has already been produced by $lazy(h')$ as well! The expected cost is therefore $\sum_{h=0}^{h'} O(2^h n^2) = O(n^2)$ time. In brief, if we can implement points (i)–(iii) in the bounds claimed, then the overall construction of T_A can be carried out in $O(n^2)$ expected time. Points (i) and (ii) are quite technical and so we discuss them in Exercises 10.18 and 10.19. We now deal with Point (iii).

10.5.1 CT'S CONSTRUCTION

There are two main steps in CT's construction in $O(n^2)$ worst-case time. As previously mentioned, CT is built on the set $\mathcal{M}'$ of distinct cL-length prefixes of $\mathcal{M}$'s macro strings.

STEP 1.   For each macro string $\alpha \in \mathcal{M}'$, we read the matrix's characters "covered" by α in the order determined by shape sequence $\mathcal{S}$ (Section 10.1). This corresponds to a regular string x of length $(cL)^2 = O(\log n)$ associated with α. We sort these strings lexicographically to obtain an ordered list $\mathcal{R}$ and group the strings sharing a common prefix together.

STEP 2.   We compute the length of the longest common prefix, LCP, between any two *adjacent* strings in $\mathcal{R}$. This can be done in constant time

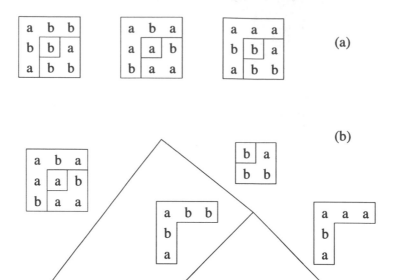

Fig. 10.19. An example of a compacted trie CT.

per string pair by means of the Four Russians' trick and some table look-ups. Next, we build CT on the macro strings in $\mathcal{M}'$ by using the ordered list $\mathcal{R}$ of associated strings along with their LCP information. Indeed, we are able to build a compacted trie in linear time, given its leaves in left-to-right order and the lowest common ancestor's depths of adjacent leaves (Exercise 10.17). In our case, the leaves correspond to the macro strings in $\mathcal{M}'$ in the order determined by their corresponding strings in $\mathcal{R}$. The lowest common ancestor's depth of two adjacent leaves is found by using the longest common prefix's length of the two relative macro strings, i.e., $\alpha, \beta \in \mathcal{M}'$. This, in turn, can be calculated by the LCP information given by the associated regular strings $x, y \in \mathcal{R}$, respectively, and by the fact that the longest common prefix's length between α and β is ℓ if and only if $\ell^2 \leq LCP(x, y) < (\ell + 1)^2$.

Example 10.33. Let $\mathcal{M}'$ contain the three macro strings illustrated in Fig. 10.19a. The shape sequence is $\mathcal{S}[1:3] = \mathcal{IN}\,\mathcal{SE}\,\mathcal{NW}$ and the associated strings are $babbababb, abaabaaba, babbabaaa$ and constitute list $\mathcal{R} = \{abaabaaba, babbababb, babbabaaa\}$. The LCP information between any two adjacent strings in $\mathcal{R}$ is 0 and 7, respectively. If we examine the compacted trie CT in Fig. 10.19b, built on the macro strings shown in Fig. 10.19a, then the macro strings appear in CT's leaves in the order determined by $\mathcal{R}$ (from left to right). In Fig. 10.19b, it can be seen that the lowest common ancestor's depth of the second and third leaf is related to the longest common prefix's length between the corresponding macro strings, i.e., $\ell = 2$

(because $2^2 \leq LCP(babbababb, babbabaaa) = 7 < 3^2$).

The details implementing Step 2 in $O(n^2)$ worst-case time are quite standard and so they are left to the reader as Exercise 10.21. In the rest of this section, we discuss the implementation of Step 1 by producing $\mathcal{R}$ from $\mathcal{M}'$.

10.5.2 SORTING $\mathcal{M}'$ TO OBTAIN $\mathcal{R}$

Given $\alpha \in \mathcal{M}'$, we want to determine its associated string x, which is used as a key to sort $\mathcal{M}'$ and produce $\mathcal{R}$. Since $|x| = O(\log n)$, we cannot explicitly compute this string for every $\alpha \in \mathcal{M}'$ because it would cost $O(n^2 \log n)$ time. Instead, we propose the following solution: We consider a string decomposition $x = x_1 \cdot x_2 \cdots x_s$, such that $1/4 \cdot L^2 \leq |x_i| \leq 1/2 \cdot L^2$ for $1 \leq i < s$ and $|x_s| \leq 1/2 \cdot L^2$. The decomposition must be *the same* for all the strings $x \in \mathcal{R}$, which are associated with the macro strings $\alpha \in \mathcal{M}'$. Sorting all the x's amounts to sorting their tuples $(x_1, x_2, \ldots, x_s)$ because we use an identical string decomposition for them. Each such string x satisfies:

- The number of strings which x is decomposed into is $s = O(1)$.
- Each x_i can be interpreted as an integer to the base $|\Sigma|$, denoted $I(x_i)$, where $I : \Sigma^* \to [0, n^2 - 1]$ is an isomorphism, such that $I(x_i) \leq I(y_i)$ if and only if x_i is *lexicographically* smaller than, or equal to, y_i (the $\$$ character is treated as the largest one).

Therefore, a constant-size tuple $(I(x_1), I(x_2), \ldots, I(x_s))$ of polynomially-bounded integers can be used instead of $(x_1, x_2, \ldots, x_s)$ for each string x to be ordered. We can now sort the integer tuples in $O(n^2)$ time and focus on the problem of associating a tuple $(I(x_1), I(x_2), \ldots, I(x_s))$ with each macro string $\alpha \in \mathcal{M}'$.

Let us fix a macro string $\alpha \in \mathcal{M}'$ and examine its associated string x. We must decide how to decompose x, i.e., we have to establish the length of the decomposition's members x_i. We use the shapes in $\mathcal{S}[1 : cL]$ to do this. We actually decompose the sequence $\mathcal{S}[1 : cL]$ into its contiguous subsequences $\mathcal{S}_1, \ldots, \mathcal{S}_s$. We assign weight $2k - 1$ (the number of covered matrix elements) to shape $\mathcal{S}[k]$, for $1 \leq k \leq cL$, so that each $\mathcal{S}_i$'s weight is defined as the sum of the weights of the shapes contained in it. We require that $\mathcal{S}_i$'s weight be between $1/4 \cdot L^2$ and $1/2 \cdot L^2$ except for $\mathcal{S}_s$'s weight, which can be smaller. This shape decomposition can always be carried out in $O(L) = O(\sqrt{\log n})$ time because each shape's weight is upper bounded by $1/2 \cdot L^2$ (since $c > 1$), and $\mathcal{S}[k+1]$'s weight is equal to $\mathcal{S}[k]$'s weight plus two. Consequently, we set $|x_i|$ equal to $\mathcal{S}_i$'s weight, for $1 \leq i \leq s$.

We must now determine x_i and find $I(x_i)$ by using the length $|x_i|$. We use a trick for it because finding $I(x_i)$ directly would take us a total of $O(n^2 \log n)$ time (see Example 10.34): We compute another integer $I(x_i')$

where string x_i' is obtained by permuting the characters in x_i, and then compute $I(x_i)$ from $I(x_i')$ without any loss in efficiency. We let ρ_i be the mapping between the characters in x_i' and x_i according to their permutation (which we define further on). Exercise 10.21 shows that we can compute a table by the Four Russians' trick with an $O(n^2)$ preprocessing time, such that a table look-up of $I(x_i')$ produces $I(x_i)$ in constant time. This means that $(I(x_1), I(x_2), \ldots, I(x_s))$ can be determined from $(I(x_1'), I(x_2'), \ldots, I(x_s'))$ by $s = O(1)$ table look-ups. In this way, we only have to define x_i' and compute $I(x_i')$.

We use $S_1 S_2 \cdots S_s = S[1:cL]$ to define x_i'. We first define α_i as α's chunk obtained by concatenating the macro characters corresponding to S_i's shapes so that we can decompose α as $\alpha_1 \cdot \alpha_2 \cdots \alpha_s$. We can see that x_i is the string obtained from α_i by reading the matrix's characters in the order determined by S_i. We then define x_i' as the string obtained by reading these characters in column-major order and ρ_i as the permutation that relates the characters in x_i and x_i' to each other. The advantage of using x_i' instead of x_i is that $I(x_i')$ can be computed more efficiently, as follows.

Example 10.34. For two macro strings $\alpha = \alpha_1 \cdot \alpha_2 \cdots \alpha_s$ and $\beta = \beta_1 \cdot \beta_2 \cdots \beta_s$, let α_i be the chunk highlighted in Fig. 10.20a and β_i be the one highlighted in Fig. 10.20b. As previously, $S[1:cL] = \mathcal{IN}\ \mathcal{SE}\ \mathcal{NW}\ \mathcal{SE} \cdots$. The matrix entries covered by these chunks are illustrated in Fig. 10.20c and 10.20d, respectively, and their associated strings can be determined by reading the characters clockwise according to the macro characters illustrated in Fig. 10.20a,b. We have $x_i = bbcaccaacbbabcccabaabcaabcc$ for α_i, and $y_i = baabaccaaaabcccabbbacbcaabc$ for β_i. It is worth noting that β_i is the "right" shift of α_i in the matrix shown in Fig. 10.20a,b. At this point, we might consider expressing y_i as a sequence of "edit" operations on x_i to compute $I(y_i)$ from $I(x_i)$ but this is not possible because the number of these operations is proportional to the number of S_i's shapes, which can be $cL/s = \Theta(L)$. We therefore examine the strings obtained by reading the characters in Fig. 10.20c,d in column-major order, i.e., $x_i' = abbcacbacccbccacbbcaaabaabc$ and $y_i' = baaaacccbccacaaabaabcbbbacb$. Now y_i' can be obtained from x_i' by a constant number of "edit" operations, namely *split* and *concatenate* (see Fig. 10.20e). The sequence of splits and concatenates depends on which S_i is chosen and on the fact that β_i is a "right" shift of α_i. We perform these operations by encoding the strings x_i' and y_i' as integers $I(x_i')$ and $I(y_i')$ to the base $|\Sigma|$ ranging in $[0, n^2 - 1]$. Splitting a string consists of computing the quotient and the remainder of the division between the encoding integer and a proper (precomputed) power of $|\Sigma|$ (we recall that the string is encoded to the base $|\Sigma|$). Merging two strings means multiplying the integer encoding the first string by some power of $|\Sigma|$, and by then adding the integer encoding the second

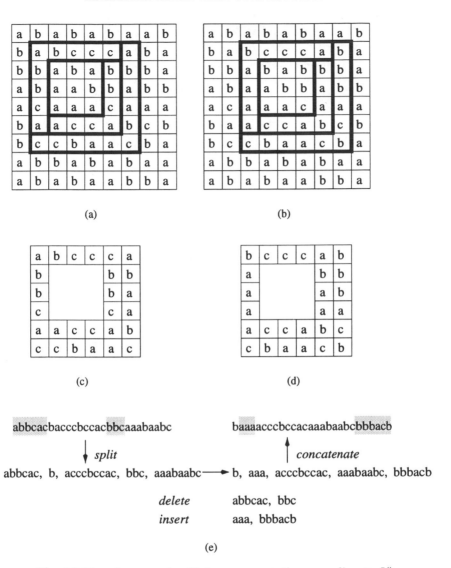

Fig. 10.20. An example of integer computation according to $I()$.

string. Therefore, if we assume that $I(x_i')$ is known and all the subcolumns of length 3 and 6 have been encoded as integers to the base $|\Sigma|$, $I(y_i')$ can be computed with splits and concatenates, according to the edit sequence shown in Fig. 10.20e. We delete the integers encoding columns *abbcac* and *bbc* from $I(x_i')$, and insert the integers encoding *aaa* and *bbbacb*. The "down" shift can be handled the same way as the "right" shift.

Example 10.34 shows us that, for a given $i \in [1, s]$, $I(y_i')$ can be obtained from $I(x_i')$ by a constant number of operations, including integer division and multiplication for a precomputed power of $|\Sigma|$. In general, for each $i = 1, \ldots, s$, we compute all the integers $I(x_i')$ by the property that an integer is either the right or the down shift of another. We then compute the integers $I(x_i)$. At the end, each $\alpha \in \mathcal{M}'$ has an associated tuple $(I(x_1), I(x_2), \ldots, I(x_s))$ and the process takes a total of $O(n^2)$ worst-case time. This can be seen as a generalization of the Karp-Rabin *fingerprint* computation for matrices, with the significant exceptions that: (a) our computation is deterministic because we work with an isomorphism from n^2 "short" strings into integers in $[0, n^2 - 1]$; (b) we do not need to bound the range of the integers resulting from an operation because (in our case) the integers always belong to $[0, n^2 - 1]$; and (c) we work with chunks rather than submatrices. This completes the description of both the sort of $\mathcal{M}'$ in $O(n^2)$ worst-case time and the construction of CT in $O(n^2)$ worst-case time.

In summary, we proved the following result:

Theorem 10.35. *According to the Logarithmic-Expected-Size hypothesis, the suffix tree T_A for an $n \times n$ matrix A can be built in $O(n^2)$ expected time for a constant-size alphabet Σ.*

10.6   Exercises

1. Reduce the node fan-out in suffix tree T_A from $O(n^2)$ to $O(|\Sigma|)$, for the $n \times n$ matrix A, by starting out from the fact that the first macro characters in the sibling arcs are different from each other, and each macro character has a string representation obtained by concatenating a subrow and a subcolumn of A. Devise an on-line search of an $m \times m$ pattern matrix B to find its occurrences as a submatrix of A in $O(m^2 \log |\Sigma| + occ)$ time, where occ is the number of occurrences.

2. Design linear-time algorithms that, given T_A, allow the computation of the following two-dimensional statistics for A:

   a) *The largest repeated square submatrices:* Find the largest square submatrices of A that occur at least twice in A. Prove and use the fact that these repeated submatrices are stored in the internal nodes of T_A.

   b) *Submatrix identifiers:* For each position (i, j) of matrix $A\hat{\$}$, with $1 \le i, j \le n$, find the smallest submatrix whose origin is only there. The matrix $A\hat{\$}$ is defined as in Section 10.1.

   c) *Compact weighted vocabulary:* For any submatrix A' of A, find the number of occurrences of A' in A in $O(\log n)$ time. [*Hint:* Preprocess the shapes in $\mathcal{S}$ such that, for any submatrix A', its origin (i, j) can be found in constant time. Take leaf (i, j) in T_A and perform a binary search on (i, j)'s ancestors assuming that the h-th ancestor can be found in constant time.]

3. For a fixed sequence S of shapes and a given matrix A, prove that the suffix trees obtained by varying the array Π of permutations are all isomorphic.

4. Extend the definition of suffix tree to d-dimensional matrices (i.e., matrices whose entries are addressed by $d > 2$ indices). What is a macro character? How can the node fan-out in the suffix tree be reduced to $O(|\Sigma|)$? [*Hint:* Sibling arcs start with different macro characters that can be treated as matrices of dimension $d - 1$. Build a compacted trie for dimension $d - 1$ recursively.]

5. **Suffix automata and directed acyclic word graphs (DAWGs) can be used for on-line string searches in a given text string (see the bibliographic notes). Is it possible to extend these notions to square matrices?

6. **Let Σ be a general alphabet. For every $n \geq 1$, prove that there are $n \times n$ matrices A whose corresponding sets $\mathcal{M}$ (Definition 10.4) contain macro strings with $\Omega(n^3 \log n)$ distinct chunks of a power-of-two length. [*Hint:* Choose A whose entries are all distinct.]

7. *Devise some efficient algorithms for the Concurrent-Read Concurrent-Write Parallel Random Access Machine (CRCW PRAM) to build the suffix tree for matrices, and to search for matrices on-line.

8. Let L be a library of square matrices having different sides. Extend the definition of suffix trees to library L, and examine the special case of Lsuffix trees. Devise some efficient algorithms that allow updating the Lsuffix tree after inserting a matrix into L or deleting it. [*Hint:* Use McCreight's construction and the Lsuffix tree.]

9. Preprocess the s-trees for an $n \times m$ matrix in $O(nm^2 \log n)$ time in order to reduce their node fan-out and then perform pattern matching (see Exercise 10.1). Devise some efficient CRCW PRAM algorithms for the construction of the s-trees and their on-line search.

10. **Devise an $O(nm^2)$-time construction of the s-trees for a constant-size alphabet Σ.

11. **Find a new index definition for rectangular matrices (alternative to Definition 10.18) for which the $\Omega(nm^2)$ lower bound in Theorem 10.21 does not hold. The asymptotic time performance of the construction of the new index should be significantly better than the $O(nm^2 \log n)$ obtained in Theorem 10.22.

12. Consider a matrix M (of a power-of-two side) treated by NOD-processing (Section·10.4.1). Note that M is decomposed into smaller and smaller submatrices (case $k > 0$) until we get characters (case $k = 0$). Let s_M be the string obtained by reading the characters in

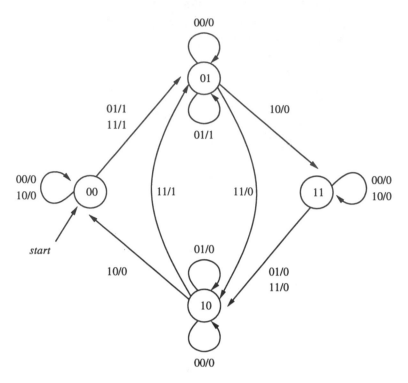

Fig. 10.21. The transducer $\mathcal{A}$ used for computing names by the succinct representation. For each triple of binary digits on the transitions, the first digit comes from B_k, the second from C_k, and the third is the output for D_k.

M in the order determined by its decomposition. Prove the following *Prefix Decomposition* property:

For any two matrices M and M' of a power-of-two side, M' occurs in the top left corner of M if and only if $s_{M'}$ is a prefix of s_M.

13. Prove the statements in:

   a) Fact 10.6. [*Hint:* Each submatrix is represented by a prefix of some macro string in $\mathcal{M}$.]

   b) Lemma 10.11, with reference to Chapter 3.

   *c) Lemma 10.14. [*Hint:* Both the submatrices of M_{α_u} and M_{α_v} that are covered by $\mathcal{S}[1:p-1]$ must be stored in u's and v's common parent.]

   d) Claim 10.27, by induction on step k.

14. Prove that the transducer $\mathcal{A}$ illustrated in Fig. 10.21 correctly produces the binary sequence D_k for any two given binary sequences B_k and C_k (see Section 10.4.2). Note that $\mathcal{A}$ has four states. Two states are "waiting" (00 and 11) and two are "coloring" (10 and 01):

State 00 encodes the fact that $\mathcal{A}$ is "waiting" for the next group of
1s in C_k to start and that this group must be assigned color 1. This
is the initial state. There is a transition out of 00 into "coloring"
state 01 when a group starts. State 01 encodes the fact that $\mathcal{A}$ is
"currently scanning" a group of 1s in C_k and that this group must
be assigned color 1. There is a transition out of 01 when the end of
a span in B_k is detected. This corresponds to the end of a group in
C_k. The next state is either "waiting" state 11 (no new group starts)
or "coloring" state 10 (a new group starts). The definitions of states
11 and 10 are symmetric to those of 00 and 01, respectively.

15. The Four Russians' trick is based on packing m consecutive charac-
    ters $a_{m-1}, \ldots, a_0 \in \Sigma$, which are interpreted as an m-digit integer
    $I(a_{m-1}, \ldots, a_0) = \sum_{i=0}^{m-1} a_i |\Sigma|^i$ to the base $|\Sigma|$. Solve the following
    problems in $O(N)$ time, where N is the input size and $|\Sigma|^m = N$.
    [*Hint:* Traverse a complete $|\Sigma|$-ary tree of m height, in which there is
    a path from the root to the leaf numbered $I(a_{m-1}, \ldots, a_0)$ for each
    distinct configuration of $a_{m-1} \ldots, a_0$.]

    a) Build a table $AND[I(a_{k-1}, \ldots, a_0), I(b_{k-1}, \ldots, b_0)]$ to compute
       the 'bitwise and' between any two sequences $a_{k-1}, \ldots, a_0$ and
       $b_{k-1}, \ldots, b_0$, where $\Sigma = \{0, 1\}$, $m = 2k$, and $2^{2k} = N$. (A
       similar table can be built for the 'bitwise or'.)

    b) Compute a table $AUT[I(s_1, s_0), I(b_{k-1}, \ldots, b_0), I(c_{k-1}, \ldots, c_0)]$
       $= I(s_1', s_0'), I(d_{k-1}, \ldots, d_0)$, with reference to the transducer $\mathcal{A}$
       described in Exercise 10.14 so that if any two sequences $b_{k-1}, \ldots,$
       b_0 and $c_{k-1}, \ldots, c_0$ are given as input to $\mathcal{A}$, and the current state
       is $s_1 s_0$, then $\mathcal{A}$ outputs the sequence $d_{k-1}, \ldots, d_0$ and reaches
       state $s_1' s_0'$. (In other words, AUT encodes all possible transitions
       of $\mathcal{A}$ on binary sequences of length k starting from any state.)
       We require that $\Sigma = \{0, 1\}$, $m = 2k + 2$, and $2^{2k+2} = N$.

    c) Given a permutation ρ of the integers in $[0, k-1]$, compute a ta-
       ble $PERM[I(a_{k-1}, \ldots, a_0)] = I(a_{\rho(k-1)}, \ldots, a_{\rho(0)})$ to permute
       the characters in any sequence according to ρ, where $m = k$ and
       $|\Sigma|^k = N$.

    d) Build a table $LCP[I(a_{k-1}, \ldots, a_0), I(b_{k-1}, \ldots, b_0)] = \ell$, such
       that $\ell \le k$ is the length of the longest common prefix between
       $a_{k-1} \cdots a_0$ and $b_{k-1} \cdots b_0$, where $m = 2k$ and $|\Sigma|^{2k} = N$.

16. Implement Step 2 of a NOD-query with vectors $\hat{B}_k$, $\hat{C}_k$, and $\hat{D}_k$
    (Section 10.4.2) by using Exercises 10.15a–b. The complexity must
    be $O(p^2 / \log p + q_k)$ time and space for each iteration k of Step 2,
    where q_k is the number of matrices in the list $\mathcal{L}_k$.

17. Build a compacted trie in linear time in its size, with your only in-
    put being the leaves in left-to-right order and the lowest common
    ancestor's depths of the adjacent leaves. [*Hint:* Use a stack.]

18. * Implement NOD-processing in $O(n^2)$ expected time (see Point (i) in Section 10.5) by using the following two ideas: (1) Simulate the first $\log L$ steps by the Prefix Decomposition property given in Exercise 10.12. Sort the strings s_M lexicographically for all F's submatrices M having side L (they are n^2 at most). Since $L = O(\log n)$, the sorting can be done in $O(n^2)$ time by Exercise 10.15c. [*Hint:* Compute the integer packing the characters in M in column-major order for all M and then use $PERM$ to obtain $I(s_M)$.] Group the equivalent submatrices together whose sides are a power of two smaller than, or equal to, L by means of a *sort history tree SHT*. This tree has $\log L + 2$ levels of nodes, numbered from -1 (the root, corresponding to the empty matrix) to $\log L$ (its leaves). There is a node at level $k \le \log L$ for each group of equal matrices of side 2^k (except for the root, when $k = -1$). A node containing a matrix, say M', is an ancestor of another node containing a matrix, i.e., M, if and only if M' occurs in the top left corner of M (i.e., $s_{M'}$ is a prefix of s_M). There are no one-child nodes except the root. Build SHT in $O(n^2)$ time by using Exercises 10.15d and 10.17. [*Hint:* Exploit the relationship between SHT and the compacted trie built on the strings s_M.] (2) Run the other steps in NOD-processing in a lazy fashion, i.e., stop executing when all equivalence classes are singletons and you obtain a "reduced" succinct representation in a total of $O(n^2)$ expected time.

19. Implement a NOD-query in $O(n^2)$ worst-case time (see Point (ii) in Section 10.5). [*Hint:* Let Q be the set of matrices to be named. Partition Q into two sets $Q_1 = \{[\![i, j]\!]^k \in Q : k \le \log L\}$ and $Q_2 = Q - Q_1$. The equivalence classes for Q_1 are obtained by grouping its matrices together by traversing SHT. The classes for Q_2 are found as indicated in Section 10.4; use the "reduced" succinct representation computed in Exercise 10.18.]

20. Extend the definition of SHT given in Exercise 10.18 to all of A's submatrices having a power-of-two side. Label each node at level k of SHT with h, h' if the equivalence class stored in this node is represented by $B_k[h{:}h'] = 10 \cdots 0 \cdots 01$ (Definition 10.25). Show that an alternative succinct representation can be given by ranking β and the extension of SHT (instead of $\hat{B}_0, \ldots, \hat{B}_{\log p}$). Also describe how to modify NOD-processing and a NOD-query.

21. Refer to Step 1 of CT's construction (Point (iii) in Section 10.5.1). Show how to transform $(I(x_1'), \ldots, I(x_s'))$ into $(I(x_1), \ldots, I(x_s))$ by using Exercise 10.15c. Also describe how to implement Step 2 by Exercises 10.15d and 10.17.

22. * Consider the following L'-hypothesis, which is a variation of the L-hypothesis for a general alphabet Σ (Section 10.5):

Each of A's largest repeated submatrices is no more than $(cL)^2$ expected size for some constant $c > 1$, where L is the largest power of two such that $L^2 \leq \lfloor \log n^2 \rfloor$ (the difference is that the logarithm is to the base two, whereas in the L-hypothesis, it is to the base $|\Sigma|$).

Show that if the L'-hypothesis holds, then the algorithms in Section 10.5 run in $O(n^2 \log |\Sigma|)$ expected time. [*Hint:* Sort and number the characters in $O(n^2 \log |\Sigma|)$ time; replace each character by the $\log |\Sigma|$ bits of its binary representation. Implement Points (i)–(iii) as follows: NOD-processing in $O(n^2 \log |\Sigma|)$ expected time, NOD-query in $O(n^2)$ worst-case time, and CT's construction in $O(n^2 \log |\Sigma|)$ worst-case time.]

23. ** Design a suffix tree construction for $n \times n$ matrices that works in $O(n^2 \log |\Sigma|)$ worst-case time for a general alphabet Σ. Say which macro strings such a fast construction does not exist for.

24. ** Devise an efficient algorithm for building the suffix tree by using some string representations other than macro strings (e.g., use row- or column-major order).

10.7   Bibliographic notes

The study of suffix tree data structures for matrices is motivated by the pattern-matching applications arising in low-level image processing (Rosenfeld and Kak [1982]), visual databases in multimedia systems (Jain [1992]) and data compression (Storer [1996]). Gonnet [1988] was the first to introduce the notion of suffix tree for a matrix by using spiral strings (also see Gonnet and Baeza-Yates [1991]), called PAT-tree—slightly different from the definition given in Section 10.1. Spiral strings were also discussed by Mark and Goodchild [1986]. The first efficient suffix tree construction for square matrices was given by Giancarlo [1993a, 1995], who introduced the Lsuffix tree and the Lstrings. An equivalent notion of Lstrings was independently proposed by Amir and Farach [1992]. Giancarlo [1993b] introduced the abstract notion of rectangular matrix index described in Definition 10.18 and he proved the lower bound in Theorem 10.22. He also defined s-trees and devised their construction. Both the s-trees and the Lsuffix tree can support a wide range of queries, many of which can be answered in optimal time (see Giancarlo [1993a, 1993b]). Both in these papers and in Choi and Lam [1995], some algorithms for the dynamic maintenance of a library of matrices (see Exercise 10.8) are proposed. Giancarlo and Grossi [1993a, 1993b] proposed some CRCW PRAM algorithms for the construction of both Lsuffix trees and s-trees. Giancarlo and Grossi [1994, 1995] introduced the general framework of macro strings and their related suffix tree families, along with an efficient suffix tree construction method, all described in this Chapter.

The definition of compacted trie can be found in Knuth [1973]. The

suffix tree construction for strings was proposed in Weiner [1973] and Mc-
Creight [1976], and the *AILSV* algorithm was introduced in Apostolico,
Iliopoulos, Landau, Schieber and Vishkin [1988] (also see Chapter 3 and
JàJà's book [1992]). The naming technique was devised by Karp, Miller
and Rosenberg [1972] and is described in Chapter 2 (the technique presented in Section 10.4 improves the amount of space required). With regard
to CRCW PRAM algorithms, Crochemore and Rytter [1991] discuss the
application of the naming technique to several problems, such as the on-
line search in pattern-matching problems involving pattern matrices having a power-of-two side (some more references for two-dimensional pattern
matching are given in Chapters 2 and 9). Linear-time lexicographic sorting algorithms are discussed in many textbooks (see, for instance, Aho,
Hopcroft and Ullman [1974]). The Four Russians' trick was devised by
Arlazarov, Dinic, Kronrod and Faradzev [1970] (see Exercise 10.15). The
L-hypothesis on the expected sizes of the largest repeated submatrices (Section 10.5) holds under mild probabilistic models, which have all been introduced and discussed for strings (see Szpankowski [1993], equations (2.3b)
and (2.10) with $b = 1$, and point (iv), p.1185), but they also generalize
to square matrices (Szpankowski [1994]). The expected-time construction
was partially inspired by the one given for suffix arrays by Manber and
Myers [1990] (e.g., the sort history tree SHT and the use of the Four
Russians' trick). The Karp-Rabin fingerprint technique for strings and
matrices is described in Karp and Rabin [1987]. De Bruijn sequences are
defined in de Bruijn [1946]. The technique for finding the longest common
prefix in constant time (proof of Theorem 10.22 and Exercise 10.1) by using the suffix tree and some lowest common ancestor (LCA) queries was
introduced by Landau and Vishkin [1989] (also see Chapter 6). The best-
known algorithms for LCA queries are described in Harel and Tarjan [1984]
and Schieber and Vishkin [1988]. The algorithm for finding a leaf's h-
th ancestor (Exercise 10.2c) was devised by Berkman and Vishkin [1994].
The directed acyclic word graphs and suffix automata mentioned in Exercise 10.5 were introduced by Blumer, Blumer, Haussler, Ehrenfeucht,
Chen and Seiferas [1985], Blumer, Blumer, Haussler, McConnell and Ehrenfeucht [1987], and Crochemore [1986].

Bibliography

AHO, A. V., J. E. HOPCROFT, AND J. D. ULLMAN [1974]. *The De-
    sign and Analysis of Computer Algorithms*, Addison-Wesley, Reading,
    Mass.

AMIR, A., AND M. FARACH [1992]. "Two-dimensional dictionary match-
    ing," *Information Processing Letters* **44**, 233-239.

APOSTOLICO, A., C. ILIOPOULOS, G. LANDAU, B. SCHIEBER, AND U.
    VISHKIN [1988]. "Parallel construction of a suffix tree with applica-

tions," *Algorithmica* **3**, 47-365.

ARLAZAROV, V. L., E. A. DINIC, M. A. KRONROD, AND I. A. FARADZEV [1970]. "On economical construction of the transitive closure of a directed graph," *Soviet Math. Dokl.* **11**, 1209-1210.

BERKMAN, O., AND U. VISHKIN [1994]. "Finding level ancestors in trees," *Journal of Computer and System Sciences* **48**, 214-230.

BLUMER, A., J. BLUMER, D. HAUSSLER, A. EHRENFEUCHT, M. T. CHEN, AND J. SEIFERAS [1985]. "The smallest automaton recognizing the subwords of a text," *Theoretical Computer Science* **40**, 31-55.

BLUMER, A., J. BLUMER, D. HAUSSLER, R. MCCONNELL, AND A. EHRENFEUCHT [1987]. "Complete inverted files for efficient text retrieval and analysis," *J. ACM* **34**, 578-595.

DE BRUIJN, N.G. [1946]. "A combinatorial problem," *Nederl. Akad. Wetensch. Proc.* **49**, 758-764.

CHOI, Y., AND T.W. LAM [1995]. "Two-dimensional pattern matching on a dynamic library of texts," *COCOON 95*, D-Z. Du and M. Li eds, LNCS 959, 530-538.

CROCHEMORE, M. [1986]. "Transducers and repetitions," *Theoretical Computer Science* **45**, 63-86.

CROCHEMORE, M., AND W. RYTTER [1991]. "Usefulness of the Karp-Miller-Rosenberg algorithm in parallel computations on strings and arrays," *Theoretical Computer Science* **88**, 59-82.

GIANCARLO, R. [1993a]. "The suffix tree of a square matrix, with applications," *Proc. Fourth ACM-SIAM Symposium on Discrete Algorithms*, 402-411.

GIANCARLO, R. [1993b]. "An index data structure for matrices, with applications to fast two-dimensional pattern matching," *Proc. Workshop on Algorithms and Data Structures*, LNCS 709, Springer-Verlag, 337-348.

GIANCARLO, R. [1995]. "A generalization of the suffix tree to square matrices, with applications," *Siam J. on Computing* **24**, 520-562.

GIANCARLO, R., AND R. GROSSI [1993a]. "Parallel construction and query of suffix trees for two-dimensional matrices," *Proc. of the 5-th ACM Symposium on Parallel Algorithms and Architectures*, 86-97.

GIANCARLO, R., AND R. GROSSI [1993b]. "Parallel construction, and query of suffix trees for square matrices," AT&T Bell Labs Technical Memorandum, submitted to journal.

GIANCARLO, R., AND R. GROSSI [1994]. "On the construction of classes of index data structure for square matrices: Algorithms and applications," AT&T Bell Labs. Technical Memorandum, submitted to journal.

GIANCARLO, R., AND R. GROSSI [1995]. "On the construction of classes of suffix trees for square matrices: Algorithms and applications," *22nd Int. Colloquium on Automata, Languages, and Programming*, Z. Fulop and F. Gecseg eds, LNCS 944, 111-122.

GONNET, G. H. [1988]. "Efficient searching of text and pictures- Extended Abstract," Tech. Report, University Of Waterloo- OED-88-02.

GONNET, G .H., AND R. BAEZA-YATES [1992]. *Handbook of Algorithms and Data Structures*, Addison-Wesley, Reading, Mass., 2nd edition.

HAREL, D., AND R.E. TARJAN [1984]. "Fast algorithms for finding nearest common ancestors," *SIAM J. on Computing* 13, 338-355.

JAIN, R. [1992]. Workshop Report on Visual Information Systems, National Science Foundation.

JÀJÀ, J. [1992]. *An Introduction to Parallel Algorithms*, Addison-Wesley, Reading, Mass.

KARP, R., R. MILLER, AND A. ROSENBERG [1972]. "Rapid identification of repeated patterns in strings, arrays and trees," *Proc. 4th ACM Symposium on Theory of Computing*, 125-136.

KARP, R. M., AND M.O. RABIN [1987]. "Efficient randomized pattern-matching algorithms," *IBM J. Res. Dev.* 31, 249-260.

KNUTH, D. E. [1973]. *The Art of Computer Programming, VOL. 3: Sorting and Searching*, Addison-Wesley, Reading, Mass.

LANDAU, G., AND U. VISHKIN [1989]. "Fast parallel and serial approximate string matching," *J. of Algorithms* 10, 157-169.

MANBER, U., AND E. MYERS [1990]. "Suffix arrays: a new method for on-line string searches," *SIAM Journal of Computing* 22, 935-948.

MARK, D. M., AND M.F. GOODCHILD [1986]. "On the ordering of two-dimensional space: Introduction and relation to tesseral principles," in B. Diaz and S. Bell Editors, *Spatial Data Processing Using Tesseral Methods, NERC Unit for Thematic Information Systems*, 179-192.

MCCREIGHT, E. M. [1976]. "A space economical suffix tree construction algorithm," *J. of ACM* 23 , 262-272.

ROSENFELD, A., AND A.C. KAK [1982]. *Digital Picture Processing*, Academic Press.

SCHIEBER, B., AND U. VISHKIN [1986]. "On finding lowest common ancestors: Simplification and parallelization," *Siam J. on Computing* 17, 1253-1262.

STORER, J. [1996]. "Lossless image compression using generalized LZ1-type methods," *Proc. IEEE Data Compression Conference*, to appear.

SZPANKOWSKI, W. [1993]. "A generalized suffix tree and its (un)expected asymptotic behaviour," *SIAM J. on Computing*, 22 1176-1198.

SZPANKOWSKI, W. [1994]. Personal communication.

WEINER, P. [1973]. "Linear pattern matching algorithm," *Proc. 14-th IEEE SWAT* (now, *Symposium on Foundations of Computer Science*), 1-11.

11
Tree Pattern Matching

Most of this book is about stringology, the study of strings. So why this chapter on trees? Why not graphs or geometry or something else? First, trees generalize strings in a very direct sense: a string is simply a tree with a single leaf. This has the unsurprising consequence that many of our algorithms specialize to strings and the happy consequence that some of those algorithms are as efficient as the best string algorithms.

From the point of view of "treeology", there is the additional pragmatic advantage of this relationship between trees and strings: some techniques from strings carry over to trees, e.g., suffix trees, and others show promise though we don't know of work that exploits it. So, treeology provides a good example area for applications of stringologic techniques.

Second, some of our friends in stringology may wonder whether there is some easy reduction that can take any tree edit problem, map it to strings, solve it in the string domain and then map it back. We don't believe there is, because, as you will see, tree editing seems inherently to have more data dependence than string editing. (Specifically, the dynamic programming approach to string editing is always a local operation depending on the left, upper, and upper left neighbor of a cell. In tree editing, the upper left neighbor is usually irrelevant — instead the relevant cell depends on the tree topology.) That is a belief not a theorem, so we would like to state right at the outset the key open problem of treeology: can all tree edit problems on ordered trees (trees where the order among the siblings matters) be reduced efficiently to string edit problems and back again? [1]

The rest of this chapter proceeds on the assumption that this question has a negative response. In particular, we discuss the best known algorithms for tree editing and several variations having to do with subtree removal, variable length don't cares, and alignment. We discuss both sequential and parallel algorithms. We present negative results having to do with unordered trees (trees whose sibling order is arbitrary) and a few approximation algorithms. Finally, we discuss the problem of finding commonalities among a set of trees.

---

[1] Since the editing problem for unordered trees is NP-complete, we can say that it is not possible to map it into a string problem.

11.1   Preliminary definitions and early history

11.1.1   TREES

A *free tree* is a connected, acyclic, undirected graph. A *rooted tree* is a free tree in which one of the vertices is distinguished from the others and is called the root. We refer to a vertex of a rooted tree as a *node* of the tree. An *unordered tree* is just a rooted tree. We use the term unordered tree to distinguish it from the rooted, ordered tree defined below. An *ordered tree* is a rooted tree in which the children of each node are ordered. That is, if a node has k children, then we can designate them as the first child, the second child, and so on up to the kth child.

Unless otherwise stated, all trees we consider are either ordered labeled rooted trees or unordered labeled rooted trees.

Given a tree, it is usually convenient to use a *numbering* to refer to the nodes of the tree. For an ordered tree T, the left-to-right postorder numbering or left-to-right preorder numbering are often used to number the nodes of T from 1 to $|T|$, the size of tree T. For an unordered tree, we can fix an arbitrary order for each of the node in the tree and then use left-to-right postorder numbering or left-to-right preorder numbering. Suppose that we have a numbering for each tree. Let $t[i]$ be the ith node of tree T in the given numbering. We use $T[i]$ to denote the subtree rooted at $t[i]$.

11.1.2   A BRIEF REVIEW OF ALGORITHMIC RESULTS IN EXACT TREE MATCHING

We distinguish between exact and approximate matching as follows. A match between two objects o and o' is *exact based on a a matching relation* R if o' is a member of $R(o)$. It is in this sense, in strings, that $w*ing$ matches both "willing" and "windsurfing" where R is defined so that * can match any sequence of non-blank characters. A match between two objects o and o' given a matching relation R is inexact or approximate if it isn't exact. For example, $w*ing$ matches "widen" only approximately. In the case of an approximate match, the *distance* is normally based on some monotonic function of the smallest changes to o and/or o' that result in objects p and p' respectively such that p' is a member of $R(p')$. Using edit distance $w*ing$ matches "widen" with distance three, the number of changes to "widen" to transform it to "wing."

Most of our work has concerned approximate matching in trees, so our review of the results of exact matching in trees is extremely brief, serving mostly to give pointers to some of the important papers with the barest hint of algorithmic idea.

Exact tree matching without variables   Let pattern P and target T be ordered labeled trees of size m and n respectively, P matches T at node

v if there exists a one-to-one mapping from the nodes of P into the nodes of T such that

1. the root of P maps to v,
2. if x maps to y, then x and y have the same labels, and
3. if x maps to y and x is not a leaf, then the ith child of x maps to the ith child of y. (This does not imply that P maps to the subtree rooted at v, but merely that the degree of y is no less than the degree of x.)

The obvious algorithm takes $O(nm)$ time. A classic open problem was whether this bound could be improved. Kosaraju broke the $O(nm)$ barrier for this problem with an $\tilde{O}(nm^{0.75})$ algorithm. (Note that $\tilde{O}(f(n,m)) = O(f(n,m)polylog(m))$) He introduced three new techniques: a suffix tree of a tree; the convolution of a tree and a string; and partitioning of trees into chains and anti-chains. More recently, Dubiner, Galil and Magen improved this result giving an $\tilde{O}(n\sqrt{m})$ algorithm. Their result was based on the use of "k-truncated" suffix trees that, roughly speaking, shorten the representation of paths from the root of the pattern P to descendants of the root to have length no more than k. They also used periodical strings. (A string α is a *period* of a string β if β is a prefix of α^k for some $k > 0$.)

Dubiner, Galil and Magen first construct a $3\sqrt{m}$-truncated suffix tree, Σ, in $O(m\sqrt{m})$ time. Depending on how many leaves Σ has, there are two cases:

- Σ has at least $\sqrt{m}$ leaves. They show that there are at most $n/\sqrt{m}$ "possible roots" in the target tree. They can find these "possible roots" and then check to see if there is a match in $O(n\sqrt{n})$ time.

- Σ has at most $\sqrt{m}$ leaves. They show that by using the properties of periodical strings, a matching can be found in $\tilde{O}(n\sqrt{m})$ time. This gives an $\tilde{O}(n\sqrt{m})$ time algorithm.

Exact pattern matching with variables   Exact pattern matching has many applications in term-rewriting systems, code generation, and logic programming, particularly as a restricted form of unification. In this application, patterns are constructed recursively from a single "wild-card" variable v, a constant c, or a function $f(p_1, ..., p_k)$ where the arguments $p_1, ..., p_k$ are patterns in the language. Thus, v, $f(c)$, $f(f(v), c, v)$ are all patterns. The recursion induces a tree: the expression $f(p_1, ..., p_k)$ is the parent of the arguments $p_1, ..., p_k$ and the p_i's are children or "subpatterns" of $f(p_1, ..., p_k)$.

Pattern p_1 *matches* p_2 if it is "more general" (i.e., $\geq$) than p_2. This holds if either

1. p_1 is v or

2. p_1 is $f(x_1, ..., x_k)$, p_2 is $f(y_1, ..., y_k)$ and $x_i \geq y_i$ for all i between 1 and k inclusive.

Note that this allows a variable to match an entire subtree, but if p_1 isn't a variable, then p_1 and p_2 must begin with the same function symbol.

Given a set of patterns P and a "subject" pattern t, the *multi-pattern matching problem* is to find the set of elements in P which match some subpattern (i.e., subtree) in t.

There are two approaches to this problem: algorithms that start from the roots of the trees (top-down) and those that start from the leaves (bottom-up). The bottom-up approaches require significant preprocessing time of the patterns, but handle each subject faster (in time proportional to the size of the subject plus the number of matches). In rewriting systems, the subject is constantly changing, so bottom-up is more attractive. However, in the *development* of rewriting systems and in the construction of conventional compilers (which use pattern matching in back-end code generation phases), patterns change frequently. Once the compiler is constructed, the patterns become static.

The basic technique in the bottom-up algorithms is to construct the set PF of all subpatterns of P. Since this can be exponential in the size of P, the auxilliary space and time requirement can be large and much effort has gone into finding good data structures to hold this set.

The basic algorithm for pattern matching with variables is due to Hoffman and O'Donnell. Improvements using better data structures or variations of the algorithm have been proposed by Chase and Cai, Paige and Tarjan. Recent work by Thorup presents a short algorithm (with a rather subtle amortized analysis) that improves the space complexity and usually the time complexity for preprocessing simple patterns of size p to $O(p \log p)$ time and $O(p)$ space.

11.1.3 EDIT OPERATIONS AND EDIT DISTANCE

Edit operations We consider three kinds of operations for ordered labeled trees. *Changing* a node n means changing the label on n. *Deleting* a node n means making the children of n become the children of the parent of n and then removing n. *Inserting* is the complement of deleting. This means that inserting n as the child of m will make n the parent of a *consecutive subsequence* of the current children of m.

We can consider the same kind of operations for unordered labeled trees. In this case, in the insertion operation, we have to change *consecutive subsequence* to *subset*.

Suppose each node label is a symbol chosen from an alphabet $\sum$. Let λ, a unique symbol not in $\sum$, denote the null symbol. We represent an edit operation as $a \rightarrow b$, where a is either λ or a label of a node in tree T_1 and b is either λ or a label of a node in tree T_2. We call $a \rightarrow b$ a change

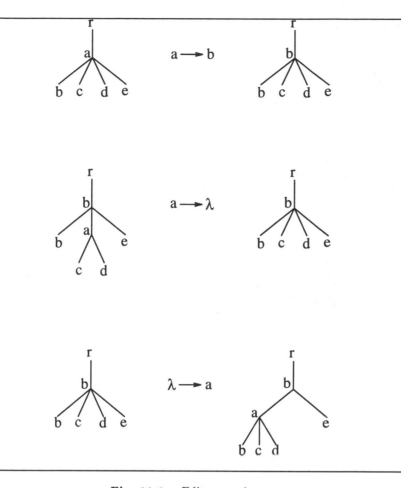

Fig. 11.1. Edit operations

operation if $a \neq \lambda$ and $b \neq \lambda$; a delete operation if $b = \lambda$; and an insert operation if $a = \lambda$. Let T_2 be the tree that results from the application of an edit operation $a \rightarrow b$ to tree T_1; this is written $T_1 \rightarrow T_2$ via $a \rightarrow b$.

Let S be a sequence $s_1, ..., s_k$ of edit operations. An S-derivation from tree A to tree B is a sequence of trees $A_0, ..., A_k$ such that $A = A_0$, $B = A_k$, and $A_{i-1} \rightarrow A_i$ via s_i for $1 \leq i \leq k$. Let γ be a cost function which assigns to each edit operation $a \rightarrow b$ a nonnegative real number $\gamma(a \rightarrow b)$.

We constrain γ to be a distance metric. That is, i) $\gamma(a \rightarrow b) \geq 0$, $\gamma(a \rightarrow a) = 0$; ii) $\gamma(a \rightarrow b) = \gamma(b \rightarrow a)$; and iii) $\gamma(a \rightarrow c) \leq \gamma(a \rightarrow b) + \gamma(b \rightarrow c)$.

We extend γ to the sequence of edit operations S by letting $\gamma(S) = \sum_{i=1}^{|S|} \gamma(s_i)$.

Edit and alignment distances   The *edit distance* between two trees is defined by considering the minimum cost edit operations sequence that transforms one tree to the other. Formally the edit distance between T_1 and T_2 is defined as:

$$D_e(T_1, T_2) = \min_S \{\gamma(S) \mid S \text{ is an ed it operation sequence taking } T_1 \text{ to } T_2\}.$$

The *alignment distance* between two trees is defined by considering only those edit operation sequences such that all the insertions precede all the deletions. The reason why this is called alignment distance will be clear when we discuss it later.

Note that *edit distance* is in fact a distance metric while *alignment distance* is not since it does not satisfy the triangle inequality.

11.1.4   EARLY HISTORY OF APPROXIMATE TREE MATCHING ALGORITHMS

Tai's classical   Kuo-Chung Tai gave the definition of the edit distance between ordered labeled trees and the first non-exponential algorithm to compute it. The algorithm is quite complicated, making it hard to understand and to implement. The space complexity is too large to be practical. We sketch the algorithm here.

Tai used preorder number to number the trees. The convenient aspect of this notation is that for any $i, 1 \le i \le |T|$, nodes from $T[1]$ to $T[i]$ is a tree rooted at $T[1]$.

Given two trees T_1 and T_2, let $D_t(T_1[1..i], T_2[1..j])$ be the edit distance between $T_1[1]$ to $T_1[i]$ and $T_2[1]$ to $T_2[j]$.

We can now use the same approach as in sequence editing. Assume that $D_t(T_1[1..i-1], T_2[1..j-1])$, $D_t(T_1[1..i-1], T_2[1..j])$ and $D_t(T_1[1..i], T_2[1..j-1])$ are already known, we now extend them into $D_t(T_1[1..i], T_2[1..j])$. If either $t_1[i]$ or $t_2[j]$ is not involved in a substitution, then it is exactly the same as in sequence editing. That is, we just need to use either $D_t(T_1[1..i-1], T_2[1..j])$ or $D_t(T_1[1..i], T_2[1..j-1])$ plus the cost of deleting $t_1[i]$ or inserting $t_2[j]$.

The difficult case occurs when we substitute $t_1[i]$ by $t_2[j]$. In this case, there must be $t_1[r]$ and $t_2[s]$ such that $t_1[r]$ is an ancestor of $t_1[i]$, $t_2[s]$ is an ancestor of $t_2[j]$, and we substitute $t_1[r]$ by $t_2[s]$. Furthermore, all the nodes on the path from $t_1[i]$ to $t_1[r]$ are deleted and all the nodes on the path from $t_2[j]$ to $t_2[s]$ are inserted.

However in the optimal edit sequence for $T_1[1..i-1]$ and $T_2[1..j-1]$ we may not find such a pair $t_1[r]$ and $t_2[s]$. This means that in general we cannot derive $D_t(T_1[1..i], T_2[1..j])$ from $D_t(T_1[1..i-1], T_2[1..j-1])$.

In order to deal with this difficulty, Tai introduces another two measures between trees and the resulting algorithm is quite complex with a time and space complexity of $O(|T_1| \times |T_2| \times depth(T_1)^2 \times depth(T_2)^2)$.

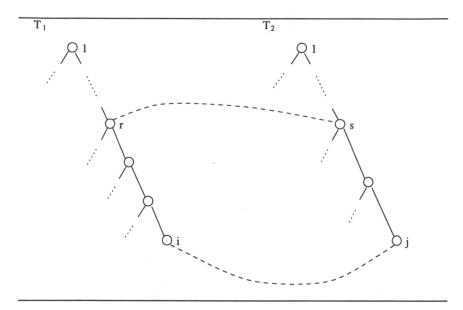

Fig. 11.2.   The difficult case

Lu's algorithm   Another edit distance algorithm between ordered trees is reported by Lu. Lu's definition of the edit operations are the same as Tai's. However the algorithm given by Lu does not compute the edit distance as it defined. Nevertheless it does provide another edit based distance.

We will briefly discuss this algorithm and show its properties. Let $t_1[i_1], t_1[i_2], ..., t_1[i_{n_i}]$ be the children of $t_1[i]$ and $t_2[j_1], t_2[j_2], ..., t_2[j_{n_j}]$ be the children of $t_2[j]$. the algorithm consider the following three cases.

1. $t_1[i]$ is deleted. In this case the distance would be to match $T_2[j]$ to one of the subtrees of $t_1[i]$ and then to delete all the rest of the subtrees.

2. $t_2[j]$ is inserted. In this case the distance would be to match $T_1[i]$ to one of the subtrees of $t_2[j]$ and then insert all the rest of the subtrees.

3. $t_1[i]$ matches $t_2[j]$. In this case, consider the subtrees $t_1[i_1], t_1[i_2], ..., t_1[i_{n_i}]$ and $t_2[j_1], t_2[j_2], ..., t_2[j_{n_j}]$ as two sequences and each individual subtree as a whole entity. Use the sequence edit distance to determine the distance between $t_1[i_1], t_1[i_2], ..., t_1[i_{n_i}]$ and $t_2[j_1], t_2[j_2], ..., t_2[j_{n_j}]$.

From the above description it is easy to see the difference between this distance and the edit distance. This algorithm considers each subtree as a whole entity. It does not allow one subtree of T_1 to map to more than one subtrees of T_2. Using the definition of edit distance, we can delete the root of one subtree and then map the remaining subtrees of this subtree to more than one subtrees.

Figure 11.3 shows an example. the edit distance is 1 since we only need to delete node b. The distance according to Lu's algorithm is 2 since we

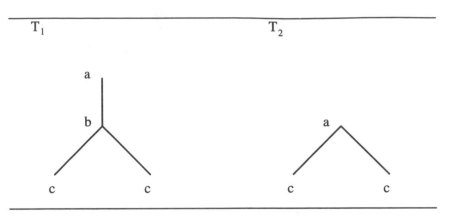

Fig. 11.3.   Lu's distance are different from edit distance

can delete node *a* of tree T_1 and than replace node *b* by *a*. We cannot directly delete node *b* since if we map *a* to *a*, then subtree rooted at *b* can only map to one of the two subtrees of tree T_2, resulting a distance of 3. For two level trees, this algorithm does in fact compute the edit distance between two ordered trees, but not for trees with more levels.

Variants of the problem   Selkow gave the another tree edit algorithm in which the insertions and deletions are restricted to the leaves of the trees. Only leaves may be deleted and a node may be inserted only as a leaf.

In this case, it is easy to see that if $t_1[i]$ maps to $t_2[j]$ then the parent of $t_1[i]$ must map to the parent of $t_2[j]$. The reason is that if $t_1[i]$ is not deleted, its parent can not be deleted or inserted. This means that if two nodes are matched, then their parents must also be matched. Yang later give an algorithm to identify the syntactic differences between two programs. His algorithm is basically a variation of Selkow's.

It is easy to design an algorithm using string edit algorithm as a subroutine to solve this problem. The time complexity is $O(|T_1| \times |T_2|)$.

Kilpelainen and Mannila introduced the tree inclusion problem. Given a pattern tree P and a target tree T, tree inclusions asks whether P can be embedded into to T. An alternative definition is to get P by deleting nodes of T. Both ordered trees and unordered trees are considered.

Since there may be exponentially many ordered embeddings of P to T, they used a concept called left embedding to avoid searching among these embeddings. Assume that the roots of P and T have the same label, their algorithm tries to embed P into T by embedding the subtrees of P as deeply and as far to the left as possible in T. The time complexity of their algorithm is $O(|T_1| \times |T_2|)$.

They showed that the unordered inclusion problem is NP-complete.

11.2 Tree edit and tree alignment algorithms for ordered trees

11.2.1 NOTATION

While computing the tree-to-tree edit distance, we must compute, as subroutines, the distance between certain pairs of subtrees and between certain pairs of ordered subforests. An ordered subforest of a tree T is a collection of subtrees of T appearing in the same order as they appear in T.

Specifically, we use a left-to-right postorder numbering for the nodes in the trees. For a tree T, $t[i]$ represents the ith node of tree T We use $T[i]$ to represent subtree of T rooted at $t[i]$ and $F[i]$ to represent the ordered subforest obtained by deleting $t[i]$ from $T[i]$. We use $desc(i)$ to denote the set of descendants of $t[i]$

We use $T[i..j]$ to denote the substructure of T induced by the nodes numbered i to j inclusive. In general $T[i..j]$ is an ordered forest.

Let $t[i_1], t[i_2], ..., t[i_{n_i}]$ be the children of $t[i]$. We use $F[i_r, i_s]$, $1 \leq r \leq s \leq n_i$, to represent the forest consisting of the subtrees $T[i_r], ..., T[i_s]$. $F[i_1, i_{n_i}] = F[i]$ and $F[i_p, i_p] = T[i_p] \neq F[i_p]$.

Let $l(i)$ be the postorder number of the leftmost leaf descendant of the subtree rooted at $t[i]$. When $t[i]$ is a leaf, $l(i) = i$. With this notation $T[i] = T[l(i)..i]$ and $F[i] = T[l(i)..i - 1]$.

We use $depth(T)$ to represent the depth of tree T; $leaves(T)$ to represent the number of leaves of tree T; and $deg(T)$ to represent the degree of tree T.

11.2.2 BASIC TREE EDIT DISTANCE COMPUTATION

Mapping and edit distance The edit operations give rise to a *mapping* which is a graphical specification of which edit operations apply to each node in the two trees (or two ordered forests). The mapping in Figure 11.4 shows a way to transform T_1 to T_2. It corresponds to the edit sequence (delete(node with label c), change(node with label g to label h), insert(node with label c)).

Formally we define a triple (M, T_1, T_2) to be a mapping from T_1 to T_2, where M is any set of pair of integers (i, j) satisfying:

(1) $1 \leq i \leq |T_1|, 1 \leq j \leq |T_2|$;
(2) For any pair of (i_1, j_1) and (i_2, j_2) in M,
    (a) $i_1 = i_2$ iff $j_1 = j_2$ (one-to-one)
    (b) $t_1[i_1]$ is to the left of $t_1[i_2]$ iff $t_2[j_1]$ is to the left of $t_2[j_2]$ (sibling order preserved)
    (c) $t_1[i_1]$ is an ancestor of $t_1[i_2]$ iff $t_2[j_1]$ is an ancestor of $t_2[j_2]$ (ancestor order preserved)

We will use M instead of (M, T_1, T_2) if there is no confusion. Let M be a mapping from T_1 to T_2, the cost of M is defined as follows:

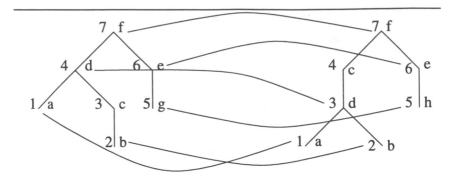

Fig. 11.4. Mapping

$$\gamma(M) \quad = \quad \sum_{(i,j)\in M} \gamma(t_1[i] \rightarrow t_2[j])$$

$$+ \sum_{\{i|\ \nexists\ j\ s.t.\ (i,j)\in M\}} \gamma(t_1[i] \rightarrow \lambda)$$

$$+ \sum_{\{j|\ \nexists\ i\ s.t.\ (i,j)\in M\}} \gamma(\lambda \rightarrow t_2[j])$$

Mappings can be composed. Let M_1 be a mapping from T_1 to T_2 and let M_2 be a mapping from T_2 to T_3. Define $M_1 \circ M_2 = \{(i,j) \mid \exists\ k\ s.t.\ (i,k) \in M_1$ and $(k,j) \in M_2\}$ It is easy to show that $M_1 \circ M_2$ is a mapping and $\gamma(M_1 \circ M_2) \leq \gamma(M_1) + \gamma(M_2)$.

The relation between a mapping and a sequence of edit operation is as follows: given S, a sequence $s_1,\ \dots\ ,s_k$ of edit operations from T_1 to T_2, there exists a mapping M from T_1 to T_2 such that $\gamma(M) \leq \gamma(S)$; conversely, for any mapping M, there exists a sequence of editing operations such that $\gamma(S) = \gamma(M)$. This implies that $\gamma(T_1, T_2) = \min\{\gamma(M) \mid M$ is a mapping from T_1 to $T_2\}$. Specifically, nodes in T_1 that are untouched by M correspond to deletions from T_1, nodes in T_1 connected by M to T_2 correspond to null edits (if the connected nodes have the same label) or relabelings (if the connected nodes have different labels), and nodes in T_2 that are untouched by M correspond to insertion operations. We will use the mapping idea to design the algorithm in the next subsection since the concept of mapping is easy to visualize and is order-independent.

General formula   The distance between $T_1[i'..i]$ and $T_2[j'..j]$ is denoted $forestdist(T_1[i'..i], T_2[j'..j])$ or simply $forestdist(i'..i, j'..j)$ if the context is clear. We use a more abbreviated notation for certain special cases. The distance between $T_1[i]$ and $T_2[j]$ is sometimes denoted $treedist(i, j)$.

We first present three lemmas and then give the algorithm.

Lemma 11.1. (i) $forestdist(\theta, \theta) = 0$
(ii) $forestdist(l(i_1)..i, \theta) = forestdist(l(i_1)..i - 1, \theta) + \gamma(t_1[i] \to \lambda)$
(iii) $forestdist(\theta, l(j_1)..j) = forestdist(\theta, l(j_1)..j - 1) + \gamma(\lambda \to t_2[j])$
where $i \in desc(i_1)$ and $j \in desc(j_1)$

Proof: Trivial. $\square$

Lemma 11.2. Let $i \in desc(i_1)$ and $j \in desc(j_1)$. Then

$$forestdist(l(i_1)..i, l(j_1)..j) =$$
$$\min \begin{cases} forestdist(l(i_1)..i - 1, l(j_1)..j) + \gamma(t_1[i] \to \lambda) \\ forestdist(l(i_1)..i, l(j_1)..j - 1) + \gamma(\lambda \to t_2[j]) \\ forestdist(l(i_1)..l(i) - 1, l(j_1)..l(j) - 1) \\ + forestdist(l(i)..i - 1, l(j)..j - 1) + \gamma(t_1[i] \to t_2[j]) \end{cases}$$

Proof: We compute $forestdist(l(i_1)..i, l(j_1)..j)$ for $l(i_1) \leq i \leq i_1$ and $l(j_1) \leq j \leq j_1$. We are trying to find a minimum-cost map M between $forest(l(i_1)..i)$ and $forest(l(j_1)..j)$. The map can be extended to $t_1[i]$ and $t_2[j]$ in three ways.

$t_1[i]$ is not touched by a line in M. Then $(i, \lambda) \in M$. In this case we have $forestdist(l(i_1)..i, l(j_1)..j) = forestdist(l(i_1)..i-1, l(j_1)..j) + \gamma(t_1[i] \to \lambda)$.

$t_2[j]$ is not touched by a line in M. Then $(\lambda, j) \in M$. In this case we have $forestdist(l(i_1)..i, l(j_1)..j) = forestdist(l(i_1)..i, l(j_1)..j - 1) + \gamma(\lambda \to t_2[j])$.

$t_1[i]$ and $t_2[j]$ are both touched by lines in M. Then $(i, j) \in M$. Here is why. Suppose (i, k) and (h, j) are in M. if $l(i_1) \leq h \leq l(i) - 1$, then i is to the right of h so k must be to the right of j by the sibling condition on mappings. This is impossible in $forest(l(j_1)..j)$. Similarly, if i is a proper ancestor of h, then k must be a proper ancestor of j by the ancestor condition on mappings. This too is impossible. So, $h = i$. By symmetry, $k = j$ and $(i, j) \in M$.

Now, by the ancestor condition on mappings, any node in subtree $T_1[i]$ can only be touched by a node in subtree $T_2[j]$. Hence, $forestdist(l(i_1)..i, l(j_1)..j) = forestdist(l(i_1)..l(i) - 1, l(j_1)..l(j) - 1) + forestdist(l(i)..i - 1, l(j)..j - 1) + \gamma(t_1[i] \to t_2[j])$.

Since these three cases express all the possible mappings yielding $forestdist(l(i_1)..i, l(j_1)..j)$, we take the minimum of these three costs. Thus the lemma is proved. $\square$

Lemma 11.3. Let $i \in desc(i_1)$ and $j \in desc(j_1)$. Then
(1) if $l(i) = l(i_1)$ and $l(j) = l(j_1)$

$$forestdist(l(i_1)..i, l(j_1)..j) =$$

$$\min \begin{cases} forestdist(l(i_1)..i-1, l(j_1)..j) + \gamma(t_1[i] \rightarrow \lambda) \\ forestdist(l(i_1)..i, l(j_1)..j-1) + \gamma(\lambda \rightarrow t_2[j]) \\ forestdist(l(i_1)..i-1, l(j_1)..j-1) + \gamma(t_1[i] \rightarrow t_2[j]) \end{cases}$$

(2) if $l(i) \neq l(i_1)$ or $l(j) \neq l(j_1)$ (i.e., otherwise)

$$forestdist(l(i_1)..i, l(j_1)..j) =$$

$$\min \begin{cases} forestdist(l(i_1)..i-1, l(j_1)..j) + \gamma(t_1[i] \rightarrow \lambda) \\ forestdist(l(i_1)..i, l(j_1)..j-1) + \gamma(\lambda \rightarrow t_2[j]) \\ forestdist(l(i_1)..l(i)-1, l(j_1)..l(j)-1) + treedist(i, j) \end{cases}$$

Proof: Immediately from Lemma 11.2. □

Algorithm   Lemma 11.3 has three important implications.

First the formulas it yields suggest that we can use a dynamic programming style algorithm to solve the tree distance problem.

Second, from (2) of Lemma 11.3 we observe that in order to compute $treedist(i_1, j_1)$ we need in advance almost all values of $treedist(i, j)$ where i is the root of a subtree containing i_1 and j is the root of a subtree containing j_1. This suggests using a bottom-up procedure for computing all subtree pairs.

Third, from (1) in Lemma 11.3 we can observe that when i is in the path from $l(i_1)$ to i_1 and j is in the path from $l(j_1)$ to j_1, we do not need to compute $treedist(i, j)$ separately. These subtree distances can be obtained as a byproduct of computing $treedist(i_1, j_1)$.

These implications lead to the following definition and then our algorithm. Let us define the set $LR\_keyroots$ of tree T as follows:

$$LR\_keyroots(T) = \{k \mid \text{there exists no } k' > k \text{ such that } l(k) = l(k')\}$$

That is, if k is in $LR\_keyroots(T)$ then either k is the root of T or $l(k) \neq l(p(k))$, i.e. k has a left sibling. Intuitively, this set will be the roots of all the subtrees of tree T that need separate computations.

It is easy to see that there is a linear time algorithm to compute the function $l()$ and the set $LR\_keyroots$. We can also assume that the result is in array l and $LR\_keyroots$. Further in array $LR\_keyroots$ the order of the elements is in increasing order.

We are now ready to present a simple algorithm for computing edit distance.

We use dynamic programming to compute $treedist(i, j)$. The forestdist values computed and used here are put in a temporary array; that is freed once the corresponding treedist is computed. The treedist values are put in the permanent treedist array.

Algorithm: EDIT(T_1,T_2)

> **begin**
>> Preprocessing:
>> (To compute $l()$, $LR\_keyroots(T_1)[]$ and $LR\_keyroots(T_2)[]$)
>> **for** $s := 1$ **to** $|LR\_keyroots(T_1)|$
>>> **for** $t := 1$ **to** $|LR\_keyroots(T_2)|$
>>>> $i = LR\_keyroots(T_1)[s]$;
>>>> $j = LR\_keyroots(T_2)[t]$;
>>>> Compute $treedist(i, j)$;
>
> **end**

Output: $tree\_dist(T_1[i], T_2[j])$, where $1 \le i \le |T_1|$ and $1 \le j \le |T_2|$.

Fig. 11.5.   Computing $treedist(T_1, T_2)$.

The computation of $treedist(i, j)$ makes strong use of the above lemmas. From the algorithm, it is easy to see that for any subtree pair $T_1[i]$ and $T_2[j]$ the time complexity for $treedist(i, j)$ is $O(|T_1[i]| \times |T_2[j]|)$ provided all the necessary treedist() values are available are available. If we compute all the $treedist()$ bottom up, we can compute the distance between T_1 and T_2. Therefore the time complexity of the algorithm can be bounded by

$$O(\sum_{i=1}^{|T_1|} \sum_{j=1}^{|T_2|} |T_1[i]| \times |T_2[j]|) = O(\sum_{i=1}^{|T_1|} |T_1[i]| \times \sum_{j=1}^{|T_2|} |T_2[j]|)$$

$$= O(|T_1| \times |T_2| \times depth(T_1) \times depth(T_2)).$$

In fact the complexity is a bit better than this. After more careful analysis, we can show that the complexity is $O(|T_1| \times |T_2| \times min(\ depth(T_1),\ leaves(T_1)) \times min(\ depth(T_2),\ leaves(T_2)))$. where $leaves(T_1)$ is the number of leaves in T_1. One implication is that this algorithm can be used to compute the distance between two strings in time $O(|T_1| \times |T_2|)$.

11.2.3   PATTERN TREES WITH VARIABLE LENGTH DON'T CARES

Many problems in strings can be solved with dynamic programming. Similarly, our algorithm applies not only to tree distance but also to a variety of tree problems with the same time complexity.

Approximate tree matching with variable length don't cares   Approximate tree matching is a generalization of approximate string matching. Given two trees, we view one tree as the pattern tree and the other as the data tree. We want to match, approximately, the pattern tree to the

---

Procedure: $treedist(i, j)$

> **begin**
> $forestdist(\theta, \theta) = 0$;
>   **for** $i_1 := l(i)$ **to** i
> $forestdist(T_1[l(i)..i_1], \theta) = forestdist(T_1[l(i)..i_1 - 1], \theta)$
> $+ \gamma(t_1[i_1] \rightarrow \lambda)$
>   **for** $j_1 := l(j)$ **to** j
> $forestdist(\theta, T_2[l(j)..j_1]) = forestdist(\theta, T_2[l(j)..j_1 - 1])$
> $+ \gamma(\lambda \rightarrow t_2[j_1])$
>   **for** $i_1 := l(i)$ **to** i
>   **for** $j_1 := l(j)$ **to** j
>   **if** $l(i_1) = l(i)$ and $l(j_1) = l(j)$ **then**
>   Calculate $forestdist(T_1[l(i)..i_1], T_2[l(j)..j_1])$
>   as in Lemma 11.3 (1).
> $treedist(i_1, j_1) = forestdist(T_1[l(i)..i_1], T_2[l(j)..j_1])$
>   /* put in permanent array */
>   **else**
>   Calculate $forestdist(T_1[l(i)..i_1], T_2[l(j)..j_1])$
>   as in Lemma 11.3 (2).
> **end**

Output: $treedist(T_1[s], T_2[t])$,
      where $s \in desc(i)$ and $t \in desc(j)$, $l(s) = l(i)$ and $l(t) = l(j)$.

Fig. 11.6.   Computing $treedist(i, j)$.

data tree. In the match, we allow the pattern tree to match only part of the data tree. For this purpose we allow subtrees of the data tree to be cut freely. Also we allow the pattern tree to contain *variable length don't cares* index variable length don't cares to suppress the details of the data tree which are not interested. Intuitively, these VLDC's match part of a path with or without the subtrees branching off that path. We now give the formal definitions for cut, variable length don't cares, and approximate tree matching.

Cutting at node $t[i]$ means removing the subtree rooted at $t[i]$. Let C be a set of nodes. We define C to be a set of *consistent subtree cuts* if $t[i], t[j] \in C$ implies that neither is an ancestor of the other. We use $Cut(T, C)$ to represent the tree T with all subtrees in rooted at nodes of C removed. Let $subtree(T)$ be the set of all possible sets of consistent subtree cuts. The term approximate tree matching (without VLDC's) is defined as computing

$$tree\_cut(P, T) = \min_{C \in subtree(T)} \{treedist(P, cut(T, C))\}.$$

Intuitively, this is the distance between the pattern tree and the cut data tree, where the cut yields the smallest possible distance.

We consider two VLDC's: $|$ and $\wedge$. A node with $|$ in the pattern tree can substitute part of a path from the root to a leaf of the data tree. A node with $\wedge$ in the pattern tree can substitute part of such path and all the subtrees emanating from the nodes of that path, except possibly at the lowest node of that path. At the lowest node, the $\wedge$ symbol can substitute for a set of leftmost subtrees and a set of rightmost subtrees. We call $|$ a path VLDC and $\wedge$ an umbrella VLDC, because of the shape they impose on the tree.

Let P be a pattern tree that contains both umbrella-VLDCs and path-VLDCs and let T be a data tree. A VLDC-substitution s on P replaces each path-VLDC in P by a path of nodes in T and each umbrella-VLDC in P by an umbrella pattern of nodes in T. We require that any mapping from the resulting (VLDC-free) pattern $\bar{P}$ to T map the substituting nodes to themselves. (Thus, no cost is induced by VLDC substitutions.) The approximate matching between P and T w.r.t. s, is defined as $tree\_vldc(P, T, s) = tree\_cut(\bar{P}, T, s)$. Then,

$$tree\_vldc(P, T) = \min_{s \in S}\{tree\_vldc(P, T, s)\}$$

where S is the set of all possible VLDC-substitutions.

The algorithm   The following lemma shows that the two kinds of VLDCs are the same in the presence of free subtree cuts.[2]

Lemma 11.4. *A path-VLDC can be substituted for an umbrella-VLDC or vice versa without changing the mapping or the distance value when we allow subtrees to be cut freely from the text tree.*

Proof: Trivial. □

We compute $tree\_vldc(i, j)$ for $1 \leq i < |P|$ and $1 \leq j \leq |T|$. In the intermediate steps, we need to calculate $forest\_vldc(l(i)..i_1, l(j)..j_1)$ for $l(i) \leq i_1 \leq i$ and $l(j) \leq j_1 \leq j$. The algorithm considers the following two cases separately: (1) $P[l(i)..i_1]$ or $T[l(j)..j_1]$ is a forest; (2) both are trees. The overall strategy is to try to find a best substitution for the VLDCs in $P[l(i)..i_1]$, and ask whether or not $T[j_1]$ is cut. (Note that in the algorithm, $\gamma(p[i_1] \rightarrow \lambda) = 0$ and $\gamma(p[i_1] \rightarrow t[j_1]) = 0$ when $p[i_1] = |$.)

---

[2]The case for matching without cuttings is much more involved. In that case, we have to consider the two kinds of VLDCs separately and need an auxiliary suffix forest distance measure when dealing with umbrella-VLDCs.

Lemma 11.5. *If $P[l(i)..i_1]$ or $T[l(j)..j_1]$ is a forest, then*

$$forest\_vldc(l(i)..i_1, l(j)..j_1) =$$

$$\min \begin{cases} forest\_vldc(l(i)..i_1, l(j)..l(j_1) - 1), \\ forest\_vldc(l(i)..i_1 - 1, l(j)..j_1) + \gamma(p[i_1] \rightarrow \lambda), \\ forest\_vldc(l(i)..i_1, l(j)..j_1 - 1) + \gamma(\lambda \rightarrow t[j_1]), \\ forest\_vldc(l(i)..l(i_1) - 1, l(j)..l(j_1) - 1) + tree\_vldc(s, t) \end{cases}$$

Proof: If $T[j_1]$ is cut, then $forest\_vldc$ $(l(i)..i_1,\ l(j)..j_1) = forest\_vldc$ $(l(i)..i_1,\ l(j)..l(j_1) - 1)$. Otherwise, consider a minimum-cost mapping M between $P[l(i)..i_1]$ and $T[l(j)..j_1]$ after performing an optimal removal of subtrees of $T[l(j)..j_1]$. The distance is the minimum of the following three cases.

(1) $p[i_1]$ is not touched by a line in M. (This includes the case where $p[i_1] = |$ is replaced by an empty tree.) So, $forest\_vldc(l(i)..i_1, l(j)..j_1) = forest\_vldc(l(i)..i_1 - 1, l(j)..j_1) + \gamma(p[i_1] \rightarrow \lambda)$.

(2) $t[j_1]$ is not touched by a line in M. So, $forest\_vldc(l(i)..i_1, l(j)..j_1) = forest\_vldc(l(i)..i_1,\ l(j)..j_1 - 1) + \gamma(\lambda \rightarrow t[j_1])$.

(3) $p[i_1]$ and $t[j_1]$ are both touched by lines in M. (This includes the case where $p[i_1] = |$ is replaced by a path of nodes in T.) By the ancestor and sibling conditions on mappings, (i_1, j_1) must be in M. By the ancestor condition on mapping, any node in $P[i_1]$ (the subtree of P rooted at i_1) can be touched only by a node in $T[j_1]$. Hence, $forest\_vldc(l(i)..i_1, l(j)..j_1) = forest\_vldc(l(i)..l(i_1) - 1, l(j)..l(j_1) - 1) + tree\_vldc(i_1, j_1)$. □

Lemma 11.6. *If $p[i_1] \neq |$ or $j_1 = l(j)$, then*

$$forest\_vldc(l(i)..i_1, l(j)..j_1) =$$

$$\min \begin{cases} forest\_vldc(l(i)..i_1, \emptyset), \\ forest\_vldc(l(i)..i_1 - 1, l(j)..j_1) + \gamma(p[i_1] \rightarrow \lambda), \\ forest\_vldc(l(i)..i_1, l(j)..j_1 - 1) + \gamma(\lambda \rightarrow t[j_1]), \\ forest\_vldc(l(i)..i_1 - 1, l(j)..j_1 - 1) + \gamma(p[i_1] \rightarrow t[j_1]) \end{cases}$$

Proof: If $T[j_1]$ is cut, then the distance should be $forest\_vldc(l(i)..i_1, \emptyset)$. Otherwise, consider a minimum-cost mapping M between $P[l(i)..i_1]$ and $T[l(j)..j_1]$ after performing an optimal removal of subtrees of $T[l(j)..j_1]$. There are two cases.

(1) $p[i_1] \neq |$. Depending on whether $p[i_1]$ or $t[j_1]$ is touched by a line in M, we argue similarly as in Lemma 11.5.

(2) $p[i_1] = |$ and $j_1 = l(j)$. Then, in the best substitution, either $|$ is replaced by an empty tree, in which case $forest\_vldc(l(i)..i_1, l(j)..j_1) = forest\_vldc(l(i)..i_1 - 1, l(j)..j_1) + \gamma(p[i_1] \rightarrow \lambda)$, or $|$ is replaced by $t[j_1]$, in

which case $forest\_vldc(l(i)..i_1, l(j)..j_1) = forest\_vldc(l(i)..i_1 - 1, l(j)..j_1 - 1) + \gamma(p[i_1] \rightarrow t[j_1])$. The distance is the minimum of these two cases.

Since $j_1 = l(j)$, $forest\_vldc(l(i)..i_1, l(j)..j_1 - 1) + \gamma(\lambda \rightarrow t[j_1]) = forest\_vldc(P[l(i)..i_1], \emptyset) + \gamma(\lambda \rightarrow t[j_1]) \geq forest\_vldc(P[l(i)..i_1], \emptyset) = forest\_vldc(P[l(i)..i_1 - 1], \emptyset) = forest\_vldc(l(i)..i_1 - 1, l(j)..j_1 - 1) + \gamma(p[i_1] \rightarrow t[j_1])$. Thus, we can add an additional item $forest\_vldc(l(i)..i_1, l(j)..j_1 - 1) + \gamma(\lambda \rightarrow t[j_1])$ to the minimum expression, obtaining the formula asserted by the lemma. $\square$

Lemma 11.7. *If $p[i_1] = |$ and $j_1 \neq l(j)$, then*

$$forest\_vldc(l(i)..i_1, l(j)..j_1) =$$

$$\min \begin{cases} forest\_vldc(l(i)..i_1, \emptyset), \\ forest\_vldc(l(i)..i_1 - 1, l(j)..j_1) + \gamma(p[i_1] \rightarrow \lambda), \\ forest\_vldc(l(i)..i_1, l(j)..j_1 - 1) + \gamma(\lambda \rightarrow t[j_1]), \\ forest\_vldc(l(i)..i_1 - 1, l(j)..j_1 - 1) + \gamma(p[i_1] \rightarrow t[j_1]), \\ \min_{t_k}\{tree\_vldc(i_1, t_k) | 1 \leq k \leq n_{j_1}\} \end{cases}$$

where t_k, $1 \leq k \leq n_{j_1}$, are children of j_1.

Proof: Again, if $T[j_1]$ is cut, the distance should be $forest\_vldc(l(i)..i_1, \emptyset)$. Otherwise, let M be a minimum-cost mapping between $P[l(i)..i_1]$ and $T[l(j)..j_1]$ after performing an optimal removal of subtrees of $T[l(j)..j_1]$. There are three cases.

(1) In the best substitution, $p[i_1]$ is replaced by an empty tree. So, $forest\_vldc(l(i)..i_1, l(j)..j_1) = forest\_vldc(l(i)..i_1 - 1, l(j)..j_1) + \gamma(p[i_1] \rightarrow \lambda)$.

(2) In the best substitution, $p[i_1]$ is replaced by a nonempty tree and $t[j_1]$ is not touched by a line in M. So, $forest\_vldc(l(i)..i_1, l(j)..j_1) = forest\_vldc(l(i)..i_1, l(j)..j_1 - 1) + \gamma(\lambda \rightarrow t[j_1])$.

(3) In the best substitution, $p[i_1]$ is replaced by a nonempty tree and $t[j_1]$ is touched by a line in M. So, $p[i_1]$ must be replaced by a path of the tree rooted at $t[j_1]$. Let the path end at node $t[d]$. Let the children of $t[j_1]$ be, in left-to-right order, $t[t_1], t[t_2], \ldots, t[t_{n_{j_1}}]$. There are two subcases.

(a) $d = j_1$. Thus, $|$ is replaced by $t[j_1]$. So $forest\_vldc(l(i)..i_1, l(j)..j_1) = forest\_vldc(l(i)..i_1 - 1, l(j)..j_1 - 1) + \gamma(p[i_1] \rightarrow t[j_1])$.

(b) $d \neq j_1$. Let $t[t_k]$ be the child of $t[j_1]$ on the path from $t[j_1]$ to $t[d]$. We can cut all subtrees on the two sides of the path. So, $forest\_vldc(l(i)..i_1, l(j)..j_1) = tree\_vldc(i_1, t_k)$. The value of k ranges from 1 to n_{j_1}. Therefore, the distance is the minimum of the corresponding costs. $\square$

These lemmas suggest the following algorithm. We omit the initialization steps.

Procedure: $tree\_vldc(i,j)$

> **begin**
>> **for** $i_1 := l(i)$ **to** i **do**
>>> **for** $j_1 := l(j)$ **to** j **do**
>>>> **if** $l(i_1) \neq l(i)$ or $l(j_1) \neq l(j)$ **then**
>>>>> Calculate $forest\_vldc(T_1[l(i)..i_1], T_2[l(j)..j_1])$
>>>>>> as in Lemma 11.5;
>>>> **else begin**   /* $l(i_1) = l(i)$ and $l(j_1) = l(j)$ */
>>>>> **if** $(p[i_1] \neq \,\mid\,$ or $j_1 = l(j))$ **then**
>>>>>> Calculate $forest\_vldc(T_1[l(i)..i_1], T_2[l(j)..j_1])$
>>>>>>> as in Lemma 11.6;
>>>>> **if** $(p[i_1] = \,\mid\,$ and $j_1 \neq l(j))$ **then**
>>>>>> Calculate $forest\_vldc(T_1[l(i)..i_1], T_2[l(j)..j_1])$
>>>>>>> as in Lemma 11.7;
>>>>> $tree\_vldc(i_1, j_1) := forest\_vldc(T_1[l(i)..i_1], T_2[l(j)..j_1]);$
>>>> **end**
> **end**

Fig. 11.7.   Computing $tree\_vldc(i,j)$.

11.2.4   FAST PARALLEL ALGORITHMS FOR SMALL DIFFERENCES

In our research, we have often imported technology developed for strings to develop fast tree algorithms. A particularly blatant example is our algorithm for the unit cost edit distance (unit cost means that node deletions, node relabellings, and node insertions all have the same cost). The algorithm starts from Ukkonen's 1983 technique of computing in waves along the center diagonals of the distance matrix. At the beginning of stage k, all distances up to $k-1$ have been computed. Stage k then computes in parallel all distances up to k. We use suffix trees as Landau and Vishkin to perform this computation fast.

In the string case, if $S_1[i..i+h] = S_2[j..j+h]$, then the distance between $S_1[1..i-1]$ and $S_2[1..j-1]$ is the same as between $S_1[1..i+h]$ and $S_2[1..j+h]$. The main difficulty in the tree case is that preserving ancestor relationships in the mapping between trees prevents the analogous implication from holding. In addition, to compute the distance between two forests at stage k sometimes requires knowing whether two contained subtrees are distance k apart.

We overcome these problems by studying the relationship between identical subforests and distance mappings. We find the relevant identical forests by using suffix trees corresponding to different traversals.

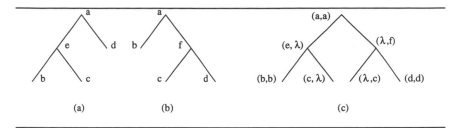

Fig. 11.8. (a) Tree T_1. (b) Tree T_2. (c) The optimal alignment of T_1 and T_2.

The preprocessing time complexity is dominated by the cost of constructing suffix trees. It is bounded by $O(\log(|T_1| + |T_2|)) \leq O(\log(2 \times \min(|T_1|, |T_2|) + k)) \leq O(\log(\min(|T_1|, |T_2|)) + \log(k))$. The time complexity of the algorithm is: $O(k \times \log(k) \times \log(\min(|T_1|, |T_2|)))$ where k is the actual distance between T_1 and T_2.

11.2.5 TREE ALIGNMENT PROBLEM

It is well known that edit and alignment are two equivalent notions for sequences. In particular, for any two sequences x_1 and x_2, the edit distance between x_1 and x_2 equals the value of an optimal alignment of x_1 and x_2. However, edit and alignment turn out to be very different for trees, see Figure 11.8. Here, we introduce the notion of *alignment of trees* as another measure of similarity of labeled trees. The notion is a natural generalization of alignment of sequences.

Definitions Let T_1 and T_2 be two labeled trees. An alignment $\mathcal{A}$ of T_1 and T_2 is obtained by first inserting nodes labeled with λ into T_1 and T_2 such that the two resulting trees T_1' and T_2' are topologically isomorphic, i.e., they are identical if the labels are ignored, and then T_1' is *overlaid* on T_2'. An example alignment is shown in Figure 11.8. An edit cost is defined for each pair of labels. The *value* of alignment $\mathcal{A}$ is the sum of the costs of all pairs of corresponding labels. An *optimal* alignment is one that minimizes the value over all possible alignments. The *alignment distance* between T_1 and T_2 is the value of an optimal alignment of T_1 and T_2.

It is easy to see that in general the edit distance is smaller than the alignment distance for trees. The reason is that each alignment of trees actually corresponds to a restricted tree edit in which all the insertions precede all the deletions. Note that, the order of edit operations is not important for sequences. Also, it seems that alignment charges more for the structural dissimilarity at the top levels of the trees than at the lower levels, whereas edit treats all the levels the same.

The notion of alignment can be easily extended to ordered forests. The only change is that it is now possible to insert a node (as the root) to join a consecutive subsequence of trees in the forest. Denote the alignment distance between forests F_1 and F_2 as $A(F_1, F_2)$. Let θ denote the empty tree, and $\gamma(a, b)$ denote the cost of the opposing letters a and b. Let T_1 and T_2 be two fixed ordered labeled trees throughout this section.

Formulas Let $t_1[i]$ be a node of T_1 and $t_2[j]$ a node of T_2. Suppose that the degrees (number of children) of $t_1[i]$ and $t_2[j]$ are m_i and n_j, respectively. Denote the children of $t_1[i]$ as $t_1[i_1], \ldots, t_1[i_{m_i}]$ and the children of $t_2[j]$ as $t_2[j_1], \ldots, t_2[j_{n_j}]$. For any s, t, $1 \leq s \leq t \leq m_i$, let $F_1[i_s, i_t]$ represent the forest consisting of the subtrees $T_1[i_s], \ldots, T_1[i_t]$. For convenience, $F_1[i_1, i_{m_i}]$ is also denoted $F_1[i]$. Note that $F_1[i] \neq F_1[i, i]$. $F_2[j_s, j_t]$ and $F_2[j]$ are defined similarly.

The following lemmas form the basis of our algorithm. The first lemma is trivial.

Lemma 11.8.

$A(\theta, \theta) = 0;$

$A(F_1[i], \theta) = \sum_{k=1}^{m_i} A(T_1[i_k], \theta); \quad A(T_1[i], \theta) = A(F_1[i], \theta) + \gamma(t_1[i], \lambda);$

$A(\theta, F_2[j]) = \sum_{k=1}^{n_j} A(\theta, T_2[j_k]); \quad A(\theta, T_2[j]) = A(\theta, F_2[j]) + \gamma(\lambda, t_2[j]).$

Lemma 11.9.

$$A(T_1[i], T_2[j]) =$$
$$\min \begin{cases} A(\theta, T_2[j]) + \min_{1 \leq r \leq n_j}\{A(T_1[i], T_2[j_r]) - A(\theta, T_2[j_r])\} \\ A(T_1[i], \theta) + \min_{1 \leq r \leq m_i}\{A(T_1[i_r], T_2[j]) - A(T_1[i_r], \theta)\} \\ A(F_1[i], F_2[j]) + \gamma(t_1[i], t_2[j]) \end{cases}$$

Proof: Consider an optimal alignment (tree) $\mathcal{A}$ of $T_1[i]$ and $T_2[j]$. There are four cases: (1) $(t_1[i], t_2[j])$ is a label in $\mathcal{A}$, (2) $(t_1[i], \lambda)$ and $(t_1[k], t_2[j])$ are labels in $\mathcal{A}$ for some k, (3) $(t_1[i], t_2[k])$ and $(\lambda, t_2[j])$ are labels in $\mathcal{A}$ for some k, (4) $(t_1[i], \lambda)$ and $(\lambda, t_2[j])$ are labels in $\mathcal{A}$. We actually need not consider Case 4 since in this case we can delete the two nodes and then add $(t_1[i], t_2[j])$ as the new root, resulting in a better alignment.

Case 1. The root of $\mathcal{A}$ must be labeled as $(t_1[i], t_2[j])$. Clearly, $A(T_1[i], T_2[j]) = A(F_1[i], F_2[j]) + \gamma(t_1[i], t_2[j])$.

Case 2. The root of $\mathcal{A}$ must be labeled as $(t_1[i], \lambda)$. In this case k must be a node in $T_1[i_r]$ for some $1 \leq r \leq m_i$. Therefore, $A(T_1[i], T_2[j]) = A(T_1[i], \theta) + \min_{1 \leq r \leq m_i}\{A(T_1[i_r], T_2[j]) - A(T_1[i_r], \theta)\}$.

Case 3. Similar to Case 2. $\square$

Note, the above implies that $A(F_1[i], F_2[j])$ is required for computing $A(T_1[i], T_2[j])$.

Lemma 11.10. *For any* s, t *such that* $1 \leq s \leq m_i$ *and* $1 \leq t \leq n_j$,

$$A(F_1[i_1, i_s], F_2[j_1, j_t]) =$$

$$\min \begin{cases} A(F_1[i_1, i_{s-1}], F_2[j_1, j_t]) + A(T_1[i_s], \theta) \\ A(F_1[i_1, i_s], F_2[j_1, j_{t-1}]) + A(\theta, T_2[j_t]) \\ A(F_1[i_1, i_{s-1}], F_2[j_1, j_{t-1}]) + A(T_1[i_s], T_2[j_t]) \\ \gamma(\lambda, t_2[j_t]) \\ \quad + \min_{1 \leq k < s}\{A(F_1[i_1, i_{k-1}], F_2[j_1, j_{t-1}]) + A(F_1[i_k, i_s], F_2[j_t])\} \\ \gamma(t_1[i_s], \lambda) \\ \quad + \min_{1 \leq k < t}\{A(F_1[i_1, i_{s-1}], F_2[j_1, j_{k-1}]) + A(F_1[i_s], F_2[j_k, j_t])\} \end{cases}$$

Proof: Consider an optimal alignment (forest) $\mathcal{A}$ of $F_1[i_1, i_s]$ and $F_2[j_1, j_t]$. The root of the rightmost tree in $\mathcal{A}$ is labeled by either $(t_1[i_s], t_2[j_t])$, $(t_1[i_s], \lambda)$, or $(\lambda, t_2[j_t])$.

Case 1: the label is $(t_1[i_s], t_2[j_t])$. In this case, the rightmost tree must be an optimal alignment of $T_1[i_s]$ and $T_2[j_t]$. Therefore $A(F_1[i_1, i_s], F_2[j_1, j_t]) = A(F_1[i_1, i_{s-1}], F_2[j_1, j_{t-1}]) + A(T_1[i_s], T_2[j_t])$.

Case 2: the label is $(t_1[i_s], \lambda)$. In this case, there is a k, $0 \leq k \leq t$, such that $T_1[i_s]$ is aligned with the subforest $F_2[j_{t-k+1}, j_t]$. A key observation here is the fact that subtree $T_2[j_{t-k+1}]$ is not split by the alignment with $T_1[i_s]$. There are three subcases.

2.1 ($k = 0$) I.e., $F_2[j_{t-k+1}, j_t] = \theta$. Therefore,
$A(F_1[i_1, i_s], F_2[j_1, j_t]) = A(F_1[i_1, i_{s-1}], F_2[j_1, j_t]) + A(T_1[i_s], \theta)$.

2.2 ($k = 1$) I.e., $F_2[j_{t-k+1}, j_t] = T_2[j_t]$. This is the same as in Case 1.

2.3 ($k \geq 2$) This is the most general case. It is easy to see that

$$A(F_1[i_1, i_s], F_2[j_1, j_t]) = \gamma(t_1[i_s], \lambda)$$
$$+ \min_{1 \leq k < t}\{A(F_1[i_1, i_{s-1}], F_2[j_1, j_{k-1}]) + A(F_1[i_s], F_2[j_k, j_t])\}.$$

Case 3: the label is $(\lambda, t_2[j_t])$. Similar to Case 2. □

Algorithm It follows from the above lemmas that, for each pair of subtrees $T_1[i]$ and $T_2[j]$, we have to compute $A(F_1[i], F_2[j_s, j_t])$ for all $1 \leq s \leq t \leq n_j$, and $A(F_1[i_s, i_t], F_2[j])$ for all $1 \leq s \leq t \leq m_i$. That is, we need align $F_1[i]$ with each subforest of $F_2[j]$, and conversely align $F_2[j]$ with each subforest of $F_1[i]$. Note that we do not have to align an arbitrary forest of $F_1[i]$ with an arbitrary forest of $F_2[j]$. Otherwise the time complexity would be higher.

For each fixed s and t, where either $s = 1$ or $t = 1$, $1 \leq s \leq m_i$ and $1 \leq t \leq n_j$, the procedure in Figure 11.9 computes $\{A(F_1[i_s, i_p], F_2[j_t, j_q])|s \leq p \leq m_i, t \leq q \leq n_j\}$, assuming that all $A(F_1[i_k], F_2[j_p, j_q])$ are known, where $1 \leq k \leq m_i$ and $1 \leq p \leq q \leq n_j$, and all $A(F_1[i_p, i_q], F_2[j_k])$ are known, where $1 \leq p \leq q \leq m_i$ and $1 \leq k \leq n_j$.

Input: $F_1[i_s, i_{m_i}]$ and $F_2[j_t, j_{n_j}]$.

Procedure: $forest\_align()$

begin
  $A(F_1[i_s, i_{s-1}], F_2[j_t, j_{t-1}]) := 0;$
  for $p := s$ **to** m_i
    $A(F_1[i_s, i_p], F_2[j_t, j_{t-1}]) := A(F_1[i_s, i_{p-1}], F_2[j_t, j_{t-1}]) + A(T_1[i_p], \theta);$
  for $q := t$ **to** n_j
    $A(F_1[i_s, i_{s-1}], F_2[j_t, j_q]) := A(F_1[i_s, i_{s-1}], F_2[j_t, j_{q-1}]) + A(\theta, T_2[j_q]);$
  for $p := s$ **to** m_i
    for $q := t$ **to** n_j
      Compute $A(F_1[i_s, i_p], F_2[j_t, j_q])$ as in Lemma 11.10.
end

Output: $A(F_1[i_s, i_p], F_2[j_t, j_q])$, where $s \leq p \leq m_i$ and $t \leq q \leq n_j\}$.

Fig. 11.9. Computing $\{A(F_1[i_s, i_p], F_2[j_t, j_q]) | s \leq p \leq m_i, t \leq q \leq n_j\}$ for fixed s and t.

Hence we can obtain $A(F_1[i], F_2[j_s, j_t])$ for all $1 \leq s \leq t \leq n_j$ by calling Procedure $forest\_align$ n_j times, and $A(F_1[i_s, i_t], F_2[j])$ for all $1 \leq s \leq t \leq m_i$ by calling Procedure $forest\_align$ m_i times. Our algorithm to compute $A(T_1, T_2)$ is given in Figure 11.10.

For an input $F_1[i_s, i_{m_i}]$ and $F_2[j_t, j_{n_j}]$, the running time of Procedure $forest\_align$ is bounded by

$$O((m_i - s) \times (n_j - t) \times (m_i - s + n_j - t)) = O(m_i \times n_j \times (m_i + n_j)).$$

So, for each pair i and j, Algorithm ALIGN spends $O(m_i \times n_j \times (m_i + n_j)^2)$ time. Therefore, the time complexity of Algorithm ALIGN is

$$\sum_{i=1}^{|T_1|} \sum_{j=1}^{|T_2|} O(m_i \times n_j \times (m_i + n_j)^2)$$

$$\begin{aligned} &\leq &&\textstyle\sum_{i=1}^{|T_1|} \sum_{j=1}^{|T_2|} O(m_i \times n_j \times (deg(T_1) + deg(T_2))^2) \\ &\leq &&O((deg(T_1) + deg(T_2))^2 \times \sum_{i=1}^{|T_1|} m_i \times \sum_{j=1}^{|T_2|} n_j) \\ &\leq &&O(|T_1| \times |T_2| \times (deg(T_1) + deg(T_2))^2) \end{aligned}$$

If both T_1 and T_2 have degrees bounded by some constant, the time complexity becomes $O(|T_1| \cdot |T_2|)$. Note that the algorithm actually computes $A(T_1[i], T_2[j])$, $A(F_1[i], F_2[j])$, $A(F_1[i_s, i_t], F_2[j])$ and $A(F_1[i], F_2[j_s, j_t])$. With these data, materializing an optimal alignment can be found using back-tracking. The complexity remains the same.

Algorithm: ALIGN(T_1, T_2)

begin
$A(\theta, \theta) := 0$;
for $i := 1$ **to** $|T_1|$
    Initialize $A(T_1[i], \theta)$ and $A(F_1[i], \theta)$ as in Lemma 11.8;
for $j := 1$ **to** $|T_2|$
    Initialize $A(\theta, T_2[j])$ and $A(\theta, F_2[j])$ as in Lemma 11.8;
for $i := 1$ **to** $|T_1|$
    for $j := 1$ **to** $|T_2|$
        for $s := 1$ **to** m_i
            Call Procedure *forest_align* on $F_1[i_s, i_{m_i}]$ and $F_2[j]$;
        for $t := 1$ **to** n_j
            Call Procedure *forest_align* on $F_1[i]$ and $F_2[j_t, i_{n_j}]$;
        Compute $A(T_1[i], T_2[j])$ as in Lemma 11.9.
end

Output: $A(T_1[i], T_2[i])$, where $1 \leq i \leq |T_1|$ and $1 \leq j \leq |T_2|$.

Fig. 11.10. Computing $A(T_1, T_2)$.

11.2.6 TREE PATTERN DISCOVERY PROBLEM

We briefly discuss the pattern discovery problem. In matching problems, we are given a pattern and need to find a distance between the pattern and one or more objects; in discovery problems, by contrast, we are given two objects and a "target" distance d and are asked to find the largest portions of the objects that differ by at most that distance. Specializing the discovery problem to a pair of trees, we want to find the largest connected component from each tree such that the distance between them is under the target distance value.

Let us consider the connected component in one of the trees. Since it is connected, it must be rooted at a node and is generated by cutting off some subtrees. This means that a naive algorithm for tree pattern discovery would have to consider all the subtree pairs and for each subtree pair all the possible cuts of its subtrees. Since the number of such possible cuts is exponential, the naive algorithm is clearly impractical.

Instead we use a compound form of dynamic programming. By compound, we mean that dynamic programming is applied (1) to compute sizes of common patterns between two subtree pairs given a set of cuts; (2) to find the cuttings that yield distances less than or equal to the target one; (3) to compute the optimal cuttings for distance k, $1 \leq k \leq d$, given the optimal cuttings for distances 0 to $k - 1$.

In the computation of an optimal solution for distance value k, we also have to solve a problem which is unique for trees. Consider a pair of subtrees s_1 and s_2 whose roots map to one another in the optimal solution for distance value k. Then, in general, there are several subtree pairs of s_1 and s_2 that map to one another. We have to determine how the distance value k should be distributed to these several subtree pairs so that we can obtain the optimal solution. We solve this problem by partitioning the subtrees of s_1, respectively s_2, into a forest and a subtree. We then compute the distance and size values from forest to forest and from subtree to subtree.

Using this general framework, we can solve the tree pattern discovery problem for edit and alignment distance measures. Given a target distance value d, the time complexity of the algorithm for edit distance measure is $(d^2 \times |T_1| \times |T_2| \times min(depth(T_1), leaves(T_1)) \times min(depth(T_2), leaves(T_2)))$, and the time complexity of the algorithm for alignment distance measure is $O(d^2 \times |T_1| \times |T_2| \times (deg(T_1) + deg(T_2))^2)$.

11.3   Algorithms and hardness results for unordered trees

Recall that unordered labeled trees are rooted trees whose nodes are labeled and in which only ancestor relationships are significant (the left-to-right order among siblings is not significant). Such trees arise naturally in genealogical studies, for example, or in parts explosions. For many such applications, it would be useful to compare unordered labeled trees by some meaningful distance metric. The editing distance metric, used with some success for ordered labeled trees, is a natural such metric. The alignment distance is another metric. This section presents algorithms and complexity results for these metrics.

11.3.1   HARDNESS RESULTS

We reduce Exact Cover by 3-Sets to the problem of computing the edit distance between unordered labeled trees. This means that computing the edit distance between unordered labeled trees is NP-hard. We assume that each edit operation has unit cost, i.e. $\gamma(a \rightarrow b) = 1$ if $a \neq b$.

Exact Cover by 3-Sets

INSTANCE: A finite set S with $|S| = 3k$ and a collection T of 3-element subsets of S.

QUESTION: Does T contain an exact cover of S, that is, a subcollection $T' \subset T$ such that every element of S occurs in exactly one member of T'?

Given $S = \{s_1, s_2, ... s_m\}$, where $m = 3k$ and $T = T_1, T_2, ... T_n$ where $T_i = \{t_{i1}, t_{i2}, t_{i3}\}$, $t_{ij} \in S$, we construct the two trees as in Figure 11.11.

The following lemmas show that $treedist(T_1, T_2) = 3n - 2k$ if and only if there exists an exact 3-cover. Since the problem is clearly in NP, the lemmas show that the problem is NP-complete. The proofs of these lemmas are left as exercises.

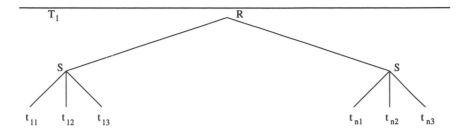

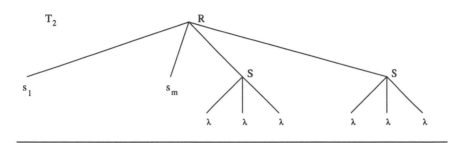

Fig. 11.11.   The reduction

Lemma 11.11. *Let M be a mapping between T_1 and T_2. If there are $d \geq 0$ nodes of T_2 not in mapping M, then $\gamma(M) \geq 3n - 2k + d$.*

Lemma 11.12. *treedist$(T_1, T_2) \geq 3n - 2k$.*

Lemma 11.13. *If there is an exact 3-cover, then treedist$(T_1, T_2) = 3(n - k) + k = 3n - 2k$.*

Lemma 11.14. *If treedist$(T_1, T_2) = 3n - 2k$, then there exists an exact 3-cover.*

In fact there are stronger results concerning the hardness of computing the edit distance and alignment distance for unordered labeled trees. Computing the edit distance between two unordered labeled trees is MAX SNP-hard even if the two trees are binary. Computing the alignment distance between two unordered labeled trees is MAX SNP-hard when at least one of the trees is allowed to have an arbitrary degree. The techniques for these proofs are similar to the one we just presented. The reduction is from Maximum Bounded Covering by 3-sets which is an optimization version of Exact Cover by 3-sets.

Algorithm: ALIGN(T_1, T_2)

> **begin**
>   **for** $i := 1$ **to** $|T_1|$
>   **for** $j := 1$ **to** $|T_2|$
> $A(F_1[i], F_2[j]) := \min\{$
> $\gamma(t_1[i_2], \lambda) + A(F_1[i_2], F_2[j]) + A(T_1[i_1], \theta),$
> $\gamma(t_1[i_1], \lambda) + A(F_1[i_1], F_2[j]) + A(T_1[i_2], \theta),$
> $\gamma(\lambda, t_2[j_2]) + A(F_1[i], F_2[j_2]) + A(\theta, T_2[j_1]),$
> $\gamma(\lambda, t_2[j_1]) + A(F_1[i], F_2[j_1]) + A(\theta, T_2[j_2]),$
> $A(T_1[i_1], T_2[j_1]) + A(T_1[i_2], T_2[j_2]),$
> $A(T_1[i_1], T_2[j_2]) + A(T_1[i_2], T_2[j_1]) \};$
>
> $A(T_1[i], T_2[j]) := \min\{$
> $\gamma(t_1[i], t_2[j]) + A(F_1[i], F_2[j]),$
> $\gamma(t_1[i], \lambda) + A(T_1[i_1], T_2[j]) + A(T_1[i_2], \theta),$
> $\gamma(t_1[i], \lambda) + A(T_1[i_2], T_2[j]) + A(T_1[i_1], \theta),$
> $\gamma(\lambda, t_2[j]) + A(T_1[i], T_2[j_1]) + A(\theta, T_2[j_2]),$
> $\gamma(\lambda, t_2[j]) + A(T_1[i], T_2[j_2]) + A(\theta, T_2[j_1]) \};$
> **end**

Output: $A(T_1[|T_1|], T_2[|T_2|])$.

Fig. 11.12.   Aligning unordered binary trees.

11.3.2   ALGORITHM FOR TREE ALIGNMENT AND A HEURISTIC ALGORITHM FOR TREE EDIT

When the degrees are bounded, we can compute the alignment distance using a modified version of Algorithm ALIGN. Lemmas 11.8 and 11.9 still work. The only difference is in the computation of $D(F_1[i], F_2[j])$. We have to revise the recurrence relation in Lemma 11.10 as follows: for each (forest) $C \subseteq \{T_1[i_1], \ldots, T_1[i_{m_i}]\}$ and each (forest) $D \subseteq \{T_2[j_1], \ldots, T_2[j_{n_j}]\}$,

$$
A(C, D) = \min \begin{cases}
\min_{T_1[i_p] \in C, T_2[j_q] \in D} & \{A(C - \{T_1[i_p]\}, D - \{T_2[j_q]\}) \\
& + A(T_1[i_p], T_2[j_q])\}, \\
\min_{T_1[i_p] \in C, D' \subseteq D} & \{A(C - \{T_1[i_p]\}, D - D') \\
& + A(F_1[i_p], D') + \gamma(t_1[i_p], \lambda)\}, \\
\min_{C' \subseteq C, T_2[j_q] \in D} & \{A(C - C', D - \{T_2[j_q]\}) \\
& + A(C', F_2[j_q]) + \gamma(\lambda, t_2[j_q])\}
\end{cases}
$$

Since m_i and n_j are bounded, $A(C, D)$ can be computed in polynomial time. If T_1 and T_2 are both in fact binary trees, the algorithm can be much simplified, as shown in Figure 11.12 It is easy to see that the time complexity of this algorithm is $O(|T_1| \cdot |T_2|)$.

For the edit distance, we have an efficient enumerative algorithm. The algorithm runs in polynomial time when one of the trees has a bounded number of leaves.

For the more general cases, we have developed heuristic algorithms based on probabilistic hill-climbing. Another way to deal with the hardness results is to add more constraints on the way in which we transform one tree to the other. This leads to a constrained edit distance between two unordered trees. The complexity of this algorithm is $O(|T_1| \times |T_2| \times (deg(T_1) + deg(T_2)) \times \log_2(deg(T_1) + deg(T_2)))$.

11.4   Conclusion

As we have discovered since making our tree comparison software generally available,[3] many applications require the comparison of trees. In biology, RNA secondary structures are topological characterizations of the folding of a single strand of nucleotides. Determining the functionality of these structures depends on the topology and therefore comparing different ones based on their topology is of interest. In neuroanatomy, networks of connections starting at a single point often describe trees. Comparing them may give a hint as to structure. In genealogy, unordered trees are of interest and may give hints about the origins of hereditary diseases. In language applications, comparing parse trees can be of interest. Finally, we are currently developing a package to enable users to compare structured documents based on tree edit distance. This should be more informative than utilities such as UNIX diff.

Algorithmically, tree comparison bears much similarity to string comparison. Tree comparison uses dynamic programming, suffix trees, and, in parallel versions, counter-diagonals. We often reason by analogy to stringologic work when developing new algorithms. For this reason, we believe that treeology may be a good discipline to study for talented stringologists who are tired of one dimensional structures. But the tree and string problems are different and no reduction appears possible — certainly not for unordered trees (because of the NP-completeness result) and we conjecture not for ordered trees.

Besides pursuing new applications and letting them lead us to new algorithms, we are currently working on the problem of tree pattern discovery. The philosophy of this work is best shown by distinction to the work we have described so far. Our work to date has consisted primarily of finding the distance between a given pattern tree and a given data tree given a pattern metric. By contrast, tree pattern discovery consists of *producing* a pattern tree that, according to a given distance metric, is close to a col-

---

[3]Send us email if you're interested.

lection of data trees. Such tree "motifs" could characterize a collection of trees representing some phenomenon in nature. We are currently working on the secondary structure of viruses.

11.5 Exercises

1. A counter-diagonal in a dynamic programming matrix extends from location (i,0) to (0,i). For trees as well as for strings, all elements in a counter-diagonal can be computed in parallel. Design a parallel version of Algorithm EDIT? Hint: The complexity should be $O(|T_1| + |T_2|)$.

2. Suppose you were only interested in the editing distance between two trees assuming they differed by no more than d. That is, your algorithm would return the exact distance if it is less than or equal to d, but would return "very different" otherwise. What would the time complexity be in that case? Hint: The complexity should be proportional to the square of d.

3. Pruning a tree at node n means removing all its children, but not removing n itself. Define the optimal pruning distance between a pattern tree P and a data tree T to be the minimum distance between P and tree T' where T' is T followed by pruning. Hint: The algorithm should be a variant of the algorithm with cuts.

4. Consider the Procedure $tree\_vldc$ in which eliminating a path was free if it is matched to a variable length don't care. Consider a metric in which all inserts, deletes and replacements cost one and in which deletions of paths in the text tree along with their subtrees also had unit cost. Design an algorithm to compute that cost.

5. Prove Lemma 11.3.1 to Lemma 11.3.1.

6. Try to show the MAX SNP-hardness result mentioned in section 11.3 by reduction from Maximum Bounded Covering by 3-sets.

7. Geographical data structures such as quadtrees are not rotation-invariant, but suppose we wanted to find the editing distance between two trees where we allow rotations among the children of the roots. That is, given two ordered rooted trees T_1 and T_2, find the distance between R_1 and R_2, where R_1 is T_1 but perhaps with a rotation among the children of the root of T_1; R_2 is T_2 but perhaps with a rotation among the children of the root of T_2, such that the distance is minimum among all such rotations of T_1 and T_2. Hint: If the degree of the root of the trees is no greater than the depth of the trees, then the complexity should be no greater than Algorithm EDIT.

8. Suppose we have a pair of ordered rootless trees T_1 and T_2. Define the edit distance between those two trees to be the edit distance between the rooted trees R_1 and R_2 where R_1 is isomorphic to T_1 and R_2 is isomorphic to T_2 and the distance between R_1 and R_2 is the

minimum edit distance of any pairs of rooted trees R'_1 and R'_2 where R'_1 is isomorphic to T_1 and R'_2 is isomorphic to T_2. Hint: Use the algorithm you developed for the previous question as a subroutine.

11.6 Bibliographic notes

The first attempt to generalize string edit distance to ordered trees was due to Selkow [1977]. He gave an tree edit algorithm in which the insertions and deletions are restricted to the leaves of the trees. The edit distance between ordered trees was introduced by Tai [1979]. Another edit base distance was introduced by Lu [1979]. Lu treated each subtree as a whole entity and did not allow one subtree to match more than one subtrees in the other tree. Tanaka and Tanaka [1988] introduced the strongly structure preserving mapping and gave an algorithm based on this kind mapping. Their algorithm is the same as Lu's algorithm. Yang [1991] gave an algorithm based on a mapping where two nodes in the mapping implies their parents are in the mapping. Edit distance between unordered tree was considered by Zhang, Statman and Shasha [1992]. Jiang, Wang and Zhang [1994] considered the tree alignment distance problem. Tree inclusion problem was introduced by Kilpelainen and Mannila.

The algorithm for edit distance presented in this chapter is due to Zhang and Shasha. The alignment distance algorithm is due to Jiang, Wang and Zhang. It is open whether the time complexity of these algorithm can be improved. There is no non-trivial lower bound result for these problems.

The parallel algorithm for unit cost edit distance discussed in this chapter is due to Shasha and Zhang.

The approximate tree match was considered by Zhang and Shasha. This was later extended to handle the case where pattern tree can have variable length don't cares. The algorithm presented is due to Zhang, Shasha and Wang.

The NP-completeness results for edit distance between unordered trees is due to Zhang, Statman and Shasha. The MAX SNP-hard result is due to Zhang and Jiang. It is open whether these problems can be approximated within a constant.

Bibliography

CAI, J., R. PAIGE AND R. TARJAN [1992]. "More efficient bottom-up multi-pattern matching in trees", *Theoretical Computer Science*, **106**, pp. 21-60.

CHASE, D. [1987]. "An improvement to bottom-up tree pattern matching", *Proceedings of the 14th Annual CM Symposium on Principles of Programming Languages*, pp. 168-177.

DUBINER, M., Z. GALIL AND E. MAGEN [1994]. "Faster tree pattern matching", *JACM*, **14**, (2), pp. 205-213.

HOFFMAN, C. AND J. O'DONNEL [1982]. "Pattern matching in trees", *JACM*, **29**, (1), pp. 68-95.

JIANG, T., L. WANG AND K. ZHANG [1994]. "Alignment of trees - an alternative to tree edit", *Proceedings of the Fifth Symposium on Combinatorial Pattern Matching*, pp. 75-86.

KILPELAINEN, P. AND H. MANNILA [1991]. "Ordered and unordered tree inclusion", To appear *SIAM J. on Computing*.

KOSARAJU, S.R. [1992]. "Efficient tree pattern matching", *Proceedings of the 30th annual IEEE Symposium on Foundations of Computer Science*, pp. 178-183.

LANDAU, G.M. AND U. VISHKIN [1989]. "Fast parallel and serial approximate string matching", *J. Algorithms*, **10**, pp.157-169.

LU, S.Y. [1979]. "A tree-to-tree distance and its application to cluster analysis", *IEEE Trans. PAMI*, **1**, pp.219-224.

SELKOW, S.M. [1977]. "The tree-to-tree editing problem", *Information Processing Letters*, **6**, pp.184-186.

SHAPIRO B.A. AND K. ZHANG [1990]. "Comparing multiple RNA secondary structures using tree comparisons", *Comput. Appl. Biosci.* **6**, (4), pp.309-318.

SHASHA, D., J.T.L. WANG AND K. ZHANG [1994]. "Exact and approximate algorithms for unordered tree matching", *IEEE Trans. Systems, Man, and Cybernetics*, **24**, (4), pp.668-678.

SHASHA, D. AND K. ZHANG [1990]. "Fast algorithms for the unit cost editing distance between trees", *J. Algorithms*, **11**, pp.581-621.

TAI, K.C. [1979]. "The tree-to-tree correction problem", *J. ACM*, **26**, pp.422-433.

TANAKA, E. AND K. TANAKA [1988]. "The tree-to-tree editing problem", *International Journal of Pattern Recognition and Artificial Intelligence*, **2**, (2), pp.221-240.

THORUP, M. [1994]. "Efficient Preprocessing of Simple Binary Pattern Forests", *Proceedings of the 4th Scandinavian Workshop on Algorithm Theory, Lecture Notes in Computer Science*, **824**, pp. 350-358.

UKKONEN, E. [1985]. "Finding approximate patterns in strings", *J. Algorithm*, **6**, pp.132-137.

WANG, J.T.L., K. ZHANG, K. JEONG AND D. SHASHA [1994]. "A system for approximate tree matching", *IEEE Trans. Knowledge and Data Engineering*, **6**, (4), pp.559-571.

YANG, W. [1991]. "Identifying syntactic differences between two programs", *Software – Practice and Experience*, **21**, (7), pp.739-755.

ZHANG, K. [1994]. "A constrained editing distance between unordered labeled trees", To appear *Algorithmica*.

ZHANG, K. AND T. JIANG [1994]. "Some MAX SNP-hard results concerning unordered labeled trees", *Information Processing Letters*, **49**, pp.249-254.

ZHANG, K. AND D. SHASHA [1989]. "Simple fast algorithms for the editing distance between trees and related problems", *SIAM J. Computing* **18**, (6), pp.1245-1262.

ZHANG, K., D. SHASHA, AND J.T.L. WANG [1994]. "Approximate tree matching in the presence of variable length don't cares", *J. of Algorithms*, **16**, pp.33-66.

ZHANG, K., R. STATMAN AND D. SHASHA [1992]. "On the editing distance between unordered labeled trees" *Information Processing Letters* **42**, pp.133-139.

Index